THE CAMBRIDGE COMPANION TO ENGLISH POETS

This volume provides lively and authoritative introductions to twenty-nine of the most important British and Irish poets from Geoffrey Chaucer to Philip Larkin. The list includes, among others, Shakespeare, Donne, Milton, Wordsworth, Browning, Yeats, and T. S. Eliot, and represents the tradition of English poetry at its best. Each contributor offers a new assessment of a single poet's achievement and importance, with readings of the most important poems. The essays, written by leading experts, are personal responses, written in clear, vivid language, free of academic jargon, and aim to inform, arouse interest, and deepen understanding.

CLAUDE RAWSON is Maynard Mack Professor of English at Yale University. One of the most distinguished eighteenth-century scholars working today, he has published widely on Swift, Pope, Fielding, and many other authors and topics. He is Founding General Editor of *The Cambridge History of Literary Criticism* and General Editor of *The Cambridge Edition of the Works of Jonathan Swift*.

A complete list of books in the series is at the back of this book.

THE CAMBRIDGE COMPANION TO ENGLISH POETS

EDITED BY
CLAUDE RAWSON

CAMBRIDGE UNIVERSITY PRESS
Cambridge, New York, Melbourne, Madrid, Cape Town, Singapore,
São Paulo, Delhi, Dubai, Tokyo, Mexico City

Cambridge University Press
The Edinburgh Building, Cambridge CB2 8RU, UK

Published in the United States of America by Cambridge University Press, New York

www.cambridge.org
Information on this title: www.cambridge.org/9780521697033

First published 2011

Printed in the United Kingdom at the University Press, Cambridge

A catalogue record for this publication is available from the British Library

Library of Congress Cataloguing in Publication data
The Cambridge Companion to English Poets / [edited by] Claude Rawson.
p. cm. – (Cambridge Companions to Literature)
Includes bibliographical references and index.
ISBN 978-0-521-87434-2 (hardback) – ISBN 978-0-521-69703-3 (paperback)
1. English poetry–History and criticism. 2. English poetry–Irish authors–History and criticism. I. Rawson, Claude (Claude Julien), 1935– II. Title. III. Series.
PR503.C36 2011
821′.009–dc22
2010045710

ISBN 978-0-521-87434-2 Hardback
ISBN 978-0-521-69703-3 Paperback

CONTENTS

ILLUSTRATIONS

NOTES ON CONTRIBUTORS

PAUL BAINES is a Professor in the School of English, University of Liverpool. He is the author of *The House of Forgery in Eighteenth-Century Britain* (1999), *The Complete Critical Guide to Alexander Pope* (2000), and many articles in the *Oxford Dictionary of National Biography*. *Edmund Curll, Bookseller*, co-written with Pat Rogers, was published in 2007. He is currently working on issues of crime and punishment in the poetry of Pope.

ANNE BARTON is a Fellow of Trinity College, Cambridge. Although most of her scholarly work has been on early modern drama, particularly Shakespeare, she has published numerous articles on Byron and the other Romantics, and a short book on Byron's *Don Juan*. Her essay 'Byron and Shakespeare' was published in *The Cambridge Companion to Byron* (ed. Drummond Bone) in 2004.

DAVID BEVINGTON is the Phyllis Fay Horton Distinguished Service Professor Emeritus in the Humanities at the University of Chicago, where he has taught since 1967. His studies include *From 'Mankind' to Marlowe* (1962), *Tudor Drama and Politics* (1968), *Action Is Eloquence: Shakespeare's Language of Gesture* (1985), and *This Wide and Universal Theater: Shakespeare in Performance Then and Now* (2007). He is the editor of *Medieval Drama* (1975), the Bantam Shakespeare, in 29 paperback volumes (1988, recently re-edited), and *The Complete Works of Shakespeare*, fifth edition (2003), as well as the Oxford *1 Henry IV* (1987), the Cambridge *Antony and Cleopatra* (1990), and the Arden Shakespeare Third Series *Troilus and Cressida* (1998). He is a senior editor of the Revels Student Editions, the Revels Plays, the forthcoming Cambridge edition of the works of Ben Jonson, and the *Norton Anthology of Renaissance Drama* (2002).

DINAH BIRCH is a Professor of English Literature at Liverpool University and the general editor of the *Oxford Companion to English Literature*, 7th edn (2009). Her books include *Ruskin's Myths* (1988), *Ruskin and the Dawn of the Modern* (1999), and *Our Victorian Education* (2007). She has also edited texts by George Eliot, Anthony Trollope, and John Ruskin, and reviews regularly for the *Times Literary Supplement* and the *London Review of Books*.

COLIN BURROW is a Senior Research Fellow at All Souls College, Oxford. He has published widely on Renaissance literature. He edited *The Complete Sonnets and Poems* for the Oxford Shakespeare and the poems for the forthcoming *Cambridge Edition of the Works of Ben Jonson*. He is presently writing the Elizabethan volume for the Oxford English Literary History.

J. A. BURROW, Fellow of the British Academy, is Emeritus Professor and Senior Research Fellow at the University of Bristol. Of his publications, chiefly on medieval English poetry, the most recent are *Gestures and Looks in Medieval Narrative* (2002), a revised edition of *Medieval Writers and their Work* (2008), and *The Poetry of Praise* (2008).

JAMES CHANDLER is Barbara E. and Richard J. Franke Distinguished Service Professor in the Department of English and in the Committee on Cinema and Media Studies at the University of Chicago, where he also serves as Director of the Franke Institute for the Humanities. His publications include *England in 1819* (1998) and *Wordsworth's Second Nature* (1984). He is co-editor of *Questions of Evidence* (1992) and *Romantic Metropolis* (2005). Recent publications include *The Cambridge History of British Romantic Literature* (2009, ed.) and, with Maureen McLane, *The Cambridge Companion to British Romantic Poetry* (2008, ed.). He is now finishing a book about the history of the sentimental mode in literature and cinema.

MARTIN EVANS is the William R. Kenan Jr. Professor in the Stanford University Department of English, where he has taught since 1963. His publications include: *Paradise Lost and the Genesis Tradition* (1968), *Paradise Lost IX–X* (Cambridge University Press, 1973), *The Road from Horton: Looking Backward in 'Lycidas'* (1983), *Milton's Imperial Epic* (1996), *The Miltonic Moment* (1998), and *John Milton: Twentieth-Century Perspectives* (2003). He was selected by the Milton Society of America as Honored Scholar for 2004.

ROLAND GREENE is Mark Pigott OBE Professor in the School of Humanities and Sciences, Stanford University. He is the author and editor of several books on early modern literature and poetics, most recently *Unrequited*

Conquests: Love and Empire in the Colonial Americas (1999). His recent work concerns the baroque, the relations between landscape and rhetoric in the colonial period, and early modern cultural semantics.

ACHSAH GUIBBORY, Professor of English at Barnard College, is the editor of the *Cambridge Companion to John Donne* (2006). She is the author of numerous articles on Donne and seventeenth-century English literature and culture, as well as *The Map of Time: Seventeenth-Century English Literature and Ideas of Pattern in History* (1986) and *Ceremony and Community from Herbert to Milton: Literature, Religion, and Cultural Conflict in Seventeenth-Century England* (1998; paperback, 2006).

DAVID HOPKINS is Professor of English Literature at the University of Bristol. Among his recent publications are the Longman Annotated Poets edition of Dryden (with Paul Hammond, 5 volumes, 1995–2005; one-volume selection, 2007) and (with Stuart Gillespie) an edited facsimile of *The Dryden–Tonson Miscellanies, 1684–1709* (2008).

SIMON JARVIS is Gorley Putt Professor of Poetry and Poetics at the University of Cambridge and a Fellow of Robinson College. He is the author of *Scholars and Gentlemen: Shakespearian Textual Criticism and Representations of Scholarly Labour, 1725–1765* (1995), *Adorno: Critical Introduction* (Cambridge University Press, 1998), and *Wordsworth's Philosophic Song* (Cambridge University Press, 2007), as well as of many articles on Wordsworth, on prosody, and on philosophical aesthetics. He is currently working on a study of Pope's versification.

ALAN JENKINS is deputy editor and poetry editor at the *Times Literary Supplement*. He has taught creative writing in England, France, and the United States. Volumes of his poetry include *Harm* (Forward Prize for Best Collection, 1994), *The Drift* (2000), *A Shorter Life* (2005), and *The Lost World* (2010). His edition of *Ian Hamilton: Collected Poems* was published in 2009.

JAMES LONGENBACH is the author of several books of poems, including *Draft of a Letter* (2007), and several works of criticism, including *Stone Cottage: Pound, Yeats, and Modernism* (1988) and *The Resistance to Poetry* (2004). He is the Joseph H. Gilmore Professor of English at the University of Rochester.

RICHARD A. MCCABE is Professor of English Language and Literature at Oxford University and a Fellow of Merton College. He was elected Fellow of the British Academy in 2007. He is author of *Joseph Hall: A Study in Satire and Meditation* (1982), *The Pillars of Eternity: Time and

Providence in 'The Faerie Queene' (1989), *Incest, Drama, and Nature's Law 1550–1700* (1993), and *Spenser's Monstrous Regiment: Elizabethan Ireland and the Poetics of Difference* (2002, 2005). He has edited *Edmund Spenser: The Shorter Poems* (1999) and, with Howard Erskine-Hill, *Presenting Poetry: Composition, Publication, Reception* (1995). He is currently editing the forthcoming *Oxford Handbook of Edmund Spenser* and working on a monograph on patronage.

EDWARD MENDELSON is Lionel Trilling Professor in the Humanities at Columbia University and the literary executor of the Estate of W. H. Auden. His books include *Early Auden* (1981), *Later Auden* (1999), and *The Things That Matter: What Seven Classic Novels Have to Say about the Stages of Life* (2006).

J. HILLIS MILLER is UCI Distinguished Research Professor at the University of California at Irvine. His most recent books are *Literature as Conduct: Speech Acts in Henry James* (2005), *For Derrida* (2009), and *The Medium is the Maker* (2009). *The Conflagration of Community: Fiction Before and After Auschwitz* is forthcoming in 2011. He has published many books and essays about nineteenth- and twentieth-century literature and about literary theory. He is a Fellow of the American Academy of Arts and Sciences and a member of the American Philosophical Society, and received the MLA Lifetime Scholarly Achievement Award in 2005.

KARL MILLER was literary editor of the *Spectator* and the *New Statesman* and editor of the *Listener*. He founded and for several years edited the *London Review of Books*. From 1976 to 1992 he was Lord Northcliffe Professor of Modern English Literature at University College London. His books include *Cockburn's Millennium* (1975), *Doubles* (1985), *Rebecca's Vest* (1993), and *Electric Shepherd* (2003).

MICHAEL NORTH is Professor of English at the University of California, Los Angeles. His most recent books are *Camera Works: Photography and the Twentieth-Century Word* (2005), *Reading 1922: A Return to the Scene of the Modern* (1999), and the Norton Critical Edition of T. S. Eliot's *The Waste Land* (2001).

MORTON D. PALEY has written extensively on Romantic-period writers and artists. Among his books are *Samuel Taylor Coleridge and the Fine Arts* (2008), *The Traveller in the Evening: The Last Works of William Blake* (2003), *Coleridge's Later Poetry* (1996), *The Apocalyptic Sublime* (1986), and *Apocalypse and Millennium in English Romantic Poetry* (1999). He has been awarded two Guggenheim Fellowships, the Distinguished

Scholar Award of the Keats–Shelley Association of America, and an Andrew F. Mellon Foundation Emeritus Fellowship. He is co-editor of *Blake: An Illustrated Quarterly*.

MARJORIE PERLOFF is Sadie D. Patek Professor Emerita of Humanities at Stanford University and Florence R. Scott Professor Emerita at the University of Southern California. She is the author of many books on twentieth-century poetry and poetics, including *The Poetics of Indeterminacy: Rimbaud to Cage* (1981), *The Futurist Moment* (1986), *Wittgenstein's Ladder: The Strangeness of the Ordinary* (1996), *Differentials: Poetry, Poetics, Pedagogy* (2004), a cultural memoir, *The Vienna Paradox* (2004) and, most recently, *Unoriginal Genius: Poetry by Other Means in the New Century*.

SEAMUS PERRY is a Fellow of Balliol College and a Lecturer in the English Faculty at the University of Oxford. His books include *Coleridge and the Uses of Division* (1999), *Alfred Tennyson* (2005), and a selected edition of *Coleridge's Notebooks* (2002). He is an editor of the Oxford journal *Essays in Criticism*.

LINDA H. PETERSON is Niel Gray, Jr. Professor of English at Yale University. She has written *Victorian Autobiography* (1986), *Traditions of Victorian Women's Autobiography: The Poetics and Politics of Life Writing* (1999), and *Becoming a Woman of Letters: Myths of Authorship, Facts of the Market*. She has edited *The Life of Charlotte Brontë* by Elizabeth Gaskell for *The Complete Works of Elizabeth Gaskell* (2006) and Harriet Martineau's *Autobiography* (2007).

CLAUDE RAWSON is Maynard Mack Professor of English at Yale University and general editor of the Cambridge Edition of the Works of Jonathan Swift. His publications on Swift include *Gulliver and the Gentle Reader* (1973), *Order from Confusion Sprung* (1985), and *God, Gulliver, and Genocide* (2001). He is the editor, with Ian Higgins, of the Oxford World's Classics *Gulliver's Travels* (2005) and of the Norton Critical Edition of *Essential Writings of Jonathan Swift* (2009).

PETER ROBINSON is Professor of English and American Literature at the University of Reading. He is the author of many books of poetry, translations, and literary criticism, including *Selected Poems* (2003), *Twentieth Century Poetry: Selves and Situations* (2005), *Selected Poetry and Prose of Vittorio Sereni* (2006), *The Greener Meadow: Selected Poems of Luciano Erba* (2007), *The Look of Goodbye: Poems 2001–2006* (2008), *Poetry and Translation: The Art of the Impossible* (2010), and *English Nettles and Other Poems*.

NIGEL SMITH is Professor of English and Director of the Center for the Study of Books and Media at Princeton University. He is the author of *Perfection Proclaimed: Language and Literature in English Radical Religion 1640–1660* (1989), *Literature and Revolution in England, 1640–1660* (1994), and *Is Milton Better than Shakespeare?* (2008). He has edited Andrew Marvell's *Poems* in the Longman Annotated English Poets series (2003, 2006) as well as the Ranter tracts and George Fox's *Journal*. A biography of Andrew Marvell is forthcoming.

HERBERT F. TUCKER teaches at the University of Virginia, where he is John C. Coleman Professor, associate editor of *New Literary History*, and series co-editor in Victorian literature and culture for the University Press. His books include *Tennyson and the Doom of Romanticism* (1988) and *Critical Essays on Alfred Lord Tennyson* (1993, ed.). To his 1991 and 1992 articles on *Idylls of the King* he has lately added several discussions included in *Epic: Britain's Heroic Muse 1790–1910* (2008). Leading arguments from that book inform his chapter on 'Epic' in the forthcoming Victorian volume (ed. Kate Flint) of the new *Cambridge History of English Literature*.

HELEN WILCOX is Professor of English at Bangor University, Wales, and Director of the Institute for Medieval and Early Modern Studies at the universities of Aberystwyth and Bangor. She has published widely on Herbert's poetry and its reception, and is the editor of the fully annotated *English Poems of George Herbert*, published by Cambridge University Press in 2007. Her further research interests are in early modern autobiography, seventeenth-century women's writing, and Shakespeare. She is currently completing an edition of *All's Well That Ends Well* for the Arden Shakespeare Third Series.

SUSAN J. WOLFSON, Professor of English at Princeton University, is the editor of *The Cambridge Companion to Keats* (2002) and editions of Keats, Mary Shelley's *Frankenstein*, and Felicia Hemans. She has published widely on writers, issues, and texts in British Romanticism. Her books include *Formal Charges: The Shaping of Poetry* (1997) and *Borderlines: The Shiftings of Gender* (2006), and *Romantic Interactions* (2010).

PREFACE AND ACKNOWLEDGEMENTS

The idea of this volume is to provide lively and authoritative introductions to twenty-nine of the most important British and Irish poets writing in English. The list is a mainstream or 'traditional' one, running from Chaucer to Larkin, and might be said non-controversially to include some of the best poetry in the world. The selection is restricted to poets of what used to be called the British Isles, though one or two exceptions have been allowed, where there is dual nationality or a distinct and historical British identity, as in the variously special cases of Eliot and Auden. No living writer has been included, as in the case of the parallel *Cambridge Companion to English Novelists*, in accordance with the practice of this series of Cambridge Companions.

I have incurred many debts. My assistant Cynthia Ingram has contributed more to the shaping of this book than I can easily describe. Colleagues and friends who have given help and advice include Linda Bree, Colin Burrow, Achsah Guibbory, Stephen Karian, James McLaverty, Ed Mendelson, Marjorie Perloff, Maartje Scheltens, James Woolley, and John Worthen.

Claude Rawson

CLAUDE RAWSON

Introduction

This volume begins with Geoffrey Chaucer, whom Dryden called 'the Father of *English* Poetry'.[1] Although there is a distinguished tradition of Old and Middle English poetry, from the eighth-century epic *Beowulf* to the anonymous chivalric romance of *Sir Gawain and the Green Knight* in Chaucer's own time, Chaucer occupies a special place. He had, long before Dryden, been regarded (in the words of the sixteenth-century rhetorician George Puttenham) as holding 'the first place' and 'as the most renowmed' of the earlier English poets.[2] He was one of the first to use the word 'poete' in English, applying it to the Italians Dante and Petrarch, as well as to the classical writers Virgil and Lucan. Though he did not use it of himself, or other English writers, he was called poet by others in the sense in which he himself spoke of the great foreign masters as poets. He is, in J. A. Burrow's description, the first English poet with a distinct personality and a substantial body of work.[3]

Puttenham's *Arte of English Poesie* (1589) appeared four years before Shakespeare's first poem, *Venus and Adonis* (1593), from the same printer, Richard Field.[4] Like other poets of his time, Shakespeare wrote with a conscious awareness of the forms and devices codified in rhetorical handbooks like Puttenham's, an example of the interplay between poetic expressiveness and a set of technical prescriptions which is part of the tension between creativity, convention, and constraint in the poetic process. The application of stylistic formulae and 'rules', as well as the 'imitation' of earlier poets, were seen as strengths in a way not always appreciated in a later intellectual climate, whose standards emphasize the importance of original genius (though Shakespeare is not often denied the possession of that faculty).

Even if the dates had made it possible, however, Shakespeare was unlikely to have been a candidate for extended discussion in Puttenham's treatise, whose brief considerations of drama mention some Greek and Latin playwrights, but reflect a contemptuous view of popular entertainments, of 'the schoole of common players' and the 'lasciuious' matter 'vttered by ... buffons or vices in playes'.[5] The fact that the greatest poet in the language is chiefly admired by posterity for his plays, and that it is in these plays that his greatest poetry is to be found, would not have qualified Shakespeare for official recognition in a learned discussion of poetry. David Bevington points out that writing plays had something of the status of ephemeral scriptwriting for film or television today. It was done for money rather than reputation. Sir Thomas Bodley expressly excluded plays, as 'idle bookes, & riffe raffes', from the Bodleian Library at Oxford (founded 1602), so that a wealth of quartos was passed over in spite of an agreement of 1610 that one free copy of each book registered with the Stationers' Company would be deposited in the library.[6] Though his name on the title-page of a play was sometimes considered a marketable asset, Shakespeare did not attach much importance to the publication of his plays, and seems to have preferred to be regarded as a poet, not a playwright.[7]

Poetry, as the oldest of verbal arts, has always enjoyed a privileged status, above the more popular media. (This may seem paradoxical if we remember that poetry has often been linked with the earliest or most primitive forms of human expression.) When, three centuries after Shakespeare, Thomas Hardy was questioned about giving up novel-writing, he declared that he wanted 'to be remembered as a poet', a position provocatively reversed in Auden's remark in 'A Letter to Lord Byron' (1936) that 'novel writing is / A higher art than poetry altogether'.[8] Auden's witty contrariness tends if anything to confirm a prevailing sense of poetry's elite status, in a downbeat oracular mode to which he sometimes reverted ('poetry makes nothing happen').[9]

The example of Hardy's poems shows the large trace of narrative fiction in poetry, including lyric poetry, ever since the emergence of the novel as a major form of literary expression, a lowly Cinderella medium growing to princely status through creative evolution rather than, as in the case of Elizabethan drama, through a process of critical awakening. Much of English poetry since the eighteenth century, including lyrics by Hardy and Auden, and satirical scenes by Eliot, tell or imply a story with partially visible novelistic contours, in a manner quite distinct from the non-narrative verse of lyric or satiric poets before 1750. The same is true of the wry lyrics of Philip Larkin, the last poet treated in this book, who was also the author of two novels in his early years, and wanted to be a novelist rather than a poet, unlike his friend the novelist Kingsley Amis, who, reversing Auden's words, thought poetry the 'higher art'.[10]

Neither this fact, nor the roll-call of novelistic masters summoned up by Auden's 'Letter to Lord Byron', changes the reality of poetry's special place in the literature of all periods. Shakespeare's wish that his reputation should rest on his poems, though triumphantly overridden by the plays, guided what we know of his chosen mode of self-promotion. The only two works he published with dedications that bear his signature were not his sonnets (now the most admired of his non-dramatic works) but his two Ovidian poems, *Venus and Adonis* and *The Rape of Lucrece* (1594).

The Rape of Lucrece was on a theme Chaucer had also treated, in *The Legend of Good Women*, and written in the stanza-form known as rhyme royal, which Chaucer used in *Troilus and Criseyde*, itself a source of Shakespeare's *Troilus and Cressida* (*c.*1602), his play set in the Trojan War. *The Rape of Lucrece* itself includes an extended account of a tapestry or painting (lines 1366–1568) depicting the Trojan War, which brings out the treachery of the Greek Sinon (lines 1520ff.) and portrays Helen as 'the strumpet that began this stir' (line 1471).[11] This in turn looks forward to the later description of Helen, in *Troilus and Cressida*, as 'a pearl / Whose price hath launched a thousand ships, / And turned crown'd kings to merchants' (II. ii. 80–2), sarcastically rephrasing a famous line in Marlowe's *Dr. Faustus*, which is itself probably echoing a Chorus from Aeschylus's *Oresteia*.[12] Shakespeare's critiques of the heroic ethos, expressed especially in his plays on classical themes, are often bitter. They do not constitute an unvarying rejection of grand styles or even heroic themes, but they put the latter under a degree of critical pressure which later made Shakespeare a model for plays by Jarry, Brecht, and Ionesco, creating a more ambivalent 'heroic' standard than the epics of Homer and Virgil had provided, until the eighteenth century, for writers portraying the decline of heroic values in modern times.

Shakespeare himself never wrote or attempted an epic, though his poems were reprinted more often than any of his plays, and he had a serious reputation as a non-dramatic poet in his lifetime. When Shakespeare dedicated *Venus and Adonis* to the Earl of Southampton, he promised that it would be followed 'with some graver labour', a gesture which might be thought to carry some suggestion of a future great work, possibly of the epic kind, though Shakespeare seems to have been alluding to *The Rape of Lucrece*.[13] (The *Sonnets*, 1609, nowadays regarded as his greatest non-dramatic achievement, may have been published without Shakespeare's cooperation.)[14] The Virgilian *cursus*, a poetic progress from the lowly genre of pastoral to the heights of poetic accomplishment in a great national epic, was not Shakespeare's pathway to greatness, though it was a common aspiration for Renaissance poets, and expressly and self-consciously adopted by both Spenser and Milton. As late as Pope, who made his literary debut by publishing four *Pastorals* in 1709, exactly a century after the publication of Shakespeare's *Sonnets*, the epic aspiration was visibly advertised, and though Pope never completed an epic either, the ambition remained to the end of his life. In Pope's lifetime, it was Milton, the author of *Paradise Lost*, and not Shakespeare, who had the status of an honorary classic, named and used as a live poetic model alongside Homer and Virgil. At the time of his 'Preface to Shakespeare' (1765), Samuel Johnson thought Shakespeare was beginning, through the passage of time, to acquire 'the dignity of an ancient'.[15] As the classical hierarchy of literary genres gradually loosened, Shakespeare's reputation as the great national poet, not only of England but of humanity (if the paradox may be permitted), began to develop.

Milton was the last great European poet successfully to fashion his career on the Virgilian programme, though his way of doing so was characteristically conflicted, one of several intellectual and spiritual oppositions (between his Puritan religious convictions and a profoundly humanist outlook, or his political radicalism and a deep attachment to classical values and traditional literary forms) which mark Milton's imagination.[16] He expressed at the age of nineteen his ambitions as a poet, the ultimate or 'last' of which was to sing 'of Kings and Queens and Hero's old', on the model of the bard at King Alcinous's court in Homer's *Odyssey*, and spoke more than once of future epic plans, whether on a national (Arthurian) theme or a classical or scriptural subject.[17] When *Paradise Lost* (1667–74) appeared, the last great epic in the Homeric-Virgilian manner, it embodied a stinging attack on the epic for its celebration of martial valour and battlefield carnage. Milton's creation of an epic that rejected the epic was responding to a moment when anti-war sentiment, and a variety of other social and cultural forces, were making it impossible for good poets to write epics, as for example the great poets of the two succeeding generations, Dryden and Pope, also aspired, but unlike Milton failed, to do. Milton's War in Heaven in *Paradise Lost*, VI, where no one gets hurt in human terms because they are celestial beings 'incapable of mortal injurie', provided a blueprint for English mock-heroic, which tended to be more protective of the high epic, with its tarnished militarist reputation, than Milton was himself.[18]

Neither Dryden nor Pope completed an epic, however, and both displaced the epic impulse in translations of Virgil and Homer, writing epics as it were by proxy, or in mock-heroic poems in which high styles could to some extent be preserved behind a cordon sanitaire of irony. The mock-heroic, in *Mac Flecknoe* and later in Pope's *Dunciad*, attempts (as Dryden suggested in his 'Discourse Concerning Satire' of 1693) to retain the majesty of heroic originals even as it misapplies them to subheroic subjects.[19] Throughout its brief history as a dominant literary form, mock-heroic attempted to transcend the parodic joke that brought it into being, and never quite succeeded, though it achieved exceptional triumphs of its own. As Auden said, '*The Dunciad* is not only a great poem but also the only poem in English which is at once comic and sublime.'[20] The attempt to find a style commensurate with the epic, which could only be found in satirical imitations of the epic, coexisted with an urge to jettison the satiric note. This, in turn, could only be achieved when the epic impulse itself ceased to exercise its ambivalent and contending pressures. We see the result in Johnson's *Vanity of Human Wishes* and the learned allusive gravity of Eliot's *Waste Land*. The grim urban sublimities of Baudelaire's Paris and T. S. Eliot's London have a significant kinship with the lofty disorders of Dryden's Barbican and the London of the *Dunciad*, as Eliot himself recognized.[21]

The epic was a principal poetic repository for elevated styles, which sometimes imitated the grammatical inflections as well as the rhetorical formulae of the Greek and Latin poets. As the sustainability of epic style became problematic, an important resource of eloquence became increasingly unavailable to poets. Milton had every intention of retaining epic grandeur when he rejected epic morality, and he forged a style that accentuated a Latinized syntax and diction whose eccentric majesty proceeded from a combination of archaism, exotically elaborate syntax remote from colloquial usage, and an orchestration of emphases more natural to the periodic structure of Latin sentences than to the forms of English speech.

The opening sentence of *Paradise Lost* runs to sixteen lines:

> Of Man's First Disobedience, and the Fruit
> Of that Forbidden Tree, whose mortal tast
> Brought Death into the World, and all our woe,
> With loss of *Eden*, till one greater Man
> Restore us, and regain the blissful Seat,
> Sing Heav'nly Muse, that on the secret top
> Of *Oreb*, or of *Sinai*, didst inspire
> That Shepherd, who first taught the chosen Seed,
> In the Beginning how the Heav'ns and Earth
> Rose out of *Chaos*: or if *Sion* Hill
> Delight thee more, and *Siloa*'s Brook that flow'd
> Fast by the Oracle of God; I thence
> Invoke thy aid to my adventrous Song,
> That with no middle flight intends to soar
> Above th' *Aonian* Mount, while it pursues
> Things unattempted yet in Prose or Rhime. (I. 1–16)

This style, in which the conclusions or finalities are delayed by an intricate syntactical elaboration, has been compared to musical orchestrations. We are held in suspense for the first six lines as to what is to be done or said of man's first disobedience, until the Heav'nly Muse is instructed to 'sing' this great theme. The capacious digressiveness of the entire sixteen-line passage, full of apparent diversions, fresh starts, and afterthoughts, is an extended preparation for the bold finality of 'Things unattempted yet in Prose or Rhime' (16). The claim itself is less an expression of poetic arrogance than an assertion of the grandeur of the poem's theme. It is perhaps the last time such a claim would be made by a serious poet without irony, and it is arguable that Ariosto, the earlier Italian poet Milton was echoing almost word for word, had himself used the words with an extravagant and un-Miltonic flourish of self-irony (*Orlando Furioso*, I. ii. 2).

There is no sign of self-irony in Milton's righteous confidence in 'the highth' of his 'great Argument' (I. 23–4). Nor is there any self-doubt in the prefatory claim that his poetic 'measure', namely 'English *Heroic Verse without Rime, as that of* Homer *in* Greek *and of* Virgil *in* Latin', is an affirmation '*of ancient liberty recover'd to Heroic Poem from the troublesom and modern bondage of Rimeing*' ('The Verse'). Milton was experiencing irritation at the growing vogue of the heroic couplet which had acquired a revived currency, and a fresh allure of polished correctness, partly modelled on the urbanity of seventeenth-century France, which Milton regarded as a 'jingling' courtier foppery. Milton deplored this new correctness, which he identified with a post-Restoration Frenchified tyranny. His militant adoption of 'English *Heroic Verse without Rime*' for *Paradise Lost* was not only a return to classical decencies (Homer and Virgil, he reminds us, did not use rhyme), but a cry of freedom from a '*troublesom and modern bondage*'. Pope, referring some forty years later to two contemporaries of Milton who wrote couplets, spoke by contrast of the urbane freedom of the couplet, of 'the *Easie Vigor* of a Line / Where *Denham*'s Strength, and *Waller*'s Sweetness join'.[22] The 'easie vigour' of couplets coexists with, and depends on, a tight metrical order. It differs from Milton's rigorously controlled syntactical elaborations, but the verse of *Paradise Lost* displays an almost ostentatious fluidity of its own in avoiding the couplet's end-stopped metre. The enjambment (or continuation of the sentence beyond the end of the line), a metrical looseness proscribed by French purists like Boileau and discouraged among the practitioners of 'correct' couplets in English, is used with determination from the start.

Pope subjected Milton's practice of enjambment to genial loyalist parody. Describing his heroine Belinda's two locks of hair, one of which is going to be 'raped' (stolen), he wrote:

> This Nymph, to the Destruction of Mankind,
> Nourish'd two Locks, which graceful hung behind
> In equal Curls, and well conspir'd to deck
> With shining Ringlets the smooth Iv'ry Neck.
>
> (*Rape of the Lock*, II. 19–22)

The trick is in contrast to the self-contained sense structures expected of the couplet, and exemplified here in the relaxed but disciplined closure of the fourth line. A more audacious mimicry occurs in the cloacal episode in Book II of the *Dunciad*, quoted below in another connection.[23] Neither *The Rape of the Lock* nor the *Dunciad* is attacking Milton, who is treated in both poems, alongside Homer and Virgil, as a primary model for a loyalist parody, deriding not the epic itself, but a lowered modern reality exposed by grandeurs of style which are no longer appropriate to it. But in mimicking the Miltonic trick, Pope is also signalling that his own correct couplets are a norm which he could playfully violate in affectionate parody, though it is only right to observe that when, at the very end of his life, Pope contemplated an epic on Brutus, the mythical founder of Britain, the few lines that survive of the attempt are in a Miltonizing blank verse, modified by some end-stopped unrhymed pentameters.[24]

Pope, the greatest master of the English couplet, rephrased Milton's claim to 'justify the ways of God to men' (*Paradise Lost*, I. 26) in the 1730s with all the tight syntactical, metrical, and rhyming symmetries Milton himself had deplored almost seventy years before:

> Laugh where we must, be candid where we can;
> But vindicate the ways of God to Man.
>
> (*Essay on Man*, I. 15–16)

Pope was being corrective rather than subversive of Milton. Milton's scorn of being 'tagged' in this manner would have matched all the arrogance of couplet superiority implied by Pope's practice.

Auden spoke of blank verse as the heroic couplet's 'only serious rival in English verse as a standard form'.[25] Shakespeare and Milton used both in varying degrees, and both are forms of the decasyllabic or ten-syllable line which has long been the normative metre in English poetry. T. S. Eliot once observed that much English verse, however 'free', is written in its shadow or played off against this presumptive norm.[26] Its notional iambic beat (in which each 'foot' is accented in the second syllable) exists, like all prescribed rhythms, in tension with the natural cadences of speech and the movement of feeling. This is true even (or perhaps especially) within the stricter constraints of the rhymed couplet, which seems first to have been used in the *Canterbury Tales*, but was brought to its most exquisite perfection by Pope. This tension becomes evident if we try to read Pope's couplets according to strict metronomic prescription, accenting each second syllable as below:

> Know thén thysélf, presúme not Gód to scán;
> The próper stúdy óf Mankínd is Mán.
>
> (Pope, *Essay on Man*, II. 1–2)

No one with an ear for the English language would read the lines strictly according to the stresses indicated by the presumed iambic beat. At the same time no natural reading of the lines is free of an unspoken relation to this presumed beat, and the unceasing silent conversation between the prescribed and the actual or natural cadences is an essential element of the vitality of poetic expression.

Eliot's view that metrical 'freedom is only truly freedom when it appears against the background of an artificial limitation' is put under acute pressure in the chapter on that poet.[27] Such sweeping pronouncements can never be absolute. Eliot occasionally contradicted himself on such issues. Nevertheless the principle retains a broad validity, even in relation to so-called 'free verse', whose rhythms, when not formally played against an identifiable traditional metre, are shaped by nuanced imitations of such metres, 'unheard' cadences that answer to the emphases of meaning and emotion. Eliot said in 1917 that any 'so-called *vers libre* which is good is anything but "free"'.[28] Eliot's own best poems, from 'The Love Song of J. Alfred Prufrock' to *The Waste Land*, show a constant dialogue between strict metrical forms and more variable and unprogrammed rhythms. Of the poets discussed in this volume, Lawrence, as Marjorie Perloff writes, was the most insistent in complaining that 'the constriction of fixed verse forms was inhibiting', but his own poems often accept the constrictions or are played off against them.[29]

The English couplet, in the form in which Pope perfected it, and stamped it as the dominant style for his age, had become fashionable in Milton's day, in the teeth of Milton's dislike of it, in the work of Waller, Denham, and Dryden. As Milton seems to have felt, it was to some extent a French import. Although the metre had existed since Chaucer, it acquired some of its formal allure (symmetry, antithesis, strictness of metre and rhyme) from the twelve-syllable alexandrine practised by Racine and Boileau, and served as a manifest icon of correctness, urbanity, and order. The famous sketch by Boileau of French poetic history (*Art Poétique*, I. 111–46) was rewritten with English examples by Dryden and Soame (1683). Boileau's announcement of the arrival of correctness ('Enfin Malherbe vint', I. 131) was changed in the English narrative to: '*Waller* came last, but was the first whose Art / Just Weight and Measure did to Verse impart.'[30]

In reality, the couplet differed from the alexandrine as much as it resembled it, and English attitudes towards the French model were ambivalent. It served as a cultural analogue, evoking order and politeness. But Dryden thought the French metre was intrinsically weaker than the English. The use of occasional alexandrines by English poets, including Dryden himself, as an ornamental flourish or as closure for sequences of pentameter couplets, was sometimes mocked.[31] Swift parodied the 'licentious Manner of modern

Poets' (meaning especially Dryden) for their use of rhyming 'triplets', in which 'the last of the three [lines], was two ... Syllables longer, called an *Alexandrian*'.[32] Adam Smith noted that the alexandrine, the official serious metre of French poetry, which is the French counterpart to the English heroic couplet, generally produces bathos in English verse, as the pentameter often does in French.[33]

There is a sense in which the Augustan couplet, for all its French allure, was thought of as an English metre. Samuel Wesley, who took pride in 1700 in belonging to 'our *Augustan* days', affirmed the superiority of the English metre: 'More *num'rous* the *Pentameter* and *strong*'.[34] By this he meant the modern refined and metrically stricter version. Like Pope and others, he found Chaucer's couplets unpolished.[35] The normative pressure of the pentameter in English has been such that other metres, both shorter and longer (the eight-syllable tetrameter, for example, as well as the alexandrine, or the eleven-syllable, hendecasyllabic, line often practised in English 'light' verse, notably by Swift),[36] have, with certain exceptions, tended to be restricted to less serious genres.[37] Roland Greene describes how, 'between the death of Chaucer *c.*1400 and the publication of *Tottel's Miscellany* in 1557, iambic pentameter, the dominant line in English verse, was often unsettled as poets – knowingly or not – experimented with varying arrangements of stresses and syllables'. Wyatt, whom he describes as 'perhaps the last poet of that phase', seemed 'ignorant or clumsy' to contemporaries, and his poems were subject to metrical regularization in Tottel's anthology.[38]

In fact, the tug of war between metrical constraint and deregulation has never ceased or even stood still. The phase of regularization associated with Tottel was itself temporary, a living and properly unstable phase in a natural process. In the 1590s, when Donne composed his five 'Satyres' (not published until 1633), a much less regulated view of the iambic pentameter is in evidence. He is writing, in Satyre II, about poetry and poets:

> One, (like a wretch, which at Barre judg'd as dead,
> Yet prompts him which stands next, and cannot reade,
> And saves his life) gives ideot actors meanes
> (Starving himselfe) to live by'his labor'd sceanes;
> As in some Organ, Puppits dance above
> And bellows pant below, which them do move.
> One would move Love by rimes, but witchcrafts charms
> Bring not now their old feares, nor their old harmes:
> Rammes, and slings now are seely battery,
> Pistolets are the best Artillerie.
> And they who write to Lords, rewards to get,
> Are they not like singers at doores for meat? (Satyre II, 11–22)[39]

The metre of the lines is so dislocated, the rhymes so deliberately 'inexact' (in a manner less like the comic rhyming of Swift or Byron than the painful dissonances of Wilfred Owen and other modern poets), the syntax so gnarled and tortuous, that it comes as a jolt to modern readers to realize that the formal metre, even of this poem, is the iambic pentameter, and indeed the rhyming couplet. Donne's satiric manner was developed partly under the influence of a widespread notion (still subscribed to by Puttenham) that satire derived from the part-bestial woodland deities known as satyrs, who made up the chorus of Greek satyr plays (like Euripides's *Cyclops*). But it was also largely modelled on the 'difficult' Roman poet Persius, known for a thrusting, dislocated, and cryptic style, as well as on the harshness of Juvenal.[40]

Donne's decision to frame such stylistic purposes in a metrical form whose boundaries it restlessly defies or transgresses was itself overtaken throughout the ensuing century by a progressive tightening and purification of the rhyming couplet, culminating in Pope. Here is how Pope 'translated' Donne's lines:

> Here a lean Bard, whose wit could never give
> Himself a dinner, makes an Actor live:
> The Thief condemn'd, in law already dead,
> So prompts, and saves a Rogue who cannot read.
> Thus as the pipes of some carv'd Organ move,
> The gilded Puppets dance and mount above,
> Heav'd by the breath th'inspiring Bellows blow;
> Th'inspiring Bellows lie and pant below.
> One sings the Fair; but Songs no longer move,
> No Rat is rhym'd to death, nor Maid to love:
> In Love's, in Nature's spite, the siege they hold,
> And soon the Flesh, the Dev'l, and all but Gold.
> These write to Lords, some mean reward to get,
> As needy Beggars sing at doors for meat.
>
> (Pope, *Donne's Second Satyre*, 13–26)

This version was written around 1713, and published with revisions a century after Donne's, in 1735–40, as *The Second Satire of Dr. John Donne, ... Versifyed*. Pope had given the same treatment to the Fourth Satire (published 1733) and also published his friend Thomas Parnell's version of the Third Satire in 1738, with the subtitle 'Versifyed by Dr. PARNELLE. In Imitation of Mr. POPE' added in 1739.[41] 'Versifyed' in all these subtitles expresses the full arrogance of a cultural superiority towards a poetic disorderliness which, though powerfully in control of its recording of turbulent doings and states of mind, appears to fall short of a newer conception of order and politeness, precisely the phenomenon Milton was already deploring in 1668. Pope has introduced lucidities and symmetries of syntax and metre which Donne had no concern for, imposing summations and finalities where Donne renders the raw heavings of a restless human absurdity. Like Donne, Pope alludes to folk beliefs and satirical magic, but wants us to know with an even more emphatic aplomb that they no longer have their old force ('No Rat is rhym'd to death', a power attributed to Irish bards). The underlying formal evocation of a satyr's roughness has been ironed out, and the crabbed obscurities from Persius are homogenized to a contemporary English idea of Horatian urbanity (whose original model had been described, not without irony, by Persius himself, an irony that Dryden elaborated into a famous phrase about Horace's 'sly, insinuating Grace'; Persius, I. 116–18; Dryden, trs. I. 228–30).

For all Milton's status as a venerated model, the heroic couplet became established as the dominant style for serious English verse in the hands of Waller (1606–87) and Denham (1615–69), and then, more triumphantly, of Dryden and Pope. Pope especially made sure that it continued so, as part of the apparatus of his own publicized pre-eminence. When he wrote his *Imitations of Horace* in the 1730s, part of his agenda was to create continuities that established him, with precisely calibrated qualifications and adjustments, as a major poet in a great classical tradition. The genre of 'imitation' had become, especially since the Restoration, a regular mode of self-definition for modern poets by means of a sophisticated allusive dialogue with ancient predecessors.

Pope was simultaneously affirming an English tradition of correctness and polite letters. His perfecting of the couplet, from the brilliant discursive vitality of the *Essay on Criticism* (1711) to the triumphs of character observation in the satires of the 1730s and the sombre resonances of the dark negative epic of the *Dunciad*, is one of the high achievements of English poetry. The elements of cultural snobbery and self-serving reputation-management which are sometimes associated with it take little away from the substantive achievement. Nevertheless, Pope's standing went into a decline at the hands of the Romantic poets (excluding Byron), from which it has never fully recovered, though a revived understanding of his greatness was re-established in the last century.

The couplet, however, acquired a reputation for metronomic monotony which does little justice to the variety and delicacy of Pope's uses of that form. The sense of containment of unruly energies which it offers in the satiric portraits of Dryden and Pope has not answered to the demands of later outlooks. T. S. Eliot, whose *Waste Land* partly originally contained a pastiche of *The Rape of the Lock*, discarded (on Pound's advice) as an unsuccessful attempt at Popeian couplets, offers an interesting and conflicted case history.[42] In 1917, five years before the publication of *The Waste Land*, Eliot wrote that 'the heroic couplet has lost none of its edge since Dryden and Pope laid it down', and that the form was only awaiting 'the coming of a Satirist – no man of genius is rarer'.[43] What was in Milton's day assumed to be the default metre for serious verse, to the extent of provoking Milton's statement of defiance, had now been reshaped in Pope's shadow, as a metre proper to satire in a high sense (though Eliot was to become uneasy at acquiring a reputation as a satirist himself, a charge subsequently levelled at him in Yeats's *Oxford Book of Modern Verse*).[44]

Eliot understood that the adoption of the couplet for the rather badly executed Popeian pastiche in *The Waste Land* was misguided, though he thought it 'an excellent set of couplets' at the time. Recollecting that episode in 1928, Eliot remarked 'that the man who cannot enjoy Pope as poetry probably understands no poetry'.[45] But in 1933, having presumably taken Pound's comments to heart, he also said that a 'writer to-day who was genuinely influenced by Pope would hardly want to use that couplet at all'.[46] At all events, the continuing versatility of the couplet has always been manifest in some surprising ways, including the fact that it is the almost 'invisible' metre of Donne's satires, as well as of Pope's 'versifyed' versions. Two and a half centuries after Donne, as J. Hillis Miller points out, the couplet accommodates both the gnarled and obscure energies of Browning's *Sordello* and the insolent conversational bravura of his 'My Last Duchess'. Couplets are used by Eliot himself, often with witty and tactical finesse, throughout the metrically varied 'Portrait of a Lady'. By the same token, Eliot's pronouncement in 'Reflections on *Vers Libre*' (1917) that traditional forms like the sonnet were no longer available to modern poets seems, as Edward Mendelson observes, to have provoked Auden into writing sonnets and indeed sonnet-sequences.[47]

As the epic lost its status as the highest poetic form, the value and even the possibility of the long poem itself came to be questioned, notably by Coleridge, whose oracular pronouncement that 'a poem of any length neither can be, or ought to be, all poetry' was elaborated, in a notorious extended statement, by the American poet Edgar Allan Poe. Poe's argument was that poetic 'intensity' could only be achieved in short bursts, and that a long poem like *Paradise Lost* was in reality a series of short lyrics held together by a connective tissue of versified prose. He also argued that the intensities of *Paradise Lost* might in fact be revealed in varying places in separate readings, so that the realization of a truly poetic moment might be the product of a reader's experience, and not solely of the process of composition or of the poem's intrinsic character. Poe even attempted an arithmetical computation for what he thought of as the optimal length of a poem, coming up with a hundred or so lines, which happened to correspond to the 'hundred and eight' lines of his own poem 'The Raven', the making of which was the subject of his essay 'The Philosophy of Composition' (1846).[48]

Poe's influence on subsequent poetic theory was considerable, if only because the issue of the long poem, though not created by him, sometimes crystallized round his formulations. He made a powerful impression on some French poets, including Baudelaire and Mallarmé, whose limited knowledge of English may have led to an inflated sense of his quality, a view variously held by Yeats, Pound, and Eliot, whose contempt for Poe's verse was stinging (though Eliot expressed the most nuanced view of the three, in an effort at sympathetic understanding of the French poets' view of Poe).[49] But Poe's questionings about the long poem hover insistently in the background of Ezra Pound's oscillating views as to whether a long poem was possible, whether his *Cantos* might count as an epic, and whether the epic ambition was compatible with the sequence of high-intensity local effects he described as 'luminous details'.[50] Even Poe's concern with a permissible arithmetic in the lyric economy of a poem found an echo in the continued preoccupation of Pound and Eliot over the exact length, in pages and lines, of Eliot's *Waste Land*. It is one of the progenitors of Pound's comment that, after the poem had abolished its 'superfluities' and reached its eventual total of '19 pages' (433 lines), *The Waste Land* was 'the longest poem in the Englisch langwidge', and must not be 'prolonged'.[51]

Pound's fluctuations on the subject of the long poem, and the allusive concentration and scope of *The Waste Land*, show the survival of the epic impulse, even as its forms and pretensions are seen to be unsustainable. Both *The Waste Land* and *Cantos* are self-consciously built on 'fragments', acknowledging poetical intensities of perception as having a force or truth denied to the classically ordered and completed work. As early as the middle of the eighteenth century, in fiction and poetry, as well as in antiquarian pseudo-mythologies like the poems of Ossian, the fragment had come to occupy an increasingly privileged place, in some ways comparable to that of lyric, which, by the time of Wordsworth and Coleridge, came to be regarded as among the highest forms of poetic expression. One of the implications of the *Lyrical Ballads*, as described by Wordsworth, is that they were poems in which the feelings gave 'importance to the action and situation', and not the other way round.[52] Not only were story or plot subordinated to 'feeling', but the word 'lyric', originally denoting something sung to the music of the lyre, itself came to imply emotional charge rather than musical accompaniment. The lyric, which occupied a modest place in the hierarchy of literary kinds, was now acquiring a dignity that challenged and overtook that of the epic. As W. K. Wimsatt and Cleanth Brooks have pointed out, a genre which in the seventeenth century might not have rated the name of poem, being referred to perhaps as a mere 'paper of verses', was henceforward to be regarded as a norm of serious poetic expression.[53] When someone says they are writing or reading a poem today, the presumption is that they are referring to a short poem; in the seventeenth century, the associations of the term normally included one of the more formally dignified genres. Matthew Arnold, who fought a rearguard action in the middle of the nineteenth century to re-establish standards of classical form and heroic dignity, complained that English poetry had become corrupted by a brilliance of local effects and single lines, a vice to be identified with Keats among others, and which Arnold attributed largely to the influence of Shakespeare.

The old idea of a poetic progression culminating in the epic could not in a simple sense remain unchanged by these developments. If the centre of poetic value was to be found not in a traditionally ordained genre but in a truth to inner feeling, or if access to universal values was to come from an imagination 'whose fountains are within' (Coleridge, *Dejection*, 46), the growth of a poet's mind would be expected to follow changes in the inward make-up of the poet himself rather than a conventionally prescribed sequence. Growing older, more mature, more learned or more experienced, no longer offered natural pathways for poetic endeavour. From Wordsworth and Coleridge to Yeats, Wallace Stevens, and T. S. Eliot, the notion of a culturally sanctioned progression like that of the Virgilian *cursus* gave way to a model of self-renewal.

It is in the Romantic period that the theme of a crisis of imagination, attendant on the ageing process, or emotional disturbance or exhaustion, becomes a central preoccupation. The predicament of writer's block, treated satirically in Pope's *Dunciad* as a product of untalented pretension, becomes a poignant subject of self-exploration. Wordsworth's and Coleridge's experiences of the loss of the youthful powers of intensity, joy, or creativity threaten their existence as poets. Their poetic survival depends on the ability to find a new, sometimes chastened, voice to match a new inner reality, as in Wordsworth's 'Immortality Ode' (1807) or Yeats's 'The Tower' (1927). Renewal may seem less glamorous than the lost radiance of an earlier state, taking 'a sober colouring from an eye / That hath kept watch o'er man's mortality', altered but offering a new if greyer form of the 'vision splendid' ('Immortality Ode', 197–8, 73). Or it may fail to occur, as in Coleridge's 'Dejection', his counter-poem to Wordsworth's 'Immortality Ode', where the feeling is that poetry has been lost to the poet, giving way to the devitalized pursuits of abstract intellect. Coleridge despairingly called this 'abstruse research' (89). Yeats in 'The Tower' contemplated the possibility that his imagination might become 'content with argument and deal / In abstract things'. After affirming a more defiant resurgence into creativity, a rebellious counterthrust ('I mock Plotinus' thought / And cry in Plato's teeth'), Yeats eventually settles for 'compelling' his soul 'to study / In a learned school', concluding that poetry could be made out of that too. In Yeats, whom James Longenbach describes as a 'notorious remaker of himself', the process was indeed a continuous one, including radical rewriting of old poems ('The Sorrow of Love', 1892, 1925), and poems in dialogue with alternative selves.[54]

The impossibility of writing a poem has become, since the time of Coleridge's 'Dejection', a recurrent preoccupation of later poets, from Tennyson to Larkin.[55] It has been said that writer's block became 'a central theme in the early Romantic period' (the phrase 'writer's block', in its English form, seems to have been coined in the 1940s).[56] The epic inhibition, or awe of classical or Renaissance predecessors, may have seemed daunting to English Augustan writers, but also provided a sense that models existed for 'imitation', though in a scaled-down form, purified by 'correctness' or protected by irony. There is no sense of creative paralysis, a condition which Swift or Pope are quick to deride as the mark of the incompetent and insolvent scribbler, still less a sense of personal travail or defeat, which could itself be the subject of high poetic expression, as in Coleridge's 'Dejection' or even Wordsworth's *Prelude*.[57]

The sense that this experience, painful as it might be, is itself an honourable state, a fit subject for poems, contrasts markedly with the satirized figure of the hack who cannot write, the starving author of Swift's *Tale of a Tub*, or Pope's untalented Laureate, surrounded by the embryos and abortions of his starving Muse:

> Swearing and supperless the Hero sate,
> Blasphem'd his Gods, the Dice, and damn'd his Fate.
> Then gnaw'd his pen, then dash'd it on the ground,
> Sinking from thought to thought, a vast profound!
> Plung'd for his sense, but found no bottom there,
> Yet wrote and flounder'd on, in mere despair.
> Round him much Embryo, much Abortion lay,
> Much future Ode, and abdicated Play.
>
> (*Dunciad*, 1743, I. 115–22)

What for Pope is a comic indignity would become a matter of huge pathos for Coleridge. Here as elsewhere, there is in Pope a satirical intuition of a predicament, viewed as in some sense damagingly 'modern', which was later revalued as a central and honourable element of the writer's condition. (This pessimistic foreshadowing of the modes of modern writing was probably acquired from Pope's old friend and collaborator Jonathan Swift, to whom the *Dunciad* is dedicated, and whose *Tale of a Tub* is purportedly composed by a scribbler who writes about nothing when he has nothing to say. This scribbler's subject-matter is the fact that he is starving in his garret, writing of the present moment in which he is writing, an image of egocentric garrulousness whose trivial ephemerality was soon to be revalued and redefined as the creative immediacy of writing 'to the Moment' in both fiction and poetry.)[58]

The *Dunciad*'s Miltonic abyss of mental vacuity, which for Pope translates into bottomless stupidity, is also a measure of depths of despair, for which the sufferings of Milton's Satan provided a Titanic prototype, variously assimilated by Romantic poets in portrayals of their own interior states. Pope's *Dunciad* is about the disintegration of a culture, not personal defeat (its great descendant, Eliot's *Waste Land*, was to combine the two themes). The Laureate who can't write is the culpable symptom of this disintegration, not an innocent victim, still less a morally victorious martyr. In the generation of Swift and Pope, poverty and poetry had none of the honorific flavour bestowed on the conjunction by the Bohemian cultures of the nineteenth century, when that high place of poets, the garret, was 'boasted of', in Yeats's words, by young men 'in Paris and in London', who 'claimed to have no need of what the crowd values'.[59] In Swift's *Tale of a Tub* or Pope's *Dunciad*, the high place is a low place, the site of deserved humiliation for hacks who write for money, but have none because they can't write. In the next generation, Samuel Johnson, in the *Life of Savage*, and Fielding, in *The Author's Farce* and *Joseph Andrews*, wrote with sympathy of the struggling writer driven to poverty and debt by the unscrupulousness of patrons and publishers. But the idea of a proud poetic fraternity, wearing its poverty as a badge of integrity and independence, rests on a conception of the artist as adversarial to the prevailing culture, rather than complicit with it, which did not develop fully until the nineteenth and twentieth centuries, and has in its way remained with us ever since.

NOTES

1 Dryden, Preface to *Fables* (1700), in *The Works of John Dryden*, eds Edward Niles Hooker, H. T. Swedenberg Jr, *et al.*, 20 vols (Berkeley, Los Angeles, and London: University of California Press, 1956–2000), VII, p. 33. Hereafter *CE*.

2 George Puttenham, *The Arte of English Poesie* (1589), I. xxxi; eds Gladys Doidge Willcock and Alice Walker (Cambridge: Cambridge University Press, 1936), p. 61.

3 See below, p. 22.

4 William Shakespeare, *The Complete Sonnets and Poems*, ed. Colin Burrow, The Oxford Shakespeare (Oxford: Oxford University Press, 2002), pp. 6, 12.
5 Puttenham, *Arte of English Poesie*, I. viii, xi; III. v (pp. 16, 25, 148) on classical playwrights; II. ix, xiv (pp. 83–4, 127) on popular entertainments.
6 *Letters of Sir Thomas Bodley to Thomas James*, ed. G. W. Wheeler (Oxford: Clarendon Press, 1926), pp. 219, 222.
7 David Scott Kastan, *Shakespeare and the Book* (Cambridge: Cambridge University Press, 2001), pp. 14–49, esp. 20, 31–40.
8 Hardy, see below, p. 440; Auden, 'Letter to Lord Byron' (1936), in *Collected Poems*, ed. Edward Mendelson (New York: Vintage, 1991), p. 83.
9 Auden, 'In Memory of W. B. Yeats' (1939), in *Collected Poems*, p. 248.
10 Philip Larkin, 'The Art of Poetry XXX' (interview), *Paris Review* 84 (1982), 11–12; Dale Salwak, 'An Interview with Kingsley Amis', *Contemporary Literature* 61.1 (1975), 16.
11 Shakespeare, *Complete Sonnets and Poems*, pp. 315–26.
12 Christopher Marlowe, *Dr. Faustus*, V. i. 91–2; Aeschylus, *Agamemnon*, 681ff.
13 See *Complete Sonnets and Poems*, p. 173 n. 12.
14 See the discussion in *Complete Sonnets and Poems*, pp. 91–103.
15 Samuel Johnson, 'Preface to Shakespeare' (1765), in *Johnson on Shakespeare*, ed. Arthur Sherbo, 2 vols (New Haven: Yale University Press, 1968), I, p. 61.
16 On some of these oppositions, see below, pp. 154ff.
17 'At a Vacation Exercise' (1628), 47–52; 'Mansus' (1638), 78–84; also 'Epitaphium Damonis' (1639–40), 161–71; Book II of *The Reason of Church-Government* (1642), in *The Riverside Milton*, ed. Roy Flannagan (Boston: Houghton Mifflin, 1998), pp. 922–3.
18 *Paradise Lost*, VI. 434. See Claude Rawson, 'Mock-Heroic and English Poetry', in *The Cambridge Companion to the Epic*, ed. Catherine Bates (Cambridge: Cambridge University Press, 2010), pp. 170–3.
19 John Dryden, 'Discourse Concerning Satire', in *CE*, IV, p. 84.
20 W. H. Auden, 'Introduction', in *Poets of the English Language III: Milton to Goldsmith*, eds W. H. Auden and Norman Holmes Pearson (London: Eyre and Spottiswoode, 1952), p. xxv.
21 On this, see Rawson, 'Mock-Heroic and English Poetry', pp. 187–8.
22 Pope, *Essay on Criticism* (1711), 360–1.
23 See below, p. 243.
24 See below, p. 235.
25 Auden, *Poets of the English Language III*, p. xviii.
26 T. S. Eliot, 'Reflections on *Vers Libre*' (1917), in *Selected Prose*, ed. Frank Kermode (New York: Harcourt Brace Jovanovich/Farrar, Straus and Giroux, 1975), p. 33.
27 Eliot, 'Reflections on *Vers Libre*', p. 35; see below, pp. 491, 496.
28 'Reflections on *Vers Libre*', p. 32; see also Eliot's 'Introduction' to Ezra Pound, *Selected Poems* (1928) (London: Faber and Faber, 1956), p. 8.
29 See below, p. 478.
30 Dryden, in *CE*, II, p. 128. See Claude Rawson, 'Poetry in the First Half of the Eighteenth Century: Pope, Johnson, and the Couplet', in *The Cambridge History of English Poetry*, ed. M. S. C. O'Neill (Cambridge: Cambridge University Press, 2010), pp. 333–57, esp. 333–6.

31 Dryden, 'Dedication of the *Aeneis*' (1697), in *CE*, V, p. 322.
32 Swift, Note to 'A Description of a City Shower' (1710), lines 61–3.
33 Adam Smith, *Theory of Moral Sentiments* (1759), V. i. 6.
34 Samuel Wesley, *An Epistle to a Friend, Concerning Poetry*, 1700, lines 621, 466.
35 Wesley, *An Epistle to a Friend*, lines 446–7.
36 See 'A Note on Rhythm and Rhyme', in Jonathan Swift, *Complete Poems*, ed. Pat Rogers (Hardmondsworth: Penguin, 1983), pp. 37–40.
37 Rogers, 'A Note on Rhythm and Rhyme', p. 38.
38 See below, pp. 49–50.
39 John Donne, *Satires, Epigrams and Verse Letters*, ed. W. Milgate (Oxford: Clarendon Press, 1987), p. 7.
40 Robert C. Elliott, *The Power of Satire: Magic, Ritual, Art* (Princeton: Princeton University Press, 1960), pp. 102ff.; Raman Selden, *English Verse Satire 1590–1765* (London: George Allen and Unwin, 1978), pp. 43, 50–3, 59.
41 Pope, *Imitations of Horace*, in the Twickenham Edition of the Poems of Alexander Pope, eds J. Butt *et al.*, 11 vols in 12 (London: Methuen, 1939–69), IV, pp. xli–xliii, 23–49, 129–45; Thomas Parnell, *Collected Poems*, eds Claude Rawson and F. P. Lock (Newark: University of Delaware Press, 1989), pp. 312–19, 586–7.
42 T. S. Eliot, *The Waste Land: A Facsimile and Transcript of the Original Drafts Including the Annotations of Ezra Pound*, ed. Valerie Eliot (London: Faber and Faber, and New York: Harcourt Brace Jovanovich, 1971), pp. 22–7, 38–41, 127n.; 'Introduction' to Pound, *Selected Poems*, p. 18.
43 Eliot, 'Reflections on *Vers Libre*', p. 36.
44 W. B. Yeats, 'Introduction' to *The Oxford Book of Modern Verse* (Oxford: Clarendon Press, 1936), pp. xxi, xxii.
45 Eliot, 'Introduction' to Pound, *Selected Poems*, p. 18.
46 Eliot, *The Use of Poetry and the Use of Criticism* (London: Faber and Faber, 1959), p. 39.
47 See below, pp. 508–9; Eliot, *Selected Prose*, p. 36.
48 Coleridge, *Biographia Literaria* (1817), ch. 14; eds James Engell and W. J. Bate, 2 vols (Princeton: Princeton University Press, 1983), II, p. 15; Poe, 'The Philosophy of Composition' (1846), 'The Poetic Principle' (1850), in *Essays and Reviews*, ed. G. R. Thompson (New York: Library of America, 1984), pp. 15–16, 71–94.
49 See for example W. B. Yeats to W. T. Horton, 3 September 1899, in *Collected Letters of W. B. Yeats. Vol. 2: 1896–1900*, ed. John Kelly (Oxford: Clarendon Press, 1997), pp. 447–8; Pound, 'The Renaissance' (1914), in *Literary Essays*, ed. T. S. Eliot (London: Faber and Faber, 1954), p. 218; Eliot, 'From Poe to Valéry' (1948), in *To Criticize the Critic* (London: Faber and Faber, 1965), pp. 27–42.
50 Ezra Pound, *Selected Prose 1909–1965*, ed. William Cookson (London: Faber and Faber, 1973), pp. 21–3.
51 Ezra Pound to T. S. Eliot, 24 January 1922, in *Letters of T. S. Eliot. Vol. I: 1898–1922*, ed. Valerie Eliot and Hugh Haughton, rev. edn (London: Faber and Faber, 2009), p. 626; see also Eliot to Scofield Thayer, 20 January 1922, and to John Quinn, 25 June 1922, pp. 623, 681.
52 Wordsworth, 'Preface' to *Lyrical Ballads*, in *Poems*, ed. John O. Hayden, 2 vols (Harmondsworth: Penguin, 1977), I, p. 872.

53 W. K. Wimsatt, Jr, and Cleanth Brooks, *Literary Criticism: A Short History* (New York: Knopf, 1957), p. 197 and n. 4.
54 See below, pp. 457–65, 471.
55 See below, p. 319.
56 Zachary Leader, *Writer's Block* (Baltimore: Johns Hopkins University Press, 1991), pp. ix, 254 n. 4.
57 On the *Prelude* as a response to writer's block, and to the poet's despair that his great project of *The Recluse* would 'ever be completed', see Leader, *Writer's Block*, pp. 184–5.
58 Jonathan Swift, *A Tale of a Tub* (1704), Preface and 'Conclusion', ed. Herbert Davis (Oxford: Blackwell, 1965), pp. 27, 133; the phrase 'to the Moment' comes from the Preface to Samuel Richardson's *Sir Charles Grandison* (1753).
59 W. B. Yeats, *Per Amica Silentia Lunae* (London: Macmillan, 1918), p. 93.

I

J. A. BURROW

Geoffrey Chaucer

Geoffrey Chaucer has long held the prime position that he occupies among English poets in this volume. Already, soon after his death in 1400, successors spoke of him as 'my master Chaucer', 'flower of poets', 'father and founder of ornate eloquence', and the like; and in the following century George Puttenham gave Chaucer, along with John Gower, pride of place in his sketch of the English poetic tradition. Puttenham found 'nothing worth commendation' before the reigns of Edward III and Richard II, and 'those of the first age were Chaucer and Gower both of them as I suppose Knightes'.[1] He evidently regarded these two as 'courtly makers', like Wyatt and Surrey mentioned later in his sketch, and he had reason to do so. Although Chaucer was born, in the early 1340s, into the family of a London vintner and was certainly never a knight, the earliest documentary evidence shows him already in 1357 serving as page in the household of the wife of Edward III's second son Lionel, and in the 1360s, following a customary progression for young gentlemen, he is acting as 'valettus' and esquire at the court of Edward himself.[2]

This early career introduced the poet into circles whose literary tastes were predominantly French: the thirteenth-century *Roman de la rose* and also modern poems such as the lyrics and longer narrative 'dits amoreux' of Guillaume de Machaut (d. 1377). Machaut's poetic disciple Jean Froissart was Chaucer's contemporary in the English court, acting as secretary to his countrywoman, Edward's Queen Philippa of Hainault, from 1361 to 1367; and another continental poet, Oton de Granson, also spent much time in England: it was Granson that Chaucer later, translating three of his balades, described as 'flour of hem that make in Fraunce'.[3] None of Chaucer's surviving poems can be dated earlier than 1368, when he was already some twenty-five years old; but long before that he must have tried his hand at some of those courtly love-lyrics which his friend Gower said he composed 'in the flowers of his youth'. Perhaps the result was something like this:

Your yen two wol slee me sodenly,
I may the beautee of hem not sustene,
So woundeth hit thourghout my herte kene.

And but your word wol helen hastily
My hertes wounde while that hit is grene,
  Your yen &c.

Upon my trouthe I sey you feithfully
That ye ben of my lyf and deeth the quene,
For with my deeth the trouthe shal be sene.
  Your yen &c.

This little roundel, probably by Chaucer, exemplifies that 'French art' which Ezra Pound, in his *ABC of Reading*, praised so highly for its musicality or 'melopoeia'.

Certainly by the late 1360s Chaucer had become an expert courtly maker in the French manner, on the evidence of his *Book of the Duchess*, a long dream-poem written in commemoration of John of Gaunt's wife Blanche, who died in 1368. Readers who look for the lineaments of a later Chaucer in this poem will be disappointed. There is very little in the way of irony or comedy here. In the opening lines, closely modelled on one of Froissart's poems, the narrator presents himself as a conventionally unhappy lover, and in his ensuing dream he behaves like a conventional courtly gentleman throughout his encounter with the figure representing John of Gaunt, the bereaved knight in black. Yet the poem is, in its own way, as accomplished as any of Chaucer's later creations. Its loose-woven octosyllabic couplets, like those of French 'dits amoreux', have little time for any striking local felicities of expression, but the great beauty of the poem lies elsewhere, in its approach to those most delicate of subjects, death and bereavement. Following a hunt in his dream, the narrator comes upon a solitary stranger, the knight in black, in a woodland glade and overhears him lamenting the death of his beloved. The dreamer is moved to approach him by pity, but courtesy forbids that he should presume to acknowledge what he has accidentally overheard. In their long ensuing conversation, the knight recalls his first meeting with his lady and describes her perfections; but it is not until the very end of the poem, when he at last does speak of her plainly as 'dead', that the dreamer feels free to recognize the fact:

'She ys ded!' 'Nay!' 'Yis, be my trouthe!'
'Is that youre los? Be God, hyt ys routhe!' (lines 1309–10)

This little exchange, in its context, has behind it a pressure built up by all the long evasions that have gone before. Now at last the dreamer is free to address the true state of affairs. His single expression of 'routhe', pity, may seem bald and inadequate; but what more can anyone really offer a mourner? Not on this occasion, certainly, the consolations of religion.

So, no sooner has the dreamer spoken these words than a horn sounds in the encircling woods to summon the hunt home, and the dream unravels.

The Book of the Duchess is a beautifully conceived piece; but I guess that, had Chaucer persisted in this vein of courtly making throughout his career, his work might mean little more to English or American readers today than do the poems of Machaut or Froissart in France. It seems to have been the poetry of Italy that did most, in the 1370s, to open up for him new horizons. In that decade Chaucer paid two visits to Italy on the king's business, in 1372–3 and 1378, acquainting himself with Dante's *Commedia*, Petrarch's *Canzoniere*, and Boccaccio's long narrative poems, *Il Filostrato* and *Il Teseida*. Chaucer refers to two of these poets by name in the *Canterbury Tales*: Dante as 'the wise poete of Florence' and 'the grete poete of Ytaille', Petrarch as 'the lauriat poete' who has 'enlumyned al Ytaille of poetrie' (*Canterbury Tales*, III. 1125, VII. 2460, IV. 31–3). These are among the very first recorded uses in English of the loan-word 'poet', a term which Chaucer elsewhere applies only to classics such as Virgil or Lucan – writers with whom, evidently, Dante and Petrarch could bear comparison. His early readers were happy to call Chaucer a 'poet', but he himself never claims the honour. On the contrary: unlike the laurel-crowned Petrarch, he can do no more, he says, than humbly kiss a nearby laurel tree (*House of Fame*, lines 1107–8); and unlike Dante, who imagined the great poets of antiquity greeting him with the cry 'onorate l'altissimo poeta!' (*Inferno*, 4.80), Chaucer asks only that his *Troilus* may be worthy to kiss the footprints (not even the feet) of those same classical masters (*Troilus and Criseyde*, 5.1791–2). Yet Chaucer was evidently what Aristotle called an *eiron*, a self-depreciating type of person; and his modest disavowals surely mask an ambition that his own poetic achievement be judged according to standards set by the Italian, and perhaps even the Roman, poets. He is the first English poet to leave behind him a substantial and varied body of work marked, like Dante's, by the imprint of its maker's personality, and also the first, with John Gower, to claim for himself a personal Muse (*Envoy to Scogan*, lines 38–40). These are among the many qualifications that allow him to keep company with the other poets in the present book.

It is in his next dream-poem, *The House of Fame*, composed some time in the 1370s after his first visit to Italy, that Chaucer the *eiron* first clearly emerges. By comparison with its predecessor, *The House of Fame* is a ramshackle affair – lacking a conclusion, as we have it – but it is also full of promise for the future. The first of its three 'Books' (a neo-classical form of division, found here for the first time in English) seems to offer its subject as love, for it introduces the dreamer to the temple of Venus, where he reads off from its walls the story of Virgil's *Aeneid*, paying particular attention to the affair between Aeneas and Dido; but the much more remarkable Liber Secundus turns the poem to its more unusual subject, which is 'tydynges' or reports of all kinds – news, gossip, rumour, and the like. Jupiter has sent a golden eagle to compensate the bookish 'Geoffrey' for his ignorance of what is going on around him by carrying him up to the House of Fame, an Ovidian edifice in outer space to which all 'tydynges' come and from which all reputations are determined. But Liber Tertius, which opens with a lofty Dantesque invocation to Apollo as 'god of science and of lyght', shows Fame to be a quite unreliable goddess, like her sister Fortune, for she pays no attention to truth or justice in the reports that she transmits. No source of tidings can be trusted, it appears, not even the great poets of antiquity who occupy places of honour in Fame's hall. So when a bystander in that hall asks Geoffrey whether he has himself come seeking reputation, he denies it:

> 'I cam not hyder, graunt mercy,
> For no such cause, by my hed!
> Sufficeth me, as I were ded,
> That no wight have my name in honde.
> I wot myself best how y stonde;
> For what I drye, or what I thynke,
> I wil myselven al hyt drynke,
> Certeyn, for the more part,
> As fer forth as I kan myn art.' (lines 1874–82)

In the Second Book, the dreamer cut a comic figure, terrified by his space-flight and forced by the loquacious eagle (who comes out of Dante's *Commedia*) to receive instruction about the stars; but here he speaks with mysterious self-possession. His experiences (*drye* means 'suffer') and thoughts are his own business, not to be handled by others, and he will keep them to himself so far as he can – even in his poetry, perhaps, if that is the 'art' to which he refers. These are the first appearances of Chaucer's very distinctive representation of himself, as one whose comic self-depreciations leave so much unsaid.

The Parliament of Fowls, composed after Chaucer's second Italian journey, exhibits two of his main technical contributions to the art of English poetry as practised by his successors. In place of the short, four-stress lines of the two earlier dream-poems, the *Parliament* employs a longer line of five stresses. This, the iambic pentameter, had no clear precedent in English, and Chaucer appears to have developed it himself out of the French decasyllabic or Italian hendecasyllabic line. He was also, most probably, the first English user of 'rhyme royal', a stanza-form common in the short French ballade but adopted by Chaucer for many of his long poems, in imitation perhaps of Boccaccio's *ottava rima*. The pattern of rhymes in rhyme royal, *ababbcc*, hinges on its fourth member, which can either complete a quatrain (*abab*) or else begin a pair of couplets (*bbcc*) – as it does in the opening stanza of the *Parliament*:

> The lyf so short, the craft so long to lerne,
> Th'assay so hard, so sharp the conquerynge,
> The dredful joye alwey that slit so yerne:
> Al this mene I by Love, that my felynge
> Astonyeth with his wonderful werkynge
> So sore, iwis, that whan I on hym thynke
> Nat wot I wel wher that I flete or synke. (lines 1–7)

One can see here Chaucer's precocious mastery of the iambic pentameter and of rhyme royal. The Man of Law was comically mistaken when he spoke in the *Canterbury Tales* of Chaucer as one who 'kan but lewedly / On metres and on rymyng craftily' (II. 47–8).

Considering its declared subject, the 'wonderful werkynge' of love, the *Parliament* opens oddly, with its narrator reading Cicero's *Somnium Scipionis*, since that text proves to concern high matters of public good and notices sexual love only to condemn in passing lecherous folk who neglect the 'commune profit'; but the narrator learns more from his ensuing dream, for this is prompted by the planet Venus (Cytherea, line 113). So he enters a Garden of Love there and encounters, first, the goddess Venus herself in her temple of brass and then another goddess, Nature, holding her Valentine's Day parliament of birds outside in the garden. These two scenes resemble, and must have helped to inspire, the symbolical 'pageants' in Spenser's *Faerie Queene*, such as his House of Pride or Garden of Adonis.[4] Chaucer's description of the temple and its environs, drawn from Boccaccio's *Teseida*, displays such a variety of love-personifications, good and bad, that it is hard to know what to make of them; but the presence of Priapus holding his erect penis in the temple's 'sovereyn place' (lines 253–9) and the sensuous description of Venus that follows clearly highlight the part played by the indulgence of physical desire. The dreamer, however, simply reports what he sees without comment before returning to the garden and encountering Nature. The various classes of bird assembled for her 'parliament' there display, as the Canterbury pilgrims do later, their differing attitudes to love, from the romantic devotion of the aristocratic eagles down to the no-nonsense realism of the goose ('But she wol love hym, lat hym love another!', line 567). Like the *Canterbury Tales*, this poem passes no judgement on the rival views that the birds display; nor does it offer any moral gloss on its two juxtaposed goddesses. Perhaps Nature is to be understood as superior to Venus – this Venus – because she is concerned to direct sexuality towards what the *Somnium Scipionis* called 'commune profit' or the general good, that is, the perpetuation of species through the annual mating of birds. But the poem does not say so.

In John Gower's *Confessio Amantis*, the goddess Venus speaks of Chaucer as 'my disciple and my poet', and it seems that Chaucer's early readers did think of him as above all a poet of love – not a love-poet like John Donne, but one who tells stories about love and reflects upon it. He does this in the greatest of his poems, *Troilus and Criseyde*. Chaucer composed *Troilus* in the 1380s, basing it on the *Filostrato* of Boccaccio. That Italian poem evidently attracted Chaucer as a rare example of a long poetic narrative devoted to just one simple, unbranching story, Troiolo's love and loss of Criseida. He saw in it the opportunity to produce in English verse a really extended love-story, registering all those minutiae of feeling and behaviour that the usual shorter narratives had no time for. In the event, he expanded the Italian from 5,704 lines of *ottava rima* to 8,239 of rhyme royal, amplifying Boccaccio's scenes, inventing new ones, and incorporating new materials both historical and philosophical. The new materials mark Chaucer's different relationship to his subject – less close, though not less sympathetic, than Boccaccio's. The Italian poet in his Proem announced that the sorrows of Troiolo mirrored his own, for he was himself a lover; but Chaucer, here as in the *Parliament*, disavows all personal experience of love (*Troilus*, II. 12–21, for instance). Hence he can write, from outside the charmed circle, with an eye to larger issues.

Since Chaucer, like Boccaccio, concentrates on just three main characters, he has ample opportunity to notice in detail not only what they say and do but also what they feel and think. The most straightforward of the three is the hero, Troilus, for once he has fallen in love his whole being is governed by his passion. Like Troilus in Shakespeare's play, he is 'as true as truth's simplicity' (*Troilus and Cressida*, III. ii. 167); and he expresses the joys and sorrows of true love in all its phases, from initial frustration through ecstatic fulfilment to ultimate loss. The poetry of his soliloquies, speeches, songs, and love-letters impressed Chaucer's successors as high models of the kind, to be imitated by them; but many readers find it hard not to feel impatience with a hero so utterly submissive to Love and to his mistress. Chaucer's Troilus is in fact also a great warrior and scourge of the Greeks, as the poet takes occasion to insist; but, since his declared subject is the hero's 'aventures in lovynge', he sets battlefields aside as 'collateral' matter, evidently relying on his audience to recognize the wider knightly ideal expressed in a medieval proverb: Troilus is 'a lamb in the chamber, a lion in the field'. A seventeenth-century reader, Sir Francis Kinaston, saw this, for in a note to his ill-fated attempt to preserve the poem for posterity by translating it into Latin, he described Troilus as 'a most compleat knight in Armes and Courtshippe [courtesy], and a faithfull constant lover'.[5]

A similar concentration on the single relevant role marks Chaucer's treatment of Pandarus. Offstage, Pandarus is himself a lover, faithful to his own mistress but unable to win her, as Troilus points out in one of his more spirited utterances:

> 'Thow koudest nevere in love thiselven wisse.
> How devel maistow brynge me to blisse?' (I. 622–3)

But his only role in the poem is to act as the confidant and helper of the hero, advising and comforting him, working on the mind and feelings of Criseyde, and engineering trysts between them. In Boccaccio's poem Pandaro plays the same part, but Chaucer makes something new out of him, investing him with a comic energy quite absent from the Italian. Whereas Pandaro is Criseida's cousin, in *Troilus* he is her uncle, and he adopts a manner towards her, jocular and flirtatious, that one recognizes as avuncular. This is most amply displayed in the long scene (II. 50–595) where he calls upon Criseyde, intending to tell her of Troilus's love. Criseyde is reading with two other ladies in her parlour when her uncle enters:

> Quod Pandarus, 'Madame, God yow see,
> With youre book and all the compaignie!'
> 'Ey, uncle myn, welcome iwys,' quod she;
> And up she roos, and by the hond in hye
> She took hym faste, and seyde, 'This nyght thrie,
> To goode moot it turne, of yow I mette.'
> And with that word she doun on bench hym sette.
>
> 'Ye, nece, yee shal faren wel the bet,
> If God wol, al this yeer,' quod Pandarus;
> 'But I am sory that I have yow let
> To herken of youre book ye preysen thus.
> For Goddes love, what seith it? telle it us!
> Is it of love? O, som good ye me leere!'
> 'Uncle,' quod she, 'youre maistresse is nat here.'
>
> With that thei gonnen laughe. (II. 85–99)

Scenes such as these display complexities of behaviour and character on a scale unprecedented in English poetry at that time; and Pandarus is certainly no simple case. The pleasures that he takes in furthering the affair are not untouched by suggestions of vicarious sexuality, nor are his methods at all scrupulous. Yet the poem never seems to question the generosity of his main motive: 'to help his frend, lest he for sorwe deyde' (IV. 429).

In his *Legend of Good Women*, Chaucer has the God of Love accuse him of traducing womankind by choosing to narrate Criseyde's betrayal of Troilus (G Prologue, lines 264–6); and the story, of course, dictated that outcome. Yet comparison with the Italian source shows Chaucer persistently adapting the narrative in Criseyde's favour and making narratorial interventions on her behalf. His Criseyde is a very much more dignified and substantial lady than Boccaccio's (or Shakespeare's). Thus, in Book Two, Chaucer takes pains to establish that her responses, after Pandarus has broken the news about Troilus's love, are neither 'light' nor 'sudden' (II. 667ff). She does 'incline to like him', but under pressure from what seems to be a fated concatenation of circumstances. After Pandarus has left, she sees Troilus happening to ride under the window of her mansion, hears her companion Antigone sing in praise of love, and falls asleep to the seductive music of a nightingale:

> A nyghtyngale, upon a cedre grene,
> Under the chambre wal ther as she ley,
> Ful loude song ayein the moone shene,
> Peraunter in his briddes wise a lay
> Of love, that made hire herte fressh and gay.
> That herkned she so longe in good entente,
> Til at the laste the dede slep hir hente. (II. 918–24)

And in that dead sleep she dreams of a painless exchange of hearts with an eagle, 'feathered white as bone'. In the last phase of the action, too, things conspire to put Criseyde under pressure. The exchange of prisoners, an 'infortune' both for the lovers and also, as it turns out, for Troy itself (IV. 183–210), exposes her to the advances of Diomede, an operator as expert in his way as Pandarus himself. Criseyde's promise to return from the Greek camp within ten days was made, the poem insists, with 'good entente' (IV. 1415–18); but circumstances prove too much for her, and the narrator can no longer excuse her conduct, much as he would like to: 'I wolde excuse hire yet for routhe' (V. 1099). Accordingly, unlike Robert Henryson in his *Testament of Cresseid*, he turns away from whatever lay ahead for her in her relationship with the unscrupulous Diomede: 'Men seyn – I not – that she yaf hym hire herte' ('I not' means 'I do not know', V. 1050). So, as the poem moves towards its end, the narrative concentrates more and more on the painful spectacle of the hero's despair and death, leaving Criseyde with her bleak last word: 'But al shal passe; and thus take I my leve' (V. 1085).

Chaucer's contemporary Thomas Usk, in the course of a discussion of free will, refers the reader to the treatment of that subject in *Troilus*, speaking of its author as 'the noble philosophical poete in Englissh'.[6] *Troilus* is indeed chief among those of Chaucer's works that impressed his early readers as 'philosophical'. He evidently came to write it shortly after completing his translation of the *De Consolatione Philosophiae* of Boethius, a dialogue in five books (like *Troilus*) on fortune, free will, and God's foreknowledge; and Boethius, here as elsewhere, is the poet's chief source for his passages of philosophy. When Chaucer puts such passages into the mouth of a character, they very often do no more than reflect the circumstances of the moment and are to be read accordingly. So when Criseyde has been persuaded by Pandarus that Troilus is angry with her, she responds in her distress with a Boethian lament on the fragility of human joys:

> 'O God,' quod she, 'so worldly selynesse,
> Which clerkes callen fals felicitee,
> Imedled is with many a bitternesse!' (III. 813–15)

Very true – but quickly forgotten once things turn out all right. In Book Four, again, Troilus, now faced with the prospect of losing his love, responds with a long soliloquy arguing that 'al that comth, comth by necessitee' (IV. 958). The source is Boethius once more, but in this case readers such as the 'moral Gower' and 'philosophical Strode' to whom Chaucer directed the poem in its penultimate stanza could be trusted to recall that Troilus's gloomy predestinarianism, attributed in the *Consolatio* dialogue to the suffering figure of Boethius, was refuted there by the authoritative figure of Philosophia.

That refutation by Philosophy, turning on a distinction between the 'perpetual' and the 'eternal', finds no expression in *Troilus*. The poem is not to that degree philosophical. Its version of sublunary life shows human plans and intentions going along with fortuitous, even fated, circumstances in a rather familiar kind of muddle to produce the changes and mutability of which Criseyde spoke: 'But al shal passe.' It is that modest pronouncement, in fact, that heralds the grand conclusion of the poem. Faced at last with sure proof of Criseyde's infidelity, Troilus seeks his own death in epic battles with the Greeks – the Wrath of Troilus – and dies at the hands of Achilles. But that event, very briefly reported, is quite overshadowed by what follows. In three stanzas taken over from Boccaccio's *Teseida*, referring there to Arcita, Troilus's soul flies up to the sphere of the moon, which in medieval cosmology marked the frontier between the changeable and the changeless.[7] Looking up, he sees the planets and hears the perpetual music of their spheres; looking down, he sees the littleness of the earth and condemns our foolish pursuit of things that cannot last. In the remaining six stanzas of the poem, Chaucer restates this thought in the homiletic terms of contemporary Christianity:

> O yonge, fresshe folkes, he or she,
> In which that love up groweth with youre age,

Repeyreth hom fro worldly vanyte,
And of youre herte up casteth the visage
To thilke God that after his ymage
Yow made, and thynketh al nys but a faire,
This world that passeth soone as floures faire. (V. 1835–41)

Most modern readers are happy enough to find rather little such direct religious discourse in Chaucer's poems, and many have balked at this conclusion. How can the joys of human love, so vividly evoked in Book Three of the poem, be so summarily condemned as vanity? Yet one does not have to believe in a lasting Christian 'home' to allow that such joys do indeed, sooner or later, 'pass', however intense they may have been at the time.

Chaucer's next big project, *The Legend of Good Women*, was evidently left uncompleted. In its long Prologue, he reverts to the courtly Anglo-French tradition of love-vision, imagining himself confronted with the God of Love and his companion Queen Alceste. Faced with Cupid's anger at his traducing of women in the *Troilus*, Chaucer can only grovel; but Alceste comes to his defence: Chaucer just likes 'making books', quite regardless of their subject; and anyway, she says, many of his other writings should incline Cupid to look favourably upon him – an argument which allows the poet, perhaps for the first time in English, to lay claim to a lifetime's oeuvre, listing his earlier works at F Prologue, lines 412–30. So Alceste persuades Cupid to impose only a light penance for the offence: Chaucer is to write some 'glorious legends' of faithful women – and of the false male lovers who betray them. Chaucer completed only eight of these, praising female 'martyrs' such as Dido and blaming betrayers such as Aeneas. The fact that this has been imposed upon him as a penitential exercise casts a shadow of doubt across the whole performance; but questions of sincerity hardly arise here. The poem is best understood as a piece of courtly making in the old style, calculated to amuse readers such as Richard's Queen Anne, to whom it was first directed by Alceste:

'And whan this book ys maad, yive it the quene,
On my behalf, at Eltham or at Sheene.'
(F Prologue, lines 496–7)

Yet the *Legend* looks forward as well as back. By contrast with the expansive manner of *Troilus*, the legends represent an exercise in what medieval poetics called the *via brevitatis*, that short way of telling stories which Chaucer was to practise in the *Canterbury Tales*. The poem also seems to be the first English work composed entirely in pentameter couplets, a form to be employed in the majority of the Canterbury stories, as in so many poems since.

In one of the very rare personal anecdotes about Chaucer, John Lydgate reports that, when the poet was asked by others to comment on their writings, he refrained from criticism and 'seide alweie the best'.[8] One may recognize here the same Chaucer who speaks in the *Canterbury Tales*, one who praises others and depreciates himself, as an *eiron* will. The 'well-saying', as Lydgate calls it, prevails in the General Prologue from the moment when Chaucer arrives at the Tabard Inn, praising its spacious stables and rooms and its first-class service; and in the ensuing portraits of his fellow-pilgrims he seems to find everything good that can be said about them, beginning with the 'verray, parfit gentil knyght'. They are all in their different ways nonpareils, 'worthy' representatives of their various occupations, and it is left for the reader to judge where the praise may be misdirected. Is it right, for instance, to single out the Prioress's exquisite table-manners for particular notice? The pilgrim Chaucer has good words to say even of the nastiest of his fellow-travellers, the Summoner:

> He was a gentil harlot and a kynde;
> A bettre felawe sholde men noght fynde. (I. 647–8)

The ironies come and go without, it seems, the speaker ever noticing them – or only very rarely – and negative judgements remain unspoken. Faced with the Monk's very worldly view of his own vocation, the narrator can only sympathize: 'And I seyde his opinion was good' (line 183).

But how, then, was Chaucer to represent himself? When he decided that there should be a prize for the pilgrim who told the best tales, he set himself an intriguing problem. Who was to judge the competition? The obvious candidate would be Chaucer the pilgrim, acknowledged as a prolific writer of stories by the Man of Law (II. 45–89); but the Man of Law does not think much of his work. It was not Chaucer's way to take pride of place in his creations, and in fact he cuts an ignoble figure among the pilgrims. When the Host – noticing him, it seems, for the first time – calls upon him for a tale, he can offer only 'a rym I lerned longe agoon' (VII. 709); and his Tale of Sir Thopas turns out to exemplify much that was worst in the English poetry of his day, as Chaucer saw it: shoddy diction, thumping rhythms, ramshackle structure. So the Host interrupts him, dismissing his performance as 'rym dogerel' – for it is he, Harry Bailey, whom the company has appointed to be their leader and judge of their tales. The Host is a forthright and dominating character, as innkeepers often are; but his various responses to other tales hardly suggest that Chaucer intended to conclude the *Canterbury Tales* with anything in the way of an authoritative literary judgement from him.

In the event, Chaucer fell far short of any such conclusion. The work survives only in discontinuous Fragments (as editors call them), evidently assembled by admirers after the poet's death. Instead of the more than a hundred tales promised in the General Prologue – four from each pilgrim, two on the road to Canterbury and two on the way back – there are only twenty-four, two of them unfinished and two interrupted. Yet the work was a great success in its time, surviving in more than eighty manuscripts, and it has since come to displace *Troilus* as the poem by which Chaucer is best known. Its appeal depends in large part upon the sheer variety of the tales that are told, a variety which matches the characters and occupations of the 'sondry folk' brought together by chance at the Tabard Inn (I. 23–6). Chaucer may have known the *Decameron*, but, whereas the tales in Boccaccio's collection are told by a homogeneous group of young ladies and gentlemen, the Canterbury pilgrimage provided a setting in which sundry folk could plausibly be represented as spending, for their common security on the road, several days together. There are no great lords, who would have travelled in their own retinues, nor any urban or rural destitutes, for whom Chaucer, unlike Langland, had no time; but the social range is otherwise wide enough, from the Knight down to the Plowman. The pilgrims pair off with their tales on a variety of principles. The Prioress's Tale, a miracle of the Virgin, is the sort of thing that a nun would read, and the 'churls' tales' may be taken to represent such funny stories of sex and trickery as might appeal to men like the Miller and the Reeve. The Merchant, recently and unhappily married, tells a tale that reflects his personal mortification, and the Wife of Bath's Tale expresses her distinctive views on relations between men and women. There is also at work a purely literary principle of decorum, for pilgrims tend to tell the kinds of story in which they themselves might figure. So the pilgrim Miller virtually reappears in the Reeve's angry response to his tale; and, in another quarrel, the Friar and the Summoner both use their stories to picture their adversary in the most unflattering terms.

The first two tales, of the Knight and the Miller, establish the poles between which the secular stories are to lie. For the Knight, Chaucer turned, not to Anglo-French romances of knightly adventure, which seem to have interested him little, but to the *Teseida* of Boccaccio – a twelve-book Italian epic that attaches itself as a kind of sequel to the *Thebaid* of Statius. Boccaccio's story of the fraternal rivalry between Palemone and Arcita for the love of Emilia might seem less appropriate for the Knight than for his amorous young son, the Squire; yet the spirit of his tale is far from youthful, for it portrays a world in which human fortunes are shaped, often cruelly, by chance, destiny, or the pagan gods. When Duke Theseus decrees that the equal claims of the two lovers can only be decided by a tournament, Arcite prays to Mars for victory and Palamon prays to Venus for Emily. Since both prayers are granted, it is left for another divinity, Saturn, to resolve the dilemma by equivocation: Arcite does win the tournament but dies immediately after in a fall from his horse, allowing Palamon eventually to marry Emily. But this happy ending is quite overshadowed by the dying words of his rival:

> 'What is this world? What asketh men to have?
> Now with his love, now in his colde grave
> Allone, withouten any compaignye.' (I. 2777–9)

In the face of this dark, Saturnine world, men can hope only to 'maken vertu of necessitee', as Duke Theseus puts it. Like his namesake in Shakespeare's *Midsummer Night's Dream*, Chaucer's Theseus takes a humorously sympathetic view of the young lovers; but his particular concern, as 'lord and governour' of Athens, is to make the best of bad jobs. It is in this mature role that he dominates the tale, making it, more than Boccaccio's poem, a true 'Theseid'.

Like the Knight's Tale, the Miller's opens with a story-teller's 'Whilom', but his story is set, not in ancient Athens, but in modern Oxford. It is the first of a number of 'churl's tales', including also those of the Reeve, the Cook (fragmentary), the Shipman, and the Merchant, all of which conform more or less closely to the literary tradition of fabliau in earlier French poetry. Fabliau plots typically concern the winning of sex, goods, or money by trickery, as the monk so elegantly does in the Shipman's Tale. Their contemporary settings offered Chaucer the chance to do some scenes from the common life of his own time: an Oxford carpenter and his student lodger, a Cambridgeshire miller, a French merchant capitalist. One can see in the Reeve's Tale, for instance, how much he relished the new challenge, taking over a well-engineered plot from some French source and realizing it with many loving details. The two Cambridge students, John and Aleyn, who carry their college's wheat to be ground at the mill in nearby Trumpington speak the northern dialect of their origins; and, when they lose their horse, it is through the soggy Cambridgeshire fenland that they have to chase it. Their eventual victim, the thieving miller, is gleefully portrayed by the Reeve, with one eye on his pilgrim enemy, as a foolish boaster with nothing but contempt for the university boys by whom he is to be outwitted. The finale of the Tale, taking place in the dark and cramped mill-house just before dawn, is vividly imagined, as John's shifting of the baby's cradle directs, first, the miller's wife into his own bed and then Aleyn into the miller's – with violent results. It is a fine bit of farce, which has gone well in modern staged versions.

The Canterbury project opened up for Chaucer several other new kinds of writing for him to attempt. So for the Pardoner and the Wife of Bath he composed long individual prologues in which their ensuing narratives – a preacher's moral *exemplum* and a romance tale, respectively – could be embedded. The relationship between the Pardoner's Prologue and his Tale is paradoxical. The Tale demonstrates the fatal consequences of *cupiditas*, love of money, yet in his Prologue the Pardoner boldly confesses that his own motive in telling it is just the same: 'I preche of no thyng but for coveityse' (VI. 424). Evidently such moral stories may fail to affect the behaviour even of those who tell them. The tale itself makes its point, as *exempla* should, with Euclidean clarity: three nameless young debauchees (A, B, and C, as it were) set out to trick each other out of the gold that they have found and all end up dead as a result. Yet its action takes place in a strange, unfocused world. The drunken 'rioters' behave as if Death were personally present in their plague-stricken neighbourhood; and the old man who directs them to the hoard, and so to the death for which he himself longs in vain, strikes all readers as indefinably other than he seems:

> 'Now, sires,' quod he, 'if that yow be so leef
> To fynde Deeth, turne up this croked wey,
> For in that grove I lafte hym, by my fey,
> Under a tree, and there he wole abyde;
> Noght for youre boost he wole him no thyng hyde.
> Se ye that ook? Right there ye shal hym fynde.' (VI. 760–5)

It seems right that Chaucer should have reserved this, his one exercise in the uncanny, for the most sinister of the Canterbury pilgrims.

The Wife of Bath, like the Pardoner, devotes her Prologue entirely to her designated occupation, as a Wife, recalling her life with five husbands and defending herself and her sex against slanders put about by men in writings such as the 'book of wikked wyves' from which her fifth husband Jankyn delighted to read:

> And whan I saugh he wolde nevere fyne
> To reden on this cursed book al nyght,
> Al sodeynly thre leves have I plyght
> Out of his book, right as he radde, and eke
> I with my fest so took hym on the cheke
> That in oure fyr he fil bakward adoun. (III. 788–93)

It may well seem that Alison herself belongs in just such a Book of Wicked Wives. She is a termagant, mercilessly 'chiding' her husbands; and her Tale affirms the sovereignty of women over men – for that is the lesson taught by the old hag to the rapist knight there. Yet this confrontational version of male–female relations is challenged, in both Prologue and Tale, by glimpses of something quite different, where women and men come together on a footing of mutual kindness. It is so in the aftermath of the fist-fight with Jankyn (III. 811–25) and also more distinctly at the end of the Tale. There the knight accepts the old woman as 'my lady and my love, and wyf so dere', terms which define her relation to him as at once superior ('lady'), equal ('love'), and subordinate ('wife'). The Wife here – if only at the end of her fairy story – dreams of something not unlike the relationship of mutuality that unites Dorigen and Arveragus in the Franklin's Tale.[9]

The Canterbury Tales, fragmentary as Chaucer left it, has what looks like a stop-gap ending in the Parson's prose exposition of the Sacrament of Penance. Yet the General Prologue had projected a quite different conclusion, a celebratory supper back at the Tabard Inn, and most readers feel that this would have been more in keeping with the prevailing mood of the whole. The collection does of course include a good deal of 'moralitee and hoolynesse' (I. 3180) besides the Parson's Tale – the tales of the Prioress and the Clerk, as well as less familiar pieces like the Second Nun's beautiful legend of St Cecilia – but its general spirit is one of holiday festivity, a spirit upheld, as one might expect, by the landlord of the Tabard. So, after the Monk's series of gloomy 'tragedies' has been cut short by the Knight's protest ('litel hevynesse / Is right ynough to muche folk, I gesse'), Harry Bailey calls on the Nun's Priest to 'make our hearts glad', and the Priest responds with what must be among the most purely comic of English poems. In his tale, Chantecleer's ominous dream provokes a long debate with Pertelote in which he proves, citing authorities and examples, that dreams do foretell future events. Since there is indeed a fox in the widow's yard, the cock's fears are to prove well founded; but he forgets all about his arguments – as Chaucer's people often do – once dawn brings the promise of food and sex. So he flies down from the safety of his perch, just as if Pertelote had been right in her scepticism. This prompts the Priest to descant on the perils of 'wommannes conseil' in a passage that represents Chaucer's always elusive treatment of the Woman Question at its most comically opaque:

> Passe over, for I seyde it in my game.
> Rede auctours, where they trete of swich mateere,
> And what they seyn of wommen ye may heere.
> Thise been the cokkes wordes, and nat myne;
> I kan noon harm of no womman divyne. (VII. 3262–6)

The ensuing capture of Chantecleer by the fox is rendered in high rhetorical style, as if it were another of the Monk's tragedies; but the cock in fact escapes, by persuading the fox to open his jaws to taunt the pursuers, and the poem ends with what can only be a joke pairing of morals, enunciated by cock and fox – respectively, 'Keep your eyes open' and 'Keep your mouth shut.'

Modern interpretations of Chaucer's poetry have tended to concentrate on its moral meanings (and also, more recently, on its historical bearings), and they commonly neglect that vein of comedy which so often surfaces in it, in such figures as the eagle in *The House of Fame* or Pandarus in *Troilus and Criseyde*. At the end of the latter poem, Chaucer expressed the hope that he might be able, before he died, to compose 'som comedye'; and he fulfilled that ambition in the Nun's Priest's Tale and also in the whole festive project of the Canterbury pilgrimage.

NOTES

1 George Puttenham's *Arte of English Poesie* (1589), eds Gladys Doidge Willcock and Alice Walker (Cambridge: Cambridge University Press, 1936), I, p. xxxi.

2 See Derek Pearsall, *The Life of Geoffrey Chaucer: A Critical Biography* (Oxford: Blackwell, 1992).

3 *The Complaint of Venus*, line 82. All quotations are taken from *The Riverside Chaucer*, ed. Larry D. Benson, 3rd edn (Boston: Houghton Mifflin, 1987).

4 On Spenser's 'pageants' of symbolical figures, see C. S. Lewis, *Spenser's Images of Life*, ed. Alastair Fowler (Cambridge: Cambridge University Press, 1967). On the *Parliament* and other dream-poems, see A. J. Minnis, V. J. Scattergood, and J. J. Smith, *The Shorter Poems*, Oxford Guides to Chaucer (Oxford: Clarendon Press, 1995).

5 Cited by Richard Beadle, 'The Virtuoso's *Troilus*', in Ruth Morse and Barry Windeatt (eds), *Chaucer Traditions: Studies in Honour of Derek Brewer* (Cambridge: Cambridge University Press, 1990), p. 219.

6 Usk's *Testament of Love*, III. iv. On Boethius in the poem, see Barry Windeatt, *Troilus and Criseyde*, Oxford Guides to Chaucer (Oxford: Clarendon Press, 1992), pp. 96–109.

7 See John Steadman, *Disembodied Laughter: 'Troilus' and the Apotheosis Tradition* (Berkeley: University of California Press, 1972).

8 Lydgate's *Troy Book*, ed. H. Bergen, EETS e.s. 97–126 (1906–20), V. 3519–26. Lydgate knew Chaucer's son Thomas.

9 See Jill Mann, *Feminizing Chaucer* (Cambridge: Brewer, 2002), on Chaucer's representations of women. On the *Canterbury Tales* generally, see Derek Pearsall, *The Canterbury Tales* (London: George Allen and Unwin, 1985), and Helen Cooper, *The Canterbury Tales*, Oxford Guides to Chaucer (Oxford: Clarendon Press, 1989).

SELECTED FURTHER READING

Benson, Larry D. (ed.), *The Riverside Chaucer*, 3rd edn, Boston, Houghton Mifflin, 1987

Boitani, Piero, and Jill Mann (eds), *The Cambridge Companion to Chaucer*, 2nd edn, Cambridge, Cambridge University Press, 2003

Cooper, Helen, *The Canterbury Tales*, Oxford Guides to Chaucer, Oxford, Clarendon Press, 1989

Gray, Douglas (ed.), *The Oxford Companion to Chaucer*, Oxford, Oxford University Press, 2003
Mann, Jill, *Feminizing Chaucer*, Cambridge, Brewer, 2002
Minnis, A. J., V. J. Scattergood, and J. J. Smith, *The Shorter Poems*, Oxford Guides to Chaucer, Oxford, Clarendon Press, 1995
Muscatine, Charles, *Chaucer and the French Tradition*, Berkeley, University of California Press, 1957
Pearsall, Derek, *The Canterbury Tales*, London, George Allen and Unwin, 1985
The Life of Geoffrey Chaucer: A Critical Biography, Oxford, Blackwell, 1992
Windeatt, B. A., *Troilus and Criseyde: A New Edition of 'The Book of Troilus'*, Harlow, Longman, 1984
Troilus and Criseyde, Oxford Guides to Chaucer, Oxford, Clarendon Press, 1992

2

ROLAND GREENE

Thomas Wyatt

In the Egerton manuscript, the poet and diplomat Thomas Wyatt begins a poem in his own hand:

> Prove whether I do change, my dear,
> Or if that I do still remain
> Like as I went or far or near,
> And if ye find ...[1]

The earliest texts of Wyatt's poems come to us in several manuscripts and two books published after his death; the Egerton, with some poems in his hand, is the most authoritative of the manuscripts. The poem was not completed in any extant manuscript, and – because it cuts close to the concerns that animate much of Wyatt's work, speaking directly to preoccupations that appear more obliquely elsewhere – perhaps it could not have been completed. Across several ranges of experience, Wyatt's poetry is engrossed with change. The poet's life took place against the background of the turbulent first fifty years of the sixteenth century, when an Englishman born into Roman Catholicism became Protestant, the regime of Henry VIII adjusted English ambitions towards the world, and the empire of Charles V – to which Wyatt was Henry's ambassador – absorbed the new reality of global reach. These historical factors, especially Henrician absolutism and the Reformation, show up everywhere in Wyatt's poems, but they are not so much examined directly as braided with a deeply felt personal outlook. Wyatt's understanding of the relations between persons is based on the conviction that men and women are profoundly unlike one another, with a sharp division of experience between them – their capacity to make entirely different meanings of common events such as love – and an utterly different orientation to change. To his jaded eye, the sexes might as well be different species, occupying adjacent but separate realities. And finally, there is poetry, which Wyatt wrote in most of the available modes of his time: psalms, epigrams, lute songs, satires, and sonnets. The most important English poet born in the first half of the century, he is usually remarked for bringing one variety of intellectual and stylistic change, that of Petrarchism – the Italianate idiom fashionable across Europe throughout the sixteenth century – to his national poetry. But he is not strictly a Petrarchan so much as a poet of several discrete voices, some of which have been barely described by criticism even as others have been rendered deceptively familiar, even into period cliché. The complexity of his work is that of his distinctive moment, in which poetry was still near to fulfilling its power as a medium of thought that flowed into philosophy, law, and other disciplines, and as an indispensable commentary on the world of affairs. A self-reflexive poetry, involved only in its own fictions, is unknown to Wyatt and his contemporaries. They sing and write to find out how language can manage the world of change they inhabit, to counterpose the poem as an artefact of controlled vicissitude against the political, religious, and interpersonal instability of their time. The present essay recovers this Wyatt of many voices and contexts.

Because his poetry was not published until after his death, it is impossible to date with certainty the phases of Wyatt's career. But it seems likely that a poet born about 1503 would have discovered continental modes in the lyric and other poetic genres sometime during the 1520s and 1530s, when a generation of European poets – many of them in military or diplomatic service across the Europe of the king of France Francis I, the Holy Roman Emperor Charles V, and the king of England Henry VIII – exchanged influences, especially in the light of the Italian models that brought new resources into the other vernaculars. In France, Spain, Portugal, Germany, and elsewhere, poetry conceived in maturity by the generation of 1500 differed strikingly from what the preceding generation wrote, thought, and felt; we might suppose that the widened world of the sixteenth century – with a vastly expanded trade system, a geography expanded by Christopher Columbus and his successors, an imperial politics – made any number of literary and other representational conventions seem suddenly outmoded. A career like Wyatt's (or those of contemporaries such as Thomas Vaux, Nicholas Grimald, John Cheke, and Henry Howard, Earl of Surrey) arose around the question of how to negotiate among several converging traditions: native English verse practice, humanist translation and adaptation of the classics, and the new Italianate writing, especially in lyric. Wyatt's choices in this matter proved to be the most influential of his cohort, establishing conditions for English poetry that lasted at least until the end of the century. More than fifty years after Wyatt's death, the theorist George Puttenham observes that Wyatt and Surrey are

> the two chief lanterns of light to all others that haue since employed their pens vpon English Poesie, their conceits were loftie, their stiles stately, their

> conueyance cleanly, their termes proper, their meetre sweete and well proportioned, in all imitating very naturally and studiously their Maister *Francis Petrarcha*.[2]

Through all of Wyatt's verse, there is a fundamental voice and stance that emerged, presumably early in his career, out of the native English tradition. The mode is epitomized by the song 'Blame not my lute':

> Blame not my lute for he must sound
> Of this or that as liketh me.
> For lack of wit the lute is bound
> To give such tunes as pleaseth me.
> Though my songs be somewhat strange
> And speaks such words as touch thy change
> Blame not my lute.[3]

This plain style – direct in its rhetoric, sparing in its figuration, often monosyllabic in its diction – comes to Wyatt as an indigenous English mode that can seem impoverished next to the more expansive poetries of the early sixteenth century.[4] In his hands, however, the mode is transformed, and when he passes it on to successors such as George Gascoigne and Walter Ralegh, it has become not so much a style as an intellectual and emotional redoubt: a self-imposed discipline, a commentary on other modes, a vantage point on the passing world. In six stanzas, 'Blame not my lute' acknowledges its plainness and claims a moral force in its directness:

> My lute, alas, doth not offend
> Though that perforce he must agree
> To sound such tunes as I intend
> To sing to them that heareth me.
> Then though my songs be somewhat plain
> And toucheth some that use to feign
> Blame not my lute.
>
> My lute and strings may not deny
> But as I strike they must obey.
> Break not them then so wrongfully
> But wreak thyself some wiser way.
> And though the songs which I indite
> Do quit thy change with rightful spite
> Blame not my lute.[5]

Perhaps most strikingly, the poem makes a virtue of its limitations. In this world, 'spite asketh spite and changing change', but a poem such as this one, stripped of ornamental figures and unusual diction, can only 'quit thy change' – requite the lady's inconstancy – with an insistent repetition of that same word, 'change', regardless of cause or context. The lady is invited to view her reflection in two dimensions, in the straitened outlook and limited vocabulary of a self-consciously 'plain' song; the inadequacy of the single word becomes a devastating indictment. If one of the hallmarks of this sort of poetry is its ruthless deployment of sympathy behind an uneven vocabulary – ideas such as truth and faith are often treated as the property of the first person, while the motives of others are distorted as 'change' and the like – Wyatt's innovation is to acknowledge that imbalance in the poem itself. He renders the plain style aware of its own limits, and makes the typical poem of this stance look outwards, struggling to account for something beyond its representational capacities, before returning to itself.

Within this stance, the tones vary from determination,

> Though time doth pass, yet shall not my love.
> Though I be far, always my heart is near.
> Though other change, yet will not I remove.[6]

to resignation,

> To seek by mean to change this mind,
> Alas, I prove it will not be;
> For in my heart I cannot find
> Once to refrain, but still agree,
> As bound by force, alway to serve,
> And other have that I deserve.[7]

to anger:

> Ye old mule that think yourself so fair,
> Leave off with craft your beauty to repair,
> For it is true without any fable
> No man setteth more by riding in your saddle.
> Too much travail so do your train appair,
>   Ye old mule.[8]

But in its most powerful vein, the turn towards what cannot be represented through plainness makes a break in the surface of the poem, a fissure through which other representational modes become visible. This is not only to turn the plain style towards the wider world of poetry and affairs, but to introduce an irruption of ethical consciousness into a kind of poem that has usually traded such considerations for moral certainty. 'Madam, withouten many words', translated from Dragonetto Bonifacio's madrigal 'Madonna non so dir tante parole', introduces such a disturbance at the centre of the poem:

> Madam, withouten many words
> Once I am sure ye will or no.

And if ye will then leave your bourds
And use your wit and shew it so

And with a beck ye shall me call.
And if of one that burneth alway
Ye have any pity at all
Answer him fair with yea or nay.

If it be yea I shall be fain.
If it be nay friends as before.
Ye shall another man obtain
And I mine own and yours no more.[9]

In the middle lines of the second stanza, the turn to the third person (as well as the feminine ending of line 6 and the trochees of line 7) marks the point at which Wyatt forces the poem to acknowledge its limits, to speak outside its mode. Or consider the rondeau 'Help me to seek', in which thirteen lines concerning lost property are suddenly complicated by an unexpected ending:

Help me to seek for I lost it there;
And if that ye have found it, ye that be here,
And seek to convey it secretly,
Handle it soft and treat it tenderly
Or else it will plain and then appair.
But rather restore it mannerly
Since that I do ask it thus honestly,
For to lose it it sitteth me too near.
    Help me to seek.

Alas, and is there no remedy
But have I thus lost it wilfully?
Iwis it was a thing all too dear
To be bestowed and wist not where:
It was mine heart! I pray you heartily
    Help me to seek.[10]

The 'here' and 'there' of the poem's topography amount to more than the conventional oppositions (e.g. 'then … now') of the amatory lyric: they corroborate the speaker's awareness that his 'here' is not everywhere, that this poem is spoken from within a kind of retreat away from a larger, more complex world. When the climax arrives at line 14 – 'It was mine heart! I pray you heartily' – one is obliged to wonder not only how the lover is able to speak heartily without a heart, but if he can, whether any of the preceding adverbs that have been disposed epistrophically throughout the poem have any tenderness or mannerliness or honesty behind them. Without compromising its character as a love-lyric, the poem discloses its liabilities as an emotionally rich statement – it recognizes its own one-sidedness – and the narrowness, perhaps even the poverty, of its mannerisms. Only in the light of such self-awareness can the penultimate line overcome its oxymoronic semantics, reaching out to us from within a prison of style and attitude to ask, movingly, for our understanding.

The pressure to admit other poetic models into Wyatt's plain style implies what the poet must have encountered when he travelled to France, Italy, Spain, Portugal, and the Low Countries in his embassies of the late 1520s and 1530s. This was the age of Petrarchism in its first wave, and Wyatt was only the first Englishman to join a cohort of European poets during these two decades who adapted Petrarch's example to their vernaculars. There is, we might say, a counterpart to Wyatt in nearly every European vernacular from Portugal to Poland.[11] It is worth pausing to ask how a medium conceived by a Florentine poet dead for more than 150 years could have become coded as modern in the early sixteenth century; how a body of lyric poetry that extends from Francisco Sá de Miranda in 1520s Portugal to John Donne in seventeenth-century England can be gathered under the single rubric of Petrarchism; and what kinds of ideas and beliefs accompanied the style of Italianate lyric.

Influential though it was in its own time, Petrarch's work as an instigation to humanism was forward-looking: conceived in the fourteenth century, it finally exploded in the early sixteenth, when the humanist values Petrarch had first articulated came to fruition out of means – the invention of movable type, the fall of Constantinople, the discovery of America – he could not have anticipated. To the degree that his poetry and his humanist programme were conceived together by Petrarch, the former embodied the assumptions of the latter; a poetic mode that might well have seemed retrograde fifty years after Petrarch's death became utterly contemporary 150 years after, in the age of educational reform, revival of the classics, and international diplomacy. For poets of Wyatt's generation, the Italianate spark represented a renewed attention to love, not as an entirely literal topic, but as a metonymy for the humanist interest in several related challenges such as the adaptation of classical mythology to the present, the articulation of a personal psychology, and the discovery of the political within the interpersonal. In the early sixteenth century, entire volumes of learned argument were devoted to these topics, but Petrarchism allowed a poem of fourteen lines to do the work of such a volume suggestively and elegantly. Moreover, Petrarchism proved to be adaptable over at least three generations of European thought. It was adjusted to changes in politics, philosophy, and geography, drawing topicality from these disciplines even as it held to timelessness from its investment in romantic love. Through all of these phases, Petrarchism remained more a mode of thinking than a poetic fashion. It showed these European generations how to weigh difference, how to recognize the weakness of power, how to accept the limits of representation. From the Spanish soldier and historian Gonzalo Fernández de Oviedo in the beginning of the sixteenth century to the English colonist Edmund Spenser at the end, Petrarchism persisted precisely until the rise of a discrete literature concerning these issues in philosophical, social, and international terms. We might think of Petrarchan lyric, apart from its vivid appeal as poetry, as loaning an imaginative programme to ideas that awaited their proper expression in other discourses.[12]

If Wyatt's plain style shows the pressure of other poetic discourses infiltrating it from outside, his Petrarchism likewise distinguishes itself from the Italianate adaptations of many of his continental contemporaries. In the first place, unlike the majority of European Petrarchans, Wyatt does not write amatory poems in sequences or even collections. His sole experiment with sequential lyric is his translation of the penitential psalms, which he adapted from Pietro Aretino and was the first published work to appear under Wyatt's name, in 1549. Instead of being embedded in a sequence like the sonnets of Ronsard or Garcilaso de la Vega, Wyatt's love-poems – thirty of them are sonnets – are enmeshed in a broader world of discourses; instead of holding a place within an array of coordinated poems, each one must make its own way, a fiction in itself. Even those poems that respond to originals by Petrarch seem remarkably fresh and unencumbered, belonging more to their contemporary world than to the fourteenth century. One of the most successful of the amatory poems is this sonnet, which is adapted from Petrarch's *Canzoniere* 190, 'Una candida cerva':

> Whoso list to hunt, I know where is an hind,
> But as for me, helas, I may no more.
> The vain travail hath wearied me so sore,
> I am of them that farthest cometh behind.
> Yet may I by no means my wearied mind
> Draw from the deer, but as she fleeth afore
> Fainting I follow. I leave off therefore
> Sithens in a net I seek to hold the wind.
> Who list her hunt, I put him out of doubt,
> As well as I may spend his time in vain.
> And graven with diamonds in letters plain
> There is written her fair neck round about:
> '*Noli me tangere* for Caesar's I am,
> And wild for to hold though I seem tame.'[13]

In Petrarch's original, an unattainable white doe inspires the speaker to abandon his labour until he falls abruptly into a river and she disappears; Petrarch treats the Caesarean inscription, a citation of John 20:17 ('noli me tangere'), as a reproach to the speaker's lassitude and desire – she would be the sign of his redemption if only he saw her that way – as well as a harbinger of Laura's death. As a parable of spiritual blindness, the sonnet represents a brokered subjectivity, in which the poem's nominal attention to the deer ('a white doe on the green grass [who] appeared to me') lightly masks its interest in the speaker himself. Such a diversion, while it can be accommodated in a sequence of 366 poems, must be made virtual in a sonnet that stands apart, present in effect if not in substance. In other words, Wyatt's sonnet must treat the speaker's condition more directly – in the isolated sonnet *c.*1530, the genre demands as much – and it must assemble its own context. Thus Wyatt introduces a fourth standpoint into the poem to complement the speaker, the doe, and the unseen Caesar: a prospective hunter who may bring a sense of wonder to the encounter, allowing Wyatt's speaker to dwell on his 'wearied mind' and vain pursuit. This hypothetical hunter may well feel the surprise and attraction of Petrarch's speaker, but to Wyatt's speaker this is a twice-told tale. Moreover, the Caesarean context has been rendered more absolutist than Christian, and the awakening in Petrarch's original replaced by a sense that the words on the collar are not allegorical but literal. In fact, in Wyatt's sonnet nothing follows those words. They hang in the air with the unmistakable sense that in this poem's world, kings and emperors do proscribe desire, and lusts have consequences outside the mind.

In general, these are the sorts of revision that accompany Wyatt's venture in Englishing Petrarchism: fresh standpoints, a reduced quotient of allegory and a reweighing of figures such as collars, shipwrecks, and lutes to render them literal, and a further degree of recension and weariness. Direct adaptations such as 'My galley charged with forgetfulness' (from *Canzoniere* 189) and 'The long love that in my thought doth harbour' (from *Canzoniere* 140) take a revisionary stance considerably different from, on the one hand, those of the Italian poets of the fifteenth and sixteenth centuries who stay close to Petrarch's originals, sometimes producing *contrafacta* (that is, parodic revisions that employ much of the same language as the originals) more than new poems; and on the other hand, those of the vernacular sequence-makers in French, Spanish, or Portuguese who carry out more diffuse adaptations of the *Canzoniere* across thirty or fifty sonnets.

One can only speculate about what Wyatt and his English and continental contemporaries saw in the Petrarchan sonnet, but in his case the form seems to be the poetic expression of a strategy to manage change – the experience of personal and social upheaval – by counterposing a stanza that renders such change virtual, controlling it through language and perspective. Each sonnet imagines a condition out of history ('Caesar, when that the traitor of Egypt'), moral philosophy ('Love and Fortune and my mind, rememb'rer'), natural philosophy ('Some fowls there be that have so perfect sight'), or simply courtship ('If amorous faith in heart unfeigned'), and broaches a problem that proves to be essentially moral: for instance, whether dissembling is justified, how much of one's self to give over to love, how to respond to inconstancy. If the typical sonnet of Wyatt's begins by adducing a dynamic, often untenable situation, it develops by showing the speaker's adjustments to that reality – a conception of lyric poetry that must have seemed exquisitely adapted to a highly volatile moment in European culture and society. The making of these adjustments is the sonnets themselves, and there are nearly as many kinds of adjustment as sonnets: these stances include self-possession ('My heart I gave thee, not to do it pain'), resignation ('I find no peace and all my war is done'), steadfastness ('Each man me telleth I change most my device'), reproof ('Such is the course that nature's kind hath wrought'), despair ('The pillar perished is whereto I leant'), and accommodation ('The long love that in my thought doth harbour'). Between the opening conceit often adapted not merely from the stock themes of poetry but from some branch of knowledge, and the concluding recalibration that tended to show the operations of both the mind and the emotions against that conceit, Wyatt and his contemporaries must have seen this sort of poetry as continuous with all their other intellectual projects – philosophical, educational, diplomatic – under the common purpose of not preventing but mastering change. Among other values, such sonnets showed Wyatt's readers how to live in a world of contingency. When to build a moral or emotional stay against change, when and how to lose, when to revise one's principles – this is the repertory of stances that Richard Tottel, the first publisher of Wyatt's amatory poetry, recognized when he titled many of the poems with abstract descriptions such as 'Of duteous love' ('Avising the bright beams of these fair eyes') and 'The wavering lover willeth, and dreadeth, to move his desire' ('Such vain thought as wonted to mislead me').

The most successful artefact of Wyatt's adaptation of Petrarch is 'They flee from me', a ballade that is one of many attempts in the period to capture the psychic dynamism of the sonnet in a longer, more fluid form.

They flee from me that sometime did me seek
With naked foot stalking in my chamber.
I have seen them gentle, tame, and meek
That now are wild and do not remember
That sometime they put themselves in danger

To take bread at my hand; and now they range
Busily seeking with a continual change.

Thanked be fortune it hath been otherwise
Twenty times better, but once in special,
In thin array after a pleasant guise,
When her loose gown from her shoulders did fall
And she me caught in her arms long and small,
Therewithal sweetly did me kiss
And softly said, 'Dear heart, how like you this?'

It was no dream: I lay broad waking.
But all is turned thorough my gentleness
Into a strange fashion of forsaking.
And I have leave to go of her goodness
And she also to use newfangleness.
But since that I so kindly am served
I would fain know what she hath deserved.[14]

If scholars have often reduced Wyatt's scope by seeing him as merely a poet of the bedchamber and the court, of frustrated love and ambition, this poem seems to address such misconceptions. Its bedchamber is turned inside out to become a forest in which wild game run, while the tortured speaker shows romantic rejection to be not simply an emotional blow but a habitable stance that calls up properly moral questions: how to 'serve' fickleness, whether 'gentleness' means anything in the absence of requital, and how love masks the transactions of power. Reflecting the conditions of his lifetime, during which resistance to authority in matters of religion and empire grew increasingly commonplace, and in which kings, governors, and diplomats struggled to redraw the boundaries between wildness and civility from Ireland to Asia to America, 'They flee from me' emplots a Petrarchan situation in the wider world of the 1530s. Anticipating John Donne, Wyatt brings that world into the bedchamber; ahead of Robert Browning, he allows the poem to raise larger issues than those seen by its speaker, a feat of dramatic irony that makes the concluding couplet,

But since that I so kindly am served,
I would fain know what she hath deserved,

not merely a rejoinder to infidelity but a meditation on the connection between 'kind' (which can mean nature, species, character), service (requital, obligation, right), and deserving, or the moral condition that responds to kind and makes service reciprocal. Wyatt's rumination settles on a problem that we know from many different contexts of the period: the obedience owed to an absolute monarch, the deserts of a retainer in service, the rights of conquered people in the face of imperial authority. The poem finds its power when, by refusing to exclude any of these, it gives licence to the three concepts in the couplet – kind, service, deserving – to combine in many different statements by which the reader may answer the speaker's request for knowledge ('I would fain know'). It belongs to Wyatt's poetic strategy across all genres to foreground concepts under revision – among them truth, liberty, virtue, faith, service – and to locate them at points of emotional, rhetorical, and even metrical tension. (If in his time some of these terms, because of semantic ambiguity or Romance origins, might have had uncertain pronunciation in English, that fact only augments his strategy.) With its climactic couplet, 'They flee from me' carries this approach further than any other of his poems.

In some ways Wyatt's amatory lyrics help us to understand the discursive poems because one recognizes in the latter – at 90–110 lines, Wyatt's most extensive poems – many of the concerns that give substance and topical weight to his songs and sonnets about love. Thus the canzone 'In Spain' presents 100 lines of poulter's measure – or alternating six- (hexameter) and seven-stress ('fourteener') lines – on the part of a speaker separated from his beloved, with more scope for reflection on the nature of desire and mortality than any sonnet offers; when we inquire further, for instance as to why the speaker is away from home, we realize that 'In Spain' belongs to the set of mid-century poems that deplore, and often indirectly criticize, the absences caused by diplomatic or imperial service and the griefs suffered by the agents of absolutism. All of the elements that are compressed otherwise into a sonnet or a song are visible here but without the intensity of expression or the sudden reversals of conceit and context. The satire 'Mine own John Poyntz', an adaptation of Luigi Alamanni's *satira* addressed to Tommaso Sertini, goes beyond 'In Spain' to indict not only Henrician court culture but 'the press of courts whereso they go', an indication that Wyatt's speaker draws his convictions from a European as well as an English setting.[15] What follows is a review of the political and moral vices of several courts: where the amatory lyrics often disclose how these settings seem through the glass of romantic love with its summits and nadirs of feeling, a satire such as 'John Poyntz' affords another view of the same courts through their quotidian activities of conversing, drinking, and boasting.

In a passage that Wyatt sharply revises from Alamanni's original,

> No man doth mark whereso I ride or go;
> In lusty leas in liberty I walk.
> And of these news I feel nor weal nor woe,
> Save that a clog doth hang yet at my heel.
> No force for that, for it is ordered so
> That I may leap both hedge and dike full well.[16]

he adds the acknowledgement of what was probably Henry's order banishing him from the court, 'a clog', but then evokes the compensatory freedoms of the English countryside, the site of a return to personal autonomy. What are the conditions of such a mental state of quietness and self-rule? Wyatt's longer poems tend to insist on the power of men, through reflection and self-knowledge, to arrive at autonomy regardless of their location in court or country, but none the less these poems cultivate an imaginative landscape quite at odds with that of the shorter lyrics. The concluding lines of 'John Poyntz', with the stirring statement of the speaker's planting 'in Kent and Christendom', made this satire an exemplar of nativist poetry of the later sixteenth century, notably including some of the work of George Gascoigne, whose 'Woodmanship' is heavily in its debt. The similar satire 'My mother's maids when they did sew and spin' compares urban and rural life, and concludes – after a parable about a country mouse who goes to the city and is caught by a cat – with an injunction that seems to favour the country as a site of self-possession:

> Thyself content with that is thee assigned
> And use it well that is to thee allotted.
> Then seek no more out of thyself to find
> The thing that thou hast sought so long before,
> For thou shalt feel it sitting in thy mind.[17]

But inasmuch as Wyatt in principle esteems a personal autonomy that can be had in court as well as countryside – 'each kind of life hath with him his disease', the satire's speaker observes – we have to notice that the rural English landscape of many of the discursive poems is hardly by itself a sign of moral value, as it will be for some of the later nativist poets. Instead, it is the topographical correlative of the discursive logic, conversational tone, and long lines that distinguish the satires from the shorter lyrics – a different way of looking at the same world, where value and purpose are still constituted inwardly. While the amatory personae speak in code and are confined in the tight stanzas or rooms-turned-worlds of their sonnets or ballades, these speakers, who name names and choose their settings from the real map of England, reveal the life that exists around those courtly and Italianate milieus. Just as each sort of speaker depends on the others (or is the others in alternative circumstances), each kind of poem lends meaning to the others as part of a broad survey of the pathologies of the desiring mind. His contemporaries and near successors (and some modern critics) may have variously celebrated one of Wyatt's modes at the expense of the others (some preferring the amatory poems, some the plain-style lyrics), but we could not do without any of them.

The question of Wyatt's verse rhythms, though often seen as impossibly complicated, demands some attention here. In a long phase between the death of Chaucer *c.*1400 and the publication of *Tottel's Miscellany* in 1557, iambic pentameter, the dominant line of English verse, was often unsettled as poets – knowingly or not – experimented with varying arrangements of stresses and syllables. Wyatt is perhaps the last poet of that phase. Surrey, the younger poet with whom he is often contrasted, established a fashion for regularity in the decasyllabic line that held sway from the appearance of Tottel until the later nineteenth century. For many of his immediate successors, Wyatt's variations from this assumed norm seemed ignorant or clumsy, and the poems were often criticized or emended on this score. One of the set pieces of recent undergraduate curricula in early modern English poetry is to compare the concluding couplet of 'They flee from me', quoted earlier in this essay, with Tottel's revision:

> But, sins that I vnkyndly so am serued:
> How like you this, what hath she now deserued?[18]

By regularizing the rhythms according to a Surreyan model, the revision does away with the possibility of a reader's lingering uncertainly over words such as 'kindly' and (the now missing) 'know'. In 'They flee from me' and indeed many of Wyatt's poems, such words are sometimes distended to compensate for what appear to be missing stressed or unstressed syllables. Poets and scholars have offered many explanations for Wyatt's practice, but in recent years the most convincing accounts have emphasized his expressive purposes, especially in the sonnets: as one critic contrasts him with his forerunners,

> Wyatt, no doubt because of his wider acquaintance with Continental models, especially with Petrarch ... [regards] meter as an expressive material whose departures from exact metronomic repetition can reflect the changing emotions of a troubled speaker and incorporate some of the syllabic texture of Italian verse.[19]

Of course there is an intellectual as well as an expressive dimension to Wyatt's rhythms, since his exploratory play with contestable terms and ideological ambiguities often coincides with his 'departures' from metrical regularity. Moreover, his work is so much a product of its distinctive moment that it hardly surprises when readers and editors even fifteen years after his death suppressed or overlooked these irregularities. Wyatt's kind of inquisitiveness, adjusted to the tensions of the Henrician and Holy Roman courts, must have seemed out of tune with the Marian era in which Tottel published his songs and sonnets, and in revising the poems towards a Surreyan regularity the editor was probably smoothing their edges in more than rhythm. Moreover, Tottel is the inventor of the style of reading that sees love as not the first but the final horizon of these poems, that treats Wyatt as a poet of national more than international interests, convictions more than questions. Even as he presents a Wyatt who decisively refreshes English poetry, Tottel leaves it to the twentieth century to rediscover a Wyatt at once more attuned to his own age and more legible to recent – that is, modernist and later – ideas of what poetry is and can be.

In a song included in the Devonshire and Arundel Harington manuscripts and often attributed to Wyatt, the speaker announces

> Now all of change
> Must be my song
> And from my bond now must I break
> Since she so strange
> Unto my wrong
> Doth stop her ears to hear me speak.
>
> Yet none doth know
> So well as she
> My grief which can have no restraint.[20]

The graduated but limitless emotion to which he refers even in this poem of the plain style – the searching of 'the innermost reaches of one's being' that critics have called Wyatt's inwardness – is developed or at least acknowledged in nearly all his poems, from the translations of the penitential psalms to the sonnets to the satires.[21] While he receives inwardness as a capacity of poetry from a number of English and continental models, he is perhaps the first early modern figure in English to extend it from devotional to amatory and social poems, and to treat it as a criterion of lyric intelligence and power. Without Wyatt's example, it is hard to imagine the success of those later poets such as Donne and George Herbert who explore the inner reaches of consciousness through meditation or less formal means. Inwardness is many things for Wyatt, but it always responds to the social world, the conditions of contingency and change over which his poems obsess. An inward poem, or even a plain-style poem that glances towards an inwardness it cannot fully express, discovers an axis of attention that draws speaker and reader away from the external world and into an idiom in which social facts are reweighed and transfigured. Belonging to a moment and a setting where 'change' was an ineluctable force, Wyatt's contribution was to adapt and invent new modes – formal, intellectual, and psychic – of managing change in the service of a renovated poetry.

NOTES

1 Sir Thomas Wyatt, *The Complete Poems*, ed. R. A. Rebholz (Harmondsworth: Penguin, 1978; rptd New Haven: Yale University Press, 1981), p. 150.
2 George Puttenham, *The Arte of English Poesie* (1589), eds Gladys Doidge Willcock and Alice Walker (Cambridge: Cambridge University Press, 1936), p. 62.
3 Wyatt, *Complete Poems*, p. 129.
4 Yvor Winters, 'The Sixteenth-Century Lyric in England: A Critical and Historical Reinterpretation', *Poetry* 53 (1939), 258–72, 320–5, and 54 (1939), 35–51; rptd in *Elizabethan Poetry: Modern Essays in Criticism*, ed. Paul Alpers (New York: Oxford University Press, 1967), pp. 93–125; C. S. Lewis, *English Literature in the Sixteenth Century, Excluding Drama*, Oxford History of English Literature 3 (Oxford: Oxford University Press, 1954), pp. 223–30; Kenneth J. E. Graham, *The Performance of Conviction: Plainness and Rhetoric in the Early English Renaissance* (Ithaca, NY: Cornell University Press, 1994).
5 Wyatt, *Complete Poems*, p. 130.
6 Wyatt, *Complete Poems*, p. 131.
7 Wyatt, *Complete Poems*, p. 157.
8 Wyatt, *Complete Poems*, p. 74.
9 Wyatt, *Complete Poems*, p. 132.
10 Wyatt, *Complete Poems*, p. 73.
11 Ernest Hatch Wilkins, 'A General Survey of Renaissance Petrarchism', in *Studies in the Life and Works of Petrarch* (Cambridge, MA: Mediaeval Academy of America, 1955), pp. 280–99.
12 William J. Kennedy, *Authorizing Petrarch* (Ithaca, NY: Cornell University Press, 1995); Roland Greene, *Unrequited Conquests: Love and Empire in the Colonial Americas* (Chicago: University of Chicago Press, 1999); William J. Kennedy, *The Site of Petrarchism: Early Modern National Sentiment in Italy, France, and England* (Baltimore: Johns Hopkins University Press, 2003).
13 Wyatt, *Complete Poems*, p. 77.
14 Wyatt, *Complete Poems*, pp. 116–17.
15 Wyatt, *Complete Poems*, p. 186.
16 Wyatt, *Complete Poems*, p. 188.
17 Wyatt, *Complete Poems*, p. 191.
18 *Tottel's Miscellany (1557–1587)*, ed. Hyder Edward Rollins, rev. edn, 2 vols (Cambridge, MA: Harvard University Press, 1965), 1, p.39.
19 George T. Wright, 'Wyatt's Decasyllabic Line', *Studies in Philology* 82 (1985), 129–56, p. 144.
20 Wyatt, *Complete Poems*, pp. 314–15.
21 Stephen Greenblatt, *Renaissance Self-Fashioning: From More to Shakespeare* (Chicago: University of Chicago Press, 1980), p. 117.

SELECTED FURTHER READING

Editions

Collected Poems, eds Kenneth Muir and Patricia Thomson, Liverpool, Liverpool University Press, 1969. An influential edition with valuable notes that place Wyatt in his continental as well as English contexts

The Complete Poems, ed. R. A. Rebholz, New Haven, Yale University Press, 1981. A reliable modern-spelling edition that sorts the poems by genre

Harrier, Richard C., *The Canon of Sir Thomas Wyatt's Poetry*, Cambridge, MA, Harvard University Press, 1975. The most rigorous edition for identifying the Wyatt canon, based on a diplomatic transcription of the Egerton manuscript

Rollins, Hyder Edward (ed.), *Tottel's Miscellany (1557–1587)*, 2 vols, rev. edn, Cambridge, MA, Harvard University Press, 1966. The standard edition of the collection in which many of Wyatt's poems were first published

Secondary works

Crewe, Jonathan, *Trials of Authorship: Anterior Forms and Poetic Reconstruction from Wyatt to Shakespeare*, The New Historicism 9, Berkeley and Los Angeles, University of California Press, 1990

Ferry, Anne, *The 'Inward' Language: Sonnets of Wyatt, Sidney, Shakespeare, Donne*, Chicago, University of Chicago Press, 1983

Greenblatt, Stephen, *Renaissance Self-Fashioning: From More to Shakespeare*, Chicago, University of Chicago Press, 1980

Greene, Roland, *Unrequited Conquests: Love and Empire in the Colonial Americas*, Chicago, University of Chicago Press, 1999

Greene, Thomas M., *The Light in Troy: Imitation and Discovery in Renaissance Poetry*, New Haven, Yale University Press, 1982

Lewis, C. S., *English Literature in the Sixteenth Century, Excluding Drama*, Oxford History of English Literature 3, Oxford, Oxford University Press, 1954

Southall, Raymond, *The Courtly Maker: An Essay on the Poetry of Wyatt and His Contemporaries*, Oxford, Blackwell, 1964

Spearing, A. C., *Medieval to Renaissance in English Poetry*, Cambridge, Cambridge University Press, 1985

Thomson, Patricia, *Sir Thomas Wyatt and His Background*, Stanford: Stanford University Press, 1964

Tillyard, E. M. W., *The Poetry of Sir Thomas Wyatt: A Selection and a Study*, London, Scholartis Press, 1929

Winters, Yvor, 'The Sixteenth-Century Lyric in England: A Critical and Historical Reinterpretation', *Poetry* 53 (1939), 258–72, 320–5, and 54 (1939), 35–51. Rptd in Paul Alpers (ed.), *Elizabethan Poetry: Modern Essays in Crviticism*, New York, Oxford University Press, 1967, pp. 93–125

3

RICHARD A. McCABE

Edmund Spenser

When *The Shepheardes Calender*, Spenser's first major work, appeared in 1579 it did so anonymously, but when its author died a mere twenty years later he was widely recognized as 'the Prince of Poets in his time'. The various stages in that rapid journey from anonymity to fame trace the trajectory of a very public and highly controversial career. Spenser conducted his relationship with his readers, and indeed with his patrons, through a series of carefully manipulated personae. He was constantly auto-referential but seldom autobiographical. The 'selves' that he offered to public view were richly complex, poetic constructs acutely responsive to the demands of genre. And his generic range was dazzling: he wrote pastoral, heroic, mock heroic, panegyrical, satiric, visionary, and amatory verse.

Spenser introduced himself to the reading public in 1579 as the 'new poet', and innovation is the hallmark of his canon. He experimented with a wider range of metres, dialects, and stanza-structures than any English poet prior to John Donne, and his stylistic and generic inventions invariably purveyed unsettling social or political comment. Although he has frequently been accused, most notably, perhaps, by W. B. Yeats, of producing propaganda, it would be truer to say that his relationship to contemporary power-structures was one of conflicted fascination.[1] He found equal inspiration in Elizabethan public life for epic and satire. The anonymity of *The Shepheardes Calender* was occasioned, at least in part, by its dangerous political content, and the *Complaints* (1591) were officially censored. The first edition of *The Faerie Queene* (1590) won him a royal pension, but the second (1596) was banned in Scotland by Elizabeth's eventual successor, James VI. Whereas propaganda is most commonly characterized by an unrelenting singleness of vision, the Spenserian canon affords a bewildering diversity of perspectives. Ten of *The Shepheardes Calender*'s twelve eclogues (pastoral poems) are cast in the form of dialogue, and even in the remaining two the 'voice' of Colin Clout, Spenser's alleged alter ego, is carefully distinguished from that of the narrator or 'author', who goes by the distinct pseudonym of 'Immeritô'. *Colin Clouts Come Home Againe* is similarly cast in the form of dialogue as is the prose tract *A View of the Present State of Ireland*, and many of the *Complaints* involve dialogue or dramatic monologue. Although he often signals his ambition to become England's Virgil, the most disconcerting feature of Spenser's imaginative universe is its Ovidian fluidity – and Ovid was the poet exiled by Augustus, Virgil's imperial patron. Within the world of *The Faerie Queene* anything may mutate into anything else, even praise into parody. The very architecture of the work, combining Virgil's 'books' with Ariosto's 'cantos', the linear structure of Latin epic with the twists and turns of Italian romance, signals a multiplicity of viewpoints, a constant revisioning of image and theme. If Gloriana is the most elusive figure in *The Faerie Queene*, she is very much cast in her creator's image.

The prefatory material to *The Shepheardes Calender* constitutes no less than a manifesto for the renewal of English verse, as revolutionary in its day as the preface to the *Lyrical Ballads* two hundred years later. The 'new poet' introduced by the mysterious 'E. K.' is a literary and linguistic reformer, but like most reformers of the sixteenth century a devotee of 'antiquitie'. The 'new poet' affords the shock of the old: 'he hath laboured to restore, as to theyr rightfull heritage such good and naturall English words, as have ben long time out of use and almost cleare disherited'. His model may be Virgil but he dissociates himself from those who have 'made our English tongue, a gallimaufray or hodgepodge of al other speches' by indiscriminately borrowing their vocabularies from French, Italian, and Latin. By contrast, he seeks to demonstrate that 'our Mother tonge ... is both ful enough for prose and stately enough for verse' despite being commonly accounted 'most bare and barrein of both'.[2] His is a work in which the Renaissance ideal of emulation of the classics melds with the Reformation ideal of rediscovering a national identity that is at once political, spiritual, and linguistic. Within the pages of the *Calender* he creates a community of very English shepherds who discuss the most topical religious, political, and aesthetic issues of the day in a manner designed to demonstrate how all three are indissolubly interrelated – and how, when properly acknowledged and nurtured, the 'English poet' can act as the guardian of his countrymen's true inheritance. Unlike any former set of eclogues, Spenser's poems are attuned to the passage of time, one pastoral per month. But the goal, as Immeritô tells us at the end of the volume, is to transmute temporal mutability into lasting artistic achievement: 'Loe I have made a Calender for every yeare, / That steele in strength, and time in durance shall outwear.' Yet there remains something teasingly incongruous about the notion that any sort of 'calender' can outlast 'time'. As so often in Spenser, the language of assertion is laced with irony.

It was the first duty of an ancient commentator to identify the author and give some account of his life. E. K., the *Calender*'s anonymous commentator, confounds all such expectations by failing to name either his author or himself. In fact, his own identity is a rhetorical function of the text upon which he comments, and he remains as much a creation of the work's imaginative world as any of the shepherds he introduces. In the Spenser–Harvey *Letters* published – again anonymously – the following year, verses supposedly translated by E. K. are directly attributed to 'Immeritô' himself (*Maye*, line 69; *Prose*, p. 16). A clever presentational game is being played here and one which is designed to cultivate a hermeneutics of suspicion and doubt. Covert allusion was traditionally attributed to Virgil's *Eclogues*, and the new poet will not be found lacking in that respect. Political pressures may have necessitated caution but Spenser makes an aesthetic virtue of political necessity by consciously infusing the eclogues with the allure of the mysterious and occult.

E. K.'s 'gloss' serves to explain difficult words, call attention to classical analogues and sources, and identify particularly striking tropes or figures, but it also makes a point of holding much in reserve and being seen to do so. As a result, Spenser's 'new' poetry appeared with the ready-made equivalent of generations of accumulated classical commentary and encouraged its readers to make their own annotations by addressing the problems that E. K. left unresolved. In all of the early editions the verse is set in traditional black-letter or Gothic typeface while the commentary (including E. K.'s 'arguments' to the eclogues) is set in contemporary roman (Fig. 1). The effect is to endow the printed 'voice' of Immeritô with a visual signature distinct from that of E. K., thereby strengthening the impression that two authors are at work rather than one. Yet despite this illusion, the verse and the commentary are actually contemporaneous and inextricable. Properly understood *The Shepheardes Calender* is more than just the twelve eclogues. The 'editorial' material – dedicatory letters, prose arguments, scholarly annotations, and analyses of cryptic 'emblems'– amounts to roughly half the volume. The 'meaning' of the work is to be sought not in any single component but in the subtle interaction of verse, commentary, *and woodcut*: this being the earliest example of an illustrated collection of original verse by a living English poet. Everything about the production of the volume proclaims that its author is anything but 'Immeritô' or 'Unworthy'. Quite the contrary: he has set his foot on the first rung of the Virgilian *rota*, a career path designed to lead from pastoral to epic.

His claim to such eventual eminence is staked through the self-proclaiming virtuosity of his verse. His range of metres and stanza-forms is quite stunning, from the relatively simple six-line stanza of *Januarye* to *August*'s

Januarye. *Fol.*1

Ægloga prima.

ARGVMENT.

IN *this fyrst Æglogue* Colin cloute *a shepheardes boy complaineth him of his vnfortunate loue, being but newly (as semeth) enamoured of a countrie lasse called* Rosalinde: *with which strong affection being very sore traueled, he compareth his carefull case to the sadde season of the yeare, to the frostie ground, to the frosen trees, and to his owne winterbeaten flocke. And lastlye, fynding himselfe robbed of all former pleasaunce and delights, hee breaketh his Pipe in peeces, and casteth him selfe to the ground.*

COLIN Cloute.

A Shepeheards boye (no better doe him call)
when Winters wastful spight was almost spent,
All in a sunneshine day, as did befall,
Led forth his flock, that had bene long ypent.
So faynt they woxe, and feeble in the folde,
That now vnnethes their feete could them vphold.

All as the Sheepe, such was the shepeheards looke,
For pale and wanne he was, (alas the while,)
May seeme he lovd, or els some care he tooke:
Well couth he tune his pipe, and frame his stile.

A.1. Tho

Figure 1 *Januarye* from *The Shepheardes Calender* (1579). By permission of the Bodleian Library, Oxford.

highly formalized variant of the Provençal sestina in which the concluding words of each line are redeployed throughout the poem in a challenging numerical pattern (123456, 612345, 561234 etc.). In *Aprill* the opening dialogue between Thenot and Hobbinol introduces the famous 'laye / Of fayre Elisa, Queen of shepheardes all' with its complex interaction of pentameter, dimeter, and concluding tetrameter rhyming *ababccddc* (or *ababccaac*):

> See, where she sits upon the grassie greene,
>   (O seemely sight)
> Yclad in Scarlot like a mayden Queene,
>   And Ermines white.
> Upon her head a Cremosin coronet,
> With Damaske roses and Daffadillies set:
>   Bayleaves betweene,
>   And Primroses greene
> Embellish the sweet violet. (lines 55–63)

Ostensibly the 'laye' constitutes a formal eulogy of Queen Elizabeth, yet the primary reason that Hobbinol gives for rehearsing it here is to demonstrate Colin Clout's poetic skill, the same skill that E. K. attributes to 'Immeritô': 'round without roughnesse, and learned wythout hardnes, such indeed as may be perceived of the leaste, understoode of the moste, but iudged onely of the learned'.[3] The excited rhythms of the verse seek to capture something of the electrifying effect that Elizabeth generated on her various progresses when she offered herself to public gaze. 'See, where she sits ... / O seemely sight': the splendour of the court, with its gorgeous scarlets and ermines, intrudes upon pastoral rusticity like an other-worldly vision. The 'learned' may realize that the riot of colour and foliage is richly symbolic but even the 'leaste' will appreciate its visually dramatic effect.

In explaining the significance of the 'bayleaves' E. K. alludes to Petrarch's laurel: 'Victorious triumphal tree / The honour of Emperors and of Poets' (*Rime Sparse*, 263), and the conjunction of poetry and politics is telling. In *October* Piers urges Cuddie (a persona of Colin's) to write epic, and in the woodcut he wears a laurel crown. The implication is quite clear: poet and prince need each other. If she will make him her Laureate, he will make her famous by capturing forever the otherwise transient glory of mortal majesty. But how far might a Laureate go before praise became flattery? The 'laye of fayr Eliza' is often quoted out of context as an example of unalloyed panegyric, but Spenser was meticulously attentive to context. At the time of publication the Virgin Queen had rendered herself remarkably unpopular by planning to marry the French and Catholic Duke of Anjou, widely denounced as an 'alien' in religion, nationality, and tongue. Eliza is '*like* a mayden Queene' but for how long? The accompanying woodcut shows her surrounded by her ladies-in-waiting but ominously positioned under the sign of Taurus, the mythical 'bull from the sea' that carried off the virgin Europa (Fig. 2). The lay is carefully located as a poem-within-a-poem, a vision of happier times recited on behalf of what the argument describes as an 'alienated' Colin Clout, and the eclogue that contains it forms part of a sequence of poems which supply a very troubled vision of Eliza's England.[4] In charting the corruption of the contemporary church, the 'moral' eclogues of *Maye*, *Iulye*, and *September* imply the failure of Elizabeth's reformation and look forward to the vicious satire of *Mother Hubberd's Tale* (1591). In a similar vein *October* complains of the court's 'contempt' for the arts and looks forward to *The Teares of the Muses* (1591) and *Colin Clouts Come Home Againe* (1595). In other words, *The Shepheardes Calender* inaugurates Spenser's career as both eulogist and satirist, as the supreme upholder of the ideals of the Elizabethan court and one of its most uncompromising critics. One of the principal reasons that no one ever meets the fairy queen within *The Faerie Queene* is Elizabeth's perceived failure to become Gloriana, a failure indicative of the unbridgeable gap between the ideal and the real. Indeed the very creation of Gloriana serves to insulate royal iconography from the activities of the capricious and petulant Belphoebe, in whom (as in the Belphoebe of Sir Walter Ralegh's *Oceans Love to Scynthia*) the person of the queen is more closely 'shadowed'.

Spenser wrote the poetry not of political and aesthetic complacency but of what the *Amoretti* (1595) terms the 'unquiet mind'. *The Faerie Queene* is a peculiarly troubled epic and draws much of its poetic power from its failures of resolution, from the constant deferral of an ending that comes to seem ever more improbable with every passing canto. What begins in Book I, 'The Legend of Holinesse' (1590), as an overt demonstration of the morality of politics becomes by Book V, 'The Legend of Iustice' (1596), a dark exploration of the politics of expediency. Spenser had moved to Ireland in 1580 and that move was as aesthetically significant for him as the departure from Rome to Tomis was for Ovid. Spenser was not, of course, an exile in the Ovidian sense but ingeniously adapted the Ovidian poetics of exile to express his increasing sense of dislocation from, and disenchantment with, the homeland. For him, Ireland provided all of the political challenge and artistic opportunity that the 'barbarous' shores of the Black Sea afforded to his Roman predecessor. It is not just that the imaginative topography of *The Faerie Queene* benefits immensely from direct experience of the 'wild' terrain and 'savage' peoples chronicled in *A View of the Present State of Ireland* (*c*.1596), but that the poem's central concepts of civility, nationality, and renewal undergo a profound transformation. As he tells us in the

Aprill.

Ægloga Quarta.

ARGVMENT.

THis Æglogue is purpoſely intended to the honor and prayſe of our moſt gracious ſoueraigne, Queene Elizabeth. The ſpeakers herein be Hobbinoll and Thenott, two ſhepheardes: the which Hobbinoll being before mentioned, greatly to haue loued Colin, is here ſet forth more largely, complayning him of that boyes great miſaduenture in Loue, whereby his mynd was alienate and with drawen not onely from him, who moſte loued him, but alſo from all former delightes and ſtudies, aſwell in pleaſaunt pyping, as conning ryming and ſinging, and other his laudable exerciſes. Whereby he taketh occaſion, for proofe of his more excellencie and ſkill in poetrie, to recorde a ſonge, which the ſayd Colin ſometime made in honor of her Maieſtie, whom abruptely he termeth Elyſa.

Thenot. Hobbinoll.

Tell me good Hobbinoll, what garres thee greete?
What? hath ſome Wolfe thy tender Lambes ytorne?
Or is thy Bagpype broke, that ſoundes ſo ſweete?
Or art thou of thy loued laſſe forlorne?

Or bene thine eyes attempred to the yeare,
Quenching the gaſping furrowes thirſt with rayne?

Like

Figure 2 *Aprill* from *The Shepheardes Calender* (1579). By permission of the Bodleian Library, Oxford.

explanatory 'Letter to Ralegh' that accompanies the first edition, Spenser has written a consciously allegorical epic, and allegory, as the etymology of the word suggests, entails 'a speaking of the other'. What this involves at its most basic level is the persistent implication of some moral or political tenor beyond the vehicle of the story, but on a deeper level Spenser's allegory involves a persistent sense of otherness or contrariety pervading the whole structure of the poem. For every virtue there is a demonic alter ego almost indistinguishable from the real thing, for every St George there is a 'false' St George, for every Florimel a false Florimel. The reader must remain ever alert to subtle nuances of distinction. When the false St George rides into Book I his description parodies the poem's famous opening stanzas in minute linguistic detail (as indicated in bold):

In **mighty armes** he was **yclad** anon:
And **silver shield**, upon his coward **brest**
A bloody crosse, and on his craven crest
A bounch of haires discolourd diversly;
Full iolly knight he seemde, and well addrest,
And when he **sate** upon his **courser free**,
Saint George himself ye would have deemed him to be.

(I. 2. 11)

The point, of course, is that the 'true' St George is in some respects just as false. Like many of the poem's questing knights he is portrayed as a foundling ignorant of his own identity, 'a tall clownishe younge man' who sits on the floor at Gloriana's feast 'unfitte through his rusticity for a better place'. He is St George only in potential and the trials he experiences along the way test that potential severely. The ultimate Spenserian quest is for self-knowledge. Before overcoming the dragon George will strut in the House of Pride, languish in the Dungeon of Ignorance, and attempt suicide in the Cave of Despair. In the world of *The Faerie Queene* there is always the fear that polar opposites may coalesce if moral energy fails, and what was true of the individual Englishman was also true of the nation. By espousing a version of the Arthurian legend, Spenser attempted to provide for Elizabethan England a myth of national identity equivalent to that created for the Romans by Virgil. But the Virgilian thrust of the poem is complicated by Ovidian anxiety, by the fear of regressive transformation. For Spenser's contemporaries Ireland, like the New World, was as much a state of mind as a place. Holinshed's *Chronicles* compared it to the Homeric island of Circe.[5] According to *A View*, it is what England once was and might again become. The English allegory of *The Faerie Queene* constantly invokes an Irish 'otherness'. In Ireland, Spenser alleged, 'civil' Englishmen 'degenerated' into 'animals', just as questing knights are habitually transformed into beasts in the 'Bowre of Blisse'. Yet therein lay the rub. So far as the second book of *The Faerie Queene* is concerned, temperance may be the avowed ideal but intemperance appears to inspire the best verse. The Bowre is imaginatively compelling precisely because it is tempting and transformative:

> So passeth, in the passing of a day,
> Of mortall life the leafe, the bud, the flowre,
> Ne more doth florish after first decay,
> That earst was sought to decke both bed and bowre,
> Of manye a Ladie, and many a Paramowre:
> Gather therefore the Rose, whilest yet is prime,
> For soone comes age, that will her pride deflowre:
> Gather the Rose of love, whilest yet is time,
> Whilest loving thou mayst loved be with equall crime.
>
> (II. 12. 75)

This famous 'song of the rose' derives from Tasso's *Gerusalemme Liberata* (16. 14–15) but with a crucial difference. In Tasso the love on offer is genuine and ultimately benign. At the heart of Spenser's skilfully divergent adaptation lies a cunning piece of orthography. This is the sole instance in the entire Spenserian canon where 'paramour' is spelled 'paramowre'. The central image is one of vegetation – leaf, bud, and flower – but this lover, far from preserving the magic of a fleeting moment, will 'mow' it down. She is actually akin to love's great enemy, 'wicked Time, who with his scythe addrest, / Does mow the flowring herbes and goodly things' (III. 6. 39). Everyone agreed that love should be mutual but the Bowre affords only criminal reciprocity: 'Whilest loving thou mayst loved be with equall crime'. In the Gardens of Adonis, conceived as a counter-image to the Bowre, the matter is quite different: 'Franckly each paramour his leman knowes' (III. 6. 41). It is this 'knowing' that distinguishes the Bowre from the Gardens. The two locations are structurally similar: each boasts an entrance guarded by a porter, a spacious garden, and a private arbour. But the porter to the Gardens of Adonis is Genius 'to whom the care / Of life, and generation of all, / That lives, pertaines in charge particulare' and who empowers self-knowledge; the porter to the Bowre, falsely called 'Genius', is 'the foe of life, that good envyes to all / That secretly doth us procure to fall' (II. 12. 47–8). Both arbours are inhabited by a male and female figure: in the Bowre, Verdant lies in the arms of the Circe-like Acrasia in a state of deadly degradation; in the Gardens, Adonis lies in the arms of Venus in a state of constant renewal:

> All be he subiect to mortalitie,
> Yet is eterne in mutabilitie,
> And by succession made perpetuall,
> Transformed oft, and chaunged diverslie. (III. 6. 47)

In the Gardens of Adonis the poetics of transformation are reappropriated to life and virtue. What is represented in Verdant is the abandonment of self to sexuality, in Adonis the discovery of self through sexuality. Both the Bowre and the Gardens function as sites of sexual pleasure, but in passing from one to the other we move from the self-indulgent to the self-fulfilling, from sexuality as an impediment to the heroic quest to sexuality as the dynamo of dynastic history. The spatial and temporal parameters of *The Faerie Queene* are accordingly opaque. External landscape frequently segues into moral topography, and even the most apparently precise chronology has symbolic implications. The 'distance' from the Bowre of Bliss to the Gardens of Adonis can be measured only in units of desire.

The first three books of *The Faerie Queene* with their legends of Holiness, Temperance, and Chastity afford plentiful instances of idealized 'atchievement', yet each one also entails a compromise with lived experience. No matter how ardently St George yearns for the New Jerusalem that he glimpses from the Mount of Contemplation, he is fated to return to the earthly service of the church militant. His great enemy Duessa survives to fight another day. Sir Guyon destroys the Bowre of Blisse but Acrasia (Intemperance), its guiding spirit, lives on. As a 'knight of maidenhead', a dedicated male virgin, he is fated to experience sexuality only as temptation, only as a 'bowre of blisse'. At the beginning of Book III he is therefore unhorsed by Britomart, whose quest entails marital sexuality, an eventual entrance to the Gardens of Adonis where Amoret, the lady she saves from the delusive House of Busyrane, is taken by Venus to be 'upbrought in goodly womanhed' (III. 6. 28). The ending to the 1590 edition of *The Faerie Queene* sees the liberated Amoret embrace her lover Scudamour so closely that they resemble a statue of Hermaphroditus (III. 12. 46), a figure here symbolic of the complementarity of male and female sexuality and ideally antithetical to the merely cross-dressed porter of the Bowre of Blisse (II. 12. 46). This emphasis on sexual fulfilment is characteristic of the Spenserian canon despite its overt praise of the queen's virginity. Alone of the major Elizabethan sonneteers he concludes the *Amoretti* with an epithalamion, a public celebration of married love wholly at odds with the unrequited, if spiritually sublimated, love of Petrarch for Laura. Queen Elizabeth may be the dedicatee and titular heroine of *The Faerie Queene* but she is not its primary inspiration. In the account of Colin Clout's vision of the Graces in the sixth book she is displaced by the shepherd poet's own love (VI. 10. 25–8).

Technically speaking, of course, Colin should never have appeared in *The Faerie Queene*. The Virgilian *rota* demands a subordination of pastoral to epic, and to readers mindful of classical precedent the generic shock of Colin's reappearance must have been as great as if the Tityrus of Virgil's

Eclogues had reappeared in his *Aeneid*. But the second instalment of *The Faerie Queene* (1596) is very different from the first, and the Colin who intrudes into it has more in common with the protagonist of *Colin Clouts Come Home Againe* (1595) than *The Shepheardes Calender*. In *Colin Clouts Come Home Againe* Spenser had utilized his residence in Ireland to allow 'Colin' to visit England as an inquisitive stranger, an age-old satiric device employed to defamiliarize the homeland by affording a distancing perspective upon its customs and values. He also employs the classical device, found in Statius and others, of juxtaposing extravagant praise of the prince with savage criticism of the court, but without any explanation of how such a contradictory state of affairs might be explained. The tone of *Colin Clouts Come Home Againe* signalled a calculated change of authorial outlook on Spenser's part prior to the publication of the second instalment of his epic. The most remarkable feature of the dedicatory sonnets to the first edition of *The Faerie Queene* is their inclusiveness. All the major factions of court life are encompassed in what looks like an effort to create a sort of national community through poetry, to promote political accord through a carefully crafted myth of assimilation and unification: 'thenceforth eternall union shall be made / Betweene the nations different afore' (III. 3. 49). The second edition begins on a very different note by implying that this project has failed owing to the poem's poor reception by Lord Burghley, Elizabeth's Lord Treasurer:

> The rugged forhead that with grave foresight,
> Welds kingdomes causes, and affaires of state,
> My looser rimes (I wote) doth sharply wite,
> For praising love, as I have done of late.

It is important to recognize how devastating such a critique would be to Spenser. A national epic was expected to engage with 'kingdomes causes, and affaires of state', and an allegorical epic was supposed to cultivate moral stamina. The allegation that Spenser had derogated from epic values into the sort of wanton ethos 'by which fraile youth is oft to follie led, / Through false allurement of that pleasing baite' is tantamount to identifying the poem itself as a Bowre of Blisse, an impediment rather than an encouragement to national heroism (4 Proem 1). By way of reply Spenser defends the link between love and heroism, eros and heroes, but the damage is already done. Classical theory, descending from Aristotle, demands an impersonal narrator for epic, but Spenser's narrator becomes increasingly intrusive and embittered. The second instalment of *The Faerie Queene* constitutes as much a revisioning of the first as a continuation. That is not to say that the first three books are substantially altered. With the one significant exception discussed below, they are not. It is rather that when re-read in the context of the three books added in 1596, the first three take on a different complexion. Spenser's technical term for such a procedure was 'retractation'. In publishing his *Fowre Hymnes* that same year he tells us that finding himself unable to recall two hymns of love and beauty written in 'the greener times of my youth', he has decided 'by way of retractation to reforme them, making in stead of those two Hymnes of earthly or naturall love and beautie, two others of heavenly and celestiall'. The two early 'hymnes' are alleged to contain precisely the sort of material that 'the rugged forhead' finds objectionable, yet they are not suppressed, despite the assertion that two new hymns have been written 'in stead' of them. The business of 'retractation', which Spenser derived from St Augustine, is quite distinct from that of retraction. By constructing a new sequence of four hymns Spenser devises a series of verbal and structural correspondences that illuminate the often paradoxical relationship between matter and spirit, producing a sequence of poems which explores both the sensuality of the soul and the spirituality of the body. What I am suggesting in this essay is that the principle of 'retractation' applies to *The Faerie Queene* no less than to the *Fowre Hymnes*. Just as their recontextualization within a four-part structure modifies the two early hymns, the recontextualization of the first three books of *The Faerie Queene* within a new six-book structure produces a similar effect. As presented in 1596, the structure of the poem more closely resembles that of medieval romance than Virgilian epic, and Helen Cooper has reminded us that 'it had long been a practice to use the second half of the structure of romance to comment on the first half'.[6]

The problematical relationship between the two 'halves' of *The Faerie Queene* is perhaps best characterized by the cancellation of the original ending to Book III. In 1590 Amoret emerges from the House of Busyrane to be reunited with her lover. In 1596 she emerges to find him gone, and the deletion of the powerful symbolism of sexual union alters not only the way in which we read Book III but the way in which we react to the ongoing business of calculated deferral across the new six-book structure. The legends of Friendship, Justice, and Courtesy which were added in 1596 are even less amenable to resolution than those of Holiness, Temperance, and Chastity. As the proem to the fourth and fifth books indicates, the world view of the poem is much darker because the era to which the political allegory alludes, the Elizabethan era, is now regarded as 'a stonie one': 'Right now is wrong, and wrong that was is right' (5 Proem 4). The allegedly poor reception of *The Faerie Queene* is proffered as a case in point because lack of aesthetic judgement is considered to be indicative of lack of moral fibre: 'Therefore do you my rimes keep better measure, / And seeke to please, that now is counted wisemans threasure' (VI. 12. 41). By allowing Book VI to conclude on the word 'threasure' Spenser ironically frames the whole of the second instalment in Burghley's displeasure. Not only does the Blatant Beast escape into the world of the narrative, it escapes into the world of the narrator, 'ne spareth he the gentle Poets rime' (VI.12. 40). This is quite unprecedented in the epic tradition and, when read in conjunction with the sudden dissolution of Colin's vision of the Graces on Mt Acidale, suggests that if epic poetry is to be written at all it may well be written in opposition to the prevailing regime rather than under its patronage.

Readers of the *Amoretti* and *Epithalamion* published just one year previously might not be surprised. The sonnet-sequence twice comments on the difficulties Spenser experienced in writing *The Faerie Queene* and sends out mixed signals as to whether or not it can be completed (Sonnets 33 and 80). Such generic cross-referencing indicates how relentlessly self-reflexive the Spenserian canon actually is. Because of the implicit association between verse-making and nation-making, the struggle to compose becomes a theme in itself. And just as the epic verse has a dialectical relationship with Virgil and Ovid, the amatory verse displays a similarly complex engagement with Petrarch. Despite verbal and thematic reminiscences of his Italian predecessor, Spenser does not write a 'Petrarchan' sequence or employ the Petrarchan sonnet form. Instead he fashions an independent fourteen-line structure, the first nine lines of which exactly replicate the stanza he designed for *The Faerie Queene*: *ababbcbcc-dcdee*. It is as if the stanzas are curtal sonnets or the sonnets expanded stanzas. The sequence Spenser presents as impeding the continuation of *The Faerie Queene* incorporates the stanzas it impedes. Epic is hereby implicit in amatory verse – and heroism in love – just as amatory conventions infuse the epic. The amatory narrator is no less concerned than his epic counterpart to find the universal in the particular:

Leave lady in your glasse of christall clene,
  Your goodly selfe for evermore to vew:
  And in my selfe, my inward selfe I meane,
  Most lively lyke behold your semblant trew.
Within my heart, though hardly it can shew
  Thing so divine to vew of earthly eye:
  The fayre Idea of your celestiall hew,
  And every part remains immortally. (Sonnet 45)

Although the opening lines read like a rebuke to female Narcissism, the speaker had recently referred to himself as Narcissus 'whose eyes him starv'd: so plenty makes me poore' (Sonnet 35). The idea was already familiar to Spenser's readers. According to E. K.'s gloss to *September*'s emblem the phrase 'plenty makes me poor', borrowed from Ovid's Narcissus (*Metamorphoses* 3. 466), was 'much used of the author, and to suche like effecte, as fyrste Narcissus spake it'. Ironically, in redirecting the lady's gaze to himself the speaker risks confirming such a reputation. Yet the lady's gaze is directed not at his body but at the 'inward selfe' which contains her own 'fayre Idea'. The problem is that this 'fayre Idea' is hard to 'shew', in image or in words. And even if it were possible to shew it, the act of gazing upon one's own 'fayre Idea' would appear to involve another form of Narcissism. The self seems inescapable. Despite gestures towards objectivity and universalism, love and art remain intensely subjective – even in heroic verse where Gloriana is invited, like the lady of the sonnets, to view her 'true glorious type' (1 Proem 4) in the 'faire mirrhour' of Spenser's verse (2 Proem 4). The point is consciously emphasized in the *Amoretti* by the repetition of Sonnet 35 as Sonnet 83. It is yet another case of 'retractation': although the sonnet is repeated virtually verbatim the act of repetition and relocation alters its significance. The lover and lady appear to have reached some form of polite accord by Sonnet 82, but the sudden recurrence of a sonnet of unsatisfied sexual longing from the earlier part of the sequence graphically signals the persistence of bodily desire. Neoplatonists interpreted the myth of Narcissus as the seduction of the soul by the body, and the introduction of Platonic ideas into Sonnet 45 looks like an attempt to counteract this. The supreme irony, however, is that Sonnet 45 constitutes an act of seduction in itself because its speaker is most emphatically not a 'Platonic' lover. His eyes, as Sonnets 35 and 83 both tell us, are 'hungry eyes' and the image of the lady's 'fayre Idea' is 'dimmed and deformd' by that hunger. All she need do in order to see her true glorious type is surrender to his love: 'But if your selfe in me ye playne will see, / remove the cause by which your fayre beames darkned be' (Sonnet 45). As this is the central sonnet of the sequence, everything is carefully structured to hinge upon this great paradox. Petrarch never enjoyed his Laura, or Sidney's Astrophil his Stella, but the *Amoretti* moves towards an *Epithalamion*, or wedding hymn. The genre was ancient, with splendid examples in Catullus, Statius, and Claudian, but this, quite characteristically, is the sole instance in which the speaker celebrates his own wedding, and his intensely personal engagement is marked from the outset. Spenser was, in fact, celebrating his marriage to Elizabeth Boyle the previous year:

> Ye learned sisters which have oftentimes
> Beene to me ayding, others to adorne …
> Helpe me mine owne loves prayses to resound,
> Ne let the same of any be envied,

So Orpheus did for his owne bride,
So I unto my selfe alone will sing,
The woods shall to me answer and my Eccho ring. (stanza 1)

According to Ovid, Orpheus's epithalamion for Eurydice was singularly ill-omened (*Metamorphoses*, 10. 1–10), and while Narcissus languished over his image in the pool, Echo, the nymph who loved him, pined away until her voice became a mere reverberation of the Narcissist's own unrequited passion. The speaker attempts to avert both catastrophes by summoning the Muses to bless his song and embracing 'Eccho' herself within the artistic design (hence the capitalization). Although he begins by announcing that 'I unto my selfe alone will sing' – consciously 'echoing' the unrequited Colin of *The Shepheardes Calender* (*Iune*, line 72) – it soon becomes clear that his marriage is a public, ceremonial matter involving the whole community. As a religious rite, matrimony transforms the wedding day into a 'holy' day, thereby offering a potential resolution to the evident conflict between the bodily and the spiritual explored by Petrarch and his followers. As the speaker looks forward to the generation of offspring, the 'boure' of his bliss is transformed into the Gardens of Adonis through a careful pattern of allusion to figures and images already familiar from *The Faerie Queene*:

And thou glad Genius, in whose gentle hand,
The bridale bowre and geniall bed remaine,
Without blemish or staine,
And the sweet pleasures of theyr loves delight
With secret ayde doest succour and supply,
Till they bring forth the fruitful progeny,
Send us the timely fruit of this same night. (stanza 22)

The marital bed is 'geniall' not only because it gratifies the speaker's desire but, as Spenser's clever wordplay on the root 'gen' demonstrates, because the true 'Genius' presides over it in order to ensure the production of 'progeny'. Yet the sheer eroticism of the moment is fully captured by the verse-form, an unpredictable effusion of long and short lines with ever-changing rhyme-schemes adapted from the Italian canzone. The poem's twenty-four sections allude to the passing hours of the wedding day, and its 365 long lines to the days of the year. In this respect the structure of the poem complements the temporal movement of the *Amoretti*, which is charted against *both* the seasonal and the ecclesiastical calendars (natural and spiritual time), moving from 'sad Winters night' (Sonnet 4) through spring (Sonnet 19) and Lent (Sonnet 22) to Easter (Sonnet 68), and onwards towards the summer solstice on St Barnabas' Day (11 June), the day of the wedding.

The *Epithalamion* is a masterpiece by any standards but even it was soon subjected to a form of 'retractation'. The following year saw the publication of the *Prothalamion*, its unfamiliar title newly coined to mark the creation of a radically different form of 'spousal' poem, a poem of anticipation rather than fulfilment. Ostensibly written in celebration of the future weddings of the two daughters of the Earl of Worcester, Elizabeth and Katherine Somerset, the poem introduces a speaker who is almost the exact antithesis of the *Epithalamion*'s joyous bridegroom, a disappointed observer who uses the occasion of the Somerset betrothals to reflect upon his own blighted hopes. The poem begins in a mood of dejection:

> When I whom sullein care,
> Through discontent of my long fruitlesse stay
> In Princes court, and expectation vayne
> Of idle hopes, which still do fly away,
> Like empty shaddowes, did afflict my brayne,
> Walkt forth to ease my payne
> Along the shore of silver streaming *Themmes*. (stanza 1)

'Expectation' is clearly a key term. Towards the end of the *Amoretti* the speaker had declared how, in the absence of his lady, 'I the time with expectation spend, / And faine my griefe with chaunges to beguile' (Sonnet 87), only to rejoice soon after in the 'night so long expected' (*Epithalamion*, line 315). As he follows the swans upstream to London, *Prothalamion*'s initially dejected speaker begins to share in the increasingly heightened expectation of 'loves couplement' until the moment of climax when, through a particularly daring piece of Spenserian orthography, the 'birdes' morph into 'brides'. His progressive involvement in the scene is hastened by the approach to Essex house, the former home of his erstwhile patron the Earl of Leicester, 'whose want too well, now feeles my freendles case' (line 140). But this note of sadness 'fits not well' with celebration and is soon dispelled by the dramatic emergence of the Earl of Essex 'like Radiant *Hesper*' to receive the future brides and bridegrooms. The effect here is complex and works more by insinuation than assertion. The question is whether the 'freendles' speaker will also be received at Essex house. The swan was, of course, an ancient image of the poet. A confident Horace employs it to predict his own literary immortality (*Odes*, 2. 20), while a despairing Ovid presents himself as a dying swan (*Tristia*, 5. 4. 1). Which was to be Spenser's case? There are, so to speak, potentially three 'swans' in the *Prothalamion*, not two, and the destiny of the third 'swan' is constantly kept before us in the haunting refrain that ends each of the ten stanzas, 'sweete Themmes runne softly, till I end my Song'.[7] The *Prothalamion* draws much of its poetic resonance from its conscious reminiscence of the *Epithalamion* in stanza-form, diction, and tone, and from the progressively emotional engagement of its speaker in the events he observes and describes. By the end of the poem he too sets all of his 'expectation' on the possibility of 'spousal' at Essex House, the possibility that as the swans become brides, the speaker may, like Horace, become an immortal swan.

When Spenser died prematurely in 1599 the Earl of Essex paid for his funeral, but his lifelong self-characterization as the 'alienated' Colin Clout fuelled the myth of a death in poverty. So powerful was the image that many of the elegies lamenting Spenser are cast as elegies for 'Colin'. This should not surprise us. The search for patronage was one of Spenser's most insistent themes and his successors responded to it precisely because it was seen to join private to public concerns, the fate of Spenser's poetry with that of English literature in general. It also forms a powerful leitmotif in the two works that appeared posthumously, *The Mutabilitie Cantos* (1609) and *A View of the Present State of Ireland* (1633). While contemporary commentators were unanimous in regarding Ireland as disastrous for Spenser, the *Mutabilitie Cantos* (1609), like Ovid's *Epistulae ex Ponto* and *Tristia*, serve as a final reminder of the poetic capital it provided. Their meticulously detailed Irish topography is transformed into a mythical landscape in which the Giantess and her antagonists debate no less than the viability of allegory itself, the possibility of identifying some form of 'meaning' or value in the complex narratives of myth, literature, and life. It is Spenser's last great fairytale, 'registred of old / In Faery lond mongst records permanent', an ironically enduring record to the artistic possibilities offered by mutability, disappointment, and imperfection. In the inset fable of Faunus and Molanna, which draws directly upon the aetiological legends of *Colin Clouts Come Home Againe*, the grimly dichotomized politics of *A View of the Present State of Ireland* are translated into a vibrant poetics of diversity in seeming defiance of the narrator's melancholy tone. The apparent contradiction serves to remind us that while Spenser reinvented the epic narrator, bequeathing to Milton a more lyrical, vulnerable, and interventionist speaker than he found in the classical or Italian tradition, he never allowed any of his various personae or voices to be more than single components of a greater design. In Spenser the relation of narrator to narrative never exactly mirrors that of author to poem. Within his canon everything, even the face of Narcissus, must be viewed 'in mirrours more then one'.

NOTES

1 W. B. Yeats (ed.), *Poems of Spenser* (Edinburgh, 1906), p. xxxiv.

2 *The Works of Edmund Spenser*, eds Edwin Greenlaw *et al.*, Variorum Edition, 11 vols (Baltimore: Johns Hopkins University Press, 1932–58), IX, p. 27. All quotations cited as '*Prose*' are taken from this volume.

3 *Edmund Spenser: The Shorter Poems*, ed. R. A. McCabe (Harmondsworth: Penguin, 1999), p. 27.
4 See Richard McCabe, '"Little booke: thy selfe present": The Politics of Presentation in *The Shepheardes Calender*', in *Presenting Poetry: Composition, Publication, Reception: Essays in Honour of Ian Jack*, eds Howard Erskine-Hill and Richard A. McCabe (Cambridge: Cambridge University Press, 1995), pp. 15–40.
5 Raphael Holinshed, *Chronicles of England, Scotland and* Ireland, 6 vols (London, 1808), VI, p. 69.
6 Helen Cooper, *The English Romance in Time: Transforming Motifs from Geoffrey of Monmouth to the Death of Shakespeare* (Oxford: Oxford University Press, 2004), p. 364.
7 For Spenser as a swan, see also *The Shepheardes Calender*, *October*, 90 and gloss.

SELECTED FURTHER READING

Editions

The standard edition of the *Complete Works*, although outdated, is *The Works of Edmund Spenser*, eds Edwin Greenlaw *et al.*, Variorum Edition, 11 vols (Baltimore: Johns Hopkins University Press, 1932–58). The following are more accessible: for the epic verse *The Faerie Queene*, ed. T. P. Roche (Harmondsworth: Penguin, 1978), or *The Faerie Queene*, ed. A. C. Hamilton, rev. edn (London: Longman, 2001); for the rest of the poetic canon either *The Yale Edition of the Shorter Poems of Edmund Spenser*, eds William A. Oram *et al.* (New Haven: Yale University Press, 1989), or *Edmund Spenser: The Shorter Poems*, ed. R. A. McCabe (Harmondsworth: Penguin, 1999). The ninth volume of the Variorum Edition (which I cite by page in the present essay) contains the best available text of Spenser's prose works including *A View of the Present State of Ireland*. For a reprint of the censored text published by Sir James Ware in 1633 see *A View of the State of Ireland*, eds Andrew Hadfield and Willy Maley (Oxford: Blackwell, 1997). A wealth of information on the texts, contexts, and biography may be found in the standard reference work *The Spenser Encyclopedia*, ed. A. C. Hamilton (Toronto: University of Toronto Press, 1990). See also *The Oxford Handbook of Edmund Spenser*, ed. R. A. McCabe (Oxford: Oxford University Press, 2010).

Secondary works

Alpers, Paul, *The Poetry of The Faerie Queene,* Princeton, Princeton University Press, 1967

Anderson, Judith, Donald Cheney, and David A. Richardson (eds), *Spenser's Life and the Subject of Biography,* Amherst, University of Massachusetts Press, 1996

Gregerson, Linda, *The Reformation of the Subject: Spenser, Milton and the English Protestant Epic,* Cambridge, Cambridge University Press, 1995

Hadfield, Andrew, *Spenser's Irish Experience: Wilde Fruit and Savage Soyl,* Oxford, Oxford University Press, 1997

Helgerson, Richard, *Self-Crowned Laureates: Spenser, Jonson, Milton, and the Literary System,* Berkeley, University of California Press, 1983

King, John N., *Spenser's Poetry and the Reformation Tradition,* Princeton, Princeton University Press, 1990

McCabe, Richard A., *Spenser's Monstrous Regiment: Elizabethan Ireland and the Poetics of Difference*, 2nd edn, Oxford, Oxford University Press, 2005

Murrin, Michael, *The Allegorical Epic,* Chicago, University of Chicago Press, 1980

O'Connell, Michael, *Mirror and Veil: The Historical Dimension of Spenser's 'Faerie Queene'*, Chapel Hill, University of North Carolina Press, 1977

Norbrook, David, *Poetry and Politics in the English Renaissance*, rev. edn, Oxford, Oxford University Press, 2005

Shore, D. R., *Spenser and the Poetics of Pastoral: A Study of the World of Colin Clout,* Kingston, McGill-Queen's University Press, 1985

Van Es, Bart (ed.), *A Critical Companion to Spenser Studies,* London, Palgrave Macmillan, 2006

Waller, Gary, *Edmund Spenser: A Literary Life,* Houndmills, Macmillan, 1994

4

DAVID BEVINGTON

William Shakespeare

In Don Marquis's enduringly funny *Archy and Mehitabel*, Archy interviews a parrot named pete who once belonged to the fellow who ran the Mermaid Tavern back around 1600, and who claims to have overheard Bill Shakespeare muttering one night over his pints of sack to Ben Jonson and Frankie Beaumont about his keen disappointment in having been obliged to earn his livelihood as a playwright when he might have been a poet. Archy reports this interview all in lower-case letters and without punctuation, because he is a cockroach pounding out his ruminations night by night on Marquis's old typewriter, jumping from key to key.

> ... any mutt can write
> plays for this london public
> says bill if he puts enough
> murder in them what they want
> is kings talking like kings
> never had sense enough to talk
> and stabbings and stranglings
> and fat men making love
> and clowns basting each
> other with clubs and cheap puns
> and off colour allusions to all
> the smut of the day oh i know
> what the low brows want
> and i give it to them
> ...
> to think i am
> debasing my talents with junk
> like that oh god what i wanted
> was to be a poet
> and write sonnet serials
> like a gentleman should[1]

Don Marquis is of course having his fun. He is also reflecting a once-popular stereotype about Shakespeare: that he was first and foremost a poet, whose incomparable genius was marred by the demands of a commercial theatre and a rowdy, unsophisticated theatre-going public. Did Shakespeare entertain such a fantasy himself? We can certainly hope that he was ultimately proud of his achievements as a successful playwright. Yet even here the evidence may hint that he thought of himself as a poet first and commercial playwright second. Several of his best plays, including *Hamlet* and *King Lear*, are so long that they may well have proved unplayable in their entirety in their original staging. However approximate the reference in *Romeo and Juliet*'s opening may be to 'the two hours' traffic of our stage', it does not say 'three hours' traffic', and reminds us of the constraints placed on London's acting companies operating south of the River Thames in winter afternoons when spectators would need to get back to the city before dark. Perhaps Shakespeare wrote *con amore* when the poetry was flowing from him and then collaborated with his acting company to produce shorter acting versions as a matter of practical necessity. This procedure, if it took place, does not make him any less a dramatist, to be sure, but it does suggest that he wrote as a dramatic poet.

Was Shakespeare even a bit ashamed of his profession as actor and writer for the public stage? Meredith Skura has evocatively raised that question in her *Shakespeare the Actor and the Purposes of Playing* (1993), using as a primary text these lines from Sonnet 111:

> Oh, for my sake do you with Fortune chide,
> The guilty goddess of my harmful deeds,
> That did not better for my life provide
> Than public means which public manners breeds.
> Thence comes it that my name receives a brand,
> And almost thence my nature is subdued
> To what it works in, like the dyer's hand.[2]

Granted that one cannot assume an autobiographical reading of the Sonnets, Skura finds this set of images so arrestingly particular as to invite speculation about the writer. What 'public means' and 'public manners' could Shakespeare be alluding to other than his own catering to public tastes? What occupation other than a life in the theatre could subdue his very nature, conferring on it a brand of shame and leaving an indelible mark, as if the writer for the stage were a kind of cloth dyer forever stained by the dye of his trade? Is this image a continuation of the poet's lament in Sonnet 110, 'Alas, 'tis true, I have gone here and there / And made myself a motley to the view'? Skura's larger argument is that acting is a profession of which the practitioner is unavoidably both proud and ashamed; the pull of narcissism invites the actor to take pleasure in displaying himself before audiences while at the same time cringing in self-abnegation for being so needful of applause. If actors are generally like that, was Shakespeare so? And does the rueful reflection on a professional life ill-spent in public self-display apply to Shakespeare's career as a dramatist as well as actor? We should remember that when Thomas Bodley established a library at the University of Oxford and instructed that it was to acquire a copy of all books printed in England, he made one striking exception: the library need not bother to include printed plays.

These intriguing speculations may invite us to wonder if Shakespeare would have preferred to be a writer of lyric and perhaps epic poetry, like Edmund Spenser or Samuel Daniel or Michael Drayton, supported, if he were lucky, by an aristocratic patron. The siren call of writing for the stage in the 1590s in London was financially very tempting. It was all a bit like writing for Hollywood today. Shakespeare soon established himself as quite a success. Thomas Nashe attested to the popularity of Shakespeare's *1 Henry VI* and its hero, Lord Talbot, in 1592, when he wrote that it would 'have joyed brave Talbot (the terror of the French) to think that after he had lain two hundred years in his tomb, he should triumph again on the stage'.[3] In that same year, Robert Greene enviously acknowledged Shakespeare's rising reputation by accusing him (without naming him directly) of being an 'upstart crow, beautified with our feathers', that is, having plagiarized materials from his fellow-dramatists.[4] Shakespeare's plays began to find their way into print in 1594 (*Titus Andronicus*) and then in 1597–8, when *Richard II*, *Richard III*, *1 Henry IV*, *Love's Labours Lost*, and an unauthorized text of *Romeo and Juliet* appeared in quarto, followed soon by others. Shakespeare presumably consented to the publication of at least some of these, but he seems not to have concerned himself with proofreading or otherwise assisting the process of publication.

On the other hand, he took great pains to establish himself as a poet. His *Venus and Adonis* appeared in print in 1593, having been entered in the Stationers' Register on 18 April of that year by the printer and publisher Richard Field, formerly of Stratford-upon-Avon and the son of an associate of Shakespeare's father. The handsomely printed quarto was dedicated 'To the Right Honourable Henry Wriothesley, Earl of Southampton, and Baron of Titchfield', in language that is strongly suggestive of a plea for continued patronage. The poet deprecates his own poetic effusion as unworthy of so noble a sponsorship, fearing that 'the world will censure me for choosing so strong a prop to support so weak a burden', but has the hardihood to offer to honour Southampton 'with some graver labour' in the near future unless 'the first heir of my invention', that is, *Venus and Adonis*, prove too 'deformed'. All this is couched in the conventionally hyperbolic language of such dedications, but it does bespeak an earnestness of hope for aristocratic endorsement. That Shakespeare should speak of *Venus and Adonis* as 'the first heir of my invention' is implicitly dismissive of the plays he had already written as somehow sub-literary. *Venus and Adonis* is his first acknowledged work in the sense of being the first to be printed and the first to aspire to the sophisticated literary genre of poetry.

The Rape of Lucrece was published in the following year, 1594, as 'printed by Richard Field, for John Harrison'. Clearly this was the 'graver labour' promised in the dedication of *Venus and Adonis* to Southampton, for this second poem too is dedicated to the young earl, and in language that is manifestly more confident of a warmly mutual relationship. 'The love I dedicate to Your Lordship is without end', wrote Shakespeare, 'whereof this pamphlet without beginning is but a superfluous moiety. The warrant I have of your honourable disposition, not the worth of my untutored lines, makes it assured of acceptance. What I have done is yours; what I have to do is yours; being part in all I have, devoted yours.' The offer here of more writings to come must refer to more formal poetry, for an earl would not ordinarily deign to sponsor a mere play; not until Ben Jonson do we encounter a playwright (also, of course, a poet) who would have the effrontery to dedicate a play to an aristocratic patron. Shakespeare never dedicated any of his plays in quarto in this fashion (though the posthumous First Folio of 1623 would be dedicated by Heminges and Condell to the Earls of Pembroke and Montgomery). The two poems of 1593–4 are unique in this way, and are the only published works of Shakespeare prefaced by dedications that bear his name. 'Your honour's in all duty, William Shakespeare', concludes the dedication to *Venus and Adonis*, and that of *The Rape of Lucrece* is essentially the same: 'Your Lordship's in all duty, William Shakespeare'.

Shakespeare was renowned as a poet no less than as a dramatist. *Venus and Adonis* had been reprinted nine times by the time Shakespeare died in 1616. None of his plays enjoyed a more brilliant record of publication. *Venus and Adonis* was heralded as among the bright gems of English poetry by Francis Meres, Richard Barnfield, John Weever, Gabriel Harvey, and Edmund Spenser among others. Meres's praise (in *Palladis Tamia*, 1598) takes the form of comparing Shakespeare with the greatest of the ancient writers: 'As the soul of Euphorbus was thought to live in Pythagoras, so the sweet, witty soul of Ovid lives in the mellifluous and honey-tongued Shakespeare; witness his *Venus and Adonis*, his *Lucrece*, his sugared sonnets among his private friends.' Meres thus begins with praise of Shakespeare the poet before going on to his achievements as a dramatist. John Weever, in his epigram *Ad Gulielmum Shakespeare* (in *Epigrams in the Oldest*

Cut and Newest Fashion, 1599), similarly apostrophizes 'Honey-tongued Shakespeare' as the creator of

> Rose-cheeked Adonis, with his amber tresses,
> Fair fire-hot Venus, charming him to love her;
> Chaste Lucretia virgin-like her dresses,
> Proud lust-stung Tarquin seeking still to prove her;
> *Romeo, Richard* – more whose names I know not.

Again, the poems take priority over the plays; Weever can hardly remember the names of the plays. Richard Barnfield, in his *Poems in Divers Humours* (1598), also waxes eloquent about the 'honey-flowing vein' of *Venus and Adonis* and *The Rape of Lucrece*. Even the classical scholar and friend of Spenser, Gabriel Harvey, though condescending to *Venus and Adonis* as an amorous poem, greets Shakespeare (in a marginal comment to a copy of Speght's *Chaucer*, 1598–1601) as worthy of comparison with the very best: 'The younger sort takes much delight in Shakespeare's *Venus and Adonis*, but his *Lucrece* and his tragedy of *Hamlet, Prince of Denmark*, have it in them to please the wiser sort.'

Today one would hardly expect to hear *The Rape of Lucrece* mentioned in the same breath with *Hamlet*, but to Shakespeare's contemporaries the comparison was apt. The poem was reprinted five times during Shakespeare's lifetime. In addition to the tributes cited in the previous paragraph by Meres, Weever, and Barnfield, all of whom pair the poem favourably with *Venus and Adonis*, we can add Henry Willobie, W. Har, and Michael Drayton (all in 1594), William Covell (1595), and perhaps Edmund Spenser. *Willobie His Avisa* (1594) describes how Collatine's most precious treasure, his 'fair and constant wife', is violated by the poem's villain:

> Yet Tarquin plucked his glittering grape,
> And Shakespeare paints poor Lucrece' rape.

Spenser seems to have Shakespeare the poet in mind when, in *Colin Clouts Come Home Againe* (1595) he praises 'Aetion' as 'last though not least' among the twelve contemporary poets that Spenser celebrates, concluding,

> A gentler shepherd may nowhere be found,
> Whose muse, full of high thought's invention,
> Doth like himself heroically sound.

To an extent we may find surprising, Shakespeare's early reputation was based to a considerable extent on his narrative and lyric poems.

Francis Meres's reference in 1598 to Shakespeare's 'sugared sonnets among his private friends' provides evidence that part of this reputation depended on sonnets that were privately circulated, just as sonnets and other poems by Donne and others were frequently handed about. We do not know how many of Shakespeare's sonnets this may have included, but the allusion does at least suggest that Shakespeare was not unwilling to be seen as a kind of inspired amateur whose literary aspirations could rise above the sullied image of commercial publication. Perhaps that is why he apparently did not collaborate in Thomas Thorpe's seemingly unauthorized publication of Shakespeare's sonnet-sequence in 1609. They were not reprinted until 1640, long after the vogue of the sonnet-sequence had passed.

What do the early poems suggest about Shakespeare's craft as a narrative poet? *Venus and Adonis* is filled with instances of metaphors and rhetorical figures of the sort that an ambitious young poet would learn how to master. Indeed, one can imagine Shakespeare at work with a copy of George Puttenham's *The Arte of English Poesie* (1589) or Thomas Wilson's *Art of Rhetoric* (1560 and many subsequent editions) close at hand, or at least firmly imbedded in his artistic consciousness through repeated study. An essential method of composition for Shakespeare and other poets of his generation was to devise a fictional narrative or argument of an edifying and entertaining sort into which rhetorical devices could then be inserted by way of poetic ornamentation.

To start with *Venus and Adonis*, Shakespeare chose the mythological story of the goddess Venus's infatuation with a mortal and reluctant male, young Adonis. The story had potential relevance to the life of the Earl of Southampton, who was, by all accounts, a youth of nearly feminine beauty and a hesitation to marry. Shakespeare may have celebrated this reluctant beauty in the first sonnets of his sonnet-sequence, possibly written about the same time. *Venus and Adonis* is filled with exhortations to savour amorous pleasure even while it also crosses those importunities with the wish of the young man to avoid erotic entanglement so that he may excel in manly pursuits. The poem is manifestly responding to a current vogue for Ovidian erotic verse, as exemplified in Thomas Lodge's *Scilla's Metamorphosis* (1589), in which a lovestruck nymph pursues a reluctant young man, and in Christopher Marlowe's *Hero and Leander*, left unfinished at his death in 1593 and later completed by George Chapman (1598). Marlowe's poem, which probably circulated in manuscript in 1592–3, offered a piquant model of intense erotic longing thwarted by tragic destiny. Michael Drayton's *Endymion and Phoebe*, published in 1595 but quite possibly available earlier in manuscript, told the familiar legend of the moon goddess and her earthly lover that had been the subject earlier of John Lyly's play *Endymion* (1588).

Behind these and other poetic accounts was the much-loved poetry of Ovid. His *Metamorphoses* offered to Shakespeare three mythological legends that he could combine in his poem: Venus's pursuit of Adonis (Book 10), the similar pursuit by the nymph Salmacis of the reluctant Hermaphroditus (Book 4), and Echo's vain attempt to win the love of Narcissus (Book 3). Hermaphroditus's name is suggestive of a sexual ambivalence that results, in this Ovidian account, in his being transformed with Salmacis into a single person embodying both sexes. Narcissus's name is no less revealing; his escape from the clutches of the nymph Echo is the consequence of his falling in love with his 'shadow' in the brook (see lines 161–2). The composite portrait, for Shakespeare, emphasizes male coyness in the face of the erotic feminine body. The young man feels the call of male pursuits, especially hunting; the poem's narrator revels in amorous dalliance while at the same time suggesting a suffocating maternal threat of engulfing and emasculating the young man.

The plot element of the poem is deliberately slight. Adonis encounters Venus, is courted avidly by her, and eventually manages his escape from her amorous clutches. She then suffers pangs of anxious fear for his safety that are ultimately justified by the young man's death in a boar hunt. He is transformed into an anemone flower, purple and white in token of his blood and pale cheeks. Venus retires disconsolately to Paphos, her dwelling in Cyprus, where she refuses to see anyone. This slender fiction provides occasion for poetic adornment: for passages of sensuous eroticism, for epic-style digressions and lengthy metaphors, for sententious reflections on what is happening, and for ingenious rhetorical tropes. At heart, the poem is a debate, much in the style of John Lyly's disquisitions on courtly topics. Venus represents the female ideal of pulchritude and desire, Adonis the male ideal of manly achievement. In the tradition of such courtly debates, neither side can be seen to win: the polarities are complementary and also incommensurate. The pleasure of the debate lies in the wittiness of the comparisons and contrasts. Each side is given its opportunity to score points.

The eroticism is cleverly deployed, for example, in an extended metaphorical comparison of Venus's enticing body to the landscape of an enclosed deer park (lines 229–40). The park itself becomes the enclosure of Venus's embrace in which she longs to hold her lover. There Adonis will be her 'deer', that is, her dear. She invites him to feed where he wishes, 'on mountain or in dale', as he wanders over the pleasing rise and fall of her body. Once he has kissed her lips, he may 'Stray lower, where the pleasant fountains lie', kissing and fondling her breasts. Within the 'limit' or boundary of this graceful park he will find 'Sweet bottom grass [pubic hair, perhaps] and high delightful plain [the Mons Veneris?], / Round rising hillocks [buttocks], brakes obscure and rough [the hair-adorned vagina], / To shelter thee from tempest and from rain'. The reader, especially the male reader perhaps, is invited to imagine a similar journey for himself; the indirectness, the wit of the extended metaphor, adds to the pleasure of erotic fantasizing. No wonder the poem was so popular. (The story goes that the copy of the 1623 Folio at Cambridge was so worn out in the love-scene passages of *Romeo and Juliet* that the library had to replace that copy with a second folio in 1640.)

Epic-style digressions can be illustrated by the poem's account of Adonis's horse being sexually aroused by the sudden appearance, from forth a neighbouring copse, of a 'breeding jennet', that is, a mare in heat (lines 259–324). The stallion, tied to a tree, breaks his rein and commences his suit. Every part about him is alert and rigid with desire: his ears are up-pricked, his mane stands on end, his nostrils drink the air, his eyes glister like fire. For her part, the mare, 'Being proud, as females are', 'puts on outward strangeness' even as she coyly signals her willingness to be wooed. Subjected thus to female scorn and even to her kicking at him with her heels, the stallion becomes a 'melancholy malcontent', his tail falling limply onto his 'melting buttock' in a telling image of frustrated male desire. Yet when Adonis attempts to catch his horse, both stallion and mare dash off into the wood, leaving us to imagine what happens next. The tone is ably controlled by the poem's narrator: ironic, amused, aware of the metaphorical implications of his story, teasing the reader with little puzzles as to what translations are to be applied. Another epic digression lengthily describes a 'timorous flying hare' attempting to escape the subtle fox, listening for signs of danger, torn by the 'envious brier' (lines 673–708). The language of epic simile is similarly invoked by the archaic expression, 'Look how', meaning 'Just as', as in 'Look how a bird lies tangled in a net, / So fastened in her arms Adonis lies' (lines 67–8; see also lines 529 and 925, and 'Look when', line 289).

Sententious observations are rife in the poem, as uttered not only by the narrator but by Venus and Adonis as well. 'What though the rose have prickles, yet 'tis plucked', ventures the narrator, by way of generalizing the observation that erotic desire perseveres in the face of daunting obstacles. 'Were beauty under twenty locks kept fast, / Yet love breaks through and picks them all at last' (lines 574–6). The narrator is repeatedly astonished by the accounts of compulsive amorous behaviour that he is chronicling. 'Oh, hard-believing love, how strange it seems / Not to believe, and yet too credulous!' the narrator exclaims, having described Venus's unstable oscillations between 'dire imagination' of Adonis's misfortune in the hunt and her 'reviving joy' at the sound of hope. 'Thy weal and woe makes thee ridiculous: / The one doth flatter thee in thoughts unlikely; / In likely thoughts the other kills thee quickly' (lines 975–90). Venus is no less given to sententious thought. 'Make use of time, let not advantage slip; / Beauty within itself should not be wasted' (lines 129–30), she urges, appealing to the timeless '*carpe diem*' commonplace that we should seize the moment of pleasure before our ageing takes from us the ability to enjoy. 'Be prodigal', she insists. 'The lamp that burns by night / Dries up his oil to lend the world his light' (lines 755–6). Adonis for his part is armed with corresponding proverbial wisdom. 'No fisher but the ungrown fry forbears', he argues, making his point that he is too young for adult sexual encounter. 'The mellow plum doth fall, the green sticks fast' (lines 526–7). When Venus counsels the young man to eschew the dangerous boar hunt, she does so with a proverb: 'Danger deviseth shifts; wit waits on fear' (line 690). Adonis of course has his answer: 'What have you urged that I cannot reprove? / The path is smooth that leadeth on to danger' (lines 787–8). The very form of their discourse is that of debate *in utramque partem*, in which the skill of the speakers (and of the poet) lies in rhetorical swiftness and appositeness of the repartee. Schoolboy training readily lent itself to this art of rhetorical parry and thrust.

Venus and Adonis is a virtual anthology of rhetorical tropes. They are generally antithetical in a way that mirrors the two-sided debate structure of the poem as a whole. Venus, when deprived of her youth's company, sings *ex tempore* a 'wailing note' of

> How love makes young men thrall and old men dote,
> How love is wise in folly, foolish witty. (lines 837–8)

The rhetorical handbooks would note here the *parison* or symmetrical repetition of words in grammatically parallel phrases: 'young men thrall' is echoed in 'old men dote' by substituting antithetically the adjective 'old' for 'young' and the verb 'dote' for 'thrall', while retaining the noun 'men' in its central position. The effect is also one of *isocolon*, since the repetitions are of equal length and vowel value. 'Wise in folly, foolish witty' illustrates the rhetorical figure of antimetabole, in which the symmetrical repetition places the words in inverted order; here the effect of inversion is enhanced by the variatio of 'wise/witty' and changing parts of speech from the nominal 'folly' to the adjectival 'foolish'. Another example of *antimetabole* occurs in line 995: 'She clepes him king of graves and grave of kings.' See also Venus's

> But now I lived, and life was death's annoy;
> But now I died, and death was lively joy. (lines 497–8)

Anaphora arranges lines of verse into groups by the insistent repetition of the first line of each verse, as in this:

> Even as the wind is hushed before it raineth,
> Or as the wolf doth grin before he barketh,
> Or as the berry breaks before it staineth,
> Or like the deadly bullet of a gun. (lines 458–61)

Here, to the effect of anaphora is added the parison and isocolon of parallel phrases of equal grammatical structure and length: 'as the *wind* [wolf, berry] *is hushed* [doth grin, breaks] before it *raineth* [barketh, staineth]'. We hear also the *alliteration* of repeated initial consonants: 'wind/wolf', 'before he barketh', 'berry breaks before', and the near-rhyme effect of 'raineth', 'barketh', 'staineth'. Similar combined rhetorical effects occur in the following:

> 'Give me my hand', saith he. 'Why dost thou feel it?'
> 'Give me my heart', saith she, 'and thou shalt have it.'
>
> (lines 373–4)

Rhetorical inversions are common. *Anadiplosis* occurs when a phrase begins with the final words of the previous phrase: 'Oh, thou didst kill me; kill me once again!' (line 499). *Epanalepsis* is still another rhetorical inversion, one in which a word or phrase occurs at the beginning and also at the end of a verse line: 'He sees his love, and nothing else he sees' (line 287). *Ploce* is the insistent repetition of a word within the same line or phrase, but not at beginning and end: 'Then why not lips on lips, since eyes in eyes?' (line 120), or 'For shame', he cries, 'let go, and let me go' (line 379). *Epizeuxis* is an intensified form of ploce, repeating the word without any intervening language:

> 'Ay me!' she cries, and twenty times, 'Woe, woe!'
> And twenty echoes twenty times cry so. (lines 833–4)

These examples are also rich in instances of parison, isocolon, and antimetabole. The rhetorical figures reinforce one another and provide strong rhythmic cadences that iambic pentameter by itself does not necessarily provide.

A different group of rhetorical figures involves wordplay, punning, double entendre. *Antanaclasis* is such a figure, in which the meaning of a repeated word shifts from one definition to another. 'My love to love is love but to disgrace it' (line 412) means something like 'My only inclination towards love is a desire to render it contemptible or to disgrace it', where 'love' signifies, in rapid succession, 'inclination or attitude', 'strong amorous affection', and 'wish or intention'. When Venus pauses in her petition to Adonis and is interrupted saucily by him, the lines read:

> 'Where did I leave?' 'No matter where', quoth he,
> 'Leave me, and then the story aptly ends.' (lines 715–16)

Here the meaning of 'leave' shifts from 'leave off, cease' to 'depart from'.

The linking of nouns and proper names with a fixed or predictable adjectival phrase is a characteristic of a certain kind of conventional poetic diction. It commonly occurs in *Venus and Adonis* from the poem's very start:

Even as the sun with *purple-coloured face*
Has ta'en his last leave of the *weeping morn*,
Rose-cheeked Adonis hied him to the chase.
Hunting he loved, but love he laughed to scorn.
Sick-thoughted Venus makes amain unto him,
And like a *boldfaced suitor* 'gins to woo him.

Similar instances of poetic diction include the 'sweating palm', the 'lusty courser', the 'tender boy', the 'glowing fire', the 'studded bridle', the 'empty eagle' (lines 25–55), and so on throughout.

Image patterns appropriately lay stress on objects like torches and jewels that burn or shine (see line 163), and on bright colours in contrasting patterns of red and white. The red of the rising sun is akin to the rose, to Adonis's blushing complexion, to Mars's warlike ensign (line 107), and the blood on the boar's mouth (line 901) that is also the blood of the dying Adonis; the whiteness of Venus's alabaster hand is like the white dove, or bed linen, or 'ashy-pale' anger (line 76), or the 'wonted lily white' of Adonis's pure complexion. Water and fire are inveterate opposites, as in line 94: 'She bathes in water, yet her fire must burn'; see also line 494. So are day and night, as in lines 122 ('And I will wink; so shall the day seem night') and 481, 'coal-black clouds' and 'heaven's light' (line 533), youth and age (lines 133–44), moist, soft plumpness and the 'barren, lean, and lacking juice' of old age (lines 136, 142–3), softness and the hardness of flint or steel (lines 199–200), heat and cold (lines 337–8), earth and heaven (lines 493–8), life and death (see lines 211–12).

Venus invokes all the five traditional senses to describe the beauty of Adonis: her ears drink the 'deep sweet music' of his 'mermaid's voice', her eyes perceive the perfect symmetry of his form, her 'sense of feeling' yields the exquisite pleasure of touch, her sense of smell enables her to savour the 'breath perfumed' that issues from the 'stillitory' of Adonis's person, and taste comes to her aid as the 'nurse and feeder of the other four' (lines 427–50). Allegorized personification enriches the treasury of this poem's roster of rhetorical devices, as when Venus imagines how her five senses, luxuriating in their feasting on Adonis's beauty, might

bid Suspicion double-lock the door,
Lest Jealousy, that sour unwelcome guest,
Should, by his stealing in, disturb the feast.
(lines 448–50; see also lines 649–57)

The art of *The Rape of Lucrece* is similar, though applied to a more serious and even lugubrious subject. The story of the ravishment of the chaste Lucretia, wife of Collatinus, by the insolent and cruel Sextus Tarquinius, son of the tyrannical Lucius Tarquinius Superbus, in the early days of Rome, was well known in antiquity and the Renaissance. The outrage had provoked the aristocrats of the city, led by Junius Brutus and Publius Valerius, to take up arms against the Tarquins in 509 BC and to institute a form of government more favourable to the oligarchical families of the city; as 'The Argument' to Shakespeare's poem puts it, 'with one consent they all vowed to root out the whole hated family of the Tarquins', so that 'with one consent and a general acclamation the Tarquins were all exiled and the state government changed from kings to consuls'. Although Shakespeare's poem does not devote much attention to this seismic political shift, the poem ends on this note in its final stanza, reminding the reader that the story of Lucrece is essentially one of the founding of republicanism in ancient Rome. Most readers would know that Junius Brutus, who at the end of the poem (lines 1847–8) reiterates his vow to avenge the outrage and death of Lucrece, was reputed to be the great ancestor of the Marcus Brutus who, in 44 BC, joined a conspiracy to assassinate Julius Caesar in the name of republican resistance to one-man single rule. The poem alludes briefly to Junius Brutus's feigning of madness to escape the fate of his brother, whom the father of the Tarquin in this poem had put to death (see lines 1734 and 1810–19). Shakespeare probably knew Livy's account in his *History of Rome*, Chapters 57–9.

Yet the poem is far more deeply invested in the personal tragedy of Lucrece. For this part of the story Shakespeare was particularly indebted to Ovid's *Fasti* (2.721–852). The story had been retold often, as in Chaucer's *The Legend of Good Women* and in William Painter's translation of Livy in *The Palace of Pleasure* (1566, 1575). Shakespeare must also have known other poems in the 'complaint' tradition of the *Fasti*, in *A Mirror for Magistrates* (1559) and in Samuel Daniel's *The Complaint of Rosamond*, for it is to this genre that *The Rape of Lucrece* belongs. The verse-form employed by Shakespeare for his poem, the so-called rhyme royal in seven lines rhyming *ababbcc*, was the stanza of choice for tragic poetry of high seriousness; Chaucer had used it in his *Troilus and Criseyde* (1380s) and in the more formal of his *Canterbury Tales*, and so had John Lydgate in his *The Fall of Princes* (1430–8). It was used also in the continuation of the *Fall of Princes* story in *A Mirror for Magistrates*, and in Daniel's *The Complaint of Rosamond*. Shakespeare's choice of verse pattern announced that he was moving up to the 'graver labour' promised by Shakespeare to the Earl of Southampton in his dedication of *Venus and Adonis*.

Shakespeare's Lucrece is a model of Roman matronly virtue, presumably with implied relevance for Elizabethan readers. She is the 'perfect' wife in a patriarchal society that values wifely obedience and chaste loyalty above all other qualities in women. The rape is so deeply offenceful in the poem because it violates a husband's right to the exclusive ownership of his wife. Although Lucrece is entirely innocent as a victim, she acquires a stain to her purity that she must resolve in suicide because her shame has become her husband's shame as well. We might suppose today that her husband, Collatine, is at fault in boasting of her incomparable chastity in such a way as to arouse the lust of Sextus Tarquinius, but the poem does not seem to blame him for this. Collatine accepts the decorousness of her suicide as necessary for the preservation of his honour, however much he may grieve at the loss of her. He and his supporters are resolved to avenge the rape as an offence against their patriarchal value system. Lucrece is the heroic upholder of that system, while Tarquin is the embodiment of everything that the system holds in abhorrence.

The poem accordingly emphasizes the huge contrast between, on the one hand, Lucrece's chaste loyalty, her beauty, her innocent trustingness, her experience of shame, and her heroic resolution to die, and, on the other hand, Tarquin's furtiveness, dishonesty, and uncontrollable lust. As the villain prepares to enter her chamber at night, having lied his way into her confidence by praising Collatine to her, we are told at length of his emotional turmoil. He is 'madly tossed between desire and dread' (line 171), compulsively lusting for Lucrece but assailed by fear of detection. He is painfully aware that what he is about to do is a 'shame to knighthood and to shining arms' (line 197). The deed, he knows, is 'vile' and 'base', so much so that the scandal will live forever with his name. His posterity will curse his bones and wish he had never existed (lines 202–10). He is all too aware that his gain will be nothing but a 'fleeting joy', and perceives that it is mad folly to 'sell eternity to get a toy' (lines 212–14), and yet he cannot help himself. The very locks to her chamber seem to cry out to him in outrage; a puff of wind threatens to extinguish his torch, as though Nature herself inveighs against the deed. The contrast between attacker and victim grows more intense as he enters her chamber.

The poem dwells sensuously on Lucrece's chaste beauty as she lies in her bed. One 'lily hand' lies under her 'rosy cheek'; the other is displayed in its perfect whiteness on the green coverlet. Wisps of her golden hair are gently played with by her breath; they are both 'modest wantons' and 'wanton modesty'. She is like the Lucretian Venus invoked by Enobarbus in his description of Cleopatra as both sensuous and transcendently holy. 'Her breasts', the narrator tells us, were 'like ivory globes circled with blue', that is, with the delicate veins visible beneath her translucent skin (lines 386–407). The reader is invited to fantasize about Lucrece's vulnerable sexual being while at the same time being insistently reminded that the violation of such beauty is an indictment of male importunity. When Tarquin's hand ventures to touch her bare breast, her 'ranks of blue veins, as his hand did scale, / Left their round turrets destitute and pale'. His hand, still remaining on her breast, is a 'Rude ram, to batter such an ivory wall' (lines 439–64). Later, when she commits suicide in the presence of her husband and his friends, the blood bubbling from her breast divides 'In two slow rivers, that the crimson tide / Circles her body in on every side' (lines 1737–9). The poem thus retains some of the erotic appeal of *Venus and Adonis*, but circumscribes that eroticism with moralizations that sternly disapprove of the voyeurism in which we have been invited to indulge.

Another shared feature of *Venus and Adonis* and *The Rape of Lucrece* is the use of the antithetical structure of debate. Just as Tarquin and Lucrece are opposites, in a similar way we encounter in this poem a series of disquisitions on lust versus chaste honour, rude will versus moral restraint, rampant desire versus rational self-government, vile evil versus pure good, and so on. Accordingly, in a series of debates, Tarquin struggles unsuccessfully with his own depraved nature, and Lucrece endeavours to persuade him to choose the good rather than ravish her. Left alone and desolate, Lucrece ponders the instructive contrasts of 'comfort-killing Night, image of hell', and the 'telltale Day' that will simply reveal and proclaim her undoing (lines 764–812). The 'hateful, vaporous, and foggy Night' is Tarquin's realm; it is a 'furnace of foul reeking smoke', hiding itself from 'jealous Day'. Lucrece's apostrophe to Opportunity similarly contrasts the terrible ways in which Opportunity invites the violations of all oaths with everything that 'Truth and Virtue' seek vainly to uphold (lines 876–924). 'Misshapen Time, copesmate of ugly Night', is paired by Lucrece with Time's servant, Opportunity, and is thus unable to fulfil the functions that Time ought to bring about: the unmasking of falsehood, the bringing of truth to light, the bringing of wrongdoers to justice, and the like. Time, the 'tutor both to good and bad', has become a 'ceaseless lackey to Eternity' when it could be such a force for good (lines 925–1022). In all these set pieces concerning Night, Opportunity, and Time, the rhetorical structure of antithesis controls the argument and reinforces the poem's attentiveness to the contrastive opposites of good and evil.

The poem's most elaborate set piece is a description of a tapestry on the fall of Troy (lines 1366–1568), viewed by Lucrece as she ponders her sad fate. The passage is, first of all, a brilliant example of *ekphrasis*, as defined in the observation of Simonides of Ceos (and reiterated by Philip Sidney in his *Defence of Poetry*) that poetry is a speaking picture and painting a silent poem. *Lucrece*'s tapestry on the fall of Troy is an instance of the latter, a silent poem. Shakespeare is fascinated with the ways in which art can convey both truth and falsehood through images. Great commanders convey 'grace and majesty' in their facial expressions; youths embody 'quick bearing and dexterity'. Conversely, 'Pale cowards' march on with 'trembling paces' like 'heartless peasants', so vividly depicted 'That one would swear he saw them quake and tremble'. Ajax's eyes show 'blunt rage and rigor'; 'sly Ulysses's' mild glances glances show 'deep regard and smiling government'. Nestor's age is suggested by his 'silver white' beard that wags 'up and down'. His listeners, caught by the ingenious artist in various characteristic poses, press forward to hear Nestor's words. Throughout, the art of representation manages to suggest, by means of metonymy and synecdoche, much more than is actually shown:

> For much imaginary work was there,
> Conceit deceitful, so compact, so kind,
> That for Achilles' image stood his spear
> Gripped in an armèd hand; himself, behind,
> Was left unseen, save to the eye of mind.
>   A hand, a foot, a face, a leg, a head,
>   Stood for the whole to be imaginèd. (lines 1422–8)

Such art is 'deceitful' in its artifice. This is both its strength and its potential harm, for the deceit is painfully close to the perfidy with which Tarquin has ruined Lucrece. His perfidy is like that of 'perjured Sinon', deceiver of Troy with his cunning device of the Trojan horse. Sinon is the perfect illustration of art's ability to deceive.

> In him the painter laboured with his skill
> To hide deceit and give the harmless show
> An humble gait, calm looks, eyes wailing still.
> (lines 1506–8)

Lucrece is distressed that the artist can succeed so in masking an evil intent: she

> chid the painter for his wondrous skill,
> Saying, some shape in Sinon's was abused. (lines 1528–9)

She is aware, too, that the Trojan War itself began with a quarrel among men over the possession of a woman:

> Show me the strumpet that began this stir,
> That with my nails her beauty I may tear.
> Thy heat of lust, fond Paris, did incur
> This load of wrath that burning Troy doth bear.
> (lines 1471–4)

The story of Troy is, for Lucrece, a series of object lessons in all that she has had to suffer.

Image patterns in *The Rape of Lucrece* mirror the antithetical structure of the poem, and in many cases are recognizably those of *Venus and Adonis* as well. The paired opposition of red and white appears in the 'heraldry' embedded in Lucrece's beautiful face, and is linked to the 'silent war of lilies and roses' (lines 11, 65–71). Again we find the contrasts of dove and owl (lines 58, 165), lamb and wolf or 'thievish dog' (lines 165–7, 677, 736–7, 878), lions and their prey (line 421), falcons or hawks and new-killed birds (lines 457, 506, 694), the 'cockatrice' or basilisk and its prey (line 540), cuckoos and sparrows (line 849), coal-black crows and snow-white swans (lines 1009–11), daylight and darkness (lines 547–51), sunny and cloudy weather (lines 372–3), fountains and muddy or toad-infested water (lines 577, 850), 'repentant cold' and 'embracing flames' (lines 4–6, 48), 'corn' (i.e., grain) and weeds (line 281), Tereus and Philomel (lines 1128–34), frightened deer and their hunters (line 1149–52), and still more.

Epic-like similes provide suitable ornament for a poem cast in the mode of elevated, serious poetry, as in the comparison of Collatine's speechless woe to a torrent of water, beginning:

> As through an arch the violent roaring tide
> Outruns the eye that doth behold his haste …
>
> (lines 1667–73)

Rhetorical figures abound, as in the *antanaclasis* or wordplay in the description of Lucrece's suicide:

> Even here she sheathèd in her harmless breast
> A harmful knife, (lines 1723–4)

where again the play on *harmless/harmful* catches the antithesis of Lucrece's innocence and tainted tragedy. Apostrophes are common, as in Lucrece's appeals to Night, Opportunity, and Time (lines 764, 876, 995, 1765). Throughout, studied rhetorical artifice, learned at least in part from the rhetoric books of the time, is enlisted in the cause of portraying uncontrollable lust and genuine grief.

The Sonnets are Shakespeare's major achievement as a lyric poet. Dating them is difficult, owing to the fact that they were not published until 1609, and then seemingly without the collaboration of the author. We cannot be sure about the order of the Sonnets, or whether they are in any sense autobiographical. Critical consensus of late, none the less, is that the order of the poems is, on the whole, intelligible and could conceivably represent what Shakespeare had intended at some point in time. We do know that some sonnets must have been in existence by 1598, when Francis Meres declared his approval of Shakespeare's 'sugared sonnets among his private friends'. Moreover, the first seventeen sonnets or so (out of a total of 154), addressed to a young friend advising him repeatedly to assure his immortality by marrying and breeding a male heir, make plausible sense as friendly counsel to the Earl of Southampton on behalf of his family and friends. Two sonnets, numbers 138 and 144, had been printed (seemingly without authority) by William Jaggard in *The Passionate Pilgrim* in 1599. If the order of the Sonnets in the 1609 quarto has any relation to dates of composition, these do turn up fairly late in the sequence, raising the possibility that most of the sonnets were written by that time.

The first of these two sonnets is not deeply related in theme or prosody to its neighbouring sonnets, many of which, beginning with 127 and including 144, seem to form a group describing the narrator's disillusioning experience with the 'Dark Lady'. The reference in Sonnet 107 to the 'mortal moon' that 'hath her eclipse endured' and to 'the sad augurs' that 'mock their own presage' is often taken to allude to the death in 1603 of Queen Elizabeth (who was identified with Diana and Cynthia as moon goddesses) and to anxious prognostications in her last years which then yielded to triumphant optimism at the ascent to the English throne of the Protestant King James VI of Scotland and I of England. Sonnet 123's reference to 'pyramids built up with newer might' may or may not refer to an obelisk erected in London in 1603; similar structures erected in Rome in 1586 offer another possibility. Sonnet 145 is in an uncharacteristic eight-syllable metre rather than the ten-syllable iambic pentameter line of the great majority. Sonnet 99 has fifteen lines, unlike the fourteen-line norm of the standard Shakespearean sonnet. The last two sonnets, 153 and 154, derived imitatively from Renaissance adaptations of the *Greek Anthology*, are not connected with the preceding sonnets and may have been added by the publisher as an afterthought.

Despite these anomalies, the sonnet-sequence as a whole reveals a persuasive coherence. It begins, as we have seen, with seventeen sonnets of advice to a young man urging him to marry and sire a male heir. These sonnets repeatedly stress the youth of the person addressed. 'Forty winters' will not besiege his brow until some distant time (Sonnet 2). In his great beauty, he is the image of his mother (3.9). He appears to be reluctant to marry (9.1–2), thus neglecting his duty to sire a son and heir (13.14). His only fault is that he is a 'tender churl', a 'beauteous niggard', an 'Unthrifty' and 'Profitless usurer' in his prodigal waste of a beauty that will too soon be spent unless an heir is produced (1, 4). This is the familiar *carpe diem* theme that Shakespeare expressed so eloquently, for example, in Feste's song in *Twelfth Night*:

What is love? 'Tis not hereafter;
Present love hath present laughter;
  What's to come is still unsure.
In delay there lies no plenty.
Then come kiss me, sweet and twenty;
  Youth's a stuff will not endure. (II. iii. 47–52)

Indeed, the early sonnets seem well fitted to the 1590s when Shakespeare was writing most of his romantic comedies.

The *carpe diem* sonnets merge gracefully into a number of sonnets celebrating the young man's beauty and youth, and the power of poetry to eternize the person being celebrated. These ideas are linked: the two means of aiming at an eternity of remembrance are to sire a male heir and to be praised in poetry. 'Thy eternal summer shall not fade', promises the narrator to the young man. 'So long as men can breathe or eyes can see, / So long lives this, and this gives life to thee' (18). 'This' is the very sonnet being thus presented to the young man. The gift is a loving one; the poet is inspired by his deep affection for the subject of his verse. Such an achievement in poetry will defeat 'Devouring Time', able otherwise to deface human achievement and human memory (19). This thought is intensified by the argument that the young man's beauty is indeed subject to Time, and therefore occupies the realm of sexual coupling and reproduction; that part of the young man belongs to women, or more particularly to some woman who will bear the young man a son or sons and thereby preserve his beauty. The goddess Nature, doting on the young man, has provided him with 'one thing to my purpose nothing', that is to say, his male sexual organ. 'But since she pricked thee out for women's pleasure', Sonnet 20 concludes, 'Mine be thy love and thy love's use their treasure.' The pun on 'pricked' underscores the erotic character of Nature's gift. This sensual part of the young man is emphatically not what the poet claims as his due. The sonnet-sequence thus defines their relationship as deeply loving but not sexual.

These themes persist in the sonnets that follow, but are soon darkened by more troubling thoughts. The poet knows that he is old. Death threatens, despite the consolations of beauty in the younger man. The poet fears that his own powers of expression will be inadequate to say what he wants to say. Because Fortune has barred him from 'public honor and proud titles', he relies, a little desperately at times, on a loving relationship that can compensate for worldly loss (25). The weariness of daily toil bids him seek refuge in the thoughts of his beauteous friend (27). Physical separation from the friend lengthens his sorrows (28). Finding himself 'in disgrace with fortune and men's eyes' and envious of those who excel him in handsomeness and ability, the poet can find comfort only in 'thy sweet love remembered' (29).

The loss of friends through death is another burden that can be compensated for only 'while I think on thee' (30). The young man is

> the grave where buried love doth live,
> Hung with the trophies of my lovers gone. (31)

Painfully aware that some other poets write with a more ingratiating style than he can command, the poet has no hope other than that the friend will read the poet's lines for their love, passing over their rude expression (32).

All these disappointments are endurable so long as the comforts of the loving relationship remain strong, but increasingly that fortress of hope begins to crumble. Just as the sun must suffer the indignity of being obscured by 'the basest clouds' (33), just as the expectant traveller must submit to 'let base clouds o'ertake me in my way' (34), the poet must confront the nightmare reality of rival claims on the young man's affection. He blames himself for being unworthy and makes excuses for the friend's 'sins' and 'sensual fault', producing a 'civil war' of 'love and hate' in the poet (35). A separation seems inescapable:

> Let me confess that we two must be twain.

The poet abases himself by confessing that his own failures deserve no less:

> I may not evermore acknowledge thee,
> Lest my bewailèd guilt should do thee shame. (36)

The poet's very love for the young man thus necessitates a separation, lest the friend suffer harm. At times the separation, though painful, is alleviated by thoughts of loving friendship that can transcend absence, but even this is a sweet deception (39). More serious still, perhaps, is the painful suggestion that the young man uses sexually a woman with whom the poet is in love (40). That relationship is a double wrong for the poet:

> Hers, by thy beauty tempting her to thee,
> Thine, by thy beauty being false to me. (41)

The 'loss in love' that touches the poet most grievously is not 'That thou hast her', but the fear of losing the friend's loyalty; only by a kind of bitter-sweet sophistry can the poet momentarily persuade himself that the woman, in loving the friend, loves in effect the poet too, since 'my friend and I are one' (42). These three sonnets anticipate the 'Dark Lady' sequence commencing with Sonnet 127.

Even when sexual desertion is not troubling the poet's peace of mind, he is obsessed with distance and physical separation. If 'the dull substance' of his flesh 'were thought', 'Injurious distance should not stop my way', but, alas, 'thought kills me that I am not thought'. The flesh and its demands are too insistent. His physical being condemns him to the heavy elements of 'earth and water', that is, to melancholy and tears (44). Only the young man is capable of dwelling in the lighter elements of 'slight air and purging fire' (45). Eye and heart are 'at a mortal war' as to whether the physical sight of the young man's beauty or the 'inward love of heart' will offer a more lasting reward to the poet (46–7). Actual journeys that remove the poet from the friend are 'heavy' and 'weary', affecting even 'The beast that bears me on' (50–1). Interspersed in these melancholic reflections are brighter thoughts of the friend's extraordinary beauty, outshining that of Adonis and of Helen and more enduring than that of the rose (53–4). The poet finds genuine comfort in the thought that his own 'powerful rhyme' will bestow on the young man an eternity not to be shared by 'marble nor the gilded monuments / Of princes' (55).

Still, the poet is too aware that he is the young man's 'slave', destined to 'tend / Upon the hours and times of your desire' (57). He is doomed to wait in this fashion, 'though waiting so be hell', nor can he blame the young man's choice of pleasure, 'be it ill or well' (58). Life, the poet sees, is an unceasing process towards death, even 'as the waves make towards the pebbled shore' (60). He fears that the friend takes cruel pleasure in the poet's weary sleeplessness at night, dwelling anxiously on the image of his inconstant friend (61). He deplores the solipsism of his own self-love (62). He dreads the thought that his friend will some day be as 'crushed and o'erworn' by 'Time's injurious hand' as the poet himself (63). This thought is 'as a death' (64). Only poetry can hope to hold out against Time's decay (65). Wearied with the meaningless round of daily life, with its profound inequalities enabling the undeserving to prosper, the poet yearns for the surcease of death (66). Self-pityingly, he urges the friend to forget him as soon as he has heard 'the surly solemn bell' ringing the news of his death (71). In himself the poet can see only the depressing tokens of advancing years

> When yellow leaves, or none, or few, do hang
> Upon those boughs which shake against the cold,
> Bare ruined choirs where late the sweet birds sang. (73)

The threat of a rival poet, better able than the speaker himself to extol the graces of the young friend, is an intolerable burden. The poet is distressed to realize that his own verse is 'barren of new pride' and 'far from variation or quick change' (76). Accordingly, he must suffer the agony of seeing his 'sick Muse' 'give another place', that is, yield place to another poet (79). It pains him to know that 'a better spirit doth use your name' (80). This rival poet, never convincingly identified in terms of Shakespeare's own biography (Marlowe? Spenser?), is a daunting prospect.

The proud full sail of his great verse,
Bound for the prize of all-too-precious you,

seems almost to have struck the poet dead (86). The loss of the friend appears to be irreversibly final:

Farewell! Thou art too dear for my possessing. (87)

Self-loathingly, the poet determines to concur in the friend's scornful estimate of him, thereby proving the friend 'virtuous, though thou art forsworn' (88). If the friend complains of the poet's lameness, the poet will obediently 'halt' in order to confirm the friend's words; the friend cannot disgrace the poet half so much as the poet will disgrace himself (89). The poet invites the friend to

hate me when thou wilt; if ever, now;
Now, while the world is bent my deeds to cross. (90)

More than anything, perhaps, the poet fears that his friend will be false without the poet's knowing of it, leaving the poet to live in an illusory dream of hope (92–3). Bitterly, the poet reflects that 'sweetest things' (such as the friend's loveliness) are all the more sour when disfigured by ungraceful deeds;

Lilies that fester smell far worse than weeds. (94)

The poet fears that he has drunk of sweet poisons and siren tears,

Distilled from limbecks foul as hell within, (119)

in his adoration of the young man. He disconsolately recalls that the friend and he have both known what it is to be unkind to the other (120).

The so-called Dark Lady sonnets, beginning with Sonnet 127, elaborate the suggestion in Sonnets 40–2 of a sexual liaison between the friend and the woman with whom the poet is in love. Most of these sonnets are addressed to the woman. The poet's feelings about her are deeply conflicted even without this rivalry: she is a 'black beauty', that is, dark-countenanced (127), and, though the poet is ready to defend her physical defects against the idealizations of most sonneteers in praise of their imaginary mistresses (130), he concedes that there is something obsessive about his devotion to a woman who can be 'tyrannous' and fully capable of tormenting him with 'disdain' (131–2). The poet is disgusted with the act and the after-effects of love-making. 'Lust in action' is an 'expense of spirit in a waste of shame', and, leading up to sexual consummation,

Is perjured, murderous, bloody, full of blame,
Savage, extreme, rude, cruel, not to trust. (129)

No sooner is the fleeting moment of desire enjoyed than the perpetrator despises himself for having sought it. Lust is 'Past reason hunted, and no sooner had / Past reason hated':

> All this the world well knows; yet none knows well
> To shun the heaven that leads men to this hell. (129)

'Hell' is an image of the woman's sexual body.

The poet plays bitterly on the word 'Will', connoting sexual desire, temper, passion, and the poet's own name (134–6, 143). The poet willingly deceives himself by believing in the truthfulness of his mistress when his reason assures him that she is lying. Punning on the word 'lie' reinforces the bitter truth of this self-deception:

> Therefore I lie with her, and she with me,
> And in our faults by lies we flattered be. (138)

The worst of it is that the woman bestows her sexual favours on both the poet and the friend:

> So, now I have confessed that he is thine.
> ...
> Him have I lost, thou hast both him and me;
> He pays the whole, and yet I am not free. (134)

'Pays' hints at the sexual act of spending his seed in intercourse. The poet hates himself for being enslaved to sexual desire. He acknowledges that he perjures himself whenever he swears that his love is 'fair' (152). He finds himself caught between two loves 'of comfort and despair', one being the 'better angel', 'a man right fair', the other being a 'worser spirit', 'a woman coloured ill' (144). His love is

> as a fever, longing still
> For that which longer nurseth the disease. (147)

We cannot know if these sonnets record an actual series of events in Shakespeare's life. He was, after all, a consummate dramatist, able to bring life to stories of political ambition and murder that can hardly have been drawn from his own experience. We can say, none the less, that the power of expression in these sonnets and early poems is in keeping with what he wrote for the theatre during the presumed same years. *Venus and Adonis* and *The Rape of Lucrece* display the techniques of verse-writing that he also exploited in his early comedies, from *The Comedy of Errors* and *The Two Gentlemen of Verona* down to *The Taming of the Shrew* and *A Midsummer Night's Dream*, all of these written by about 1595. The earlier poems in the sonnet-sequence, quite plausibly early in composition as well, concern themselves with courtship and the prospect of marriage. The increasing complexities of jealous rivalry and fears of desertion as the sonnet-sequence proceeds correspond nicely with the potentially tragic circumstances that obtrude upon romantic happiness in *The Merchant of Venice*, with the dark plot of Shylock to kill Antonio, or *Much Ado About Nothing*, with Don John's nearly successful attempt to ruin the intended marriage of Claudio and Hero, or *As You Like It*, with the malice of Oliver and Duke Frederick, or *Twelfth Night*, with the unremitting antagonism of Malvolio to romantic happiness.

Especially when we come to the so-called problem plays of 1601–4, *Troilus and Cressida*, *All's Well That Ends Well*, and *Measure for Measure*, we encounter a world in which sexual inconstancy, prostitution, and male fears of sexual intimacy remind us of the Dark Lady and the unfaithful friend in the latter end of the sonnet-sequence. As Richard Wheeler has persuasively argued,[5] the Sonnets occupy, with the problem plays and with *Hamlet*, a crucial and pivotal position in the development of Shakespeare's art. Having worked his way forward in the comedies towards a romantic solution to the multiple anxieties of courtship, and (in the history plays) towards male maturation enabling a young man to come to terms with the image of his father, Shakespeare evidently found himself ready to venture onto the challenging terrain of tragedy, of womanly infidelity, of jealous rage and murderous ambition. The Sonnets encapsulate this transition in a chronology that is uncertain and yet suggestive of a great mind attempting to depict the shape of human life in its perilous trajectory from hopeful youth to wary maturity.

Along with the Sonnets in his 1609 quarto, Thorpe also published a poem called *A Lover's Complaint*. The poem is not mentioned on the title-page of the volume, but does have its own headtitle on sig. Kv: 'A Louers Complaint. BY William Shakespeare'. This ascription is Thorpe's, and should not be taken too seriously, since Thorpe seems not to have had authority from Shakespeare to publish the Sonnets and may have added the last two sonnets on his own initiative. *A Lover's Complaint* was not assigned to anyone other than Shakespeare during his lifetime, and has generally been allowed to be his, albeit with sceptical reservation. A recent exception is Brian Vickers, who argues for John Davies of Hereford as the author.[6] Vickers's promotion of Davies as the author is perhaps less convincing than his earlier campaigns against Shakespeare's putative authorship of 'A Funeral Elegy for Master William Peter' (now assigned to John Ford) and the short 'Shall I fly, shall I die', but he does raise serious questions as to whether *A Lover's Complaint* is really by Shakespeare.

Even if Shakespeare's authorship still remains open to question, *A Lover's Complaint* deserves our attention for its complex and ironic reworking of the pastoral tradition. Its handling of multiple points of view is innovative. After the poet-narrator has presented to the reader the forlorn maiden of the poem's title, he brings on an old shepherd as sympathetic audience for the bulk of the maiden's sad lament of having been seduced and then abandoned by an attractive and smooth-talking young man. The main portion of the poem is in the form of her story as told to the old man. We also hear the voice of the male wooer as he subdues the maiden to his manly charm.

Framed thus, the three participants come before us in considerable subtlety and range of expression. The male wooer is given his opportunity to appeal to our sympathy, or at least our willingness to appreciate his consummate skill as a seducer. The young woman as teller of her own tale is eloquent on how easy it was for her to hearken to such a beautiful seduction. The old man comes alive as a character too, in his sympathy, his regret for the young woman's misfortune, and his inability finally to be of much help. The language is often metaphorically dense and vivid, as in the young woman's outcry,

> Oh, father, what a hell of witchcraft lies
> In the small orb of one particular tear! (288–9)

Whoever wrote those two lines was certainly a poet of no small talent.

Shakespeare is generally accepted as the author of a short poem called 'The Phoenix and Turtle', published by Robert Chester in a collection of poems entitled *Love's Martyr: Or, Rosalins Complaint* in 1601. The idea of the volume was to offer various poetic exercises on the theme of the phoenix and the turtledove 'by the best and chiefest poets of our modern writers'. Probably Shakespeare's contribution was written shortly before the publication date of 1601, since it is aimed so specifically at the theme of the collection. The phoenix, a mythical bird that was thought to live in the Arabian desert for some five or six hundred years and then be consumed in fire, only to be reborn in its own ashes, was regarded as a symbol of immortality. The turtledove symbolized constancy in love. Together, in Shakespeare's poem, they are subsumed in a 'mutual flame' of eternal union.

Shakespeare beautifully pairs the two in a repeated mystical paradox of two in one and one in two.

> So they loved, as love in twain
> Had the essence but in one,
> Two distincts, division none;
> Number there in love was slain. (25–8)

Distance cannot mar their love even when they are asunder. Reason itself is 'confounded' by a division that grows together and by a singleness of being that is mysteriously 'compounded'. Reason is indeed supplanted by Love in these two that have been subsumed, even immolated, into one another's essence. Beauty, truth, and rarity unite to grace, in utter simplicity, the urn where lie enclosed the ashes of these two that are forever one. These paradoxes are familiar from Neoplatonic tradition, as splendidly expressed for example in John Donne's 'The Extasie', but here they achieve an exalted sublimity that is all the more remarkable for the unadorned purity of the language. No one poem better illustrates the perfect elegance in Shakespeare's poetic control of language and metaphor.

This essay has focused on Shakespeare's narrative and non-dramatic poems, but something needs to be said about Shakespeare the poet in his plays. The early plays especially are predominantly in verse. Plays like *A Comedy of Errors*, *The Two Gentlemen of Verona*, and *The Taming of the Shrew* quite regularly use iambic pentameter blank verse for the conversations of the major characters in the love-plots and prose for the comic scenes involving their servants. *A Midsummer Night's Dream* follows this pattern. It also provides further versatility by introducing four-stress or tetrameter patterns in the speeches of Puck, Oberon, and other fairies, sometimes with trochaic or inverted iambic feet stressing the first syllable: 'Through the forest have I gone, / But Athenian found I none', and so forth (II. ii. 72–3). The many songs use freer lyric forms. The mid-1590s are sometimes referred to as Shakespeare's 'lyric' period because of this exuberance of poetic forms.

Romeo and Juliet (1594–6) is very much in this lyric mode. It introduces sonnets into the discourse, as when Romeo and Juliet first meet at the Capulets' masked ball. Romeo leads off with a quatrain or four-line passage alternately rhymed *abab* ('If I profane with my unworthiest hand / This holy shrine, the gentle sin is this: / My lips, two blushing pilgrims, ready stand / To smooth that rough touch with a gentle kiss', I. v. 94–7). Juliet counters with a quatrain of her own, after which they volley with one-line exchanges (and one two-line speech) until they reach the final two lines of the Shakespearean sonnet form, lines 13 and 14, which they rhyme as a couplet ('JULIET Saints do not move, though grant for prayers' sake. / ROMEO Then move not, while my prayer's effect I take'). At this point they kiss. The opening Prologue is also a sonnet, and the Chorus introducing Act II (which, however, may be spurious). Shakespeare is looking for ways to meld poetic and dramatic discourse. Even the Nurse speaks mainly in blank verse, though the other comic servants in the Capulet household speak mainly in prose. Mercutio is master of both verse (as in his Queen Mab speech, I. iv. 53–95) and prose (in his conversation with Benvolio about Romeo's lovesickness and Tybalt as the prince of cats, and so forth, II. iv. 1–98). The earlier *Titus Andronicus* is predominantly in blank verse.

The early history plays, from *1 Henry VI* to *Richard III*, follow a similar pattern of blank verse for the many scenes of political conflict occasionally interspersed with bouts of low comedy in prose, as in the Jack Cade rebellion of *2 Henry VI* (IV. ii–iii, IV. vi–viii, x). *1* and *3 Henry VI* have no prose at all. *Richard III* is in blank verse throughout except for the talk of the two murderers sent to execute the Duke of Clarence (I. iv. 85–169), and even they shift into verse as their colloquy with Clarence grows more serious. The anonymous citizens of London discussing the plight of their country in II. iii speak in blank verse. *King John* is in blank verse throughout, even in the comic dialogue of Philip the Bastard. Appropriately enough in a play about an ill-fated king of refined poetic temperament, *Richard II* never varies from its blank verse pattern, even when two anonymous gardeners are comparing views on the state of the commonwealth (III. iv).

The verse in these early plays is, moreover, quite metrically regular as compared with what is to follow. Run-ons without punctuation past the ends of lines are not common; so too with pauses, or caesuras, in the middle of verse lines. Hypermetric verse feet are relatively scarce, though some pleasing variation is needed to avoid a drum-beat monotony of stressed and unstressed. Accents usually fall on the syllables of multisyllabic words where we would expect the accents to occur. As one example, consider what Duke Theseus says to Hermia in *A Midsummer Night's Dream*, asking her whether, if she yields not to her father's choice,

> You can endure the livery of a nun,
> For aye to be in shady cloister mewed,
> To live a barren sister all your life. (I. ii. 70–2)

This is perfectly regular, if 'livery' is understood to be pronounced in two syllables. The stresses in 'SHADy CLOISter' and 'BARren SISter' land where they should land. Each line ends with punctuation. No significant pauses occur in mid-line. At the same time we should note that Theseus's next line, 'Chanting faint hymns to the cold fruitless moon', is pleasingly irregular, with an opening stress on 'Chant-' and with two stressed syllables placed side by side (called 'spondee') in 'faint hymns' and 'cold fruit-' to underscore perhaps the laboriousness of what a nun's life would be like.

As Shakespeare undertook the writing of his second tetralogy of history plays and the great romantic comedies of the late 1590s, his poetic style became notably more free. Movement back and forth between verse and prose sometimes leaves an ambiguous sense as to which is which, in subtle ways that can be symptomatic of character development. In *1 Henry IV* (1596–7), Prince Hal joshes with Falstaff in rich and splendidly colloquial prose as he and Falstaff converse in the Prince's apartments and in the tavern. These magnificent scenes of prose comedy are regularly interspersed with verse scenes at court in which King Henry IV contends with the opposition of the Percies. A prose episode at an innyard on the London–Canterbury road (II. i), prior to the Gadshill robbery, is a vibrant glimpse of life on that dangerous pilgrimage route, with two carriers or haulers of produce into London warily fending off the attempts of one of the robbers' spies to find out their itinerary.

The tavern scene, one of Shakespeare's greatest artistic achievements up to this point in his writing career, is in prose except for the sobering moment when Prince Hal must give the Sheriff some account of his relationship to Falstaff (II. iv. 507–20). The devastating dressing-down that Hal receives next morning from his father (III. ii), and the son's reply, in verse, are immediately followed by Falstaff's banter with Bardolph and Mistress Quickly in the tavern. Hal and Falstaff are separated now, and so are the idioms in which they speak. When they come together once more at Shrewsbury, some of Falstaff's witticisms seem as ill-timed as his offering Hal a bottle of sack when the Prince has asked for a sword (V. iii). In this interchange, Hal speaks in blank verse and Falstaff in prose. Falstaff's disquisitions on his abusing of his recruitment authority (IV. ii. 11–47) and on honour (V. i. 129–40) are incomparably fine; the distinguishing of prose and verse is not simplistically one of roguery versus chivalry. Even so, it does demarcate the drifting apart of Hal and Falstaff and suggests the inevitability of the ultimate rejection of Falstaff.

As that rejection approaches, near the end of *2 Henry IV*, the prose scenes of Falstaff with Justices Shallow and Slender, and the tawdry business of Doll Tearsheet and Mistress Quickly being apprehended by the Beadle to be whipped, are meaningfully juxtaposed with the new King Henry's banishment of his former companion (in verse) and his embracing of the Lord Chief Justice as his new counsellor. The hero-king of *Henry V* amply displays his powers as a verse rhetorician in defying the French ambassador or addressing his adoring troops at Harfleur and Agincourt, but he also has not forgotten how bewitchingly he can speak in prose, as when he converses with his soldiers on the night before the battle (IV. i) and when he woos Katharine of France (V. ii).

The romantic comedies of the late 1590s differ similarly from the earlier comedies in their use of prose and verse. In *Much Ado About Nothing*,

Beatrice and Benedick spar and quip in brilliant prose, and most of the comic business of tricking them (especially Benedick) into admitting love for each other is also in prose. So of course are the ridiculous antics of Dogberry and the watch. Verse is saved for Claudio's conversation with Don Pedro about his longing to marry Hero (I. i. 278–316), for an occasional song, for Margaret and Ursula's deception of Beatrice (pointedly contrasted in this respect with the tricking of Benedick by Leonato and the other men), for the abortive wedding ceremony in which Claudio throws Hero back to her father (IV. i), for a serious moment in which Leonato and his brother nearly come to blows with Don Pedro and Claudio over the defaming of Hero (V. i), and for most of the final scene of discovery and reconciliation – though even here, appropriately, Benedick ends the play in prose. *The Merry Wives* is extensively in prose, except for some of the conventional love-plot about Master Fenton and Anne Page and in a poetic tribute to Windsor Castle (V. v). The wooing scenes and the comic bravura of Touchstone in *As You Like It* give us Shakespeare at the top of his form as a prose-writer; verse is saved mainly for the court of Duke Frederick, for the plight of old Adam, for the Petrarchan follies of Silvius and Phoebe, the conversion of Oliver from villain to loving forester, and once again the finale. *Twelfth Night* is effortless in its blending of prose, blank verse, and song.

Shakespeare's protean flexibility as a poet is so vast, and seemingly so carefully controlled (though we can doubt that Shakespeare himself was always conscious of his progression towards freer forms), that scholars have been able to construct charts detailing some significant shifts. The total of run-on lines, for example, in which the verse ends without a punctuation stop or pause, changes from 12.9 per cent in *The Comedy of Errors* and 9.5 per cent in *Titus Andronicus* to 43.3 per cent in *Antony and Cleopatra*, 41.5 per cent in *The Tempest*, and 46.3 per cent in *Henry VIII*. These figures of course concern verse only, not prose. The number of light or so-called 'feminine' endings in which the last foot of a verse line concludes in an unaccented syllable (e.g., 'Of sulphurous roaring the most mighty Neptune / Seem to besiege and make his bold waves tremble', *The Tempest*, I. ii. 204–5) goes up from practically none in the *Henry VI* plays and *The Comedy of Errors* to a remarkably high percentage in *Cymbeline*, *The Winter's Tale*, and *The Tempest*.

The ending of one character's speech and the commencement of another character's reply in the middle of a blank verse line similarly increases from virtually none in the early plays to common occurrence in the late plays, sometimes involving the entrance of the second speaker in mid verse line. Here is an instance when Leontes is speaking remorsefully in *The Winter's*

Tale of his guilt for having accused his wife and his friend Polixenes of having committed adultery:

> And how his piety
> Does my deeds make the blacker!
> [*Enter Paulina.*]
> PAULINA Woe the while!
> Oh, cut my lace, lest my heart, cracking it,
> Break too!
> FIRST LORD What fit is this, good lady? (III. ii. 171–4)

This passage also illustrates another marked trend, towards pauses in the midst of blank verse lines in the late plays. In part, this development may have resulted from the influence of John Fletcher and other Jacobean dramatists, whose style gravitates in this direction; Fletcher was Shakespeare's successor as chief playwright for the King's Men and his collaborator in writing *The Two Noble Kinsmen* and *Henry VIII*. But the development was also surely integral to Shakespeare's growth as poet and dramatist.

The plays for which Shakespeare is most famed are also, not coincidentally, the plays in which his extraordinary capacity as a poet is at its height. The richness of poetic imagery, ably studied by Caroline Spurgeon and others,[7] invites the spectator or view to ponder the clustering of images in *Hamlet* having to do with decay, disease, human frailty, incest, poison, graveyards, skulls, suicide, drowning, and much more. Images prevail in *Othello* of an old black ram and a white ewe, apes and monkeys, devils and angels, damnation and salvation, witchcraft, green-eyed monsters, meshes and nets, and a pearl thrown away by a 'base Indian' (V. ii. 357). *King Lear* dwells on images of the natural versus the unnatural as variously interpreted, on obedience and disobedience, on astrological signs and whether they are to be believed, on blasts and fogs and wolves, on thunder, and on the gods – if they exist. Macbeth concludes at last that his life 'Is fall'n into the sere, the yellow leaf', beyond the reach of purgative drugs that might restore health (V. iii. 23). Life is 'but a walking shadow, a poor player / That struts and frets his hour upon the stage / And then is heard no more' (V. v. 24–6). *Antony and Cleopatra*, despite its tragic tale, culminates in a triumphant celebration of the power of imaginative poetry to conjure up an Antony whose 'legs bestrid the ocean' and whose 'reared arm / Crested the world', so greatly that there was no winter in his bounty. His delights were 'dolphinlike' in the way they 'showed his back above / The elements they lived in' (V. ii. 81–91).

Shakespeare's powerful images often seem intensely aware of their theatrical context. Macbeth compares himself to an incapable actor, strutting and fretting. Hamlet sharply advises the visiting players at Elsinore not to saw the air with their hands or 'tear a passion to tatters, to very rags, to split the ear of the groundlings'; instead they should work to acquire temperance so that they can hold a mirror up to nature, 'show virtue her feature, scorn her own image, and the very age and body of the time his form and pressure' (*Hamlet*, III. ii. 4–24). The fact that these incisive meta-dramatic images are in a prose passage makes the point that Shakespeare is entirely capable of being poetic in his prose. All the world is a stage, as Jaques observes in *As You Like It* (II. vii. 138–65), borrowing a metaphor from a commonplace but transforming it into memorable verbal beauty.

Shakespeare loves oxymoron, or inherent contradiction, as a figure of speech designed to accentuate the paradoxes that haunt our human condition. 'Love is a smoke made with the fume of sighs', observes Romeo sadly of his own lovesick condition. 'What is it else? A madness most discreet, / A choking gall, and a preserving sweet' (*Romeo and Juliet*, I. i. 190–4). He sees signs everywhere of opposite forces tearing themselves apart, especially in the feuding of Verona's two families:

> Why, then, O brawling love, O loving hate,
> O anything of nothing first create,
> O heavy lightness, serious vanity,
> Misshapen chaos of well-seeming forms,
> Feather of lead, bright smoke, cold fire, sick health,
> Still-waking sleep that is not what it is! (176–81)

To Friar Laurence is given the saintly wisdom of seeing these paradoxes on the cosmic scale of a battle between good and evil:

> Two such opposèd kings encamp them still
> In man as well as herbs – grace and rude will;
> And where the worser is predominant,
> Full soon the canker death eats up that plant. (II. iii. 27–30)

As Juliet says, 'My only love sprung from my only hate!' (I. v. 139). The lovers are sacrifices to their families' enmity. The whole play is in effect an oxymoron, making the point of the inseparable nature of Shakespeare's gifts as dramatist and as poet.

Shakespeare deftly knits the substance of his reading into the poetic texture of his plays. Hamlet compares his father and his uncle to Hyperion and a satyr; he remembers his father as having 'An eye like Mars to threaten and command' and 'A station like the herald Mercury / New-lighted on a heaven-kissing hill' (I. ii. 140, III. iv. 57–60). Hamlet and the First Player recite some lines from an old play about the death of Priam and the grief of Hecuba as told by Virgil (II. ii. 434–518) by way of gaining some perspective on Hamlet's own story of the death of his father. The whole of *Troilus and Cressida* is a meditation on the devastations of the Trojan War as told by Homer, Chaucer, and John Lydgate. Ovid's story of Pyramus and Thisbe serves as a foil for that of the lovers in *A Midsummer Night's Dream*. In such poetic choices and methods, we see again and again the craftsmanship of the author of the non-dramatic poems as well, who learned to be a poet by applying metaphors and illustrations to his verse as meaningfully integrated ornament. The poet and the dramatist are one.

NOTES

1 Don Marquis, *Archy and Mehitabel* (London: Faber and Faber, 1931, rptd 1954).

2 Meredith Skura, *Shakespeare the Actor and the Purposes of Playing* (Chicago: University of Chicago Press, 1993). Shakespeare quotations in this essay are from *The Complete Works of Shakespeare*, ed. David Bevington, 6th edn (New York: Pearson Longman, 2008).

3 Thomas Nashe, *Pierce Penniless His Supplication to the Devil* (London, 1592), in *The Works of Thomas Nashe*, ed. R. B. McKerrow (London: A. H. Bullen, 1910).

4 Robert Greene, *Greene's Groatsworth of Wit Bought with a Million of Repentance* (London, 1592).

5 Richard Wheeler, *Shakespeare's Development and the Problem Comedies: Turn and Counter-Turn* (Berkeley: University of California Press,1981).

6 Brian Vickers, *Shakespeare, 'A Lover's Complaint', and John Davies of Hereford* (Cambridge: Cambridge University Press, 2007).

7 Caroline Spurgeon, *Shakespeare's Imagery and What It Tells Us* (Cambridge: Cambridge University Press, 1935).

SELECTED FURTHER READING

Editions

The Complete Works of Shakespeare, ed. David Bevington, 6th edn, New York, Pearson Longman, 2008

The Complete Sonnets and Poems, ed. Colin Burrow, The Oxford Shakespeare, Oxford and New York, Oxford University Press, 2002

The Poems, ed. F. T. Prince, The Arden Shakespeare, 2nd series, London, Methuen, and Cambridge, MA, Harvard University Press, 1960

Shakespeare's Sonnets, ed. Katherine Duncan-Jones, The Arden Shakespeare, 3rd series, Walton on Thames, Thomas Nelson, 1997

Secondary works

Asals, Heather, 'Venus and Adonis: The Education of a Goddess', *Studies in English Literature* 13 (1973), 31–51

Booth, Stephen, *An Essay on Shakespeare's Sonnets*, New Haven, Yale University Press, 1969

Donaldson, Ian, 'A Theme for Disputation: Shakespeare's *Lucrece*', in *The Rapes of Lucretia: A Myth and Its Transformations*, Oxford: Oxford University Press, 1982

Dubrow, Heather, *Captive Victors: Shakespeare's Narrative Poems and Sonnets*, Ithaca, NY, Cornell University Press, 1987

Echoes of Desire: English Petrarchism and Its Counterdiscourses, Ithaca, NY, Cornell University Press, 1995

Fineman, Joel, *Shakespeare's Perjured Eye: The Invention of Poetic Subjectivity in the Sonnets*, Berkeley, University of California Press, 1986

Hulse, Clarke, *Metamorphic Verse: The Elizabethan Minor Epic*, Princeton, Princeton University Press, 1981

Kahn, Coppélia, 'The Rape in Shakespeare's Lucrece', *Shakespeare Studies* 9 (1976), 45–72

Man's Estate: Masculine Identity in Shakespeare, Berkeley, University of California Press, 1981

Kapitaniak, Pierre (ed.), *Shakespeare poète*, Paris, Société Française Shakespeare, 2007

Keach, William, *'Venus and Adonis', Elizabethan Erotic Narratives: Irony and Pathos in the Ovidian Poetry of Shakespeare, Marlowe, and Their Contemporaries*, New Brunswick, NJ, Rutgers University Press, 1977

Marquis, Don, *Archy and Mehitabel,* London, Faber and Faber, 1931, rptd 1954

Maus, Katharine Eisaman, 'Taking Tropes Seriously: Language and Violence in Shakespeare's The Rape of Lucrece', *Shakespeare Quarterly* 45 (1994), 66–82

Mortimer, Anthony, *Variable Passions: A Reading of Shakespeare's'Venus and Adonis',* New York: AMS, 2000

Schiffer, James (ed.), *Shakespeare's Sonnets: Critical Essays*, New York, Garland, 1999

Shakespeare Survey 15 (1962). Devoted chiefly to the poems and music, including the Sonnets

Vendler, Helen, *The Art of Shakespeare's Sonnets*, Cambridge, MA, Harvard University Press, 1997

Vickers, Brian, *'Counterfeiting' Shakespeare: Evidence, Authorship, and John Ford's 'Funerall Elegy'*, Cambridge, Cambridge University Press, 2002

Shakespeare, 'A Lover's Complaint', and John Davies of Hereford, Cambridge, Cambridge University Press, 2007

5

ACHSAH GUIBBORY

John Donne

John Donne (1572–1631) has been called the greatest love-poet in the English language, but this category does not adequately describe either the variety or the complexity of his poetry. Indeed, in the late seventeenth and the eighteenth century, his 'metaphysical wit' was thought to compromise his stature as a love-poet. Deaf to the seductive effect that intellect or wit can have on readers (female as well as male), John Dryden condemned Donne for 'perplex[ing] the Minds of the Fair Sex with nice Speculations of Philosophy, when he shou'd engage their hearts'. Later, Samuel Johnson coined the term 'the metaphysical poets' and described metaphysical wit as a kind of '*discordia concors*' that discovered 'occult resemblances in things apparently unlike', yoking together 'the most heterogeneous ideas ... by violence'.[1]

Donne lived and wrote when people were more likely to see correspondences between things that would come to seem discrete (for example, the human body or microcosm and the macrocosm of the world), when the line between the private and public realms had not yet been sharply drawn, when spiritual and secular realms were intertwined. But there were challenges to the older order, and resulting scepticism about received truths. Galileo confirmed Copernicus's hypothesis that the earth was not the centre of the universe. A new experimental science was developing, that sought to discover natural laws according to which the physical world worked. People were interested in the discovery of the heavens, of nature, of the Americas. It was also a time of religious change and instability. The Protestant Reformation had split the western Christian church, and that instability touched England, which was in Donne's time a Protestant country, making life fraught for Catholic families.

Fascinated with exploration and discovery, acutely aware of instability and danger in a world where 'change' seemed the only constant, Donne and his poetry were products of their time. His interest in the issues of his day is evident. But most of his poetic explorations and discoveries concern not the external world, but the more circumscribed, yet significant world of intimate, personal experience to which he bent his prodigious linguistic, poetic, and intellectual talents. Donne's attempt to articulate the mysteries of the heart and mind, of human desire, makes his poetry continue to speak to us. Whether in his secular love-poems or in religious devotional poems, whether in poems to friends and patrons or in poems to a beloved (real or imagined) or hymns to God, Donne charts a challenging terrain of experience. He does so in fresh, exciting language, as if he is the first to have passed this way. He gives voice to erotic desires which cannot always be separated from the soul, and to the desire for something beyond the self, for something more permanent than the mutable world – the desire for the divine, which often seems quite removed from the world of disease, decay, and death, but might occasionally be glimpsed as present in earthly experience.

Born into an English Catholic family, Donne had a strong sense of being both an insider and an outsider, drawn to the public world but also conscious of standing at a certain distance. His mother was descended from Thomas More, who was executed by Henry VIII for opposing the king's divorce from the Church of Rome. Many of Donne's family, including his brother Henry, suffered for their loyalty to the Roman church. Being a Catholic was difficult in post-Reformation England. English Protestants thought of Catholics, no matter how ancient their English lineage, as potential traitors and dangerous outsiders in what was now officially a Protestant country. Attendance in the Church of England was compulsory, and Catholics were fined for being 'recusant' if they failed to attend. 'Pursuivants' or spies hunted down and interrogated Catholics who sheltered the Jesuit priests who came to England to strengthen the faith. If a Catholic priest were caught, he could suffer a horrific death that included hanging and being disembowelled while alive. No wonder Donne's poetry is haunted by an obsession with death, secrecy, and martyrdom, and by a preference for private spaces.

People sometimes say, 'once a Catholic, always a Catholic'. But Donne did not remain in the Roman church, even if he retained a Catholic sensibility, and a sense of loyalty to his Catholic family. Around 1593, after he had left Oxford University and was studying law at the Inns of Court, which groomed ambitious English gentlemen for 'advancement' in society and at court, Donne read deeply in the theological controversies between Catholic and Reformed theologians. By 1598, Donne probably had, at least outwardly, conformed to the English church, for he now was secretary to Thomas Egerton, who had a high position in the government of Elizabeth I.

While living with Egerton, Donne fell in love with and secretly courted Egerton's young niece, Anne More. If Donne was uncertain about choosing a church, he was decisive about Anne. In December 1601 they eloped, marrying without the parental permission that was expected in an age of arranged marriages. In less than two months, the marriage was exposed, Anne's father had his son-in-law briefly jailed, and Donne lost his job. The marriage prospered, but he would spend years trying unsuccessfully to find employment, sometimes afflicted with illness and depression, seeking patronage from wealthy and powerful persons. Later, in 1615, Donne took orders in the Church of England, becoming a priest, and eventually Dean of St Paul's, as well as one of the most powerful preachers of his day.

Donne's poetic output is relatively small. He wrote five formal verse satires in the vein of Horace and Juvenal exposing frivolity, corruption, and injustice in England, fewer than twenty love-elegies modelled on Ovid's *Amores*, short epigrams in the style of classical epigrammatists, a long, unfinished satirical poem *Metempsychosis*, and occasional poems and verse letters to friends or patrons, including two *Anniversaries* on the death of Elizabeth Drury, the fifteen-year-old daughter of his patron Sir Robert Drury. Of thirty-five divine poems, the most important are his twenty-one 'holy sonnets', 'Goodfriday, 1613. Riding Westward', and three hymns to God. The *Songs and Sonets*, just under sixty poems, constitute his largest, most varied group of poems, and those for which Donne is most famous. We do not know when Donne wrote individual poems (with the exception of 'Goodfriday, 1613' and the two *Anniversaries*, 1611–12), and thus we cannot tie them to events in his life. The *Elegies* are presumed to be among his earliest, written in the early or mid-1590s when he was at Lincolns Inn; the *Satires*, too, are thought to date from the 1590s. His *Songs and Sonets* probably date from the 1590s and early 1600s, though one might be as late as 1617. Most of the holy sonnets may have been composed in 1608–9, long before his ordination, but dating remains a matter of speculation.[2] Despite the fact that the secular love-poems as a group are earlier than the devotional ones, there may be some chronological overlap, and we find religious images in the erotic poems and analogies to erotic love in the religious. With the exception of the *Anniversaries*, Donne did not publish his poetry. Rather, poems circulated more intimately in manuscript among coterie audiences who might be expected to appreciate his distinctive wit, to get references others might miss, and even to share his values.[3] Circulation of poetry in manuscript was considered proper for a gentleman but would also be appropriate for private poetry, or for potentially dangerous or subversive poems or sentiments one might want to keep hidden.

And there certainly is a subversive aspect to Donne's poetry. His writing is marked by paradox, which in Donne's time meant, 'A statement or tenet contrary to received opinion or belief' (*OED*, 1.a.). Whether he is writing satires, elegies, love-lyrics or religious poems, we typically find an anti-authoritarian stance, an irreverence, even when he is addressing God. Self-consciously positioning themselves against authority figures, the speakers of Donne's lyric poems establish their own authority, claim independence, and delight in flouting established, traditional powers. The pose is edgy – and helps explain why Donne kept most of his poems relatively private and later feared they would hurt his reputation as a priest.

Perhaps the *Elegies* and *Satires* seemed the most dangerous. Dramatic addresses by a male speaker to a woman or another man, the *Elegies* defy figures of authority or try to outwit them. The speaker of 'The Perfume' carries out a clandestine affair with an unmarried young woman, hoping to get her father's 'goods' (line 11) and at the end fantasizes about the father's death. 'Jealousie' and the elegy beginning 'Natures lay Ideot' concern adulterous affairs, in which the husband's authority is mocked or despised. The male voice in these poems is dominant; he insists on control, though such power often remains a wish rather than an accomplishment. In 'Natures lay Ideot', he complains that his married mistress has learned the art of deceptive love so well from him that she is now leaving him for a new lover. The patriarchal power of parents and husbands was believed to be the foundation of society, even during the reign of Elizabeth. Thus Donne's speakers suggest a broader antagonism towards the established social order.

Donne's Ovidian elegies are anti-Petrarchan. A dominant literary form in the 1580s and 1590s, Petrarchan poetry derived from Petrarch's earlier sonnet-sequence about his love for Laura, a woman he had loved from a distance for years after first seeing her. With its elevation of the soul and idealization of the worshipped mistress, Petrarchism became the language of the court. Elizabeth enjoyed being seen as the powerful, adored mistress, dispenser of grace.[4] Donne's *Elegies* parody Petrarchan conventions, preferring Ovidian earthiness and cynicism to abject servility, and thus suggest Donne's alienation from Elizabeth's court, at the very time that he hoped to gain a position. Parodying the conventional 'blazon' praising the mistress's beauty, the speaker in 'The Comparison' describes the 'sweat drops' on his 'Mistris breast' as 'pearle carcanets' (lines 4, 6), contrasting them with the 'Ranke sweaty froth' of his supposed friend's mistress which is 'Like spermatique issue of ripe monstrous boiles' (lines 7–8).[5]

Whereas the Petrarchan lover is subservient and long-suffering, Donne's speakers in the *Elegies* are bold. They proclaim their 'libertinism' in love. Refusal to be tied to one woman becomes an assertion of freedom in life. 'Variety' begins, 'The heavens rejoyce in motion, why should I / Abjure my so much lov'd variety, / And not with many youth and love divide?' (lines 1–3). The speaker in 'Change' at first rails against such inconstancy, accusing his mistress of infidelity natural to women, who are 'more hot, wily, wild' than 'beasts' (lines 11–12). By the end of the elegy the speaker has changed his mind, and vows to pursue a middle course between Petrarchan long-suffering faithfulness and indiscriminate promiscuity. He will instead practise serial monogamy, like a river that remains 'purest' when it 'kisse[s] one banke, and leaving this / Never looke[s] backe, but the next banke doe[s] kisse' (lines 33–5).

Donne's elegies are frank about sex. They are written from a distinctly masculine, sometimes misogynist point of view, though the exception is 'Sapho to Philaenis', a poem about lesbian love featuring a female speaker. Still, all Donne's elegies reject or mock current fashions of love that sublimated male desire, forcing it (as Donne says in 'Loves Progress') 'new strange shapes to take' (line 5). In Donne's most famous elegy, 'Going to Bed', an ardent lover addresses his mistress, urging her: 'Come, Madam, come, all rest my powers defie, / Until I labour, I in labour lie' (lines 1–2). This elegy, like so many of Donne's poems, gives the feeling of naturalness, with its conversational, colloquial language and tone, the rhythms of speech, the directness, which draw the reader in. He commands his mistress to undress, labelling the various articles of clothing (and restraint) that he sees or imagines her removing, and then describing how he wants to explore her body, 'O my America! my new-found-land' (line 27). 'Licence my roaving hands, and let them go, / Before, behind, between, above, below' (lines 26–7). Love-making is compared to the exploration and possession of new lands, but also to religious experience. The 'soft bed' is a 'hallow'd temple' (line 18). Are we to take the religious language seriously, or is it just a seduction tactic? At the end, the reader discovers that the speaker is already naked: 'To teach thee I am naked first; why than / What needst thou have more covering then a man?' (lines 47–8).

In Donne's witty poetry, we see a clever, creative mind at work. The wit – the precise yet equivocal, densely figurative language – is seductive. It pulls the reader in, establishing an intimate relation between poet and reader, which mirrors the relation between the speaker and his addressee, who often assumes a role (if not a voice) in the poem. Donne makes demands on the reader. His images are not decorative, but the substance of his poetry, the vehicles of argument, and we must follow the logic of his poems. Donne's sense of the variety, mutability, and instability of the world finds its counterpart in the difficult syntax of his poems, the sometimes dizzying metaphorical language of poems which, despite their strong endings, resist firm closure. We find ourselves going back for more.

Though 'Going to Bed' is unusual among Donne's elegies for idealizing the woman and glorifying sex through religious imagery, it shares with his other elegies the assumption that sexual activity is natural and legitimate, that men and women are bodily creatures of natural desires, that love is about sex and the body, a skilful art to be learned and practised. He advises a friend in 'Loves Progress' that the best way to seduce a woman is not to spend time praising her hair and face but to 'practice my Art' and begin 'below' (line 73), at the foot, and work up since that is the quickest passage to her virginal/vaginal '*India*' (line 65). Donne's elegies seem written for young Inns of Court men, who would appreciate the analogy between success in love and getting ahead in the world. 'Oh, let mee not serve so, as those men serve / Whom honours smoakes at once fatten and sterve' (lines 1–2), he tells his mistress. He wants to be rewarded for his faithful service. He ends warning her not to let her 'deepe bitternesse' (intense coldness, animosity) create 'carelesse despaire' in him (lines 35–6). For then he would 'fall' from her love, 'As nations do from Rome' (line 42).

My hate shall outgrow thine, and utterly
I will renounce thy dalliance: and when I
Am the Recusant, in that resolute state,
What hurts it mee to be'excommunicate?

Love, politics, and religion come together, as the speaker asserts that his loyalty is contingent upon his mistress (whether it is a woman, a monarch, or a church) repaying and returning his love. There might be criticism of Queen Elizabeth, but the broader implication that loyalty is conditional, that allegiances can be changed, explains why such an elegy could be considered politically dangerous and subversive enough not to be published until 1669.

Donne's *Satires* are more overtly political, as they critique corruptions and inadequacies of the society in which he presents himself as an ambivalent participant. One gets the feel of London, but also of London as synecdoche for England. The first satire announces ambivalence about the public world that haunts all five satires. The speaker of this first poem is a scholar, apparently happily 'coffin'd' (line 4) in his study with his books, but pulled out into the street with its fashions, dirt, and materiality by his friend, the sycophantic courtier who is 'monstrous' in his 'refin'd manners' (lines 27–8). The speaker expresses both disgust and fascination as he chronicles the absurd actions of his inconstant 'lost sheep' (line 93), who 'greet[s] / Every fine silken painted foole we meet' (lines 71–2), and deserts the speaker 'Violently ravish'd to his lechery' (line 108), only to return home injured and penitent. The satirical spirit becomes sharper and the assessment of England grimmer in the following satires, which concern law, religion, and the system of justice (or rather, injustice) Donne sees in England. Satire II attacks the 'ravenous maw' (line 26) of the court of law, and lawyers who 'practice for meere gaine' (line 63), concerned with money, not justice; Satire IV describes his visit to the royal court as a 'sinne' (line 1) punished by the experience of the court itself, which has been his 'Purgatorie' (line 3), filled with 'strange' creatures (courtiers), whose talk makes him sick, and 'Pictures of vice' which 'teach' him 'virtue' (line 72). It is a place of vanity, corruption, disease, a place where 'my Mistresse Truth' (line 163) cannot be found, and, as in the first satire, he longs to be 'At home in wholesome solitarinesse' (line 155). The fifth satire is most despairing: it presents England as a 'Court' (both royal and legal), filled with suitors seeking patronage, who 'run' to their ruin as the 'Officers' prey on them and devour them (lines 13–21). The world of England is divided between those who seek sustenance or justice, and those who might be able to distribute it but refuse to. Donne lives not in the Iron Age but in an 'Age of rusty iron' (line 35) in which 'Injustice is sold'. Behind the poem lies not just Horace or Juvenal but Deuteronomy, which insists that judges must judge justly, not respecting persons or taking gifts (Deut. 16:18–20), for law is the foundation of a society's health, human justice mirroring God's. Greed has corrupted England's entire society; and the speaker asks Elizabeth, 'Greatest and fairest Empresse, know you this?' (line 28). She is ignorant or complicit – either possibility is damning.[6]

The third and best-known satire is on 'Religion'. Here the questions Donne raises (which is the true church? is there a 'true' church on earth?) seem related to his own situation. Though most scholars believe the poem dates from the 1590s, the poem suggests a desire for an inclusive church that Donne retained even after he became a priest in the Church of England. The speaker condemns a world devoted to the 'Realme' of the 'Devill' which will 'wither away and passe', indeed which is now 'In her decrepit wayne' (lines 33, 35, 36, 38). Addressing himself, as if he stands alone in this decadent world, the only one devoted to 'Our Mistresse faire Religion' (line 5), the speaker urges, 'Seeke true religion', only to ask 'O where?' (line 43). Describing religion as a mistress, he invokes the biblical metaphor of God's people or the church as beloved bride. But as he surveys the possibilities – the Church of 'Rome' (line 45), 'Geneva' (Calvinism, line 50), and the one which 'dwells with us' (the Church of England, line 58) – each seems insufficient, though Donne is also criticizing the misguided reasons by which people choose (or reject) a religion. His satire expresses the dilemma of living at a time when people believed you could only be saved if you chose the true church, but also when there were multiple options within Christianity and when you could be punished, with fines, imprisonment, even with loss of life, if you were true to a faith that was outlawed by the state. Insisting that he cannot allow his 'Soule' to be 'tyed / To mans lawes, by which she shall not be tried / At the last day' (lines 93–5), the speaker tells himself to 'Be busie to seeke' truth (line 74).

> doubt wisely; in strange way
> To stand inquiring right, is not to stray;
> To sleepe, or runne wrong, is. On a huge hill,
> Cragged, and steep, Truth stands, and hee that will
> Reach her, about must, and about must goe. (lines 77–81)

The search is what matters, and Donne has faith that eventually he will 'winne' the hill (line 82), that some of 'the truth' will be 'found' (line 89), even if the journey can never be completed in this life.

This passion for truth, this restless inquiry, drives Donne's poetry. Writing seemed the expression of his soul, if we are to believe his verse letter to Henry Wotton which begins, 'Sir, more than kisses, letters mingle Soules; / For thus, friends absent speake' – a remark that acknowledges the intimacy in male friendship, long thought superior to marriage as it was a relation among equals. All Donne's poems are provisional attempts to reach truth, and to capture that truth in language. The hyperbolic verse letters to prospective or current patrons such as Lucy Countess of Bedford or the Countess of Huntingdon might seem an exception. Donne recognizes they could be thought 'flatteries' ('To the Countesse of Huntingdon', 'Man to Gods image', line 49), but insists that flattery can 'worke' to 'raise' or improve a person (lines 51–2). Hyperbole seems most excessive in the long *Anniversaries*, where his praise of Elizabeth Drury as the soul of the world, the only perfect creature, whose death has caused the death of the world, was so extreme that it caused Ben Jonson to remark that such praise would have been appropriate had the subject been the Virgin Mary, but was incommensurate for a fifteen-year-old girl, whom Donne had never met.[7] Still, Donne was concerned not only to please Sir Robert Drury but to articulate spiritual truth. In *The First Anniversary*, 'An Anatomy of the World', mourning Elizabeth becomes a vehicle for mourning the death of virtue, the prevalence of corruption and decay in the world. Donne describes a world which has lost integrity, health, wholeness, spirit, godliness, virtue. It was as if he and the few who had any memory of virtue left were lonely survivors, anticipating a cosmic, catastrophic end.

The *Anniversaries* are public poems, the *Songs and Sonets* much more private. They vary in stanza-form and rhyme-scheme (none is a formal 'sonnet') but also in the attitudes towards love and women they display. With a couple of exceptions, the speakers are male. Although some poems have been thought connected to Donne's clandestine courtship of and marriage to Anne More,[8] his lyrics are not autobiography – they are fictional, made things. Still, Donne's speakers present their poetic utterances as more real or 'true' than the love-poems of others. In 'Loves Growth', the speaker mocks poets who 'have no Mistress but their Muse' (line 112) and write poetry that is false to the experience of life, which is unpredictable, full of the surprise of either disappointment or happiness.

> I scarce believe my love to be so pure
> As I had thought it was,
> Because it doth endure
> Vicissitude, and season, as the grasse. (lines 1–4)

Donne's *Songs and Sonets* present conflicting perspectives on women and love. One 'Song' ('Sweetest love') addresses his beloved, reluctant to leave, since she is 'the best of mee' (line 32). Another ('Goe, and catche a falling starre') proclaims: 'No where / Lives a woman true, and faire' (17–18). Perhaps Donne is trying out poses, with different speakers. Perhaps the inconsistencies, the contradictions, are simply consonant with the flux of experience and the vagaries of desire, whose ebbs and flows he traces.

Some readers have wondered about Donne's 'sincerity' since his poetry seems contradictory in several senses – contradicting conventional opinions of his society, employing equivocal arguments and syntax, but also making seemingly definitive but contradictory pronouncements. 'Hope not for minde in women' (line 23), says the speaker of 'Loves Alchymie', who does not believe there is a 'centrique happinesse' (line 2) in human love. Women are 'but *Mummy*, possest' – once enjoyed, they are like embalmed bodies, inert, devoid of spirit, though perhaps of medicinal value (as 'mummy' was thought to be – *OED*). Then there is 'The Relique', which concludes, 'All measure, and all language, I should passe, / Should I tell what a miracle shee was' (lines 32–3). The tone of these two poems is very different, and yet in each the speaker makes his final pronouncement with confidence in the rightness of his perception. One of Donne's best readers has remarked: 'Does Donne believe what he so often passionately asserts? Absolutely at the moment of its articulation, one feels, although not necessarily beyond the poem's last words.'[9]

Some *Songs and Sonets*, like the Ovidian elegies, articulate an emotional and intellectual detachment about love. Love and women do not seem worth what Shakespeare in Sonnet 129 would call the 'expense of spirit'.[10] 'Communitie' suggests that women are 'things indifferent' which 'all' men may 'use' but 'neither love, nor hate' (lines 3, 12, 4). What some might call 'love' is only an appetite and not even a very necessary or keen one: 'they are ours as fruits are ours / He that but tasts, he that devours, / And he that leaves all, doth as well' (19–21). The speaker in 'Farewell to love', having discovered that there is no 'Deitie in love' (2), that we lose our appetite for things once we get them, and that sexual consummation leaves only a 'sorrowing dulnesse to the minde' (20), has decided not to 'pursue things which had indammag'd me' (line 34). Love is a 'sport' (line 27), but Donne's men want to avoid losing freedom, or even the life-force (spirit) that was thought to be spent with ejaculation. In 'Confined Love', the female speaker voices a similar desire for freedom:

> Are Sunne, Moone, or Starres by law forbidden,
> To smile where they list, or lend away their light?
> Are birds divorc'd, or are they chidden
> If they leave their mate, or lie abroad a night? (lines 8–11)

Both sexes share the same basic nature, which has been perverted by society's laws. Still, the desire for freedom in love is usually associated with men in Donne's poems, which obliquely express discomfort at being a political subject, with restricted freedom. The speaker in 'The Indifferent' chafes at confinement. Asserting that he 'can love both faire and browne' (line 1), that he 'can love any, so she be not true' (line 9), he asks, 'Rob mee, but binde me not, and let me goe. / Must I, who came to travaile thorow you, / Grow your fixt subject, because you are true?' (lines 16–18). Monogamy is like being a 'fixt subject', and the ability to choose a different lover analogous to choosing a new monarch.

Paradoxically, these anti-romantic, libertine poems offer the 'truth' that there is no 'truth' in this world, that even if one woman is true she will soon turn out to be false. In 'The Indifferent', Venus pronounces that the exceptional woman who (unlike her mother) is 'true' (line 26) will be cursed with being 'true to them, who'are false to you' (line 27). But in contrast to the lyrics that are sceptical about women and love stand a group of poems describing the thoughts and feelings of a lover who thinks he has finally experienced 'true' love, who has found a constant woman and soul-mate, and who hopes this special love might be the exception and antidote to the world of disappointment, corruption, and decay.

'The Good-morrow', an aubade that takes place in the lovers' bed after a night of love, expresses a sense of wonder, undiminished by the wit of a speaker who can admit previous sexual conquests:

> I Wonder by my troth, what thou, and I
> Did, till we lov'd? were we not wean'd till then?
> But sucked on countrey pleasures, childishly? (lines 1–3)

'The Sunne Rising' challenges the 'unruly Sunne' (line 1), which marks time and calls men to business, to leave these lovers in their bed, which is the centre of their alternative universe:

Looke, and to morrow late, tell mee,
Whether both the'Indias of spice and Myne
Be where thou leftst them, or lie here with mee.
Aske for those Kings whom thou saw'st yesterday,
And thou shalt heare, All here in one bed lay. (lines 16–20)

Donne's private world of love contains everything that is necessary, and seems the source of all satisfaction. There is a modern feel to such poems, with their privileging of love and privacy. Aware of the explorations of his day, Donne instead turns to the intimate geography of love and asks the sun, at the end of 'The Sunne Rising', to 'shine here to us, and thou art every where' (line 29). As the speaker in 'The Good-morrow' declares:

Let sea-discoverers to new worlds have gone,
Let Maps to others, worlds on worlds have showne,
Let us possesse one world, each hath one, and is one.
(lines 12–14)

This love, like the soul, is transcendent, not tied to time and space (like the body), yet it embraces the body and sexual desire. 'The Extasie' defines love as something that grows in souls but requires 'Our bodies' (line 50). Donne's verse letter to Henry Wotton had spoken of how the souls of friends mingle, and the similarity between Donne's descriptions of male friendship and heterosexual love is notable. His letter to Wotton draws on the classical assumption that friendship is a masculine prerogative and can only be between equals and thus not between men and women, who were identified more closely with the body and bodily desires. But in some *Songs and Sonets* Donne extends the longstanding tradition of male homoerotic friendship between equals to the realm of heterosexual love, enhancing the value of heterosexual love but also placing new demands on it. As 'The Extasie' begins, the lovers are lying like 'sepulchrall statues' (line 18) on a bank, their 'soules' (line 15) having risen above their bodies. But, lest we think that transcendence of the body is the goal, the speaker then argues that, since they recognize that their changeless souls are the substance of their love, they now can confidently 'turne' (line 69) to their bodies: 'Loves mysteries in soules doe grow, / But yet the body is his booke' (lines 71–2). This may be a witty seduction poem – like Donne's more famous 'The Flea' – but it expresses a serious view of the interrelation of body and soul that underpins much of Donne's writing. That view echoes the Catholic understanding that life is sacramental, but Donne's celebration of sexual love is revolutionary, for it defies the dominant Christian tradition that distrusted the body and sexuality and associated sex with sin.[11]

In contrast to Neoplatonic dualism that splits the soul from the body, or the unconsummated longings of the Petrarchan lover, Donne is preoccupied with the interrelation of bodies and souls.[12] The speaker in 'The Good-morrow' greets the 'waking soules' (line 8) of these lovers, which have been brought to life by a love that embraces sexual desire. These lovers lie so close that 'My face in thine eye, thine in mine appears' (line 15). This physical phenomenon mirrors the emotional and spiritual one, and Donne's comparisons must be understood literally as well as figuratively for the poem's logic to work. The vehicle of the metaphor can no more be left behind than the body.

The lovers are a little world that contains and transcends the larger world. Donne's hope is that the world of the lovers, an alternative to the corruption of the external world, will not be ruled by time and death. 'The Sunne Rising' boasts, 'Love, all alike, no season knowes, nor clime, / Nor houres, dayes, moneths, which are the rags of time' (lines 9–10). 'The Good-morrow' ends,

> What ever dyes, was not mixt equally;
> If our two loves be one, or, thou and I
> Love so alike, that none doe slacken, none can die.
> (lines 19–21)

'The Anniversarie' celebrates the lovers' first anniversary, and though the speaker acknowledges that eventually their bodies will lie in graves, he declares:

> All other things, to their destruction draw,
> Only our love hath no decay;
> This, no to morrow hath, nor yesterday. (lines 6–8)

These celebratory poems treasure the bond between the lovers, and express the faith (or hope) that love will last, defying the laws of the physical universe. The lovers are committed to each other, united, though not necessarily by marriage. They stand outside society's institutions. There is often a sense of secrecy or at least alienation. In 'The Canonization', the speaker challenges the institution of the church, arguing that he and his beloved deserve to be '*Canoniz'd* for Love' (line 36): they have been exemplary, 'dye[ing] and ris[ing] the same' (line 26) (in an imitation of Christ? made one in the act of love-making?), even embracing martyrdom: 'Wee can dye by it, if not live by love' (line 28).

Here, as in 'The Good-morrow' or 'The Sunne Rising', the speaker describes a sense of completeness that contrasts with the fragmentation that characterizes the world and ordinary experience. That wholeness feels transcendent, as it integrates body and soul as well as two people. It is thus no wonder that, in contrast to the scepticism voiced by 'Loves Alchymie' or 'The Indifferent', the so-called 'mutual love' poems in the *Songs and Sonets* use religious imagery to describe this experience of love, often referring to Catholic practices that Protestantism had prohibited. The lovers are saints who will be prayed to as intercessors ('The Canonization'); they are priests, elevated above the 'layetie' of ordinary lovers ('A Valediction: forbidding mourning', line 8); they leave behind relics ('a bracelet of bright haire') that might be 'adored' by later generations ('The Relique', lines 6, 19).[13]

Donne captures a sense of awe at the miraculous, transformative potential of loving, the feeling (however fleeting) that one is no longer alone, the prisoner of the self, but completely connected with another human being. Fearing that in some indeterminate future his grave will be disturbed, the speaker in 'The Relique' is moved to record the 'miracles wee harmelesse lovers wrought' by loving 'well and faithfully' (lines 22–3), chastely, despite the sexually suggestive 'bracelet of bright hair about the bone'. The lovers in 'The Good-morrow' are two 'hemispheres' (line 17) who have miraculously found their matching halves. In 'The Extasie' we learn that the union of their 'two soules' has produced an 'abler soule' which 'Defects of lonelinesse controules' (lines 414–44).

Some poems are about beginnings. Some are about the difficult middle time in a relationship. 'Aire and Angels' ponders the problem that, once his love has taken shape and 'fixe[d]' (line 14) itself in the beloved's body, he feels overwhelmed – 'I saw, I had loves pinnace overfraught' (line 18), he complains, and tries to understand the 'disparitie' between 'womens love, and mens' (lines 26, 28). The speaker in 'A Lecture upon the Shadow', finding their love at high noon, wonders whether 'shadowes' (line 15) of deceit will come between them, whether 'loves day' (line 24) will be short. The speaker in 'Loves growth' is more hopeful, having seen his love survive the winter and even grow in spring, though that growth has brought complications and pain.

But many poems are about endings, sometimes feared, sometimes imagined, and sometimes (it seems) experienced. Donne wrote numerous 'valedictions', poems of farewell in which the speaker contemplates an imminent journey. In 'A Valediction: forbidding mourning', the parting of the lovers is compared to death, a separation of soul and body. Here the famous extended image or 'conceit' of the compass offers hope that they will continue to be connected and that he will return home. So many poems – with different degrees of seriousness – imagine the speaker's death – 'The Dampe', 'The Funerall', 'The Apparition' – or the death of both lovers ('The Anniversarie', even 'The Exstasie') – or the death of the woman. But the most powerful and disturbing is 'A nocturnall upon S. Lucies day, Being the shortest day', in which the speaker expresses his despair at the death of the woman (perhaps Donne's wife, who died in childbirth in 1617) who has been his soul and his life, and hence the soul of his world. ''Tis the years midnight, and it is the dayes' (line 1). The speaker's depression mirrors the darkness of the natural world, but he is cut off from that world, since he will not revive. Numb with grief, dead to all pleasure (yet still fecund in his bitter wit, which multiplies analogies, seeking to find a way to express his situation), he has been 'ruin'd' by love, 're-begot / Of absence, darknesse, death; things which are not' (lines 17–18). His lover's departure has left him in a state of living death, only able to 'prepare towards her' (line 43), keeping 'her Vigill' (line 44) and hoping to meet her in heaven.

Some have seen Donne turning here from earthly, profane life to heaven, but actually the turn is to the beloved, not God. At the end of the 'Nocturnall', the speaker is still longing for the woman (his 'Sunne', not the Son), which both Augustine and Petrarch would consider idolatry. In his devotional poems, Donne turns to God, and struggles to find in God satisfaction for his desires.

The idea of a turn or 'conversion' preoccupies Donne's religious poems, which are obsessed with his sinful state and his anxious desire for salvation. In 'Goodfriday, 1613. Riding Westward', the speaker worries that he is going in the wrong direction, riding 'westward' on 'pleasure or business' (line 7) rather than going to church, or east to the site of the crucifixion that Good Friday commemorates. He begins comparing his soul to a heavenly 'Spheare' (line 1) moved by 'forraigne motions' (line 4), but then imagines what he 'should see' were he to witness 'Christ on this Crosse' (lines 11, 13). In this meditation, he visualizes the crucifix that Protestants had outlawed, making it 'present ... unto my memory' (line 34). At the end, he asks his 'Saviour' (line 36) to

> ... punish mee,
> Burne off my rusts, and my deformity,
> Restore thine Image, so much, by thy grace,
> That thou may'st know mee, and I'll turn my face.

The submissive posture, presenting himself for punishment, jars with the insolence of turning one's back on a person of higher position. Donne turns what seemed originally a movement away from God into a return to God.

Behind the logical and verbal gymnastics of this poem is a fearful anxiety about salvation, a sense of unworthiness that also characterizes Donne's Holy Sonnets. These are the only formal sonnets Donne wrote, as if reserving this traditional form of love-poetry for God. God is at once the Father, Christ, and a lover, a power Donne woos, argues with, even tries to seduce with his wit as he wrestles with uncertainty about whether he is saved. 'Thou hast made me, And shall thy worke decay? / Repaire me now, for now mine end doth haste' (lines 1–2). Directly addressing a divine power, he questions God's wisdom, challenges God to act. He hopes God 'like Adamant' (the magnetic lodestone) will 'draw mine iron heart' (line 14). Imagining death or judgement, the sonnets paint a Calvinist universe, in which God has predestined some to be saved, but more to be damned, and the speaker is uncertain where he belongs. He desires salvation. He thirsts for God ('Since she whom I lov'd'), but is pulled by the world and contrary desires ('Oh to vex me, contraryes meet in one'). He can only be saved by God's grace, not by any effort of his own. The sonnet beginning 'Oh my blacke Soule' expresses the 'catch-22' of Calvinism when at the 'volta' or 'turn' of the sonnet, he announces, 'Yet grace, if thou repent, thou canst not lacke; / But who shall give thee that grace to beginne?' (lines 9–10). Donne's speakers feel both a terrible sinfulness and a helplessness that sometimes leaves them on the verge of despair.

As in 'Goodfriday', Donne's speaker asks for extreme, even physical measures, so that he can experience the presence of a God who seems remote, absent. Whereas the Church of Rome taught that God was present in the sacraments, the reformed church, particularly under the influence of Calvin, stressed inward spirituality and held that the sacraments were only signs or symbols (not effective instruments) of grace. God was not present physically in the world, Christ having ascended to heaven after his Resurrection. Donne's language expressive of spiritual desire is very corporeal, as if, in his relation with God as in his relation with an earthly lover, he wants an embodied experience. In one sonnet, he declares his sinful self 'must be burnt' ('I am a little world', line 10). In 'Batter my heart', he longs for God but is helpless, 'betroth'd' (line 10) unto Satan. His 'Reason' is 'captiv'd', 'weake or untrue, / Yet dearely I love you, and would be lov'd faine' (lines 7–9). The intensity of desire is provocatively expressed in this sonnet which pushes the analogy between earthly and heavenly love to the edge of blasphemy, as if Donne wants to startle the reader and delight himself with his final, witty paradox that, in reworking the trope of God as the bridegroom, brings the language of sex and violence into the arena of religion:

> Divorce mee, 'untie, or breake that knot againe,
> Take mee to you, imprison mee, for I
> Except you'enthrall mee, never shall be free,
> Nor ever chast, except you ravish mee. (lines 11–14)

Modern readers might think his wit transgressive, but maybe Donne thought God would appreciate it. His *Devotions Upon Emergent Occasions* (written in late 1623 when he was very ill) describes God as a witty God, 'a *figurative*, a *metaphorical God* ... in whose words there is such a height of *figures*, such *voyages*, such *peregrinations* to fetch remote and precious *metaphors*'.[14] Perhaps he thought his own wit was a divine gift, even as he worried it might get him into trouble.

Whether reading the *Elegies* or *Satires*, the *Songs and Sonets* or his devotional poems, we see a mind continually at work, trying to capture and figure out the significance of experiences that are always about to slip away. Even the proximity of death did not stop him from writing. In 'Hymne to God my God, in my sicknesse' (1623?), he stands aside from his body, describing it as a map. Where the physicians only see the passages of death, Donne finds 'joy', realizing that just 'As West and East / In all flatt Maps (and I am one) are one, / So death doth touch Resurrection' (lines 11, 13–15). In 'An Hymne to God the Father' (1631?), Donne's irrepressible wit surfaces in what may be his last poetic confession. The first two stanzas conclude with Donne punning on his name and perhaps his wife's: 'When thou hast done, thou hast not done / For, I have more' (lines 5–6, 11–12). There is a fine line here between humility and pride. But the tone changes in the third stanza. He confronts the demon of despair in a powerful image:

> I have a sinne of feare, that when I have spunne
> My last thred, I shall perish on the shore.
> But sweare by thy selfe, that at my death thy sonne
> Shall shine as he shines now, and heretofore
> And having done that, Thou haste done,
> I feare no more. (lines 13–18)[15]

In these remarkable lines, fear is resolved by a sense of divine presence, as if Donne has finally completed the journey and come home.

NOTES

1 For Dryden's and Johnson's comments, see A. J. Smith (ed.), *John Donne: The Critical Heritage* (London: Routledge, 1975), pp. 151, 217–18.

2 On dating, see *The Variorum Edition of the Poetry of John Donne*, gen. ed. Gary A. Stringer, vol. 7, pt 1 (The Holy Sonnets) (Bloomington: Indiana University Press, 2005), pp. lxxxviii–ci.

3 Arthur F. Marotti, *John Donne, Coterie Poet* (Madison: University of Wisconsin Press, 1986); Dennis Flynn, 'Donne and a Female Coterie', *Lit: Literature Interpretation Theory* 1 (1989), 127–36.

4 Arthur F. Marotti, '"Love is not love": Elizabethan Sonnet Sequences and the Social Order', *ELH* 49 (1982), 396–428.

5 Achsah Guibbory, '"Oh, let me not serve so": The Politics of Love in Donne's *Elegies*', *ELH* 57 (1990), 811–33.

6 See M. Thomas Hester, *Kinde Pitty and Brave Scorn: John Donne's Satyres* (Durham, NC: Duke University Press, 1982); Annabel Patterson, 'Satirical Writing', in *The Cambridge Companion to John Donne*, ed. Achsah Guibbory (Cambridge: Cambridge University Press, 2006), pp. 117–31.

7 Jonson's comments are reprinted in Smith, *John Donne*, p. 69.

8 See e.g. Ilona Bell, '"If it be a shee": The Riddle of Donne's "Curse"', in *John Donne's 'Desire of More': The Subject of Anne More Donne in His Poetry*, ed. M. Thomas Hester (Newark: University of Delaware Press, 1996), pp. 106–39.

9 Judith Scherer Herz, 'Rereading Donne's Poetry', in *The Cambridge Companion to John Donne*, pp. 101–15, at 112.

10 William Shakespeare, *The Complete Sonnets and Poems*, ed. Colin Burrow, The Oxford Shakespeare (Oxford and New York: Oxford University Press, 2002), p. 639.

11 On that tradition, see Elaine Pagels, *Adam, Eve, and the Serpent* (New York: Vintage, 1989).

12 See A. J. Smith, *The Metaphysics of Love* (Cambridge: Cambridge University Press, 1985), ch. 3 on 'The Extasie'; Ramie Targoff, 'Traducing the Soul: Donne's *Second Anniversarie*', *PMLA* 121 (2006), 1493–1508.

13 See M. Thomas Hester, '"This cannot be said": A Preface to the Reader of Donne's Lyrics', *Christianity and Literature* 39 (1990), 365–85, on Donne's 'recusant' poetics.

14 John Donne, *Devotions Upon Emergent Occasions*, ed. Anthony Raspa (Oxford: Oxford University Press, 1987), Expostulation 19, p. 99.

15 Important manuscript variations appear, among which is 'thy Sunn' (rather than 'son'), and the last line, 'I have noe more.' Grierson prints a second version as 'To Christ'.

SELECTED FURTHER READING

Editions

The Variorum Edition of the Poetry of John Donne, gen. ed. Gary A. Stringer, Bloomington, Indiana University Press, 1995–

Vol. 2: *The Elegies* (2000)

Vol. 7, pt 1: *The Holy Sonnets* (2005)

Vol. 6: *The Anniversaries and the Epicedes and Obsequies* (1995)

Until the Variorum edition is completed, the best edition for the other poetry remains *The Poems of John Donne*, ed. Herbert J. C. Grierson, 2 vols, *Vol. 1: The Text of the Poems, with Appendixes*, London, Oxford University Press, 1912; rptd 1968

Secondary works

Guibbory, Achsah (ed.), *The Cambridge Companion to John Donne*, Cambridge, Cambridge University Press, 2006

Haskins, Dayton, *John Donne in the Nineteenth Century*, Oxford, Oxford University Press, 2007
Hester, M. Thomas, '"This cannot be said": A Preface to the Reader of Donne's Lyrics', *Christianity and Literature* 39 (1990), 365–85
Low, Anthony, 'John Donne and the Reinvention of Love', *English Literary Renaissance* 20 (1990), 465–86
Marotti, Arthur F., *John Donne, Coterie Poet*, Madison, University of Wisconsin Press, 1986
(ed.), *Critical Essays on John Donne*, New York, G. K. Hall, 1994
Post, Jonathan F. S., 'Irremediably Donne', in *English Lyric Poetry: The Early Seventeenth Century*, New York, Routledge, 1999
Ricks, Christopher, 'Donne After Love', in Elaine Scarry (ed.), *Literature and the Body*, Baltimore, Johns Hopkins University Press, 1988, pp. 33–69
Stachniewski, John, 'John Donne: The Despair of the "Holy sonnets"', in *The Persecutory Imagination: English Puritanism and the Literature of Religious Despair*, Oxford, Oxford University Press, 1991, pp. 254–91
Summers, Claude, and Ted-Larry Pebworth, *The Eagle and the Dove: Reassessing John Donne*, Columbia, University of Missouri, 1986
Targoff, Ramie, *John Donne, Body and Soul*, Chicago, University of Chicago Press, 2008

6

COLIN BURROW

Ben Jonson

The reputation of Ben Jonson's poetry has had its ups and downs. To his contemporaries and immediate successors he was 'Saint Ben', one of the greatest English poets, who, with his friend John Donne, dominated English poetry until the end of the seventeenth century. By the late eighteenth century readers were finding his style crabbed and unnatural; and by the nineteenth he was known chiefly as the author of plays and of a handful of charming lyrics which were extracted from them. His three major collections of verse – *Epigrams*, *The Forest*, and *The Underwood* – not to mention his uncollected dedicatory poems, were rarely read, and, if read, were often abused. The poet A. C. Swinburne said of the *Epigrams* 'the worst are so bad, so foul if not so dull, so stupid if not so filthy, that the student stands aghast with astonishment'.[1]

Jonson's verse began its slow revival in the later twentieth century, but still was often praised in ways which were either grudging or a touch off-putting. He was commended as a master of the plain style, as an artful imitator of classical verse, and as the advocate of a 'centred self', which resists the distractions of passion and roots itself in a larger community of the virtuous. The terms of praise which came to be applied to his verse all suggest that there is something, in a pejorative sense, monumental about him – a vast classical corpus of a poet, who tells his readers just what they should find in what he writes. The suspicion that Jonson is just a little too controlled comes through very strongly in Stanley Fish's extremely influential essay on the poetry. Fish argued that Jonson's poems create a 'community of the same': that is, they praise patrons and friends in ways that unite author, patron, and readers in a single community of virtue. All are good, and since all of them are good there is no need to define what that word might mean.[2] Jonson becomes the poet of the monumental tautology:

> I do but name thee, Pembroke, and I find
> It is an epigram on all mankind,
> Against the bad, but of, and to the good.
> (Epigram 102, lines 1–3)

Some of Jonson's more routine verse can work in this way, by assuming a set of shared values. But his more sophisticated poems contain a whole welter of uncontrolled cross-currents within an apparently monumental exterior. 'On My First Son' (Epigram 45), which is often regarded as Ben Jonson's best poem (partly because it seems to say it is – readers do tend to take Jonson literally), illustrates this point:

Farewell, thou child of my right hand, and joy;
My sin was too much hope of thee, loved boy.
Seven years thou wert lent to me, and I thee pay,
Exacted by thy fate, on the just day.
Oh, could I lose all father now! For why
Will man lament the state he should envy?
To have so soon 'scaped world's and flesh's rage,
And, if no other misery, yet age?
Rest in soft peace, and, asked, say here doth lie
BEN. JONSON his best piece of poetry.
For whose sake, henceforth, all his vows be such,
As what he loves may never like too much.

The poem was prompted by the death of Jonson's son Benjamin in 1603. There is plenty to resist or even dislike in it. 'Benjamin', the name of both Jonson son and Jonson father, means in Hebrew 'son of the right hand'. The etymological pun seems scripted to lead inevitably towards the conceit that the son is 'BEN. JONSON his best piece of poetry', as much a poem produced by the father's right hand as a person. The chiselled capitals of the father's name (which is how it appears in the Folio of 1616) seem to turn the poem into something like a tombstone, and to turn the tombstone of the child into a mark not of its own identity, but of the father's authorship. The effect is slightly chilling: Jonson the possessive author turns the death of his own flesh into a chiselled monument to his art, 'his best piece of poetry'.

But in this, as in all of Jonson's best work, there is a restlessness beneath the surface. The apparently impersonal exclamation 'For why / Will man lament the state he should envy?' allows at least two reasons for 'envying' the state of death. One is the general and pious thought that death is an escape from care. The other is that the bereaved person is so miserable that they want to die too. The secondary sense insists that a father who has lost a son, and his joy, is wrecked. The force of that secondary sense comes through in the strange asymmetrical opposition in the final line, 'As what he loves may never like too much'. This seems at first to be the wrong way round. Surely liking is *less* than loving? The rhetorical structure tries to make it appear that to 'like' means to have 'merely mortal affection', while 'love' must, in order to make the opposition work, mean something like 'to adore disinterestedly'. The apparent reversal of the two terms keeps the father's misery alive in the poem: what you love will always be missed, and perhaps missed too much, since even if you can control 'liking' you cannot alter the fact that you love what is lost. The opposition between liking and loving has a further layer of complexity. It derives from a poem by the Latin epigrammatist Martial, whose lament for a slave boy (6. 29) concludes 'quidquid ames, cupias non placuisse nimis', 'Whatever you love, pray that it not please too much.' The final line sits awkwardly between various options: is it an expressively botched statement of restraint, in which fatherly love breaks out of the monumental structure erected to contain it? Or does the grammatical structure of a classical poem break through accidentally to emphasize the sense of loss? Either way Jonson is not the controlled, classicizing poet which his popular reputation would have him to be.

Early career

How did Jonson's career as a poet begin and develop? This is a curiously difficult question to answer because of the way he worked. He did not write for a single community or even for a single medium, or, indeed, for a single time. His poems began life in manuscript, and many were written to mark particular occasions, or for presentation to a patron. Many of these occasional poems were subsequently printed, sometimes as much as forty years later, in one or other of the three major printed collections of his verse. *Epigrams* appeared in the Folio of Jonson's *Works* in 1616, and was followed by another book of fifteen poems called *The Forest*. These two collections were retrospective gatherings put together by the poet himself, and it is impossible to be sure when many poems which they include were composed. *The Underwood* appeared in the Folio of 1640, three years after Jonson's death, and it is not certain how strong a role he played in the construction of that volume. This habit of belated publication, however, has a number of consequences for our understanding of Jonson the poet. The first is that it strongly indicates that he was not interested in creating a 'community of the same' or single ethical perspective in his verse. Many of his poems were designed for an amphibious existence in manuscript and print. As a result they had to address both an immediate audience – the person whom they praise or describe – and a wider body of unknown people who might read them in print, and whose responses to them would be far harder to predict than those of their immediate addressee. The poems also often address a number of contexts at once. Jonson was very good at making light revisions to his poems, which took account of the passage of time between composition and publication. He was also a master of positioning an old poem in print beside a newer one in order to release new senses from both.

The other major consequence of Jonson's habit of retrospective publication is that 'Ben Jonson the poet' refers to at least two distinct agents. The first is a poet who had a probably rather haphazard career, which involved several false starts, many revisions to his poems, and confusions about the overall direction of his oeuvre. The second is the editorial Jonson who revised and ordered his poems retrospectively into verse collections. Friction between these two Jonsons is part of what makes his poems electric, since Ben the editor is frequently curbing, checking, and attempting to centre the energies of Ben the poet. Although Ben the editor left such a strong mark on his poems that it is very hard to reconstruct the order in which Jonson the poet wrote them, it is certain that in the late 1590s Jonson the poet was very unlike the received image of staid, centred, plain Ben. His first datable poem was not printed in his lifetime, and was prefixed to a manuscript treatise on the properties of herbs and plants by the Catholic Thomas Palmer. It compares Jonson's wonder at the book with the circles within circles created when a stone is dropped into water:

> So in my brain the strong impression
> Of thy rich labours worlds of thoughts created,
> Which thoughts, being circumvolved in gyre-like motion,
> Were spent with wonder as they were dilated;
> Till giddy with amazement I fell down
> In a deep trance * * * *
> * * * * * (lines 21–7)

The vocabulary here ('circumvolved in gyre-like motion') is as far removed from the textbook clichés about Jonson's plain style as one could imagine, and its subject-matter – a wordless, inspired rhapsody which lapses into asterisks – is completely at odds with the traditional picture of Jonson as a classically controlled poet. Jonson in the late 1590s was avant-garde. He was experimenting with how to represent poetic inspiration. In the same period he also experimented with the classical form of the ode. His use of this form enabled him to associate his art with that of the Roman poet Horace, with whom he repeatedly identified himself during his career. It also allowed him to experiment with irregular line-lengths, sudden jumps of argument, reverberating mythological allusions. The short-line declamatory manner which emerged from these early experiments runs in and out of Jonson's later verse, from the 1629 ode on the death of Sir Henry Morison through his stinging attack on the insensibility of audiences to his late play *The New Inn* from the same year. And it was a form which Jonson never fully integrated into his poetic career. In 1601 he joined with Shakespeare, Marston, and Chapman to produce verses appended to Robert Chester's allegorical poem called *Love's Martyr*. These included Shakespeare's uncategorizable and mystifying 'Let the bird of loudest lay', as well as Jonson's 'Ode Enthusiastic' on the phoenix:

> Splendour! O more than mortal,
> For other forms come short all
> Of her illustrate brightness,
> As far as sin's from lightness. (lines 1–4)

A high proportion of the early odes, including this one, were not reprinted in his lifetime. Jonson was not a poetic juggernaut who relentlessly pursued a predetermined career as a Laureate poet.[3] He was always hypersensitive to criticism, and he almost certainly suppressed his own vestigial early career as an inspired writer of odes because he was teased about it. Thomas Dekker's *Satiromastix* (1601) represented the inspired Horace – who is meant to be Jonson – searching desperately for a rhyme:

> For I to thee and thine immortall name –
> In – sacred raptures flowing, flowing, swimming, swimming,
> In sacred raptures swimming,
> Immortal name, game, dame, tame, lame, lame, lame ...[4]

The suppression of the early odes is a good indication of how Jonson tended to bury part of himself when he set about preparing his poems for the press.

The *Epigrams*

Jonson's first great retrospective attempt to make sense of his own miscellaneous career as satirist, panegyrist, and author of commendatory verses, *Epigrams, the I Book*, appeared in the Folio of his *Works* printed in 1616. There are some indications that a lost edition may have appeared as early as 1612, and despite the promissory 'the I Book' there never was a second. Jonson described the poems it contained as 'the ripest of my studies'. Some of the epigrams to named individuals – Epigram 91 to the soldier Sir Horace Vere, and the poems to Robert Cecil – survive in manuscript copies which Jonson presented to their addressees years before the *Epigrams* were printed. These provide some evidence of how he reshaped his earlier poems when he prepared them for printing. Jonson the editor lightly worked over the Cecil poems (Epigrams 43 and 63) to make them suit a book rather than a personal presentation: the printed version reads 'When in my book men read but Cecil's name' (43. 9), while the manuscript has 'When in my *verse* ...'.

The final poem to Robert Cecil is followed in the *Epigrams* volume by Jonson's address 'To My Muse':

Away, and leave me, thou thing most abhorred,
That hast betrayed me to a worthless lord,
Made me commit most fierce idolatry
To a great image through thy luxury. (65, lines 1–4)

The 'worthless lord' is not identified directly, but Jonson was clearly insinuating that Cecil – from whom he became estranged for reasons which remain obscure – was the target of the whoreish/abhorred muse's affections. In the autograph version of Epigram 63 his 'voice' addresses Cecil with the intimacy of personal address; in the printed version, as though to cement the link with Epigram 65, it is his 'muse'. Jonson the editor was clearly at work in the *Epigrams*, shifting the emphases and overall impact of old poems so that a new and wider audience might find in them tonalities which were not available to their original addressees. This suits the peculiar characteristics of an epigram, which George Puttenham described as

> but an inscription or writing made as it were upon a table, or in a windowe, or upon the wall or mantell of a chimney in some place of common resort, where it was allowed every man might come, or be sitting to chat and prate, as now in our tavernes and common tabling houses, where many merry heades meete, and scrible with ynke with chalke, or with a cole such matters as they would every man should know, & descant upon. Afterward the same came to be put in paper and in bookes, and used as ordinarie missives, some of frendship, some of defiaunce, or as other messages of mirth.[5]

Although Puttenham is describing the historical development of the epigram form from graffiti to print, his description exactly captures the progress of Jonson's epigrams through sociable and haphazard origins towards their eventual dissemination in books. The art of the epigram as it was developed by Jonson was an art of retrospect. Many of his epigrams breathe *esprit de l'escalier*, the noble art of thinking up stunning put-downs after the event. In 'To Lord Ignorant' the very name of the addressee is obliterated in an act of revenge ('Thou call'st me "poet" as a term of shame, / But I have my revenge made in thy name', Epigram 10, lines 1–2). And Epigram 58, 'To Groom Idiot', is a similarly crushing retrospective act:

Idiot, last night I prayed thee but forbear
To read my verses; now I must to hear.
For, off'ring with thy smiles my wit to grace,
Thy ignorance still laughs in the wrong place.
And so my sharpness thou no less disjoints
Than thou didst late my sense, losing my points.

So have I seen at Christmas sports one lost,
And, hoodwinked, for a man embrace a post.

The rehearsed witty remark was a great feature of social life in the 1590s: diarists frequently record sharp and supposedly impromptu observations which were performed at dinner or other occasions. This is the social genre to which many of Jonson's epigrams belong, and, like anecdotes which reflect a little too well on the person who is telling them, they can seem like history rewritten to the author's advantage for a group of friends who might know that the real historical encounter had not gone quite so well as the report of it would suggest. The editorial function – reshaping experiences to fit new modes of dissemination – is in this sense a deep part of Jonson's art in the *Epigrams*: a combative social encounter becomes in an epigram a performance before an audience, or a 'message of mirth' to carry home.

'Inviting a Friend to Supper' (Epigram 101) is one of the most arresting of the *Epigrams*. It splices together details from a number of poems by Martial, which invite friends to ostentatiously humble dinners, and is therefore partly driven by Jonson's lifelong ambition to digest the substance of classical poetry into his own poetic identity. But it begins in the present, with a direct address to an unnamed friend: 'Tonight, grave sir, both my poor house and I / Do equally desire your company' (1–2). This locates the poem in the here and now, and flatters a reader of the printed volume into thinking that it might be an address to me, here, now. Since it is an invitation poem the entertainment it offers lies in the future, and is therefore uncertain and contingent. Jonson offers his unnamed guest perhaps no more than a verbal feast:

a short-legged hen,
If we can get her, full of eggs, and then
Lemons and wine for sauce: to these a cony
Is not to be despaired of for our money;
And, though fowl now be scarce, yet there are clerks,
The sky not falling, think we may have larks.
I'll tell you of more, and lie, so you will come:
Of partridge, pheasant, woodcock, of which some
May yet be there, and godwit, if we can:
Knat, rail, and ruff too. (lines 11–20)

In a way this presents a prospective epigram: it imagines the open space before a group of wits have sat down to exchange pointed anecdotes, and before members of this group go their separate ways to write epigrams about each other. That allows it to breathe uncertainty, not just about how many fowl of what kinds will grace the plates of the diners (and an early version of the epigram offers the rather less exotic 'duck and mallard' in place of the 'Knat, rail, and ruff'), but about quite how the relationship between the author and his addressee will play out in the evening. The poem tries to create a zone of freedom through anticipation. At its ending, however, it cannot escape the fear that the words freely exchanged by the guests at dinner might eventually be more widely disseminated, and bring harm to their authors:

> And we will have no Poley or Parrot by,
> Nor shall our cups make any guilty men:
> But, at our parting, we will be as when
> We innocently met. No simple word
> That shall be uttered at our mirthful board
> Shall make us sad next morning, or affright
> The liberty that we'll enjoy tonight. (lines 36–42)

'Poley' and 'Parrot' were government informers who may have spied on Jonson when he was imprisoned in 1597 for his part in writing a supposedly seditious play called *The Isle of Dogs*. Although these threatening presences are excluded from the feast, their names cast a chill over the end of the invitation: they remind its reader that words can be repeated, recycled, and re-presented to the wrong audience. And that alarming thought is emphasized by the way in which the poem itself recirculates the word 'Tonight'. As the first word of the poem it offers immediate welcome; when it is repeated as the final word it rhymes with 'affright'. Jonson's poems are not closed systems. 'Inviting a Friend to Supper' invites us in to join a conversation, to imagine what we will eat, to become members of the tribe of Ben in a moment of social freedom. But it is also partly about what might happen to this kind of free exchange once it reaches a wider audience, through publication or through being written down on a table or a window in the way that Puttenham describes. Will words once they are repeated or shaped into writing or print remain innocent? The *Epigrams* volume artfully fashions social and imagined encounters into printed form, but it is not free from Jonson's uneasy attempt to position his poetry between a social act and the fixity of writing and print.

The Forest

Jonson's art of retrospect takes on a further dimension in *The Forest*. The title of this gathering of fifteen miscellaneous poems derives from classical collections of '*silvae*' ('woods') – a term said by the rhetorician Quintilian to mean rough drafts intended for revision. *The Forest* is a masterly combination of artistry and apparently modest disorder. Its structure is sometimes said to suggest a moralized progress akin to Dante's passage through the '*selva oscura*' ('dark wood') of human life, beginning with a renunciation of love ('Why I write not of Love'), to a dark central trio of erotic poems imitated from Catullus and Philostratus, two of which (before minor revision) had originally been used by the predatory Volpone in his attempt to seduce the innocent Celia. The final poem in the collection, 'To Heaven', suggests an aspiration towards divine love.[6] The volume, however, also keeps more literal forests in its readers' minds: Penshurst, the home of the Sidney family which is the subject of the second poem, has its well-kept orchards and copses for deer, as well as having within its grounds an oak which was believed to have been planted at the birth of Sir Philip Sidney. Sir Robert Wroth is praised for his retreat from the masqueings and shows of court into his own estate among 'the curled woods and painted meads', while the penultimate poem, an 'Ode to Sir William Sidney, on His Birthday', celebrates that occasion with a fire, as the living wood of the forest is turned first into a source of warmth, and then into a metaphor for the burning love of Sidney's friends: 'Then / The birthday shines, when logs not burn, but men' (14. 59–60).

Several of these poems are panegyrics to members of the family of Sir Philip Sidney. Jonson's idea of praise was that it functioned as exhortation rather than description. As he put it in his 'Epistle to Master John Selden' (*Underwood*, 14):

> Though I confess (as every muse hath erred,
> And mine not least) I have too oft preferred
> Men past their terms, and praised some names too much;
> But 'twas with purpose to have made them such. (lines 19–22)

The poems in *The Forest* are characteristic of Jonson in being able to talk to a variety of readers, and to a variety of times, at once. They also create a warm and edgy blend of praise and admonition. The ending of the ode on William Sidney's birthday is not simply festive: the phrase 'when logs not burn but men' creates a flickering suggestion of the burning of the wicked in the afterlife. Given that Sir William was a tearaway who had stabbed one of his tutors – and was dead by the time the poem was published – the suggestion of a warning within the festive praise becomes louder when the poem was printed than it would have been to its twenty-one-year-old dedicatee when he received a copy of it. Jonson tends, as it were, to take his readers in, in both senses of that phrase. He can persuade us that he has created a poem which embodies an ethical or communal ideal, and he can invite us to join it, as when he describes himself feasting vastly in the hall of Penshurst:

Here no man tells my cups; nor, standing by,
　　A waiter, doth my gluttony envy;
But gives me what I call, and lets me eat. (2. 67–9)

The poet seems part of the larger Penshurst community, which draws in all classes, from the local farmers' daughters to the king and his son. But Jonsonian ethical ideals and communal structures are always shifting artfully, sometimes deceptively, around their readers. His extraordinary 'Epistle to Elizabeth, Countess of Rutland' (*Forest*, 12) is a prime example of this. The poem was addressed to the daughter of Sir Philip Sidney on New Year's Day 1600. This was the day on which gifts were regularly exchanged between patrons and clients. In a virtuosic nineteen-line first sentence Jonson confesses he has no gold to give his patroness, but that she, the living heir of Sir Philip Sidney, will value poetry above lucre:

　　With you, I know, my off'ring will find grace.
For what a sin 'gainst your great father's spirit
　　Were it to think that you should not inherit
His love unto the muses, when his skill
　　Almost you have, or may have, when you will?
Wherein wise nature you a dowry gave
　　Worth an estate, treble to that you have.
Beauty, I know, is good, and blood is more;
　　Riches thought most: but, madam, think what store
The world hath seen, which all these had in trust,
　　And now lie lost in their forgotten dust.
It is the muse alone can raise to heaven,
　　And, at her strong arm's end, hold up and even
The souls she loves. (lines 31–44)

Jonson's verbs here are apparently guileless (know, find, think, inherit, have, will, gave, know, thought, seen, had, lie, raise, hold), and it is easy to suppose that because its words are short this passage is easy. It appears to say that poets alone can preserve the true merit of their patrons. But it is far from straightforward. He 'knows' that his poem will be rewarded by the Countess of Rutland. But he knows that because it would be a sin against the spirit of Sidney to believe that she would not value poetry as highly as he did, given that she is almost as good a poet as her father – and here the argument tails off: she is almost, or could be, perhaps, if she wants, as good a poet as her father. And that word 'even' at the end of line 43, what does it do? Is it an adverb paired with 'up' ('hold steady and level')? Is it a verb in parallel with 'hold up' ('level out')? Or does it add a note of incredulity to the claim that the muse can *even* sometimes elevate people whom she actually loves, rather than those who pay her or to whom she feels bound? The outward plain praise offered by the poem is unsettled by uncertainty. Even plain words, even 'even', seem multifaceted.

And as the poem moves on, Jonson imagines a point when 'time shall bring / To curious light' his poems – presumably when they are published:

> Then all that have but done my muse least grace
>   Shall thronging come, and boast the happy place
> They hold in my strange poems, which, as yet,
>   Had not their form touched by an English wit.
> There, like a rich and golden pyramid,
>   Borne up by statues, shall I rear your head
> Above your under-carvèd ornaments,
>   And show how, to the life, my soul presents
> Your form impressed there. (lines 80–8)

Jonson's patrons and addressees here become the ones who praise *him*, as they gather together to boast that they have been praised by him. But as so often in Jonson's verse, what appears to be a public monument proves on reflection to be something shifting and mobile. Who is 'like a rich and golden pyramid'? Is Jonson like an architect or stone-mason building a monument which will raise up the worth of his patron? Or is he himself 'like a rich and golden pyramid / Borne up by statues', building a monument of his own praise? The grammatical uncertainty here presents two alternatives which, taken individually, would justify either one of the most popular reasons for disliking Jonson: either he is slavishly praising the Countess of Rutland or he is egomaniacally turning himself into a monument to his own genius. What the poem succeeds in doing, however, is to allow both of these alternatives to coexist. They do not simply cancel each other out, nor does the poem become more nauseating because it accommodates both possibilities. They together create the effect of what might be called a social monument, a poem which looks as though it stands in monumental stillness, but which actually includes a number of distinct perspectives and reading possibilities within it – a community, not of the same, but of diverging perspectives, in which either the patron or the poet could be the final source of value.

The Underwood

After *The Forest* most of Jonson's contemporaries would have perceived an enormous hiatus in his poetic career. With the exception of dedicatory verse he printed no poems between 1616 and the posthumous second folio of 1640. This twenty-four-year silence was not as complete as it might appear, however. During this period Jonson circulated his poems in manuscript, and evidently relished their progress from small, socially elevated coteries of readers to a wider public. A poem from the early 1630s, 'An Epigram: To My Muse' (*Underwood*, 78), describes Lady Venetia Digby passing Jonson's poems in manuscript to the Lord Treasurer, Richard Weston, and thence to a wider circle of readers:

Oh, what a fame 'twill be!
What reputation to my lines and me,
When he [Kenelm Digby] shall read them at the Treasurer's board!
The knowing Weston, and that learnèd lord
Allows them! Then what copies shall be had,
What transcripts begged! (78. 25–30)

The Underwood includes a hundred or so poems by Jonson, as well as three which are known to be by other authors (one by Donne, one by Sidney Godolphin and another by Sir Henry Wotton – these Jonson may have copied out into his own manuscripts). It is likely that Sir Kenelm Digby put together and perhaps reordered gatherings of poems from Jonson's papers which the poet might have grouped together but not finally arranged. The collection in its surviving form seems arranged partly according to dates of composition, partly by groups of addressees, and partly to create internal symmetries. The series of love-lyrics, 'The Celebration of Charis', which appears third in the collection seems to be balanced by the (incomplete) sequence of poems to Lady Venetia Digby, which is positioned close to the end. The whole volume begins with divine poems and ends with a series of translations of classical works on the good life, as though God and Horace round Jonson's poetical career.

The Underwood is prefixed by a note signed by Jonson which describes its contents as 'lesser poems of later growth', mere shrubs in comparison to the noble trees of *The Forest*. This note has meant that *The Underwood* (along with the majority of Jonson's later works) has often been undervalued as a product of Ben's late dotage. The effects of the note have been compounded by the subject-matter of many of the poems. Jonson writes about ageing, 'My hundreds of grey hairs', 'My mountain belly, and my rocky face' (9. 14–17), his weight of nearly twenty stone, which is enough to 'crack a coach' (56. 10). He vainly courts Charis early in the collection, and is rejected by her for not being enough of a curly-haired courtling. The stirring defence of a short but intensely lived life in the ode 'To the Immortal Memory and Friendship of That Noble Pair, Sir Lucius Cary and Sir H. Morison' does nothing to help the cause of old age:

It is not growing like a tree
In bulk doth make man better be;

Or standing long an oak, three hundred year,
To fall a log at last, dry, bald, and sear:
A lily of a day
Is fairer far, in May,
Although it fall, and die that night;
It was the plant and flower of light. (70. 65–72)

Whether or not Jonson's old age was 'dry, bald, and sear' there is no doubt his predilection for targeted manuscript circulation later in his career could restrict the tonal range of his verse. Some of *The Underwood*'s panegyrics to Charles I and Queen Henrietta Maria acknowledge the growing murmurs of discontent which surrounded the Stuart court in the late 1620s and early 1630s, but usually these are presented as ungrateful noises off, rather than voices of criticism that might be found within the poems themselves by a wider print audience. In *Underwood*, 62, the king is thanked for sending Jonson a hundred pounds, and thereby curing 'the poet's evil, poverty' in the same way that he was believed to cure by touch the King's Evil, scrofula. The poem concludes with a reference to the deep disagreements between king and people which had led to the dissolution of Parliament in 1629: 'What can the poet wish his king may do, / But that he cure the people's evil too.' Increasingly the communities Jonson evokes are linked together less by reciprocal ties of gratitude and praise than by immediate material debts and obligations: 'the people's evil' grows outside the charmed circle in which poems are sent in grateful return for a gift of money, and that makes the phrase mean more 'the wickedness of the people' than 'the people's unfortunate illness'.

The poem to Sir Edward Sackville (*Underwood*, 13, written around 1620–3) transforms the poet's debts to a patron into an ethical bond between giver and recipient (and the poem underwrites its argument by its own extensive debts to Seneca's *De Beneficiis*). But elsewhere in *The Underwood* Jonson becomes the poet-petitioner, urgently in need of cash. He complains to a clerk to the Exchequer, John Burgess, that unless he receives the pension of a hundred pounds and the tun (keg) of wine which he had been granted by Charles I, then 'No plover, or cony / Will come to the table, / Or wine to enable / The muse or the poet' (57. 22–5). The jolly, short rhyming lines (which imitate the style of the early sixteenth-century poet John Skelton) do not counteract the unhappy inversion of the epigram 'Inviting a Friend to Supper': here there is not even the hope of a cony, let alone a lark. Jonson seems in some of his later verse to be a figure condemned to negotiate on the edges of the royal household, rather than someone who heaps the voluntary gift of praise onto noble figures in order 'to have made them such'.

But it would be misleading to present old Ben in *The Underwood* as a half-dead epicurean, poet-petitioner, and master of senescent twitches of passion. The volume also reprints poems which suggest quietly resistant forms of nostalgia, praising a number of men who had fallen out of favour in the Jacobean and Caroline courts, such as Sir Walter Ralegh, Bishop John Williams, and Francis Bacon[7] – and in doing this *The Underwood* set the tone for a large number of retrospective and posthumously printed collections of poems which appeared in the 1640s to look back nostalgically to the days before the Civil War. The losses recorded are also personal, and perhaps cast a wistful eye out towards the permanence of print: 'An Execration upon Vulcan' (*Underwood*, 43) was written after a fire destroyed a number of Jonson's manuscript writings in November 1623. Presented as a curse on the god of fire, the poem effectively invents a lost canon of Jonson's works, which include his 'journey into Scotland sung, / With all th'adventures' (lines 94–5) and a commentary on Horace's *Ars Poetica*. That record of lost works makes the poem stand for a larger concern of *The Underwood* volume as a whole: that of memorializing through loss. The 'Execration' makes a poetic canon out of works so completely ephemeral that they have actually been eaten up by fire. Building Jonson's poetic identity out of destruction, basing vitality on ephemera, seems to be one function of *The Underwood*.

But the collection also has a satirical bite that sinks deeper into English society than any verse Jonson had composed before the 1620s. The 'Epistle to a Friend, to Persuade him to the Wars' savagely attacks citizen and courtly wives for turning sex into another form of financial exchange: 'Adulteries, now, are not so hid, or strange: / They're grown commodity upon exchange' (15. 85–6). The friend is urged to 'fly from hence' to join those enlisting early in what was to become the Thirty Years War.[8] Late Jonson is incandescent ('let these kindled rhymes / Light thee from hell on earth', 15. 162–3), and the balance of his interests is shifting away from the ethical life of the individual towards a wider political vision, in which warfare abroad might be one means of resisting corruption at home. A few years later in 'A Speech According to Horace' (*Underwood*, 44) from 1626 Jonson develops this distinctive concern of his later verse. He (ostensibly at any rate) praises the Artillery Company, which was established by citizens in order to train informal militias – and which was seen by the increasingly anti-Spanish Charles I as one means of advancing England's standing abroad. Jonson's praise of these trooplets cannot quite escape from a sense of their absurdity:

Thou canst draw forth thy forces, and fight dry
    The battles of thy aldermanity,
Without the hazard of a drop of blood,
    More than the surfeits in thee that day stood.

(44. 45–8)

The idea here is that fighting is like a form of bodily purgation, which the armed bands cannot quite achieve because they are too reluctant to shed their own blood. The poem then moves on to attack not just the 'aldermanity' of the citizen militia, but also the ancient nobility, who spend their hours curling their hair and making up their faces rather than emulating the martial activity of their ancestors. And here it becomes an aggressive dialogue – almost a civil war – between different elements of London society:

> What love you then? Your whore? What study? Gait,
> Carriage, and dressing. There is up of late
> The academy, where the gallants meet –
> 'What, to make legs?' 'Yes, and to smell most sweet;'
> 'All that they do at plays.' 'Oh, but first here
> They learn and study, and then practise there.' (44. 87–92)

It's easy here to register the vigour with which Jonson records a variety of voices and clashing moral perspectives. An attempt to press a nobleman into joining up with the citizen militias ('The academy') turns into a joke about how theatrical the militia men are. But it is much harder to be sure when each of these voices stops and another begins (the speech-marks in the quotation above are editorial). In these later satires Jonson uses his dramatist's ear for the opposing styles of different voices, while also exploiting the way that a poem can allow those voices to blend together. The satires (or '*sermones*', 'conversations') of Horace had taught him the art of writing on the boundaries between direct and indirect speech, and the skill of leaving his readers unsure of whose voice they are hearing. This does not produce the art of the 'centred self', nor does it create a 'community of the same' between Jonson's readers and the author: it is, effectively, city-speak. In these poems Jonson sits on the cusp between several communities: he is friends with, and partly writing for, city wits who might find the military aspirations of urban citizens comical, but he is also attempting to feel his way into the pro-war sentiments of Charles I and his advisers. In his city satires of the 1620s Jonson does everything that makes him a great poet: within a framework deriving from classical satire he generates a number of conflicting voices, and creates the effect that he is talking not alone but for and within a larger community of which the different parts fail fully to understand each other. It is as though he is simultaneously trying to stand apart from a crowd and absorb its energies into himself, to hear and respond to the politics of the nation while accommodating the tastes and concerns of his friends and immediate addressees. And a semi-public epistle – an 'Epistle to a Friend' which finds its way to a larger community of readers – is the ideal form in which to present that project.

A satirist is often someone who cannot comfortably locate his own voice within the larger community of voices around him, all of which he dislikes, and who gradually realizes that by catching those voices and refusing to align himself with any one of them he can sound most like himself – a person absent, registered as a pattern of antipathies. Jonson became such a satirist, and, with his sharp ear for both the arguments of high politics and the squabbles of the streets, made himself into the poet who came to matter most to the great masters of poetry which is simultaneously public and conversational, Dryden and Pope. We could as a result think of Jonson's as a poetic identity shaped by patterns of aversion or by attempts to differentiate himself from the mass, or to unite himself with elite patrons in the construction of value. But it is more accurate to regard him as a poet of multiple voices, who registers the widest possible variety of social and historical demands upon himself, and turns them into poems which are monuments to diversity.

NOTES

1 Algernon Charles Swinburne, *A Study of Ben Jonson* (London: Chatto and Windus, 1889), p. 94.
2 Stanley Fish, 'Author-Readers: Jonson's Community of the Same', *Representations* 7 (1984), 26–58.
3 Richard Helgerson, *Self-Crowned Laureates: Spenser, Jonson, Milton and the Literary System* (Berkeley: University of California Press, 1983).
4 Jesse Franklin Bradley and Joseph Quincy Adams, *The Jonson Allusion-Book* (New Haven: Yale University Press, 1922), p. 16.
5 George Puttenham, *The Arte of English Poesie* (1589), eds Gladys Doidge Willcock and Alice Walker (Cambridge: Cambridge University Press, 1936), p. 54.
6 Alastair Fowler, 'The Silva Tradition in Jonson's *The Forrest*', in *Poetic Traditions of the English Renaissance*, eds Maynard Mack and George deF. Lord (New Haven: Yale University Press, 1982), pp. 163–80.
7 See Annabel Patterson, *Censorship and Interpretation: The Conditions of Writing and Reading in Early Modern England* (Madison, 1984), pp. 128–52.
8 See Martin Butler, 'The Dates of Three Poems by Ben Jonson', *Huntington Library Quarterly* 55 (1992), 279–94.

SELECTED FURTHER READING

Editions

The forthcoming *Cambridge Edition of the Works of Ben Jonson* (from which quotations are taken here) and the unmodernized Oxford English Texts edition by Mark Bland will incorporate much new manuscript material.

Works, eds. C. H. Herford, P. Simpson, and E. M. Simpson, vol. 8, Oxford, Clarendon Press, 1947. The standard scholarly old-spelling edition

Poems, ed. Ian Donaldson, Oxford, Oxford University Press, 1975, updated and rev. in Ian Donaldson (ed.), *Ben Jonson*, Oxford, Oxford University Press, 1985. The most reader-friendly version

Secondary works

Barton, Anne, *Ben Jonson: Dramatist*, Cambridge, Cambridge University Press, 1984

Booth, S., *Precious Nonsense: The Gettysburg Address, Ben Jonson's Epitaphs on His Children, and Twelfth Night*, Berkeley, University of California Press, 1998

Donaldson, Ian, *Jonson's Magic Houses*, Oxford, Clarendon Press, 1997

Evans, Robert C., *Ben Jonson and the Poetics of Patronage*, Cranbury, NJ, Associated Universities Press, 1989

Greene, Thomas M., *The Light in Troy: Imitation and Discovery in Renaissance Poetry*, New Haven and London, Yale University Press, 1982

Loewenstein, Joseph, *Ben Jonson and Possessive Authorship*, Cambridge, Cambridge University Press, 2002

Patterson, Annabel, *Censorship and Interpretation: The Conditions of Writing and Reading in Early Modern England*, Madison, University of Wisconsin Press, 1984

Peterson, Richard S., *Imitation and Praise in the Poems of Ben Jonson*, New Haven, Yale University Press, 1981

Riggs, David, *Ben Jonson: A Life*, Cambridge, MA, Harvard University Press, 1989

Sanders, Julie, *Ben Jonson's Theatrical Republics*, Basingstoke, Macmillan, 1998

Trimpi, Wesley, *Ben Jonson's Poems: A Study of the Plain Style*, Stanford, University of Stanford Press, 1962

van den Berg, Sara J., *The Action of Ben Jonson's Poetry*, Newark, University of Delaware Press, 1987

Wayne, D. E., *Penshurst: The Semiotics of Place and the Poetics of History*, Madison, University of Wisconsin Press, 1984

7

HELEN WILCOX

George Herbert

The date 1633 is a significant one in the history of English poetry. In that year, two remarkable collections of verse were published posthumously: the poems of John Donne, and *The Temple* by George Herbert. Donne was well known in his lifetime as a distinguished preacher and Dean of St Paul's Cathedral; he is now widely admired for his witty love-poetry, dynamic satires, and religious verse and prose. Herbert, by contrast, ended his life in relative obscurity as the rector of a rural parish near Salisbury, and some modern readers may have assigned him an equivalent place in the landscape of English poetic achievement. Since his verse output consisted of just one modest book containing nothing but devotional poetry, does Herbert's work really deserve to be placed alongside that of the other major names celebrated in this volume? This essay, not surprisingly, will answer that question with a resounding affirmative.

My aim is to demonstrate the greatness of Herbert's poetry by focusing on four key features of his work, each of which is discussed in general terms and explored in one representative poem. While Herbert's volume of verse consists of three main parts – 'The Church-porch', 'The Church' and 'The Church Militant' – it is the lyric poems in the extensive middle section that are now most frequently read and acclaimed. These will form the basis of the following celebration of Herbert's poetry, the 'utmost art'[1] which he himself offered in praise of God.

'I resolved to be bold': plainness and profundity

Let us begin with the enticing quality of Herbert's beginnings. To start reading a lyric poem from *The Temple* is to be drawn immediately into a dialogue, a drama, a narrative, or an arresting mood. 'Mattens', for example, begins by asserting – and resuming – the perpetual interaction of creature and creator: 'I cannot ope mine eyes, / But thou art ready there to catch / My morning-soul and sacrifice' (p. 226). At the opening of 'Man' we overhear an almost gossipy conversation between the speaker and God: 'My God, I heard this day, ... ' (p. 332), while in the first line of 'Content' the speaker grumpily addresses his own rebellious self: 'Peace mutt'ring thoughts' (p. 250). The poems launch into life with apparent effortlessness, offering the experience of a human relationship with God as though it were a friendship or love-affair. This is spirituality expressed in down-to-earth ordinariness. Herbert's lyrics open in a great variety of ways, but his beginnings have in common their accessibility to the reader. 'Love unknown' invites us into the poem with gentle courtesy: 'Deare Friend, sit down, the tale is long and sad:' (p. 453). 'It cannot be', asserts the opening phrase of 'The Temper' (II) with disarming bluntness, lamenting the sudden disappearance of 'that mightie joy, / Which just now took up all my heart' (p. 196). The beginning of 'Dulnesse' directly and honestly explores a heavy-hearted mood: 'Why do I languish thus, drooping and dull, / As if I were all earth?' (p. 410). The voice is puzzled, and the complaint all too human; the poem has a psalm-like quality, bringing devotion directly into the realm of the familiar.

With such openings, it is evident that Herbert's poems have an immediate and apparently uncomplicated appeal. However, it would be wrong to underestimate the subtlety that the lyrics also embody. The continuing satisfaction of reading Herbert's poems is that their clarity and directness go hand in hand with a complexity of thought and expression. His sonnet 'Prayer' (I), for instance, begins in a no-nonsense manner – 'Prayer the Churches banquet, Angels age' – but then spends thirteen-and-a-half of its fourteen lines searching for appropriate metaphors for prayer, ranging from 'The soul in paraphrase, heart in pilgrimage' to the serenely reciprocal idea of prayer as 'Church-bels beyond the starres heard'. However, in the last half line the poem suggests that no words are sufficient to evoke prayer, and it closes with the achieved simplicity of the resonant phrase, 'something understood' (p. 178). The poem is packed with thought-provoking images, but ends with profound plainness. The lyrics of *The Temple* move between the humdrum and the holy with such ease that those distinctions blur and ultimately dissolve. As Herbert writes in 'The H. Communion', passing from earth to heaven should be as straightforward as moving 'from one room t'another' (p. 183).

The impact of Herbert's plainness may be clearly seen in 'Redemption', a poem which entices the reader with its conversational mode, yet contains the whole of biblical history within its narrative and concludes with a brilliant and unexpected change of perspective:

> Having been tenant long to a rich Lord,
> Not thriving, I resolved to be bold,

And make a suit unto him, to afford
A new small-rented lease, and cancell th' old.

In heaven at his manour I him sought:
They told me there, that he was lately gone
About some land, which he had dearly bought
Long since on earth, to take possession.

I straight return'd, and knowing his great birth,
Sought him accordingly in great resorts;
In cities, theatres, gardens, parks, and courts:
At length I heard a ragged noise and mirth

Of theeves and murderers: there I him espied,
Who straight, *Your suit is granted*, said, & died. (p. 132)

Like many of Herbert's personae, the speaker has a misplaced confidence in his own sense of God's relationship with humankind. Bustling and 'bold', he sets out to make new demands of God, but these are based on false assumptions: 'knowing his great birth', the plaintiff sets off with absolutely no sense of the unsparing humility of the divine. God is not to be found in heaven, or in 'great resorts', but dying on the cross amid 'theeves and murderers'. The speaker's 'suit' is granted before it can be requested; the true action of the story is not the quest by the misguided human, but the love offered by a self-sacrificing incarnate God.

'Redemption' is a brief parable, finely tuned in tone and in the drama of its denouement; it explores the shift from the earthly meaning of its title as a legal and economic transaction to its spiritual reinterpretation as the astonishing gift of grace. With characteristic lightness of touch, Herbert suggests the complexity of the Old and New Covenants, spanning events from the creation to the first Good Friday and hinting at the overlapping of past and present in the redemptive scheme of things – yet the poem remains straightforward in its story-telling and graspable human scenario. It ends with the speaker surprised to find himself amidst the 'ragged noise and mirth' which is both the chaos of the crucifixion and the joy of being set free, with the 'lease' of sin 'redeemed'. The layers of meaning reward many re-readings of 'Redemption', but even on a first encounter the poem's complexity within transparency holds our attention from beginning to startling end.

'And mend my ryme': command of lyric form

'Redemption' is one of only fifteen sonnets in 'The Church', which contains 162 lyric poems. This alone suggests something of the formal ingenuity of Herbert's 'utmost art': in an era when most poets were drawn to write sonnet-sequences, Herbert created a sequence of devotional poems avoiding the repetition of lyric forms; his poetry demonstrates such virtuoso skill in the construction of stanzas that the same structures (apart from his few sonnets) are hardly ever used more than once. The only major English precursor of this phenomenon is the late sixteenth-century translation of the Psalms by Philip and Mary Sidney, the most significant influence on *The Temple* apart from the Bible and the *Book of Common Prayer*. Like the Sidney Psalms, Herbert's poems fully exploit the expressive potential of line-lengths, metres, and rhyme patterns. As a practising musician, Herbert also exploited the lyric effectiveness of rhythms and rests, as paralleled in the lute songs of Dowland and Campion. He refers to his own verse as 'a hymne or psalme' (p. 576), a sacred equivalent of the 'window-songs' written to worldly lovers (p. 411), and in 'Easter' he concludes that the apt response to the resurrection is for 'heart and lute' to 'consort' joyfully together and 'twist a song / Pleasant and long' (p. 140). The poems which result from this intertwining of devotion and art are among the finest English examples of lyric craftsmanship.

A preliminary glance at the titles of Herbert's lyrics also suggests something of the range of lyric forms he created, from the implied simplicity of 'A true Hymne' and 'The 23 Psalme' to the complexity of an 'Antiphon' and 'A Dialogue-Antheme'. The choice of alternating and answering structures is indicative of Herbert's knowledge of liturgical music, but also stresses his experience of devotion as conversation with God, as one might talk with a 'friend' (pp. 339, 367). The final poem in 'The Church' – the deservedly well-known 'Love' (III) – is an accomplished combination of controlled lyric elegance and reported speech, in which the 'sweetly questioning' Christ engages in gentle conversation with a hesitant speaker who is all too conscious of being 'Guiltie of dust and sinne' (p. 661). 'Heaven' is ingeniously constructed as an echo poem in which the 'delight' is 'light', 'pleasure' is 'leisure', and heavenly joys 'persever' for 'ever' (p. 656). This is not a display of rhetorical skill for its own sake, but a declaration of the power of form. 'Trinitie Sunday' honours the three-personed God in three three-line stanzas containing trios rather than pairs of rhyme-sounds, as a means of expressing the speaker's endeavour to use 'heart, mouth, hands' in order to 'runne, rise, rest with thee' (p. 249).

One of the best examples of Herbert's expressive control of lyric structure is 'Deniall', in which metaphorical language, syntax, and rhyme combine magnificently to explore the apparent failure of prayer:

When my devotions could not pierce
Thy silent eares;
Then was my heart broken, as was my verse:
My breast was full of fears
And disorder:

...

O that thou shouldst give dust a tongue
To crie to thee,
And then not heare it crying! all day long
My heart was in my knee,
But no hearing.

Therefore my soul lay out of sight,
Untun'd, unstrung:
My feeble spirit, unable to look right,
Like a nipt blossome, hung
Discontented.

O cheer and tune my heartlesse breast,
Deferre no time;
That so thy favours granting my request,
They and my minde may chime,
And mend my ryme.

(pp. 288–9)

In every stanza except the last, the form is an epitome of dysfunction and 'disorder', with final lines which do not rhyme. The music of the verse is thus 'broken', like the speaker's heart; its harmonies are 'Untun'd'. The parts of the speaker's body seem dislocated – a human being is mere 'dust' given a 'tongue', and fruitless hours of attempted prayer are suggested by the notion of the 'heart' in the 'knee' – while the absence of God is powerfully suggested in the dumbness and deafness of 'silent eares'. Even the line breaks suggest the melancholic mood: like the word 'hung' which dangles disconsolately at the end of a line, the speaker's 'feeble spirit ... hung / Discontented'. Only in the last stanza is harmony restored; the speaker ceases to accuse God of denying him any contact and instead begins to pray, thereby ending his own 'Deniall'. As soon as the conversation begins, with the speaker's urgent plea for a retuning of their relationship, the harmony of the lyric form is restored: for once, the last line of the stanza does indeed rhyme, as an expression of the renewed 'chime' of the soul with God. Just as in the conclusion of 'Redemption', the desired effect is achieved before the speaker has been able to express or complete his request.[2]

'Louely enchanting language': multidimensional words

Related to Herbert's command of lyric form is a third major feature of his poetic art: an awareness of all the dimensions of language. We have noted that Herbert was deeply conscious of the aural impact of words; metre and rhythm, rhymes and echoes, cadences and silences are all so vital that he refers to his poetry as 'My musick' (p. 316). This is the first dimension of the language of poetry, which works on the ear of the listener before the intellect is engaged. But written poetry is also a visual form, drawing out the significance of shapes and patterns as they meet the eye of the reader, and Herbert makes more of this second dimension of language than most poets. Building on his commitment to the connection between form and meaning, he creates unique 'shaped poems' as visual complements to the ideas explored. In these seventeenth-century precursors of concrete poetry, the poem becomes an expressive object, a visual image striking the eye as well as a melody sounding in the ear.

Among the most famous of Herbert's shaped poems is 'The Altar' (Fig. 3), taking the form of a stone altar or pillar and acting as the symbolic place of sacrifice on which Christ's passion is offered. The subject of the poem is the human heart, made of stone but broken by sin and suffering; the poet's words are designed to form a 'frame' in which 'These stones to praise thee may not cease' (p. 92). There is a sense of the visual dimension of the poem being effective even if the poet should 'chance to hold [his] peace'. Like the rhymes of 'Deniall' which almost supersede the poem's meaning, the shape of 'The Altar' is granted its own efficacy. This is also true of 'Easter wings', Herbert's celebration of the resurrection expressed in two stanzas shaped like pairs of angels' wings. In the narrowest parts, the poem speaks of contracted human experience as 'Most poore' and 'Most thinne', while the longest lines expand to contain the hope of resurrection: 'Then shall the fall further the flight in me' (p. 147). With its metaphors of feathers and wings, as well as its association of the resurrection with the flight of a bird, the poem unites sight and mind, stasis and movement, using everything that words have to offer.

Although 'The Altar' and 'Easter wings' have not always met with critical approval,[3] they embody a principle which underlies all the lyrics of *The Temple*. In 'Coloss. 3.3', the biblical paraphrase, 'My life is hid in him that is my treasure', is embedded within the poem's syntax but picked out in italics to be read diagonally from the first to the last words of the lyric (p. 305). As poem and biblical motto both point out, two dimensions function simultaneously, the one hidden and the other overt. While this suggests the mingling of earthly and spiritual lives, it also makes clear Herbert's attitude towards words. The human capacity to use language is God-given, and the devotional poet celebrates the giver and the gift, knowing that they constitute the poet's art: 'Thy word is all, if we could spell' (p. 568). For Herbert, writing is the discovery of the original creating 'Word' and a revelation of the full riches 'compacted' (p. 316) within language.

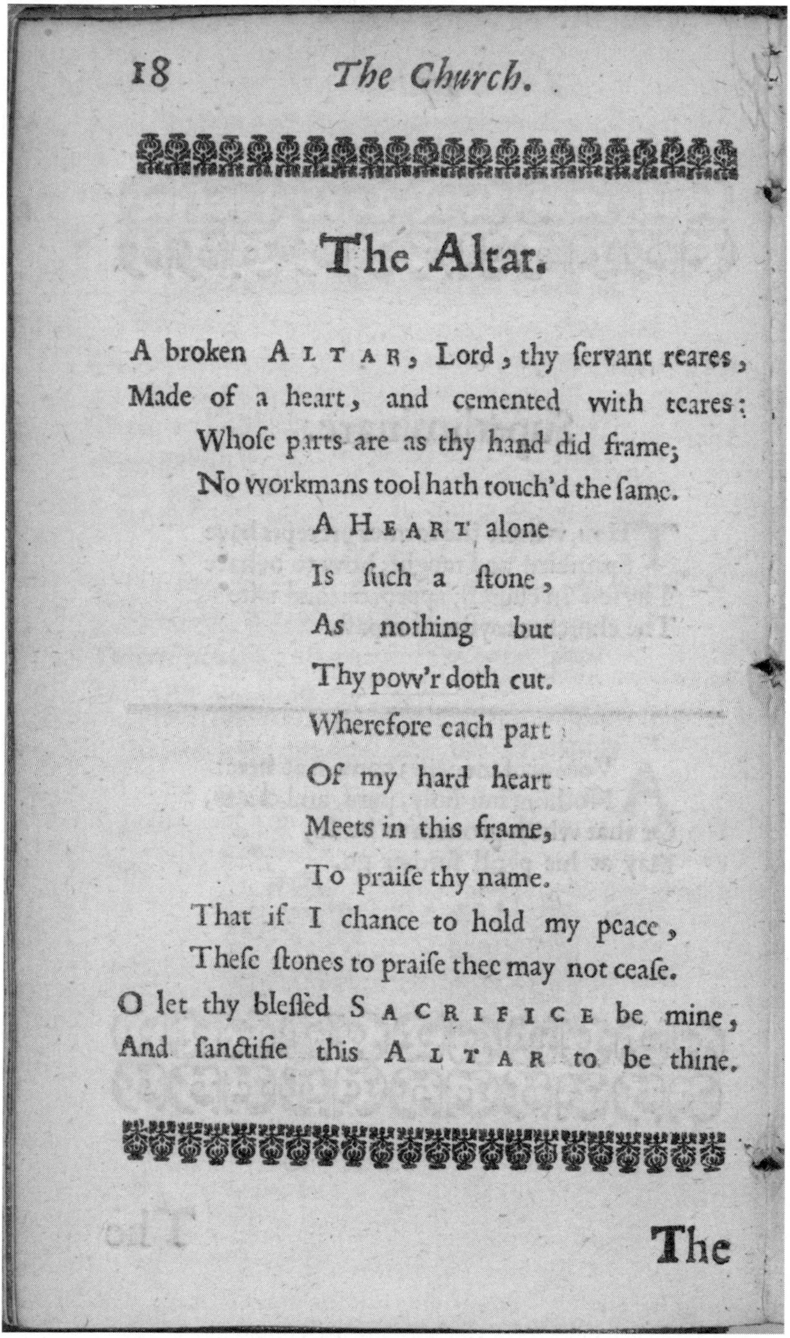

18 *The Church.*

The Altar.

A broken A L T A R, Lord, thy ſervant reares,
Made of a heart, and cemented with teares:
Whoſe parts are as thy hand did frame;
No workmans tool hath touch'd the ſame.
A H E A R T alone
Is ſuch a ſtone,
As nothing but
Thy pow'r doth cut.
Wherefore each part
Of my hard heart
Meets in this frame,
To praiſe thy name.
That if I chance to hold my peace,
Theſe ſtones to praiſe thee may not ceaſe.
O let thy bleſſed S A C R I F I C E be mine,
And ſanctifie this A L T A R to be thine.

The

Figure 3 'The Altar' by George Herbert, from the first edition (1633) of *The Temple*, p. 18, reproduced by kind permission of the Syndics of Cambridge University Library.

The words at work in *The Temple* are multidimensional, working on sound and sight, literal and metaphorical meanings, horizontal and vertical ways of reading, and appealing to the intellectual as well as the sensual faculties of the reader. 'I like our language', exclaims the speaker of 'The Sonne': 'How neatly doe we give one onely name / To parents issue and the sunnes bright starre!' (p. 573). The possibility of punning on 'sun' and 'son' – a bonus for a witty devotional poet – is yet one more sign of the expressive potential within words. It is not surprising that Herbert uses language in all these possible dimensions within his lyrics, since he was highly trained in the skills of rhetoric and had been Public Orator of the University of Cambridge before being ordained. As he wrote in the opening of 'The Pearl', 'I know the wayes of learning' (p. 322); but after an exploration of those 'wayes' the first stanza concludes, 'Yet I love thee.' There is an implicit contradiction here between worldly 'learning' and spiritual 'love', as though the first must be abandoned in favour of the second – a great difficulty for the rhetorician who wishes to express love for God by means of 'utmost' and highly learned 'art'. Indeed, many of Herbert's poems foreground the dilemma of the devotional poet who finds himself 'Decking the sense, as if it were to sell' ('Jordan' (II), p. 367); the temptation to 'excell' with 'quaint words' is always in danger of pre-empting the sacred purpose for which the poem was intended. This focus on words as not only the medium but the subject of devotional poetry is the ultimate dimension of language at work in *The Temple*.

Herbert's ambivalent fascination with beautiful language is the focus of his poem 'The Forerunners', in which he reports seeing the first 'harbingers' of ageing, some chalk-white hairs, and contemplates the consequences for the 'sparkling notions' in his poet's brain:

> The harbingers are come. See, see their mark;
> White is their colour, and behold my head.
> But must they have my brain? Must they dispark
> Those sparkling notions, which therein were bred?
>   Must dulnesse turn me to a clod?
> Yet have they left me, *Thou art still my God.*
>
> ...
>
> Farewell sweet phrases, lovely metaphors.
> But will ye leave me thus? when ye before
> Of stews and brothels onely knew the doores,
> Then did I wash you with my tears, and more,
>   Brought you to Church well drest and clad:
> My God must have my best, ev'n all I had.

Louely enchanting language, sugar-cane,
Hony of roses, whither wilt thou flie?
Hath some fond lover tic'd thee to thy bane?
And wilt thou leave the Church, and love a stie?

...

Let follie speak in her own native tongue.
True beautie dwells on high: ours is a flame
    But borrow'd thence to light us thither.
Beautie and beauteous words should go together.

Yet if you go, I passe not; take your way:
For, *Thou art still my God*, is all that ye
Perhaps with more embellishment can say.
Go birds of spring: let winter have his fee,
    Let a bleak palenesse chalk the doore,
So all within be livelier then before. (pp. 611–12)

At times the speaker seems to ache with an almost sensual longing for the words which are about to leave him – the 'sweet phrases, lovely metaphors' of his 'enchanting language', delicious as sugar and the scent of roses. Herbert delights in the words even as he claims to let them go, resigned to the idea that rich poetic language belongs solely in the world of secular love. But there are two compensations for his impending loss: the knowledge that heavenly values are themselves 'beautie', and the fact that the kernel of his praise, '*Thou art still my God*', will remain. In the relationship between complexity and simplicity, the plain biblical statement appears to have triumphed. However, with knowing irony the poet allows an element of uncertainty into the last stanza, using the word 'Perhaps' to leave the attractions of language intact. The poem ends with a reassertion of what the multidimensional words of *The Temple* are attempting to convey: the life 'within' in all its liveliness.

'Shall I ever sigh and pine?': vagaries of the human heart

The conclusion of 'The Forerunners' is a reminder of the prevailing concern of Herbert's poems: the spiritual life of ordinary human beings as they struggle with their mortality. Although his book was given the title *The Temple* and its subsections refer to parts of the church, Herbert's lyrics are not predominantly doctrinal, political, or historical, but devotional. The original title-page cites Psalm 29:8, 'In his Temple doth every man speak of his honour', reminding the reader that the Jewish temple was a place of worship and praise. The poems are concerned with the yearning of the human spirit for God, and the title finds its full significance in St Paul's metaphor of the individual as a living 'temple' of the Holy Spirit.[4] Herbert's understanding of God is inward and intimate rather than external or grand; as 'Sion' suggests, the undoubted glories of Solomon's temple are 'not so deare to [God] as one good grone' (p. 382). Herbertian spiritual encounters do not take place in a temple made of 'brasse and stones', but in the heart: 'now thy Architecture meets with sinne; / For all thy frame and fabrick is within' (p. 382).

The Temple is a treasury of the life 'within' – Aldous Huxley characterized Herbert as a great poet of 'the inner weather'.[5] There are many days when that climate is warm and sunny, as the speaker celebrates the 'mirth' of redemption (pp. 132, 273) and feels the 'sugred strange delight' caused by one glance from a loving God (p. 589). However, there are also days of storms and bitter emotional weather. It is significant that, while Herbert includes three lyrics entitled 'Love' in his collection, and another three entitled 'Praise', there are five (the largest single group) bearing the title 'Affliction'. There is a strong sense that affliction can lead to even greater joys – 'We are the trees, whom shaking fastens more' (p. 350) – but these poems of suffering, regret, and longing form a substantial part of *The Temple*, threaded throughout the sequence. Herbert's biographer Izaak Walton reported that the poet had described his lyrics as 'a picture of the many spiritual Conflicts ... betwixt God and my Soul',[6] and it is true that they portray a variety of moods from anger and frustration to submission and love, with all the unpredictability of an intense relationship. As 'Bitter-sweet' declares, the poet matches his 'deare angrie Lord' by vowing to 'complain, yet praise': 'And all my sowre-sweet dayes / I will lament, and love' (p. 587).

Unlike devotional poets such as Donne and Hopkins, whose dark days often end with unresolved despair, Herbert's poems of 'lament' are never far from confidence and hope, however much those anchors may seem to have disappeared. Consider the outspoken complaint entitled 'The Collar':

> I struck the board, and cry'd, No more.
> I will abroad.
> What? shall I ever sigh and pine?
> My lines and life are free; free as the rode,
> Loose as the winde, as large as store.
> Shall I be still in suit?
> Have I no harvest but a thorn
> To let me bloud, and not restore
> What I have lost with cordiall fruit?
> ...
> Away; take heed:
> I will abroad.

Call in thy deaths head there: tie up thy fears.
He that forbears
To suit and serve his need,
Deserves his load.
But as I rav'd and grew more fierce and wilde
At every word,
Me thoughts I heard one calling, *Childe*:
And I reply'd, *My Lord*. (p. 526)

The opening represents an outburst of such furious frustration that it borders on the sacrilegious – for the 'board' is the altar itself. The 'collar' of apparent enslavement to God's service is too restricting, and the speaker resents the losses and suffering that it entails. The poem is a cry of rebellion, a bid for freedom from burdens and constraints; yet it is actually only the distance of one word, '*Childe*', from the renewal of a devoted relationship with God. The significance of that word is enormous: until the last two lines, the speaker's error is to consider himself a slave, rather than the child of a loving '*Lord*'.

While 'The Collar' gives an idea of the spectrum of moods to be found within *The Temple*, it is also a fine example of the other qualities of Herbert's verse that I have so far sought to highlight. Its opening is arresting and its impact immediate, but it goes on to explore complex doctrines and emotions. Something of this may be gleaned from the emblematic title, in which several meanings are combined and the progression of the poem is condensed. The speaker is driven by a burst of anger or 'choler', caused by resentment of the 'collar' of service to God. The discovery enacted by the poem is that the speaker's choleric reaction was based on an error, since the collar is not the iron shackle of a slave but the 'easy' yoke of a child of God.[7] In addition, the pun on 'caller' refers at first to the speaker's outcry to God, 'I will abroad', but by the conclusion it is clear that the true and effective caller is in fact the 'one calling, *Childe*'.

'The Collar' also displays Herbert's inventiveness with lyric form, in a continuous structure which some readers have seen as a precursor to twentieth-century free verse. In fact, there is a pattern to the metre, line-lengths, and seemingly inconsistent rhymes, but one brilliantly devised to display the speaker's ravings. And at the poem's most intensely 'wilde' moment, four lines from the end, the intervening divine voice calling '*Childe*' completes the rhyme and restores order, both structurally and spiritually. Herbert's awareness of all the potential of language is once more revealed. The puns in the title exploit the relationship between the aural and semantic dimensions of words, while the messy visual impact of the poem reflects the speaker's emotional chaos. Above all, the vocabulary used by the protesting speaker conveys earthly and heavenly meanings inseparably. He desires to be 'free as the rode', an expression suggesting the 'road' of departure and release but also unwittingly recalling the 'rood' or cross of Christ, which the poem goes on to reveal as the source of true spiritual freedom. When the speaker complains of 'thorns' and 'bloud', his own miseries are expressed in the language of the passion of Christ: the crown of thorns, and the wine of the Last Supper which becomes the 'blood of the new covenant' in the Eucharist. Even as he speaks of his own suffering, therefore, the spiritual overtones of the vocabulary are a hidden reminder that Christ has suffered before his followers, and is with them in their distress even when that leads them to reject him. At the end of the poem, the speaker may grow 'more fierce and wilde / At every word', but it is also, quite literally, in 'every word' that he has uttered that God's voice can be heard, 'calling'.

'And now in age I bud again': Herbert's enduring greatness

Herbert is a poet of paradoxes. He writes with simultaneous plainness and complexity, and conveys colloquial inner dialogues with lyrical and rhetorical dexterity. His poems are crafted and apparently fixed constructions, yet to read them is to participate in what seems like an organically developing experience. Herbert delights in multivalent language which works on the eye and the ear as well as the heart and mind, yet among his most powerful moments are the final words of 'Jordan' (I) – the biblical phrase '*My God, My King*' (p. 200) – and the monosyllabic climax of 'Love' (III), 'So I did sit and eat' (p. 661). The speakers of poems such as 'Love' (III) struggle to accept God's freely given love, yet the poems as a whole are full of its 'sweet' impact. And while there is plenty of sorrow and frustration in *The Temple*, its 'pulse' is 'praise' (p. 436). Ironically, the poems celebrate God's goodness and grace 'at every word', even while asserting that 'eternitie is too short' to do so (p. 507).

This range of contradictory features may go some way towards explaining the appeal of Herbert's poetry to readers of differing backgrounds and attitudes. In the seventeenth century, when *The Temple* was so popular that it went through eleven editions, Herbert's admirers included prominent figures on opposite sides of the religio-political divide: Charles I read *The Temple* when imprisoned before his execution, and Oliver Cromwell's chaplain recommended that his son should read the works of 'Mr Herbert'.[8] Readers favouring a sacramental approach to devotion continue to be drawn to Herbert's evocation of God's presence in immediate and sensual experience, as suggested in the conclusion to his Good Friday poem 'The Agonie': 'Love is that liquour sweet and most divine, / Which my God feels as bloud; but

I, as wine' (p. 119). Those preferring a Calvinist approach, emphasizing the biblical inheritance and the dependence of sinful humanity on God's grace, also find inspiration in *The Temple*; as the speaker in 'The Holdfast' learns, 'to have nought is ours, not to confesse / That we have nought' (p. 499). The poems' varied tones and concerns, from angst to joy both personal and liturgical, echo the range and intensity of the Psalms, placing Herbert in the ranks of the greatest devotional poets. His admirers among writers, who include Vaughan, Coleridge, Christina Rossetti, T. S. Eliot, R. S. Thomas, and Seamus Heaney, attest to the poetic skills and metaphysical insights that characterize the work of this 'sweet singer of the Temple'.[9]

In the spirit of these and many others, I have suggested that the greatness of Herbert's work may be seen in its mingling of the everyday and the holy, its imaginative use of poetic forms and of linguistic potential, and its exploration of the shifting and often contradictory nature of spiritual experience. Crucially, these features are not separate but intertwined, so that the very process of writing is a means to, and metaphor for, the poet's relationship with God. As we have seen, the 'verse' of 'Deniall' and the 'lines' of 'The Collar' are respectively 'broken' and 'free', a reference to the emotional as well as structural context of each poem. As Herbert writes in 'The Flower', celebrating the wondrous spring-like 'returns' of God into his barren spiritual life,

> And now in age I bud again,
> After so many deaths I live and write;
> I once more smell the dew and rain,
> And relish versing: O my onely light,
> It cannot be
> That I am he
> On whom thy tempests fell all night. (p. 568)

The joyous lucidity of this stanza derives from the qualities we have already observed, but also from the inseparability of the spiritual and poetic recovery: the writer's rediscovered 'relish' in 'versing' is absolutely integral to his renewed friendship with God.

Herbert's accessible lyricism and profound yet intimate devotion continue to appeal to readers in the twenty-first century. One of his most recent admirers, the novelist and poet Vikram Seth, astutely summed up the 'very Herbertian attributes' that he discerned in the work of another modern writer: 'I am grateful for its wit, its intensity of feeling, its enlightening juxtapositions, its clear yet complex structure and its decorous colloquiality.'[10] Countless readers are indeed grateful for all these qualities – and more – in Herbert's poetry.

NOTES

1 George Herbert, 'Praise' (II), in *The English Poems of George Herbert*, ed. Helen Wilcox (Cambridge: Cambridge University Press, 2007), p. 507. All further references to Herbert's poems are to this edition.
2 See Isaiah 65:24: 'And it shall come to pass, that before they call, I will answer; and while they are yet speaking, I will hear.'
3 See Dryden's mockery of the altars and wings of 'Acrostick Land' in *Mac Flecknoe*, line 207.
4 1 Corinthians 6:19.
5 Aldous Huxley, *Texts and Pretexts* (New York: Harper, 1933), p. 13.
6 Izaak Walton, *The Life of Mr. George Herbert* (London, 1670), p. 74.
7 See Matthew 11:30, 'For my yoke is easy, and my burden is light.'
8 Charles's prison reading was said to have included '*Herbert*'s divine Poems', and Sterry urged his son to read 'Mr. Herbert' alongside the scriptures; see Robert H. Ray (ed.), *The Herbert Allusion Book: Allusions to George Herbert in the Seventeenth Century*, *Studies in Philology* 83.4 (1986), pp. 128, 65.
9 Barnabus Oley, preface to *Herbert's Remains* (1652), a11v.
10 Vikram Seth, 'Foreword', in Ronald Blythe, *George Herbert in Bemerton* (Salisbury: Hobnob Press, 2005), p. 9.

SELECTED FURTHER READING

Primary works

The Bible: Authorized King James Version, eds Robert Carroll and Stephen Prickett, Oxford, Oxford University Press, 1997

The Book of Common Prayer 1559: The Elizabethan Prayer Book, ed. John E. Booty, Charlottesville, University Press of Virginia, for the Folger Shakespeare Library, 1976

Slater, Ann Pasternak (ed.), *The Complete English Works of George Herbert,* London, Dent, 1995

Tobin, John (ed.), *George Herbert: The Complete English Poems,* London, Penguin, 1991

Walton, Izaak, *The Life of Mr. George Herbert* (1670), in *Lives*, Menston, Scolar Press, 1969

Wilcox, Helen (ed.), *The English Poems of George Herbert,* Cambridge, Cambridge University Press, 2007

Secondary works

Bloch, Chana, *Spelling the Word: George Herbert and the Bible*, Berkeley, University of California Press, 1985

Blythe, Ronald, *George Herbert in Bemerton*, Salisbury, Hobnob Press, 2005

Charles, Amy M., *A Life of George Herbert*, Ithaca, NY, Cornell University Press, 1977

Fish, Stanley, *The Living Temple: George Herbert and Catechizing*, Berkeley, University of California Press, 1978

Guibbory, Achsah, *Ceremony and Community from Herbert to Milton: Literature, Religion, and Cultural Conflict in Seventeenth-Century England*, Cambridge, Cambridge University Press, 1998

Hodgkins, Christopher, *Authority, Church, and Society in George Herbert: Return to the Middle Way*, Columbia, University of Missouri Press, 1993

Lewalski, Barbara K., *Protestant Poetics and the Seventeenth-Century English Lyric*, Princeton, Princeton University Press, 1979

Malcolmson, Cristina, *George Herbert: A Literary Life*, New York, Palgrave Macmillan, 2004

Martz, Louis L., *The Poetry of Meditation*, New Haven, Yale University Press, 1954

Nuttall, A. D., *Overheard by God: Fiction and Prayer in Herbert, Milton, Dante and St. John*, London, Methuen, 1980

Patrides, C. A. (ed.), *George Herbert: The Critical Heritage*, London, Routledge, 1983

Ray, Robert H. (ed.), *The Herbert Allusion Book: Allusions to George Herbert in the Seventeenth Century*, *Studies in Philology* 83.4 (1986)

Schoenfeldt, Michael C., *Prayer and Power: George Herbert and Renaissance Courtship*, Chicago, University of Chicago Press, 1991

Strier, Richard, *Love Known: Theology and Experience in George Herbert's Poetry*, Chicago, University of Chicago Press, 1983

Summers, Joseph H., *George Herbert: His Religion and Art*, London, Chatto and Windus, 1954

Tuve, Rosemond, *A Reading of George Herbert*, Chicago, Chicago University Press, 1952

Vendler, Helen, *The Poetry of George Herbert*, Cambridge, MA, Harvard University Press, 1975

8

MARTIN EVANS

John Milton

For a variety of reasons, Milton has acquired over the years a somewhat intimidating reputation as a poet. Thanks largely to his association with Puritanism, he is often thought to be a grim, humourless, unfeeling religious zealot, remote from the joys and sorrows of everyday human experience. In fact, although he could certainly sound as fierce and uncompromising as any hell-fire preacher, he could also be as sensuous as Keats, as passionate as Shakespeare, as rapturous as Gerard Manley Hopkins, and as playful as Donne.[1] Of all our non-dramatic poets he is perhaps the most various, the most fully and richly human.

Yet beneath this bewildering variety of voices and moods there is one characteristic that seems to me to be quintessentially Miltonic: the poet's contrariness. From the very beginning of his career, Milton evidently delighted in pitting one set of values or beliefs against another. An extraordinary number of his poems, that is to say, consist essentially of two antithetical movements based on diametrically opposed premises. In the opening stanzas of his first original English poem, 'On the Death of a Fair Infant', for instance, the speaker assumes (a) that the child is dead, (b) that she was human, and (c) that her fate was caused by the descent of a pagan divinity:

> O fairest flower, no sooner blown but blasted,
> Soft silken primrose, fading timelessly,
> Summer's chief honour if thou hadst outlasted
> Bleak Winter's force that made thy blossom dry;
> For he being amorous on that lovely dye,
> That did thy cheek envermeil, thought to kiss
> But killed alas, and then bewailed his fatal bliss.

But beginning in stanza five the speaker proceeds to reverse all these assumptions. The fair infant, he asserts, is not dead but alive, 'Yet can I not persuade me thou art dead' (line 29), she is not human but divine, 'for something in thy face did shine / Above mortality' (34–5), and her departure from the world is to be explained not by the descent of a destructive figure such as

Winter or Aquilo but by the ascent of a creative one – one of the four daughters of God, perhaps, or a member of 'the golden winged host' (57).

Over and over again this binary pattern is repeated in Milton's poetry – in the opposition between the Christian story of Christ's birth in the first half of the ode 'On the Morning of Christ's Nativity' and the mythological references to the pagan oracles in the second, between the lamentation for Edward King's death in the first part of 'Lycidas' and the celebration of his resurrection in the second, between the anguished questions in the octave of 'Sonnet XVI' and the confident answer provided by Patience in the sestet. What is more, the same fundamental pattern also informs the relation that many of Milton's individual poems have to each other. Thus the 'Nativity Ode' is counterbalanced by 'The Passion', 'L'Allegro' by 'Il Penseroso', *Paradise Lost* by *Paradise Regained*, which in turn was juxtaposed with *Samson Agonistes* when the two poems were published together in 1671. Milton's poems argue with each other as well as with themselves. As E. M. W. Tillyard suggested over fifty years ago,[2] Milton's entire poetic production might be modelled on the antithetical structure of the scholastic disputations and declamations in which he was trained to participate as a young student at Cambridge. Contradiction is the very essence of his poetic identity.

No less remarkable is the complete absence in his poems of any transition between the opposing elements. He seems to get from the thesis to the antithesis not by any progressive argument but rather by an implicit or explicit infusion of fresh insight, a conceptual leap signalled in many cases by a single adversative conjunction, 'but' or 'yet', as in the fifth stanza of 'On the Death of a Fair Infant': 'Yet can I not persuade me thou art dead.' Indeed, the shift from one side of the argument to the other is so abrupt, so violent, that it often requires the entrance of a completely new speaker: 'But wisest Fate says no, / This must not yet be so' ('Nativity Ode', lines 149–50); 'But not the praise, / Phoebus replied, and touch'd my trembling ears' ('Lycidas', lines 76–7); 'But Patience to prevent / That murmur soon replies' ('Sonnet XVI', lines 8–9). Dr Johnson complained famously that *Samson Agonistes* lacks a middle. It does, and so do the majority of Milton's poems. That is what makes them so different from Donne's notoriously disputatious *Songs and Sonets*, say, or Marvell's syllogistic love-lyrics. This is the poetry of a continually self-contesting personality. Even his final work is an *agon*.

Puritan/humanist

As a result, both the man and his poetry defy straightforward categorization. They simply will not fit into any one of the various compartments which literary and intellectual historians of the seventeenth century have constructed to hold them. To begin with, although he was unquestionably a Puritan in certain respects, in other respects Milton was also a committed humanist. To be sure, Christian humanism was a common phenomenon during the Renaissance, but for Milton the effort to reconcile the two belief systems with each other seems to have been a continual source of intellectual and poetic tension.

The key to the difference between the two ideologies is to be found in their opposing views about the effect of the Fall of Man. Puritans believed that Adam's disobedience in the garden of Eden had so thoroughly corrupted human nature that his descendants were utterly incapable of performing any virtuous act of their own volition. Totally dependent upon the grace of God, fallen humanity was consequently incapable of contributing anything to its own salvation. Everything now rested in the hands of the Almighty, and the only way to achieve salvation was through the God-given gift of faith; any attempt to approach the Creator by rational means was doomed from the start. The true source of wisdom, therefore, was to be found in the divinely inspired scriptures rather than in the unenlightened speculations of human reason enshrined in the philosophy and literature of classical antiquity.

Humanists, on the other hand, believed that despite the ravages inflicted on it by the Fall of Man, human nature was still essentially rational, and to that extent still perfectible by education. In Sir Philip Sidney's words, 'the ending end of all earthly learning' was 'virtuous action'. Knowledge, as Socrates had claimed, was the gateway to virtue, and knowledge was to be found in the great works of the ancient philosophers and poets whose writings could turn fallen men and women into active moral agents, well equipped to participate in the civic life of their society.

From his earliest years, Milton was exposed to both these belief systems. As a small boy he was taught by Thomas Young, a Scottish Calvinist hired by his father to serve as his son's private tutor. Then, from the age of nine or thereabouts, he attended one of the finest humanist schools in England, St Paul's, where he studied a variety of classical authors ranging from Ovid, Cicero, and Virgil to Theocritus, Homer, and Euripides. From there he proceeded in 1625 to Cambridge University, the intellectual headquarters of the Puritan movement in England, in preparation for a career in the ministry. But the insistence of the ecclesiastical authorities on conformity to Anglican doctrine and practice made it impossible for him to enter the church without violating his conscience. So after graduating with an MA in 1632, he spent the next six years at the Milton family home, first in Hammersmith and then in Horton, where he embarked on a self-designed reading programme in classical and ecclesiastical history, philosophy, theology, and literature.

The result of this double exposure can be seen over and over again in Milton's writings. For instance, the influence of Puritanism may well be responsible for Milton's refusal to admit any intermediaries between the reader and the Christ-child in the 'Nativity Ode', where all the usual human presences at the manger – the shepherds, the wise men, Mary and Joseph – are erased from the scene along with the traditional animals, with the result that the reader is forced, like a good Puritan, to encounter the Redeemer face to face. Puritanism again finds expression in the Lady's critique of 'lewdly pampered luxury' in 'Comus' (line 770) and even more vehemently in St Peter's famous tirade against the 'corrupted clergy' of the Anglican church in 'Lycidas' (113–31). Less obviously, it may well have shaped Milton's selection of the Fall of Man, the seminal event in the Puritan version of Christian history, as the subject of his most ambitious poem. And it surely lies behind Christ's rejection of classical philosophers and poets in Book IV of *Paradise Regained*:

> Alas what can they teach, and not mislead;
> Ignorant of themselves, of God much more,
> And how the world began, and how man fell
> Degraded by himself, on grace depending. (IV. 309–12)

The influence of humanism, on the other hand, is most immediately apparent in the sheer depth and breadth of Milton's learning. No other English poet, not even John Donne or Ben Jonson, could rival his immense command of both classical and contemporary culture (in addition to composing poems in English, Milton also wrote them in Latin, Greek, and Italian). His poetry and his prose are consequently saturated with allusions to other texts ranging from Homer's *Iliad* and Dante's *Divine Comedy* to Spenser's *Faerie Queene* and Camoens's *Lusiads*. For a modern reader who has not been exposed to such a vast range of Latin, Greek, medieval, and Renaissance literature, Milton's writings may therefore seem forbiddingly difficult on first acquaintance. Here, for example, is his description of the serpent in which Satan has disguised himself in order to tempt Eve in *Paradise Lost*:

> Pleasing was his shape,
> And lovely, never since of serpent kind
> Lovelier, not those that in Illyria changed
> Hermione and Cadmus, or the god
> In Epidaurus; nor to which transformed
> Ammonian Jove, or Capitoline was seen,
> He with Olympias, this with her who bore
> Scipio the height of Rome. (IX. 503–10)

Unless we know that Cadmus and his wife Hermione were transformed into serpents and became 'friendly snakes' that 'do not shun mankind, or do them harm' (Ovid, *Metamorphoses* XV), that when Asclepius, the god of healing, left his sanctuary in Epidaurus in the form of a snake, he did so to cure a plague in Rome, and that when Jupiter Ammon and Jupiter of the Capitol turned into snakes they begot two of the greatest heroes of classical history, Alexander the Great and Scipio Africanus, we will miss the irony of the situation. For the serpent in *Paradise Lost* does intend to do harm to mankind, his mission is to spread a plague rather than to cure one, and he begets not two great heroes but Sin and Death. On a much smaller scale, when Adam claims to 'Approve the best and follow what I approve' (*Paradise Lost* VIII. 610), the full significance of his assertion will only be apparent if we remember the famous words Ovid puts into the mouth of Medea: 'I see the better, I approve it too: / The worse I follow' (*Metamorphoses* VII. 20–1). One of the major tasks of Milton scholarship and criticism has been to bridge the vast intellectual gap that separates us from the rich and complex tradition which fertilized Milton's poetic imagination.

What is more, humanistic ideas undergird Milton's unusually exalted theory of poetry itself. Poetic abilities, he wrote in one of his prose tracts, 'are of power, beside the office of a pulpit, to inbreed and cherish in a great people the seeds of virtue and public civility, to allay the perturbations of the mind, and set the affections in right tune' (*Reason of Church Government*, 1642, preface to Book II). The implied musical image in the last phrase is highly significant, for Milton believed that thanks to the Fall of Man:

disproportioned sin
Jarred against Nature's chime, and with harsh din
Broke the fair music that all creatures made
To their great Lord. ('At a Solemn Music', lines 19–22)

Figuratively speaking, Adam's disobedience put his descendants out of tune with the universe so that they could no longer hear the music of the spheres. When they were divinely inspired, however, music and poetry could restore that harmony and resolve the dissonance between man and nature.

In order to perform this redemptive function, it followed, the poet had to be 'himself a true poem, that is, a composition and pattern of the best and honourablest things; not presuming to sing high praises of heroic men or famous cities unless he have in himself the experience and practice of that which is praise-worthy' (*An Apology against a Pamphlet*, 1642). And indeed, Milton's whole life was an attempt to realize that ambition, a long and arduous preparation for the great work he felt he had it in him to produce. He was perhaps the first poet in our language to whom the writing of poetry was a real vocation to which everything else was subordinate.

But although it is possible to identify discrete instances of Puritan and humanist elements, in most of Milton's writings the two ideologies coexist, albeit somewhat uneasily at times, as they do in his prose tract *On Education* (1644), where he declares that 'the end, then, of learning is to repair the ruins of our first parents by regaining to know God aright ... as we may the nearest by possessing our souls of true virtue, which, being united to the heavenly grace of faith, makes up the highest perfection'. The first part of the sentence is a ringing declaration of the humanist belief in the redemptive capacity of education; the final phrase, on the contrary, affirms the Puritan insistence on the saving power of faith conferred by grace. Just how the two forces can be 'united' is left unexplained.

A rather more complex example of this tension can be found in Milton's first major work to appear in print, 'Comus' (1637), an elaborate theatrical spectacle featuring music and dance as well as dialogue, written to celebrate the Earl of Bridgewater's appointment as Lord President of Wales. The entire action of this brief entertainment seems designed to illustrate, and perhaps even resolve, the ideological conflict between the Puritan emphasis on the indispensable role of divine grace and the humanist confidence in the efficacy of individual human effort. When the Lady, who has been imprisoned by the evil enchanter Comus in his palace, has been liberated and restored to her parents, the Attendant Spirit, who has assisted in her release, concludes the masque with the following tribute to virtue:

> She can teach ye how to climb
> Higher than the sphery chime;
> Or, if virtue feeble were,
> Heaven itself would stoop to her. (lines 1020–3)

The first two of these lines sound like an endorsement of the humanist belief in the redemptive function of education, as embodied in the figure of the Attendant Spirit (played by Henry Lawes, the family's music tutor) who has taught the Lady's brothers how to save her from Comus's clutches. The last two lines, however, raise the possibility that, as the Puritans held, frail human beings are incapable of acting virtuously without the assistance of heavenly grace, embodied in the figure of the water goddess Sabrina who alone was able to release the Lady from Comus's spell. The situation is complicated, however, by the fact that it is the Attendant Spirit, not Sabrina, who 'stoops' (line 1023) from Heaven 'by quick command from Sovran Jove' (41) to assist those 'favoured of high Jove' (78). Milton's point seems to be that just as his own tutor, Thomas Young, was one of those 'whom God himself sent, who bring you glad tidings from the skies, who teach you what way, when men are dust, *leads them to the stars*'

('Elegia IV', lines 92–4, my italics), so the Attendant Spirit in the masque is simultaneously a representative of humanist education *and* a vehicle of divine grace.

Impersonality/self-expression

The same problem and perhaps the same solution are evident in the second major dichotomy in Milton's writings: the conflicting stances he adopted as a poet. In several of his poems, from the 'Nativity Ode' to *Paradise Regained*, Milton made use of the well-worn classical convention of the Muse, according to which the poet is not speaking in his own person at all but simply reciting the words dictated to him by a supernatural being. The proem to the 'Nativity Ode', for instance, informs us that the 'voice' (line 27) that welcomes the Christ-child and the 'humble ode' (24) with which it celebrates his birth both belong not to Milton but to the 'Heavenly Muse' (15), singing in concert with the 'angel choir' (27). And indeed the rest of the poem contains not a single 'I', 'me', or 'my' in its entire thirty-one stanzas. The poet has effectively erased himself from his own poem. And in the prologue to Book IX of *Paradise Lost* Milton again portrays himself as the Muse's secretary, recording the utterances of:

> my celestial patroness, who deigns
> Her nightly visitation unimplored
> And dictates to me slumbering. (IX. 21–3)

If we take such statements seriously, as Milton certainly intended us to, they imply that we should read such poems as the 'Nativity Ode' and *Paradise Lost* as essentially impersonal, selfless works of art rather than autobiographical expressions of his own individuality.

But whatever else he may have been, Milton was a man endowed with an extremely strong and forceful personality, and as a result he found it difficult to remain completely detached from his poems for very long. In the companion piece to the 'Nativity Ode' we consequently find him vigorously asserting his authorial presence in the very opening stanza:

> For now to sorrow must *I* tune *my* song,
> And set *my* Harp to notes of saddest woe.
> ('The Passion', lines 8–9, my italics)

In vivid contrast to the impersonality of the 'Nativity Ode', Milton's treatment of Christ's passion is so self-referential – one stanza contains no fewer than six first-person pronouns – that we can scarcely glimpse its ostensible subject through the veil of the poet's own 'woe' (line 32).

In his later poems, the Puritan inclination to attribute his creative powers to divine grace and the humanist urge to take personal responsibility for his works often contend with each other within a single text. In the headnote to 'Lycidas', for example, we are told that the ensuing lament for Edward King is a 'monody' spoken by the 'author'. But although the elegy begins as if it were a species of personal monologue delivered by Milton himself in the dramatic present, by the fifteenth line 'the sisters of the sacred well' are invited to take over the poem. Within another four lines, however, the 'author' resumes control of the text and remains in charge of it until line 76, when the god of poetry unexpectedly interrupts the proceedings:

> 'But not the praise'
> Phoebus replied, and touched my trembling ears.
> 'Fame is no plant that grows on mortal soil,
> Nor in the glistering foil
> Set off to the world.' (lines 76–80)

Phoebus's intervention momentarily deprives the poet of his authorial function; he heard these words, but he did not compose them. And the same thing happens when the 'pilot of the Galilean lake' (line 109) appears on the scene to address not the poet, as Phoebus had done, but the dead Lycidas: 'How well could I have spared for thee, young swain' (113). Milton has virtually disappeared from his own poem. What began as a monody, a song uttered by a single voice, is beginning to turn into a drama. When St Peter has finished his attack on hireling shepherds, the speaker once again regains his authorial control, but not for long. At line 186 he is dismissed from the poem for good:

> Thus sang the uncouth swain to the oaks and rills,
> While the still Morn went out with sandals grey;
> He touched the tender stops of various quills,
> With eager thought warbling his Doric lay. (lines 186–9)

The historical 'author', John Milton, bewailing a 'learned friend', has become a fictional 'swain', and a new author begins what is essentially a new poem in a new verse-form (*ottava rima*). The unidentified voice which utters the final eight lines of 'Lycidas' belongs to a speaker we have never heard before, a speaker who seems to come from the same world as the 'sisters of the sacred well' (line 15) and Phoebus Apollo, the world of the heavenly muse. Just as the humanist educator turned out to be an emissary of divine grace in 'Comus', so the mournful 'author' of 'Lycidas' is transformed into a mere character in a new speaker's joyful narrative.

Revolutionary/conservative

Finally, the fundamentally dichotomous nature of Milton's poetry is reflected in the fact that although Milton was a revolutionary in religious and political terms, in literary terms he was one of the most conservative poets to write in our language. To begin with the revolutionary component in his work, when the social, religious, and political tensions between Charles I and Parliament finally exploded in the English Civil War that began in 1642, Milton was unequivocally and vociferously on the side of the rebels, and in fact he devoted most of his adult life from that point on until 1660 to supporting the republican cause in print, producing a vast body of polemical prose pamphlets on the burning issues of the day – the reform of the English church (*Of Reformation*, 1641, and *The Reason of Church Government*, 1642), the divorce laws (*The Doctrine and Discipline of Divorce*, 1643, and *Tetrachordon*, 1645), the freedom of the press (*Areopagitica*, 1644), the execution of Charles I (*The Tenure of Kings and Magistrates*, 1649), and the nature of a free republic (*The Ready and Easy Way to Establish a Free Commonwealth*, 1660). Indeed, of all the major English poets, Milton was by far the most deeply involved in the political and religious controversies of his time. As a reward for his services to the revolutionary cause, perhaps, in 1649 he was appointed as Secretary for Foreign Tongues, an important position in Oliver Cromwell's administration, and he continued to serve the republican government even after he became totally blind in 1652. Not surprisingly, therefore, the restoration of the monarchy in 1660 came as a tremendous blow to all his political hopes. The 'good old cause' to which he had devoted most of his mature years had come to nothing. He only narrowly escaped execution by the royal authorities in 1660, and he retired, blind and embittered, to turn all his energies to his first love, poetry. Like Dante's *Divine Comedy*, the three great works of Milton's old age, *Paradise Lost*, *Paradise Regained*, and *Samson Agonistes*, are the creations of a disillusioned political outcast.

So far as the conservative element in Milton is concerned, the first thing to notice here is the fact that almost all Milton's poems are written in a traditional genre. The 'Nativity Ode' is a Pindaric ode, 'Comus' is a court masque, 'Lycidas' is a pastoral elegy, *Paradise Lost* is a Virgilian epic, and *Samson Agonistes* is a Greek tragedy. Established forms like these are invariably characterized by a clearly defined set of literary conventions which an educated reader would expect to be observed. In a pastoral elegy like 'Lycidas', for instance, he would expect an idealized rural setting, a shepherd-poet mourning one of his companions, a procession of classical or rustic deities, and an allegorical subtext. In an epic like *Paradise Lost* he would anticipate a twelve-book structure modelled on Virgil's *Aeneid* (*Paradise Lost* was originally published in a ten-book version in 1667, but republished in twelve books in 1674, the year of Milton's death), a lofty and dignified style sprinkled with elaborate epic similes, a hero cast in the mould of Achilles or Aeneas, a story that begins *in medias res*, 'in the middle of things', recalling the first half in lengthy flashbacks, and an elaborate mechanism of divine beings overseeing and sometimes intervening in the affairs of the human characters.

Now generic structures such as these are clearly far more restrictive than a mere verse-form like the sonnet, where the only conventions are technical: the number of feet per line, the number of lines per sonnet, the pattern of the rhymes, and so on. For, as the brief account I have given of the characteristics of the pastoral elegy and the epic may suggest, traditional genres prescribe their own plot structure, their own style, and their own protagonist. Their conventions form, as it were, a distinctive and rigid mechanism within which the poet must work, a whole series of rules and regulations which the poet must obey if his poem is to be recognized as belonging to that particular genre.

At first sight, therefore, it is very strange to find a revolutionary champion of individual liberty writing most of his major works in long-established literary genres. A man who enthusiastically advocated the overthrow of the monarchy and the abolition of the episcopal structure of the church because they both infringed upon the freedom of the individual would not, we might suspect, have consented very easily to the equally authoritarian demands of traditional literary forms.[3]

And, as a matter of fact, Milton did not consent easily. When we look closely at any of his poems we can detect, I believe, a profound challenge to the form in which he is writing, a challenge so strong that on many occasions it comes close to bursting the seams of the convention altogether. It is this intense and lifelong struggle that gives Milton's poetry its extraordinary dynamism. Reading it, one has the constant sense of two powerful but opposing forces scarcely held in equilibrium, of a tremendously strong and rebellious personality striving against the limitations of established restrictions but never quite overcoming them, straining the traditional rules almost to the breaking point, but never actually shattering them.

For example, as Milton's contemporary, the poet and critic John Dryden, was the first to notice, without ever ceasing to be an epic, *Paradise Lost* is totally unlike any other epic ever written. Milton could only be said to have written a traditional epic, Dryden asserted, 'if the devil had not been his hero instead of Adam'. The idea that Satan is the poem's real hero was subsequently taken up, albeit for emotional and ideological reasons rather than formal ones, first by the English Romantic poets, Shelley and Blake, and then by modern literary critics. To take just one instance, the American poet Robert Lowell declared: 'I do not understand Milton's intention. Who or what is his Satan? He is not ultimate evil, though in Milton's myth he is the origin of human ill ... He is no devil, but a cosmic rebellious earl of Northumberland, Harry Hotspur with an intelligence and iron restraint. He is almost early American, the cruel, unconquerable spirit of freedom.'[4]

The reason for the heroic quality of the poem's villain is to be found, I would suggest, in Milton's evolving attitude towards the epic genre itself. From his earliest days as a student at Cambridge University, he seems to have intended to write an epic poem based on Homer's *Iliad* or *Odyssey*. In an academic exercise which he wrote at the age of nineteen, he declared his wish to use the English language to sing:

> of kings and queens and heroes old,
> Such as the wise Demodocus once told
> In solemn songs at King Alcinous' feast,
> While sad Ulysses' soul and all the rest
> Are held with his melodious harmony
> In willing chains and sweet captivity.
>
> ('Vacation Exercise', lines 47–52)

Over the course of the next eleven years, however, the desire to write a classical epic dealing with classical themes appears to have given way to the wish to produce a patriotic English epic, modelled on Spenser's *Faerie Queene*, involving King Arthur and the knights of the round table. His great ambition, he declared in 1638, was to celebrate 'the kings of my native land, and Arthur waging war even under the earth ... or tell of the great-hearted heroes of the Table made invincible by their fellowship' ('Mansus', lines 78–83; see also 'Epitaphium Damonis', lines 161–8).

Why, then, did Milton abandon this patriotic topic for a biblical story when he finally came to write his epic about twenty years later? First, it seems probable that his researches in British history had revealed that there was little or no factual basis for the story of King Arthur and the Knights of the Round Table. Arthur's deeds, Milton wrote in his *History of Britain* (1670), 'were more renowned in songs and romances than in true stories'. More importantly, when he began serious work on *Paradise Lost* Milton was in no mood to write a patriotic tribute to the kings of his native land or the glories of England, for it was becoming increasingly clear that the republican government to which he had dedicated some of the most productive years of his life was about to collapse, as it did shortly after. Small wonder that the great national epic was never written.

What is more, Milton may also have come to realize that the old heroic ideals of magnificent defiance and combat against overwhelming odds exemplified by characters like Homer's Achilles were not only utterly useless, but also the main obstacle that lay between man and the Christian life as he conceived it. For epic values celebrated conflict rather than harmony, pride rather than humility, the glorification of the individual rather than the submission of the individual to God. Hence the violent attack on earlier epics which Milton delivers in the prologue to Book IX of *Paradise Lost*. To describe the Fall of Man, he writes, is a

sad task, yet argument
Not less but more heroic than the wrath
Of stern Achilles on his foe pursued
Thrice fugitive about Troy wall, or rage
Of Turnus for Lavinia disespoused,
Or Neptune's ire or Juno's, that so long
Perplexed the Greek and Cytherea's son.

He is, he goes on,

Not sedulous by nature to indite
Wars, hitherto the only argument
Heroic deemed, ...
... the better fortitude
Of patience and heroic martyrdom
Unsung. (IX. 13–33)

The whole basis of epic is being condemned here. 'That which justly gives heroic name / To person or to poem' (IX. 40–1), Milton asserts, is not celebrated at all in the epics of classical antiquity or in their successors. He has finally come face to face with the fact that in the kind of universe in which Christianity had believed for the previous thousand years or so, the kind of universe described in works like Dante's *Divine Comedy*, the epic hero with his individualism, his dedication to glory, his idealization of military prowess, is in effect a villain. For the ordered hierarchical universe which Milton posits in *Paradise Lost*, and which the Christian church had believed in until the Renaissance, demands that each creature submit its own will to that of its creator and remain satisfied with its predestined place in the natural hierarchy of things. Within such a universe true freedom lies in submission to the divine will rather than in the pursuit of personal honour or glory.

As a result, *Paradise Lost* is fundamentally an anti-heroic poem, an anti-epic in which Milton deliberately sets out to subvert the values associated with the epic tradition from within the epic form itself. Ironically, the instrument he uses to accomplish this purpose is the very figure whom Dryden and his successors identified as the poem's hero: Satan. To begin with, in Books I and II, when we first meet him, the devil embodies precisely those qualities we would normally associate with a great epic hero. The tone is immediately set in his opening speech to Beelzebub:

> What though the field be lost?
> All is not lost. The unconquerable will,
> And study of revenge, immortal hate,
> And courage never to submit or yield
> And what is else not to be overcome? (I. 105–9)

This is the very archetype of heroic defiance, Achilles, Odysseus, Hector, Aeneas, all rolled into one. Nor does Satan merely talk like an epic hero. He looks like one as well:

> He above the rest
> In shape and gesture proudly eminent
> Stood like a tower. His form had yet not lost
> All her original brightness ... But his face
> Deep scars of thunder had entrencht, and care
> Sat on his faded cheek, but under brows
> Of dauntless courage and considerate pride,
> Waiting revenge. (I. 589–604)

And not merely does Satan look and sound like an epic hero. He is treated like one by his followers, and still more significantly by Milton himself. Like every epic, that is to say, *Paradise Lost* is characterized by the frequent appearance of elaborate epic similes, but it is unusual in that the vast majority of them are applied to Satan and his colleagues in Hell.

The constant application of this device to the devil's party reinforces the impression that in these early books at least, Milton consciously intended us to see in Satan the perpetuation of the heroic tradition of classical epic. There is solid ground, then, for the critical insistence from Dryden onwards that Satan is presented as a magnificent and outwardly impressive figure in the early books of the poem. What we are chiefly made to see and feel in the first two books, declares one critic, are not malice and depravity but 'fortitude in adversity, endurance, a certain splendid recklessness, remarkable powers of rising to an occasion, extraordinary powers of leadership, and striking intelligence in meeting difficulties that are novel and could seem overwhelming. What we feel most of all, I suppose, is his refusal to give in, just that.'[5]

Why, then, does Milton treat Satan so heroically in the opening books of the poem? In my view, it is a brilliantly executed tactic on Milton's part, a deliberate feint, an all too successful attempt to lead us, temporarily at least, up the garden path. In the first two books we are deliberately encouraged by Milton to identify Satan as the poem's hero so that our feelings can then be manipulated all the more effectively throughout the rest of the story. Coming to an epic poem, after all, we are naturally predisposed to expect an epic hero possessing certain qualities, so Milton gives us one with a vengeance: a hero who is engaged in fighting not just against heavy odds but against insuperable ones, a hero whose quarrel is not over the abduction of a woman or the conquest of a kingdom but about who should govern the universe, a hero whose revenge encompasses not the destruction of a person or even of a city but the damnation of the entire human race.

Moreover, a well-educated seventeenth-century reader, who had studied Virgil's *Aeneid* intensively at school, might have been even more tempted than we are to see Satan as an epic hero in the opening books. For the basic pattern of events in *Paradise Lost* parallels exactly those at the beginning of Virgil's epic. Just as Aeneas and his companions have been cast out of Troy with fire and slaughter, so Satan and his angels have been ejected from Heaven. Just as Aeneas and his companions find themselves swept up on the shore of an alien country, so Satan and his angels wake up on the shore of a fiery lake in Hell, and just as Aeneas and his companions eventually go on to found a new and greater empire in Rome, so Satan and his angels aspire to colonize the earth.

So when, during the course of the remainder of the poem, Milton shows the devil's heroic pose to be an impossible and finally a ludicrous one, the fact that we have responded positively to that pose makes its gradual deflation doubly effective. We are made to realize that we ourselves have been, in a sense, taken in by Satan, just as the sailor is deceived into mooring his frail craft to a whale in the poem's first epic simile:

> Him haply slumb'ring on the Norway foam
> The pilot of some small night-foundered skiff,
> Deeming some island, oft, as seamen tell,
> With fixed anchor in his scaly rind
> Moors by his side under the lee, while night
> Invests the sea, and wished morn delays;
> So stretched out huge in length the Arch-Fiend lay
> Chained on the burning lake. (I. 203–10)

Just as the sailor will be drowned when the whale inevitably dives back down into the depths, so we will be forced to recognize that the figure we took to be hero of the epic is in fact the most corrupt and destructive force in the poem.

Not that Milton does not give us warnings. In fact he continually offers us hints, including the above simile, that we should not take everything we see and hear at face value. So immediately after Satan's rousing first speech, the narrator comments in words that echo Virgil's description of Aeneas's initial address to his followers in Book I of the *Aeneid*:

> So spake the apostate angel, though in pain,
> Vaunting aloud but rackt with deep despair. (I. 125–6)

What is more, he puts into his hero's mouth, even in the most impressive speeches, rhetorical language whose self-contradictions and falsifications are all too apparent once we go back and analyse it. Indeed, Satan speaks some of the worst poetry in *Paradise Lost*, empty bombastic noise – it is no accident that Milton's detractors quote from Satan's speeches so often when they want to illustrate the alleged grandiloquence of his poetry. But on a first reading, we tend, like the fallen angels, to be swept along on the magnificent stream of sound without stopping to scrutinize its content too closely.

Then we come to the all-important moment at the beginning of Book IV when we meet Satan alone for the first time. Now that he has no audience to impress, no stricken followers to encourage, the devil reveals himself in his true agony, and the deep despair of which Milton gave us hints in the opening books comes out into the open:

> Which way should I fly
> Infinite wrath and infinite despair?
> Which way I fly is hell. Myself am hell.
> And in the lowest deep a lower deep
> Still threatening to devour me opens wide,
> To which the hell I suffer seems a Heaven.
> O then at last relent. Is there no place
> Left for repentance, none for pardon left?
> None left but by submission, and that word
> Disdain forbids me, and my dread of shame
> Among the spirits beneath, whom I seduced
> With other promises and other vaunts
> Than to submit. (IV. 73–85)

The heroic mask has fallen away, and underneath it we are shown the inglorious pettiness, the desperate ironies, and the whole sham of the Satanic posture. The hollow pretence in which he has indulged himself in the opening books collapses before our very eyes, and we see the real Satan for the first time. According to medieval poets and artists who illustrated the story, Satan and his followers changed from angels to demons even as they fell. Milton's point seems to be that the floor of Hell does not mark the limit of Satan's descent. His pictorial and physical fall is followed by a still heavier one in the Hell within him.

By the time we reach Book IX, indeed, the proud warrior who had dared to defy all the powers of Heaven in Books V and VI has degenerated into a furtive intruder, slipping into Eden under cover of darkness and disguising himself in the form of a serpent. And his fall continues in Book X in spite of his attempt to mimic an epic hero as he addresses his expectant followers after his return to Hell:

> Long were to tell
> What I have done, what suffered, with what pain
> Voyaged th'unreal, vast, unbounded deep
> Of horrible confusion. (X. 469–72)

He sounds for all the world like a weary Aeneas relating his 'adventure hard' (line 468) to Dido and her court. But the triumphant homecoming that he has stage-managed so carefully proves to be a fiasco as his words are greeted not with the 'high applause' (505) he is expecting but a 'dismal universal hiss, the sound / Of public scorn' (508–9). Satanic epic has turned into farce.

Satan, then, provides a vivid negative image of the epic values Milton is attempting to subvert in *Paradise Lost*. The question is, who embodies the positive values with which he hopes to replace them? Who demonstrates 'the better fortitude / Of patience and heroic martyrdom' (IX. 31–2)? Not the Son, certainly, who appears principally in the role of an invincible warrior 'in celestial panoply all armed' (VI. 760) carrying 'ten thousand thunders' (VI. 836) in his right hand and driving the rebel angels 'pursued / With terrors and with furies to the bounds / And crystal wall of Heav'n' (VI. 858–60). Not Adam and Eve either, for although they may seek a kind of martyrdom during their reconciliation in Book X (see lines 933–6, 952–7), they never achieve it.

It was the absence of a figure exemplifying 'that which justly gives heroic name / To person or to poem' (IX. 40–1) in *Paradise Lost* that may well have stimulated Milton to produce a sequel focusing on the ultimate paradigm of Christian heroism, Christ himself. This, in turn, might explain why Milton chose as the subject of *Paradise Regained* Christ's patient rejection of the devil's temptations in the wilderness. For the central temptation in the poem, the temptation of the kingdoms, is in essence a temptation to engage in precisely the kind of heroism that Milton had rejected in *Paradise Lost*. Christ confesses in Book I that in his youth:

> Victorious deeds
> Flamed in my heart, heroic acts, one while
> To rescue Israel from the Roman yoke (I. 215–17)

and it is to this boyhood ambition that Satan appeals in Book III when he invokes the memory of the great heroes of classical antiquity:

> Thy years are ripe, and over-ripe; the son
> Of Macedonian Philip had ere these
> Won Asia and the throne of Cyrus held
> At his dispose, young Scipio had brought down
> The Carthaginian pride. (III. 31–5)

But Christ will have none of it. 'They err', he declares, 'who count it glorious to subdue / By conquest far and wide, to overrun / Large countries, and in field great battles win, / great cities by assault' (III. 71–4). His model is Job, the biblical exemplar of 'saintly patience' (III. 93), rather than men like Achilles and Aeneas who pursued only glory and empire. The moral of *Paradise Regained* is the same as the lesson Patience teaches the rebellious poet in the last line of 'Sonnet XVI': 'They also serve who only stand and wait.'

The final vision

An even more emphatic statement of this theme is to be found in Milton's biblical drama, *Samson Agonistes*. Once again, the key to understanding the text is the genre in which Milton chose to write it. For in another act of cultural fusion, Milton superimposed on the Old Testament story of Samson in the Book of Judges the instantly recognizable structure of a Greek tragedy. Indeed, even before he read a single word of the play itself, a well-educated seventeenth-century reader would have realized just from the title that Milton was combining Hebraic subject-matter and Hellenic form, for while *Samson* is, of course, a Hebrew name, *Agonistes* derives from the Greek word for an athletic contest, *agon*. An *agonist* was a competitor, a contestant. (Milton makes it clear in his preface to the play that it was not written for performance. As the title-page states, *Samson Agonistes* is a 'dramatic poem' rather than a poetic drama. Recent attempts to stage it have met with varying degrees of success.)

The actual drama, moreover, contains numerous features associated with Greek tragedy. The Chorus, for example, is obviously modelled on the chorus in such plays as Sophocles's *Oedipus the King*, the detonation of the catastrophe off-stage so that it has to be reported by a messenger is common to both plays, and the Aristotelian notion of tragic catharsis or purgation receives unforgettable expression in the play's final lines. Still more significantly, the plot structure of *Samson Agonistes* conforms precisely to that of Sophocles's *Oedipus the King*. Whereas the English dramatic tradition, the tradition of Marlowe, Shakespeare, and Jonson, was essentially linear, tracing the progress of the story in chronological order from beginning to end, in *Oedipus the King* Sophocles treated only the final stages of the story, recounting the earlier events in the characters' recollections. In other words, the Sophoclean plot structure corresponds to the typical fifth act of a Shakespearean play. It consists of one long denouement.

So why did Milton decide to use this structure rather than the native English model? Because, I would suggest, the Sophoclean dramatic structure allowed him to concentrate exclusively on the final phase of Samson's life, in which he becomes a model of the 'patience and heroic martyrdom' that Milton believed to constitute true heroism, and still more to the point it also allowed him to eliminate all those episodes earlier in Samson's life which displayed the old-fashioned concept of heroic action that Milton hoped to subvert. For in the original story in the Book of Judges, Samson appears to be little more than a violent strongman who commits a whole series of atrocities before pulling down the temple on the heads of the Philistines. In *Samson Agonistes*, on the contrary, Milton does not mention any of these atrocities. As one critic puts it, 'to pass from the Book of Judges to Milton's drama is like moving into another world – certainly another and a nobler sphere. Traces of barbarism, murder, and torture are gone ... and the conceited ruffian of the Book of Judges is now revealed to us as an altered and penitent man.'[6] The Sophoclean structure, in other words, provided Milton with the precise dramatic focus he needed.

There is, however, one crucial aspect in which Milton appears to have violated the plot structure of his Sophoclean model. According to Aristotle's *Poetics*, which Milton alludes to over and over again in his preface to *Samson Agonistes*, a good plot, such as that of *Oedipus the King*, should consist of a causal sequence of interconnected events, with one action leading inevitably to another until we reach the final catastrophe. As Aristotle put it, a well-made play consists of a beginning, a middle, and an end. But if we try to apply this principle to *Samson Agonistes* we very soon discover that it simply does not fit. There seems to be no causal relationship whatsoever between the various events that precede the destruction of the temple. In Samuel Johnson's words, 'the poem has a beginning and an end, but it must be allowed to lack a middle, since nothing passes between the first act and the last that either hastens or delays the death of Samson'. In particular, a more recent scholar has noted, 'there is a dramatic improbabililty about Samson's final regeneration. His sudden resolution, due to an inner prompting, to obey after all the lords' summons, is too abrupt to be convincing. It seems to be taken too lightly.'[7] We get the impression that Samson and his author had apparently come to a dead end when God whispered the solution in their ears. Compared with the plot of Sophocles's *Oedipus the King*, the plot of *Samson Agonistes* seems on the face of it to be disjointed and episodic.

How, then, can the play be defended against Johnson's strictures? How is the middle of *Samson Agonistes* related to its beginning and its end? We may find the starting point for an answer in the passage from Aristotle's *Poetics* I alluded to earlier. The basis of Aristotle's definition of a tragic plot is the 'law of probability or necessity', as Aristotle called it, the law which in his view constituted both the unifying principle of the physical universe and the indispensable essence of a dramatic plot. For Aristotle, as for most Greek writers, the universe was a rational, orderly system of law accessible to human reason. But for Renaissance Protestants like Milton, on the contrary, the universe was an impenetrable mystery presided over by an inscrutable deity whose ways were above human understanding. The whole point of Milton's drama, therefore, is that human history is governed not by the laws of nature but by the eternal providence of God. *Samson Agonistes* was composed 'after the antient manner' of Greek tragedy for precisely the same reason that *Paradise Lost* was modelled on the classical epic: to challenge and subvert the ideology of its generic prototype. It is, in fact, what I would call an anti-tragedy. Just as *Paradise Regained* offers a revolutionary new definition of heroic virtue, so *Samson Agonistes* confutes the fundamental principle of classical tragedy as Aristotle had defined it. The events of Milton's play are unified not by the law of probability or necessity but, in the words of one critic, by 'the sovereignty of providence, undistracted by man's errors and deserts, moving invincibly towards the objective proposed'[8].

Far from being a dramatic flaw, then, the *dis*connection between Samson's initial dilemma and his ultimate victory is absolutely critical to Milton's meaning. The first phase of Samson's history is over when we first meet him; his attempts to liberate his people have ended in failure and betrayal. The second phase, which will culminate in the destruction of the temple, is just starting as he leaves the stage with the Officer. Between them there stretches neither an interlinked chain of cause and effect of the kind that Aristotle envisioned, nor a gradual ascent from despair to redemption of the kind that some modern critics have posited, but a prolonged moment of hiatus, a period of psychological and spiritual suspension at the end of which the direction of Samson's life will be utterly transformed. Up to the moment at which Samson decides to go to the temple after all, the play is an extended intermission between the first and last acts of his personal drama, during the course of which Samson's thoughts and feelings reproduce the circular motion of his labour at the mill.

Then suddenly, unexpectedly, undeservedly, he experiences the 'rouzing motions' (line 1382) that will lead him to his triumphant act of destruction in the temple. This, surely, is the kind of deus ex machina to which Aristotle objected so strongly in the *Poetics*, for nothing that has happened in the play so far serves to bring about God's intervention at precisely this point of the action, nothing Samson has done or said or felt has merited the internal illumination that allows him to realize that God wants him to obey the Officer's instructions after all. This is not to say, however, that Samson plays no role whatsoever in his own rehabilitation. Unlike Calvin, Milton did not believe in the doctrine of irresistible grace. As he had made clear in *Paradise Lost*, he believed rather that God's 'Prevenient Grace' (XI. 3) had restored to every descendant of Adam and Eve the ability to exercise a strictly limited but nevertheless real degree of free will. Samson could choose, therefore, whether or not to cooperate with divine grace; he could have ignored or disobeyed the divinely inspired 'motions' of his spirit. His heroism consists not in his rejection of the proposals presented by his visitors, as some critics have suggested, but in his acceptance of God's 'intimate impulse' (line 223) even though it had led to defeat and humiliation in the past. God may have been 'favouring and assisting to the end' (1720), as Manoa insists, but Samson's victory over the Philistines was ultimately the product of his own freely made decision.

The point that Milton thus seems to be making is an extremely radical one, namely that it is God's will, and God's will alone, that determines whether a particular action or decision is right or wrong, good or evil. There is no such thing, the play seems to imply, as an intrinsically good or evil deed. As in *Paradise Lost*, fortitude, loyalty, compassion, and all the other virtues are only virtuous if they are exercised in conformity with God's will. If they are not, then they are vices. And by the same token, cowardice, treachery, cruelty, deceit, and all the other vices are only wicked if they are exercised in opposition to God's will. If they are not, they may under some circumstances be virtuous. We simply cannot assume that certain qualities and certain actions are always either good or evil. What matters is whether they are deployed in the service of God or his adversary.

In the light of recent events, many readers will surely find this view utterly repellent. In particular, they will find it difficult to share the Chorus's pleasure in the wholesale destruction of the Philistines. Milton and his revolutionary contemporaries, however, were rather less scrupulous about destroying their enemies than a contemporary reader living in the aftermath of Hiroshima and 9/11 is likely to be. So however offensive the slaughter of the Philistines might be to our modern sensibilities, we should not allow our moral revulsion to blind us to the fact that the man who applauded

Cromwell's massacres in Ireland would have been unlikely to lose any sleep over Samson's massacre of 'his country's tyrants' (*Defence of the People of England*, 1651). In the lifelong contest between Milton the humanist conservative and Milton the Puritan revolutionary, it was the revolutionary who ultimately proved to be the stronger.

NOTES

1 See *Paradise Lost* X. 629–37, 'L'Allegro', lines 136–49, 'A Masque Presented at Ludlow Castle', lines 593–9, *Paradise Lost* V. 185–99, and 'On the University Carrier II', lines 7–14, respectively.

2 E. M. W. Tillyard, *Milton*, rev. edn (New York: Collier Books, 1967).

3 The use of traditional genres, of course, was virtually universal among poets of the sixteenth and seventeenth centuries, however revolutionary their religious and political beliefs may have been. In Milton's case, however, the practice seems to have been an acute source of conflict for most of his career, from 'Comus', with its implicit critique of the court masque, to *Samson Agonistes*, where the assumptions underlying classical tragedy are subverted by a vision of God as an inscrutable deus ex machina.

4 Robert Lowell, 'Epics', *New York Review* (21 February 1980), p. 3.

5 A. J. A. Waldock, *Paradise Lost and its Critics* (Cambridge: Cambridge University Press, 1947), p. 77. Waldock is responding to C. S. Lewis's characterization of Satan as a fool rather than a hero in *A Preface to 'Paradise Lost'* (London: Oxford University Press, 1942).

6 Chauncey B. Tinker, 'Samson Agonistes', in *Tragic Themes in Western Literature*, ed. Cleanth Brooks (New Haven: Yale University Press, 1955), pp. 64, 69.

7 Tillyard, *Milton*, p. 291.

8 G. A. Wilkes, 'The Interpretation of Samson Agonistes', *Huntington Library Quarterly* 26 (1963), 378.

SELECTED FURTHER READING

Editions

The Cambridge Milton for Schools and Colleges, ed. John Broadbent, Cambridge, Cambridge University Press, 1972–6

The Poems of John Milton, eds. John Carey and Alastair Fowler, New York, Longmans, Green, 1968

John Milton: Complete Poems and Major Prose, ed. Merritt Y. Hughes, New York, Odyssey Press, 1957

John Milton: The Complete Poems, ed. John Leonard, London, Penguin, 1999

Secondary works

Brown, Cedric, *John Milton's Aristocratic Entertainments*, Cambridge, Cambridge University Press, 1985

Burnett, Archie, *Milton's Style*, Harlow, Longman, 1981

Danielson, Dennis (ed.), *The Cambridge Companion to Milton*, rev. edn, Cambridge, Cambridge University Press, 1989

Empson, William, *Milton's God*, London, Chatto and Windus, 1961

Evans, J. Martin, *The Miltonic Moment*, Lexington, University of Kentucky Press, 1998

Fallon, Robert T., *Milton in Government*, University Park, Pennsylvania State University Press, 1993

Fish, Stanley E., *Surprised by Sin: The Reader in 'Paradise Lost'*, London and New York, Macmillan, 1967

Frye, Roland M., *Milton's Imagery and the Visual Arts*, Princeton, Princeton University Press, 1978

Hill, Christopher, *Milton and the English Revolution*, London and New York, Viking Press, 1977

Kerrigan, William, *The Sacred Complex: On the Psychogenesis of Paradise Lost*, Cambridge, MA, Harvard University Press, 1983

Lewalski, Barbara K., *The Life of John Milton*, Oxford, Blackwell, 2000

Milton's Brief Epic: The Genre, Meaning, and Art of Paradise Regained, Providence, RI, and London, Methuen, 1966

Lewis, C. S., *A Preface to 'Paradise Lost'*, London: Oxford University Press, 1942

Radzinowicz, Mary Ann, *Toward 'Samson Agonistes': The Growth of Milton's Mind*, Princeton, Princeton University Press, 1978

Ricks, Christopher, *Milton's Grand Style*, Oxford, Oxford University Press, 1963

Rumrich, John, *Milton Unbound: Controversy and Reinterpretation*, Cambridge and New York, Cambridge University Press, 1996

Turner, James G., *One Flesh: Paradisal Marriage and Sexual Relations in the Age of Milton*, Oxford, Oxford University Press, 1987

Waldock, A. J. A., *Paradise Lost and its Critics*, Cambridge, Cambridge University Press, 1947

9

NIGEL SMITH

Andrew Marvell

In 1673, the satirist Samuel Butler represented the poet, politician and prose controversialist Andrew Marvell thus:

> Being passionately in Love (you may allow him to be an *Allegorical Lover* at least) with old *Ioan* (not the *Chandlers*, but Mr. *Calvins* Widow) walks discontentedly by the side of the Lake *Lemane*, sighing to the Winds and calling upon the Woods; not forgetting to report his Mistresses name so often, till he teach all the *Eccho's* to repeat nothing but *Ioan*; now entertaining himself in his Solitude, with such *little* Sports, as *loving his Love with an I*, and then *loving his Love with an* O, and the like for the other Letters ... after he has carv'd his Mistresses Name with many *Love-knots* and *flourishes* in all the *Bushes* and *Brambles*; and interwoven those sacred Characters with many an *Enigmatical* Devise in *Posies* and *Garlands* of *Flowers*, lolling sometimes upon the Bank and sunning himself, and then on a sudden (varying his Postures with his Passion) raising himself up, and speaking all the fine things which Lovers us'd to do. His Spirits at last exhal'd with the heat of his Passion, swop, he falls asleep, and snores out the rest.[1]

Butler was attacking Marvell's own objections to Samuel Parker's high church ecclesiastical religious politics in his prose work *The Rehearsal Transpros'd* (1672), so the first part of the paragraph refers to Marvell's association with the Calvinist nonconformists, John Owen in particular (the 'old Ioan' – 'I' 'O' – of the passage), and he walks alongside Lake Geneva, Geneva being the home of Jean Calvin and his version of the Reformation.[2] But Butler also recognizes that Marvell was a love-poet who liked to cultivate his muse privately and with nature close at hand. Indeed, the landscape with the poet in it, resembling a Poussin painting, relates to the scenes in Marvell's 'The Garden', 'Upon Appleton House', or any of the Mower poems, and contains an echo of the 'echoing song' in 'To his Coy Mistress'. Then the poet sleeps, self-enclosed in his own fantasies.

Butler's statement is extremely unusual but very insightful. Very few indeed knew that Marvell was a poet. Only nine of his poems were published in print in his own lifetime, and of these only five carried his name. For this reason, the dating of most of his lyric verse is impossible to know with certainty. The circulation of his verse in manuscript was very restricted, although it was known by a significant number of poets.[3] His poetic reputation would be built after his death, and very slowly. His first collection of poems was published in 1681, three years after he died, and it was only in the later nineteenth century that his reputation as a significant poet would outstrip his fame as a politician and prose-writer. The poetry he produced for circulation in his own lifetime was written to praise his patrons. It was verse written while being a high-ranking civil servant, or someone on the way to being so. His poems were thus tokens in the economy of praise and deference, or tools of diplomatic exchange. He sought a career as a secretary and that is how he remained for most of his life, even after he became MP for Hull in 1659: an extremely well-qualified literary servant.

Such poetry was not written primarily to delight or to reflect extensively on its own construction. It was meant to serve the purpose of praise and occasionally to blame. To this extent, it followed the models set out in grammar-school precepts, classical literature being at the heart of the curriculum. Marvell's earliest known poem, written while an undergraduate at Cambridge, is a Latin imitation of Horace's Ode I. ii, with Horace's words changed round somewhat in order to meet the occasion, the birth of a royal daughter.

The discipline of following other poetry closely, altering it sometimes only slightly, was a method that Marvell developed over the course of his career. It is responsible for a sense of 'echo' observable on many levels of his verse, and particularly when the source poet's presence is felt by a discerning and knowledgeable reader. This quality also gives Marvell's prosody a distinctive precision. Although he imitated Donne, Herbert, and Milton, there is none of Donne's forthright, masculine bravado, no vigorous conversational line or fluid matching of concept with visual shapes that we find in Herbert, and none of Milton's muscular power and virtuoso experimentalism.[4] Marvell's line dwells on the very shape of the object it describes, while his stanza is a poetic embodiment of the action of that object. Which is to say that he succeeds in a total poetic imitation of and response to his subject. With Marvell you see the poetic subject on the page in refreshing, unfamiliar detail, and this has been likened to the effect of a Vermeer painting, where a familiar object is reborn in the viewer's apprehension by the arresting way in which it is painted. At the same time, Marvell's general avoidance of personal pronouns, especially the first-person 'I', has been seen as particularly responsible for his evasiveness, either denying connection with a sexual other or finding obvious partisan or national affinity. This is an effect that further casts poetic subjects in an unusual light.[5]

A good example would be 'On a Drop of Dew', where the poem falls into two mutually mirroring parts, one referring to a real dewdrop and the other its invisible analogue, the soul. The metre of the first half is almost always changing from line to line, with one exception, and in imitation of the very shape of the tiny water drop. The rhyme-scheme is equally various. By contrast, the groups of similar-length lines in the second half suggest the greater substance of the soul, just as the couplets at the end of each section imply clarity, resolution, and stasis, as opposed to the undulating movement in the opening parts of each section. The syntax of the first eighteen lines is extremely difficult, as Marvell imitates the integrity of the drop: the syntax appears to 'run round' the surface of the drop in an endless chain. The two halves of the poem interpenetrate: the dewdrop description never escaping from symbolic connotations and the soul rendered in pictorial vocabulary. This elaborate arrangement might be seen as a meditation on the nature of interpenetration itself, including the interpenetration of subject and object. Yet this itself is undermined by the impersonal nature of the speaker's voice, which never uses the first person, but which is itself undermined still further by the refined and fastidious feelings attributed to the dewdrop and the soul:

> See how the orient dew,
> Shed from the bosom of the morn
> Into the blowing roses,
> Yet careless of its mansion new;
> For the clear region where 'twas born
> Round in itself incloses:
> And in its little globe's extent,
> Frames as it can its native element.
> How it the purple flower does slight,
> Scarce touching where it lies,
> But gazing back upon the skies,
> Shines with a mournful light;
> Like its own tear,
> Because so long divided from the sphere.
> Restless it rolls and unsecure,
> Trembling lest it grow impure:
> Till the warm sun pity its pain,
> And to the skies exhale it back again.[6] (lines 1–18)

Marvell wrote poems with closer sources to English than the sacred Greek epigram usually thought to be the inspiration for this poem. None the less, that source and all the other poems that make a tradition of dew and tear poems are part of Marvell's 'repertoire of civilization' as T. S. Eliot understood it.[7]

These skills were deployed with enormous success in the different arena of praise poetry. 'An Horatian Ode upon Cromwell's Return from Ireland' has indeed been seen as the finest political poem in the language. The unusual pattern of alternating rhymed four-beat and three-beat couplets, with the delicate monosyllables of the second pair undercutting the first pair, is a singular achievement, inscribing self-reflection in the heart of the poem's structure, as if the poem had two distinct verse patterns. Many of the words chosen by Marvell have a wide semantic range. This, coupled with Latinate inversion in the word order, is responsible for the reserved, ambiguous, and ironic tone of the poem. We cannot tell whose side the poet is on, and in a way both Cromwell and Charles I are heroes, the former heroically, the latter tragically. When Cromwell 'urged his active star', was he in charge or was it the star (Providence, destiny, fate) doing the urging? We cannot easily tell. Such ambiguity is enhanced by grammatical openness: 'blast' (line 24) may be transitive or intransitive, Caesar's head subject or object; does victory crown Cromwell, or sit on his helmet (line 98)? Many verbs are conditional, and nouns and verbs could have at once a passive and active application; adjectives too can be nouns or adverbs (e.g. 'restless', line 9). Adverbs are frequently truncated (e.g. lines 31–2, 92, 101–2), and English versions of Latin idioms have the same effect (e.g.,'Nor', from Latin *nec*, for 'And not', lines 3, 61, 81, 111; 'what he may', from *qua licet*, line 87). Ellipses at lines 31–2, 92, and 101–2 complete the effect.

When Marvell fits the energy of epic imagery inside his tightly bound but loosely signifying prosodic machine the effect is electric:

So restless Cromwell could not cease
In the inglorious arts of peace,
  But through advent'rous war
  Urgèd his active star:

And like the three-forked lightning, first
Breaking the clouds where it was nursed,
  Did thorough his own side
  His fiery way divide.

(For 'tis all one to courage high,
The emulous or enemy;
  And with such, to enclose
  Is more than to oppose.) (lines 9–20)

However much Marvell may have let his remaining sympathies for Charles I and the royalists show through (he had been writing royalist verse only months before he wrote the 'Ode'), the poem by its very mould-breaking form becomes expressive of the new age taking shape as monarchy is left behind. To this extent, the poem is exploratory republican verse, feeling out the poetics of a poised situation brought about by the weakness of the old order and the strength of the new. Neither poetry nor anything else can hold this back. There is always a risk, so Marvell seems to imply, that the source of power (Cromwell) in the state will break free from his controllers (the Parliament):

> He to the Commons' feet presents
> A kingdom, for his first year's rents.
>   And, what he may, forbears
>   His fame, to make it theirs:
>
> And has his sword and spoils ungirt,
> To lay them at the public's skirt.
>   So when the falcon high
>   Falls heavy from the sky;
>
> She, having killed, no more does search,
> But on the next green bough to perch;
>   Where, when he first does lure,
>   The falc'ner has her sure. (lines 85–96)

Marvell has the ability to capture a historical moment as it appeared to contemporaries; to make poetry speak history dispassionately. Part of this was the consequence of his acute incorporation of Machiavellian political thought, the terms of which are in the poem. 'Industrious valour' is English for two key Machiavellian terms, *industria*, endless vigilance, and *virtù*, the power to overcome the stumbling blocks that *fortuna* puts in one's way. The openness of the vocabulary is thus matched by political theory's rewriting of the terms of statecraft. The poem ends 'The same arts that did gain / A pow'r must it maintain', meaning that in Machiavellian terms there is no difference between the arts of war and those of peace: Cromwell will need all of his strategic skill to survive and prosper in the peaceful future.

The significance of rhyme in 'An Horatian Ode' touches an issue that concerned Marvell not only in his later judgement of Milton and Dryden, but also in respect of his own verse. Rhyme itself becomes an echoing voice that speaks after the primary voice has spoken, and that is always present, a fraction of a second behind the lead voice. Rhyme might be regarded in this respect as a further mirror for the poet-maker. This quality has been associated with Marvell's extraordinary use of parenthesis ('the last great exploiter of brackets until the Romantic period'), and by many commentators with allusiveness.[8] They are usually figured in criticism as one kind of doubleness or another: a reversal, an instance of reflexivity or a 'self-inwoven device', even a 'boomerang' method.[9] Is there a further connection here not merely with the breaking down of boundaries between subject and object, 'I' and 'Thou', but also with the 'liberty' that John Creaser sees dramatized in the texture of the verse?[10] Such features include the combination of the highly disciplined (regular couplet rhymes, highly formed, regular stanzas) and the relatively liberal: frequent deviation from regular stress patterns, but never so much as to endanger the metrical shape of the whole. This is in contrast to harder taskmasters, like Milton, who in their epics make irregularity thematically functional.

These feats of imagery and prosody become more intricate in the two later Cromwell poems, in response in part to the increasingly complicated politics of the Cromwellian Protectorate. Much of the metaphorical, prosodic, and syntactic inventiveness of 'The First Anniversary of the Government under his Highness the Lord Protector' is devoted to the argumentative structure of the poem. Thus, while there are instances of verbal ambiguity, these are harnessed to the purpose of demonstrating the viability of the Protectorate, rather than left in the more suggestive manner of 'An Horatian Ode'. Most of the poem is notable for its clarity, and this quality is at its greatest in the passages that are related to the printed propaganda of the Commonwealth (e.g. lines 22ff.). The assured tone of the syntax (unlike that of the later Cromwell elegy) with sentence and clause breaks working confidently in and around the rhyming couplets helps to generate the poem's persuasiveness. Syntactic inversion, where it occurs, not only affects rhymes, but may also mimic the care necessary for the proper ordering of the Commonwealth (e.g. line 96), or produce an arresting effect in the reader's mind, so as to draw attention to a particular point of reason (e.g. lines 115–16, 201–2, 355).

The demonstrative rhetoric is framed by a series of powerful images that give the figure of Oliver Cromwell a dominant presence in the poem. The poem begins with the image of the sinking weight creating a maze of ripples in smooth waters: likewise, the brief tumult of a human life raises 'ripples' that are soon lost in the smooth flow of time. Cromwell transcends this limitation in order to confront the tempests of state: he 'raises' his head above malice and praise (line 399), as opposed to mere men who raise ripples when they sink in time. The poem ends with the picture of Cromwell as the angel of the Commonwealth troubling these stormy waters in order to calm them. The opening imagery of building and of stars returns in carefully deployed places later on (e.g. lines 245–8, 343). In another kind of juxtaposition, the demands upon the reader made by the musical and architectural images of construction are set against local instances of very obvious images, such as the burying of china-clay to bake it (lines 19–20). The most cryptic aspects of the poem concern the use of Old Testament prophecy. They are worked into the poem's language so deeply that they appear to be part of the historical certainty that the poem offers. Marvell creates the impression of a participatory government, the context being the summoning of the second Protectoral Parliament in September 1654:

> The common-wealth does through their centres all
> Draw the circumf'rence of the public wall;
> The crossest spirits here do take their part,
> Fast'ning the contignation which they thwart;
> And they, whose nature leads them to divide,
> Uphold, this one, and that the other side;
> But the most equal still sustain the height,
> And they as pillars keep the work upright;
> While the resistance of oppose̊d minds,
> The fabric as with arches stronger binds,
> Which on the basis of a senate free,
> Knit by the roof's protecting weight agree. (lines 87–98)

Not everyone agreed with this view: Edmund Waller wrote his panegyric on Cromwell as a riposte to Marvell's interpretation of Machiavelli.[11]

Marvell's habit of alluding to and refashioning in his own verse poetry that had recently appeared in print is not merely helpful with dating. It points to his interest in other poets, marked also by a series of poems on poets notable for their high quality and perceptiveness. There is no other poet who has so thoroughly assessed his own art against the achievements of other poets in his own poems. 'Flecknoe, an English Priest at Rome' (*c.*1646) is a humorously troubled look at the Jesuit poet Richard Flecknoe, whom Marvell met during his stay in Rome. Flecknoe is precisely the kind of poet Marvell might have become, especially if he had converted to Catholicism. Flecknoe's tiny room is presented as a coffin, and the decorations make Catholicism seem a religion of spiritual death. It is significant that Marvell alludes in this poem to Milton's great elegy 'Lycidas', where the theme of the poet's own destiny emerges from grief for the elegy's deceased subject. Marvell is supremely skilled at making sense of the similarities as well as the differences that the subject of the other poet produces. Much of Marvell's poem appears to be a riposte to Flecknoe's ideals, beliefs, behaviour, and poetry. Flecknoe's idealistic poetic sees music and poetry as a harmonious combination that reflects divine truth. If Flecknoe was interested in mock-heroic drollery as early as the time that Marvell met him, some of the poem's imagery could be seen as an appropriate mock-heroic response (e.g. lines 41–4), as well as an attack upon Flecknoe's notorious snobbery. His poverty and his ceaseless search for patronage are documented in his own poetry, the performance of which tortures Marvell's gentlemen listener: 'hideous verse … in dismal tone'.

The poem makes a series of obscure and abstruse references in the service of humour, but it does so through the voice of a supremely confident speaker: perhaps too confident by half. The rhyming couplets are executed with seeming ease and effortlessly combined with lively speech rhythms and conversational manners, which offer suspension, balance, and interruptive variety within the regular iambic pattern. As an early poem, Marvell offers what the reader is meant to take as a thoroughly virtuoso, precocious performance, over and against the awful grotesquery of Flecknoe's songs, and their tuneless performances by the youth in the poem. None the less, Flecknoe is made to stand out as an embodiment of a circumstance that all poets share: they must take from their environment and re-present it in their verse:

> But were he not in this black habit decked,
> This half-transparent man would soon reflect
> Each colour that he passed by; and be seen,
> As the chamelion, yellow, blue, or green. (lines 79–82)

If Flecknoe represents a poetic road not taken or one shunned, Marvell's hero-poet in 1648 was Richard Lovelace, the epitome of a Cavalier: urbane, well educated, romantic, loyally royalist, and a brilliant poet. Marvell's verse letter to Lovelace is a celebration of the by then lost world of pre-Civil War courtliness (albeit of literature associated with the town, London, the world of inns and theatres, and not the secluded world of the court): 'That candid age no other way could tell / To be ingenious, but by speaking well.' The Civil War has wrought a destruction of literary culture, in which journalism and controversial pamphlet wars have debased letters:

> These virtues now are banished out of town,
> Our civil wars have lost the civic crown.
> He highest builds who with most art destroys,
> And against others' fame his own employs. (lines 11–14)

Lovelace and his 'faultless' verse are the subject of Marvell's speaker's admiration, a quality that he shares in the poem's fiction with the women defenders of Lovelace. They think Marvell is one of the Puritan 'rout', but the speaker identifies with them. In so far as he is a poet (and the poem is a verse letter from one poet to another), it is the sight of Lovelace that is the object of inspiration: 'pain 'twould be to lose that sight'.

Behind Lovelace stands Ben Jonson, whose ghost speaks most of Marvell's verse satire 'Tom May's Death' (1650). And it is Jonson whom Marvell most regarded as poetic father figure, the consonance of diction between the two poets being evident, and Marvell admiring what he regarded as Jonson's ethical rectitude. This poem relies upon a series of parodic echoes, especially of Jonson mocking (sometimes gently, sometimes fiercely) May's poetic, historiographical, and polemical procedures. This is an inversion itself, since May was an early admirer of Jonson.

It was unconventional to have Jonson as opposed to a classical figure passing judgement in a Menippean satire, and because of this Jonson's authority is almost mocked (the parallel figures in Seneca's satire *Apocolocyntosis*, one of Marvell's models, are Hercules and Jupiter). At the same time, Jonson's political views are made exaggeratedly monarchical with the help of allusions to Dante (lines 17–18); Jonson's own earlier portrayal of Brutus and Cassius in *Sejanus* was as protectors of liberty, not the people's cheats.

In 'On Mr. Milton's *Paradise Lost*' (1674), Marvell again imitates Ben Jonson's prefatory poem to Thomas May's translation of Lucan and in doing so implies that Milton's poem was a Lucanic enterprise, a covert critique of empire in the name of republicanism, and a piece of resilient Stoicism, understood as resistance in retirement rather than a sacrifice of the cause. To this extent, Marvell is certainly being true to Jonson's poetic ethos as much as to Milton's, although the circumstances have clearly changed since the time of May's demise. There are many detailed imitations of the special style of *Paradise Lost* in the poem, even as Marvell contributes a major piece of early 'Augustan' verse, with imagery subordinated to the speaker's finely discriminating tone. The most significant feature here is Marvell's taking of the convention of praise by initial doubt to an extreme, 'straining praise through the sieve of doubt'. It almost seems as though Marvell's narrator is a Miltonic one, submitting himself to error, seeing events through 'Satanic' spectacles, then correcting our vision, and finally affirming the truth. The sense that Milton is to be regarded critically is unmistakably present in Marvell's adoption of Milton's own character of Samson to represent the poet (lines 9–10). Despite Marvell's qualification of the critique, it stays in the reader's mind (most famously in the image of Milton as Samson 'groping' in his blindness for the pillars in the Theatre of Dagon), alongside the repeated references to the potentially overreaching vastness of Milton's design. 'Vast' (line 2) is a word usually associated with Satan: Marvell's tactic is a fitting response to the double-sidedness of Milton's epic. The joke in the poem at lines 49–50 comparing rhyme-words to the tags and points that held clothes together refers back to the phrase Milton used when he gave Dryden permission to adapt *Paradise Lost* for the stage in rhyme ('Mr Milton received him civilly, and told him he would give him leave to tagge his verses'), but the fact that tags and points had already been superseded by hooks and eyes makes the reference also one that evidently refers to a former age.[12] Marvell knew that Milton was old (he would die later in the year), but Marvell also knew even at this stage that the poem would be extremely influential. He must also have discerned, for it is hard to imagine a more well-informed contemporary reader, that *Paradise Lost* was regarded as a seditious work when it first appeared, embodying a veiled attack on monarchy. 'On Mr. Milton's *Paradise Lost*' acknowledges all of these resonances in one of the subtlest pieces of praise ever penned.

The high point of Marvell's career as a poet is usually thought to be the period between 1649 and 1653. In addition to 'An Horatian Ode', he wrote in this period his delightful 'Upon Appleton House' (1651) while resident in Yorkshire as a tutor to Lord Fairfax's daughter Mary. This poem of surprising shifts in perspective, a landmark in landscape and prospect poetry, is no less engaged with other contemporary poets and artists. Marvell mocks Sir William Davenant's epic pretensions in his poem *Gondibert* (1651) even as he startles us with his rich representation of the plain of the River Wharfe. Marvell's intention seems to have been to make his own aesthetic grow out of the materials in and around the house, not least Lord Fairfax's own interest in libertine and occult poetry, and his translations of French poetry and Hermetic texts.

The poem is a meditation upon the meaning of the 'sober frame', by which is meant the house, the grounds, and the various perspectives offered by the associations that grow up within the 'picture' of the poem. The action fits within one day, from dawn (line 289) until dusk (line 775), but the middle of the poem, between stanzas 47 and 59, recounts at least several days' work of harvesting hay and grazing the stubble, followed by the flooding of the meadows (albeit presented as a courtly entertainment; lines 385–6). The poem is written in eight-line stanzas of octosyllabic iambic couplets, called by George Puttenham in *The Arte of English Poesie* (1589) the 'square or quadrangle equaliter', associated with the earth and the constant-minded man on account of its regularity and solidity. This was a form used by the seventeenth-century French poet Marc-Antoine Girard, sieur de Saint-Amant, whom Fairfax translated; Marvell had already used it with success in 'The Gallery' and 'The Unfortunate Lover', and he would do so again in 'The Garden'. The couplets have been noted for being both riddling and conversational and yet with an over-complicated syntax and conspicuous run-on words. They have Spenserian pace, but with casual inclusiveness.

Much of 'Upon Appleton House' is an exercise in the conjuration of Protestant magic, against the unreformed past and the continuing Catholic present. It is in this context that we are given a narrator who as magus can talk to the birds in their own language. Maria, the apotheosis of Mary Fairfax in the poem, has the power to stun nature as she becomes the object of worship, a Protestant, aristocratic goddess contrasted with the sexual impropriety of the nuns who used to live at Nun Appleton:

LXXXIV

So when the shadows laid asleep
From underneath these banks do creep,
And on the river as it flows
With ebon shuts begin to close;
The modest halcyon comes in sight,
Flying betwixt the day and night;
And such an horror calm and dumb,
Admiring Nature does benumb.

LXXXV

The viscous air, wheres'e'er she fly,
Follows and sucks her azure dye;
The jellying stream compacts below,
If it might fix her shadow so;
The stupid fishes hang, as plain
As flies in crystal overta'en;
And men with silent scene assist,
Charmed with the sapphire-wingèd mist.

LXXXVI

Maria such, and so doth hush
The world, and through the ev'ning rush.
No new-born comet such a train
Draws through the sky, nor star new-slain.
For straight those giddy rockets fail,
Which from the putrid earth exhale,
But by her flames, in heaven tried,
Nature is wholly vitrified. (lines 665–88)

The landscape is sterile none the less, despite the serene activity of nature, which fits uncomfortably with Mary's own fate (she would be largely abandoned by her future husband, the second Duke of Buckingham, and died childless), although Marvell cannot have known this at the time. The fullest objects of fertility are the mowers of the four mower poems. The sequence obliquely studies alienation from the viewpoint of the well-being that comes with an honest connection to the countryside. While being faithful to pastoral or to Horace, the poems develop the theme of lost innocence converting goodness to anarchy and violence, and so becoming 'symptomatic of disturbances in the very fabric of seventeenth-century life'.[13] Never is Marvell more powerfully succinct or more himself. A fine instance in this respect would be the single sentence that constitutes 'The Mower to the Glow-worms', with the main verb not appearing until the first line of the final stanza. The preceding stanzas are made up of apostrophes in the first line of each stanza, followed by balanced relative clauses, whose pattern is almost exactly repeated in each stanza. The poem is 'in number' precise, the word placed exactly halfway being 'fall', but the somewhat jarring expletives that complete rhymes and the contrapuntally sophisticated vocabulary produce the mood of the emotionally disorientated mower: his 'displacement'. The mower is a misfit: neither a cavalier nor a stringent Puritan, but someone with 'true knowledge' who belongs to a world outside of politics and religion. He lives in a kind of English Eden, or if you will Elysium, and Marvell is extremely interested in him.

Marvell continued to write lyric poetry after he became a Member of Parliament. In uncomfortable political circumstances, he also turned his hand from panegyric to verse satire. Although several of these, where the attribution can confidently be made to Marvell, are comparatively rough and ready compositions, and may well have been jointly authored, some evidently rework figures from the earlier verse. One in particular, 'The Last Instructions to a Painter' (1667), is a masterpiece, Marvell's longest poem, and involving intricate court and Parliamentary satire. The preceding 'Second' and 'Third Advice to a Painter' approach it, and earlier lyrics like 'The Gallery' and 'The Picture of Little T.C. in a Prospect of Flowers' show what precise knowledge Marvell had of European art and how well he could turn it to brilliant poetic effect.

'The Last Instructions to a Painter' displays considerable flexibility in its use of the rhymed decasyllabic couplet, ranging from the measuring of chaotic subject-matter with highly controlled and dignified verse (i.e. the mock-heroic) to grotesque couplets that reflect unpleasant subject-matter (e.g. lines 449–56). The poem consists of three central narrative sections: the sitting of Parliament in 1666 (lines 105–396); the attempt of the court to secure peace (lines 397–522); and the Dutch invasion of the Thames and the Medway (lines 523–884). These are preceded by pictures of courtly corruption and debauchery, and succeeded by the depiction of Charles II attempting to force erotic favours from his vision, the naked 'England or the peace', which is followed by a forty-one-line address to the king. These sections are informed by three elements: first, often fragmentary narration and description of the actual world; second, the 'instructions' through which artistic coherence is given, but which, in the debate between poet and painter (and momentarily between poetry and music), are shown to be impossible to complete; and third, a new 'tectonic' structure which abandons the known artistic forms in order to restore faith in an ideal order. Throughout the poem, media and different parts of experience are confused, in order to suggest the difficulty of describing the subject.

The entire poem is a series of modulating, intricately composed poetic pictures, imitating a variety of contemporary pictorial modes: effectively a history of vision. Each example participates in an aesthetic of inversion, just as the English fleet is unsoundly built and hence unprepared for battle, and the only 'battle' the debate over the Excise Bill in Parliament. This leads to a series of crises of representation, where either pictures or words, or both, fail to capture the subject-matter. In this context, the appeal to the king is an appeal for the restoration of the *ut pictura poesis* tradition, in which a poem is regarded as a speaking picture.

Just as the obscene 'limnings' of lines 9–11 subvert courtly portraiture, so Marvell's poem, a sexually grotesque satire circulated in manuscript, subverts the official panegyric of Edmund Waller's 'Instruction to a Painter' (which celebrated a supposed English victory in the Battle of Lowestoft in 1665), Dryden's *Annus Mirabilis* (1667), and other works of courtly panegyric. Sexual satire had been used as a way of criticizing the behaviour of courts, monarchs, parliaments, republic, Puritans, and Protector throughout the seventeenth century, though with particular vigour from the mid-1640s onwards. It has been argued that the particular treatment of sexual corruption in this poem is an acknowledgement of the 'force of sexuality in imaginative exploit, in the argument of heroic venture, in the calculation of human potential, and in the luxuries of retreat'.[14] The reign of Charles II was publicly celebrated at the Restoration as a renewal of fertility; Marvell responds by attacking the body politic on the level of sexual morality. Forms of sexual representation in the poem have been located in the context of both learned or elite and scurrilous pornography, especially in pictures, from the tradition stemming from Aretino's *Postures*.[15] Appropriately, the description of de Ruyter (lines 523–34) begins heroically and in a pastoral idyll, but degenerates until the Dutch admiral succumbs to a sexual appetite not far removed from those of the English courtiers.

The one exception to the satirical and parodic modes of the poem is the passage dealing with the heroic death of Archibald Douglas, which has been seen to contain a fusion of Christian and pagan allusions, characteristic of Rubens, as well as a baroque, fantastic mode in the style of Bernini. The visual point of Douglas's death is the distinction between his 'shape' and the fire enfolding him: 'the identification between what is without and within is complete, because the act of immolation simultaneously registers and enacts his heroism'.[16] In this way, the poem offers a poetic version of martyrological iconography – the truth in painting, in contrast to the allegorical victory painting of Cornelis de Witt, deputy Admiral to the Fleet, presiding over the raid. Douglas's demise is described in terms that are rich with associations that build out variously from martyrdom and Christology to Ovid, Roman sculpture, and beyond:

Like a glad lover, the fierce flames he meets,
And tries his first embraces in their sheets.
His shape exact, which the bright flames enfold,
Like the sun's statue stands of burnished gold.
Round the transparent fire about him glows,
As the clear amber on the bee does close,
And, as on angels' heads their glories shine,
His burning locks adorn his face divine. (lines 677–84)

Some of the martyrs immortalized by John Foxe in his very influential *Acts and Monuments of the Church*, popularly known as his *Book of Martyrs*, are described as going to sleep in suffering fiery martyrdom (e.g. Anne Askew: 'being compassed in with flames of fire, as a blessed sacrifice unto God, she slept in the Lord A. D. 1546'). However, Douglas will sink as 'relics', a clear signal of the survival of Roman Catholic martyrdom in the poem. And then, if Douglas imitates Christ with his face shining like the sun (Matthew 17:2), so also he is more literally likened to the Sun's Statue, a large statue that reputedly was brought to Rome from the east and was commonly thought to have been the Colossus of Rhodes. Marvell might well have seen the head that stood outside the Lateran Palace – the only piece of the statue that remained by the seventeenth century. But a medieval account of Rome explains that the complete statue, which behaved miraculously, in that it turned slowly through a full circle during the day so that the face always turned to the sun, was destroyed by an early pope, who lit a fire underneath it, so causing it to shatter. Marvell knew this from a book called *The Marvels of Rome* (*c.* thirteenth century) by Magister Gregorius. So behind Douglas's calm and composed end is a history of early iconoclasm and religious intolerance. The point is apt and deeply ironic: just as it was harsh for Pope Gregory (or Pope Sylvester) to destroy the miraculous statue, so it is painful for a loyal Catholic, as Douglas almost certainly was, to die fighting for a dissolute and poorly advised Protestant king. And there is still another paradox: the image of the bee in amber comes from Martial, that most profane of Latin poets, while the painterly references suggest 'a posture in the Renaissance sense, a display of copulation transmuted into art', representing a heroic death as an erotic encounter in an 'intimate domestic interior'[17] (one thinks too of an entirely different mode in Bernini's 'Ecstasy of St Theresa'). Marvell is showing how martyrdom is produced across cultural and religious divides, and produced most obviously by tyrannous behaviour. It is precisely because martyrdom so transcended national and linguistic boundaries that he was able to show this.

The erotic and the plight of the lover are at the heart of Marvell's most famous poem, 'To his Coy Mistress', but instead of the placidness with which the martyr-lover accepts his fate, the burden of the very activity of the sex act is confronted in the poem's crisis. The Epicurean overtones of the speaker's '*carpe diem*' plea to the mistress are compromised by the ever-present reality of oncoming death, and the speaker is wise enough to know this. So many love-poem clichés are lifted by the poet and recombined to make something strikingly original, both an apparently honest plea and a parody of itself, mindful of finitude yet in denial of it, both morbid and full of the joy of sex. The poem's three parts correspond generically and rhetorically to an erotic 'blazon', a naming of the lover's different bodily parts or aspects, notable for its precise but absurd arithmetical exaggeration and its sense of a slowing down of time (lines 1–20); a briefer, second section echoing an epigram from the *Greek Anthology*, and most densely indebted to emblems (lines 21–32); and the final section in which the majority of the Ovidian echoes are located, which is abundant in erotic energy (in opposition to the previous section) and verbs of (sometimes violent) action. The Ovidian infrastructure apparently invites cross-gendered perspectives since it puts the voice of Echo into that of the supposedly male speaker, and the identity of Narcissus into the mistress. It amazes us as a love-poem and yet perhaps is not one at all. The climax is thus the enigma of the expenditure of energy to which we are led, howsoever we recognize it:

> Let us roll all our strength, and all
> Our sweetness, up into one ball:
> And tear our pleasures with rough strife,
> Thorough the iron gates of life.
> Thus, though we cannot make our sun
> Stand still, yet we will make him run. (lines 41–6)

This takes us back to Butler's account of Marvell, for these lyrics are the product of extremely concentrated musing. Alongside 'To his Coy Mistress' would have to be ranked in respect of achievement the fierce logical exercise of 'The Definition of Love', the imagining of a solitary Edenic state in 'The Garden', or the clever voicing of feminine distress in 'The Nymph Complaining for the Death of her Fawn'. The musing might have required sleep afterwards, much as Marvell complained of the exhaustion he suffered sitting for long sessions in Parliament and writing up accounts of its business afterwards. Butler wanted to defame Marvell and in the same work makes some disturbing comments about the poet's sexual habits. This matter, like the unhappiness some feel is beneath the surface of the lyrics, is an issue for the biographer. But as we have them, there is no doubting the ability of the poems to make us see objects and relationships afresh, to capture moments of history, to understand literary achievement in those historical moments, to understand the path of literature's development, and in so doing to make the reader appreciate precisely literature's role in the passing of time. As Marvell grew older so he also understood that poetry was a weapon in the defence of liberty and toleration.

NOTES

1 [Samuel Butler], *The Transproser Rehears'd* (1673), pp. 137–8.

2 Samuel Parker attacked the prominent Puritan divine John Owen, sometime chaplain to Oliver Cromwell and Vice-Chancellor of Oxford University; Marvell defended him; Owen helped with the production of Marvell's *The Rehearsal Transpros'd*.

3 See Nicholas McDowell, *Poetry and Allegiance in the English Civil Wars: Marvell and the Cause of Wit* (Oxford: Clarendon Press, 2008).

4 See John Creaser, '"Service is perfect freedom": Paradox and Prosodic Style in *Paradise Lost*', *RES*, n.s. 58 (2007), 268–315.

5 See Paul Hammond, 'Marvell's Pronouns', *Essays in Criticism* 53 (2003), 219–34.

6 'On a Drop of Dew'. All quotations from Marvell's poems are from Andrew Marvell, *Poems*, ed. Nigel Smith, rev. paperback edn (Harlow and New York: Pearson Longman, 2006).

7 T. S. Eliot, 'Andrew Marvell', *TLS* (31 March 1921); rptd in *Selected Essays* (London and New York: Faber and Faber, 1932).

8 John Lennard, *But I Digress: The Exploitation of Parentheses in English Printed Verse* (Oxford: Oxford University Press, 1991), p. 82; Rosalie Colie, *'My Ecchoing Song': Andrew Marvell's Poetry of Criticism* (Princeton: Princeton University Press, 1970).

9 See Christopher Ricks, '"Its own resemblance"', and John Carey, 'Reversals Transposed: An Aspect of Marvell's Imagination', in *Approaches to Marvell: The York Tercentenary Lectures*, ed. C. A. Patrides (London and Boston: Routledge and Kegan Paul, 1978), pp. 108–35, 142–3.

10 John Creaser, '"As one scap't strangely from Captivity": Marvell and Existential Liberty', in *Marvell and Liberty*, eds W. Chernaik and M. Dzelzainis (Basingstoke and New York: Palgrave Macmillan, 1999), pp. 145–72. See also John Creaser, 'Prosody and Liberty in Milton and Marvell', in *Milton and the Terms of Liberty*, eds Graham Parry and Joad Raymond (Cambridge: Boydell and Brewer, 2002), pp. 37–55.

11 Timothy Raylor, 'Reading Machiavelli, Writing Cromwell: Edmund Waller's Copy of *The Prince* and his Draft Verses towards *A Panegryick on my Lord Protector*', *Turnbull Library Review* 35 (2002), 9–32.

12 John Aubrey, *Brief Lives*, ed. Andrew Clark, 2 vols. (Oxford: Oxford University Press, 1898), II. 72.

13 Robert Wilcher, *Andrew Marvell* (Cambridge: Cambridge University Press, 1985), p. 104.

14 Steven N. Zwicker 'Virgins and Whores: The Politics of Sexual Misconduct in the 1660s', in *The Political Identity of Andrew Marvell*, eds Conal Condren and A. D. Cousins (Aldershot and Brookfield, VT: Scolar Press, 1990), p. 86.

15 James Grantham Turner, 'The Libertine Abject: The Postures of *Last Instructions to a Painter*', in *Marvell and Liberty*, pp. 217–48.
16 Donald Friedman, 'Rude Heaps and Decent Order', in *Marvell and Liberty*, p. 139.
17 Turner, 'The Libertine Abject', pp. 240–1.

SELECTED FURTHER READING

Editions

Poems and Letters, ed. H. M. Margoliouth, 2 vols, 3rd edn, rev. Pierre Legouis, with the collaboration of E. E. Duncan-Jones, Oxford, Clarendon Press, 1971

Poems, ed. Nigel Smith, Longman Annotated English Poets, Harlow, Pearson Longman, 2003, rev. edn 2006

The Complete Poems, ed. E. S. Donno, Penguin Classics, Harmondsworth, Penguin, 1972, rev. edn 2005

The Prose Works of Andrew Marvell, eds Annabel Patterson, Martin Dzelzainis, Nicholas von Maltzahn, and N. H. Keeble, 2 vols, New Haven, Yale University Press, 2003

Secondary works

Brett, R. L., *Andrew Marvell: Essays on the Tercentenary of his Death*, Oxford and New York, Oxford University Press, 1979

Chernaik, Warren, *The Poet's Time: Politics and Religion in the Work of Andrew Marvell*, Cambridge, Cambridge University Press, 1983

Chernaik, Warren, and Martin Dzelzainis (eds), *Marvell and Liberty*, Basingstoke and New York, Macmillan and St. Martin's Press, 1999

Colie, Rosalie L., *'My Ecchoing Song': Andrew Marvell's Poetry of Criticism*, Princeton, Princeton University Press, 1970

Eliot, T. S., 'Andrew Marvell', *TLS*, 31 March 1921; rptd in *Selected Essays*, London and New York, Faber and Faber, 1932

Eyber, Vitaliy, *Andrew Marvell's 'Upon Appleton House': An Analytic Commentary*, Madison, NJ, Fairleigh Dickinson University Press, 2010

Friedman, D. M., *Marvell's Pastoral Art*, Berkeley, University of California Press, 1970

Healy, Thomas (ed.), *Andrew Marvell*. Longman Critical Readers, London and New York, Longman, 1998

Hirst, Derek and Steven N. Zwicker, *Cambridge Companion to Andrew Marvell*, Cambridge, Cambridge University Press, 2011

Holberton, Edward, *Poetry and the Cromwellian Protectorate: Culture, Politics, and Institutions*, Oxford and New York, Oxford University Press, 2008

Kelliher, Hilton, *Andrew Marvell, Poet and Politician, 1621–78: An Exhibition to Commemorate the Tercentenary of his Death*, London, British Museum Publications, 1978

McDowell, Nicholas, *Poetry and Allegiance in the English Civil Wars: Marvell and the Cause of Wit*, Oxford, Clarendon Press, 2008

Murray, Nicholas, *World Enough and Time: The Life of Andrew Marvell*, London, Little, Brown, 1999

Norbrook, David, *Writing the English Republic: Poetry, Rhetoric, and Politics, 1627–1660*, Cambridge, Cambridge University Press, 1999

Patrides, C. A. (ed.), *Approaches to Marvell: The York Tercentenary Lectures*, London and Boston, Routledge and Kegan Paul, 1978

Patterson, Annabel M., *Marvell and the Civic Crown*, Princeton, 1978, rev. as *Marvell: The Writer in Public Life*, Harlow and New York, Longman, 2000

Rees, Christine, *The Judgment of Marvell*, London and New York, Pinter, 1989

Rogers, John, *The Matter of Revolution: Science, Poetry and Politics in the Age of Milton*, Ithaca, NY, Cornell University Press, 1996

Smith, Nigel, *Andrew Marvell: The Chameleon*, New Haven and London, Yale University Press, 2009

Von Maltzahn, Nicholas, *An Andrew Marvell Chronology*, Basingstoke and New York, Palgrave Macmillan, 2005

Wallace, John M., *Destiny His Choice: The Loyalism of Andrew Marvell*, Cambridge, Cambridge University Press, 1968

Worden, Blair, *Literature and Politics in Cromwellian England: John Milton, Andrew Marvell, Marchamont Nedham*, Oxford, Clarendon Press, 2007

Zwicker, Steven N., *Lines of Authority: Politics and English Literary Culture, 1649–1689*, Ithaca, NY, Cornell University Press, 1993

10

DAVID HOPKINS

John Dryden

Readers comparing the accounts of Dryden offered by his most influential critic from the twentieth century, Mark Van Doren, and from the eighteenth, Samuel Johnson, might be forgiven for thinking that they were reading about two entirely different poets. 'Dryden', Van Doren tells us, 'was rarely successful in his descriptions of Nature and his accounts of the human passions' ('what data he did possess upon these subjects', he adds, 'he had borrowed, not very happily, from the classical poets'). Dryden's attempts at fancy or passion always result in 'absurdity and bathos'. He never displayed 'a happy gift for turning up images'. 'More journalist than artist', Dryden 'is virtually barren of illuminating comments on human life which move a reader to take new account of himself'. He was 'most at home when he was making statements'. Since he 'never got outside himself', he mostly 'failed to learn anything by his translating'. He was inspired not by 'happy perceptions of identities in the world of nature and man' but by 'circumstances'. His religious and political verse displayed no 'conspicuous principles of his own concerning Church and State'. In his ratiocinative verse he was 'a versifier of propositions rather than a philosopher resorting to poetry, or even a poet speculating'. His amatory poetry never goes 'deeper than the painted fires of conventional Petrarchan love'. He 'did not tell a story particularly well'. His *Fables* 'catered to a jaded taste that craved the strong meat of incest, murder, flowing blood, cruel and sensual unrealities'.[1]

The contrast with Johnson could not be more marked. Dryden's genius, in Johnson's view, was 'acute, argumentative, comprehensive and sublime'. His works 'abound with knowledge and sparkle with illustrations'. 'Every page ... discovers a mind' which was 'always curious, always active', 'very widely acquainted both with art and nature, and in full possession of great stores of intellectual wealth'. Dryden's mind was 'peculiarly formed' for making 'penetrating remarks on human nature'. His considerable ratiocinative and argumentative powers were often dialectical in nature: 'When once he had engaged himself in disputation, thoughts flowed on either side: he was now no longer at a loss; he had always objections and solutions at command.' Though seldom stimulated by tender or pathetic subject-matter, Dryden was a master at depicting the passions 'as they are complicated by the various relations of society, and confused in the tumults and agitations of life' – particularly love 'in its turbulent effervescence with some other desires'. His translations were crucial 'in breaking the shackles of verbal [word for word] interpretation', and were, moreover, English literary masterpieces in their own right. Some passages in his Juvenal 'will never be excelled', and any faults in his Virgil 'are forgotten in the hurry of delight'.[2]

It is Van Doren's rather than Johnson's account of Dryden that has prevailed in our time. Its admirers have included T. S. Eliot, W. H. Auden, and F. R. Leavis, and its influence persists to this day. I shall be arguing that it is misguided and misleading in almost every respect, and that Johnson presents a far truer and more reliable assessment of Dryden's artistic character and achievement. But if Van Doren's account is so erroneous, why has it commanded such widespread and continuing acceptance? The question can be answered partly with reference to the larger frameworks of ideas within which seventeenth-century English literary and political history have been interpreted, and partly with reference to the shape and pattern of Dryden's literary career itself.

A notable feature of both the Whig and Marxist interpretations of English history, which dominated the field from Lord Macaulay in the nineteenth century to Christopher Hill in the twentieth, was a marked lack of sympathy for the later Stuart monarchy, a hostility shared by the 'New Historicists' who have been so influential in recent literary studies. To both groups of scholars, Dryden has seemed a reactionary figure, opposed to the 'progressive' religious and political tendencies of his age, and deeply implicated in the attitudes and assumptions of an outmoded and unprincipled ruling class. Responses to Dryden have also been negatively prejudiced by assumptions about the literary dynamics of his period. Particularly influential has been the notion, memorably canvassed by T. S. Eliot, that mid-seventeenth-century England witnessed a 'dissociation of sensibility': a traumatic collapse of the delicate fusion of 'thought' and 'feeling' characteristic of the Elizabethan and Jacobean sensibility, when 'the intellect was immediately at the tip of the senses' and poets were effortlessly able to 'amalgamate disparate experience' to form 'new wholes'.[3] For the 'dissociationists', the Restoration marked a drastic thinning and coarsening of the national psyche: it was, for them, only to be expected that its leading poet would be myopically and complacently preoccupied with the social, the topical, and the modish, and that his stylistic staple would be a prosaic 'poetry of statement', manifesting the 'mathematical plainness' recommended by the newly founded Royal Society.

Such assumptions might seem at first sight to be confirmed by the pattern of Dryden's literary career. Dryden's literary output was largely 'occasional', having been mostly written in direct response to contemporary events or circumstances, to solicit patronage, or to generate income from performance or publication. Having decided, after his education at Westminster School and Trinity College, Cambridge, and a brief spell of employment in the Cromwellian civil service, to make his living as a writer in London, Dryden was substantially dependent on his pen for the rest of his life. His first poems after the Restoration – addressed to Sir Robert Howard (whose sister he married in 1663), the Earl of Clarendon, the antiquary Dr Walter Charleton, and the king himself – were clearly designed to canvass the patronage of the new establishment, and his lengthy 'historical poem' *Annus Mirabilis* (1667), an exuberantly patriotic depiction of events in the Second Dutch War (1665–7) and the Great Fire of London (1666), was crucial in gaining him the official positions of Poet Laureate (1668) and Historiographer Royal (1670). But his major source of income during the first two decades of his career was writing for the stage. Between 1663 and 1682, he produced, sometimes with collaborators, twenty-one plays for the King's Company, in which he was a shareholder. In these works he both exploited and developed the various styles and modes popular in the highly competitive Restoration theatrical market: 'heroic drama', courtly comedy, Shakespearean adaptation, bawdy farce. For his own plays, and those by fellow-dramatists, he wrote prologues and epilogues which engaged the audience in topical and witty banter. To the printed texts, he appended dedications and prefaces which flattered the plays' aristocratic dedicatees, and debated matters of current critical concern. Dryden's theatrical activities sometimes involved him in controversy. When his fellow-dramatist Thomas Shadwell complained that he had shown insufficient respect towards Shadwell's own dramatist-hero, Ben Jonson, Dryden took his revenge in *Mac Flecknoe* (circulating in manuscript, 1676; published, 1682 (unauthorized), 1684 (authorized)). In this mock-heroic lampoon, Shadwell is depicted as succeeding the notorious hack poet Richard Flecknoe, another self-styled disciple of Jonson, as monarch 'Through all the Realms of Non-sense absolute' (line 6). In Dryden's portrayal, Shadwell is transformed into a dunce of heroic proportions:

> The rest to some faint meaning make pretence,
> But Sh------ never deviates into sense. (lines 18–19)[4]

During the Popish Plot (1678–9) and Exclusion Crisis (1680–3) Dryden was drawn into political controversy on the king's behalf. In *Absalom and Achitophel* (1681) he satirized the attempts, led by the Earl of Shaftesbury, to block the succession to the throne of James, Charles II's Roman Catholic brother, and to replace him as heir-designate with Charles's illegitimate son, the Duke of Monmouth. Shaftesbury's machinations were likened, allegorically, to the Old Testament rebellion of Absalom against his father, King David, under the evil influence of Ahitophel the Gilonite. A second part of *Absalom and Achitophel* (with Nahum Tate) followed in 1682, together with another, harsher, satire on Shaftesbury, *The Medall: A Satire Against Sedition*. Dryden's later Laureate verse included *Threnodia Augustalis* (1685), lamenting the death of Charles II and heralding James's accession, and *Britannia Rediviva* (1688), celebrating the birth of the new king's son. Dryden's lengthy religious poem *The Hind and the Panther* (1687) defended the Roman Catholic religion to which he had been converted on the eve of the new reign. (In an earlier religious poem, *Religio Laici* (1682), he had made the case for Anglicanism, a faith which he now argued was lacking in ultimate religious authority.)

At the Revolution of 1688–9, Dryden was removed from his court posts. He returned for a few years to the stage, and wrote several poems addressed to, or commemorating, friends and contemporaries: William Congreve, Sir Godfrey Kneller, Henry Purcell. But his main income in his last decade came from translation, a medium in which he had been active since the 1680s in partnership with the enterprising and commercially astute young publisher Jacob Tonson. Dryden contributed translations to Tonson's verse miscellanies (1684, 1685, 1693, 1694), edited and contributed to a complete translation of *The Satires of Juvenal and Persius* (1692, dated 1693), and in 1697 published, as a handsome subscription folio, *The Works of Virgil*. His last volume, *Fables Ancient and Modern* (1700), consisted of translated episodes from Chaucer, Homer, Ovid, and Boccaccio, together with a handful of 'original' poems, including *Alexander's Feast*, the Ode which he had written for the London celebrations of St Cecilia's day in 1697.

Such a curriculum vitae might seem to confirm Van Doren's view of Dryden as a provider of partisan satire, bespoke entertainment, and marketable commodities for his age. And such a view might seem further supported, for modern readers, by the apparently dated nature of many of Dryden's expressed critical concerns, by the perceived unstageability of most of his plays, and by the way in which the densely topical nature of much of his verse necessitates constant recourse to explanatory notes.

But the surface pattern of Dryden's writing life gives only a very partial and superficial sense of his deeper poetic talents and imaginative interests. For, within and throughout a career shaped, at one level, by ephemeral pressure and financial necessity, the presence can be detected of a subtly interrelated set of speculations and imaginings which touch, with searching depth and power, on some of the most urgent and intractable dilemmas of the human condition – the role of fate and fortune; the nature of human reason; the relation of man to the animal and inanimate worlds; the possibility of human happiness; the difference between wise rule and brutal tyranny; the conflict between human and natural law; the glories and follies of martial heroism; the nature of love; the relations of the sexes; the dangers and lure of anarchy; the possibility of personal or artistic immortality. Dryden's 'comprehensive speculations' are detectable throughout his work, but can sometimes only be dimly glimpsed through copious circumstantial detail. They were thought by many of his early admirers to be most clearly and sustainedly apparent in his translations, where 'his genius sports at ease, freed from the shackles of a political or polemical task'.[5] But how, it may be asked, can a poet's 'own' thoughts be most clearly revealed when rendering those of others?

For Dryden, translation seems to have been as much an act of self-exploration and self-discovery as of passive reception. In the Preface to *Sylvae* (1685), he refers to the 'hot fit' of imaginative engagement which had produced translations in which he had discovered 'something that was more pleasing than [in his] ordinary productions'. Dryden asserts the need to 'maintain' the 'character' of each of his originals. In rendering the 'noble pride, and positive assertion of his opinions' to be found in Lucretius, for example, he has 'laid by' his own 'natural Diffidence and Scepticism for a while, to take up that Dogmatical way of [Lucretius], which ... is so much his Character as to make him that individual Poet'. Similarly, when translating Horace, he has endeavoured to capture the 'Briskness', 'Jollity', and 'good Humour' that form 'the most distinguishing part of all' that poet's 'Character' (*Works*, vol. 3, pp. 11, 16). At the same time, and paradoxically, Dryden says, he has been drawn to translate poets who are 'according to [his] genius' and who have 'most affected [him] in the reading'. By the end of his life, indeed, Dryden's sense of identity with his originals was so intense that he had come to see himself as a virtual reincarnation of the poets he translated.

'Good translation', wrote T. S. Eliot, 'is not merely translation, since the poet is giving the original through himself, and finding himself through the original'.[6] Translation was a particularly apt medium in which Dryden could 'find himself' because of his convictions about the mutable, malleable, and permeable nature of the human mind. In the Dedication to *Aureng-Zebe* (1676), he quoted a celebrated tag from Terence when affirming the necessary changeability of his human sympathies: '*Homo sum, humani a me nihil alienum puto* [I am a man, and consider nothing human to be foreign to me]. As I am a Man, I must be changeable ... An ill Dream, or a Cloudy day, has power to change this wretched Creature, who is so proud or a reasonable Soul, and make him think what he thought not yesterday' (*Works*, vol. 12, p. 157). In the light of such beliefs, it is perhaps not surprising that Dryden was often able to discover, mobilize, and explore his own artistic personality most fully (and unpredictably) when re-voicing the sentiments of others.

Dryden's poetry abounds in passages in which the poet, or one of his imagined characters, expresses bewilderment, anxiety, or resentment at the conditions under which human life must be lived. In one of the most celebrated of these 'complaints against life', the eponymous hero of *Aureng-Zebe* laments the 'Strange Couzenage' which impels men to a false hope of future success, only to discover that 'Tomorrow's falser than the former day' (IV. i. 33–44). In *The State of Innocence* (1677), Adam laments the 'Hard state of life' according to which 'Heav'n fore-knows' his 'will', but he is 'not ty'd up from doing ill' (IV. i. 113–14). In *The Tempest* (1670), Prospero complains, in a similar vein, that life is equally problematic whether it is governed by Fate or by free will:

> If Fate be not, then what can we foresee,
> Or how can we avoid it, if it be? (IV. v. 157–8)

The human mind, Nature tells Man in Dryden's translation of Lucretius's diatribe 'Against the Fear of Death' from Book 3 of *De Rerum Natura*, is tormented by 'Eternal troubles' whose 'cause and cure' man 'never' hopes 'to find', thus causing him to be constantly 'with' him 'self at strife', to 'wander in the *Labyrinth* of Life', and to be haunted by 'Th' avenging horrour of a Conscious mind' which 'makes a Hell on Earth, and Life a death' (lines 267–70, 231, 235). The Reason by which man attempts to comprehend the mysteries of religion provides us with but a 'glimmering Ray' (*Religio Laici*, line 5). In our religious strivings, human pride causes us to be 'wing'd with vain desires', to be 'misled by wandring fires', and to follow 'false lights' (*The Hind and the Panther*, 1. 72–3).

Dryden's epistolary and elegiac poetry also provides telling testimony to his sense of life's uncertainties and precariousness. In his elegy on John Oldham (1684) he lamented, with measured and allusive precision, the death of a young poet with whose soul he felt his own to be 'near ally'd', and concluded with a hauntingly bleak commemoration of Oldham's premature demise:

> Once more, hail and farewel; farewel thou young,
> But ah too short, *Marcellus* of our Tongue;
> Thy Brows with Ivy, and with Laurels bound;
> But Fate and gloomy Night encompass thee around.
> (lines 22–5)

In his ode on the death of the young poet Anne Killigrew (1685, dated 1686), Dryden articulated his profound sense of shame, when contrasting the chastity of Killigrew's 'Celestial Song' with the 'steaming Ordures of the Stage' with which his 'lubrique and adult'rate age' had impelled him and his contemporaries to profane God's 'Heav'nly Gift of Poesy' (lines 13, 63, 57). And in his epistle to William Congreve (1693, dated 1694), writing as a man now

> worn with Cares and Age,
> And just abandoning th' Ungrateful Stage: (lines 66–7)

he movingly begged Congreve, a man 'to better Fortune born', to

> Be kind to my Remains; and oh defend,
> Against Your Judgment Your departed Friend! (lines 72–3)

The miseries of human existence are blamed by the narrator of 'Palamon and Arcite', Dryden's version of Chaucer's 'Knight's Tale', on 'Pow'rs above' which

> move our Appetites to Good or Ill,
> And by Foresight necessitate the Will. (2. 220–1)

Such 'Pow'rs' are, as Dryden's engagement with classical literature deepens and intensifies throughout his career, increasingly identified with the Olympian deities of Greek and Roman antiquity (merged in 'Palamon and Arcite' with those of medieval astrology), who are conceived both as powers exerting 'external' influence on human and non-human nature, and, in their anthropomorphic susceptibility to human emotions and passions, as embodiments of psychological forces working 'within' the human mind. These deities are Janus-faced: they can sometimes ennoble humanity, inspiring deeds of selfless courage and eloquence, but more often contrive to make human life disturbing, demeaning, or absurd. Their ineluctable power means that they can never be dismissed or denied, and that to contemplate them always involves an element of awed wonder.

Chief among Dryden's Olympian pantheon is Venus, whose conventional designation as the 'love goddess' gives an inadequate sense of the universal force of procreative fecundity and generative passion who, in Dryden's conception, holds sway throughout the animal and inanimate worlds, as well as the human. Venus can be celebrated as a 'Delight of Humane kind, and Gods above',

> Whose vital pow'r, Air, Earth, and Sea supplies;
> And breeds what e'er is born beneath the rowling Skies.
> ('Lucretius: The Beginning of the First Book', lines 1–4)

She can also be revered as the great civilizing power that

> first invented Verse, and form'd the Rhime,
> The Motion measur'd, harmoniz'd the Chime.
> ('Cymon and Iphigenia', lines 33–4)

The 'secret Joys of sweet Coition' which she inspires are felt not only by 'Man's Imperial Race' but also by 'they'

> That wing the liquid Air, or swim the Sea,
> Or haunt the Desert, rush into the flame:
> For Love is Lord of all; and is in all the same.
> ('The Third Book of the *Georgics*', lines 376–80)

Venus's power impels the 'Mother Lion' who, 'stung' with her 'rage',

> Scours o're the Plain; regardless of her young:
> Demanding Rites of Love. (lines 382–3)

She also infects the stallion who

> snuffs the well-known Scent afar;
> And snorts and trembles for the distant Mare. (lines 391–2)

Her servants include not only the 'bristled Boar', who, having felt 'the pleasing Wound', 'New grinds his arming Tusks, and digs the Ground' (lines 397–8), but also Leander, the human lover of Hero, whose 'Liver' was 'Transfixt' and 'heart' 'inflam'd' by 'Love's unerring Dart' (lines 403–4). Venus can sometimes inspire her servants to courageous acts of bravery and eloquence. Sigismonda, the heroine of one of Dryden's translations from Boccaccio's *Decameron*, is inspired to defend her clandestine but honourable marriage to her father's squire Guiscardo by a proto-feminist appeal to natural law –

> State-Laws may alter: Nature's are the same;
> Those are usurp'd on helpless Woman-kind,
> Made without our Consent, and wanting Pow'r to bind,
> ('Sigismonda and Guiscardo', lines 418–20)

– and by a bold declaration of her sexual rights:

> Where was the Crime, if Pleasure I procur'd,
> Young, and a Woman, and to Bliss inur'd? (lines 451–2)

Venus's power can, alternatively, be a source of rich comedy, sometimes in unexpected circumstances. The satire of *Absalom and Achitophel*, as we have seen, is primarily designed to pillory those rebelling against their divinely anointed monarch. But this is how the poem begins:

> In pious times, e'r Priest-craft did begin,
> Before *Polygamy* was made a sin;
> When man, on many, multiply'd his kind,
> E'r one to one was, cursedly, confind:
> When Nature prompted, and no law deny'd
> Promiscuous use of Concubine and Bride;
> Then, *Israel*'s Monarch, after Heaven's own heart,
> His vigorous warmth did, variously, impart
> To Wives and Slaves: And, wide as his Command,
> Scatter'd his Maker's Image through the Land. (lines 1–10)

These lines perform, on one level, a strategic function within Dryden's polemic: to dispose of the awkward matters of Charles's promiscuity and Monmouth's illegitimacy, so that the poem can move securely to its defence of Charles as exemplar of divinely sanctioned order. But Dryden's sly ironies resound in more complex and equivocal ways than their satirical purpose necessitates, and raise teasing and potentially subversive questions about the amatory behaviour of gods, men, and monarchs to which Dryden provides no easy or straightforward answers. Is Charles's conduct, we find ourselves asking, *seriously* to be considered in accord with divine wishes ('after Heaven's own heart') – more 'holy' than the conduct approved of by 'Priest-craft'? If so, what god, or gods, does Charles resemble or serve? Are not the promptings of the 'Nature' that impel him closer to those instigated by Venus (as imagined by Lucretius or Virgil) than to any sanctioned by the Old Testament Jehovah? Is Charles's behaviour not uncomfortably (or delightfully) close to that of Chanticleer, the farmyard cock in Dryden's version of Chaucer's 'Nun's Priest's Tale' who 'Six Misses had beside his lawful Wife' and who was 'the wight of all the World who serv'd Venus best':

> Who true to Love, was all for Recreation,
> And minded not the Work of Propagation. (lines 690–2)

If such passages show Dryden to have been alive to the comic potential of Venus's realm, his stress falls elsewhere on the agonizing effects of the goddess's power. In 'Palamon and Arcite' the carvings on Venus's temple walls depict 'Complaints, and hot Desires, the Lover's Hell' and

Nuptial Bonds, the Ties
Of Loves Assurance, and a Train of Lies,
That, made in Lust, conclude in Perjuries. (2. 475–9)

And the lovers depicted in 'Concerning the Nature of Love', Dryden's version of the ending of Book 4 of Lucretius's *De Rerum Natura*, are desperately driven by their pursuit of an unachievable unity:

They gripe, they squeeze, their humid tongues they dart,
As each wou'd force their way to t' others heart:
In vain; they only cruze about the coast,
For bodies cannot pierce, nor be in bodies lost: (lines 75–8)

A particularly powerful presentation of the agonizing effects of Venus's power is to be found in 'Cinyras and Myrrha', Dryden's rendering of an episode from Book 10 of Ovid's *Metamorphoses*. Myrrha, a Cyprian princess consumed with incestuous desire for her father, expresses her resentment for the humanity whose laws (in apparently arbitrary conflict with those of Nature) prevent her from succumbing to her passion:

The Father-Bull his Daughter may bestride,
The Horse may make his Mother-Mare a Bride;
What Piety forbids the lusty Ram
Or more salacious Goat, to rut their Dam?
The Hen is free to wed the Chick she bore,
And make a Husband, whom she hatch'd before;
All Creatures else are of a happier Kind,
Whom nor ill-natur'd Laws from Pleasure bind,
Nor Thoughts of Sin disturb their Peace of mind.
But Man, a Slave of his own making lives;
The Fool denies himself what Nature gives: (lines 43–53)

Dryden responds to Ovid's distinctive handling of the situation, recreating and enhancing the verbal 'turns' (witty wordplay) by which Ovid allows us to appreciate the paradoxicality of Myrrha's situation, as she succumbs to desires which seem both 'natural' and, a few lines later, profoundly contrary to the 'Sanctions' which 'Nature has designed' (line 97). In his rendering, Dryden maintains a subtle and complex balance of sympathy and distance, exposing the sophistry of some of Myrrha's claims, while simultaneously alerting us to the intractable dilemmas encapsulated in her situation: incest is part of nature; incest is contrary to nature.

Venus is, in Dryden's conception, the pre-eminent power that links human to animal and inanimate nature, and his poetry abounds in passages that evoke the curious continuities between the three worlds. In *Annus Mirabilis* he blends first-hand observation with his memory of Ovid's *Metamorphoses*, when comparing Prince Rupert's pursuit of two beleaguered Dutch vessels with the pursuit of a hare by an exhausted dog:

So have I seen some fearful Hare maintain
    A Course, till tir'd before the Dog she lay:
Who stretch'd behind her, pants upon the plain,
    Past pow'r to kill as she to get away.

With his loll'd tongue his faintly licks his prey,
    His warm breath blows her flix up as she lies:
She, trembling, creeps upon the ground away,
    And looks back to him with beseeching eyes.
(lines 521–8)

Dryden here deploys a dialect word for animal fur ('flix') and tellingly observed natural details (the dog's lolling tongue, the warmth of his breath, the tremulous exhaustion of the hare) to evoke, with delicacy, pathos, and striking impartiality, a moment of uneasy calm amidst the hectic chaos of battle or the hunt: our sympathies, in this generally jingoistic poem, are at this moment as much with the beleaguered (Dutch) hare as the pursuing (English) dog – or more.

Dryden is equally responsive to continuities between the human world and that of plants and the seasons. In his evocations of spring, for example, he brings out the textures of new-growing vegetation, describing how

The Grass securely springs above the Ground;
The tender Twig shoots upward to the Skies.
('The Second Book of the Georgics', lines 451–2)

In the world of budding plants, spring witnesses a burgeoning of tentative timidity into the confident vigour of young growth, when

gentle Heat, and soft repeated Rains,
Make the green Blood to dance within their Veins.
Then, at their Call, embolden'd out they come,
And swell the Gems, and burst the narrow Room;
Broader and broader yet, their Blooms display,
Salute the welcome Sun, and entertain the Day.
('The Flower and the Leaf', lines 10–15)

Second only to the power of Venus and Nature, in Dryden's evocations of the Olympian deities, is that of Mars, the presiding deity, for Dryden (as in contemporary astrology) not only of war, but of ambition, civil strife, jealousy, crime, anger, and natural disasters. Mars's temple, in 'Palamon and Arcite', contains depictions of 'Treason lab'ring in the Traytor's Thought', of

'Hypocrisie, with holy Lear', of 'th'assassinating Wife' and 'Traytor-Friend', of 'Unpunish'd Rapine', of 'bawling Infamy' and suicide, of 'Madness laughing in his ireful Mood', of 'raging Fire', and of 'All Trades of Death that deal in Steel for Gains' (2. 560–603). Mars is the inspirer of such figures as 'Achitophel' (the Earl of Shaftesbury). But the god's power ensures that his followers cannot be glibly dismissed. In his portrait of 'Achitophel', Dryden counterpoints outright hostility to the king's enemy (Achitophel's is 'A Name to all succeeding Ages Curst') with more searching and disturbing notes which reveal him as a quasi-tragic figure, in the grip of psychosomatic impulses beyond his control. Shaftesbury's 'fiery Soul', we are told,

working out its way,
Fretted the Pigmy Body to decay:
And o'r inform'd the Tenement of Clay, (lines 156–8)

and in the famous lines that follow, Dryden evokes the mysterious mental forces that drive the body relentlessly, even to its own destruction, in a sequence of questions that seem more than merely rhetorical:

Great Wits are sure to Madness near ally'd;
And thin Partitions do their Bounds divide:
Else, why should he, with Wealth and Honour blest,
Refuse his Age the needful hours of Rest?
Punish a Body which he could not please;
Bankrupt of Life, yet Prodigal of Ease? (lines 163–8)

Urges of the kind that impel 'Achitophel' are evoked with particularly vivid mimetic effect in the remorseless strivings of Sisyphus – for Dryden (as for Lucretius, his source) not a figure from the mythical Hades, but one from the world of modern power politics:

The *Sisiphus* is he, whom noise and strife
Seduce from all the soft retreats of life,
To vex the Government, disturb the Laws,
Drunk with the Fumes of popular applause,
He courts the giddy Crowd to make him great,
And sweats and toils in vain, to mount the sovereign Seat.
For still to aim at pow'r, and still to fail,
Ever to strive and never to prevail,
What is it, but in reasons true account
To heave the Stone against the rising Mount;
Which urg'd, and labour'd, and forc'd up with pain,
Recoils and rowls impetuous down, and smoaks along the plain.
('Lucretius ... Against the Fear of Death', lines 200–11)

Mars is also the inspirer of Homer's intemperately passionate Achilles, in 'The First Book of Homer's *Ilias*', of Achilles' son Pyrrhus who, in 'The Second Book of the *Aeneis*', slaughters the aged Priam, dragging him 'Slidd'ring through clotter'd Blood, and holy Mire' and leaving his body 'on the bleak Shoar', 'a headless Carcass, and a nameless thing' (lines 749, 752–3), and of the bloodlust and intolerance inaugurated near the beginning of time by 'The murth'rer *Cain*' (*The Hind and the Panther*, 1. 275). He is also the inspirer of such natural disasters as the Great Fire of London (*Annus Mirabilis*, lines 871–88) and the gleefully destructive storm that destroys Ceyx in 'Ceyx and Alcyone'. The power of Mars is sometimes allied with that of Venus, as when Alexander the Great is inspired by his mistress Thais (and his court musician-poet Timotheus) to burn the newly conquered city of Persepolis:

The Princes applaud, with a furious Joy;
And the King seyz'd a Flambeau, with Zeal to destroy;
Thais led the Way,
To light him to his Prey,
And like another *Hellen*, fir'd another *Troy*.
(*Alexander's Feast*, lines 147–50)

Mars is also a close ally of Fortune, the classical embodiment of all that is fickle and unsettling in human life, whose capricious destructiveness is most memorably evoked in Dryden's version of Horace, *Odes* 3. 29:

Fortune, that with malicious joy,
Does Man her slave oppress,
Proud of her Office to destroy,
Is seldome pleas'd to bless.
Still various and unconstant still;
But with an inclination to be ill;
Promotes, degrades, delights in strife,
And makes a Lottery of life. (lines 73–80)

Does Dryden have any consolation to offer against such formidable powers? In his 'public' poetry, his suggested remedies tend to be couched in the conventional terms of royalist rhetoric. In such poems as *Astraea Redux* (1660), *To His Sacred Majesty* (1661), *To My Lord Chancellor* (1662), and *Annus Mirabilis* Dryden celebrates the divine Providence which, he asserts, had restored the Stuart monarchy and which would continue to sanction and sanctify its affairs. To attempt 'To change Foundations' or to 'cast' the political 'Frame anew', he suggests in *Absalom and Achitophel*, is 'work for Rebels' who pursue 'base Ends' and attempt to 'controul' (challenge or dispute) both 'Divine and Humane Laws' (lines 805–7). In *Threnodia*

Augustalis (1685) the recently deceased Charles II is commemorated as 'God's Image, God's Anointed' (line 63), and in *Britannia Rediviva* (1688) James II's newborn son is likened to the 'Manna' sent to the Israelites by God (line 65).

But the forces that disrupt and disturb human life are treated in a more tentative and less straightforwardly confident way in Dryden's religious verse. In *Religio Laici* Dryden reaffirms his fear (now focused specifically on the Protestant sects) of those who 'disturb' 'the publick Peace' (line 448), but ends his plea for religious moderation – in which excessive reliance on reason (deism), church tradition (Roman Catholicism), and individual inspiration (extreme Protestantism) are rejected in favour of an Anglican *via media* – not with confident doctrinal assertion but with a plea for the 'Common quiet' which is, above all, 'Mankind's concern' (line 450). And in *The Hind and the Panther*, where Dryden (now a Roman Catholic) voices his fears about the Church of England's powerlessness to control the extremes of Protestant individualism, his faith rests on a beleaguered and solitary surrender to a mysterious unseen God whose

throne is darkness in th' abyss of light,
A blaze of glory that forbids the sight. (1. 66–7)

Rather than being written out of spiritual confidence, Dryden's poem emanates dark forebodings about the likely consequences of King James's intemperate Catholicism. And Dryden's later religious verse is frequently focused on figures, real or fictional, who commit quiet, courageous acts of pious virtue and charity in a hostile or corrupt world.

But if Dryden's Christian verse is increasingly marked by a sense of anxiety and isolation, his re-creation of consolatory poetry from the pagan world is notable for its conspicuous confidence, buoyancy, and élan. The translations from Lucretius and Horace in *Sylvae* are imbued with the spirit of Epicureanism, a philosophy devoted to the attainment of *ataraxia*: the peace of mind achieved by freeing oneself from vain ambition, fruitless desires, and groundless fears, especially the fear of death. Epicureanism is an emphatically materialist philosophy: the atoms which compose both body and soul pass into the void on the death of the individual; the gods (themselves material) take no part in human affairs, and therefore need neither to be reverenced nor feared.

In the Preface to *Sylvae*, Dryden is at pains to dissociate himself from Lucretius's mortalism. But his passionate re-creation of the hectoring vigour of Lucretius's evangelical tirades shows him to have been able to achieve, at least in the act of composition, a remarkable identification with the Roman poet's vehement materialism:

We, who are dead and gone, shall bear no part
In all the pleasures, nor shall feel the smart,
Which to that other Mortal shall accrew,
Whom of our Matter Time shall mould anew.
For backward if you look, on that long space
Of Ages past, and view the changing face
Of Matter, tost and variously combin'd
In sundry shapes, 'tis easie for the mind
From thence t' infer that Seeds of things have been
In the same order as they now are seen:
Which yet our dark remembrance cannot trace,
Because a pause of Life, a gaping space
Has come betwixt, where memory lies dead,
And all the wandring motions from the sence are fled.

('Lucretius ... Against the Fear of Death', lines 27–40)

Dryden's Lucretius offers an excoriating denunciation of the vain delusions that beset mankind. His Horace, in contrast, imagines what it might be like to speak from a position of achieved Epicurean self-possession. In his version of *Odes* 3. 29, Dryden exhorts his addressee to 'Enjoy the present smiling hour; / And put it out of Fortune's pow'r', and, after evoking the destructiveness of Fortune's activities with a fearless relish, defiantly proclaims the capacity of human beings to triumph over her assaults:

Happy the Man, and happy he alone,
He, who can call today his own:
He, who secure within, can say
To morrow do thy worst, for I have liv'd to day.
Be fair, or foul, or rain, or shine,
The joys I have possest, in spight of fate are mine.
Not Heav'n it self upon the past has pow'r;
But what has been, has been, and I have had my hour.

(lines 65–72)

Later in life, Dryden composed two poems which fused such Epicurean *ataraxia* with a quasi-Christian faith in an ultimate principle of creative benevolence. 'Palamon and Arcite' narrates events which are attributed, by the poem's narrator and its characters, to a variety of (sometimes incompatible) causes: 'destiny', 'fate', 'fortune', 'providence', 'chance', the 'powers above', the astrological position of the planets. But near the end of the poem, a year after Arcite's death in the tournament in which he and Palamon have fought for Emily's hand, Duke Theseus summons Palamon and Emily to Athens, and, in a lengthy culminating speech, proposes that they should marry, thereby transforming the sadness of recent events into joy. Behind the apparent anarchy of the sublunary world, Theseus affirms, there stands a benign 'First Mover', a 'perfect' and 'stable' figure who resembles the Christian God in his benignity and omnipotence, but is remote and mysterious, his presence consolatory to human beings not because he guarantees individual survival, but because, according to his 'Law', though 'Individuals die', 'ev'ry kind' (species) will 'by Succession live' (3. 1044–6). Theseus surveys, with scrupulous, unsentimental accuracy and stately dignity, the inexorably harsh processes of nature: the 300-year-old growth and decay of an oak tree, the wearing away of the paving stone in the street, the decline of cities, the drying up of rivers, and the development of human beings from a primal 'Drop' to the ambitious arrogance of maturity. Given such facts of existence, he affirms, the only sane attitude is one of philosophical acceptance, combining Horatian insouciance with the Stoicism of the final lines of Juvenal's tenth satire, in a gesture of existential triumph in the face of all that might cause us to despair:

> What then remains, but after past Annoy,
> To take the good Vicissitude of Joy?
> To thank the gracious Gods for what they give,
> Possess our Souls, and while we live, to live? (3. 1111–14)

'Of the Pythagorean Philosophy', from Book 15 of Ovid's *Metamorphoses*, shows that Dryden saw intimate connections both between Ovid's poem and his own life and times and between Ovid's subject-matter and the processes by which he (Dryden, the translator-poet) was communicating that subject-matter to his English readers. In rendering Ovid's evocation of the autumnal phase of human life,

> More than mature, and tending to decay,
> When our brown Locks repine to mix with odious Grey,
> (lines 314–15)

Dryden glances wryly at his own sixty-eight-year-old person. In his description of nature's changes –

> Ever in motion; she destroys her old,
> And casts new Figures in another Mold, (lines 264–5)

– he echoes Andrew Marvell's evocation of Oliver Cromwell's destruction of the old political order.[7] And in his rendering of Pythagoras's description of the passing away of all things, he glances at the supposed 'abdication' of the king he had formerly served:

> For former Things,
> Are set aside, like abdicated Kings. (lines 274–5)

But Dryden's colourings of his original go beyond the merely personal and contemporary. A little earlier in the poem, Pythagoras had offered a general celebration of the ceaseless continuity-in-flux that is Nature's domain:

> Thus are their Figures never at a stand,
> But chang'd by Nature's innovating Hand;
> All Things are alter'd, nothing is destroy'd,
> The shifted Scene, for some new Show employ'd.
> Then to be born, is to begin to be
> Some other Thing we were not formerly:
> And what we call to Die, is not t' appear,
> Or be the Thing that formerly we were.
> Those very Elements which we partake,
> Alive, when Dead some other Body make:
> Translated grow, have Sense, or can Discourse,
> But Death on deathless Substance has no force. (lines 386–97)

The sentiments of this passage are clearly connected with Dryden's paradoxical claim in the Preface to *Fables* (apropos of Chaucer's Canterbury pilgrims) that 'Mankind is ever the same, and nothing lost out of Nature, though every thing is alter'd' (*Works*, vol. 7, pp. 37–8). And Dryden's use of the word 'Translated' to describe the relocation of bodily 'Elements' applies Pythagoras's words to the very literary process by which they are being communicated. Dryden clearly sees in his rendering of Pythagoras's words both an affirmation and an enactment of the processes of poetic rebirth, renewal, and succession that are a central preoccupation of his own Preface. In his capacity to link reflections on his own life and times with processes of the most transcendent grandeur, in an imaginative re-creation of a poem from the remote past which embodies its own precepts in the 'long, majestic March'[8] of its verse-music, Dryden displays precisely the intellectual adventurousness, philosophical profundity, prosodic mastery, and comprehensive sublimity roundly denied him by Mark Van Doren, but affirmed by Samuel Johnson as essential hallmarks of his genius.

NOTES

1 Mark Van Doren, *John Dryden: A Study of his Poetry*, rev. edn (Bloomington: Indiana University Press, 1960), pp. 10, 31, 33, 37, 67, 68, 94, 107, 142, 169, 184, 209, 215, 265.

2 *Samuel Johnson on Shakespeare*, ed. H. R. Woudhuysen (Harmondsworth: Penguin, 1989), p. 238; Samuel Johnson, *The Lives of the Most Eminent English Poets*, ed. Roger Lonsdale, 4 vols (Oxford: Clarendon Press, 2006), vol. 2, pp. 101, 122, 130, 143, 148–9; vol. 4, p. 95.

3 T. S. Eliot, *Selected Essays*, 2nd edn (London: Faber, 1934), pp. 210, 287.
4 All quotations from Dryden are from *The Works of John Dryden*, eds Edward Niles Hooker, H. T. Swedenberg Jr, *et al.*, 20 vols (Berkeley, Los Angeles, and London: University of California Press, 1956–2000), cited in the text by line-reference, or as *Works* by volume and page.
5 John Aikin (ed.), *Fables from Boccacio and Chaucer* (London: T. Cadell and W. Davies, 1805), p. iii.
6 T. S. Eliot, 'Introduction: 1928', in *Ezra Pound: Selected Poems*, ed. T. S. Eliot (London: Faber, 1948), p. 13.
7 Cf. 'An Horatian Ode on Cromwell's Return from Ireland', lines 35–6.
8 Alexander Pope, *The First Epistle of the Second Book of Horace Imitated: To Augustus*, line 269, quoted with approval by Johnson, *Lives of the Most Eminent English Poets*, vol. 2, p. 153. The view of Dryden outlined in the present chapter is expounded at greater length in my *Writers and Their Work: John Dryden* (Tavistock: Northcote House and British Council, 2004).

SELECTED FURTHER READING

Editions

The Works of John Dryden, eds Edward Niles Hooker, H. T. Swedenberg Jr, *et al.*, 20 vols, Berkeley, Los Angeles, and London, University of California Press, 1956–2000

The Poems of John Dryden, eds Paul Hammond and David Hopkins, Longman Annotated English Poets, 5 vols, Harlow, Longman/Pearson, 1995–2005; one-volume selection, 2007

Secondary works

Hammond, Paul, *John Dryden: A Literary Life*, Basingstoke, Macmillan, 1991

Dryden and the Traces of Classical Rome, Oxford, Oxford University Press, 1999

Hammond, Paul, and Hopkins, David (eds), *John Dryden: Tercentenary Essays*, Oxford, Clarendon Press, 2000

Harth, Phillip, *Contexts of Dryden's Thought*, Chicago, University of Chicago Press, 1968

Pen for a Party: Dryden's Tory Propaganda in its Contexts, Princeton, Princeton University Press, 1993

Hopkins, David, *John Dryden*, Cambridge, Cambridge University Press, 1986

Writers and Their Work: John Dryden, Tavistock, Northcote House and British Council, 2004

Johnson, Samuel, 'Dryden', in *The Lives of the Most Eminent English Poets*, ed. Roger Lonsdale, 4 vols, Oxford, Clarendon Press, 2006, vol. 2, pp. 79–164, 306–76

Reverand II, Cedric D., *Dryden's Final Poetic Mode: The Fables*, Philadephia, University of Pennsylvania Press, 1988

Scott, Sir Walter, *Life of Dryden*, vol. 1 in *The Works of John Dryden*, ed. Sir Walter Scott, 2nd edn, 18 vols, Edinburgh, Archibald Constable, and London,

Hurst, Robinson, 1821; rev. George Saintsbury, Edinburgh, William Paterson, 1882–93

Winn, James Anderson, *John Dryden and His World*, New Haven and London, Yale University Press, 1987

'When Beauty Fires the Blood': Love and the Arts in the Age of Dryden, Ann Arbor, University of Michigan Press, 1992

Zwicker, Steven N., *Dryden's Political Poetry: The Typology of King and Nation*, Providence, RI, Brown University Press, 1972

Politics and Language in Dryden's Poetry: The Arts of Disguise, Princeton, Princeton University Press, 1984

(ed.), *The Cambridge Companion to John Dryden*, Cambridge, Cambridge University Press, 2004

11

CLAUDE RAWSON

Jonathan Swift

Byron said of Swift as a poet that 'he beats us all hollow, his rhymes are wonderful'.[1] Ted Hughes, a century and a half later, wrote: 'Swift is the only stylist ... his writing is the bedrock from which every writer must start.'[2] Hughes thought him the 'nearest model' for the 'fables' in his own collection *How the Whale Became* (1963), and told Kenneth Baker, then Education Secretary, that children should memorize a page of the prose *Modest Proposal*, along with some pages of Robert Frost and Eliot's 'Animula', as a 'great sheet anchor' of sensibility.[3] But it was Swift's impact on his own work as a poet that Hughes was declaring.

It is sometimes forgotten that Swift was a poet, who wrote almost as much verse as Pope, not counting the latter's translation of Homer. Swift's reputation as a poet has been higher among poets than among critics. His admirers and imitators include Byron, Yeats, and Eliot. His standing as a poet has been occluded by the towering reputation of his prose satires *A Tale of a Tub* (1704) and *Gulliver's Travels* (1726), and by the idea, fostered by Pope, that the heroic couplet, as perfected by Pope, was the normative style of serious English poetry, whose master was Pope himself. In the words of Adam Smith:

> In our own language, Mr. Pope and Dr. Swift have each of them introduced a manner different from what was practised before, into all works that are written in rhyme, the one in long verses, the other in short. The quaintness of Butler has given place to the plainness of Swift. The rambling freedom of Dryden, and the correct but often tedious and prosaic languor of Addison, are no longer the objects of imitation, but all long verses are now written after the manner of the nervous precision of Mr. Pope.[4]

We should note that Adam Smith takes seriously Swift's status as a poetic initiator, perhaps equal to Pope, but in an alternative (and not necessarily inferior) style. The reputations of both writers were often seen as competing, and nine years earlier the minor poet Shenstone, praising Swift's poetic pre-eminence, did so with an explicit dismissal of Pope: 'I must beg Mr. Pope's

Pardon so far as to esteem Dr. Swift (tho' in a way rather contemptuous of regular Poetry and therefore manly) ye Poetical *Genius* of ye Age he liv'd in. He had inconceivable Invention, wch was not remarkably ye Talent of ye other.'[5]

Shenstone, like Adam Smith in a more nuanced way, nevertheless assumes that Pope's reputation is the officially recognized one. It is in this context that Swift himself sometimes subscribed, or pretended to subscribe, to the view that he was not a poet, 'only a Man of Rhimes, ... never having written serious Couplets in my Life'.[6] There seems to have been no envy or false modesty in this remark. He would probably have accepted the common view of later generations that identified Pope as the great poet of the time and Swift as the great master of satirical prose, and would perhaps not have felt affronted at the relative neglect of his poetry by later readers. Samuel Johnson wrote a life of Swift in the *Lives of the Poets* (1779–81) which, although originally written as a preface to Swift's poems, barely mentioned the poems at all, beyond saying that 'In the Poetical Works of Dr. Swift there is not much upon which the critick can exercise his powers.'[7] There is irony in Johnson's statement, not only because he disliked Swift, partly from an unacknowledged sense of resemblance, but also because, although a poet of distinction himself, he was adopting, as a 'critick', a view which came to be more characteristic of critics than of other poets.

When the reputation of eighteenth-century writers was at a low ebb, roughly between the 1790s and 1920, it was the poet Byron, also a great admirer of Pope, who championed and imitated Swift's poetic style. When Pope began to be rehabilitated in the 1920s, it was largely a critical and academic movement, though the poet Edith Sitwell was an early enthusiast and T. S. Eliot an admirer.[8] Swift's poetry on the other hand continued to receive little attention, except from poets.[9] James Reeves, who, like Yeats, but unlike Eliot and Auden, detested Pope, wrote an entire volume, *The Reputation and Writings of Alexander Pope* (1976), denouncing what he described as an academic conspiracy to elevate Pope at the expense of better poets, notably Swift, whose poems he anthologized in his series the Poetry Bookshelf. Ted Hughes, who continued to dislike 'everything post-Restoration in Eng Lit, ... except for the generation of Blake, Wordsworth, Coleridge, Keats', made a special exception of Swift and Christopher Smart, whom he regarded as victims or casualties of an unpoetic era, perhaps with their Popeian loyalties in mind.[10] Academic recognition came later. Until recent decades, very few extended studies of Swift's poems existed, and a partial reversal of this trend from the 1970s was led by a number of women scholars, paradoxically, in the light of Swift's reputation for misogyny.

Nevertheless, Swift's autobiographical poems make it clear that he also readily thought of himself, and had a reputation, as a poet: 'Nay, 'twas affirm'd, he sometimes dealt in Rhime', he reported in 'The Author upon Himself' (1714, 1735, line 10).[11] In his *Verses on the Death of Dr. Swift* (1731, 1739), he jauntily reports that he was indeed once regarded as a 'Fav'rite of *Apollo*' (line 249), 'famous in his Time' precisely for his 'Knack at Rhyme', though fashions have changed and 'His way of Writing now is past' (lines 263–5).[12] This is ambiguously self-dismissive. It also contains self-affirmation, and the flipness reflects his habitual shyness of grand gestures. He took himself seriously as a poet in the way that he and others took seriously his predecessor in 'serious' light verse, Samuel Butler, author of *Hudibras* (1663–80). Swift did actually write decasyllabic or 'heroic' couplets, but in an idiom less tightly structured or grandiloquent than Pope's, whose 'serious Couplet' mode Swift readily accepted as a higher thing than his own versifying.

Pope was Swift's friend and collaborator, and, in the view quickly established at the time and subsequently adopted as a commonplace of literary history, the greatest poet of the day. (The traditional stereotype usually identified Swift as correspondingly the greatest prose-writer.) Pope's most ambitious poem, *The Dunciad* (1728–43), was dedicated to Swift, and Swift collaborated on it in some way. The two were allies in the culture wars and the political contentions of their time. No doubt existed in Swift's mind as to Pope's mastery, and he might be said to have shown his lack of envy freely in a genial display of mock-envy:

> In Pope, I cannot read a Line,
> But with a Sigh, I wish it mine:
> When he can in one Couplet fix
> More Sense than I can do in Six:
> It gives me such a jealous Fit,
> I cry, Pox take him, and his Wit.
>
> (*Verses on the Death of Dr. Swift*, lines 47–52)

The lines carry the ambiguous charm of affectionate autobiography in which genial self-tolerance teeters on the edge of self-regard. It is one of several attractive portrayals of Swift and his friends. But the eagerness to affirm, in the same poem, that 'Fair LIBERTY was all his Cry' (line 347), while making sure the remark is attributed not to himself but to an impartial obituarist, is an essential feature. The attractions of a companionable self-approbation, repudiating grand statements about himself while simultaneously making sure they are made, are precariously close to a benign bad faith. Pope would have no difficulty making such statements grandly and overtly, and Swift fully accepted the rightness of his doing so.

A similarly self-exculpating coyness, pretending to some discreditable moral lapses but indicating thereby that he's not like that really, is more prominently apparent in the tortuously self-justifying account, in *Cadenus and Vanessa* (1713, 1726), of one of his two important love-affairs. Here too compliments to another are oblique compliments to himself, the compliment resting awkwardly on a seeming self-depreciation. The moral convolutions of that poem, to which I return later, have a mincing self-consciousness Swift himself would normally be quick to disown, but also a sign of the satirist's intimate inwardness with the human frailties he deplores. There are other such moments, a small wrinkle in a great writerly achievement. But despite the affected indirections, there seems for the most part neither envy nor malice in the 'jealous Fit' about Pope's couplets, only admiration and an unquestioning assumption that Pope's is the kind of poetry that really matters, and Swift freely accepted a substantially lower place in the pecking order of poetical honours.

Swift's avowed avoidance of 'serious Couplets' expresses a shrinking from all styles with pretensions to 'serousness' or dignity. But when he added that his verses were 'never without a moral View', he was affirming the claims of an alternative style, informal, self-mocking, playfully irreverent of verse conventions. The 'wonderful' rhyming praised by Byron did not consist of euphonic exactitude, but was a cheeky defiance of expected harmonious closures, as in these examples from *A Character, Panegyric, and Description of the Legion Club* (1736), a late invective on the Irish House of Commons:

> As I strole the City, oft I
> Spy a Building large and lofty,
> Half a Bow-shot from the College,
> Half the Globe from Sense and Knowledge.
>
> ... Such a Triplet could you tell
> Where to find on this Side Hell?
> *H[arrison]*, and *D[ilkes]*, and *C[lements]*,
> Souse them in their own Ex-crements.
>
> ... How I want thee, humorous *Hogart*?
> Thou I hear, a pleasant Rogue art.
>
> (lines 1–4, 183–6, 219–20)[13]

This is a style of rhyming that Byron, the Shelley of *Peter Bell the Third*, and the Auden of 'A Letter to Lord Byron' exploited with great inventiveness. 'Bad' rhyming is a witty resource, partly drawn from popular entertainments (still in evidence, for example, in calypso and reggae), much used in English demotic art from the Middle Ages onwards, in farces, heroic rants, and puppet-shows. It is exploited by a long line of non-demotic, sophisticated poets including John Skelton, Charles Cotton, Samuel Butler (one of Swift's favourite writers, 'whose comic rhymes', as Derek Mahon says, 'he imitated and surpassed'),[14] Byron, Shelley, Eliot, Auden, and more recently Gavin Ewart. It is a staple of the kind of poetry Auden anthologized in his *Oxford Book of Light Verse* (1938) and belongs to what another poet, Ronald Bottrall, described as 'the colloquial tradition in English poetry'.[15]

'Bad' or 'imperfect' rhymes are not normally the result of carelessness or inattention, though they are sometimes designed to give that impression. They are 'serious' poetic devices, in the sense in which Auden said 'light verse can be serious' (Swift's 'never without a moral View').[16] One of their elementary registers is a cavalier defiance of expectations of euphony, closure, order, the values embedded in the Popeian couplet, though it should be said again that Swift was not attacking Pope or the couplet. He may even have been paying it the tribute of suggesting, or simulating, a sense that its high standard was outside his own modest reach. At all events he was indicating a non-adversarial disengagement from its obligations, without conceding that this was relaxation of the 'moral View' he claimed for all his poems.

Some (especially later) poets have taught us that faulty rhyming can retain the 'seriousness' Swift disavowed, without necessarily sharing Swift's starting point of light-hearted parody. Wilfred Owen's poems (for example, 'Exposure', 'Insensibility', 'Strange Meeting') subvert the closures of rhyme not by jokily deflating a reader's expectations of order, but by evoking the grinding painfulness and senseless disarray of trench warfare. The systematic and protracted appearance of discordant near rhymes ('killed/cold', 'brothers/withers', 'knives us/nervous', 'wire/war', 'burn/born', 'fruit/afraid', 'grained/groined', 'hall/hell', 'moan/mourn', 'distilled/spoiled') shows the extent to which the initiating parodic joke of a bad rhyme can be discarded, in the way that some modern writers, notably T. S. Eliot in *The Waste Land*, have succeeded in discarding mockery of epic poems while availing themselves of the poetic resources provided by mock-heroic poems. Even in his most sombre poem, the *Dunciad*, Pope could not free himself from the joke implied in its very nature as a mock-*Aeneid*. Swift would not have wished to try. The horrors of the mock-Virgilian inferno of the *Legion Club* openly retain a style of robust demotic invective, rather than the dignified Virgilian majesty Pope would have sought to achieve while travestying it.

Swift would have no truck, in his own writing, with the majestic accents of the *Dunciad*, a poem which, as I have mentioned, was dedicated to him and to which he probably contributed. His own rough way with rhyming, as in 'C[lements]/Ex-crements', remains playful, serving an aggressive political invective intended to hurt beyond the joke. One of the effects is to express intensities of indignation without surrendering composure. The model is not Juvenalian eloquence, but the accents of street balladry and rough bardic invective, into which Swift simultaneously injects a patrician loftiness. In *Traulus* (1730), Swift denounces another Irish politician, whose low ancestry is the subject of similarly high-spirited discordancies:

> Who cou'd give the Looby such Airs?
> Were they Masons, were they Butchers?
> ... This was dext'rous at his Trowel,
> That was bred to kill a Cow well. (*Traulus*, II. 25–30)

The mock-demotic clumsiness of the rhyming is brought into ironic relief by the fact that it expresses a billowing contempt for the victim's origins, and that its ritualized, drumming syncopation intermittently blends primitive incantation with a command of strict and perfect rhyme:

> TRAULUS of Amphibious Breed,
> Motly Fruit of Mungril Seed:
> By the *Dam* from Lordlings sprung,
> By the *Sire* exhal'd from Dung. (II. 1–4)

In this context the ostensible awkwardness of 'such Airs / Butchers' and 'Trowel / Cow well' becomes ostentatious, a stylish flouting of stylishness, fully under the poet's control.

Swift's late poems about Irish politicians draw additionally on traditions of magical imprecation which go back to ancient ideas of the power of words to kill. Irish bards were traditionally reputed for their ability to rhyme rats to death, a skill which was also applied to rival poets, a tradition alluded to through the ages by Ben Jonson and W. B. Yeats, as well as Swift.[17] Ben Jonson spoke of the death-dealing 'drumming rhymes' of Irish bards, a commonly invoked instance of the primitive power of satire.[18] These repetitive curses work similarly to mingle crude demotic energies with a lordly disdain of the lord's lowly origins, and an undemotic allusiveness to classical poetry (the Muse; *Atavus*, the Latin word for ancestor; etc.). The application of a low idiom to uppishness creates a witty and sophisticated comedy out of the disgraces of the physical body and social class. The invective is harsh and hyperbolic, but its excess is partly self-disarming, and the tempo's high-spirited jauntiness conveys an impression that the poet is having fun with his excessive insults and isn't going over the top.

This witty undercutting of rage is essential to Swift's manner. It extends to non-invective contexts, and is a temperamental feature which underlies his deliberate and proclaimed refusal of the 'serious Couplet', a verse-form which was sometimes called 'heroic'. Swift's praise of Pope's couplets, each able to fix more sense than Swift could do in six, not only signposts his own avoidance of a disciplined definitional style in favour of a lighter and more garrulous metre, but is also related to a shyness of high styles. This manner thrives on a sophisticated adaptation of crude and indecorous popular rhythms and vocabulary, freedoms of verbal informality which court risks of clumsiness and offer special opportunities for an exuberant irreverence unavailable in the more licensed poetic styles.

Swift's ear for the accents and cadences of popular speech and street language has been remarked on by James Reeves and other poets.[19] Swift had a connoisseur's feeling for these, as well as for the idiocies of polite conversation. This is evident in his Flaubertian mania for collecting absurdities in his brilliant prose sottisier, *A Compleat Collection of Genteel and Ingenious Conversation*, published in 1738. This late work, the product of years of obsessive recording, displays gifts that might have been used in the creation of novels or stage comedies, if Swift had been willing to convert mimicry into full fictional impersonation. But Swift held back, or declined, the full surrender of authorial presence to imaginative sympathy this would have required. He could capture brilliantly what was available for mockery, but would not seek an illusion of reality, in the manner of his despised contemporary Daniel Defoe. The snatches of conversation in the *Compleat Collection* stand as individual absurdities, with only a nugatory dimension of story or character, and no strong sense of the characters' relations with each other.

The same collecting instinct, and the same ear for characteristic speech, evident in the polite inanities of the *Compleat Collection* may be seen, stripped of some of its acerbity, in Swift's mimicry of more demotic speakers. These, unlike the polite version, come more often in verse than in prose, as in the collection of Dublin street cries, 'Verses made for Women who cry Apples, &c.', posthumously published in 1746 and doubtless also collected over time. The series begins with a buoyancy reminiscent of the energetic lyricism of Christina Rossetti's 'Goblin Market' (1862):

Come buy my fine Wares,
Plumbs, Apples and Pears,
A hundred a Penny,
In Conscience too many,
Come, will you have any.[20]

The tone darkens, not, as in Rossetti's poem, into disquieting fairy lore, but into an unillusioned social pathos:

My Children are seven,
I wish them in Heaven,
My Husband's a Sot,

With his Pipe and his Pot,
Not a Farthing will gain 'em,
And I must maintain 'em.

The pathos is harsh. The woman who wishes her seven children 'in Heaven' is not harder-souled than the child speaker in Wordsworth's lyrical ballad 'We are seven' (1798), but retains a grim gusto for life in the face of poverty and her dispiriting domestic life.

The oyster-seller's song does not engage with these dark social realities. It too pays affable attention to popular idiom, adding a satirical rundown of dietary superstitions:

Charming Oysters I cry,
My Masters come buy,
So plump and so fresh,
So sweet is their Flesh,
  No *Colchester* Oyster,
  Is sweeter and moyster,
  Your Stomach they settle,
  And rouse up your Mettle,
  They'll make you a Dad
  Of a Lass or a Lad;
  And, Madam your Wife
  They'll please to the Life;
Be she barren, be she old,
Be she Slut, or be she Scold,
Eat my Oysters, and lye near her,
She'll be fruitful, never fear her.[21]

The genially satirical treatment of folk ideas about the digestive and procreative virtues of food is more characteristic of these poems than is the realism of 'Apples'.

The poem about oranges is written in a longer hendecasyllabic (eleven-syllable) metre, which is one of the forms, sometimes favoured by Swift, through which light verse challenges the finalities of the iambic pentameter. It reveals a warm culinary gusto beneath a deceptive appearance of satirical sting:

Come, buy my fine Oranges, Sauce for your Veal,
And charming when squeez'd in a Pot of brown Ale.
Well roasted, with Sugar and Wine in a Cup,
They'll make a sweet Bishop when Gentlefolks sup.[22]

'Sweet Bishop' is a brew of mulled port, not a tart reflection on the ecclesiastical hierarchy. It is perhaps worth noticing that the warmth of feeling in the poem is focused more on the taste of the food and the luxuriance of the sales-talk than on the gentlefolk's supping. Gentlefolk are in any case a recessive presence in these poems. Altogether, this collection of demotic street cries has a good humour not usually extended to the politer classes. Even the signature sting about bad breath in the poem about onions ('lest your Kissing should be spoyl'd') is unusually benign, especially when one remembers the prominence of halitosis, in servants as well as their masters, of that other late satirical compilation, *Directions to Servants*, a prose work, published not long before the posthumous street cries, in the year of Swift's death (1745), and consisting of satirical commentary rather than mimicry.

The *Directions to Servants* reminds us that the lower orders are no more immune than their masters from the failings of the common Yahoo. It is also possible that Swift saw servants as typically tainted by their relationship to, as well as the example of, their masters. The gusto with which Swift enters into the cries of street sellers suggests something of the patrician play of sympathy which Augustan writers sometimes affected for non-competing social groups, and which Yeats (with his mind partly on Swift's writings) extended to his whole dramatis personae of wise beggars. Swift too wrote poems with wise beggars, the best-known of which is 'Mad Mullinix and Timothy' (1728), an early example of the series of poems on Irish parliamentarians which includes *Traulus* and the *Legion Club*. Mad Mullinix has something of the folly of the righteous, which is a kind of wisdom. He is a Tory adversary to the Whiggery of Dublin's governing group, and thus shares Swiftian sympathies, though he is not otherwise an expression of fondness for beggars or lunatics, or a shining example of the more exalted understanding, which Yeats attributed to Swift, 'that wisdom comes of beggary'.[23]

We know from many other writings that Swift had no more affection for beggars than, on the evidence of the *Directions*, he had for servants. The harshness of the satire against servants in the *Directions*, which Ian Higgins has described as 'a master's nightmare of household subversion and anarchy where the turpitude of servants is manic', parallels the comments in Swift's sermon on the *Causes of the Wretched Condition of Ireland* (1715) and elsewhere.[24] But the *Directions* has a force which, like the brilliant *Tale of a Tub*, derives some of its inventive energy from the 'manic' nature of the depravities it is describing. Both works are examples of a process in which an author's creative powers transfer their grace to a graceless subject-matter, and confer on unlovely material something of the virtues of sympathetic mimicry.

It is perhaps the feat of mimicry which gives a particular charm to two favourite poems by Swift in which servants are speaking, 'Mrs Harris's Petition' (1701, published 1711) and 'Mary the Cook-Maid's Letter' (1718, published 1732). Like the street cries, both poems are characterized by somewhat unexpected exactitudes of demotic ventriloquism. In this they resemble the pub scene in the 'Game of Chess' section of T. S. Eliot's *The Waste Land*, the work of an author who might seem similarly disinclined to dramatic impersonation, and whose other poems register a downbeat view of human society, strongly coloured by Swiftian influences. 'Doing the police in different voices' (the phrase Eliot recalled from Dickens's *Our Mutual Friend* (Ch. xvi) for the species of social ventriloquism exhibited in 'A Game of Chess', and which he borrowed for an early title of *The Waste Land*) is not a practice we immediately think of as characteristic of either poet.[25] It is conducted with extraordinary skill in the dialogue in *The Waste Land*, and Eliot may have been helped in its composition.[26] It is almost unique in his work, and has no equivalent in his plays. The woodenness with which Eliot rendered it in his recordings of *The Waste Land* suggests the kind of uneasiness at the prospect of a total surrender to his fictional creation which we may imagine Swift to have felt at the idea of writing a Richardsonian novel.

The brilliance of Eliot's lines resides in a dry, depressed atmosphere, captured with a precision whose gusto consists of a denial of gusto. By contrast, the servant Frances Harris, reporting the loss of her purse, containing 'seven Pound, four Shillings and six Pence, besides Farthings, in Money, and Gold ... And, *God* knows, I thought my Money was as safe as my Maidenhead' (lines 2, 11), is as far removed from Eliot's 'damp souls of housemaids' as it is possible to be (though Eliot's phrase comes from 'Morning at the Window', a poem almost certainly influenced by Swift's 'Description of the Morning').[27] This maid, portrayed as being sweet on the parson Swift ('You know, I honour the Cloth, I design to be a *Parson*'s Wife', line 60), is, despite her loss of a considerable sum, a buoyantly garrulous spirit, with a generous feeling for the misprisions and malapropisms of herself and her peers,

Then my Dame *Wadgar* came, and she, you know, is thick of Hearing;
Dame, said I, as loud as I could bawl, do you know what a Loss I have had?
Nay, said she, my Lord *Collway*'s Folks are all very sad,
For my Lord *Dromedary* [Drogheda] comes a *Tuesday* without fail,
(lines 25–8)

and a heaving amplitude about her misfortune, her suspicion of theft, and the comedy of cunningly clumsy imputation:

So I went to the Party suspected, and I found her full of Grief;
(Now you must know, of all Things in the World, I hate a Thief.)
However, I was resolv'd to bring the Discourse slily about,
Mrs. *Dukes*, said I, here's an ugly Accident has happen'd out;
'Tis not that I value the Money three Skips of a Louse;

But the Thing I stand upon, is the Credit of the House;
'Tis true, seven Pound, four Shillings, and six Pence, makes a great Hole
    in my Wages,
Besides, as they say, Service is no Inheritance in these Ages.
Now, Mrs. *Dukes*, you know, and every Body understands,
That tho' 'tis hard to judge, yet Money can't go without Hands.
The *Devil* take me, said she, (blessing her self,) if I ever saw't!
So she roar'd like a *Bedlam*, as tho' I had call'd her all to naught,
So you know, what could I say to her any more. (lines 34–46)

The metre is a loping free verse which might be the envy of that master of metrical garrulities, Ogden Nash. Her use of colourful cliché ('Tis not that I value the Money three Skips of a Louse') is the demotic counterpart of the polite inanities of the *Compleat Collection* or the funereal chatter of the fine ladies in the *Verses on the Death* – ('The Dean is dead *(and what is Trumps?)*') – but more kindly treated.[28] The self-righteous humbug of 'But the Thing I stand upon, is the Credit of the House' is rendered with a kind of Chaucerian tolerance, and the colloquial mastery even in the least colourful phrasings ('So you know, what could I say to her any more') has a geniality of accomplished performance which somehow rubs off on the character herself.

The poem ends with some reimbursement promised by Lord Berkeley, one of 'the Lords Justices of Ireland' being humbly petitioned. Frances Harris was petitioning for their 'Protection, / And that I may have a Share in next *Sunday*'s Collection, … With an Order for the *Chaplain* aforesaid; or, instead of Him, a Better' (lines 70–3). Swift portrays his female servants as having a self-interested affection for him, including marital ambitions. 'Mary the Cook-Maid's Letter to Dr. Sheridan' is written to complain that Swift's friend and fellow-parson Thomas Sheridan (grandfather of the playwright Richard Brinsley Sheridan) had 'call'd my Master a Knave' (line 5):[29]

Knave in your Teeth, Mr. *Sheridan*, 'tis both a Shame and a Sin,
And the Dean my Master is an honester Man than you and all your kin:
He has more Goodness in his little Finger, than you have in your whole Body,
My Master is a parsonable Man, and not a spindle-shank'd hoddy-doddy
And now whereby I find you would fain make an Excuse,
Because my Master one Day in anger call'd you Goose.
Which, and I am sure I have been his Servant four Years since *October*,
And he never call'd me worse than Sweet-heart drunk or sober.
(lines 7–14)

Frances Harris signalling her nuptial designs on Swift (at the time chaplain to the Earl of Berkeley, whose daughter she served), and Mary's boast that the Dean 'never call'd me worse than Sweet-heart', are comic enactments of the stereotype of the maid aspiring to raise her status by marrying the parson, though Swift did habitually call Mary 'Sweet-heart'.[30] Only a few years later, the scenario of a maid marrying her employer would be the subject of Richardson's best-selling novel *Pamela* (1740), parodied in Fielding's *Shamela* (1741), where the longings of serving-women are seen in a less generous light. The naïve marital aspirations of Mrs Harris and the Cook-Maid give way to the shameless mercenary designs and lusty profligacy of the minx Shamela, who marries the squire for his money *and* disports herself with the parson. Swift employs language (and spellings) Fielding was to turn to hostile use, and writes for once more good-naturedly than his disciple. When Mary says 'My Master is a parsonable Man, and not a spindle-shank'd hoddy-doddy', she looks forward to Shamela's protestations about her 'vartue' and her contemptuous description of her husband as a '*spindle-shanked ... Squire*'.[31] Fielding uses the phrase regularly of beaux and sexual suitors of questionable virility, presumably the meaning intended by Mary the Cook-Maid, but offered by Swift as an affectionate take-off of colloquial servant-speak, and a token of the maid's loyalty, rather than a slur on his friend Sheridan, though the poem is part of a sparring match with the latter.[32]

Like his record of polite conversation, these imitations of servant language may be described as 'realistic', but their realism is that of the take-off rather than of an extended simulation of character. Unlike the polite mimicries of the *Compleat Collection*, these two servant monologues are written with an affectionate complicity which may seem inconsistent with some of Swift's views about servants expressed elsewhere. This is enhanced by the ambiguous touch of eroticism, which in both cases shows the woman voicing what are evidently unthreatening expressions of affection. In 1713, Swift wrote a very different poem, in which a woman, who was not a servant, was deeply in love with the same dean, and which did not portray the situation as unthreatening, though a kind of self-flattery may be common to all three poems.

Cadenus and Vanessa (1713, published 1726) reports the passion of a brilliant and beautiful younger woman, Vanessa (Swift's name for Esther Vanhomrigh (1688–1723), which has passed into the language as a girl's name), for the mature clergyman Cadenus (anagram of Decanus, or Dean), who has guided her intellectual education.[33] The implication is that she thus acquired the discernment to fall in love with a man who might not otherwise have expected to be attractive to a young woman, and who now professes himself to be surprised and discomfited by the result. The poem is coy about the outcome: 'But what Success *Vanessa* met, / Is to the World a Secret yet' (lines 818–19), a self-conscious innuendo Swift would be quick to mock in others, and which anticipates the winking will-tell-won't-tell fuss over what passed between Tristram Shandy and his 'dear, dear *Jenny*' in Sterne's novel (I. xviii) half a century later.[34] The poem, which might be thought a prime exhibit in any possible imputation of contempt for women, is much admired in some feminist circles. In real life, the story ended tragically, but the facts of the relationship remain obscure.

The poem revolves around the fable of a divine plot to create a woman with all the virtues of both sexes. The male virtues are those of intellect and learning, and Vanessa's attainments are partly offered as a demonstration of Swift's genuine belief in the educability of women, and in the need for society to think of them as something other than exalted beings or pretty objects of gallantry. While also making the point that even a woman so educated could not hope to emulate male accomplishments, Swift held that the acquisition of intellectual and moral qualities was the only basis on which a woman could maintain a man's respect after the passing of her physical attractions. While this remains a male-centred position and takes disagreeable forms in this poem, it is the mainstay of a conscientious and serious conviction that 'fair-sexing', as he called it, was a falsifying feature of both social and literary behaviour, and distorted the possibility of mutual respect between the sexes.

This conviction is expressed in the prose *Letter to a Young Lady on her Marriage* (1723).[35] It is also at the centre of two important groups of poems, those addressed to Stella (1719–27), and a set of satires on the theme of female beauty whose most important examples run from 'The Progress of Beauty' (1719) to *The Lady's Dressing Room* (1730) and 'A Beautiful Young Nymph Going to Bed' (1731, published 1734), and include the famous poems about Celia and Chloe. Stella (Esther Johnson, 1681–1728) was Swift's closest and steadiest woman friend, or even (as some think) his secret wife. Their friendship, though in its way richly documented, is little understood. It is clear that he felt for her a devotion and tenderness he expressed for no one else. Like Vanessa, she was seen as the product of his tutoring, and is said in his poems to her to have risen to the standards of moral and intellectual excellence which Swift thought necessary to ensure a durable and mutually respectful friendship with a serious man.

It is only in the poems to Stella that Swift seriously risked the vocabulary of gallantry, even then lacing it with an awareness of its limits in the face of the ravages of age. In the poem for 'Stella's Birth-Day' (1725), he wrily surveys their friendship, with an acute awareness of the tension between poetic compliment and the realities of old age:

> Beauty and Wit, too sad a Truth,
> Have always been confin'd to Youth;

The God of Wit, and Beauty's Queen,
He Twenty one, and She Fifteen:
No Poet ever sweetly sung,
Unless he were like *Phœbus*, young;
Nor ever Nymph inspir'd to Rhyme,
Unless, like *Venus*, in her Prime.
At Fifty six, if this be true,
Am I a Poet fit for you?
Or at the Age of Forty three,
Are you a Subject fit for me?
Adieu bright Wit, and radiant Eyes;
You must be grave, and I be wise.
Our Fate in vain we would oppose,
But I'll still be your Friend in Prose:
Esteem and Friendship to express,
Will not require Poetick Dress;
And if the Muse deny her Aid
To have them *sung*, they may be *said*. (lines 15–34)

His final compliment to her sustains the hyperbole he considers due to her virtues, and then muses with a painful twist on the capacity of his own fading faculties to apprehend them:

But, *Stella* say, what evil Tongue
Reports you are no longer young?
That *Time* sits with his Scythe to mow
Where erst sate *Cupid* with his Bow;
That half your Locks are turn'd to Grey;
I'll ne'er believe a Word they say.
'Tis true, but let it not be known,
My Eyes are somewhat dimmish grown;
For Nature, always in the Right,
To your Decays adapts my Sight,
And Wrinkles undistinguish'd pass,
For I'm asham'd to use a Glass;
And till I see them with these Eyes,
Whoever says you have them, lyes.

No Length of Time can make you quit
Honour and Virtue, Sense and Wit,
Thus you may still be young to me,
While I can better *hear* than *see*;
Oh, ne'er may Fortune shew her Spight,
To make me *deaf*, and mend my *Sight*.[36] (lines 35–54)

He later added in the margin of a copy of the poem 'now deaf 1740'.

Contrasting with, and complementary to, the poems to Stella is a series of satires which include the 'scatological' poems of the late 1720s and early 1730s. In two of these, *The Lady's Dressing Room* (written in 1730, published in 1732, and containing a friendly parody of Belinda's toilette in Pope's *Rape of the Lock*) and 'Cassinus and Peter' (1731, 1734), a half-witted swain discovers to his dismay that his sweetheart defecates, like anyone else, a fact denied, or occluded, in romances and love-poems, as well as in the idiom of gallant compliment.[37] The refrain that '*Celia, Celia, Celia* shits' (line 118), which is echoed by a similar plaint about the mock-pastoral heroine in 'Strephon and Chloe' (1731, 1734), urinating on her wedding night, became the focus of denunciations of Swift's misogyny and body-hatred by such vocal promoters of sexual wholesomeness as D. H. Lawrence and Aldous Huxley.[38]

There is much debate over Swift's purported misogyny, but the mockery in these poems is chiefly at the expense of the besotted young men who are unable to come to terms with the obvious fact that women are subject to the same human needs as men. A poem which belongs to the same group, 'A Beautiful Young Nymph Going to Bed', offers a less light-hearted picture of an ageing prostitute, who sheds her cosmetic and prosthetic aids to beauty when going to bed.[39] It is this poem, not those with the catchy refrain about Celia, that might be thought seriously vulnerable to allegations of body-disgust. Even here there is evidence of a playful excess comparable to that of the political invectives, where an over-the-top intensity comes across to some extent as a self-disarming stylistic sport. The poem nevertheless displays a harshness or astringency not evident in the light-hearted élan of 'Cassinus and Peter' or 'Strephon and Chloe'. All these poems, including the 'Beautiful Young Nymph', are mock-pastorals, in a scabrous urban setting, with heroines bearing the pastoral names of Celia, Chloe, or Corinna (the last, however, carrying less innocent associations too).

Whatever their psycho-biographical implications, all these poems register a determination to counter the damaging absurdities of fair-sexing. On balance, their main thrust is against these, and in favour of recognition that women are neither angels nor whores, but human creatures with the frailties and some of the moral and intellectual potential that go with the territory. That their equality is in many ways that of the common Yahoo reflects the downbeat view of human nature most fully articulated in *Gulliver's Travels* (1726), where humanity is viewed as exemplifying all the vices it attributes to its own despised sexual and racial subgroups.

If Swift accepted the idea that the heroic couplet, the rhyming iambic pentameter line of ten syllables, was, as Pope practised it, the norm to aspire to, his choice of a briefer, racier, colloquial, 'low' metre makes a statement less about the standing of the couplet than about his own relationship to high, dignified speech. In his *Epistle to a Lady, Who desired the Author to make Verses on Her, in the Heroick Stile* (possibly written in 1728, published 1733), he playfully but firmly said that 'For your Sake as well as mine, / I the lofty Stile decline' (lines 217–18).[40] What was declined was not only the high rhetoric of epic or mock-epic, or the elevated discursiveness of a philosophical poem, but the high style of extravagant compliments to ladies. He often parodied the latter, because he regarded the compliments of love-poetry as a ridiculous convention. But his remarks clearly also referred to satiric indignations like those of the Roman satirist Juvenal. Swift argued that ridicule was a more effective weapon than railing, without denying the intense feelings that provoked the invective of such poems as *Traulus* and the *Legion Club*: 'In a Jest I spend my Rage: (Tho' it must be understood, I would hang them if I cou'd)' (lines 168–70).

This jesting is not a matter of witty urbanity, of the kind he uses to deflect the lady's request, but one of an exuberant excess of insult which is itself disarmed to some extent precisely because it is excessive, a rant protected by an element of mock-rant. The real agenda is not to declaim, for that involves a loss of poise. Instead, he proposes entering the dirty world of the enemy, and punishing him by undignified intimacies of humiliation resembling the *Legion Club*'s 'Souse them in their own Ex-crements' (line 186):

> Let me, tho' the smell be Noisome,
> Strip their bums; let CALEB hoys'em;
> Then, apply ALECTO's whip,
> Till they wriggle, howl, and skip. (lines 177–80)

Just as the declared objective of *Gulliver's Travels* was to 'vex the world rather th[a]n divert it', as Swift said to Pope in a letter of 29 September 1725, so the aim here is to get his victims to 'wriggle, howl, and skip', set their 'Spirits all a working' (line 205), arousing a species of panic rather than crushing them by denunciation. To conclude his rejection of high styles, Swift additionally, and only half-mockingly, confesses that he fears making a fool of himself: 'I Shou'd make a Figure scurvy' (line 219). The fear that lofty styles would make a figure scurvy, the predilection for a low-key idiom, and the affectations of light-hearted inconsequence are part of an atmosphere Auden described in later poets, for whom 'light verse', in the context of prevailing poetic pretensions, provided the only possibility of a 'sufficient intimacy with their audience to be able to forget themselves and their singing-robes'.[41]

Swift did occasionally write 'couplets', and we may try to discern what he meant about their not being 'serious':

Now hardly here and there an Hackney-Coach
Appearing, show'd the Ruddy Morns Approach.
Now *Betty* from her Masters Bed had flown,
And softly stole to discompose her own.
The Slipshod Prentice from his Masters Door,
Had par'd the Dirt, and Sprinkled round the Floor.
Now *Moll* had whirl'd her Mop with dext'rous Airs,
Prepar'd to Scrub the Entry and the Stairs.
The Youth with Broomy Stumps began to trace
The Kennel-Edge, where Wheels had worn the Place.
The Smallcoal-Man was heard with Cadence deep,
'Till drown'd in Shriller Notes of Chimney-Sweep,
Duns at his Lordships Gate began to meet,
And Brickdust *Moll* had Scream'd through half the Street.
The Turnkey now his Flock returning sees,
Duly let out a Nights to Steal for Fees.
The watchful Bailiffs take their silent Stands,
And School-Boys lag with Satchels in their Hands.
('A Description of the Morning', 1709)[42]

Swift's couplets are indeed not Popeian, and were written before Pope's appearance as an influential presence on the literary scene. The 'Description of the Morning' appeared on 30 April 1709, three days before Pope first appeared in print on 2 May.[43] While Swift always accepted that 'serious Couplets' were Pope's territory, his own practice in this form is one which goes back to Chaucer, a poet whose more informal version of this metre Pope chose to 'translate' into Popeian couplets, in a manner which W. K. Wimsatt has described as differing from Chaucer's in 'its closure or completeness, its stronger tendency to parallel, and its epigrammatic, witty, intellectual point'.[44] Arguably, Swift's array of social types, and especially the sharp but also softened castigation, similarly share Chaucerian features. The more relaxed nature of Swift's lines, their flat, incremental observation of human activity, differ from Pope's tightly structured and pointedly definitional portrayals of character. Swift's pentameters often tap older traditions, untouched by 'correctness', and are closer to 'the oblique forward movement of actions in sequence' Wimsatt perceives in Chaucer.[45]

We can see from Swift's 'Description' what he means when he says his poetry is 'never without a moral View', even when dealing with 'low' subject-matter with a good-natured drabness. But in this, as in the formal or structural sense, we also see how he would think his couplets unserious by the Popeian standard. Swift's very way of imitating or travestying his classical models also differs from Pope's. The 'Description' parodies formal descriptions of dawn in heroic or rural settings, the mundane and scabrous realities of an urban morning played off against formal models describing a battlefield sunrise or a georgic or pastoral scene. A few years later, Pope described Belinda, the heroine of *The Rape of the Lock* (1714), rising like the sun among her entourage of beautiful people:

> Not with more Glories, in th' Etherial Plain
> The Sun first rises o'er the purpled Main,
> Than issuing forth, the Rival of his Beams
> Lanch'd on the Bosom of the Silver *Thames*. (II. 1–4)

Pope's lines, like Swift's, evoke epic or georgic originals, similarly pitting them against a lowered modern reality, in this case a society of amiable and silly flirts. Pope adds the mock-gallantry of comparing the heroine's eyes to the sun, a staple of the kind of love-poetry about which Swift also wrote, both derisively and poignantly, in other poems. The blowsy elevation of Pope's mock-grandeur, however, is designed to allow an element of original grandeurs to rub off on the parody. Unlike Swift in the 'Description', he actually uses high language for his low people, allowing part of the inflation to flower into a dignity of its own, a trick cultivated in recent decades in the mock-heroic poems of Boileau, Dryden, and Garth. This procedure reinforces an element of genuine compliment to Belinda, the real beauty and charm of her person and behaviour ('graceful Ease, and Sweetness void of Pride'), so that the mock-gallantries acquire their own quality of lyricized celebration (II. 15).

This is what Swift's refusal of the lofty style is partly about, a shrinking not only from conventions of inflated compliment, but from grandeurs which survive (in the way Dryden or Pope wanted them to) in the very idiom of mock-pompous pastiche. Swift's 'Description of the Morning' offers instead a flat, hard-edged comedy of low misdemeanours, downbeat and uninflated, evoking higher styles not by misapplying them to low matter, but by highlighting the lowness where grandiose gesturing might have been expected. High originals announce themselves by an effacement rather than pretension of grandeur. Swift's friend Gay, future author of the *Beggar's Opera* (1728), was to follow Swift in composing scenes of urban busyness and squalor in forms usually applied to pastoral subjects. But Swift's manner should be distinguished from an alternative 'burlesque' style from which Pope's mock-heroic also distinguished itself, where high people speak low language instead of the other way round, providing an effect of slapstick vulgarity, as in Charles Cotton's travesty of the *Aeneid*: 'I *Sing the Man*, read it who list, / A Trojan true, as ever pist.'[46]

Swift avoids the two kinds of burlesque registered by the French poet Boileau, in a foreword to the first great mock-heroic poem, *Le Lutrin*

(1674): that in which Dido and Aeneas spoke like fishwives and porters, and that in which low people are made to speak like Dido and Aeneas.[47] Swift inserts instead a deadpan factuality, flat, precise, and sharp, avoiding the stylizations of high rant and low farce alike. The manner provides a point of departure for T. S. Eliot's early poems, 'Morning at the Window' and 'Preludes':

> They are rattling breakfast plates in basement kitchens,
> And along the trampled edges of the street
> I am aware of the damp souls of housemaids
> Sprouting despondently at area gates.[48]

What Eliot took, partly from Swift, is the idiom of flat notation, the drabness of urban mornings, played off against remembered grandeurs of poetic dawns. Swift's focus is on small-scale moral slippages (the maid sleeping with her master, the slipshod apprentice, the profiteering turnkey). This low-level scabrousness is the product of specifiable misdemeanours, though in his later prose satires Swift defined the human condition as depraved beyond specific attributions of vice. Eliot's drabness is that of demoralization rather than bad morals, lassitude rather than laxity: his housemaids have damp (not peccant) souls, sprouting despondently; his decors are a devitalized rather than depraved universe. Eliot offers the raw materials of satirical perception, formally uncoupled from the satirical project of moral inculpation, a measure of large cultural shifts in poetry in the (almost exactly) two centuries between the high age of mock-heroic and its modernist avatars.

Both poems offer a flattening or anti-climactic pay-off. Swift rounds off not with a Popeian conclusiveness or summation, but with the calculated inconclusiveness of yet another small-scale exemplar. The schoolboy follows the bailiff and turnkey, in a random list that is not finalized, but merely additive, without climax or summation. Eliot's 'Preludes, II' replaces lagging schoolboys with 'faint stale smells of beer' and 'dingy shades, / In a thousand furnished rooms', a flattening detail which leaves an atmosphere hovering inconclusively over the dismal scene.[49] 'Morning at the Window' concludes with a more literal kind of hovering:

> The brown waves of fog toss up to me
> Twisted faces from the bottom of the street,
> And tear from a passer-by with muddy skirts
> An aimless smile that hovers in the air
> And vanishes along the level of the roofs.

The hovering smile creates a lingering, indefinable mood, which acquires resonance precisely from its indefinability, the 'aimless smile that hovers in the air / And vanishes along the level of the roofs'. Here satirical verse is redirected to the quizzical suggestiveness of the mood poem, and allows a sudden lyricized turn to seep into the sourness, an effect developed in subsequent years in the satirical lyrics of W. H. Auden and Louis MacNeice. This final turn is one Swift would not take, and marks a large shift in the way poetry has managed the satirical impulse in recent centuries.

NOTES

1 *His Very Self and Voice: Collected Conversations of Lord Byron*, ed. Ernest J. Lovell, Jr (New York: Macmillan, 1954), p. 268.

2 Ted Hughes to Olwyn Hughes, *c.*1952 and August 1956, in *Letters*, ed. Christopher Reid (London: Faber and Faber, 2007), pp. 20, 46.

3 Ted Hughes to Kenneth Baker, 20 November 1988, in *Letters*, p. 546.

4 Adam Smith, *Theory of Moral Sentiments* (1759), V. i. 7, eds D. D. Raphael and A. L. Macfie (Oxford: Oxford University Press, 1976); rptd (Indianapolis: Liberty Fund, 1982), p. 198.

5 William Shenstone to Lady Luxborough, 27 June 1750, in *Letters of William Shenstone*, ed. Marjorie Williams (Oxford: Blackwell, 1939), p. 282.

6 Swift, letter to Charles Wogan, ?July–August 1732, in *Correspondence*, ed. David Woolley, 5 vols (Frankfurt: P. Lang, 1999–). All quotations from Swift's correspondence in this chapter are taken from this edition.

7 Samuel Johnson, 'Swift', in *Lives of the Most Eminent English Poets* (1779–81), ed. Roger Lonsdale, 4 vols (Oxford: Clarendon Press, 2006), para. 139, III. 214.

8 Edith Sitwell, *Alexander Pope* (1930) (Harmondsworth: Penguin, 1948).

9 See Donald M. Berwick, *The Reputation of Jonathan Swift, 1781–1882* (Philadelphia: [no publisher], 1941).

10 Ted Hughes to Nick Gammage, 7 April 1995, in *Letters*, pp. 680–1.

11 *Poems*, I. 193. Quotations from the poems are identified by line numbers in the text and are from *Poems*, ed. Harold Williams, 3 vols, 2nd edn (Oxford: Clarendon Press, 1958).

12 *Poems*, II. 551–72.

13 *Poems*, III. 827–39.

14 Derek Mahon, 'Introduction' to Jonathan Swift, *Poems* (London: Faber and Faber, 2001), p. ix.

15 Ronald Bottrall, 'Byron and the Colloquial Tradition in English Poetry', *Criterion* XVIII (1939), 204–24.

16 W. H. Auden, 'Introduction' to *Oxford Book of Light Verse* (Oxford: Clarendon Press, 1938), p. ix.

17 See Robert C. Elliott, *The Power of Satire: Magic, Ritual, Art* (Princeton: Princeton University Press, 1960), pp. 3–48.

18 Ben Jonson, *The Poetaster* (1601), 'To the Reader' ('Apologetical Dialogue'), lines 150–1; Elliott, *The Power of Satire*, pp. 3–48.

19 James Reeves, *The Reputation and Writings of Alexander Pope* (London: Heinemann, 1976), p. 56; *Selected Poems of Jonathan Swift*, ed. James Reeves (London: Heinemann, 1969), p. 12.

20 *Poems*, III. 951.

21 *Poems*, III. 952–3.

22 *Poems*, III. 953.
23 *Poems*, III. 772–82; Yeats, 'The Seven Sages' (1931).
24 *The Essential Writings of Jonathan Swift*, eds Claude Rawson and Ian Higgins (New York: W. W. Norton, 2009), p. 195 n.
25 T. S. Eliot, *The Waste Land: A Facsimile and Transcript of the Original Drafts Including the Annotations of Ezra Pound*, ed. Valerie Eliot (London: Faber and Faber, and New York: Harcourt Brace Jovanovich, 1971), p. 4.
26 *Waste Land Facsimile*, pp. 13, 127 n. 5.
27 *Poems*, I. 68–73, 103–5; *The Complete Poems and Plays of T. S. Eliot* (London: Faber and Faber, 1969), p. 27.
28 *Verses on the Death of Dr. Swift* (1739, written 1731), line 228, *Poems*, II. 562.
29 *Poems*, III. 985–7.
30 See *Poems*, III. 985 n. 14, and letters of Swift to Archdeacon Walls, 6 December 1716 and 30 March 1717.
31 Henry Fielding, *Shamela* (1741), p. 50.
32 See Irvin Ehrenpreis, *Swift: The Man, His Works, and the Age*, 3 vols (London: Methuen, 1962–83), III. 62–8.
33 *Poems*, II. 683–714.
34 *Poems*, II. 712.
35 *Prose Writings*, eds Herbert Davis *et al.*, 16 vols (Oxford: Blackwell, 1939–74), IX. 85–94.
36 *Poems*, II. 756–8.
37 *Poems*, II. 524–30, 593–7.
38 *Poems*, II. 584–93. See Claude Rawson, *Order from Confusion Sprung: Studies in Eighteenth-Century Literature from Swift to Cowper* (London: George Allen and Unwin, 1985; paperback, London: Humanities Press, 1992), pp. 168, 189 n. 30.
39 *Poems*, II. 580–3.
40 *Poems*, II. 628–38.
41 Auden, 'Introduction' to *Oxford Book of Light Verse*, p. x.
42 *Poems*, I. 123–5.
43 Pope, *Pastoral Poetry and An Essay on Criticism*, eds E. Audra and Aubrey Williams (London: Methuen, 1961), p. 58.
44 W. K. Wimsatt, Jr, *The Verbal Icon* (1954) (New York: Noonday Press, 1958), p. 157.
45 Wimsatt, *Verbal Icon*, p. 160.
46 The opening lines of Charles Cotton's adaptation (1663?) of Scarron's 'travesty' of Virgil's 'arma virumque cano', 'Arms and the Man I sing ...' (*Genuine Poetical Works of Charles Cotton*, 3rd edn, 1734, p. 1).
47 *Le Lutrin* (1674), 'Au Lecteur', prefixed to first edition.
48 T. S. Eliot, 'Morning at the Window', in *Complete Poems and Plays*, p. 27.
49 *Complete Poems and Plays*, p. 22.

SELECTED FURTHER READING

Editions

Cambridge Edition of the Works of Jonathan Swift, gen. eds Claude Rawson *et al.*, 18 vols, Cambridge, Cambridge University Press, 2007–

Correspondence, ed. David Woolley, 5 vols, Frankfurt, P. Lang, 1999–
Poems, ed. Harold Williams, 3 vols, 2nd edn, Oxford, Clarendon Press, 1958
Complete Poems, ed. Pat Rogers. Harmondsworth, Penguin, and New Haven, Yale, 1983
Prose Writings, eds. Herbert Davis *et al.*, 16 vols, Oxford, Blackwell, 1939–74
The Essential Writings of Jonathan Swift, eds Claude Rawson and Ian Higgins, New York, W. W. Norton, 2009

Secondary works

Biography

Ehrenpreis, Irvin, *Swift: The Man, His Works, and the Age*, 3 vols, London, Methuen, 1962–83

Critical studies

Barnett, Louise K. *Swift's Poetic Worlds*. Newark, University of Delaware Press, 1982
Jonathan Swift in the Company of Women, Oxford, Oxford University Press, 2007
Berwick, Donald M., *The Reputation of Jonathan Swift, 1781–1882*, Philadelphia, no publisher, 1941; rptd New York, Haskell, 1965
England, A. B., *Energy and Order in the Poetry of Swift*, Lewisburg, PA, Bucknell University Press, 1980
Fischer, John Irwin, and Donald C. Mell (eds), *Contemporary Studies in Swift's Poetry*, Newark, University of Delaware Press, 1981
Jaffe, Nora Crow, *The Poet Swift*, Hanover, NH, University Press of New England, 1977
Johnson, Maurice, *The Sin of Wit: Jonathan Swift as a Poet*, Syracuse, NY, Syracuse University Press, 1950
Karian, Stephen, *Jonathan Swift in Print and Manuscript*, Cambridge, Cambridge University Press, 2010
Mell, Donald C. (ed.), *Pope, Swift, and Women Writers*, Newark, University of Delaware Press, 1996, 1998
Rawson, Claude, *Order from Confusion Sprung: Studies in Eighteenth-Century Literature from Swift to Cowper*, London, George Allen and Unwin, 1985; paperback, London, Humanities Press, 1992
(ed.), *Jonathan Swift: A Collection of Critical Essays*, Englewood Cliffs, NJ, Prentice Hall, 1994
Schakel, Peter J., *The Poetry of Jonathan Swift*, Madison, University of Wisconsin Press, 1978
Vieth, David M. (ed.), *Essential Articles for the Study of Jonathan Swift's Poetry*, Hamden, CT, Archon, 1984
Williams, Kathleen (ed.), *Swift: The Critical Heritage*, London, Routledge, 1970
Woolley, James, *Swift's Later Poems: Studies in Circumstances and Texts*, New York, Garland, 1988

12

PAUL BAINES

Alexander Pope

In the year before he died, Pope planned an epic on the story of Brutus, grandson of Aeneas, who, in patriotic legend, had voyaged from Troy to found Britain. *Brutus* consists of a fragment, one sentence long:

> The Patient Chief, who lab'ring long, arriv'd
> On Britains Shore and brought with fav'ring Gods
> Arts Arms and Honour to her Ancient Sons:
> Daughter of Memory! from elder Time
> Recall; and me, with Britains Glory fir'd,
> Me, far from meaner Care or meaner Song,
> Snatch to thy Holy Hill of Spotless Bay,
> My Countrys Poet, to record her Fame.[1]

This is not the familiar Pope of expertly weighted ironic couplets, but a Pope of epic aspirations, engaging with the national myth in Miltonic guise. The fragment is a reverse of Shelley's later sonnet 'Ozymandias', the toe of a monument never built; so far as the verse goes, nothing beside remains. Yet *Brutus* represents a key element of Pope's imagination, harnessing the energy of classical legend for national purposes, as Virgil used Aeneas to found Rome through the appropriation of Greek epic. Where Keats consoled himself with the thought that he would be among the English poets after his death, Pope's is the rare instance of a poetic career which seems single-mindedly devoted from the outset to ensuring a position in the kind of canon which this book represents. Labouring like his own 'Patient Chief', Pope had always appeared determined to build a literary monument – akin to the 'monumentum aere perennius', the 'monument more lasting than bronze', that Horace claimed to have erected (*Odes* 3. 30, line 1) – as 'My Countrys Poet', however vexed his Englishness sometimes needed to be.

'First in these Fields I try the Sylvan Strains'

Pope was born in 1688, almost at the moment of the 'Glorious Revolution', which displaced the Catholic James II in favour of the Protestant William and

Mary, and thus ensured that, as a Catholic, Pope could never occupy Dryden's official post of Poet Laureate; as with that poet's later career, everything would have to be done through sheer literary effort in the marketplace. The early poems established mastery in different but related modes. Pope began with three contributions to a high-class miscellany published by Dryden's paymaster, Jacob Tonson, in 1709. 'January and May', a cleaned-up version of Chaucer's 'Merchant's Tale', was the first of the 'Imitations of English Poets' that Pope published to indicate his speeded-up poetic evolution, while the 'Episode of Sarpedon', from Homer's *Iliad*, signalled epic intentions, the first of many translations from Greek and Roman poets. The volume concluded with Pope's *Pastorals*, in homage to the masters of eclogue, Theocritus and Virgil. But classical shepherds (Damon, Alexis) now inhabit a mythologized English landscape: '*Albion*'s Cliffs resound the Rural Lay' (*Spring*, line 6). Hawthorns and daisies decorate a sward cooled by Zephyrs; Apollo finds himself charmingly introduced to the poet Edmund Waller (*Spring*, lines 45–6). Despite the rural theme, there is a built, geometric quality to the poems, which form an orderly sequence from morning to night and from Spring to Winter; the four last lines summarize the four poems as a whole.

Spring consists of a singing match between Daphnis and Strephon, who exchange perfectly matched quatrains; they both win. None the less it is significant that Pope opens with a poetry match, for the Anglicization has a competitive element:

> First in these Fields I try the Sylvan Strains,
> Nor blush to sport on *Windsor*'s blissful Plains.
>
> (*Spring*, lines 1–2)

It is a claim to territory. 'First' suggests the innovative manner of yoking classical pastoral with the landscape of the Thames valley: the river Po is specifically subordinated to Thames, while '*Cynthus* and *Hybla* yield to *Windsor*-shade' (*Spring*, lines 61–8). But 'First' also gives the hint that pastoral will be followed by epic. In *Summer* (lines 39–40), Pope explicitly claims the 'flute' of Colin Clout, that is Spenser, the poet for whom pastoral led to the (also unfinished) epic of Albion, *The Faerie Queene*.

The *Pastorals* were carefully examined by a group of mentors before they saw print, and Pope conspicuously defers to their supposedly greater talents, suggesting a poet waiting to emerge and claim his place in the English line. This patronage, like the poems, was centred in Windsor Forest; Pope was born in the commercial heart of London, but his sense of self and mission was formed in the mixed landscape around Binfield, his Forest home from about 1700 to 1716. Next in line, on the Virgilian model, should have been Georgic, which deals directly with agricultural labour. *Windsor-Forest*

(1713) does portray the seasonal round of farming, hunting, and fishing, and its ending quotes the opening of the *Pastorals*, as if completing a project. But it is closer to the form of 'prospect poem', a vision of England on the verge of emerging as a world power. The landscape is explicitly offered as an aesthetic paradigm, in an early example of Pope's desire to keep both ends of any spectrum of experience in busy correspondence:

> Here Hills and Vales, the Woodland and the Plain,
> Here Earth and Water seem to strive again,
> Not *Chaos*-like together crush'd and bruis'd,
> But as the World, harmoniously confus'd:
> Where Order in Variety we see,
> And where, tho' all things differ, all agree. (lines 11–16)

In this special place, 'At once the Monarch's and the Muse's seats' (line 2), we find a model of forces and desires checked and balanced by each other, a display of energetic stasis. However, it transpires that this optimistic fusion is historically contingent, based on the political fulcrum represented by the last of the Stuarts. Queen Anne's symbolic role as patron of 'Peace and Plenty' is celebrated (line 42) but offset by historical contrast with 'Ages past', a grim counter-landscape of tyranny and oppression associated with 'William' – ostensibly the 'Conqueror', though close enough to the ultra-Protestant William III, Anne's immediate predecessor. Pope's historical summary brings us back to an age of gold in Anne, aligned with 'Fair *Liberty*, *Britannia*'s Goddess' (line 90), but the threat of dissolution lurks.

According to Pope, the 'rural' section of the poem was written 'at the same time with the Pastorals', the latter part being added to celebrate the Treaty of Utrecht, which ended the War of Spanish Succession in 1713. An architectural doubleness (static countryside, the flux of history) has the effect of making symmetries both more important and less secure than those of the *Pastorals*: more is riding on the see-saw. In an inset Ovidian interlude the nymph Lodona strays from the protected zone of the Forest and is pursued by Pan, representing untrammelled energies, perhaps of political rapacity. She is metamorphosed into a river, the Loddon, bearing strange, beautiful, inverted reflections of the landscape of reality:

> Oft in her Glass the musing Shepherd spies
> The headlong Mountains and the downward Skies,
> The watry Landskip of the pendant Woods,
> And absent Trees that tremble in the Floods;
> In the clear azure Gleam the Flocks are seen,
> And floating Forests paint the Waves with Green.
> (lines 211–16)

The victimized Lodona is redeemed into briefly held aesthetic order by a poetry which appears to be commenting on its own compromised processes here. As a tributary, none the less, Loddon adds to the flow of the Thames; stasis becomes sequence again, and Pope makes his poem flow from Windsor to the seats of power in the city, compiling a poetic history of Britain (including poets whom Pope had imitated, like Cowley and Denham) along the voyage. Pope draws on the allegorical, patriotic masques and poems of Drayton and Jonson to transform Father Thames into a classical river god who claims superiority over the European rivers stained by the bloodshed of the war just ending and grandly prophesies a new role for British commerce in the adventure of Empire.

This sense of a tide of history flowing in patriotic directions had had its counterpart in Pope's *Essay on Criticism* (1711).[2] In the history of critical discourse that Pope supplies at the end of the poem, we fast-forward from Aristotle through Horace, Quintilian, and Longinus, finding ourselves brought by the Renaissance out of monkish gloom into the light of a particularly British Enlightenment. Chased out of Italy, like Brutus from Troy, the arts of criticism flourish in France but are resisted by 'brave Britons':

> Fierce for the *Liberties of Wit*, and bold,
> We still defy'd the *Romans*, as *of old*. (lines 717–18)

The position is both (positively) 'unconquer'd' and (negatively) 'unciviliz'd' (line 716). Pope's final self-definition, modelled on English poet-critics able to mediate between independence and submission, is that of a supreme tightrope-walker:

> Careless of *Censure*, nor too fond of *Fame*;
> Still pleas'd to *praise*, yet not afraid to *blame*;
> Averse alike to Flatter, or Offend;
> Not *free* from faults, nor yet too vain to *mend*.
> (lines 741–4).

The whole poem is structured by this flexible, juggled weighing-up of opposite qualities: light against dark, soul against body, licence against law, liberty against rule, English against French, ancients against moderns, male against female, poetry against criticism. Couplings of this kind suggest a full scope being scanned and arrayed.

But this is not merely a regular neo-classical monument. While the poem invokes abstractions that seem absolute or transcendent – Wit, Nature, Judgment, Sense – its processes repeatedly align critical discourse with actual living: 'like' may be its key word. Key concepts (poetry, language, criticism) find themselves resembling the soul, the body, army manoeuvres, getting drunk, medicine, clothing, sex, buildings, climbing the Alps, flirting with noble women or with their more easily available handmaids. The critic must be a gentleman, and there is a strongly masculine tone to the imagery, perhaps emphasizing a coming-of-age (Pope was 23). Critics are the sexual rivals of poets; those who cannot write are, explicitly, eunuchs (line 31); bad poets 'Rhyme with all the *Rage* of *Impotence*' (line 609); obscenity in verse is as shameful as '*Impotence* in *Love*' (line 533). Along with manly authority goes a potential for satirical attack. The miserable position of the client author, 'A constant Critick at the Great-man's Board, / To *fetch and carry* Nonsense for my Lord' (lines 416–17), prefigures the anti-patronage satire of the *Epistle to Dr Arbuthnot*. The bookstalls of Duck Lane (line 445) are in *Dunciad* territory, as is the 'Bookful Blockhead' with his '*Learned Lumber*' (lines 610–25). The poem is happily energetic in its comic negations.

Also in urbane mode, *The Rape of the Lock* (1712/14) was Pope's most distinctive early synthesis of classical and modern (and the first to bear his name). Its defining strategy is well exemplified in the vision of Hampton Court (to which the heroine Belinda sails, reversing *Windsor-Forest*'s directional flow of power).

Here *Britain*'s Statesmen oft the Fall foredoom
Of Foreign Tyrants, and of Nymphs at home;
Here Thou, Great *Anna*! whom three Realms obey,
Dost sometimes Counsel take – and sometimes *Tea*.

(III. 5–8)

Power and sex slip their separate moorings, and high and low swap status in comically abrupt shifts of scale. The sovereign whose fiat ends years of European war in *Windsor-Forest* now sips Bohea. The world of commercial venturing, so epic in the imagining of Father Thames, is miniaturized into the luxurious 'mystic order' of Belinda's dressing table:

This Casket *India*'s glowing Gems unlocks,
And all *Arabia* breathes from yonder Box.
The Tortoise here and Elephant unite,
Transform'd to *Combs*, the speckled and the white.

(I. 133–6).

Belinda's cosmetic preparations mimic the arming of Achilles; the sylphs who guard her stand as miniature epic 'machinery', in place of Miltonic and Homeric gods, spliced with the English 'fairy' tradition. The animated card game of Canto II draws on epic warfare (as well as more recent battles); Belinda's visit to the 'cave of spleen' internalizes the underworld journeys of Odysseus and Aeneas as hysteria. The battle between the belles and the beaux has Jove raising the scales of Fate to decide the issue, though here it is wit against hair rather than Trojan against Greek.

The result is a preposterous poise, superbly held together, as in Ariel's sense of impending disaster:

> Whether the Nymph shall break *Diana*'s Law,
> Or some frail *China* Jar receive a Flaw,
> Or stain her Honour, or her new Brocade,
> Forget her Pray'rs, or miss a Masquerade,
> Or lose her Heart, or Necklace, at a Ball;
> Or whether Heavn' has doom'd that *Shock*
> must fall. (lines 105–10)

It is as if the oppositions of the earlier poems have been pushed beyond the limits of any power but poetry itself to refocus. The point of the 'rape' (abduction) of the lock is that while Paris stole Helen (breaking 'Diana's law'), the baron has 'only' taken an inanimate lock of hair (damaging the 'frail China jar'). But in the context that Pope has set up, at once telescopic and microscopic, where minor gestures carry major weight, the loss of hair signifies that the baron has, in all the ways that actually matter, sexually possessed her: Belinda's is not simply a moral case of over-reaction.

Like the 'glitt'ring forfex' which cuts off the lock, couplets can divide things 'for ever, and for ever!', as well as join them together. Belinda has no way to return to independent power or intactness; disordered and unbalanced (one lock missing), she can only become the central figure of a unitary poem ('*this* Lock'); based on the appropriation and transformation of a metonymic piece of her, which is then handed to her as compensation. Like Lodona, what she gets back is art; the masculine aspirations of the *Essay on Criticism* are realized in a poem of visual transformations which showcase the powers of its creator. Indeed, *The Rape of the Lock* was not alone in being centred on female vulnerability, passion, and suffering, a zone where imagination meets hysteria. Belinda was one of a number of 'problem' female figures haunting Pope by stepping over some sort of line: Chaucer's wanton wives, Jane Shore, Cleopatra, Sappho. *Eloisa to Abelard* and the *Elegy to the Memory of an Unfortunate Lady* (1717) also promote stories of female transgression and both end by foregrounding the male poet and his gallant, if ventriloqual, narrative attentions.

'Here she beholds the Chaos dark and deep'

These poems, rural and urban, appropriating classical models for English themes, seeking out areas of transgression and trouble to capture in assured artistic form, established Pope as the successor to Dryden. The next decade produced the enormous achievement of the Homer translations, lucrative enough for Pope to build himself a neo-classical villa in five acres of land on the banks of the Thames at Twickenham. Only nine years after the *Pastorals*, Pope was publishing his *Works* (1717), with commendatory verses, engraved headpieces, and a beautifully engraved portrait as frontispiece (no poet before Pope was so carefully, and so plentifully, represented in portraiture). Though the Preface wrily poses the question 'whether to look upon my self as a man building a monument, or burying the dead', the *Works* was something like the monument of classic permanence he had envisaged himself approaching in *The Temple of Fame*, his heavily trimmed version of Chaucer's *House of Fame* (1715).[3] From one perspective, Pope already was his country's poet.

It was, however, a troubled position. Pope's first major poems were produced in the last years of Queen Anne, while Pope's friends the Tory politicians Robert Harley, Earl of Oxford, and Henry St John, Viscount Bolingbroke, together with their main propagandist, Jonathan Swift, were running the country. She died in 1714, ushering in the ultra-Protestant Hanoverians, and thirty years of Jacobite agitation. *The Temple of Fame* was laced with political anxiety in the face of anti-Catholic fervour, while the *Iliad* translation was repeatedly denounced as 'Popish' (Addison had tried to undermine it by promoting a rival 'Whig' version). A jibe in the *Essay on Criticism* had provoked the critic John Dennis into attacks on Pope's diminutive physique and Catholic background, published by the scandal-mongering bookseller Edmund Curll – whom Pope poisoned with an emetic in 1716, writing up the results in two scabrous and funny pamphlets which were not included in the *Works*. (Also excluded were Pope's other prose squibs, as well as the unofficial but embarrassingly ribald poems that Curll had got hold of, such as the notorious 'Roman Catholick Version of the First Psalm'.) The life of a wit, at least of a Catholic wit in England, was, as Pope put it in the Preface to his *Works*, 'a warfare upon earth'. Perhaps Pope was happier that way. Pope's *Works* coincided with the death of his father, and one of his intellectual mentors, Bishop Francis Atterbury, took this opportunity to suggest a prudent conversion to Anglicanism. In a brilliantly measured refusal, Pope constructed a sense of Englishness at once unimpeachable (even if, as it transpired, Atterbury was a leading Jacobite agent) and exempt from the oaths of loyalty:

> If I was born under an absolute Prince, I would be a quiet subject; but I thank God I was not. I have a due sense of the excellence of the British constitution. In a word, the things I have always wished to see are not a Roman Catholick, or a French Catholick, or a Spanish Catholick, but a true Catholick: and not a King of Whigs, or a King of Tories, but a King of England. Which God of his mercy grant his present Majesty may be, and all future Majesties![4]

Whilst it suggests a transcendent or centrist position, Pope was actually constructing his own dominion, a zone where disqualification is a kind of enfranchisement, a platform for denunciation.

In 1728 appeared (anonymously) *The Dunciad. An Heroic Poem. In Three Books*. The proximate cause of this dystopian epic of British cultural life was Lewis Theobald's *Shakespeare Restor'd* (1726), which had holed the scholarship of Pope's edition of Shakespeare (1725) below the waterline. For vandalizing the monument, Pope installed Theobald (a poet-critic not in the gentlemanly mould of the *Essay on Criticism*) as the unheroic hero, the favoured son of the Goddess Dulness, herself a mock-epic descendant from the pre-literate zone of Milton's Chaos (I. 9–16). In her returning manifestation she is the sort of protecting goddess that Aeneas has in his mother Venus, inflated into a monstrously suffocating and infantilizing parody of female power. The productions of literary London indicate that the time is right for her to resume 'her old empire' (I. 15); Dulness watches with unalloyed pleasure the teeming generic miscegenations and mixed metaphors that (according to Pope) characterize modern writing (I. 53–76). In the final book, the hero falls asleep on Dulness's lap and dreams of her future empire, a parody of the optimistic future Pope had envisioned for Britain in *Windsor-Forest*, the rickety, pantomime ineptitude of Duncely writings representing an impiously 'uncreating word'. The generic hybrid mock-epic, Pope indicates, is the only kind of epic Britain deserves.

Pope sets himself up as the only conscious agent of resistance to Dulness's gravitational sway, able to mimic and indulge in but crucially to control the attractive but delusory excesses and irregularities that Dulness delights in. The measure of control is the inventive appropriation of stock Homeric situations, splicing them with scenes of a London which more closely resembles the amusingly mucky back streets of his early Spenserian imitation 'The Alley' than it does the polished drawing rooms of Belinda's London. The results are gleefully grotesque. The insalubrious street-map – Rag Fair, Bedlam, Moorfields, Fleet Ditch, Tyburn, the Strand, and above all Grub Street – underpins the mythopoeic transition from the City to the seats of power in Westminster, parodying the journey of Aeneas from Troy to Rome: Theobald will bring 'the Smithfield Muses to the Ear of Kings' (I. 2) in a gross travesty of that cultural movement.

In Book II, the coronation of Theobald is celebrated by Games, in parody of the funeral games for Aeneas's father in *Aeneid* V. Virgil's footrace is grossly transformed into contests between Bernard Lintot, Pope's former publisher, whose corpulence is cruelly caricatured, and Curll. First prize is the 'phantom poet', an allusion to the illusory Aeneas created by Juno as a decoy in battle, here an exemplification of the book trade's habitual deceits. Where a runner in the *Aeneid* slips on the blood of holy sacrifices, Curll 'fortun'd to slide' in 'a lake' (urine or excrement) deposited with absurd delicacy by Elizabeth Thomas, the 'Corinna' who had sold Curll some racy Pope letters. Nothing abashed, Curll prays to Jove, who receives Curll's petition at the hands of Cloacina (goddess of the sewer) while retired 'for ease', and signs it 'with that Ichor which from Gods distills'. It is perhaps the most elaborate euphemism for going to the toilet that poetry has ever come up with. It works for Curll:

Renew'd by ordure's sympathetic force,
As oil'd with magic juices for the course,
Vig'rous he rises; from th' effluvia strong
Imbibes new life, and scours and stinks along. (II. 95–8)

The Dunces all behave with utter lack of humour, as if they were engaged in genuine epic activity, oblivious to smell, disaster, degradation, pain. Curll simply does not notice 'the brown dishonours of his face', used to fishing Cloacina's 'nether realms' as he is. Curll also wins the pissing contest (II. 149–82) thanks to his 'vigor and superior size', claiming as his prize 'yon Juno of majestic size', the writer Eliza Haywood, 'two babes of love' (illicit amorous novels) 'close clinging to her waste', leaving the loser to crown himself with a chamber pot. In Virgil, this had been a boxing match.

Subsequently the Dunces indulge in a mud-diving contest at the point where Fleet Ditch

with disemboguing streams
Rolls the large tribute of dead dogs to Thames,
The King of Dykes! than whom, no sluice of mud
With deeper sable blots the silver flood. (II. 259–62)

The tributaries which decorously add to London's 'silver flood' in *Windsor-Forest* (where 'sable' is used for its rich heraldic suggestions, not its suggestion of pollution) have here become a toxic parody. The winner returns with an elaborate narrative of his sojourn among the 'Mudnymphs', a category unknown to classical authors and invented here to fuse the language of romance with the contents of the sewer: while 'black', 'brown', and 'soft' might conventionally refer to women's characteristics or hair colours, here they suggest excrement.[5] As excremental visions go, it is verbally unimpeachable; everything is narrated in high periphrasis, demonstrating that Pope can do this with consummate control while the Dunces actually belong in Fleet Ditch.

'A mighty maze! but not without a plan'

Pope is not mentioned in the poem. *The Dunciad Variorum* (1729) extended his assault on Theobald by providing prefaces, mock-commentaries, notes, indexes, and testimonies of authors, in parody of the bone-headed apparatus which, by implication, normally beset a classic text once editors got their hands on it. Much of the material was derived from the Dunces themselves, absorbing their protests on the publication of the original poem into the material of his satiric project in an extraordinary act of cultural stage-management.[6] These paratexts convey in parodic voice much information on the Dunces accurate enough to be damaging without being fair enough to be above malice. They protest (too much, perhaps) against the pamphlet war waged against Pope. As a whole, the exercise drew a line between the Dunces and Pope's own status as the self-governing aristocrat of poetry, above the economic neediness and political subservience which leads them to fish in the sewer and libel their betters.

Pope set up his own printer and bookseller in order to control the production details and the manner of release of his work according to his own agenda. From this position he planned an 'opus magnum' (of which *Brutus* was perhaps the last vestige) to supplement the inverted grandeur of *The Dunciad* with more directly ethical work. The first block of material was the *Essay on Man*, published in four epistles (1733–4). The poem sought to steer a course 'betwixt the extremes of doctrines seemingly opposite' and to form 'a *temperate* yet not *inconsistent*, and a *short* yet not *imperfect* system of Ethics'. In proposing to 'vindicate the ways of God to Man' (line 16), Pope conspicuously alludes to Milton's epic attempt to 'justify the ways of God to men', but in place of Milton's intense psychological narrative of fall and redemption, we have a static diagram of universal truths. Quashing the Adamic desire for celestial knowledge, which is identified with the sin of Pride (I. 123–40), Pope leaves the vision of the whole system to the providential eye,

> Who sees with equal eye, as God of all,
> A hero perish, or a sparrow fall,
> Atoms or systems into ruin hurl'd,
> And now a bubble burst, and now a world. (I. 87–90).

Such extremes are not, as in *The Rape of the Lock*, evidence of moral indifference to scale, though they must still register as that for us to understand that God has a different perspective on the whole. We have our appropriate place within, and limited perception of, the 'vast Chain of Being' which links everything from nothingness to infinity, because only God, the supreme artist, can see the whole work.

From this pattern, reminiscent of the artistic paradigms of the *Essay on Criticism*, Pope explores the more dynamic aspects of human psychology, seeking out a providentially guaranteed balance between self-love, which urges action, and reason, which curbs and restrains it. As Pope analyses it, psychology, while apparently chaotic, boils down to a kind of couplet, or series of couplets, acting in harmonious concert, as self-love urges us to action and reason sets a limit to its force. Providence also sees to it that we are supplied with 'one master Passion in the breast', a particular, characteristic desire which is itself poised between virtuous and vicious manifestations (prudence/avarice; philosophy/sloth; love/lust), with reason acting to turn the scale virtue's way.

> This light and darkness in our chaos join'd,
> What shall divide? The God within the mind. (II. 203–4).

This microcosmic appropriation of God's wisdom, controlling the oscillations of behaviour without recourse to Sin, or Grace, was designed in part to avoid factional controversy; few would have expected the Catholic prophet of cultural apocalypse to produce something so acceptable. Yet the poetry is not content with its rationally argued limits; it is always glimpsing over the edge of what is decorous, feeling for what it suppresses; and like the *Essay on Criticism*, the poem is stuffed with satiric observations and postures, as if looking for windmills to tilt at.

Pope's 'Design' promised that the *Essay on Man* was merely the '*general Map* of MAN', the '*fountains*' of ethics; 'charts' showing the course of humanity's '*rivers*' would follow. The four *Moral Essays* (1731–5) gave Pope a personal space to explore some of this 'mighty Maze', in a less formal setting. The *Epistle to Cobham*, 'on the Knowledge and Characters of Men', picks up the problem of determining the properties of mental life, touched on in the *Essay on Man*, rendering in even-handed detail the 'puzzling Contraries' of mental states and expanding his theory of the 'ruling passion' to establish core stability within a flux of contradictory appearances. In *To a Lady*, this solution will not work, because women – the argument goes – are simply too various in the way they present themselves to suggest any stable character at all. Pope presents a scandalously vivid gallery of contradictory female attitudes, as if all women did was adopt roles from an art gallery: 'Here Fannia, leering on her own good man, / Is there, a naked Leda with a Swan.'

> Pictures like these, dear Madam, to design,
> Asks no firm hand, and no unerring line;
> Some wand'ring touches, some reflected light,

> Some flying stroke alone can hit 'em right:
> For how should equal Colours do the knack?
> Chameleons who can paint in white and black?
>
> (lines 151–6)

Again, poetry must produce order out of this chaos, must find the (accidental) grace beyond the reach of art to bring things under control. There is a ghostly echo of Pope's (at least ostensibly) sympathetic portrayal of erring, passionate women in the early poems, as 'Narcissa' veers between extremes of conscience and passion just as Eloisa had done: 'A very Heathen in the carnal part, / Yet still a sad, good Christian at her heart' (lines 67–8). 'Lucretia's dagger, Rosamonda's bowl' (92) mocks a gothic passion reminiscent of Pope's own 'Unfortunate Lady'. The 'Ghosts of Beauty' who glide 'round and round', haunting 'the places where their Honour dy'd' (241–2), remind us that the belles of *The Rape of the Lock* are now twenty years older. Offered in place of that risky identification with passionate women is the exceptional figure of Martha Blount, Pope's closest female friend and the unnamed 'Lady' to whom the poem is addressed as a kind of gift, and who is granted stability and transcendence in the form of a strangely androgynous model femininity, a 'softer man' combining the best 'passions' of both sexes.

In the two epistles 'Of the Use of Riches', the balancing act is different, though some of the same psychological drives are still operative. In the *Epistle to Bathurst*, Pope enters a fantasy domain in which money has now become, in the form of paper credit, a zone of powerful, amoral imagination:

> Gold imp'd by thee, can compass hardest things,
> Can pocket States, can fetch or carry Kings;
> A single leaf shall waft an Army o'er,
> Or ship off Senates to a distant Shore;
> A leaf, like Sibyl's, scatter to and fro
> Our fates and fortunes, as the winds shall blow:
> Pregnant with thousands flits the Scrap unseen
> And silent sells a King or buys a Queen. (lines 71–8)

Pope restores control by summoning the providential ordering of the *Essay on Man*, which asserts that between them, avarice and prodigality contribute, through a systole/diastole rhythm, to economic regularity. Old Cotta is a miser, refusing the stewardship obligations of the landed gentry; Young Cotta, inheriting the fortune, ruins himself with prodigal support for the Hanoverian regime. Between these extremes Pope cites the example of the Man of Ross, supporting an entire rural community in a one-man social security system; he in turn is contrasted with the city-based tale of Sir

Balaam, a compact character study in the corrupting power of riches, taking sly vengeance on a type of Whig grandee in a bravura display of observational comedy narrative.

In the *Epistle to Burlington*, Pope cites the Earl's architectural work as an example of the proper application of wealth, not for magnificence, but for use, and again the model is rural – indeed, as gardening (one of Pope's own favourite studies) is combined with building as a model of art, we might almost be back in the golden landscape of *Windsor-Forest*. Financial disaster intrudes here in the shape of Timon's Villa (lines 99–168), a parvenu monstrosity, the kind of disastrous mismatch of scale that mere money brings to landscape. The true mode of operation in the country is benign patronage:

> His Father's Acres who enjoys in peace,
> Or makes his Neighbours glad, if he encrease;
> Whose cheerful Tenants bless their yearly toil,
> Yet to their Lord owe more than to the soil;
> Whose ample Lawns are not ashamed to feed
> The milky heifer and deserving steed;
> Whose rising Forests, not for pride or show,
> But future Buildings, future Navies grow:
> Let his plantations stretch from down to down,
> First shade a Country, and then raise a Town.
>
> (lines 181–90)

Once again, Pope identifies a chaotic problem and supplies a balancing solution.

'I cough like Horace, and tho' lean, am short'

But this vision of commerce founded on English rural virtues was even less neutral in 1735 than it had been in *Windsor-Forest*. Pope never left England, though he travelled extensively on his 'rambles', staying with friends on their country estates. These landscape gardens, sculpture-heavy and inscription-laden, were highly politicized sites of interpretation; Cobham's garden at Stowe, celebrated in *To Burlington*, was strongly associated with the 'Patriot' opposition to the prime minister, Sir Robert Walpole. Pope's own ground at Twickenham was leased, since as a Catholic he could not own land, but it was leased with his own money, whereas Horace's Sabine farm, on which its iconic image is based, was the fruit of patronage. Pope's home became a highly visible locus of personal, virtuous independence. 'Twit'nam', as Pope familiarizes it, is the setting of the *Epistle to Dr Arbuthnot* (1735); the poem opens with Pope telling his gardener to shut the door against the tide of visitors who invade the private space – not exactly the deranged masses of *The Dunciad*, but rather the sycophantic crowds of amateur writers who beset Pope, the beleaguered Great Man of English letters, with demands for advice, tuition, and cash. (The reader is, by contrast, invited in.)

> What Walls can guard me, or what Shades can hide?
> They pierce my Thickets, thro' my Grot they glide,
> By land, by water, they renew the charge,
> They stop the Chariot, and they board the Barge. (lines 7–10)

It is a comically exaggerated picture, with Pope fending off the troublesome incursions of 'All *Bedlam*, or *Parnassus*', poetasters so desperate that Pope finds them flattering even his notorious bodily deformities. The self-depreciation absorbs and converts the abuse routinely deployed against Pope: so far from being the outcast cripple of hostile pamphleteers, Pope has only too much admiration.

This is Pope's space. At the heart of the poem lie three set-piece satiric portraits representing other kinds of one-man court, from which Twit'nam, and Pope, were to be differentiated. The 'Atticus' (Addison) portrait (lines 193–214) settles an old score by rendering the leading writer of Pope's early youth, 'Blest with each Talent and each Art to please', an envious and devious figure, presiding over 'his little Senate' and sitting 'attentive to his own applause', in marked contrast to the closing critical balances of the *Essay on Criticism*. While Addison could 'bear no brother near the throne', Pope's own (monarchic) position is different:

> I sought no homage from the Race that write;
> I kept, like *Asian* Monarchs, from their sight. (lines 219–20)

He never needed the company of aristocratic patrons such as Bufo, the conceited peer, 'fed with soft dedication all day long' (lines 231–50); still less Sporus (305–33), Pope's contemptuous name for the courtier Lord Hervey, whose sexual ambiguity and superficial glamour Pope dismantles and exposes in an extraordinary virtuoso display:

> His Wit all see-saw, between *that* and *this*,
> Now high, now low, now Master up, now Miss,
> And he himself one vile Antithesis. (lines 323–5)

It is close, of course, to the kind of allegation made against Pope's own witty manner and compromised manliness, and it is at this exact point that Pope inserts his definition of (one) poet's role, by negation of these others:

> Not Fortune's Worshipper, nor Fashion's Fool
> Not Lucre's Madman, nor Ambition's Tool,

Not proud, nor servile; be one Poet's praise,
That, if he pleas'd, he pleas'd by manly ways. (lines 334–7)

The poems of the 1730s increasingly identify 'Pope' with the role, name, and function 'poet', as here. 'Wit, and Poetry, and Pope' (line 26) become synonymous, Pope no doubt enjoying the phonetic proximity of his name with his function.[7]

Pope's first Horatian imitation, *The First Satire of the Second Book of Horace Imitated* (1733), had begun this process of offering a personal 'Pope' to the world. His lawyer offers Pope some prudential health and safety advice: 'if you needs must write, write CÆSAR's Praise, / You'll gain at least a *Knighthood*, or the *Bays*' (lines 21–2). Slily eluding once more the offer of accommodation to the court, Pope declares, not quite with a straight face, that he loves to 'pour out all myself', 'My Head and Heart thus flowing thro' my Quill' (lines 51, 63); personally speaking, satire is all mere honesty. In a similar way, ironic self-depreciation functioned as a kind of claim: acknowledging that he is 'Far from a Lynx, and not a Giant quite' (*The First Epistle of the First Book of Horace Imitated*, line 50) is less a means of defusing attack than of reminding us of what he can see, and the ways in which he is a (literary) giant. The 'Horatian' range of voices includes Swiftian mediations, 'versifications' of Donne's imitations, and the smutty *Sober Advice from Horace*, 'imitated in the manner of Mr. Pope', but all have this ironic mastery. Pope lives within an inverted Penshurst, the luxuriating landscape of patronage replaced by one of unglamorous but resilient self-sufficiency:

Content with little, I can piddle here
On Broccoli and mutton, round the year ...
'Tis true, no Turbots dignify my boards,
But gudgeons, flounders, what my Thames affords:
To Hounslow-heath I point and Bansted-down,
Thence comes your mutton, and these chicks my own:
From yon old wallnut-tree a show'r shall fall;
And grapes, long ling'ring on my only wall,
And figs, from standard and Espalier join;
The dev'l is in you if you cannot dine.

(*The Second Satire of the Second Book of Horace Paraphrased*, lines 137–48)

This is frugal, even 'low', in language as in food: poets before Pope had not written much about broccoli. Thames is no longer the demi-God of *Windsor-Forest* but a homely provider in Old England; the ancient, maturing fruits of the English garden replace the empire of the world.

From this degree-zero Englishness, Pope claims the right to say what he likes; in *The First Epistle of the Second Book of Horace Imitated* (1737), he addresses his sovereign '*with a decent Freedom ..., with a just Contempt of his low flatterers, and with a manly Regard to his own Character*' – or, as readers might understand it, with a flagrantly insulting irony which was none the less unreachable by law. The invited comparison between George II and the emperor from whom he took his middle name – and between the Roman and the English poet – finds poetry emerging rather better from the exercise than monarchy. Pope envisages a kind of canon of English poetry, set alongside the erratic course of British history, with a strong sense of their superiority to any 'monster of a King'. The two dialogues of the *Epilogue to the Satires* likewise begin in suave conversational exchange about the responsibilities of satire and end in steely condemnation of national corruption. Heavy with the names of the big political players, and a fair number of outlaws and criminals (the categories are not, for Pope, mutually exclusive), the poems declaim against the 'corruption' of 'Old *England*'s Genius' (I. 152). Coolly displaying his familiarity with the private character of Walpole, Pope's own role becomes that of the biblical prophet:

> *Fr*. You're strangely proud.
> *P*. So proud, I am no Slave:
> So impudent, I own myself no Knave:
> So odd, my Country's Ruin makes me grave. (II. 205–7)

Pope appoints himself the Laureate of internal exile, the 'Last of Britons' (line 250), refusing to accept the sovereignty of any power beyond that of poetry.

'One Mighty Dunciad of the Land'

'My Country's Ruin' is the theme of the revised *Dunciad*, fully refitted in 1743 after the publication of the engagingly shameless autobiography of Colley Cibber (comic actor and Poet Laureate) in 1740, together with some damaging anecdotes about Pope's early life, had provided Pope with sufficient personal excuse to expunge Theobald and install Cibber as the greater 'hero' of his inverse epic. But the new fourth book in fact has nothing to do with the hero, who is already overwhelmed by the mother goddess Dulness. She summons all her devotees, here not so much professional hacks as representatives from the worlds of intellectual regulation that Pope considered himself lucky to have escaped: public schools, the universities (which as a Catholic he could not attend), the Grand Tour. The court is gradually weighed down by their sheer material presence, a parody of Newtonian 'gravity'. Education hangs a 'jingling padlock' (IV. 162) on the mind by concentrating on letter rather than spirit, text rather than meaning. 'Aristarchus' (the classical scholar Richard Bentley) boasts:

> For thee we dim the eyes, and stuff the head
> With all such reading as was never read:
> For thee explain a thing till all men doubt it,
> And write about it, Goddess, and about it. (IV. 249–52)

As Bentley determines to destroy the aspirations of the *Essay on Criticism* with the tools of Theobald, Pope deliberately has the Dunces invert the values of his own earlier poems. The opening vision of Science, Wit, Logic, and Rhetoric bound beneath the throne of Dulness (IV. 21–30) is an inversion of the subjugation of Envy, Faction, Rebellion, and Furies at the conclusion of *Windsor-Forest*. The virtuoso's concentration on parts rather than wholes, and material aspects of creation rather than the creative wisdom behind them, breaks the rules espoused in the *Essay on Criticism* and *Essay on Man*. The Wizard's Cup of self-love (IV. 517) lacks the antidote of reason that controlled it in the *Essay on Man*. Annius's fake coins travesty the patriotic aspirations of the patriotic medal, as Pope had celebrated them in the epistle 'To Mr. Addison'. The youth who returns from the Grand Tour in the company of his paramour and tutor constitutes an ironic 'young Æneas' (IV. 290), blazing a trail of cultural decadence round Europe: 'All Classic learning lost on Classic ground' (IV. 321). The poem ends in apocalyptic inertia; the nightmare vision of the earlier poem, originally a prophecy, is fulfilled, as Dulness's cack-handed travesty of Milton's Chaos swamps the creations of poetry.

It is still, just, a joke. From all of these disasters Pope, as the controlling artist, is by definition exempt, not least because of the surviving comic prose of the mock-commentary, doubling as parody and as claim to classic status. It may be a spoof monument, but it is still a monument, a Temple of British Infamy testifying to the greatness of its architect. Pope had expertly blown what he sniggeringly alluded to as 'Fame's posterior Trumpet' (*Dunciad*, IV. 71), a suitably raucous type of Aeolian wind. But *Brutus* remained to invert the mock-epic once again, to summon the national poet from 'meaner care' and 'meaner song' (the intoxications of Dulness). All classic learning might still be recovered on English ground. That hopeful, and bereft, first line is full of echoes: 'Elder time', 'Ancient Sons', 'Daughter of Memory', 'spotless Bay', and of course 'Fame' have a ghostly ring if read immediately after the four-book *Dunciad*. 'Snatch', conversely, reminds us of that Promethean urge to '*snatch* a *Grace* beyond the Reach of Art' (*Essay on Criticism*, line 155). The sentence suggests a path into something non-oppositional

(Walpole had resigned in 1742), sinuous rather than symmetrical, not even couplet-bound: beyond anything he had done before – even if it would have required him to cleanse the English language of the ambivalent richness he had himself contributed to its spectrum of meaning.

NOTES

1 Cited, as are all quotations from Pope unless otherwise stated, from the text in *The Poems of Alexander Pope: A One-Volume Edition of the Twickenham Text with Selected Annotations*, ed. John Butt (London: Methuen, 1963, rptd 1968). Some lines of a youthful epic, *Alcander*, destroyed by Pope, survive.

2 See also 'To Mr. Addison, Occasion'd by his Dialogues on Medals': 'Oh when shall Britain, conscious of her Claim, / Stand emulous of Greek and Roman fame?' (lines 53–4).

3 For the Preface see *The Prose Works of Alexander Pope*, vol. I: *The Earlier Works 1711–1720*, ed. Norman Ault (Oxford: Blackwell, 1936), pp. 289–302.

4 Pope to Atterbury, 20 November 1717, in *Selected Letters of Alexander Pope*, ed. Howard Erskine-Hill (Oxford: Oxford University Press, 2000), p. 120.

5 Pope uses these adjectives for female character, without apparent contamination, in the opening of the *Epistle to a Lady*: 'Matter too soft a lasting mark to bear, / And best distinguish'd by black, brown, or fair' (lines 3–4).

6 Pope was following the practice of Swift (dedicatee of the poem) in the fifth and final edition of *A Tale of a Tub* (1704).

7 Compare 'To you gave Sense, Good-humour, and a Poet', *Epistle to a Lady*, line 292; 'Convict a Papist He, and I a Poet', *The Second Epistle of the Second Book of Horace Imitated*, line 67; 'Dare they to hope a Poet for their friend', *Epilogue to the Satires*, II. 115.

SELECTED FURTHER READING

Editions

The Twickenham Edition of the Poems of Alexander Pope, eds J. Butt *et al.*, 11 vols, London, Methuen, 1938–68

The Poems of Alexander Pope: A One-Volume Edition of the Twickenham Text with Selected Annotations, ed. J. Butt, London, Methuen, 1963, rptd 1968

Alexander Pope: Selected Poetry, ed. P. Rogers, Oxford, Oxford University Press, 1996

The Dunciad: In Four Books, ed. V. Rumbold, Harlow, Longman, 1999

The Poems of Alexander Pope, Vol. III: The Dunciad (1728) and The Dunciad Variorum (1729). ed. V. Rumbold, London, Longman, 2007. The first instalment to be published of a five-volume edition in the Longman Annotated English Poets series

Secondary works

Deutsch, H., *Resemblance and Disgrace: Alexander Pope and the Deformation of Culture*, Cambridge, MA, Harvard University Press, 1996

Fairer, David, *Pope's Imagination*, Manchester, Manchester University Press, 1984
Griffin, D. H., *Alexander Pope: The Poet in the Poems*, Princeton, Princeton University Press, 1978
Mack, M., *The Garden and the City: Retirement and Politics in the Later Poetry of Pope 1731–1743*, Toronto, University of Toronto Press, 1969
Collected in Himself: Essays Critical, Biographical, and Bibliographical on Pope and Some of His Contemporaries, London, Associated University Presses, 1982
Alexander Pope: A Life, New Haven, Yale University Press, 1985
McLaverty, J., *Pope, Print, and Meaning*, Oxford, Oxford University Press, 2001
Rogers, P., *The Alexander Pope Encyclopedia*, Westport, CT, Greenwood Press, 2004
Essays on Pope, Cambridge, Cambridge University Press, 2006
(ed.), *The Cambridge Companion to Alexander Pope*, Cambridge, Cambridge University Press, 2007
Rumbold, V., *Women's Place in Pope's World*, Cambridge, Cambridge University Press, 1989
Stack, F., *Pope and Horace: Studies in Imitation*, Cambridge, Cambridge University Press, 1985
Williams, C. D., *Pope, Homer, and Manliness: Some Aspects of Eighteenth Century Classical Learning*, London, Routledge, 1993
Wimsatt, W. K., *The Portraits of Alexander Pope*, New Haven, Yale University Press, 1965

13

MORTON D. PALEY

William Blake

William Blake is one of the very few great poets to have devoted himself to art and to writing with equal commitment. Apprenticed for seven years to an engraver, he made his living in that trade all his life. He also studied in the Royal Academy schools; he painted in water colour and in tempera, made 'colour printed drawings', and devised a mode of relief etching in order to incorporate text and image into what we now call his illuminated books. This discussion must necessarily be limited to his poetry, but we should remember that Blake conceived most of his poems in conjunction with designs.

Blake's first book, however, was printed, though never published. Produced in 1783 at the expense of friends, *Poetical Sketches* was presumably circulated among the members of a small circle, and some copies were kept by Blake himself. The book was not seen by a wider readership until Richard Herne Shepherd's edition of 1868. An anonymous 'Advertisement' told the reader that the poems were 'the production of an untutored youth, commenced by the author in his twelfth, and occasionally resumed by the author till his twentieth year' (E 846).[1] As his time since then had been occupied with 'the attainment of excellence in his profession', he had not had 'the leisure requisite to such a revisal of these sheets, as might have rendered them less unfit to meet the public eye'. This sounds like faint praise indeed, but we should realize that the deprecatory or self-deprecatory preface to a first book was in its time a sub-genre, especially when the author was self-educated. When John Taylor published John Clare's *Poems Descriptive of Rural Life and Scenery* (1820), the publisher wrote that these poems were 'the genuine productions of a young Peasant, a day-labourer in husbandry, who has had no advantages of education beyond others of his class' (p. i). Blake's friends did not necessarily think of his poems as full of faults, and it is hardly likely that Blake himself did.

Some of the *Poetical Sketches* read like trial runs: among these the melodramatic ballads 'Fair Elenor' and 'Gwin, King of Norway', the Ossianic purple prose piece 'The Couch of Death', and six scenes of an historical drama called *King Edward III*, so puzzling in its attitude to war that scholars debate about whether it is satirical or a piece of youthful jingoism (but which nevertheless shows a good ear for the cadences of Shakespeare's early history plays). Several of the lyrics called 'Song' are very fine, and the one beginning 'How sweet I roam'd from field to field' prefigures in its ironical closing Blake's later theme of entrapment by love. However, some poems in this book are neither promising, nor aspiring, nor important for Blake's development, but simply magnificent. These include four addresses to the seasons in unrhymed iambic pentamenter, sixteen to nineteen lines in length. The lines are presented as strophes, strengthening a sense of regularity: the two sixteen-line ones are divided into four groups of four lines each, the eighteen-line one into three groups of six, with only 'Summer' having the slight irregularity of 6 + 7 + 6. Each begins with a vocative O, addressing the season personified. That last word is important, because of Blake's love of personifications. His poetry frequently employs them, and so does his art, as in some of the water colours illustrating Edward Young's *Night Thoughts*, and the colour printed drawing *Pity*. For Blake the personification was often halfway between a figure of speech and a mythical being, often shading off more in the direction of the latter, as in his addresses to the seasons.

'To Spring' is an invocation in erotic language redolent of the Song of Songs: our eyes are 'longing', our winds will 'kiss' her 'perfumed garments', we will 'taste' her 'morn and evening breath'; and the verbs attached to her are imperative: 'turn ... Thine eyes', 'issue forth', 'let thy holy feet visit' (E 408). In the first three stanzas a speaker who represents the whole 'lovesick land' importunes Spring, while in the fourth a single lover is ordered to 'deck her forth', 'pour / Thy soft kisses on her bosom', and 'put / Thy golden crown' upon her. She too is lovesick, or why would her head be 'languished'? Summer enters as a potent lover, with his 'ruddy limbs and flourishing hair', and is invited to 'throw thy / Silk draperies off, and rush into the stream'. Autumn, rich with fruit, displays a certain ambiguity in being 'stained / With the blood of the grape' (E 409) – life intertwined with death. To him alone is given his own song, nine lines that recapitulate the two preceding seasons' 'narrow bud' followed by blossoms and flowers. 'Autumn' ends with a wonderful anti-climax: he 'rose, girded himself, and o'er the bleak / Hills fled from our sight; but left his golden load'. We can't help thinking of the poet to come who will picture Autumn sitting on a granary floor – both looking back to James Thomson's 'Autumn, nodding o'er the yellow plain, / Comes jovial on.'[2] 'To Winter', like the other three poems, begins as an address with strong, single-syllable imperatives – three in the first four lines – but the difference here is in their lack of effect. 'He hears me not', says the speaker, and goes on to describe the depredations of 'the direful monster'. In a parody of the erotic actions of the other three seasons, 'his hand / Unclothes the earth, and freezes up frail life'. Yet as we read we are made conscious of the conventional: 'To Winter' is not frightening but like a storm scene in an eighteenth-century theatre with its wave machine and papier-mâché rocks. The mariner is a 'Poor little wretch! That deal'st / With storms', but he survives when 'heaven smiles' in what Geoffrey Hartman aptly calls 'an inspired period cliché',[3] 'and the monster / Is driv'n yelling to his caves beneath mount Hecla' (E 410). Together these four poems compose a masterpiece of the age of sensibility.

In 1783, the year that *Poetical Sketches* was printed, Blake wrote a prose satire now called *An Island in the Moon*. Most of this manuscript fragment (in the Fitzwilliam Museum, Cambridge) involves foolish conversations among a group of people with fanciful names, and it displays a mordant wit for which Blake is not often enough credited: 'she seemd to listen with great attention while the Antiquarian seemd to be talking of virtuous cats, but it was not so. she was thinking of the shape of her eyes & mouth & he was thinking, of his eternal fame' (E 449). *An Island* is full of sharp contrasts, none more dramatic than when a song is performed, beginning: 'Upon a holy thursday their innocent faces clean / The children walking two & two in grey & blue & green' (E 462–3). Even this silly, superficial group is struck by the lyric's beauty. 'After this they all sat silent for a quarter of an hour' (E 462–3).

This song is the first known version of the poem entitled 'Holy Thursday' that Blake published in his *Songs of Innocence* in 1789, and it is a good example of Blake's method in *Innocence* and its complementary *Songs of Experience*. (*Songs of Experience* is dated 1793; the combined *Songs* were issued with a new title-page in 1794.) The subject is the annual choral concert of the charity school children at St Paul's Cathedral on Holy Thursday, an event famous throughout Europe. When Franz Josef Haydn heard the children perform in 1791, he wrote in his notebook: 'In all my life, no music moved me so powerfully as this reverent and innocent [music].'[4] The children in their school uniforms, the seeming purity of the beadles as expressed by their white wands, the simile of 'multitudes of lambs' with its inevitable suggestion of the Lamb of God, and the reverend men sitting as guardians all give the sense of a divinely ordered universe. This is reinforced by the simile of 'a mighty wind' for the children's song, which recalls how when the disciples gathered at Pentecost, 'suddenly there came a sound from heaven as of a rushing mighty wind, and it filled all the house where they were sitting' (Acts 2:2). What seems the moral conclusion of the poem echoes Hebrews 13:2: 'Be not forgetful to entertain strangers: for thereby some have entertained angels unawares.' This in turn calls to mind how Abraham and Sarah extended their hospitality to three strange men in the plains of Mamre (Genesis 18:1–10), to which the speaker finds the activity of the charity schools a parallel.

Like Haydn, the speaker regards the concert as an example of human benevolence. However, charity school children were, as Blake well knew, brought up to occupy the lowest rung of society as servants and seamstresses, and the abusive conditions in some charity schools had recently been a subject of public discussion. This is seen clearly by the speaker in the 'Holy Thursday' of *Songs of Experience*, who sees 'Babes reduced to misery, / Fed with cold and usurous hand' (E 19), and asks 'Is that trembling cry a song?' When we return from *Experience* to *Innocence*, we may see the first poem with different eyes. The design can now strike us as showing an enforced regularity – the children in pairs wearing their school uniforms, the beadles, one with a staff, leading the boys in the top margin, a bonneted dame leading the girls at the bottom (**Fig. 4**). The beadles' wands now suggest the power to intimidate, and we note how the children are 'seated in companies', their 'wise guardians' with their backs to them. The rhythm of line 3 reinforces the sense of regimentation, comprising seven iambic feet that become more obviously regular as the stresses fall on monosyllables five times.

– ´ / – ´ / – ´ / – ´ / – ´ / – ´ / – ´
The children walking two & two in red & blue & green

A similar contrast occurs in the two 'Chimney Sweeper' poems. After reading the child of Experience's bitter denunciation of his parents' clothing him in 'the clothes of death' (E 23), we are not likely to endorse the Innocent sweep's conclusion 'So if all do their duty, they need not fear harm' (E 10). Indeed the *then* or *so* in the last line of each poem exhibit the power of ratiocination to reach false conclusions. In some other paired poems the oppositions are explicitly stated. In the first 'Nurses Song' the speaker, who says 'my heart is at rest within my breast'(E 15), allows the children to play until sundown. In the second, the Nurse bitterly remembers 'the days of my youth' (E 23) and orders the children home with the miserable reflection that 'Your spring & your day, are wasted in play / And your winter and night in disguise.' 'The Divine Image' declares that humanity incarnates the divine attributes of 'Mercy Pity Peace and Love', while 'The Human Abstract' sees Pity as contingent on the poverty of others, Mercy on their unhappiness, peace on 'mutual fear', and love as being 'selfish' (E 27). 'Infant Joy' gives us a happy two-day-old whose name is Joy; in 'Infant Sorrow' the baby is 'Like a fiend hid in a cloud' (E 28). The Blossom is happy sheltering the Sparrow and the Robin 'Near my Bosom', but in 'The Sick Rose' the flower

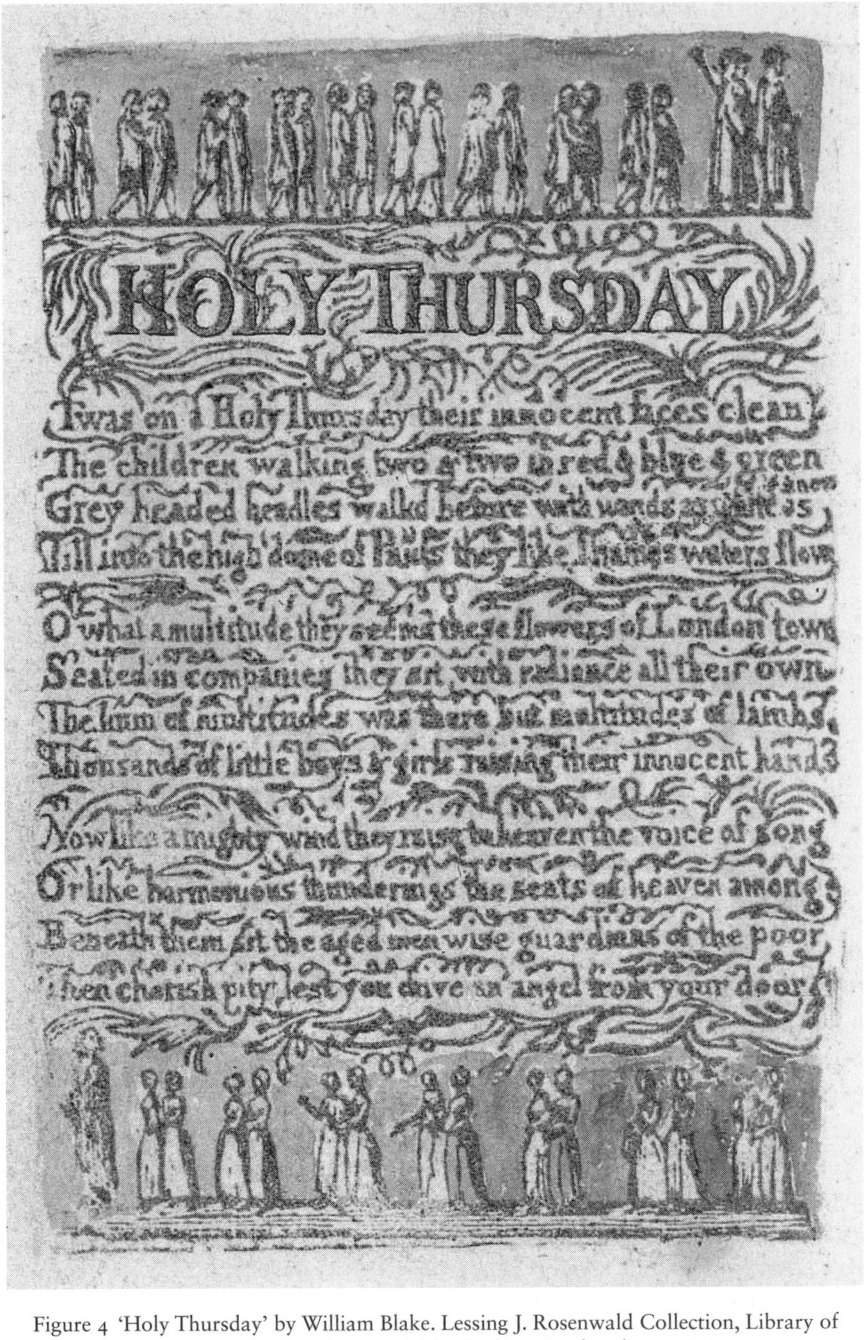
HOLY THURSDAY
Twas on a Holy Thursday their innocent faces clean
The children walking two & two in red & blue & green
Grey headed beadles walkd before with wands as white as snow
Till into the high dome of Pauls they like Thames waters flow
O what a multitude they seemd these flowers of London town
Seated in companies they sit with radiance all their own
The hum of multitudes was there but multitudes of lambs
Thousands of little boys & girls raising their innocent hands
Now like a mighty wind they raise to heaven the voice of song
Or like harmonious thunderings the seats of heaven among
Beneath them sit the aged men wise guardians of the poor
Then cherish pity, lest you drive an angel from your door

Figure 4 'Holy Thursday' by William Blake. Lessing J. Rosenwald Collection, Library of Congress © 2008 the William Blake Archive. Used with permission.

is destroyed by the 'dark secret love' of 'The invisible worm' (E 10, 23). In contrast to the 'merry Sparrow' who flies 'swift as arrow' into the Blossom's bosom, the worm is invisible and flies in the night.

Some *Songs of Experience* contain in themselves their own antitheses. In 'The Clod & the Pebble', the softly yielding Clod embodies Love as a giving of Self that creates a heaven, the hard-edged Pebble as a possessive gratification that creates a hell. The speaker of 'The Garden of Love' once played on the green where a chapel is now built with 'Thou shalt not. writ over the door' (E 26). The Little Black Boy in his Innocence imagines serving in heaven as on earth, but the Experienced reader should realize that there is something lacking in the 'little English boy' who can love only someone who will 'be like him' (E 9). And each of the iconic beasts, Lamb and Tyger, embodies an attribute of God in the particular world it inhabits. Neither world is self-contained or self-sufficient. As Northrop Frye memorably put it, 'The *Songs of Experience* are satires, but one of the things they satirize is the state of innocence ... Conversely, the *Songs of Innocence* satirize the state of experience, as the contrast which they present to it makes its hypocrisies more obviously shameful. Hence the two sets of lyrics show two *contrary* states of the soul, and in their opposition there is a double-edged irony, cutting into both the tragedy and the reality of fallen existence.'[5]

Even when he first published *Songs of Innocence*, Blake aspired beyond lyric poetry. He wanted to write narrative poems as well. The first of these is *The Book of Thel* (1789), also produced by relief etching. Thel is a shepherdess who inhabits a seeming paradise, 'the vales of Har' (2:1, E 4). Oppressed by thoughts of transience and of death, Thel is addressed in turn by the Lilly of the valley, the Cloud, the Worm, and the Clod of Clay, each of whom (there is no 'which' in this animated universe) teaches her that 'we live not for ourselves' (4:10, E 5), that change leads only to a higher end, and that every death contributes to new life. Thel is allowed to view existence on the plane that Blake will soon call Experience and later Generation: 'A land of sorrows & of tears where never smile was seen' (6:5, E 6). After hearing a 'voice of sorrow' come from 'her own grave plot', Thel 'with a shriek. / Fled back unhinderd till she came into the vales of Har' (6:22, E 6). This *anima* has refused to be born, which leads S. Foster Damon to suggest a personal element to the story: 'Might not [William's wife] Catherine have given birth to a stillborn girl? Perhaps *The Book of Thel*, with its strange ending, was an elegy to the Blakes' dead daughter, their only offspring.'[6]

In the years 1789–93 Blake produced three further narrative poems, each conceived for a different mode of publication. Each has as its major theme one aspect of tyranny. The first, *Tiriel*, exists as a manuscript (British Museum) on eight foolscap pages, accompanied by twelve finished drawings, now scattered.[7] The verse is iambic septameter, the metre of George Chapman's great translation of the *Iliad*. Perhaps it was the 'ancient' associations of the septenary that attracted Blake, for he used it for much of his work, including his three longest poems. Tiriel, a blind old tyrant whose oppressed sons have rebelled against him, enters a false paradise inhabited by Har and Heva, a parodic Adam and Eve who never left Eden but instead degenerated into a prolonged infantilism. His wanderings continue until he falls dead after a deeply pessimistic speech, part of which describes the development of the boy child in a world like that of Experience:

> The father forms a whip to rouze the sluggish senses to act
> And scourges off all youthful fancies from the newborn man.
>
> (8:14–15, 16–18, E 285)

Although conceived of as embodying the aftermath of a struggle between primal father and band of brothers,[8] *Tiriel* suffers from arbitrariness in its characters and episodes and fails to achieve the universality that Blake desired. Its production as a manuscript precluded its reaching any appreciable audience. (The text was first printed in William Michael Rossetti's *The Poetical Works of William Blake, Lyrical and Miscellaneous*, 1874.)

Meant for a larger readership, but known only through a single set of proofs (1791, Huntington Library), is *The French Revolution*, which bears the imprint of Joseph Johnson, the publisher for whom Blake did a considerable amount of engraving work. It is declared as the first of seven books, although there were to be no others. We may think of it as Blake's response to the debate initiated by Edmund Burke's *Reflections on the Revolution in France* (1790) and Thomas Paine's reply to Burke, *Rights of Man* (1791). Very sympathetic to the Revolution at this point, Blake offers a mythologized presentation of events from the convening of the three estates through the meeting of the National Assembly, the king's mustering his troops, the dismissal of Jacques Necker, the establishment of a National Guard with La Fayette as its commander, the Assembly's demand that the troops be removed, and the king's assent to this.[9] These pivotal events, which actually took place over more than two months (4 May to 15 July 1789), are presented as occurring in rapid, dramatic succession.

Among the dramatis personae are the names of historical characters like Lafayette, the Duc d'Aumont, the Duke of Orleans, 'the Abbe de Seyes', and the king himself. Also present are the Duke of Burgundy, who did not literally exist, and Henri IV, come from another world. All these move on the same plane, as do powerful forces embodied in fire, fog, darkness, cold, and the sun. Blake creates eloquent fictitious speeches for his participants, and describes the movements of crowds of troops and of civilians in highly charged language laden with similes. His intention is to render not versified history but an archetypal conflict between the forces of life and death:

For the Commons convene in the Hall of the Nation; like spirits of fire in the beautiful
Porches of the Sun, to plant beauty in the desart craving abyss, they gleam
On the anxious city ... (E 288)

... the ancientest Peer, Duke of Burgundy, rose from the Monarch's right hand, red as wines
From his mountains, an odor of war, like a ripe vineyard, rose from his garments. (E 289)

Of course, if Blake actually wrote this in 1791, he would have had no way of knowing what would happen in the following books of *The French Revolution*, although these are declared 'finished' (E 286). Why the first book was not issued separately is puzzling, for even according to the stringent laws of the day there was nothing actionable in it. In any event, after this Blake never attempted publication in typographical form again. In his next narrative he returned to etching text and design in a composite form.

After *Thel* Blake had published another illuminated book, the prose *Marriage of Heaven* (1790), in which, through 'the voice of the Devil', he declared 'Energy is the only life and is from the Body' (E 34). In *Visions of the Daughters of Albion* (1793), he goes on to explore an aspect of this theme as it affects the women of England. His scenario has three characters, and their speeches, comprising laments, questions either rhetorical or unanswerable, and hortatory addresses, are made *at* rather than *to* one another. Oothoon, raped by the thundering Bromion, who then calls her a harlot, vainly exhorts her lover Theotormon to regard her as 'pure'. This god-tormented man prefers to weep and to ask questions like 'Tell me where dwell the thoughts forgotten till thou call them forth / Tell me where dwell the joys of old! & where the ancient loves?' (4:4, E 48). As for Bromion, he senses the limitations of his own existence, asking:

And are there other joys, beside the joys of riches and ease?
And is there not one law for both the lion and the ox?
And is there not eternal fire, and eternal chains? (4:21–3, E 48)

Oothoon asks questions too, but she alone of the three is also capable of declarations, like:

Infancy, fearless, lustful, happy! nestling for delight
In laps of pleasure; Innocence! honest, open, seeking
The vigorous joys of morning light; open to virgin bliss. (6:4–6, E 49)

It may be the magnificence of lines like these that once caused readers to overlook a disturbing aspect of Oothoon's eroticism. She will do anything for Theotormon:

> But silken nets and traps of adamant will Oothoon spread,
> And catch for thee girls of mild silver, or of furious gold;
> I'll lie beside thee on a bank & view their wanton play
> In lovely copulation bliss on bliss with Theotormon
>
> (7:23–6, E 50)

These are disquieting lines, indicating the total subservience of female to male, and calling attention to the problematic nature of sexuality at some points in Blake's later works, when androgyny and partriarchy appear to alternate as ideals, or even intermix.[10] *Visions* ends in stasis, with its final line repeating one that has occurred twice before: 'The Daughters of Albion hear her woes, & eccho back her sighs' (8:13, E 51).

In 1790 William and Catherine Blake had moved to Lambeth, into a house with a garden and plenty of space for William's rolling press and tools of his trade. The illuminated books produced there are often referred to as 'the Lambeth books', especially the six that bear 'Lambeth' on their title-pages and that can be taken as parts of a single narrative. Executed from 1793 to 1795, these six books describe a myth of the world from creation to fall – or more precisely creation *as* fall – through human history to apocalypse.

America and its sequel, *Europe*, are the only books that Blake called a 'Prophecy'. They are of course prophecies in the sense not of telling the future, but of exposing the underlying meanings of events in the past and present. ('Every honest man is a Prophet', Blake wrote, 'he utters his opinion both of private & public matters / Thus / If you go on So / the result is So / He never says such a thing shall happen let you do what you will.'[11]) Both works, and especially *America*, are concerned with historical events, but are no more versified histories than is *The French Revolution*. Now, however, Blake had the advantage of writing in retrospect. *America* includes events of the American Revolution and its immediate aftermath; *Europe* begins with the birth of Christ, fast-forwards eighteen centuries to the American and French Revolutions, and concludes with the outbreak of war between England and France in February 1793. *America* is by far the more optimistic of the two books, while *Europe* culminates with a dark vision of the present.

In *America* the colonists are oppressed by 'The Guardian Prince of Albion' – George III – who appears in his 'dragon form' to bombard the coast (3:1, 15–16, E 52). But the 'fierce Americans' (15:12, E 27) are supported by a fiery figure called Orc (killer whale), who voices the promise of millennial freedom:

The morning comes, the night decays, the watchmen leave their stations;
The grave is burst, the spices shed, the linen wrapped up;

. . . .

Let the slave grinding at the mill, run out into the field:
Let him look up into the heavens & laugh in the bright air.

(6:1–2, 6–7, E 53)

No match for this powerful rhetoric, the response of Albion's Angel out-Herods Herod:

Blasphemous Demon, Antichrist, hater of Dignities;

Lover of wild rebellion, and transgresser of Gods Law;
Why dost thou come to Angels eyes in this terrific form? (7:5–7, E 53–4)

The forces of Empire, embodied in plagues, attack the fertility of America 'As a blight cuts the tender corn when it begins to appear' (14:6), but the fierce Americans and the flames of Orc drive them back to the home country. Now Britain itself is infected by what Blake saw as imminent revolution, perhaps as embodied in the figure of Thomas Paine, one of the two non-generals mentioned by name in *America* (the other is Benjamin Frankin). Paine, whom Blake probably knew, had been able 'to overthrow all the armies of Europe with a small pamphlet',[12] and had then written and published his *Rights of Man* in England before moving on to revolutionary France. Blake went farther than either Paine or the revolutionists did, in seeing the Daughters of Albion free at last, with Orc's fires 'Leaving the females naked and glowing with the lusts of youth' (15:22, E 57). The fires of Orc then threaten France, Spain, and Italy with what Blake views as a totalizing revolution. Urizen, the father god of repressive law, now manifests himself in order to rescue his royal vice-regent, but the best he can do is to freeze the situation temporarily, hiding Orc with his 'stored snows' and 'icy magazines' (16:15)

Till Angels & weak men twelve years should govern o'er the strong:
And then their end should come, when France reciev'd the Demons light.

(16:14–15, E 53–7)

Europe begins with a miraculous birth in the metre of Milton's 'On the Morning of Christ's Nativity':

The deep of winter came;
What time the secret child,
Descended thro' the orient gates of the eternal day. (3:2–4, E 61)

Ironically, this is followed by the reign of Enitharmon, who has become a composite of the goddess Diana and all the queens of the world. For the next eighteen hundred years Enitharmon sleeps, and history is her dream: 'Shadows of men in fleeting bands upon the winds: / Divide the heavens of Europe' (9:6–7). But the partition separating dream and reality is broken when 'Albions Angel smitten with his own plagues fled with his bands' (9:6–8, E 63). Enitharmon has a rude awakening when her son 'terrible Orc, when he beheld the morning in the east / Shot from the heights of Enitharmon; / And in the vineyards of red France appear'd the light of his fury' (15:1–3). So the promise of the last line of *America* is fulfilled. This is speedily followed by the 'strife of Blood' between England and France.

In *The [First] Book of Urizen*, Blake turns to cosmogony, which is for him psychology as well, in the form of a syncretic myth. Among the parallels meant to be recognized are Genesis, the rebellion and fall of Satan, the exposure of the baby Oedipus in Cithaeron, and Moses leading his people out of Egypt. In this way Blake suggests an archetypal mythology behind all existing mythologies. This is the rhetorical strategy called metalepsis, by which older accounts are made to seem posterior to an underlying (but actually new)[13] one, a true myth conveyed through the imagination of William Blake.

An initial harmony of Eternal beings is disrupted when Urizen, 'rent from Eternity', asserts dominion. Los, now 'The Eternal Prophet' (10:7), is charged with forging a material body for Urizen to contain the disruption he has caused. Los acts in anguish, for both were once part of a composite being, and Urizen has been 'rent from his side' (6:4). Further division follows, as Los's female counterpart, Enitharmon, divides from him and becomes 'the first female form now separate' (18:10). Despite her evading him in 'perverse and cruel delight' (19:12), Los embraces her and fathers the infant whom they name Orc. Jealous, Los takes Orc to a mountain top, where he and Enitharmon chain him to a rock. The scene then shifts back to Urizen, who invents measuring devices and explores his dens, and there emanates from him an enormous web that envelops whole cities. Urizen's children, led by his fiery son Fuzon, then come together, name the earth Egypt, and leave it.

There was no second *Book of Urizen*, although *The Book of Los* takes up the same subject from Los's perspective, and *The Book of Ahania* tells the further story of rebellious Fuzon. In the contest between father and son, Fuzon first wounds Urizen, causing Urizen's female component, Ahania, to separate from him. One would have thought Urizen could degenerate no further, but:

He siez'd [her] on his mountains of jealousy.
He groand anguishd & called her Sin,
Kissing her and weeping over her. (2:83–5, E 84–5)

The maimed Urizen is not, however, defeated. He makes a bow from the ribs and sinews of an enormous serpent, poisons a rock with its blood, and fires the projectile. Fuzon, thinking himself victorious, begins what will become a major theme in Blake: the transformation of revolutionary to tyrant: 'I am God. said he, eldest of things!' (3:38, E 86). At just this moment, he is struck by Urizen's rock, which then falls to earth to become 'Mount Sinai, in Arabia' (3:46). The last part of the poem belongs to Ahania, who in a beautiful lament of sixty-four lines conjures up a prelapsarian world *in illo tempore*:

> When I found babes of bliss on my beds.
> And bosoms of milk in my chambers
> Fill'd with eternal seed
> O! eternal births sung round Ahania
> In interchange sweet of their joys. (5:19–23, E 89)

But hers is a voice crying from 'the verge / Of Non-entity' (4:53–4, E 88).

Blake's other illuminated book of 1795 was *The Song of Los*, which in two parts, 'Africa' and 'Asia', supplies the remaining continents. First the misguided children of Los give Urizen's laws to the nations, imagination encoding false religious scripts. 'Moses beheld upon Mount Sinai forms of dark delusion'; the Greek philosophers obtained 'an abstract Law'; Jesus 'recievd A Gospel from wretched Theotormon'; Mahomet was given 'a loose Bible'[14] and Odin 'a Code of War' (E 67). Blake brings things into modern times when Urizen gives 'a Philosophy of Five Senses' to Newton and Locke (4:17–18), creating the basis for an Age of Reason that Blake resolutely set himself against. The last line of 'Africa' is the first line of *America* – 'The Guardian Prince of Albion burns in his nightly tent.' We have again arrived at the Age of Revolution.

Some time after completing the last Lambeth book in 1795, Blake decided to pull his material together in epic form. The new work was called *Vala*, featuring the four component powers of human identity. These Blake calls *zoas*, Greek for 'living creatures' (translated as 'beast' in the AV of the Bible, as in the 'four beasts' mentioned eleven times in Revelation). Blake imagines them as androgynous forms in a primordial paradise. Although they are far from merely allegorical, in one aspect each represents an indwelling human faculty: Urizen/Reason, Tharmas/Sensation, Luvah/Emotion, and Los/Imagination. When they struggle for domination, they divide into male and female, and also cause a deep separation of functions within the Eternal Man, who cries at one point 'O war within my members' (*Four Zoas*, 119:32, E 388). This internal war parallels the external one raging between Britain and France. Blake had hoped to end *Vala* with a re-integration of the human psyche accompanied by a millennial peace. However, by the turn of the century world events, as David Erdman shows in *Blake, Prophet Against Empire*, forestalled any such resolution. At roughly that time Blake had a series of visionary experiences that profoundly affected his poetry and art. Consequently, he interjected passages concerning the Lamb of God, a group called the Council of God, the Seven Eyes of God, and other redemptive elements. Now called *The Four Zoas*, the poem was still to culminate in an apocalypse and Last Judgement, but this would be brought about by the spiritual regeneration of Albion. At some point Blake recognized the inadequacy of overlaying his original structure with visionary Christian themes, and he abandoned the manuscript.

Milton a Poem is Blake's effort to build a long poem on his new vision. It is preceded by the great untitled lyric, beginning 'And did those feet in ancient time', in which Blake demands his 'Bow of burning gold' and 'Arrows of desire' for the 'Mental Fight' to follow (E 95). John Milton, the poet who meant the most to Blake, is imagined as 'Unhappy tho in heav'n' because of the state of his Sixfold Emanation (comprising his three wives and three daughters) 'scatter'd thro' the deep / In torment!' (2:18–20, E 96). To undo his past errors towards his female counterparts, he descends through a Vortex that is the gateway back to the natural world. Urizen opposes Milton's second coming and tries to prevent it in a parodic baptism, taking water from the Jordan and 'pouring on / To Miltons brain the icy fluid from his broad cold palm' (19:9, E 112). Milton does not reply in kind, but moulds 'the red clay of Succoth' (of which the ornaments of Solomon's temple were made) over the bones of the skeletal Urizen, 'one giving life, the other giving death / To his adversary' (19:30). Continuing his quest, Milton withstands the temptations posed by the alluring sons and daughters of Rahab and Tirzah (in this context sexual licence and frosty purity), and becomes manifest as a falling star that enters William Blake's left foot. In a beautiful image Blake expresses his new sense of being when invested with the spirit of Milton:

> And all this Vegetable World appeard on my left Foot,
> As a bright sandal formd immortal of precious stones & gold:
> I stooped down & bound it on to walk forward thro' Eternity.
>
> (21:13–15, E 115)

Milton's Emanation is named Ololon. Like Joyce's Anna Livia Plurabelle, she is both a river– 'in Eden a sweet River, of milk & liquid pearl' (21:15) – and a female being. She makes a descent parallel to Milton's, and appears in Blake's garden as a virgin of twelve years. 'Knowest thou of Milton', she asks, 'who descended / Driven from Eternity; him I seek!'

(37:1–2). This sweet simplicity contrasts with Ololon's later apocalyptic manifestation:

> ... as a Moony Ark Ololon descended to Felphams Vale
> In clouds of blood, in streams of gore, with dreadful thunderings
> Into the Fires of Intellect that rejoic'd in Felphams Vale.
>
> (42:7–9, E 143)

This event either causes or is the signal of Blake's spiritual experience outside the cottage in Felpham, Sussex, where the Blakes lived from 1800 to 1803.

> My bones trembled. I fell outstretchd upon the path
> A moment, & my Soul returnd into its mortal state
> To Resurrection & Judgment in the Vegetable Body
> And my sweet Shadow of Delight stood trembling by my side.
>
> (42:25–28, E 143)

Thus *Milton* is a deeply personal work, with its final theme being the empowerment of the poet William Blake.

If *Milton* centres on Blake's individual experience, all humanity is the centre of *Jerusalem*: *The Emanation of the Giant Albion*, which Blake probably began in 1804, producing his first complete copy in 1820, and the gloriously coloured copy E in 1826, the year before his death. Its central myth is the sleep and awakening of Albion, and his reunion with his female counterpart Jerusalem, following Revelation 21:2 – 'And I John saw the holy city, new Jerusalem, coming down from God out of heaven, prepared as a bride adorned for her husband.' The narrating voice is that of the empowered poet:

> I write in South Molton Street, what I both see and hear
> In regions of Humanity, in Londons opening streets. (34:42–3, E 180)

Jerusalem's four chapters of twenty-five plates each may lead the reader to suspect a linear development, but actually the narrative element of *Jerusalem* is relatively weak, and its meaning is established largely through the development of themes.[15] Some of these involve a back-story in which Albion falls into the power of his Spectre (the reasoning power separate from total human identity). In the 'now' of the poem Albion is described in his fallen state; the cast-out Jerusalem laments her previous existence; Los and his emanation are divided and contend with each other; Los's own Spectre rises against him and then is reconciled; the fallen Zoas are described; Jesus is incarnated, is crucified, and speaks; and Satan becomes manifest. All these thematic events are repeated, although not necessarily or to the same extent in every chapter: Jerusalem is most featured in

Chapters 1 and 4, while Jesus does not appear in Chapter 1 except for dictating his 'mild song' to Blake at the beginning, and Satan is absent from Chapter 1 and most prominent in Chapter 2. Starting with 'Time was finished!' (94:18), however, the final plates have a strong forward progression. Albion awakens, takes up his four-fold bow, and fires 'the Arrows of Intellect' at the Spectre that is Blake's Antichrist. All Human Forms find their true identities, but – and this is highly characteristic of Blake – they do not disappear undifferentiatedly into some heavenly realm but rather oscillate between 'Planetary lives' and 'the Life of Immortality' in Albion's Bosom (99:1–4).

Of course no identification of themes and recounting of events can even begin to characterize Blake's greatest illuminated book. We should, for example, be aware of the social texture of *Jerusalem* – the impressed sailors 'carried away in thousands from London' (65:33), 'the cries of War on the Rhine & Danube' (47:9), 'the slave [who] groans in the dungeon of stone' (20:16), 'Tyburns fatal Tree' (once site of the public gallows, 12:26), 'Chelsea [Hospital] / The place of wounded Soldiers' (8:3), and the oppressors who 'compell the Poor to live upon a crust of bread by soft mild arts' (44:30). It also has a deeply personal aspect, for, as in *The Four Zoas*, the contentions of Los and Enitharmon are those of William and Catherine Blake. In these and other ways, we can say of *Jerusalem* what Blake says of the Imagination's archetypal works of art:

> All things acted on Earth are seen in the bright Sculptures of
> Los's Halls & every Age renews its powers from these Works.
> (16:61–2)

NOTES

1 All references are to *The Complete Poetry and Prose of William Blake*, ed. David V. Erdman (Berkeley and Los Angeles: University of California Press, 1988). This edition is designated as E, followed by the page reference as here, or by the plate or MS page number and line number.

2 *The Complete Poetical Works of James Thomson* (1908), ed. J. Logie Robinson (London: Oxford University Press, 1963), p. 133. *The Seasons* (London: printed for J. Millan and A. Millar, 1730 (1731))., p. 5.

3 Geoffrey Hartman, 'Blake and the Progress of Poesy', in *Beyond Formalism: Literary Essays 1958–1970* (New Haven: Yale University Press, 1970), p. 204.

4 See Ian Spink, 'Haydn at St. Paul's – 1791 or 1792?', *Early Music* 33 (2005), 273–80.

5 Northrop Frye, *Fearful Symmetry: A Study of William Blake* (Princeton: Princeton University Press, 1947), p. 237.

6 S. Foster Damon, *A Blake Dictionary: The Ideas and Symbols of William Blake*, rev. edn., foreword and annotated bibliography Morris Eaves (Hanover, NH: University Press of New England, 1988), p. 401.
7 See G. E. Bentley, Jr, *Tiriel: Facsimile and Transcript of the Manuscript, Reproduction of the Drawings and a Commentary on the Poem* (Oxford: Clarendon Press, 1967).
8 Blake's works are used as major illustrations of this theme by Norman O. Brown in *Love's Body* (New York: Random House, 1966), *passim*.
9 See David V. Erdman, *Blake, Prophet Against Empire: A Poet's Interpretation of the History of His Own Times*, 3rd edn (Princeton: Princeton University Press, 1977), pp. 164–74.
10 See Anne K. Mellor, 'Blake's Portrayal of Women', *Blake: An Illustrated Quarterly*, 16 (1982–3), 148–55.
11 Annotations to *An Apology for the Bible* (1798) by Bishop Richard Watson, E 617.
12 E 617, Annotations to Watson's *Apology for the Bible* referring to Paine's *Common Sense* (Philadelphia, 1776).
13 See Harold Bloom, *Poetry and Repression: Revisionism from Blake to Stevens* (New Haven and London: Yale University Press, 1976), p. 20.
14 The word *Koran* was once thought to mean 'a collection of loose sheets'. See W. H. Stevenson, ed., *Blake: The Complete Poems*, 2nd edn (London and New York: Longman, 1989), p. 248 n.
15 See the tables in Morton D. Paley, *The Continuing City: William Blake's Jerusalem* (Oxford: Clarendon Press, 1983), pp. 308–11.

SELECTED FURTHER READING

Editions

The Complete Poetry and Prose of William Blake, ed. David V. Erdman, Berkeley, University of California Press, 1988

The Complete Writings of William Blake: with Variant Readings, ed. Geoffrey Keynes, London, Oxford University Press, 1966

Blake: The Complete Poems, ed. W. H. Stevenson, 3rd edn, London, Pearson/Longman, 2007

The Illuminated Books of William Blake, gen. ed. David Bindman, 6 vols, Princeton, Princeton University Press, 1994–8

Secondary works

Beer, John B., *William Blake: A Literary Life*, Basingstoke, Palgrave Macmillan, 2007

Damon, S. Foster, *A Blake Dictionary: The Ideas and Symbols of William Blake*, rev. edn, foreword and annotated bibliography Morris Eaves, Hanover, NH, University Press of New England, 1988

Eaves, Morris (ed.), *The Cambridge Companion to William Blake*. Cambridge. Cambridge University Press. 2003

Erdman, David V., *Blake, Prophet Against Empire: A Poet's Interpretation of the History of His Own Times*, 3rd edn, Princeton, Princeton University Press, 1977

Essick, Robert N., *William Blake and the Language of Adam*, Oxford, Clarendon Press, 1989

Frye, Northrop, *Fearful Symmetry: A Study of William Blake*, Princeton, Princeton University Press, 1947

Lincoln, Andrew, *Spiritual History: A Reading of William Blake's Vala, or, The Four Zoas*, Oxford, Clarendon Press, 1995

Paley, Morton D., *The Continuing City: William Blake's Jerusalem*, Oxford, Clarendon Press, 1983

Viscomi, Joseph, *Blake and the Idea of the Book*, Princeton, Princeton University Press, 1993

14

KARL MILLER

Robert Burns

Robert Burns came to fame during the decade that fell between the American and the French Revolutions, and his fame was itself in some ways revolutionary. He was a man from the poor who became a national poet and a patriotic icon. He was an early inhabitant of what could be known to his immediate posterity as an age of personality – a morning star. But his stardom did not save him from remaining precariously poor, and he did little to court material reward. Those who stepped into the Lowland cottages of the last century could find themselves standing before a sepia engraving of the poet, perhaps in Masonic dress, displayed in the manner that portraits of popes, leaders, and founding fathers were displayed elsewhere in the world. But these man-of-feeling, thriving-farmer images were unlikely to suggest the polemically democratic Burns who has been affirmed but also neglected in his native land, who has been both taken and left as an aspect of the Burns 'revolution'. Within living memory he could be referred to in Lowland cottages as 'Rabbie'. Rabbie spoke up for honest poverty but was not usually accounted a subversive.

He was born on 25 January 1759, fifty years after the parliamentary union of Scotland and England, a bond recently relaxed. Scotland kept its established Presbyterian church and its legal system, which meant that the political life of which the young Burns grew conscious encompassed the debates of Edinburgh's ministers and lawyers in the General Assembly of the Church of Scotland, and the *odium theologicum* of the parish and the synod. His family lived near Ayr in the west of Scotland, his father a hard-pressed cotter or small farmer who read Adam Smith's *Theory of Moral Sentiments*, with its doctrine of the primacy of fellow-feeling, and who saw to it that his sons were taught by a capable teacher, later to give English lessons to Talleyrand, the French statesman, in London. In 1786, a collection of Robert Burns's poems appeared in Kilmarnock. Thereupon he went to Edinburgh, where he was taken up and looked down on by the aristocracy and literati of the town. An enlarged Edinburgh edition of his poems was dedicated to the esquires of the Caledonian hunt.

Below the Highland line, Scotland spoke two languages, Scots and English, variants of the same speech. Many Scots were in the habit of modulating between the two, and many of Burns's poems were in an Anglo-Scots, a simultaneous Scots and English. The Scottish historian Henry Cockburn made telling reference, in 1852, to 'writers in that classic Scotch, of which much is good old English, from Gavin Douglas to Burns'.[1] In the course of the eighteenth century English gained ground among the upper class, and Burns could be commended for his ability to speak it. Much of his correspondence is in English, but many of its finest flights are not, and his best poems are in the vernacular, his cherished native tongue. English was an effort, he said, and it was an effort which learned friends advised him to make.

After Edinburgh, he returned to the west, where he soon had a wife and family to support. He farmed near Dumfries and served as a Customs officer, one of the Excise, a body he'd conventionally scorned, where he was expected to act rather than think. His last years were spent on his songs, and on the collecting and refurbishing of Scotland's store of folk lyrics. A touch that can seem unsurpassable steers, at times, the very simplest of words.

Lanely night comes on,
    A' the house are sleeping;
I think on the bonnie lad
    That has my heart a keeping.

('When I sleep I dream', p. 508, lines 5–8)

He died in Dumfries at the age of 37, after a life of hardship, 'bardship', ill-health, depression, and elation: a bipolar Burns can sometimes be surmised, in his swings, and in the 'inconsistencies' and black 'hypochondrias' he suffered from, eighteenth-century words for his (and James Boswell's) divided state. His premonitory lines 'on the death of Robert Ruisseaux' are as apt as the name he conferred on himself here, with reference to his surname and that of Jean-Jacques Rousseau.

Now Robin lies in his last lair,
He'll gabble rhyme, nor sing nae mair,
Cauld poverty, wi' hungry stare,
        Nae mair shall fear him;
Nor anxious fear, nor cankert care,
        E'er mair come near him.
To tell the truth, they seldom fasht him,
Except the moment that they crusht him.

('Elegy on the Death of Robert Ruisseaux', p. 219, lines 1–8)

His anxieties were not soothed by experience of a severe class distinction. In *The History and Social Influence of the Potato*, Redcliffe Salaman mentions 'the devices of so intensely a class-ridden society as that of 18th-century Scotland'. Burns fell victim to the devices in question, those of a society whose leading man of later years, Walter Scott, could successively say of his fellow-writers Robert Burns and James Hogg that their birth was too low for them to be expected to respond suitably to the delicate business of duelling challenges. Burns was 'a high-souled plebeian', and no coward; he had the delicacy, 'of another sort', to mind about the safety of his wife and children in such matters. But he was still a plebeian, 'untinged with the slightest shade of that spirit of chivalry which since the feudal times has pervaded the higher ranks of European society'. He lacked 'that chivalrous sensibility of honour which places reason upon the sword's point'. Scott also referred, with a degree of ambiguity, to a moral collapse of the 'later and more evil days' of this extravagant genius.[2] Despite his ascents to the company of noblemen and gentlemen, Burns never lost his resentment of unearned favour and distinction.

With reference to Church of Scotland factional discord, Thomas Carlyle called Burns 'the fighting-man of the New Light priesthood'.[3] He has also been called anti-clerical. He was schooled in the Presbyterian faith by his father, a liberal adherent, and came of age with a distaste for 'polemical divinity'[4] and a willingness to trade blows in this setting. Scotland's ministers were ranged, he found, in two camps: the liberal, or modern, and the evangelical. Self-styled 'moderates' encountered the 'wild', as evangelicals would eventually be known, in the course of an enduring theological cold war. Schism could appear an article of faith for the more zealous among these ministers, with the independence of the church from state control frequently at issue. The patronage Act of 1712 restored to the crown and to heritors, to the landowning lay patron of a kirk, the right to choose a minister. This right, upheld by the Moderate party, was an instrument of government control, as were the Moderates themselves. At one point the Burgher's Oath whereby office-bearers had to profess the religion of the state led to a dispute, which was overtaken by a further dispute between the New Licht and Auld Licht factions that do battle in Burns's satires. New Licht Moderates were Arminian, anti-predestinarian, in theological tendency, while the second faction prided itself, wrote Lockhart, Scott's son-in-law and biographer, on being the 'descendants and representatives of the haughty Puritans, who chiefly conducted the overthrow of Popery in Scotland, and who ruled for a time, and would fain have continued to rule over both king and people, with a more tyrannical dominion than ever the Catholic priesthood itself had been able to exercise amidst that high-spirited nation'.[5] They called for a fidelity to the Calvinism of the seventeenth-century Solemn League and Covenant.

Reticent on the landowner's right to appoint ministers, Burns was nevertheless aligned with the Moderates. The name 'Presbyterian' could be used by him in tones of irony or aversion, but he was in some sense a pious man. He would joke to his male friends about the 'holy Somebody that directs this world',[6] and about the chance of an afterlife, and he was expressly not 'fanatical'. One variety of his religious experience caused him to hate the very idea of 'controversial divinity', and to invoke a 'Religion of the bosom', just as James Hogg, a generation later, was to invoke a 'religion of the heart'. To such formulations – a period phenomenon barely imaginable a hundred years before – Burns elsewhere admits the concept of mind: 'We can no more live without Religion, than we can live without air; but give me the Religion of Sentiment & Reason.'[7]

Each of these writers, Burns and Hogg, could yield to a sentimental morality which sought an approximation of religious fervour and sexual love. In Burns's high-flown letters to well-born Agnes McLehose in Edinburgh the lovers – communing as Clarinda and Sylvander – are seen to share a sense of the benevolence and omnipotence of God, while Clarinda envisaged a heaven in which love would cease to be a crime: Addison's hymn, 'How are Thy servants blest, O Lord', a favourite text of Burns's from his early days, is quoted to Clarinda, who was inclined to use her religion as a means of sexual control. Meanwhile Burns and Hogg were responsible for two of the deepest and most satirically effective indictments of controversial divinity and of the Christianity of punishment and exclusion. Each was the author of the confessions of a fanatic, a title once affixed to Hogg's novel on the subject.

Burns's engagement with religious questions and with the local politics they helped to generate carried its uncertainties, and so did his engagement with political issues of national and international scope. But there can be no doubt that he was a strong democrat, hostile to titled rank, whose soirées he attended. He walked the streets of Edinburgh, 'Jacobite as he was', claimed Lockhart, in the Foxite livery of blue coat and buff waistcoat. He could seem both Jacobite and Jacobin. The praiser of the 'unfortunate' Bonny Prince Charlie (a stock designation) was also a republican. Disaffection changed shape with the outbreak of the French Revolution: 'jacobites became half-jacobins', Lockhart wrote.[8] But when war broke out with revolutionary France, he could enlist as a volunteer who demanded to know: 'Does haughty Gaul invasion threat?' The estimates and impressions of Westminster's principal politicians which appear in his writings have been thought to show a mutability partly determined by the turns and vicissitudes of their careers. Snubbed, as he felt, by the Dundas dynasty, he would never have subscribed to its command of the north, even if they'd acknowledged receipt of his poems. He alludes in his poems to the Tory potentate Henry Dundas, Scotland's so-called 'Harry the Ninth', William Pitt's minister for security, calling him shrewd and sly, at a time when a Jacobin army was officially presumed to be mustering on British soil. The spectrum of the poet's opinions ranged from Whiggish to regicidal.

The fighting man of the New Light priesthood talked in 1795 of 'coming forward with my services, as poet-laureate to a highly respectable political party'.[9] He can be accounted a constitutional or reform Whig, a 'Real Whig', siding with those, among them some of his social superiors, who wanted a more equal representation, short Parliaments, and a return to the original purity of the Constitution of 1689. During the repressions and sedition trials of 1790s Scotland, when a programme of this kind could be embodied in the judicial definition of treason, he came forward as a libertarian, endangering his post at the Excise. There were associates of his who asked shocking questions. Is Britain to be a free country? Are people to be locked up without trial? Are wars to be waged without consulting the people?

Edwin Muir called him a 'Protean figure', who could be moulded according to taste.[10] But this is too bland. Some of his best pieces say radical things ('A man's a man'). Others do not, and a number of his political pieces are uninteresting. But it is clear that his writings are those of a reformer some of whose objectives prefigured the Reform Act of 1832, and who was at once deterred and undeterred by the need to make a living and defend his family. One of his political pieces stands him apart from the conventional Whiggism of the left then prevailing. His Dumfriesshire gentleman friend Robert Riddell had kennelled a fox:

> The staunchest whig, Glenriddell was
> Quite frantic in his country's cause;
> And oft was Reynard's prison passing,
> And with his brother-whigs canvassing
> The rights of men, the powers of women,
> With all the dignity of freemen.
>
> ('On Glenriddell's Fox Breaking his Chain', pp. 548–9, lines 25–30)

Sir Reynard breaks his chain, having sat in on edifying debates as his masters, supporters of quite another fox, strolled past his prison. His kennelling suggests that 'we to scoundrels owe our freedom'.

Subversive words and actions blamed on Burns gave rise to scandal and invention, and to a habit of avoidance on the part of those of later generations who favoured an anodyne national poet. Could he have been suspected of being a French spy? A far from clandestine one: he published and proclaimed his opinions, and he told his grand friend Mrs Dunlop, whose sons were army officers, that the king and queen of France, 'a perjured Blockhead & an unprincipled Prostitute', deserved their fate. John Barrell's recent book *Imagining the King's Death* goes in great depth into the relationship, as exhibited among both loyalists and radicals, between the language of sentiment and the definition of treason devised for the security concerns of the 1790s by a government of 'alarmers and alarmists'. The sentimental subject of family life supplied metaphors for the execution of the 'unfortunate' Louis XVI, shaping its representation in print and pictorially. Burns's representation of the king's death may be thought to have suspended the language of sentiment. The man of feeling was silent on this occasion.[11]

For Burns, the notion of sympathy and that of brotherhood were a collaboration; the fellow-feeling taught by Adam Smith became an aspect of Burns's radicalism. The issues that arose for him as a 'feeler' who was also a political devotee are astutely discussed in Robert Crawford's important new biography *The Bard* and in his synoptic history *Scotland's Books*.[12]

In 1792, in the course of his official duties, Douanier Ruisseaux helped capture a smuggler brig, the *Rosamund*, and was said in his clandestinity to have purchased its carronade guns and endeavoured to send them to revolutionary France. This outlandish story may contain some truth, but if the guns were seized at Dover, as Walter Scott supposed, how could Burns have survived at the Excise?

After the affair of the carronades came 'the affair of the daggers', as Burns spoke of it to Mrs Dunlop.[13] His Dumfries friend and doctor, William Maxwell, a high-born Francophile, rumoured to have dipped his handkerchief in the blood of the guillotined king of France, attempted to send daggers to the new French army. Edmund Burke inveighed in the House of Commons against a radical arms trade, brandishing a dagger to make his point.[14] And there was an assault on Burke's behaviour in a poem originally published in the *Edinburgh Gazetteer* of 16 May 1793 which has recently been attributed to Burns, as a disproof of the idea that his oppositionist zeal had waned or been daunted towards the end of his life.[15] The attribution has been both accepted and rejected – with the poem assigned elsewhere. The diction is certainly his; the dislike of Burke is his; its 'cannons' and 'daggers' form a conjunction that might be held to point to Burns. None of this, however, is enough to admit the poem to the canon, as distinct from a circle of vernacular poets of a radical turn to which he set an example.

'The Dagger' is a song of 'paddy and his gully' – Irishman Burke and his knife – by 'ane o' the swine', Burke's 'swinish multitude'.

> But trouth I fear the Parliament
> Its ancient splendour fully,
> When chiels man back an argument
> By waving o' a gully;
> Yet some there are, wi' honest heart,
> (Whose courage never swaggers)
> Will ne'er the public cause desert,
> For cannons or for daggers,
> By night or day.

The poem condemns Burke for waving his dagger: he was making a threat that would have seen off the arguments of a Demosthenes or Tully. But the poem, too, utters a veiled threat, before protesting its loyalty to king and Constitution. The swine may one day insist on reform. Before long, in Edinburgh's rigged sedition trials, they were kept in check by transportation. Most of the swine in question were of a station somewhat above the multitude.

The poem is one of several discovered in Edinburgh and London opposition journals and presented around the turn of the present century by scholars keen to stress Burns's radicalism and to rebuke the traditional inclination to hush it up. Some of the poems have been shown to be by other writers. Some appear to be by Burns. This 'radicalizing' of the writer was the goal of the edition entitled *The Canongate Burns*, by Andrew Noble and Patrick Scott Hogg, which has led to prolonged and inflamed exchanges among Burns scholars. The editors provide chapter and verse for the concerted activities of dissenters and protesters in the 1790s, and for the existence of a radical underground (and overground). They print a long letter from Lord Daer to Charles Grey in London, a member there of the Friends of the People who was to become the Whig prime minister in charge of the Reform Bill of 1832. Burns dined in Daer's company, and wrote a flattering poem about him. Daer's letter seems practical and shrewd: 'You wish us in Scotland to come forward because we are more numerous. I believe that small as our numbers are, they are greater in proportion than in England, but far from enough to command protection from the Executors of the forms of law.' At a time when petitions and conventions, easily characterized as sedition, were tactically important for oppositionists, Daer wants Grey to come forward, and deprecates the idea of his not petitioning for Parliamentary reform.[16]

Disclaiming treason, Burns warned the provost of Dumfries, on 1 March 1790, that 'there is a dark stroke of Politics in the belly of the Piece'. The piece was a benefit-night address for delivery at the Dumfries Theatre. As for the dark stroke:

> Perhaps, if bowls row right, and Right succeeds,
> Ye yet may follow where a Douglas leads!
> ('Scots Prologue for Mrs Sutherland's Benefit-Night', pp. 243–4, lines 33–4)

The *Canongate* editors identify this as a reference to Lord Daer, 'Citizen Douglas'. A prologue written by Burns for Miss Fontenelle in 1792 proclaims, with a '*Ça ira!*', that 'the Rights of Woman merit some attention'.[17]

Then, in 2002, an excellent study by Liam McIlvanney appeared, *Burns the Radical*. Burns's radicalism has never been a secret. In 1828 Lockhart apologized for his excesses in this line – for what was deplored in him, by the literatus Hugh Blair, as the politics of the blacksmith's shop.[18] McIlvanney's study, however, a cogent if sometimes controversial work of literary criticism and of political and ecclesiastical history, adds a dimension to the understanding of the poet's democratic sympathies.

Burns, with his antipathy to 'presbyterian bigots', is placed here in a tradition of liberal Presbyterianism. McIlvanney[19] sees an inaugural Calvinism pledged to free inquiry and a tolerance of dissent. Fletcher of Saltoun, a descendant of Robert the Bruce and a leading anti-Unionist, is termed 'a great theorist of Real Whiggism': but if he believed in liberty he also believed in slavery, a slavery he thought would be good for the Scottish poor, who were already acquainted with it in the coalfields and elsewhere. McIlvanney alludes to Burns's 'nationalist strategies': but he was more of a patriot than a nationalist, and can seem resigned to the political system introduced in 1688, though his reference to a 'heavenly Hanoverianism' was a stroke of irony. In this respect, as in others, he was variable and complex, 'heterogeneous', a responder to, and an instance of, the 'intermingledoms' of 'this world' which are perceived in his letters, and in Byron's *Journal*, with its 'antithetical' Burns. This was a world in which good and bad, pure and impure, meet. 'Protean' is hardly the right word for the plurality Burns imagines and enacts.[20]

The living man is surely present in the story told by a witness at whom Burns had raised roars of laughter – 'at me an' my original sin' – but who then, in the room they shared, caught his mocker in a prayer of contrition.[21] The prayer may well have been fictional, but the story is a reminder of the range and volatility, the qualms and fierce rejections, of Burns's religious experience.

The editors of *The Canongate Burns* have been studying a set of documents which throw a painful light on the poet's life, with their talk of women in trouble, illegitimate children, and venereal infections.[22] The documents consist of new-found transcriptions of his letters to a womanizing lawyer friend, Robert Ainslie; new letters are included, and fragmentary published letters supplemented. Eyewitness accounts of Burns can appear to hail him as the incarnation of a new species, as a sensorium of well-nigh industrial strength, boiling with passion, sparkling with impulse, melting with pity, their gauge a glowing eye. His letters to Ainslie may be felt to qualify this conception.

In the summer of 1787, on a Border tour, he was informed that the servant girl May or Margaret Cameron was pregnant by him, in Edinburgh. Burns asked Ainslie to call on her at the house of James Hogg, a shoemaker, and give her some money, warning him that he was on no account to meddle with her. An appeal for help, written for her by Hogg's wife, had been received from the girl, who was in the cauld blast of misfortune: now that her pregnancy was noticeable, her mistress could not keep her in the house, for the sake of its good name. The following year, in an augmented version of a published letter dated mid-October, Burns is pleased that a child borne to him by Jenny Clow, a servant of the Agnes McLehose he had been courting, is doing well. He tells Ainslie that an illegitimate child of Ainslie's, possibly injured at birth, has a claim on his humanity, but that he can't help sharing his wish that Abraham had the little wretch in his bosom. He speaks of Jenny's child as a candidate for the protection of Mrs Dunlop, but Jenny refused to give her up. Before long, he learns from Mrs McLehose that Jenny, a moving, fleeting presence in the confused and endlessly over-investigated history of Burns's love-affairs, is dying. He undertakes to go to Edinburgh to see her. The man of feeling – who wore the cover off his copy of the iconic novel of that name by Henry Mackenzie – is thought to have fathered thirteen children, if not more.

In a new letter to Ainslie of 19 August 1787 he speaks of Jean Armour, whom he is soon to marry, and who has borne him a set of twins and is now pregnant with another set. In his poem 'The Kirk's Alarm' he describes himself as a 'priest-skelper' (pp. 142–4, line 69), and in this letter he is an amorous wife-skelper: he tells how he skelped away at her, worked away at her, till she was nearly driven through a partition separating them from four or five couples similarly engaged – by sheer good luck the commotion remained private. 'Skelp', meaning smack or slap, was a word which he enjoyed using, and which appears in sexual and in martial contexts, convergent as these often are in Burns, whose most arresting pieces of poetry can include the imagination of harm done to the female body. The following year, in a collected letter of 3 March, there occurs the triumphal passage, warmly admired by free spirits of the middle of the last century, in which he gives her 'such a thundering scalade that electrified the very marrow of her bones'.

This is to look at the realities and extremes of Burns's life, and of a society in which the Ball of Kirriemuir (Scottish folklore's principal debauch) took place from time to time, and in which infants and their mothers had many appointments with Abraham's bosom. The letters to Ainslie bring to mind Robert Louis Stevenson's class-conscious and unfeeling essay on 'Some Aspects of Robert Burns', in which he figures both as a 'country Don Juan' and as a 'professional Don Juan', who made 'desperate submissions to evil'.[23] A more humane approach, and a more historically aware one, would have been welcome. At the same time, it may seem that authenticity was an object for Stevenson in writing as he did. Most investigators of his amours have chosen to look away from the less amenable aspects of the Burns hedonism.

Burns liked to say that it was human to have faults, and his own well-known faults were human enough, bearing, as they often do, the mark of his hard times and crying needs. His sexual adventures, inspiring to so many, bear this mark.

A' that I hae endur'd,
  Lassie, my dearie,
Here in thy arms is cur'd,
  Lassie lie near me.

He endured a subsistence-level poverty. There could be a need to please – with affirmations of his honesty and sensibility, for instance – the social superiors whose outlook was in many cases foreign to his democratic art: but the posthumous charge that 'the countenance of the great' was agreeable to him ignores his needs, and has the air of a standard simplification that writers incur. He was both a writer and a bard, exposed both to booksellers and publishers and to a residual patronage. There were 'faults' of his in which his difficulties can be seen, and he was not the 'monster of vice' he was made out to be. A friend, the schoolmaster James Gray, who knew Burns in Dumfries, spoke up for him, in response to such accusations, as 'a good son, a good brother, a good father, and an affectionate husband'.[24]

Burns suffered from an imperfection of the soul, he told Ainslie: 'namely, a blundering inaccuracy of her olfactory organs in hitting the scent of craft or design in my fellow creatures'. He was deceived in the trusted Ainslie, who became disloyal to him and to his memory, as an elder of the kirk and the author of pious tracts, who published letters to him from Burns and retrieved his own letters to Burns, having at one point become a friend of Agnes McLehose. Another contentious close friend was William Nichol, a

Latin teacher at the High School of Edinburgh, and a drinker, remembered as a thrasher of the boys by two former pupils of the school, Walter Scott and Henry Cockburn. The angry Nichol feuded with his headmaster, Dr Adam, a reputedly gentle classical scholar of liberal mind, widely respected and officially disapproved of, and was rumoured to have ambushed him one dark night and knocked him down. A letter to Ainslie contains an allusion to a damaging story about Nichol, which may have originated, Burns remarks, in a 'malevolence' of Dr Adam.[25]

'To one like me, who never cares for speaking any thing else but nonsense, such a friend as you is an invaluable treasure', he told Ainslie.[26] The nonsense and candour of the letters to Ainslie have much to offer students of all registers of Burns's verse and prose, and of the ambivalence of their trade-offs between sentiment and its brutal obverse. Some of Burns's most brilliant and most uninhibited prose is to be met with here, and some of his explosive suddennesses. Certain of his letters, he writes, are

> original matter – spurt – away! zig, here; zag, there; as if the Devil that, my grannie (an old woman *indeed*!) often told me, rode on Will-o'-wisp, or, in her more classic phrase, SPUNKIE, were looking over my elbow. – A happy thought that idea has engendered in my head! SPUNKIE – thou shall thenceforth be my Symbol, Signature, & Tutelary Genius! Like thee, hap-step-&-lowp, here-awa-there-awa, higglety-pigglety, pell-mell, hither-&-yon, ram-stam, happy-go-lucky, up-tails a'-by- the-light-o'-the-moon, has been, is, & shall be, my progress through the mosses & moors of this vile, bleak, barren wilderness of a life of ours.

The letter is signed 'Spunkie' (Will-o'-the-Wisp), a meaning joined to that of a spark, a match, a human live wire, a meaning that became inseminated in later times; and Spunkie draws the letter to a close with another happy thought – that of Ainslie's having begotten another of his children against a book-press. No doubt this 'will have an astonishing effect' on the child. Mere physical contact with books can do a blockhead good. This leads to a tale about a country reading circle of which Burns was the factotum, among them 'a little, wise-looking, squat, upright, jabbering body' of a tailor.

> I advised him, instead of turning over the leaves, *to bind the book on his back*. – Johnie took the hint; and as our meetings were every fourth Saturday, & Prick-Louse having a good Scots mile to walk in coming, &, of course, another in returning, BODKIN was sure to lay his hand on some heavy Quarto, or ponderous Folio, with & under which, wrapt up in his grey plaid, he grew wise as he grew weary all the way home. – He carried this so far, that an old, musty Hebrew Concordance, which we had in a present from a neighbouring Priest, by mere dint of applying it as doctors do a blistering plaister, between his shoulders, STITCH, in a dozen pilgrimages, acquired as

> much *rational* Theology as the said priest had done by forty years perusal of the pages.

This conveys what Burns was prone to think, not just about aberrant theology, but about the piety of priesthoods.[27]

Despite the idolatry and commodification of Burns, there has been, so far as one can judge, a steady sense of the basis of his achievement, though 'The Cotter's Saturday Night', once paramount, is no longer so, and the antinomian-Brechtian song cycle 'Love and Liberty' (alias 'The Jolly Beggars') gained salience with the twentieth-century revolutions in taste. There can be few doubts about the satirical and epistolary poems, the songs, and the late narrative poem 'Tam o' Shanter'. This is poetry in which Scots is spoken, and in which Ayrshire and Nithsdale – the life Burns led there and the hard work he did there – are all-important, as Carlyle, his co-regionary, wished to emphasize (while objecting to Burns's worldliness).[28] These are the qualities of one of Burns's best and most radical poems, in which talking dogs indict the class in possession of Scotland. Such people are enough to give humanity a bad name:

> up they gat and shook their lugs,
> Rejoiced they werena men but dogs.
>
> ('The Twa Dogs', pp. 38–44, lines 235–6)

These qualities are united with a bard's love of language and story, and with a bardic integration into the community of his first readers and listeners. The community he belonged to is inspiringly evident in the class-transcending response to the Kilmarnock edition of his poems.

Human interest and a related artistic worth, literary criticism's traditional preoccupation, are by no means abundant in the political invectives, or in the perfunctory hymns of praise to lasses, ladies, worthies, and the city of Edinburgh; and literary criticism has with reason preferred his poems in Scots to those in English. In this respect, his verse is no different from that of James Boswell, his near neighbour in the country whom for class reasons he never met, and whose poems come to life in the vernacular.

A radical content is not in itself enough for literary criticism, but its practitioners could hardly refuse every passage of this description by Burns. 'The Author's Earnest Cry and Prayer', in strong Scots, is rich, too, in an at once invidious and condign bravura. It attacks the northern representation in the House of Commons, voted in by a particle of Scotland's population. These Members of Parliament are corrupt, and have let through a fiscal harm to the distilleries of the north. Freedom and whisky go together, and if these MPs don't look out free-born Scotsmen will take to the streets and stick their daggers into the first person they meet. A patriotic Postscript, which fails to look forward to the armies of Napoleon, boasts that skelping Scottish soldiers are better than wine-drinking soldiers, of whom Burns writes:

Their gun's a burden on their shouther;
They downa bide the stink o' powther;
Their bauldest thought's a hank'ring swither
To stan' or rin,
Till skelp! A shot – they're aff, a' throu'ther,
To save their skin.

But bring a Scotsman frae his hill,
Clap in his cheek a Highland gill,
Say 'Such is royal George's will,
An' there's the foe!'
He has nae thought but how to kill
Twa at a blow.

(pp. 79–84, lines 157–68)

Patriotism turns here into what could be received as a subversive sarcasm, with the suddenness of a volte-face, and the reader has to decide whether Burns loves or is grimly laughing at his native country, or both. In the last stanza Scotland wets herself, as the praise of whisky reaches its climax.

Scotland, my auld respected Mither!
Tho' whyles ye moistify your leather ... (lines 81–2)

'Leather' refers to the private parts. The poem has its swerves and its uncertainty; and its passages of very good verse, at moments ill-bestowed.

'Holy Willie's Prayer' is certain and unerring. Its ventriloquism is aimed at a local worthy, Willie Fisher; it went unpublished during the poet's lifetime, but circulated as samizdat – unauthorized or subversive writing, often in manuscript form. New Licht gentry are defended against the scandal-bearing devout, or 'unco guid'. It uses the language of the Saints – of the Covenanting tradition – and the scandals dear to the Saints, in order to incriminate them. It moves at a stately, almost sacerdotal pace, while also volted with humour; it is both sonorous and funny. Burns is, with Chaucer and Shakespeare, a poet whose most significant verse can make you laugh. There can be no more beautiful and no more comical music in Scottish poetry than the opening ironies of the 'Prayer':

O Thou, wha in the Heavens dost dwell,
Wha, as it pleases best thysel',
Sends ane to heaven and ten to hell,
A' for thy glory,
And no for ony guid or ill
They've done afore thee!

I bless and praise thy matchless might,
Whan thousands thou hast left in night,
That I am here afore thy sight,
For gifts an' grace
A burnin' an' a shinin' light,
To a' this place.
(pp. 86–9, lines 1–12)

'Death and Dr Hornbook' and the 'Address to the Deil' are conjoined comic masterpieces, each intensely local, each patterned on a hallucinatory encounter, a drunk man's dream. Death and the Devil are both working men, like many another. But an actually existing upstart pharmacist has been putting Death out of a job, rather as the incoming Irish were to be thought to do in the west of Scotland. As for the Devil's work, he may mend his ways and be spared his own hell. This work dates, of course, from the earliest of times:

Lang syne, in Eden's bonnie yard,
When youthfu' lovers first were pair'd,
And all the soul of love they shar'd,
The raptur'd hour,
Sweet on the fragrant flow'ry swaird,
In shady bow'r;

Then you, ye auld snick-drawing dog!
Ye cam to Paradise incog.
An' play'd on man a cursed brogue,
(Black be your fa'!)
An' gied the infant warld a shog,
'Maist ruin'd a'.
('Address to the Deil', pp. 71–5, lines 85–96)

Eden is in English here, by and large, while the words for Satan, the latch-lifter, are Scots. This *Paradise Lost* in little is a match for anything written by a consciously serious Burns, in any period vein of sentiment or solemnity. The idea of a spoilt or compromised human sexuality was perceptible, it would seem, to Burns, the poet of a romantic love, and it is not diminished, on this occasion, by a smiling lightness of touch, a buffo or rococo charm. 'Maist' for 'almost' comes across as an intensifier, with the force, perhaps, of 'mostly'. These are Mozartian stanzas.

'Adam Armour's Prayer', to be found in the *Canongate Burns*, from which I shall quote here, shares a target with Holy Willie's. It's a poem more gruesome than funny, but it demonstrates the superiority of the local satires over the long-distance mockeries of Westminster politicians. Adam Armour was the diminutive brother of Jean, Burns's wife. He was an adolescent vigilante who had ridden a loose woman, Geordie's jurr or servant girl, out of Holy Willie's 'place', the village and vicinity of Mauchline, on a rail, with the rail stuck between her legs in the form of a pole or stang, a shaming rather worse than the skimmington-ride witnessed in Hardy's *Mayor of Casterbridge*. Like Willie, Adam shows himself up by praying to God:

> An' now Thou kens our woefu' case,
> For *Geordie's Jurr* we're in disgrace,
> Because we stang'd her through the place,
> An' hurt her spleuchan,
> For which we daurna show our face
> Within the clachan.
> ('Adam Armour's Prayer', in *Canongate Burns*, pp. 598–9, lines 7–12)

It has already been made clear that the creative humour of Burns informs his letters as it does his poems. He flows with it and sings with it, and franks it to receptive friends, the right friends. When the cross and drunken Nicol reproved him for some indecorum, Burns Miltonically retorted: 'O thou, wisest among the Wise, meridian blaze of Prudence, full-moon of Discretion, & Chief of many Counsellors ... from the luminous path of thy own right-lined rectitude, thou lookest benignly down on an erring Wretch, of whom the zig-zag wanderings defy all the powers of Calculation, from the simple copulation of Units up to the hidden mystery of Fluxions.'[29] Spunkie was his name for his zigs and zags and innuendoes. Meanwhile his other name, Robert Ruisseaux, with its allusion to that further full moon of discretion, the French philosopher, is among the sweetest of his jokes.

Poetry and poverty took part in the dialectic of 'something' and 'nothing' that turns up in Burns's writings. His auld farmer, saluting his auld mare, hopes that after a lifetime's struggle there will in their old age be 'something yet' for them both, and poetry was a something out of nothing, a spell against poverty and the 'perpetual labor' which in Burns's early days he saw entailed on him by his father's situation. In the Hornbook poem Death itself is an eerie 'Something'. Burns possessed when he was young, he thought, 'a stubborn, sturdy something in my disposition', and was sometimes to believe in 'a certain noble, stubborn something in man', as in the possibility of a certain holy Somebody in control of the world, and of a Something beyond the grave.[30] Against such hopes and fears must be set a nihilistic poem addressed to his Ayrshire patron Gavin Hamilton, in which everything – love, sectarian controversy, the drowning of the poet himself should he sail the sea in search of salvation in the West Indies, as an overseer of slaves – comes to 'naething', the poem's refrain ('Naething', pp. 552–4).

Poetry and poverty go together in 'The Vision' of 1786, in which Burns's favourite Habbie Simson stanza is put to fine use. He has come back to his cottage tired out after a day's threshing. He sits by the fire, choking on the smoke and listening to the rats in the rafters.

All in this mottie misty clime,
I backward mused on wasted time,
How I had spent my youthfu' prime,
        An' done nae-thing,
But stringin' blethers up in rhyme
        For fools to sing.

Had I to guid advice but harkit,
I might, by this, hae led a market,
Or strutted in a bank, and clarkit
        My cash account;
While here, half-mad, half-fed, half-sarkit,
        Is a' th'amount.
('The Vision', pp. 51–8, lines 19–30)

Human interest and artistic worth go together in this memorable passage, with its hint of Pope's 'Epistle to Arbuthnot'. The poet, 'half-sarkit', is wearing a garment that abuts on the witch Nannie's mini-skirt in 'Tam o' Shanter'. A 'click!' is heard, with the resonance of that 'skelp!' in his chauvinistic war passage The latch is drawn and in slips a muse who is also a real girl who shows a real leg.

When click! the string the snick did draw;
An' jee! the door gaed to the wa';
And by my ingle-lowe I saw,
        Now bleezin' bright,
A tight outlandish hizzie, braw,
        Come full in sight. (lines 37–42)

In the 'Address to the Deil' Satan draws a snick to enter Paradise and give it a shock. Here, the muse Coila is clad in a televisual plaid on which the landscapes of Kyle are displayed. The poem is in two Duans (an Ossianic chapter division). In the course of it, a polite English takes over, and good advice is tendered by the muse. The bard must write about love and the manners of his class. He must know the place he inhabits and his own place there. The heroes, judges, and beauty spots of the neighbourhood, including, in one version, Boswell's family seat of Auchinleck, are spelt out. Auchinleck is no place for 'rustic muses such as mine' – it is the haunt, from 'classic ground', of 'th'ancient, tuneful, laurelled Nine'. Burns can't expect to throb and glow with Thomson and Shenstone and Gray. He must be meek. But then he went on to write 'Tam o' Shanter', and had already written his riotous cantata 'The Jolly Beggars': in both works, locality and transgression are one. He had not taken his own advice, and continued to disregard it.

'The Jolly Beggars' opens, as does 'The Vision', with a winter scene. Night, but no lonely night, comes on. A letter by Burns, subsequent to the cantata, refers to 'a squalid Vagabond glorying in his rags'.[31] Three years earlier his beggars had gloried in their rags. The songs they sing exult in an overthrow of decency and order. In the later twentieth century this work was experienced as a relief by readers who'd had enough of the long hegemony of 'The Cotter's Saturday Night', with its enshrining of pre-marital chastity and his father's evening service. These jolly beggars are not Ayrshire's peasants at play, but they are people he might have met at Poosie Nansie's in Mauchline, whose loose woman had to ride the stang. James Hogg remarked, in the edition of Burns's poems published with William Motherwell in 1834–6, that he had 'never heard that Burns had any intercourse with any class below' the peasantry.[32] So you have to suppose that his Nansies and Nannies were imaginary.

'Tam o' Shanter' is fundamental to the history of the country; in that sense at least, it could be considered radical. After an evening spent drinking with his friend Souter Johnny, and flirting with the landlady, Tam heads off in a storm on his mare Maggie, in the direction of a sullen wife, and at Alloway kirk he encounters a jolly coven of witches and warlocks. Satan plays the bagpipes. Tam peeps at Nannie in her cutty sark or 'scanty shirt', and utters a cry of joy which affronts the coven, who chase him from the kirk. Nannie tears off the mare's tail as she clears the bridge over the Doon. The Burns scholar David Daiches used to take a just pleasure in reciting:

> The carlin claught her by the rump,
> And left poor Maggie scarce a stump.

Another poem by Burns, 'Come rede me, dame', which is understood to make use of folk material, has a passage which is worth comparing with what happened to poor Maggie:

> The carlin clew her wanton tail
> Her wanton tail sae ready.[33]

'Tam o' Shanter' ends by advising that drink and a voyeur's attention to cutty sarks may cost you your mare's tail and your own. The 'reel o' stumpie' was a name for sexual intercourse, and 'tail' could mean both penis and vagina. In 'A Poetical Epistle to a Tailor' Burns confronts the loss of his own tail, in the form of a punishment mooted by the clergy:

> 'Na, na,' quo' I, 'I'm no for that,
> Gelding's nae better than 'tis ca't.' (pp. 192–3, lines 55–6)

Some years ago I made the following claim with reference to the moral in the poem's tail:

> It is a lesson which alerts us to the presence in Hanoverian Scotland of a dangerous and delightful phantasmagoric alternative to sexuality and marriage: Scotland's national poem, with its peeping Tam and deep potations, whispers the overthrow of the sexual act. It tells of a Scotland in which sex and Scots could both be condemned, in which tongue and tail could both be tied, in which recourses and resistances had be sought and imagined, and it predicts a Scotland in which its hero can be thought a representative figure.[34]

There was no clap of thunder at this claim from my native Scotland, but I have since wondered whether the poem really is about such a displacement, which can hardly be said to have occurred in Burns's own case. I still feel that it is. And I feel about it what a Scotswoman, a servant of Mrs Dunlop, felt about 'The Cotter's Saturday Night': 'I dinna see how he could hae tauld it ony other way.'[35]

A use and abuse of Burns have survived in Scotland. The land he knew, and the happy land he has been made to stand for, are both still current. The exemplary force of his writings and of his life-history remains – for all the debauching of his immortal memory. His words are still remembered, thrilled to, and lived by, and the Scots tongue to which they belong is still spoken, after repeated alleged demises, and has in modern times been written to great effect. Burns is still here, and now. The vernacular comedy which features Tam, Holy Willie, Spunkie, Rab the Ranter, and Robert Ruisseaux has yet to raise its last laugh.

Burns's words were remembered by the Orkney poet of the last century George Mackay Brown. A biography of him by Maggie Fergusson reveals a holy, dreamy man, a Catholic convert, often ill, a drinker, attended by muses with whom his relations were evidently in the main chaste. Some lines of his evoke the opening of Burns's 'The Vision'.[36] A writer looks at a sunset, and at a blank page.

> The latch lifted. A stranger came in.
> So beautiful
> She seemed to be a woman from the sea.

George Mackay Brown was no redivivus Tam. But there's a degree of ancestral affinity here.

Over the sea, in Northern Ireland, Ayrshire's neighbour, Burns's verse was seized on from the first, and no poet in English or Scots is closer to Burns than Seamus Heaney, who has written about him with the insight of fellowship. Each is of the soil and of the country. 'Under my window, a clean rasping sound' – Heaney's early poem about his father digging – directs a homage that can also be caught in the solemn music of 'The Cotter's Saturday Night'. With no wish to atavize the two and freeze them at the spade or plough, it might be said that the vitality of the one attests to the vitality of the other, each trenching upon a pre-industrial common ground.

NOTES

Unless otherwise noted, quotations from Burns's poems are taken from J. Logie Robertson's edition (Oxford: Oxford University Press, 1904, rptd 1950), and page numbers refer to this edition. Quotations from his letters are taken from J. De Lancey Ferguson's *Letters of Robert Burns*, 2nd edn, ed. G. Ross Roy, 2 vols (Oxford: Oxford University Press, 1985). James Kinsley's edition of the *Poems and Songs of Burns*, 3 vols (Oxford: Oxford University Press, 1968), has been consulted throughout.

1 Henry Cockburn, *Life of Lord* Jeffrey, 2 vols (Edinburgh: Adam and Charles Black, 1852), I, p. 48.
2 Redcliffe Salaman, *The History and Social Influence of the Potato* (Cambridge: Cambridge University Press, 1949), p. 371. See Walter Scott, *Quarterly Review* (Feb. 1809), and James Mackay, *Robert Burns* (Edinburgh: Mainstream, 1992), pp. 663–4. See also Karl Miller, *Electric Shepherd*, rev. edn (London: Faber and Faber, 2003), p. 177.
3 Miller, *Electric Shepherd*, p. 309.
4 Letter 125, his expansive autobiographical letter to Dr John Moore.
5 J. G. Lockhart, *Life of Robert Burns* (Edinburgh: Constable, 1828), p. 61.
6 Letter 157.
7 Letters 176 and 423, and see Miller, *Electric Shepherd*, pp. 366–7.
8 Lockhart, *Life of Robert Burns*, pp. 141, 210.
9 Letter 662.
10 Liam McIlvanney, *Burns the Radical* (East Linton: Tuckwell Press, 2002), p. 17.
11 Letter 649, and see John Barrell, *Imagining the King's Death: Figurative Treason, Fantasies of Regicide 1793–96* (Oxford: Oxford University Press, 2000), p. 232. 'Alarmers and alarmists' are the words of the Marquis of Lansdowne.
12 Robert Crawford, *The Bard: Robert Burns, A Biography* (London: Jonathan Cape, 2009), and *Scotland's Books*, London, Penguin, 2007.
13 Letter 638.
14 Barrell, *Imagining the King's Death*, pp. 87, 224.
15 Andrew Noble and Patrick Scott Hogg, eds, *The Canongate Burns* (Edinburgh: Canongate, 2001), pp. 456–62. See also Patrick Scott Hogg, ed., *Robert Burns: The Lost Poems* (Glasgow: Clydeside Press, 1997).
16 Noble and Hogg, *Canongate Burns*, pp. 632–40.
17 Ibid., pp. 733–5. For the prologue for the actress Miss Fontenelle see the Logie Robertson Oxford edition, pp. 244–5.
18 Ian McIntyre, *Dirt and Deity: A Life of Robert Burns* (London: HarperCollins, 1995), p. 123.
19 McIlvanney, *Burns the Radical*, pp. 135, 56, 227.
20 Letters 285, 505. See Byron's *Journal*, 13 December 1813, for his 'antithetical' Burns.

21 Miller, *Electric Shepherd*, pp. 308–9.
22 This material has been appraised, and prepared for circulation, by Patrick Scott Hogg. It is distinctly suggestive of Burns. See also Mackay, *Robert Burns*, pp. 317–18, 331, 390, 423.
23 Jeremy Treglown, ed., *The Lantern-Bearers* (London: Chatto and Windus, 1988), pp. 105, 107, 120.
24 'A' that I hae endur'd' comes from Kinsley's edition. Miller, *Electric Shepherd*, pp. 308, 81. The 'countenance of the great' claim appears to be James Hogg's.
25 Letters 249, 266. For Cockburn's and Scott's connection with Nicol see McIntyre, *Dirt and Deity*, pp. 117, 224.
26 Letter 122. 'I have set you down as the staff of my old age', adds Burns.
27 Letter 561.
28 Miller, *Electric Shepherd*, pp. 309–10.
29 Letter 537.
30 Letters 125, 619. McIntyre, *Dirt and Deity*, p. 144.
31 Letter 252.
32 Miller, *Electric Shepherd*, p. 308.
33 See Kinsley no. 252 and Letter 304.
34 *Robert Burns*, sel. and intro. Karl Miller (London: Weidenfeld and Nicolson, 1981), p. 27.
35 McIntyre, *Dirt and Deity*, p. 91.
36 Maggie Fergusson, *George Mackay Brown* (London: John Murray, 2006), p. 261.

SELECTED FURTHER READING

Editions

Robert Burns: Poems Selected by Don Paterson, London, Faber and Faber, 2005
Greatest Poems, arr. Andrew O'Hagan, Edinburgh, Canongate, 2008

Secondary works

Carswell, Catherine, *Life of Robert Burns*, new edn, Edinburgh, Canongate, 1990
Crawford, Robert (ed.), *Robert Burns and Cultural Authority*, Edinburgh, Edinburgh University Press, 1997
Scotland's Books, London, Penguin, 2007
The Bard: Robert Burns, A Biography, London, Jonathan Cape, 2009
Crawford, Thomas, *Burns: A Study of the Poems*, new edn, Edinburgh, Canongate, 1994
Daiches, David, *Robert Burns*, London, G. Bell, 1952
Low, Donald (ed.), *Robert Burns: The Critical Heritage*, London, Routledge, 1974
McGuirk, Carol, *Robert Burns and the Sentimental Era*, Athens, GA, University of Georgia Press, 1985
(ed.), *Robert Burns: Selected Poems*, London, Penguin, 1993
O' Hagan, Andrew (arr.), *A Night Out with Robert Burns*, Edinburgh, Canongate, 2008
Paterson, Don (sel.), *Robert Burns: Poems*, London, Faber and Faber, 2001

15

SIMON JARVIS

William Wordsworth

Here is what happened when Crabb Robinson read Wordsworth's great Ode beginning 'There was a time' (generally known after 1815 as the 'Immortality Ode') to William Blake in 1825.

> I had been in the habit when reading this marvellous Ode to friends, to omit one or two passages – especially that beginning
>
> But there's a tree of many one,
>
> lest I should be rendered ridiculous, being unable to explain precisely *what* I admired – Not that I acknowledged this to be a fair test: But with Blake I could fear nothing of the Kind, And it was this very Stanza which threw him almost into an hysterical rapture – His delight in Wordsworth's poetry was intense [And seeming undiminished *deleted*] nor did it seem less notwithstand[g] by the reproaches he continually cast on W [which I have anticipated and which he characterised as Atheism that is, in worshipping nature *deletd*] for his imputed worship of nature – which in the mind of Blake constituted Atheism.[1]

The narrative tells us a good deal about early reception of Wordsworth. Robinson is worried about appearing ridiculous. Why? Not because he doubts whether every part of Wordsworth's Ode is admirable, but because he knows that he cannot *explain* his admiration for every part of it. Perhaps Robinson had already had the experience of becoming ridiculous in this way. Yet, on this occasion, he knows not to worry. Blake, madder than even Wordsworth could ever be, experiences a near-'hysterical rapture'. 'Hysterical', of course, intimates to us Robinson's own partial scepticism about Blake and his raptures, and, in doing so, intimates that some of the ambivalence about this passage of Wordsworth's poem, that ambivalence which Robinson attributes to his auditors, may after all be Robinson's own.

> – But there's a Tree, of many one,
> A single Field which I have looked upon,

Both of them speak of something that is gone:
The Pansy at my feet
Doth the same tale repeat:
Whither is fled the visionary gleam?
Where is it now, the glory and the dream?[2]

Robinson's disquiet is understandable. Lines of this kind sometimes seemed almost insane to contemporary readers. If they rarely do to us, that is because of the extent to which we live in a poetic culture which Wordsworth made for us. The poet sounds, first of all, as though he is talking to himself, because he sounds as though he is expecting listeners to know something they can't: which tree, which field? Then there is the near-redundance so characteristic of many of Wordsworth's sublimest moments: surely *every* tree is 'of many one'? The poet tells us that he 'has looked upon' a certain field. (Well, so one might expect, if he is telling us about it!) And there is also the unembarrassed attribution of prophetic powers to the meanest of natural phenomena. A talkative pansy is trying to tell the poet something very important. After which brooding darkness we are rewarded with two lines which lend the poet's own most memorable eloquence to what he is apparently being told by a tree, a field, and a pansy. And perhaps it was just the denaturalization of these objects, their temporary conversion into personified prophets, that appealed to Blake – who, otherwise, worried that Wordsworth might be a nature-worshipper.

We lose something important about Wordsworth's poetry when we overlook the resistance which it at first produced, and sometimes continues to produce even today. The hostile reviewers were not making it up, but responding to something which was really new in the poetry and which could be found acutely painful, ridiculous, or embarrassing, as well as inducing rapture, 'hysterical' or otherwise. At the centre of what is troubling is the risk which is central to Wordsworth's poetry: its gamble that it will speak to all humankind, not by cutting out everything which would be merely accidential or peculiar to Wordsworth and which could not therefore possibly demand universal interest, but rather by looking at these apparent contingencies so steadily and trustingly that they come to seem inseparable from whatever the human would itself be. So that, in one sense, the exasperation of a critic like Francis Jeffrey, who 'begged' Wordsworth to offer 'these nobler elements of his poetry, without the debasement of childish language, mean incidents, and incongruous images' captures something about what reading Wordsworth's poetry is actually *like*, something which can be missing from the much more respectful approaches which have succeeded Jeffrey's.[3] John Stuart Mill can write that

> Wordsworth's poetry is never bounding, never ebullient; has little even of the appearance of spontaneousness: the well is never so full that it overflows. There is an air of calm deliberateness about all he writes, which is not characteristic of the poetic temperament: his poetry seems one thing, himself another; he seems to be poetical because he wills to be so, not because he cannot help it: did he will to dismiss poetry, he need never again, it might almost seem, have a poetical thought.[4]

We are a very long way from Jeffrey's ridicule, certainly, but also from Blake's 'rapture'. Yet Mill, too, is responding to something which is really there. Even though it is hard to believe that they are experiencing the same poet, Blake and Mill separately register a powerful conflict which is present in Wordsworth's writing almost from the beginning until almost to its end: the conflict between an enthusiastic 'overflow' of powerful feelings, and the disciplining and tranquillizing of those feelings. Sometimes the story of Wordsworth's poetical life is written as though a simple narrative could be found. In this way of telling the story, Wordsworth was first inspired, then tranquil, then, finally, asleep. In truth, though, the work of what Wordsworth once referred to as 'humanizing' his soul is never done. His soul keeps breaking out into ambitions and visions which are, one must presume, imagined by him as 'inhuman'. They do so especially in two modes: the Ode – although the great Ode is never again matched, it has a series of extraordinary successors such as the 'Ode to Duty' of 1805, the 'Ode, Composed upon an Evening of Extraordinary Splendour and Beauty' of 1817, and the ode 'On The Power of Sound' (1828) – and the blank verse associated with his life's work, the grand philosophical poem to be entitled 'The Recluse', a poem which he never completed, but to which his best-known work, 'The Prelude', was conceived merely as the antechamber.

'The Recluse' was the site of almost lifelong inspiration and also of almost lifelong pain for Wordsworth in part because it was so intimately connected in his mind with the man who was for many years his closest friend, and the one most important to his writing, Samuel Taylor Coleridge. Coleridge knew much more about philosophy than Wordsworth, certainly encouraged Wordsworth in his plan to write a philosophical poem, and was himself to have provided notes from which Wordsworth could work. But none of this would have mattered, nor would Wordsworth have listened to Coleridge, had he not already made a crucial breakthrough in his poetic writing. This breakthrough had less to do with a new way of thinking than with a new way of writing verse – or, rather, Wordsworth discovered a new way of writing verse which also opened up new ways of thinking. In about 1797

Wordsworth started to write passages of blank verse which did something quite new with the medium.

> I have seen the Baker's horse
> As he had been accustomed at your door
> Stop with the loaded wain, when o'er his head
> Smack went the whip, and you were left, as if
> You were not born to live, or there had been
> No bread in all the land. Five little ones,
> They at the rumbling of the distant wheels
> Had all come forth, and, ere the grove of birch
> Conceal'd the wain, into their wretched hut
> They all return'd.[5]

There is here a kind of furious fidelity to the integrity and sequence of a lived experience. Information filters through to readers in just that sequence in which it reaches the participants. The horse stops because he knows that he always delivers bread to this house. He and we are surprised together with the 'Smack' which then greets him. He moves off, and the children who have silently come out for the bread also return silently. No word has been spoken by anyone. Yet everything essential has been communicated: 'as if / You were not born to live'. The entire network of social and economic relations – and not only among humans – is implicit in movement and gesture and is activated by the blow of the whip on the horse's head. The poet completely strips himself of the opportunity for sentimental or moral commentary of the kind which would have been likely to characterize any other poet's treatment of this topic at this date. Much of the art of Wordsworth's new mode is an art of subtraction. The poet is, in one way, turned entirely inwards, to the precise sequence of his own experiences. Instead of first digesting them himself and then communicating his results to us, he invites us to take an interest in the ordering of his singular experience. Yet it is precisely by his fidelity to this sequence that he achieves an equal and answering fidelity to the interlinked social relationships implied. The turn inward, the turn towards the shape of experience, is not a turn away from the social, but a way of getting to it.

No one had written blank verse in English in quite this way before Wordsworth. In the first place, the presumptive connection between metre and diction has been completely severed. We see here what Wordsworth meant when, in the famous 'Preface' to the *Lyrical Ballads*, he insisted that metre need have no consequences for poetic lexicon. But practice came first. The 'Preface' legitimates a breakthrough in verse thinking which has already happened. Wordsworth happens upon or finds out a way of writing verse in which prose order seems at first sight almost entirely undisturbed and yet in which the tiny adjustments or mutilations imposed by verse make all the difference. Central to this is the way Wordsworth handles blank verse syntax. The often strongly suspended syntax of, say, Miltonic epic is one way of producing powerful momentum in blank verse, because readers cannot make full sense of the lines until the main verb arrives, often several lines after the beginning of the sentence (the very first sentence of *Paradise Lost* is a famous example). So they are driven strongly through the lines by syntax, whilst at the same time Milton's densely compressed thinking, frequent straddling of the sense over lines, and complex stress patterning provide a series of cognitive difficulties. This is the richness of Milton's verse: an irresistible forward propulsion which is, nevertheless, resisted by numberless traps for attention.

Wordsworth's syntax much less often makes us wait for the sense to be completed. It usually works with, rather than against, the habitual word order of English prose and of spoken English. This by itself is not what makes Wordsworth distinctive. Few eighteenth-century poets went the whole way in imitating Milton's handling of blank verse. Instead, eighteenth-century blank verse tended to become progressively less syntactically suspended, to the extent that some readers found it to be a kind of unrhymed couplet.[6] This is because of the extent of end-stopping in it, of making the end of the verse line coincide with the end of a clause or sentence. In William Cowper's *The Task*, or in Charlotte Smith's *The Emigrants*, two of the most important predecessors of Wordsworth's verse style, there is a much greater degree of end-stopping than we find in Wordsworth. In Wordsworth's blank verse, by contrast, sense continually spills over line breaks. The line end rarely coincides with a syntactic break. At the same time he pushes the refusal of unnecessary markedness of diction still further even than Cowper.

The result is the luminous medium of Wordsworth's blank verse. If you transcribe it as prose and try to read it out you are quite likely to run out of oxygen. This doesn't happen when you do the same thing with Cowper or Charlotte Smith. Transcribed as prose, Wordsworth's blank verse is breathless. In verse, the line end is serving as punctuation. Yet its force is metrical, not syntactical. The blank verse which Wordsworth discovers in 1797 is a flexible medium in which he is able to follow with close discrimination the minutest nuances of affective coloration or of deep conceptual reflection, and which at the same time is intensely and evidently melodic. It enables the completely unprecedented poetic thinking undertaken in the poem on his own life, the poem to Coleridge, which Wordsworth only much later came to call 'The Prelude'. It does not drive the reader forward, but accompanies him or her: a movement inward, a comparison with the shape of our own experience, is necessary to make the writing intelligible.

If no one had written blank verse like this before, no one had written about poverty like this before, and no one had written about the shape of experience like this before. These discoveries are all made at the same time. None comes first. If one likes one can conjecture that Wordsworth's new way of writing enabled him to see the shapes of experiences with unprecedented steadiness of attention – but one can equally conjecture that Wordsworth's steadiness of attention drove him to a new way of writing verse. And, just in case this should sound like a theory that the arts are progressive, one can remark that these achievements can also be lost, and that no one *after* Wordsworth was ever quite able to recover this note.

The severe subtractions upon which this new poetic depended were in their way not a rejection, but a continuation and a deepening of canons of taste developed through the century leading up to Wordsworth's writing. Here, once again, looking steadily at Wordsworth requires the differentiation of his activity from some of the stories soon told about it. Wordsworth did not think, with Matthew Arnold, that Pope was a classic of our prose, but, instead, that he bewitched the nation with his melody. The central characteristic of Pope's and then Johnson's critical thought, the absolute insistence that verse is not an alibi, that verse must be subject to no less exacting standards of making sense than prose, remained a key criterion for Wordsworth. In the 'Preface' to the *Lyrical Ballads* Wordsworth complained that metre had taken on an inappropriately symbolic function: it had come to seem like a sort of advertisement to the reader that a peculiar kind of diction and phraseology was to be expected. This argument was not a rejection of, or even a deviation from, the criterion of prose sense, but rather a deepening and exacerbation of it. Not only would verse no longer be an excuse for mixed metaphor or cliché or weak thinking; it would now also be no promise of any peculiarly poetical language. The difficulties following from Wordsworth's attempt to specify what language poetry would use, a language drawn from 'low and rustic life' but 'purified indeed from all lasting and rational causes of dislike and disgust', have obscured the much more significant theoretical breakthrough in Wordsworth's theory of poetry: the severing of the naturalized connection between metre and poetical diction. Wordsworth's friend Coleridge, after their friendship had cooled, mounted an influential attack on Wordsworth's theory in which he associated the issue of the class basis of language with that of the separation of metre from diction. On the whole it was Coleridge's view that 'I write in metre, because I am about to use a language different from that of prose'[7] which stuck with poets and critics, with lasting consequences for the theory and practice of poetry in English. When the modernist assault on metre itself began, metre was treated precisely as a symbol, as Coleridge had treated it, and not as a cognitive practice engaging the fundamental powers of the human mind, its ability to discern similitude in dissimilitude and dissimilitude in similitude, as Wordsworth had thought it. This, perhaps, is one reason *why* Wordsworth's blank verse style remained without real successors.

The observation that Wordsworth was in many ways a deeply classical poet and critic, returning to and developing classical canons of taste, can also occasion a reinterpretation of his thinking as well as of his verse technique. 'Romantic' may possibly have some uses as an epithet, but as a way of describing Wordsworth's writing it is misleading. The term, invented some years after Wordsworth's key technical and substantive breakthroughs, usually acquires a content not from a description of a mode of writing, but from a description of a cluster of ideas. This is a procedure of questionable validity, not only because, as Mallarmé is said to have reminded Degas, poems are not made with ideas, but with words, but also because the ideas in question are handled so differently by the poets in question as no longer to be the same ideas. Coleridge's theory of the primary and secondary imagination emphasizes, on the one hand, the primary imagination's role as a transcendental condition of the possibility of experience, and, on the other, the secondary imagination's active role in shaping, remaking, and transforming experience. Wordsworth sometimes writes in ways that can be brought into relation with these ideas, yet, in general, the most powerful appearances of the term in his verse are connected neither with the transcendental a priori, nor with the mind's creative activity, but, rather, with a moment when something happens *to* him. In one of the later fragments written towards the 'Recluse', Wordsworth writes about walking through the streets of London on a snowy day, having left Coleridge after what may well have been an unsatisfactory meeting. Wordsworth's head is bowed, but then he looks up, and is given an anchor in his distress by the surprise of seeing St Paul's cathedral 'through its own sacred veil of falling snow'. What is striking is that this is described as a 'Gift of Imagination's holy power'. If one follows the idea that Imagination is about the mind's ability to shape the world, this identification makes no sense. One might just as well say that it is a gift of the snow's holy power, or a gift of the holy power that Wordsworth has of lifting up his head and looking at the cathedral instead of staring down at the ground. Imagination, here, names not the capacity to give meaning, but the capacity to receive it. It is the capacity for experience, the capacity to be surprised, just as Wordsworth is surprised at two critical occurrences of the word in 'The Prelude': the moment at which he discovers that he has already crossed the Alps, and that at which, ascending Snowdon, the sea of mist parts and the real sea is seen through it.

In recent years, advancing scepticism about the reliability of literary-historical classifications and periodizations has enabled scholarship to rediscover the breadth and variousness of Wordsworth's interests. Duncan Wu's exhaustive work on Wordsworth's reading has shown us how broad and deep was Wordsworth's intellectual formation, despite Matthew Arnold's judgement that 'the English poetry of the first quarter of this century, with plenty of energy, plenty of creative force, did not know enough'.[8] As well as knowing English poetry by heart in quantities which would be extremely unusual today, Wordsworth read political economy, travel narratives, histories, Italian poetry, contemporary literary and philosophical reviews; he was interested in geology, theories of education, political controversy, church history, ancient Greek poetry, associationist psychology, and many other topics. This was not only miscellaneous browsing but also preparation for his central work. 'The Recluse' was initially conceived not only as a meditative poem but also as a comprehensive one, 'On Man on Nature and on Human Life'. In the elation of its first conception, Wordsworth wrote to a friend that he did not know anything which would not come within his plan. It was not to require only thinking, but also knowing: hence Wordsworth's anxiety over Coleridge's missing notes, and hence his requirement for large quantities of travel writing, the social anthropology of his day.

Part of the new interest in the range of Wordsworth's interests has been fuelled by our contemporary preoccupation with the politics of culture. The young Wordsworth was a revolutionary sympathizer who wrote a powerful attack on the Bishop of Llandaff; the old Wordsworth was a confirmed Tory of markedly hierarchical persuasions. The precise path from the first of these two positions to the second is a complex one, and has occasioned a good deal of argument. Amongst the most persuasive treatments has been David Bromwich's suggestion that the beginning of military hostilities between England and France induced in Wordsworth an intense personal crisis, a crisis which coincides (though conjunctures are not causes) with the emergence of the new verse mode of 1797.[9] Wordsworth was a committed universalist. Yet it was the peculiar characteristic of his universalism to proceed not by deleting the singular, but by paying attention to it. Two sets of intense attachments to which Wordsworth attributed a universal value – his attachment to the Lakes and to those he knew there, and that to the elation of liberty and those in France like the young officer, Michel Beaupuy, who had helped him discover it – appeared to have come into irreconcilable conflict. This would make sense of the way in which the war itself and its conduct, rather than larger and more abstract questions of political justice, were continually at the centre of Wordsworth's political reflections for the following decade. It mattered intensely to Wordsworth, for example, that the armies fighting the French in the Iberian peninsula were mountain armies. They were, for Wordsworth, fighters conducting a war of liberation on native land to which their feelings, like Michael's in Wordsworth's poem of that name, were inextricably linked. The Iberian mountains, in his mind, could be mapped onto the 'perfect equality' of the 'community of shepherds and agriculturalists' which had in his view existed until recently among the Lakes.[10] So the war could be imagined as a republican one, in a native (Harringtonian) idiom of reflection on liberty which was always at least as important to Wordsworth as any thinking coming from the continental Enlightenment. When England seemed to Wordsworth to betray Portugal in this war, Wordsworth's astonishing pamphlet on the peace treaty in question, the Convention of Cintra – a 'considerable part' of which pamphlet Coleridge aptly described as being 'almost a self-robbery from some great philosophical poem'[11] – testifies to the rage and grief which he felt at the apparent removal of this way of thinking about, of getting through, the war.

All this indicates that one quite usual way of imagining what changed in Wordsworth – that it was a retreat from public to private, from London or Paris and the hopes associated with them, to Grasmere and Rydal Mount and a progressive poetical and political sclerosis – is only partially accurate. A better understanding can be arrived at by concentrating not on the history of Wordsworth's opinions, always an item of restricted significance in the case of a poet, but on the history of his *métier*, verse-writing. The failure to complete 'The Recluse', or even, after the publication of a central pillar of it, *The Excursion*, in 1814, to make very much headway with it, was, from one point of view, a disaster. Wordsworth's vocation remained unfulfilled. Yet, from another, it may have been an index of the sharpness of his instincts as a poet. Coleridge, late in life, gave in conversation an account of the plan for the poem which made it sound like a distinctly late-Coleridgean system, one which would have 'reconciled all the anomalies'.[12] On this account, it sounded as though Wordsworth was to do little more than add verse to Coleridge's ideas. Yet the value of those portions of the poem which were completed, and especially of the 'poem to Coleridge', *The Prelude* itself, in no way lay in the verse presentation of a coherent philosophical system from which all contradiction would have been removed. It lay, rather, in the development of a particular verse idiom for thinking in which all sorts of contradictory ideas could be explored.

Wordsworth's later poetry needs to be understood in relation to the failure to complete 'The Recluse' and what that failure meant for Wordsworth. The poet, trying to understand for himself what kind of unity might underlie the great variety of his poems, resorted when he published *The Excursion* not to an organic but to an ecclesiastical and architectural metaphor. The unpublished poem on the poet's own life (later 'The Prelude') and *The Excursion*, he wrote

> have the same kind of relation to each other … as the Anti-chapel has to the body of a gothic Church. Continuing this allusion, he may be permitted to add, that his minor Pieces, which have been long before the Public, when they shall be properly arranged, will be found by the attentive Reader to have such connection with the main Work as may give them claim to be likened to the little Cells, Oratories, and sepulchral Recesses, ordinarily included in those Edifices.[13]

The analogy itself indicates one less programmatically intended, yet none the less fundamental, feature of the revolution which Wordsworth has helped to bring about in the production of verse: the relations of different kinds of verse-writing to each other can no longer adequately be understood with reference to a (however complex) series of variations on the array of classical and neo-classical genre categories, but requires instead an analogy which emphasizes, not the author's contribution to a number of kinds of writing, but the contribution of a number of kinds of writing to the overarching, cathedral-like unity of the authorship. And in the 'Preface' to his important collection of 1815, Wordsworth attempted (though with only partial success) a more rational classification of the kinds of poetry: a classification all of whose categories were related in some way to the faculties or personal history of the poet producing them: poems of the Imagination or the Fancy, but also poems of youth, old age, and so on.

These ideas of Wordsworth's about how his poems made sense in relation to each other were of course in part a retrospective projection. His shorter pieces are often entirely content to appeal to an older schedule of generic categories. There are Odes, Elegiac Stanzas, and so on, and Wordsworth continues to deploy such categories all the way through his career. 'Michael' is even subtitled 'a Pastoral Poem', although it is one in which, as it were, a dead metaphor is brought back to life, because the subject of the poem is literally the work of caring for sheep and the commitments implied by such work. Yet the need to reach for a different set of categories and analogies also reflects something new about the way Wordsworth conceives of the activity of writing poetry. Poetry is not in the first place, for Wordsworth, a material object. It is passion, feeling; so every poem comes in a way to participate, however slightly, in the projected philosophic song. 'The Recluse', although incomplete, thus introduces a new architecture sheltering even those poems which do not contribute to it.

While shorter or lower kinds of poetical work could feel (and could certainly be seen by Coleridge) as diversions from the chief work of 'The

Recluse', ways of evading an insuperable problem, they could also at the same time be understood as furnishing and enriching that work. Partly for this reason, these 'diversions' themselves result in the production, not only of some mundane and uninspired work, but also of masterpieces. One key genre here is the sonnet. After 1800, Wordsworth began to write more and more sonnets, many of which were immediate responses to developments in the conduct of the wars with France. The temptation is to read them in opposition to the project of 'philosophic song'. Yet they could also instance a poetic thinking intimately related to that project. The point can be developed by thinking about one of the greatest of all Wordsworth's poems, 'Surprized by joy', not written until 'long after' the death of his daughter Catharine in 1812, but before late October 1814 when the volume in which it first appeared was sent to the press:

Surprized by joy – impatient as the Wind
I turned to share the transport – Oh! with whom
But thee, deep buried in the silent Tomb,
That spot which no vicissitude can find?
Love, faithful love recalled thee to my mind –
But how could I forget thee? – Through what power,
Even for the least division of an hour,
Have I been so beguiled as to be blind
To my most grievous loss? – That thought's return
Was the worst pang that sorrow ever bore,
Save one, one only, when I stood forlorn,
Knowing my heart's best treasure was no more;
That neither present time, nor years unborn
Could to my sight that heavenly face restore.[14]

The poem is remarkable, in the first place, for unfolding an experience whose whole force is indissolubly connected with its temporal structure in such a way that anyone who reads it is enabled, or perhaps even compelled, to unfold that experience in the same order. This is an achievement of determined fidelity to the shape of an experience. We do not initially even know who is 'surprized'; when we find out, that person is immediately attempting to share his joy with – someone whom he only rediscovers to be dead in the very act of trying to share the joy. The discovery is instantly succeeded by an introspection which asks how this forgetting could ever have taken place. No answer is given to the question. Instead the pain of this reflection is compared to the only thing worse than it: the pain of the first bereavement itself. When you for one instant forget that someone you love deeply has died, you are both remembering (their life) and forgetting (their death).

Yet paraphrase stammers when put next to the poem itself. Paraphrase seems to retain no single fragment of the poem's power, because the poem is not only an achievement of attention, but also an achievement of verse thinking. As in 'The Baker's Cart', the ineluctable logic of a single experience of pain is unfolded in a single apparently unbroken line, a line which yet, nevertheless, is made up of a series, precisely, of breaks: of self-interruptions, -interrogations, and -reproaches. The irresistible forward momentum of the thought, driving, in a way which Wordsworth had partly learnt from Milton, through the little rooms of the sonnet, is nevertheless resisted by the forlorn echoes of the rhymes. Rhyme bodies forth that forlorn power, that failure to learn, which refuses to believe that my daughter is dead. The poem persuades readers that this isn't a willed way of suiting manner to matter, but rather a thought which could never have been thought in this way without this peculiar instrument. It closes in unbounded grief just because the rhymes are telling us that the poem is over at the very moment when the syntax and the argument are telling us that it is not. The poet has asked a question, the question through what power he could ever have forgotten his daughter. The poem has not only not answered this question, but seems itself to have forgotten about it. So the question mark's raised intonation reverberates like the voice of an unappeased spirit just at the moment when the final period's lowered one tries to lay it. No word of consolation, no attempt to extract universal significance of any kind from the disaster, is provided. The poem is of an unflinching steadiness, whose only consolation – beyond the consolation of metre itself – is that, where everything is bad, it must be good to know the worst. It might almost stand as a designed example of what Wordsworth meant when he wrote that metre renders tolerable what would otherwise be unendurably painful. Yet here the semblances of consolation and closure provided by rhyme seem rather to intensify the poet's open grief.

The mode of verse thinking which Wordsworth developed in his drafts, sketches, and fragments towards 'The Recluse' also spilled out and was itself developed, then, in all sorts of other modes, into a poetry which is in no way coextensive with the category, say, of 'imaginative literature', but which is, instead, no less unflinchingly turned to the fabric of experience than any phenomenologist could ever be. And, for anyone who might want to think that the achievement of this poem was something Wordsworth was shortly to lose touch with, we should note that one key word in the poem, a word without which the poem would now seem to us severely damaged, the word 'turned', in the second line, was added only in 1820 (the text had previously read 'wished').

The account given so far necessarily leaves out a very great deal. One thing which must not be omitted, however, is the relation of Wordsworth's poetry to the lives and working (or forcibly non-working) experiences of the rural poor. Some commentary in the last quarter century has found this engagement politically suspect, regarding it as a form of aestheticization of poverty. Wordsworth's interest in the imaginative pleasures and the spiritual experiences of the poor, as well as in their poverty, has seemed to some to be a tacit way of wishing that their poverty would continue. When this is put together with the poet's at least ambivalent view of urban experience – although here too the picture is more complicated than has sometimes been thought – it is easy to construct a view of the poet as suffering from a culpable nostalgia for unalienated labour and for organically solidary forms of social organization.

One important point to bear in mind here is Wordsworth's acute distrust for any idea that it would be easy to separate truth from illusion in the understanding of social experience. At around the same time as Wordsworth began to develop his new blank verse mode and to write his new kinds of ballad, in which ballad metre was crossed with or interfered with by the metres of art-verse lyric, he also experienced a clarification of his relation to certain kinds of social and political reasoning. A short but important prose fragment, the so-called 'Essay on Morals' (though it is really an essay on abstract moral reasoning), marks the break. Wordsworth develops an account of moral life in which 'habit' is central. Abstract moral (and, by implication, political) reasonings like William Godwin's 'are impotent over our habits; they cannot form them; from the same cause they are equally powerless in regulating our judgments concerning the value of men and things. They contain no picture of human life; they *describe* nothing.'[15] When we put this together with Wordsworth's declaration in the 'Preface' to the *Lyrical Ballads* that he has at all times endeavoured to look steadily at his subject, we can see the extent to which Wordsworth's poetical descriptions of rural habits of living, working, and feeling are intended as a kind of counter to aprioristic moral philosophy. When Wordsworth writes, in the same prose fragment, that 'I know no book or system of moral philosophy written with sufficient power to melt into our affections, to incorporate itself with the blood and vital juices of our minds, and thence to have any influence worth our notice in forming those habits of which I am speaking',[16] he is also, by implication, offering us a programme for his own writing, which *is* to find a way of melding, in this startlingly embodied incorporation with 'blood and vital juices', with our minds. The figure of Rivers, in Wordsworth's long-unpublished drama *The Borderers*, by contrast, is one who (like the young Wordsworth) precisely has experienced the power of aprioristic systems of moral philosophy, which, however, do not, in Rivers's case, place him in the position of angelic moral vantage imagined by Godwin but, instead, seduce him into a faith in his own reason which easily and rapidly becomes a self-serving solipsism.

In this light the willingness of some contemporary criticism to assume that Wordsworth's treatment of rural life is aestheticizing or nostalgic has itself something superstitious about it. It is as though, for such writing, only one mode of production (urban capitalism) is real, and as though even the very fact of attention to other modes of production and experience is already culpable. Certainly, in Wordsworth's view, those who owned the land they worked constituted an especially important category of citizen. He took the trouble to send a copy of the second edition of *Lyrical Ballads* to the leading Whig politician Charles James Fox, and especially mentioned the poems 'Michael' and 'The Brothers' as an attempt 'to draw a picture of the domestic affections as I know they exist among a class of men who are now almost confined to the North of England. They are small independent *proprietors* of land here called statesmen, men of respectable education who daily labour on their own little properties.' The poems, Wordsworth comments, are written 'to shew that men who do not wear fine cloaths can feel deeply'; property was especially important to this because 'Their little tract of land serves as a kind of permanent rallying point for their domestic feelings, as a tablet upon which they are written which makes them objects of memory in a thousand instances when they would otherwise be forgotten.'[17] The point is directly exemplified in the first verse paragraph of 'Michael':

And grossly that man errs, who should suppose
That the green Valleys, and the Streams and Rocks
Were things indifferent to the Shepherd's thoughts.
Fields where with chearful spirits he had breath'd
The common air; the hills, which he so oft
Had climb'd with vigorous steps; which had impress'd
So many incidents upon his mind
Of hardship, skill, or courage, joy or fear;
Which like a book preserv'd the memory
Of the dumb animals whom he had sav'd,
Had fed or shelter'd, linking to such acts,
So grateful in themselves, the certainty
Of honourable gains; these fields, these hills
Which were his living Being even more
Than his own Blood – what could they less? had lay'd
Strong hold on his Affections, were to him
A pleasurable feeling of blind love,
The pleasure which there is in life itself.[18]

Wordsworth sketches a view which is roughly that of many contemporary cultural sceptics: that those who make their living from the land are 'utterly unsentimental' about it. He regards this as a gross error. Yet, at the same time, he is also rejecting another kind of view – the view that pleasures may readily be divided into those which are merely self-interested, on the one hand, and those (aesthetic) which are disinterested, on the other. Wordsworth is not arguing that Michael feels a pure 'aesthetic' pleasure in nature. On the contrary, he takes care to point out that Michael's recollection of the animals he has rescued, a recollection which is attached to various parts of the landscape, is vivid partly because it is linked to Michael's own 'gain'. The poem, instead, is trying to show how difficult it would be to discriminate among self-interested 'gratification' and aesthetic 'delight' – yet not for the cynical end of showing that all delight is gratification, but for the utopian one of intimating that gratification participates in delight.

Wordsworth points this out *to Fox* partly because he hopes 'at a time when these feelings are sapped in so many ways that the two poems might co-operate, however feebly, with the illustrious efforts which you have made to stem this and other evils with which the country is labouring'.[19] He does hope, that is, that the poems may have some political effect. Yet they are to have it, not by exhortation, but by steadiness of observation. The final lines of this verse paragraph are not intended as Arcadian, but as allowing the full resonance of ambivalence to sound. The pleasurable feeling is of *blind* love. Michael's pleasure is, 'to him', 'The pleasure which there is in life itself'. The pleasure rests on what could only, if treated with literal strictness, be regarded as an illusion – the illusion that the land is his living being even more than his own blood – and yet, as the poem, and Wordsworth's work in general, implies, no one has ever yet become so perfectly undeluded as to escape from all illusions of this kind. The final line lends eloquence to this illusion, and, with it, hopes that the illusion will one day be – not deleted, but redeemed. In this it stands as a fit emblem for Wordsworth's poetry as a whole, a poetry which was always hoping that Wordsworth's own poetic bliss might one day come 'to all the Vales of earth and all mankind'.[20]

NOTES

1 G. E. Bentley, Jr, *Blake Records* (Oxford: Clarendon Press, 1969), p. 544.

2 'Ode' ('There was a time'), in *Poems, in Two Volumes, and Other Poems, 1800–1807*, ed. Jared Curtis (Ithaca, NY: Cornell University Press, 1983), pp. 269–77, 272 (lines 51–7).

3 Francis Jeffrey, from an unsigned review of *The Isle of Palms* (1812) by John Wilson, in *Wordsworth: The Critical Heritage. Vol. 1: 1793–1820*, ed. Robert Woof (London: Routledge, 2001), pp. 322–4, 323.

4 John Stuart Mill, 'Thoughts on Poetry and its Varieties', in *Dissertations and Discussions; Political, Philosophical and Historical*, 2 vols (London, 1859), p. 84.

5 Wordsworth, *The Ruined Cottage and The Pedlar*, ed. James Butler (Ithaca, NY: Cornell University Press, 1979), p. 463.
6 See Richard Bradford, *Augustan Measures: Restoration and Eighteenth-Century Writings on Prosody and Metre* (Aldershot: Ashgate, 2002), p. 158.
7 Samuel Taylor Coleridge, *Biographia Literaria*, eds James Engell and W. Jackson Bate, 2 vols (Princeton: Princeton University Press, 1983), vol. 2, p. 69 (ch. 18).
8 Matthew Arnold, 'The Function of Criticism at the Present Time', in *Lectures and Essays in Criticism*, ed. R. H. Super (Ann Arbor: University of Michigan Press, 1962), pp. 258–85, 262.
9 David Bromwich, *Disowned by Memory: Wordsworth's Poetry of the 1790s* (Chicago: University of Chicago Press, 1998), pp. 74–91.
10 *Wordsworth's Guide to the Lakes*, ed. Ernest de Sélincourt (Oxford: Oxford University Press, 1977), p. 60.
11 S. T. Coleridge to Daniel Stuart, 13. vi. 1809, in Coleridge, *Collected Letters. Vol. III: 1807–1814*, ed. E. L. Griggs (Oxford: Clarendon Press, 1959), p. 214.
12 S. T. Coleridge, *Table Talk recorded by Henry Nelson Coleridge (and John Taylor Coleridge)*, ed. Carl Woodring, 2 vols (Princeton: Princeton University Press, 1990), vol. 1, pp. 307–8 (21 July 1832).
13 '"Preface" to *The Excursion*, 1814', in *Home at Grasmere*, ed. Beth Darlington (Ithaca, NY: Cornell University Press, 1977), pp. 463–4, 464.
14 *Shorter Poems 1807–1820*, ed. Carl H. Ketcham (Ithaca, NY: Cornell University Press, 1989), pp. 112–13. I quote here the text as revised in 1820.
15 'Essay on Morals' [title editorial], in *William Wordsworth: Selected Prose*, ed. John O. Hayden (Harmondsworth: Penguin, 1988), pp. 104–6, 105.
16 Ibid.
17 Wordsworth to Charles James Fox, 14. i. 1801, in *The Letters of William and Dorothy Wordsworth*, ed. Ernest de Selincourt, rev. Alan G. Hill, 8 vols (Oxford: Clarendon Press, 1967–93), vol. 1, pp. 312–15, 314–15.
18 Wordsworth, 'Michael. A Pastoral Poem', in *'Lyrical Ballads', and Other Poems, 1797–1800*, eds James Butler and Karen Green (Ithaca, NY: Cornell University Press, 1992), pp. 252–68, 254–5 (lines 62–79).
19 Letter to Fox, p. 315.
20 Wordsworth, in *Home at Grasmere*, p. 52 (MS.B, l. 256).

SELECTED FURTHER READING

Editions

The standard scholarly edition of Wordsworth's poems is the Cornell Wordsworth, gen. ed. Stephen Parrish (Ithaca, NY: Cornell University Press, 1975–2007), now complete with the publication of the final volume, *The Excursion*. The Cornell texts provide photographs and transcriptions of relevant manuscripts, as well as a full conspectus of revisions and other variants. There are too many volumes to give bibliographical details separately for each volume here. A generous selection, in good texts, and including both the 1805 'Prelude' and some of Wordsworth's critical prose, is given in *William Wordsworth: The Major Works*, ed. Stephen Gill (Oxford: Oxford University Press, 2000). For a completer conspectus of 'The Prelude', see *The Prelude: The Four Texts 1798, 1799, 1805, 1850*, ed. Jonathan Wordsworth (London: Penguin, 1995). The standard edition of Wordsworth's prose is *The Prose Works of William Wordsworth*, ed. W. J. B. Owen and Jane Worthington Smyser

(3 vols, Oxford: Clarendon Press, 1974); see also *William Wordsworth: Selected Prose*, ed. John O. Hayden (Harmondsworth: Penguin, 1988). For the letters, see *The Letters of William and Dorothy Wordsworth*, ed. Ernest de Selincourt, rev. Alan G. Hill, 8 vols (Oxford: Clarendon Press, 1967–93). A useful selection is *Letters of William Wordsworth: A New Selection*, ed. Alan G. Hill (Oxford: Oxford University Press, 1984). There are lively biographies by Kenneth Johnston (*The Hidden Wordsworth*, New York: W. W. Norton, 2000) and Juliet Barker (*Wordsworth: A Life*, London: Viking, 2000) as well as John Worthen's *The Gang: Coleridge, the Hutchinsons and the Wordsworths in 1802* (New Haven: Yale University Press, 2001). Still useful is Mary Moorman's *William Wordsworth: A Biography* (2 vols, Oxford: Oxford University Press, 1957–65). Valuable primary information can be found in *The Journals of Dorothy Wordsworth*, ed. Ernest de Selincourt (2 vols, London, Macmillan, 1941). The materials assembled in Duncan Wu, *Wordsworth's Reading* (2 vols, Cambridge: Cambridge University Press, 1993–5) are of the first interest.

Secondary works

Abrams, M. H., *Natural Supernaturalism: Tradition and Revolution in Romantic Literature*, New York, 1971

Bewell, Alan, *Wordsworth and the Enlightenment: Nature, Man and Society in the Experimental Poetry*, New Haven, Yale University Press, 1989

Bromwich, David, *Disowned by Memory: Wordsworth's Poetry of the 1790s*, Chicago, University of Chicago Press, 1998

Chandler, James, *Wordsworth's Second Nature: A Study of the Poetry and the Politics*, Chicago, University of Chicago Press, 1984

Empson, William, 'Sense in The Prelude', in *The Structure of Complex Words*, London, Chatto and Windus, 1951, pp. 289–305

Ferguson, Frances, *Wordsworth: Language as Counter-Spirit*, New Haven, Yale University Press, 1977

Gill, Stephen (ed.), *The Cambridge Companion to Wordsworth*, Cambridge, Cambridge University Press, 2003

Hartman, Geoffrey H., *Wordsworth's Poetry 1787–1814*, New Haven, Yale University Press, 1964

Jarvis, Simon, *Wordsworth's Philosophic Song*, Cambridge, Cambridge University Press, 2007

Johnston, Kenneth, *Wordsworth and 'The Recluse'*, New Haven, Yale University Press, 1984

de Man, Paul, *The Rhetoric of Romanticism*, New York, Columbia University Press, 1984

O'Donnell, Brennan, *The Passion of Meter: A Study of Wordsworth's Metrical Art*, Kent, OH, Kent State University Press, 1995

Ricks, Christopher, *The Force of Poetry*, Oxford, Clarendon Press, 1984

Simpson, David, *Wordsworth and the Figurings of the Real*, London, Macmillan, 1982

Woof, Robert (ed.), *Wordsworth: The Critical Heritage.:Vol. 1: 1793–1820*, London, Routledge, 2001

16

SEAMUS PERRY

Samuel Taylor Coleridge

Hope and disappointment

It is difficult to think of another poet whose principal masterpieces seem so different. Auden might be one; but where Auden's endless versatility feels an integral part of his identity, the miscellaneousness of Coleridge's poetic career has struck most observers as merely unfortunate, testament to a crucial desultoriness. Coleridge's poems are actually very numerous, and his life in verse was in one way long and dedicated;[1] but, nevertheless, for no other English poet of comparable rank is a characterization of failure so central a part of the critical tradition. The list of Coleridge's unwritten poems betrays a poetic life unled: 'The Brook', 'Comforts and Consolations', an epic on the siege of Jerusalem, 'The Soother of Absence', 'The Flight and Return of Mohammed' – besides the ideas for innumerable smaller works that flit through the notebook: an ode to pleasure, a poem on suicide, a song entitled 'Transpositions', a poem on 'strange things'.[2] Hazlitt was sharp: 'Alas! "Frailty, thy name is *Genius*!" – What is become of all this mighty heap of hope, of thought, of learning and humanity?' That allows a kind of greatness (by association with Hamlet) while still damning Coleridge with a crippling absence of purpose: 'While he should be occupied with a given pursuit, he is thinking of a thousand other things; a thousand tastes, a thousand objects tempt him, and distract his mind, which keeps open house, and entertains all comers.'[3]

The most influential person to cast Coleridge as one who failed youthful hopes was Coleridge himself, repeatedly:

> The Poet is dead in me – my imagination (or rather the Somewhat that had been imaginative) lies, like a Cold Snuff on the circular Rim of a Brass Candlestick, without even a stink of Tallow to remind you that it was once cloathed & mitred with Flame. That is past by! – I was once a Volume of Gold Leaf, rising & riding on every breath of Fancy – but I have beaten myself back into weight & density, & now I sink in quick-silver, yea, remain squat and square

on the earth amid the hurricane, that makes Oaks and Straws join in one Dance, fifty yards high in the Element.[4]

Such ruinous self-depreciation is often attributed by defensive biographers to the influence of Wordsworth; but the great example of Wordsworth only illuminated what was the case anyway: 'As to Poetry', Coleridge wrote in 1800, aged only twenty-eight, 'I have altogether abandoned it, being convinced that I never had the essentials of poetic Genius, & that I mistook a strong desire for original power' (*CL*, I, p. 656). He considered it one of the shortcomings of the contemporary scene that merely 'an intense desire to possess the reputation of poetic genius' should so often take writers far;[5] and the possibility of his own poetic imposture was something he felt vividly: one consuming fear was 'that I had no real Genius, no real Depth' (*CL*, II, p. 959). Self-abasement runs the gamut from polite gesture to entrenched despair to brilliant tragicomedy, and involves an obvious paradox: for, as Humphry House put it best, 'In view of what in fact he achieved, Coleridge was quite unbelievably modest about his own poems; and the modesty was of a curious kind, sometimes rather humble and over-elaborate, sometimes apparently quite candid, because he did not see the merits that others have found since.'[6] And there is a further paradox: for as the short passage about the 'Volume of Gold Leaf' shows, lamenting the failure of imagination could itself spur Coleridge to feats of tremendous verbal vitality, which one can only think of as themselves highly imaginative.

That the disappointment of hopes should feature in much of the best Coleridgean commentary is evidence of more than just the power of a biographical myth: it is significant too because it responds to a preoccupation of the poems themselves. For Coleridge himself is repeatedly drawn by the matter of hope, its fragility and perplexity, its tenacity, its disappointment and reawakening: it was an abiding concern of his intellectual and emotional life. Our hopes, he told Humphry Davy, constitute 'the vitality & cohesion of our Being' (*CL*, I, p. 649); and the capacity to hope characterizes humanity itself: 'Our Maker has distinguished man from the brute that perishes by making hope, first an instinct of his nature, & secondly, an indispensable condition of his moral & intellectual progression.'[7] It was, he thought, one of the principal duties owed by the state to its people that they might entertain 'THE HOPE' of betterment: hope is an attribute of the free man, its lack a mark of slavery.[8]

Coleridge wrote to encourage an acquaintance: 'so I say to you, *Hope!* From hope, faith, and love, all that is good, all that is great, all lovely, and "all honourable things" proceed' (*CL*, III, p. 89). Any Christian writer should find the topic compelling, as it is one of the virtues named by Paul (1

Corinthians 13:13, to which Coleridge alludes). Hope in this sense is pious assurance rather than eager anticipation. When the Prayer Book speaks of 'sure and certain hope' (in the funeral service) it strikes a modern ear as puzzling, since any hope seems naturally to include the background idea that things might *not* work out in the way you would prefer; but the puzzle arises because a more psychological and secular conception of hope ('Expectation of something desired; desire combined with expectation': *OED*, 1) has come to complicate a theological use ('Feeling of trust or confidence': *OED*, 2). Sometimes one kind faces off the other: Cowley's 'Hope' deftly explains how hoping for things to be better only makes you more unhappy; and Crashaw offers a religious correction.[9] (Coleridge admired Crashaw's poem especially, as 'not only the wit of words, but the wit of images'.[10]) A full historical account of such developments might draw connections with the growth of speculative capitalism, as a probabilistic universe (which one might exploit) replaces a providential one (to which one is subject): anyway, the concept had an evident fascination for the post-Enlightenment mind.[11] Hume, say, writes with great suggestiveness about the psychology, seeing in hope 'grief and joy ... intermingled with each other', an instance of the 'contrariety of passions'.[12] Cowper's 'Hope' (1782), meanwhile, shows the confident religious sense still fully alive; while Campbell scored a hit with *The Pleasures of Hope* (1799), about which Coleridge was contemptuous.[13]

William Empson observed of Coleridge that he always offered you 'the fascination of the most extreme case of something';[14] and his dealings with hope occupy the full spectrum. His grown-up religious thought begins with an exuberant affirmation of 'sure and certain hope', with a universal optimism of the most embracing kind; and the early verse, especially, is preoccupied by a vision of the world's goodness and progressive moral plenitude. At the same time, Coleridge was always sharply alive to a Humean 'contrariety of passions'; and he was drawn, too, by the dark possibility of a universe subject to mere bad luck: the famous poems of his great period, chiefly the late 1790s, are astonishing not least in the way they manage to encompass both perspectives at once, as though articulating two whole world views. The Pauline virtues being faith, hope, and charity, their antitheses are as surely (as a character in Beckett observes) 'Doubt, Despair and Scrounging';[15] and Coleridge's life was replete with all three. But only gradually did disappointment itself emerge as a major theme for his art, tentatively in the 'conversation' poems, and then momentously in 'Dejection: An Ode'. What Paul called 'Hope', Geoffrey Hartman once suggested, in the Romantics 'becomes ... Imagination':[16] a ramificatory remark; and one of its ramifications is the supplementary observation that, for the Romantics, the absence of hope can become an occasion for imagination too.

Early verse

M. H. Abrams argues in a celebrated essay that the Romantic imagination was a displaced utopianism: a transference of political hope from the external world to the spirit.[17] That is how Coleridge understood Wordsworth's story: 'that dear Hope afflicted, and struck down, / So summon'd homeward, thenceforth calm and sure / From the dread Watch-Tower of man's absolute Self, / With light unwaning on her eyes, to look / Far on' ('To a Gentleman', lines 39–43). For Coleridge himself hope had always been an affair of the inner life, even when most embroiled in contemporary events. The theological background here is Unitarianism, to which he had been converted while a Cambridge undergraduate. The Unitarian ethos was radical, enlightened, and rationalist, taking most elements of Christian orthodoxy to be contaminations, including the divinity of Jesus. Rather than uniquely incarnate in Christ, God was pervasively present throughout creation: as Coleridge put it in lines contributed to Southey's *Joan of Arc*, 'Nature's vast ever-acting Energy! / In will, in deed, Impulse of All to All!' ('Destiny of Nations', lines 461–2). The exciting corollaries of God's universal agency were necessitarianism (the non-existence of individual human will) and the ultimate goodness of all things: Coleridge described the position to Southey as that of 'a Necessitarian – and (believing in an all-loving Omnipotence) an Optimist' (*CL*, I, p. 145). Hope is hard-wired: 'Reasoning strictly and with logical Accuracy I should deny the existence of any Evil', he announced in 1795, 'inasmuch as the end determines the nature of the means and I have been able to discover nothing of which the end is not good.'[18] The 'pious confidence of Optimism' was not always easy to live with: Southey nicknamed him 'Dr Pangloss' after the embattled Leibnizian sage of Voltaire's *Candide* (*CL*, I, p. 168). But Coleridge remained drawn to the idea that 'Divine Providence ... regulates into one vast harmony all the events of time, however calamitous some of them may appear to mortals' ('Ode to the Departing Year'). In 1822, after numerous reconfigurations, he was still professing it 'almost irreligious not to rely on Providence and the Life of Hope' (*CL*, V, p. 202); and his last book still maintains that contemplating history properly, as a record of unfolding providence, 'infuses hope and reverential thoughts of man and his destination' (*CS*, p. 32).

The 'Life of Hope' in Coleridge's early poetry took heart from the millennial excitements of the age and looked forward ('Argument' to 'Religious Musings') to 'Millenium. Universal Redemption. Conclusion'. Such prophetic confidence mingled for a time with plans to establish a utopian community ('Pantisocracy') in America: 'O'er the Ocean swell / Sublime of Hope I seek the cottag'd Dell' (lines 4–5), and though by the time of his first volume, *Poems, on Various Subjects* (1796), the scheme had collapsed, the temper of the collection remained headily prospective. 'Lines Composed while Climbing the Left Ascent of Brockley Coomb' is literally about a fine prospect – a favourite Coleridgean narrative, climbing to gain the view from the top of a hill: 'Ah! what a luxury of landscape meets / My gaze!' (lines 12–13). (He later recalled admiring Crowe's *Lewesdon Hill* (*BL*, I, pp.17–18).) A prospect poem is a poem about seeing a prospect but also about having prospects of your own, as you gaze into the world you are about to enter; and the book is mindful of Coleridge's own promising future as a poet: he remembered in a slightly later poem 'that divine and nightly-whispering Voice, / Which from my childhood to maturer years / Spake to me of predestinated wreaths, / Bright with no fading colours!' ('To the Rev. George Coleridge', lines 36–9). The association of poetry with such hopefulness was instinctive – as when he flattered Davy with the observation that chemistry, 'being necessarily performed with the passion of Hope ... was poetical' (*CL*, I, p. 557).

Poems, on Various Subjects declares miscellaneousness on its title-page; but hopefulness is one of the things that draws it together. The Brockley Coomb lines appear as number XXI in a sequence of thirty-six 'Effusions', a mixture of sonnets addressed to public figures and other pieces including 'To a Young Ass' (XXXIII) and the poem later entitled 'The Eolian Harp' (XXXV). 'I hail thee BROTHER – spite of the fool's scorn' (line 26): the ass is a piece of ebullient fraternity, at once heartfelt and whimsical, moved by a surprising sense of the 'federal Republic of the Universe', as Coleridge put it in his notebook (*CN*, I, p. 1073). The poem is larky, but Coleridge is perfectly serious about the theology too, and gives it a ponderously wonderful exposition in 'The Eolian Harp':

> And what if all of animated nature
> Be but organic Harps diversly fram'd,
> That tremble into thought, as o'er them sweeps
> Plastic and vast, one intellectual Breeze,
> At once the Soul of each, and God of all? (lines 44–8)

'To thee, unblinded by these outward shews, / The unity of all has been revealed', Wordsworth said to Coleridge in *The Prelude*, which was kindly.[19] The climax to the 1796 volume, 'Religious Musings', finds a language for that unity in convoluted Miltonics:

> 'Tis the sublime of man,
> Our noontide Majesty, to know ourselves
> Parts and proportions of one wond'rous whole:
> This fraternizes man, this constitutes

Our charities and bearings. But 'tis God
Diffused through all, that doth make all one whole.
(lines 135–40)

The verse is clunkily impressive: it returns, with fitting single-mindedness, to fine-tune 'one wondr'ous whole' into 'one whole'; while, more deftly, the magic of homophony has found the *one* implicit in *wonder*. Ascent here is more than climbing a hill: it is zooming through levels of being towards the revelation that all is intended and for the best: 'and thence soared to HOPE, / Strong to believe whate'er of mystic good / Th'ETERNAL dooms for his IMMORTAL Sons' (lines 43–5).

'The Ancient Mariner' and 'Christabel'

But such an insistence upon the 'unity of all' might come across as more fraught than serene; and certainly many of Coleridge's other writings show him vividly aware of quite an opposite reality. In 'The Destiny of Nations' the possibility of forces within the universe getting on with their own thing, independent of divine will, is rejected contemptuously – 'Self-working tools, uncaused effects, and all / Those blind Omniscients, those Almighty Slaves, / Untenanting Creation of its God' (lines 33–5); but the matter is more pressing than the safely unthinkable. No doubt Coleridge's early theological position spoke to him so strongly, in part, because of the curious proximity of its universe of hope to a cosmos of disorganization. (Room for doubt even appears within the sunny spaces of 'The Eolian Harp': to ask 'And what if all of animated nature ... ?', is hardly to proclaim what it *is*; and the poem ends nervously withdrawing to a safer piety.) 'Quere – How is it that Dr Priestley is not an atheist?', Coleridge asked a correspondent in 1796: 'He asserts in three different Places, that God not only *does*, but *is*, every thing. – But if God *be* every Thing, every Thing is God – : which is all, the Atheists assert –. An eating, drinking, lustful *God* – with no *unity* of *Consciousness*' (*CL*, I, pp. 192–3). God's diffusion through the multiplicity of his world does not work to gather it all into one, but rather to scatter him into its bewildering manyness. Coleridge describes an unplanned perplexity with which he was dreadfully familiar, and which features in his poetry in a wide range of moods. His first published poem was a forlorn address 'To Fortune', written after buying a ticket in the Irish lottery, in which he pines amid a chancy universe for 'One Flower of Hope!' (line 21); and several early poems indulge a sentimental melancholy of pathetic lucklessness, as 'On Observing a Blossom on the First of February 1796'. The major achievement in this vein is the 'Monody' for Chatterton (composed in 1790, revised several times) in which the allegorical figure of 'Hope' (line 51) is but one character among a cast of personifications all battling over Chatterton's body, among whom 'Penury' and 'CARE' prove victorious, leaving behind 'DESPAIR' and 'INDIGNATION' – before the poem abruptly abandons Bristol for a Pantisocratic America (line 136).[20]

The major poems written at the end of the 1790s occupy this same strange 'intermundium' (Coleridge's word: *BL*, I, p. 32) between a universe of hope and one of unpredictability and chance. The marvellousness of 'The Rime of the Ancyent Marinere' (published in *Lyrical Ballads*, co-authored with Wordsworth, in 1798, and frequently revised: I quote from Beer's later text) lies partly in the way it manages to describe a wholly plausible narrative of religious confidence while allowing for the possibility of the darkest spiritual anarchy: one evidence of this ambivalence is the starkly divergent readings that the poem provokes, some dwelling on its Christian logic, and others, with no less credibility, on its nightmarish irrationalism.[21] A religious coherence is not hard to discern. In shooting the amiable albatross, the Mariner commits a crime of unmeditated cruelty; the energies of nature turn on him with a savage reproach; and crazed by physical suffering, he feels for the creatures of the ocean a visceral disgust: 'slimy things did crawl with legs / Upon the slimy sea' (lines 125–6). But, at what seems the turning point, something in his benighted spirit is moved to recognize the sanctity of this same creation, and 'slimy things' are transformed into 'happy living things': 'A spring of love gushed from my heart, / And I blessed them unaware' (lines 284–5). The benediction marks the beginning of a return to health, and the poem draws to its close with his homely aphorisms: 'For the dear God who loveth us, / He made and loveth all' (lines 616–17).

That line of interpretation feels bolstered by the marginal commentary that Coleridge added in 1817: the notes describe a difficult but sure progression from transgression to epiphany to restoration ('The curse is finally expiated': to line 442); and such an account would exemplify Coleridge's principle that there is 'nothing of which the end is not good'. On the other hand, the poem is suspiciously full of things that don't readily fit into an optimistic scheme. Leslie Stephen observed the oddity that the only person not punished with an agonizing death is the murderer himself;[22] and it is obviously a moot point whether the curse is *ever* finally 'expiated'. It is striking, too, that the Mariner's fate is apparently decided, long before the moment with the water snakes, on the outcome of a game of dice between the ghastly figures (belatedly identified in 1817 as 'Death' and 'Life-in-Death'): dice would seem to place at the heart of things, not the authorship of providence, but an emblematic chanciness and luck. The old Mariner clings pathetically to his up-beat version, and his account has at least convinced the editorial persona who writes the marginal commentary; but the poem is fully more embracing and complicated. Even its declared catastrophe, the shooting of the albatross, has a strangely evasive connection with the events that ensue: immediately afterwards the weather actually improves, and the crew are slapping the Mariner on the back (lines 101–2). They change their tune; but the detail is enough to muddy any clear allegory.

Wordsworth remembered Coleridge as 'quite an epicure in sound'.[23] His acute sensitivity to the sound of verse also enlivened him to the creative potential of mis-sounding, and he exploits the elbow-room afforded by the pretended genre (an oral ballad) to create within 'The Rime' a brilliantly approximate aural world of mixed and missed rhymes, even when things might seem most hopefully in tune:

> Sometimes a-dropping from the sky
> I heard the sky-lark sing;
> Sometimes all little birds that are,
> How they seemed to fill the sea and air
> With their sweet jargoning! (lines 358–62)

The ballad form naturally allows for an altogether unrhymed line: Coleridge uses the effect to insinuate recurrently a sense of elements unincorporated or unaccommodated within the poem. Here, additionally, where the subject is sweet swinging, the verse resists sweetness ('air' and 'are' manage a bare off-rhyme, 'sing' and 'jargon*ing*' come together gawkily). A rhyme, as Arthur Hallam, that deeply Coleridgean thinker, once observed, combines appeals to memory and to hope;[24] a failed rhyme frustrates a hope; and a rhyme can fail in ways other than by being off. Coleridge strikingly uses reiteration where you expect rhyming:

> A spring of love gushed from my heart,
> And I blessed them unaware:
> Sure my kind saint took pity on me,
> And I blessed them unaware. (lines 284–7)

As Christopher Ricks remarks of a similar moment in Shakespeare, the repetition enacts a 'log-jam of feeling':[25] here, the effect is wonderfully suspended between the emphatic underlining of a great religious realization, and a neurotic insistence upon some belief that, however unfounded, is nevertheless overwhelmingly important.

Coleridge believed that 'Christabel', if finished, would have fulfilled his ambitions better even than the 'Mariner' (*BL*, II, p. 7); and the poem occupies much the same ambivalent territory; but its non-completion is not just a regrettable accident, but one expression of that ambivalence. The Mariner's ship was the first ever to enter the Pacific (lines 105–6); and 'Christabel', too, turns about the invasion of what had once been inviolate space: in this case, the home.

> The lady sank, belike through pain,
> And Christabel with might and main
> Lifted her up, a weary weight,
> Over the threshold of the gate:
> Then the lady rose again,
> And moved, as she were not in pain. (lines 129–34)

One of the audacities of the poem is Coleridge's decision to entrust it to a narrator so clearly out of his depth: 'For what can ail the mastiff bitch?' (line 153), he asks, and 'Alas! what ails poor Geraldine?' (line 206), when few readers can have been in much doubt; but the uncertainty that the hesitant narrator spreads about events is contagious and speaks to some genuine perplexity within the story. Geraldine's corrupting power appears irresistible, and at the startling climax of the fragment Christabel's identity appears taken over ('And passively did imitate / That look of dull and treacherous hate!': lines 605–6). But what happens next is missing. According to surviving accounts, Christabel was to end the poem not only unharmed but having exerted a redemptive influence on others, demonstrating that 'the virtuous of this world save the wicked':[26] as the poet's son realized, Geraldine would then be 'no witch or goblin, or malignant being of any kind, but a spirit, executing her appointed task with the best good-will'.[27] That would represent Coleridge's religious views at their most rosy, and might (as it were) realize the 'Christ' within the name of 'Christabel'; but her name also contains 'Abel', whose fate was less happy.[28] In the event, the poem breaks off with both hopeful and hopeless outcomes envisaged but neither achieved, perpetually suspended within the experience of what John Beer calls its 'insoluble problem'.[29]

The conversation poems

The 'conversation' poems are also mainly a product of the late 1790s, and express in their way a similar insolubility. The genre is the invention of critics, named after the subtitle to 'The Nightingale':[30] the poems were grouped by Coleridge, with others, as 'Meditative Poems in Blank Verse'.[31] Following the pattern of 'The Eolian Harp' the poems intertwine transcendence and domesticity, religious vision and the experience of landscape: their artistry lies in the way they modulate between particular observation and a subsequent movement 'beyond the particular objects of his experience', as Kelvin Everest has put it, before completing 'a return to those particular conditions, or to a different but related set of particulars, but the private context is now charged with our heightened sense of the potential that Coleridge can generate out of such moments'.[32] The theological impetus is what Coleridge calls, in 'Fears in Solitude' (1798), 'adoration of the God in nature' (line 188): the poems set out to picture a universe with 'joyance every where', and draw an important moral: 'Methinks, it should have been impossible / Not to love all things in a world so fill'd' ('The Eolian Harp', lines 29, 30–1).

'This Lime-Tree Bower My Prison' (comp. 1797) offers a good test-case for such love. The poem is addressed to Charles Lamb, whom Coleridge fondly imagines out walking, in rapture at the scenery, while he stays behind in the garden.

> My gentle-hearted Charles! when the last rook
> Beat its straight path along the dusky air
> Homewards, I blest it! deeming its black wing
> (Now a dim speck, now vanishing in light)
> Had cross'd the mighty Orb's dilated glory,
> While thou stood'st gazing; or, when all was still,
> Flew creeking o'er thy head, and had a charm
> For thee, my gentle-hearted Charles, to whom
> No sound is dissonant which tells of Life. (lines 68–76)

The young ass's 'dissonant harsh Bray of Joy' had made a terrible noise, but turned out to be in tune with God after all. The Mariner's snakes are physically revolting, but blessed all the same; and now the solitary rook, 'creeking' tunelessly, is blessed too. The latter two poems, at least, do not win their moments of optimism easily; and much of their greatness comes from Coleridge's readiness to acknowledge in his peripheral vision kinds of experience that are very far from blessings: what Hazlitt noted to deplore – that 'his mind ... keeps open house, and entertains all comers' – coarsens a fine perception into a jibe, for it was Coleridge's openness to counter-truths that distinguishes his best verse. The lime trees form a prison, keeping Coleridge from the numinous experience imagined for Charles (lines 32–43), but they also create a protected and enclosed space – 'Hope's trim bower' ('Effusion XXXVI', line 11) – as though acknowledging the presence of some dark trouble without, from which one might well wish to withdraw. The solitary rook at dusk brings with it the possibility of something wicked by way of *Macbeth* ('Light thickens, / And the Crow makes Wing to th' Rookie Wood'); and the poem mentions briefly, though with awful emphasis, Charles's own familiarity with 'evil and pain / And strange calamity' (lines 31–2): the year before, his sister Mary had killed their mother in a fit of insanity, a fact of such rebarbative horror that the wish to accommodate it within a universe of 'joyance' seems hopeless.

Coleridge's own exclusion from the visionary landscape in 'This Lime-Tree Bower' is characteristic: his remoteness from the blessedness he imagines is an important part of the way all the great conversation poems work. That one might 'be a jarring and a dissonant thing, / Amid this general dance and minstrelsy' was the nightmarish prospect raised in 'The Dungeon', published in the 1798 *Lyrical Ballads* (lines 26–7). 'Imaginative vision, in Coleridge's poetry', Lucy Newlyn observes, 'is always vicariously achieved':[33] or anyway most plausibly achieved when done vicariously. Coleridge claims it for himself in, say, 'Lines Composed while Climbing ... Brockley Coomb' and 'Reflections on Having Left a Place of Retirement'; but the effect in those cases is curiously abstract, as though stating a theoretical possibility: 'Blest hour! It was a luxury, – to be!' (line 42). 'Frost at Midnight', like 'The Nightingale' (both comp. 1798), imagines for his son a life led within an encompassing universe of love, a life that Coleridge can contemplate only from the outside:

For I was reared
In the great city, pent 'mid cloisters dim,
And saw nought lovely but the sky and stars.
But *thou*, my babe! shalt wander like a breeze
By lakes and sandy shores. (lines 51–5)

The cloisters come from an extended simile in *Paradise Lost* (IX. 445–54) describing Satan's response to the momentarily enlivening air of Eden, disabled by a loveliness he can never possess: the Satanic self-reference is quietly terrible; but the lines are not hag-ridden, for hope features here in its most generous and precarious form, which is to say hope for another. Not the least of Coleridge's achievements is an exquisite poetry of benediction. 'Therefore all seasons shall be sweet to thee' (line 65): how poignantly determined, that 'Therefore', to assert as a logical certainty something which is anything but certain; and how untainted by adult disappointment the tenderness of the wish for his boy – nothing here, for instance, to bring to mind (except by contrast) Prospero's world-weary response to Miranda's 'How many goodly creatures are there here!', ''Tis new to *thee*.'

'Dejection: An Ode'

Contemplating the national struggle against France in the *Morning Post* in September 1802, Coleridge sought to find 'sufficient of hope to preserve us from dejection'.[34] He refers to the outcome of political analysis; but secretly he draws on recent verse of private experience: 'Dejection: An Ode' was published a few days later in the same newspaper. In April 1802, Coleridge had composed a long verse 'Letter' to Sara Hutchinson, soon to be Wordsworth's sister-in-law, for whom he had contracted an impossible love. 'Dejection' recast that poem, shortening it and removing the more betraying personal references, turning a poem of complicated multiple crises into a poem about a crisis of imagination, and so creating, as Donald Davie says, 'one of the great poems in the language'.[35] 'The Poet is dead in me', Coleridge had written in a letter of March 1801; and the paradoxical brilliance of 'Dejection' was to find himself a new kind of poet in that death:

All this long eve, so balmy and serene,
Have I been gazing on the western sky,
And its peculiar tint of yellow green:
And still I gaze – and with how blank an eye!
And those thin clouds above, in flakes and bars,
That give away their motion to the stars;
Those stars, that glide behind them or between,
Now sparkling, now bedimm'd, but always seen:
Yon crescent Moon, as fixed as if it grew
In its own cloudless, starless lake of blue;
I see them all so excellently fair,
I see, not feel how beautiful they are! (lines 27–38)

These are blank eyes, yet the lines convey a painterly attentiveness ('its peculiar tint of yellow green'); the sights succeed one another in real time ('the stars; / Those stars') as though eyes were casting about for some place to rest in untroubled wonder. But whatever lingering powers the lines evince, they enact superbly too a dissipation of vitality in their faltering rhyme: first, the sonic impropriety of 'grew' and 'blue'; and then an inspired mis-hit of a couplet, 'fair'/'are'. The failure to write might seem a perverse end to which to put such writerly inventiveness, but Coleridge anticipates a creativity of a peculiarly modern kind. 'No European poet before the present century, in all probability', wrote George Watson in 1966, 'has written so many poems as Coleridge about the difficulty or impossibility of writing a poem';[36] but many have since pursued that 'difficulty or impossibility' as a theme (Tennyson, Arnold, Hopkins, Yeats, Eliot, Stevie Smith, Beckett, Larkin).

'Dejection' is as much the parody of a conversation poem as a conversation poem: it occupies a world in which hope is something of the past (lines 80–2), and where the harmonious goodness of all things has been supplanted by a cruel cacophony: 'What a scream / Of agony by torture lengthen'd out / That lute sent forth!' (lines 97–9). It is a lament for a loss of powers that, especially in its first version as the 'Letter', looks back self-elegiacally to Coleridge's experience 'While yet a Boy' (line 72) – one quality of boyishness, with fitting playfulness, is buoyancy: 'I am not the buoyant

Thing I was of yore' (line 227). (A mark of genius is 'The buoyant child surviving in the man': 'The Blossoming of the Solitary Date-Tree', line 59.) But a different kind of childhood is also visible, one of Coleridge's saddest evocations of the abandonment that 'Frost at Midnight' had allowed itself only to touch upon:

> a little child
> Upon a lonesome wild,
> Not far from home, but she hath lost her way:
> And now moans low in bitter grief and fear,
> And now screams loud, and hopes to make her mother hear.
> (lines 121–5)

Like 'Frost at Midnight', the poem ends with a benedictive turn, addressing the anonymous 'Dear Lady': 'To her may all things live, from Pole to Pole, / Their life the eddying of her living Soul!' (lines 135–6). The lines are nicely poised – between the old belief that her spirit might participate in the dynamic energy of the good world at large (so that the movements of her soul would be one expression of their larger life), and the chastened new possibility that the vitality she perceives in 'all things' might be merely her own soul's projection.[37] The complication of feeling in the lines is augmented by 'from Pole to Pole': a poetic phrase that fits the tender wish, but the Coleridgean context brings to mind an earlier appearance in the harried world of 'The Ancient Mariner' (line 293).

The later poetry

Coleridge's verse increasingly takes his own disappointment, including his poetic disappointment, as a dominant theme: it is the paradox identified by Watson as 'creative despair'.[38] The last of the conversation poems, addressed to Wordsworth after his recitation of *The Prelude* in January 1807 (published as 'To a Gentleman' in 1817), sets that disappointment against Wordsworth's triumph: a poem of gratitude and congratulation becomes one of self-lament. Wordsworth is venerated for redeeming political hope as a new mental empowerment: 'the dread Watch-Tower of man's absolute Self'. But meanwhile Coleridge finds within himself something quite different: the lines tangle themselves up in stalemate, deadlocked first by chiasmus and then by the striking immobility of an anti-rhyme, 'in vain':

> And Fears self-will'd, that shunn'd the eye of Hope;
> And Hope that scarce would know itself from Fear;
> Sense of past Youth, and Manhood come in vain,
> And Genius given, and Knowledge won in vain. (lines 68–71)

Even this poem ends with a possibility of renewal: 'And when I rose, I found myself in prayer' (line 113), as the Mariner found himself able to pray (line 288); but it is left uncertain whether the phrase conveys the confidence of having finally found one's true self (as in the Christian obligation 'to lose and find all self in GOD', *BL*, I, p. 283) or, rather, a note of self-estrangement, finding oneself doing something without having consciously purposed to do so.

Hope in the later poems is less an inherent tendency of the universe and more a piece of needy psychology: it gathers with greater and greater desperation about the transformative potential of a fully reciprocated human love, which remains necessarily quite unknown. Without such hope a creative life cannot be sustained, but 'Hope without an object' ('Work without Hope', line 13) only serves to reinforce a prevailing hopelessness – 'Sad lot, to have no Hope!' ('The Visionary Hope' (?1810), line 1): as in 'Love's Apparition and Evanishment' (1833), in which Love's fleeting reappearance wakes 'just enough of life in death / To make Hope die anew' (lines 26–7). In an eerie allegory, 'Hope and Time' (1802–7; reworked in part as 'Time, Real and Imaginary', published in 1817), Coleridge casts 'HOPE' as a girl running, looking over her shoulder towards 'TIME', her blind brother: he runs on steadily, 'And knows not whether he is first or last' (line 25). The allegory points to a Hardyish irony in the idea that some unbridgeable gap stretches between Hope and the progress of a human life.

The later poems are very various, including skits and epigrams, occasional pieces and *jeux d'esprit*, as well as more substantial pieces in which Coleridge returns to earlier preoccupations in disenchanted retrospect. At most, he advocates a tenacious endurance: in 'Love, Hope, and Patience in Education' (1829), the first two virtues cannot last the human course, and leave only Patience. At other times, he envisages with unassuaged vividness 'the mere Horror of blank Nought at all' ('Limbo', line 23):

No constellations alphabet the Sky –
The Heavens one large black Letter only shews,
And as a Child beneath its master's Blows
Shrills out at once its Task and its Affright,
The groaning world now learns to read aright,
And with its Voice of Voices cries out, O!
('The Indifference of the Heavens', lines 10–15)

The contrast with 'Frost at Midnight', where Coleridge had pictured his boy reading God in the landscape like a book, is terribly undisguised. 'Work without Hope' (1825) similarly revisits that earlier natural scene of benevolent activity: 'All Nature seems at work'; all but the poet himself, 'the sole unbusy thing' (lines 1, 5). His professed lack of creativity comes with an extra, submerged pathos, for it was Wordsworth's line, 'The thrush is *busy* in the wood', that Coleridge had once singled out as the sort of thing that only a true poet could have conceived (*BL*, II, p. 105): his own perception of unbusyness marks him out as 'no Poet'. And yet 'unbusy' is a remarkable thing to have written: no common word, Coleridge uses it with audacity to nominate a state of the spirit. Such a moment exemplifies the peculiar power of the later poetry – the 'transfiguring of weakness into strength' that Geoffrey Hill once admired in Coleridge, 'a subsuming'.[39]

'Kubla Khan' and the limits of poetry

Many of Coleridge's later poems, like 'Hope and Time', have an allegorical cast; and there is a peculiarity here since, as Morton Paley points out, Coleridge's firmly expressed preference was for 'symbolism'.[40] That discrepancy is only one way in which Coleridge's later poems evade the prescriptions of his own aesthetics. Coleridge spent much of the first two decades of the nineteenth century developing a giddily elevated conception of literary form and poetic vocation, which attributed to the aesthetic all the divine hopefulness with which he had formerly invested the universe: the perfect poem possessed an internal, self-justifying inevitability, in which all its autonomous parts were yet subservient to an overall unity, and in which no detail, not 'a word, or the position of a word', might be changed without loss (*BL*, I, p. 23). But the later poems are, by contrast, abbreviated, fragmentary, incidental, throwaway; 'The Improvisatore' (?1826) begins in prose, and wanders into verse; 'The Blossoming of the Solitary Date-Tree' offers prose paraphrases of some stanzas and invites the reader to put them into verse. Tillotama Rajan has theorized this phenomenon: 'Abjecting themselves from an aesthetic order whose expectations they cannot meet, the poems draw attention to the pathos of that abjection, and cling to the mood which is the very cause of their self-rejection';[41] and you do not need to subscribe to the Kristevan terminology to share a sense of these works as existing, knowingly, to one side of an idea of poetry that they cannot hope to fulfil.

If an oddly enabling lack of self-coincidence indeed be a feature of the late poems, then it is startling to remember just how young Coleridge was when he wrote some of them. 'For Coleridge', as Paley observes, 'the later poetry begins relatively early';[42] and once you look you can see the great 'early' works already anticipating such self-conscious developments. One of Coleridge's more gnomic utterances in *Biographia* is: 'a poem of any length neither can be, or ought to be, all poetry' (*BL*, II, p. 15), and although no doubt theoretically perplexing, it highlights an interest long implied by his own poetic practice. Quite literally, Coleridge was fond of including with his poems things that weren't poetry: prefaces, footnotes, glosses; but as a matter of idiom, too, his poetry enjoys modulating between self-consciously 'poetic' or literary and more speaking or even prosaic registers. The conversation poem, which has some claim to being Coleridge's major generic innovation, exists in a hinterland between lyrical expression and colloquial ease: this is what Davie had in mind when he referred, with guarded appreciation, to 'Coleridge's experiments in amorphous poetry'.[43] 'Reflections on Having Left a Place of Retirement' was originally subtitled 'A Poem, which affects Not to be POETRY', a literary joke that implies Coleridge's fascination with the way the artistic and the non-artistic interplay one with another.[44]

Coleridge mythologized such questions before he theorized them, in perhaps the most astonishing of all his works, 'Kubla Khan' (written, probably, in 1797; pub. 1816). The poem begins with a colossal act of creativity, the pleasure dome summoned into existence by the authority of the Khan's 'decree': the space of his artistry is 'girdled round' with 'walls and towers' (line 7), simultaneously an act of exclusion and embattlement. What is being excluded becomes abruptly clear as the poem turns, antithetically, to picture the unartistic landscape outside: 'But oh! that deep romantic chasm which slanted / Down the green hill athwart a cedarn cover!' (lines 12–13); and emerging from the violent dynamism of that sublime landscape is a threat of violence ('Ancestral voices prophesying war!': line 30). In the little third verse, Kubla's creation and Xanadu's wilderness come into a momentary reconciliation, as though balancing the claims of their competing realities: 'It was a miracle of rare device, / A sunny pleasure-dome with caves of ice!' (lines 35–6); but any sense of a unity won soon dissipates. The last verse, a sort of coda, introduces the poet himself: he recollects his moment of inspiration under the influence of a muse-like 'damsel', and looks forward (without much conviction of success) to her return – 'Could I revive within me / Her symphony and song' (lines 42–3). Played in a different key, it is a kindred narrative of imagination achieved but then lost that occurs in the seriocomic 'Preface': the 'person on business from Porlock' interrupts Coleridge's transcription of the vision witnessed within the sealed-off space of his own mind ('a profound sleep, at least of the external senses'). David Bromwich writes memorably of 'Kubla Khan' as a rare case of 'poetry unconfined by chance encounters with the actual world';[45] but while Coleridge certainly entertains the dream of such an art, something different happens in this particular work of art: in both poem and prose accompaniment, the serenity and autonomy of the imagination is shadowed and disturbed by an actuality that it cannot contain. Still, it would be odd to maintain that the landscape of Xanadu was deplorable; it gets a much more rapt description than the dome, and Coleridge is clearly very excited by it; and everyone remembers the prosy gentleman from Porlock, whose entrance is one of the great fictional inventions of the Romantic period, and whose undeflected tenacity before would-be visionary genius has a droll heroism of its own. He would certainly not affect to be 'poetry', but the text of 'Kubla Khan' makes space for him.

NOTES

1 See *Poetical Works*, ed. J. C. C. Mays, 3 vols (Princeton: Princeton University Press,, 2001). I quote here from the widely used single-volume *Samuel Taylor Coleridge: Poems*, ed. John Beer (London: Everyman, 1999).

2 *The Notebooks of Samuel Taylor Coleridge*, eds Kathleen Coburn *et al.*, 5 vols (New York/Princeton: Pantheon Books/Princeton University Press, 1957–2002), II, pp. 2091, 2510, 2072, 2334. Hereafter *CN*.

3 *The Complete Works of William Hazlitt*, ed. P. P. Howe, 21 vols (London: Dent, 1930–4), XI, pp. 34, 36.

4 *Collected Letters of Samuel Taylor Coleridge*, ed. Earl Leslie Griggs, 6 vols (Oxford: Oxford University Press, 1956–71), II, p. 714. Hereafter *CL*.

5 *Biographia Literaria*, eds James Engell and W. J. Bate, 2 vols (Princeton: Princeton University Press, 1983), I, p. 38. Hereafter *BL*.

6 Humphry House, *Coleridge: The Clark Lectures 1951–2* (London: Hart-Davis, 1962, rptd 1969), p. 57.

7 *On the Constitution of the Church and State*, ed. John Colmer (Princeton: Princeton University Press, 1976), p. 220. Hereafter *CS*.

8 *Lay Sermons*, ed. R. J. White (Princeton: Princeton University Press, 1972), pp. 216; 227. John Colmer identifies hope as 'one of the most important single themes in C[oleridge]'s works' (*CS*, p. 73 n.); and cf. Colmer's 'Coleridge and the Life of Hope', *Studies in Romanticism* 11 (1972), 332–41.

9 The poems are in *The Poems of Richard Crashaw*, ed. J. R. Tutin (London: Routledge, 1900), pp. 158–9, 159–61.

10 *Marginalia*, eds H. J. Jackson and George Whalley, 6 vols (Princeton: Princeton University Press, 1980–2001), I, p.67.

11 William Empson, *Seven Types of Ambiguity*, 2nd edn (London: Chatto and Windus, 1947, rptd 1973), p. xiii.

12 David Hume, *A Treatise of Human Nature*, ed. P. H. Nidditch, 2nd edn (Oxford: Clarendon Press, 1978), p. 441.

13 A. G. L'Estrange, ed., *The Life of Mary Russell Mitford*, 3 vols (London: Bentley, 1870), I, p. 163.

14 *Coleridge's Verse: A Selection*, eds William Empson and David Pirie (London: Faber, 1972), p. 97.

15 Samuel Beckett, *More Pricks Than Kicks* (1934 ; London: Calder and Boyars, 1970), p. 53.

16 Geoffrey Hartman, *Beyond Formalism: Literary Essays 1958–1970* (New Haven: Yale University Press, 1970), p. 158.

17 M. H. Abrams, 'English Romanticism: The Spirit of the Age', in *The Correspondent Breeze: Essays on English Romanticism* (New York: Norton, 1984), pp. 44–75, 63.
18 *Lectures 1795 On Politics and Religion*, eds Lewis Patton and Peter Mann (Princeton: Princeton University Press, 1971), p. 105.
19 1799 text, lines 255–6. *The Prelude 1799, 1805, 1850*, eds Jonathan Wordsworth, M. H. Abrams, and Stephen Gill (New York: Norton, 1979), p. 20.
20 Cf. David Fairer, 'Chatterton's Poetic Afterlife, 1770–1794: A Context for Coleridge's Monody', in *Thomas Chatterton and Romantic Culture*, ed. Nick Groom (Basingstoke: Macmillan, 1999), pp. 228–52.
21 A resourceful recent attempt to take on the spectrum of interpretations is T. Dilworth, 'Symbolic Spatial Form in *The Rime of the Ancient Mariner* and the Problem of God', *Review of English Studies* n.s. 58 (2007), 500–30.
22 Leslie Stephen, *Hours in a Library*, new edn, 4 vols (London: Smith, Elder, 1907), IV, p. 355.
23 *The Prose Works of William Wordsworth*, ed. Alexander B. Grosart, 3 vols (London: Moxon, 1876), III, p. 427.
24 *The Writings of Arthur Hallam*, ed. T. H. Vail Motter (New York: MLA, 1943), p. 222.
25 Christopher Ricks, *T. S. Eliot and Prejudice* (London/Berkeley: Faber/University of California Press, 1988), p. 135.
26 James Gillman, *The Life of Samuel Taylor Coleridge*, 1 vol. published (London: Pickering, 1838), p. 283.
27 *The Poems of Sam[ue]l Taylor* Coleridge, eds Derwent Coleridge and Sara Coleridge (London: Pickering, 1869), p. xlii.
28 Coleridge took the name 'Christabel', which is not medieval, from Percy's *Reliques*: cf. *Poetical Works*, I, p. 484 n.
29 John Beer, *Coleridge the Visionary* (London: Chatto and Windus, 1959), p. 195. Beer shows how absorbed Coleridge became in the myth of Cain, Adam's fratricidal son, around the time of writing the poem (pp. 118–24).
30 *Poetical Works*, II, p. 680.
31 *Sibylline Leaves* (London: Rest Fenner, 1817), p. 163.
32 Kelvin Everest, *Coleridge's Secret Ministry: The Context of the Conversation Poems* (Hassocks: Harvester, 1979), p. 219.
33 Lucy Newlyn, *Coleridge, Wordsworth, and the Language of Allusion* (Oxford: Clarendon Press, 1986), p. 38.
34 *Essays on his Times*, ed. David V. Erdman, 3 vols (Princeton: Princeton University Press, 1969), II, p. 324.
35 Donald Davie, *Purity of Diction in English Verse* (London: Chatto and Windus, 1952), p. 129.
36 George Watson, *Coleridge the Poet* (London: Routledge and Kegan Paul, 1966), p. 9.
37 I suggested this at greater length in *Coleridge and the Uses of Division* (Oxford: Clarendon Press, 1999), p. 144.
38 Watson, *Coleridge the Poet*, p. 136.
39 Geoffrey Hill, *The Lords of Limit: Essays on Literature and Ideas* (London: André Deutsch, 1984), p. 12.

40 Morton D. Paley, *Coleridge's Later Poetry* (Oxford: Oxford University Press, 1996), p. 29.
41 Tillotama Rajan, 'Coleridge, Wordsworth, and the Textual Abject', *Wordsworth Circle* XXXIV (1993), 61–8, p. 66.
42 Paley, *Coleridge's Later Poetry*, p. 2.
43 Davie, *Purity of Diction*, p. 131.
44 *Poetical Works*, II, p. 353.
45 David Bromwich, *Skeptical Music: Essays on Modern Poetry* (Chicago: University of Chicago Press, 2001), p. 48.

SELECTED FURTHER READING

Editions

The Collected Works of Samuel Taylor Coleridge, gen. ed. Kathleen Coburn, 16 vols, Princeton/London, Princeton University Press/Routledge, 1969–2002, of which vol. 16 of *Collected Works* is the *Poetical Works*, ed. J. C. C. Mays, 3 vols, each in two parts. Now the standard edition

The Poetical Works of Samuel Taylor Coleridge, ed. E. H. Coleridge, 2 vols, Oxford, Clarendon Press, 1912. The previous standard edition, and still useful

Samuel Taylor Coleridge: Poems, ed. John Beer, London, Everyman, 1966; rev. edn, 1999. The most accessible modern edition

Secondary works

Early accounts

Charles Lamb, 'Christ's Hospital Five and Thirty Years Ago', in *Essays of Elia*, London, Taylor and Hessey, 1823

William Hazlitt, 'My First Acquaintance with Poets', *Liberal* I (1823); 'Mr. Coleridge', in *The Spirit of the Age*, London, Colburn, 1825

Thomas De Quincey, 'Samuel Taylor Coleridge', *Tait's Magazine* I (1834–5)

Classic accounts

Leslie Stephen, 'Coleridge', in *Hours in a Library*, 1879; new edn, 4 vols, London, Smith, Elder, 1907

T. S. Eliot, *The Use of Poetry and the Use of Criticism*, London, Faber, 1933

Virginia Woolf, 'Coleridge', in *The Death of the Moth*, London: Hogarth Press, 1942

Modern works with substantial discussions of the poetry

Abrams, M. H., 'Structure and Style in the Greater Romantic Lyric', 'Coleridge's "A Light in Sound"', and 'Coleridge and the Romantic Vision of the World', in *The Correspondent Breeze: Essays on English Romanticism*, New York, Norton, 1984

Bate, Walter Jackson, *Coleridge*, London, Macmillan, 1969

Beer, John, *Coleridge the Visionary*, London, Chatto and Windus, 1959
Coleridge's Poetic Intelligence, London, Macmillan, 1979
Everest, Kelvin, *Coleridge's Secret Ministry: The Context of the Conversation Poems*, Hassocks, Harvester, 1979
House, Humphry, *Coleridge: The Clark Lectures 1951–2*, London, Hart-Davis, 1962, rptd 1969
Newlyn, Lucy, *Coleridge, Wordsworth, and the Language of Allusion*, Oxford, Clarendon Press, 1986
Watson, George, *Coleridge the Poet*, London, Routledge and Kegan Paul, 1966
Wheeler, Kathleen, *The Creative Mind in Coleridge's Poetry*, London, Heinemann, 1980

17

ANNE BARTON

George Gordon, Lord Byron

In 1937, T. S. Eliot published an essay on Byron (later reprinted in his collection *On Poetry and Poets*, 1957) in which he asserted that of all the Romantic period poets, Byron 'would seem the most nearly remote from the sympathies of every living critic'. That was scarcely true in 1937 – W. H. Auden, for instance, had composed his long 'Letter to Lord Byron' in 1936 – and it was even less true twenty years later. Byron, however, was certainly remote from Eliot's own sympathies and not just because he felt there were unthinking schoolboy enthusiasms to interrogate and overcome, or even because he deplored the lack of concentration in Byron's verse, and its sheer volume by comparison with what he judged to be its overall quality. In the two essays on Milton also reprinted in *On Poetry and Poets*, Eliot found much to cavil at too when considering the author of *Paradise Lost*. But he was clear that (despite the damage supposedly done by Milton to the English language, compounded by a deficiency of visual perception by no means attributable merely to his literal blindness) 'it must be admitted that Milton was a very great poet', even though Eliot thought him 'antipathetic' not only as a thinker but simply as a man, when judged 'by the ordinary standards of likeableness in human beings'.

Eliot never admitted that Byron was a great poet, although he did concede that, partly because of his gift for digression, and the 'torrential fluency' of his verse, he is never monotonous or dull. (He failed to mention that Byron can also be gloriously funny.) He found a few specific things to praise: the narrative skill of some of the Eastern Tales (works he preferred to *Childe Harold*) or the later, English cantos of *Don Juan* and its savage Dedication to the poet Robert Southey, together with the underworld slang Byron deployed in his obituary of Tom the foot-pad, shot dead by Juan in Canto XI:

> He from the world had cut off a great man,
> Who in his time had made heroic bustle.

Who in a row like Tom could lead the van,
  Booze in the ken, or at the spellkin hustle?
Who queer a flat? Who (spite of Bow Street's ban)
  On the high toby-spice so flash the muzzle?
Who on a lark, with black-eyed Sal (his blowing)
So prime, so swell, so nutty, and so knowing?[1] (stanza 19)

Eliot did not accuse Byron of actually damaging the English language, merely of writing it as though he had been an intelligent foreigner, basically imperceptive to the English word, capable only of crude effects. While insisting moreover that he was not in the least concerned with the facts of Byron's somewhat spectacular life, Eliot was certainly preoccupied with the poet's personality, as he interpreted it from the verse, and even with Byron's face as depicted in contemporary busts and portraits: a face in which Eliot imagined he discerned a 'restless triviality of expression' and 'that blind look of the self-conscious beauty'.

What Eliot omitted from his account of Byron was almost as perverse as what he included. One would never guess from this essay how many more tales Byron wrote after the four early ones – *The Giaour*, *The Bride of Abydos* (both 1813), *The Corsair*, and *Lara* (both 1814) – that Eliot mentions. He was totally silent about some of the best later ones: *The Prisoner of Chillon* (1816), *Mazeppa* (1818), and Byron's South Seas story *The Island* in 1823. *Beppo* (1818), the *ottava rima* predecessor of *Don Juan*, he also ignored, as he did that brilliant satire *The Vision of Judgement* (1822) and Byron's eight verse dramas, each one remarkable (including *Heaven and Earth* and *The Deformed Transformed*, the two that remained unfinished) in its own highly individual way. Of all the major Romantic period poets, Byron indeed was the only one to achieve real success with tragedy. Above all, Eliot neglected the aspect of Byron's work that engages so many critics now: his untiring concern with the political scene not only in his native England but more widely in post-revolutionary Europe, where Byron travelled, and in various countries (Greece, Switzerland, Italy) in which he lived between 1809, the year of his first 'pilgrimage' abroad, and his death in 1824, aged 36, at Missolonghi, where he went to aid the Greeks in their struggle for independence from Turkish rule. He was by far the most cosmopolitan of the English poets of his time, the one who enjoyed the most significant European reputation, as indeed he still does today.

The early poems

Byron began to circulate some of his poems while still an undergraduate at Trinity College, Cambridge. His first two collections were printed privately, intended only for the eyes of his associates and friends. In 1807, however, while still (in a somewhat desultory fashion) studying at Cambridge, he submitted *Hours of Idleness* to public perusal, equipping it with a Preface in which he stressed both his youth ('a young man who has lately completed his nineteenth year') and, somewhat unfortunately, his noble rank and lineage. Even more imprudently, he indicated that this first of his verse publications would probably be the last. It was a promise he was to make – and immediately violate – repeatedly, sometimes as here in public. In two of the editions of *English Bards and Scotch Reviewers* (1809) he rashly vowed never in future 'to stun mankind with poetry or prose',[2] and then in the Dedication to Thomas Moore of *The Corsair*, five years later, vowed silence 'for some years', only to publish *Lara* almost at once. After that, although Byron was continually trying to give up 'scribbling', as he contemptuously called it, in favour of the world of action, he recognized, however reluctantly, his psychological inability to do so and became more careful about such renunciations, confining them to his journals or to personal letters.

Hours of Idleness was not a particularly remarkable first volume, even considering Byron's tender age. It consists mostly of short poems, some of them translations, and the short poem was only occasionally something at which Byron excelled . He would, of course, produce a handful of superb lyrics in later years – 'She walks in beauty like the night', 'So we'll go no more a-roving', 'There be none of beauty's daughters', or the sonnet on Chillon. His, however, was in general a more expansive muse, and one that tended to resist closure. Byron almost always found it difficult to regard his poems as finished. He was likely to emend passages or insert additional lines after fair copies had been made, in proof, or even, as with *The Giaour*, after the initial publication. Although *Childe Harold* apparently reached a resounding conclusion at the end of Canto IV, bidding farewell to readers 'who have traced the Pilgrim to the scene / Which is his last' (stanza 186), Byron later entertained the possibility of a Canto V.

Hours of Idleness elicited a mixed bag of notices. It was, however, the one that appeared anonymously in the influential *Edinburgh Review* that stung Byron to the quick and provoked the first of his poems that really matters: the satire *English Bards and Scotch Reviewers*. The Edinburgh critic – Henry Brougham, although Byron erroneously thought it was the journal's editor Francis Jeffrey, a man whose literary judgement he later came to respect – poured scorn on the poems and also had a field day with the pretensions of their Preface. In his verse reply, Byron lashed out ferociously not only against Jeffrey and other critics but against most of the poets of his day, including (to his subsequent regret) Thomas Moore and Sir Walter Scott, both of whom were to become good friends. Towards Southey, on the other hand, and Wordsworth (whom he probably never met) the antipathy registered here was to remain almost entirely unchanged.

At the time, all of Byron's friends urged him to publish *English Bards and Scotch Reviewers* anonymously. He complied in the first edition, but added his name to those that followed. Later, he would refuse to heed advice not to publish *Don Juan* and *The Vision of Judgement* at all. (Only after death had rendered him powerless did his friends succeed, unfortunately, in obliterating another 'scandalous' work: his memoirs, which they reduced to ash in the grate of his publisher Murray's front room in London's Albemarle Street.) *English Bards and Scotch Reviewers* is an intemperate work, without the finesse and control of Byron's later verse satires, but it is full of life, and it can be very funny, as when Byron (who had clearly read and disliked Wordsworth's Preface to the 1800 edition of *Lyrical Ballads*) describes its author as a man 'who both by precept and example shows / That prose is verse, and verse is merely prose' (lines 241–2). As for Wordsworth's poem 'The Idiot Boy', it survives Byron's comic demolition of it – but only just. He was later to make very partial amends in his own poem 'Churchill's Grave', of 1816, with its note claiming that there could be few who both admired and deplored Wordsworth's verse more than himself. It is intriguing to speculate what Byron would have felt about *The Prelude*, not published until 1850, and *Don Juan*'s only rival as the greatest long poem of the Romantic period. Probably, it would have been another uneasy compound of admiration and mockery.

According to Byron, Shelley 'dosed' him with Wordsworth in 1816 when the two men were briefly neighbours in Switzerland. Wordsworth certainly believed that Byron had shamelessly imitated him in such passages as the famous one from Canto III of *Childe Harold* beginning 'I live not in myself, but I become, / Portion of that around me' (stanza 72). The allegation was false. Byron's response to the natural world, and his relationship to it, were fundamentally different from Wordsworth's, both here and elsewhere in his work. It is interesting in this context to compare Wordsworth's first sight of Mont Blanc in Book VI of *The Prelude* with Byron's response to Parnassus in Canto I of *Childe Harold*. Wordsworth regretted having actually seen the mountain and now finding 'a soulless image on the eye / That had usurped upon a living thought / That never more could be' (lines 444–6). Byron, by contrast, rejoiced in a Parnassus 'which I now survey / Not in the phrenzy of a dreamer's eye, / Nor in the fabled landscape of a lay, / But soaring snow-clad through thy native sky' (stanza 60). The reality that disappointed Wordsworth by comparison with what his imagination had previously conjured up was just what Byron treasured. This attitude, moreover, was typical.

In a period when poets glorified the Imagination as never before – 'the living power and prime agent of all human perception ... a repetition in the finite mind of the eternal act of creation' as Coleridge put it[3] – Byron stands apart. He shared neither his friend Shelley's belief that poets were 'the unacknowledged legislators of the world', nor Keats's conviction that 'what the Imagination seizes as Beauty must be truth – whether it existed before or not'. Byron was more likely to assert (as he did in a letter to Annabella Milbanke on 10 November 1813) that 'I by no means rank poetry or poets high in the scale of intellect ... I prefer the talents of action – of war, of the senate, even of science – to all the speculations of those dreamers of another existence.'[4] No one understood – and deplored – this conviction more than William Blake, a man Byron never met. Blake's last poem, *The Ghost of Abel* (1822), contains a dedication 'To Lord Byron in the Wilderness':

> What dost thou here, Elijah?
> Can a poet doubt the Visions of Jehovah? Nature has no Outline,
> But Imagination has. Nature has no Tune, but Imagination has.
> Nature has no Supernatural, and dissolves: Imagination is Eternity.

For Blake, Byron wandered in a wilderness that was not just that of foreign exile but that of error. He was a potential poet-prophet clinging perversely to the world of fact although Truth lay beyond it.

Byron would eventually make his own special peace with poetry and the imagination, indeed had already done so when Blake administered this rebuke. It was, however, to be a long struggle, and when he left England in 1809, after the initial publication of *English Bards and Scotch Reviewers*, it had only just begun. France at that time was out of bounds to English travellers because of hostilities between the two countries. Byron sailed initially to Lisbon, moved through Portugal and Spain, and then, after visiting Gibraltar and Malta, journeyed to Albania (the last still uncharted country for his English contemporaries), from there to Greece and Constantinople, and back to Greece again, where he settled in Athens for the best part of a year. There, on 14 January 1811, he announced, in a letter to his mother, that he had employed a Bavarian artist to take some views of Athens for him, something which would be 'better than scribbling, a disease I hope myself cured of' – only to confess, later in the very same letter, that he had already completed Cantos I and II of *Childe Harold's Pilgrimage: A Romaunt*.

This, of course was the poem that, on its publication later that year, after Byron had returned to England, instantly made him a celebrity. ('I awoke one morning', Thomas Moore later reported him as writing, probably in the lost Memoirs, 'and found myself famous'.[5]) For us now, these first two cantos suffer by comparison with III and IV, which he was to embark on five years later. Yet they have a freshness and spontaneity deriving in part from the fact that Byron actually wrote them in the scenes and countries they describe, partly from his own barely concealed delight in the landscapes and people he met in his travels, even when they took him – as with Greece – to countries whose current foreign occupation and enslavement he deplored. It was not really surprising that English readers, to a large extent cut off from the continent during the troubled Napoleonic period, should respond to the poem's variety and energy (the edition sold out in a matter of days) even if it was by no means clear what Byron was really trying to do.

In his Preface, Byron was at pains to remind readers of the traditional ballad meaning of 'Childe' (a youth of gentle birth) – as in 'Childe Waters' or 'Childe Roland' – lest they suppose his hero inappropriately juvenile. What he failed to explain was what they were to understand by the terms 'Pilgrimage' and 'Romaunt'. Pilgrims, after all, are by definition travelling to a specific and usually holy place, whether Canterbury, Jerusalem, Mecca, Walsingham, or Compostela. Harold is not. Like his creator, he goes at random where chance and whim may lead him, in a journey that has no destination or purpose (other than to shake off the boredom and 'satiety' that had overcome him at home) and can be indefinitely prolonged. (When, at the end of Canto IV, Byron announces that 'My pilgrim's shrine is won' (stanza 175), it is difficult to tell if that 'shrine' is supposed to be Rome, or the formless and inhuman sea.) 'Romaunt' is equally questionable as a description. Its prime appearance before, in English, had been *The Romaunt of the Rose*, adapted from the French *Roman de la rose*, and attributed for some time to Chaucer. Unlike it, however, or the romance more widely, *Childe Harold* has no plot, and very little concern with 'romantic' love. It is also remarkably uncertain about the status and function of its titular protagonist.

As early as stanza 16 of Canto II, Byron as narrator found himself asking 'But where is Harold? Shall I then forget / To urge the gloomy wanderer o'er the wave?' Where indeed. Such forgetfulness marks the poem throughout, increasing in the two subsequent cantos. Byron was always firm in his denial that Harold represented any living person – least of all himself. It was a somewhat disingenuous disavowal. Harold's relation to the narrator presents more of a problem. The ancestral abode from which Harold departs at the beginning of Canto I is transparently Byron's own Newstead Abbey, and his hero's weariness with the riot and disorder he had introduced there is Byron's own. Harold both was and was not Byron, and his creator never seems quite sure what to do with him, any more than he was of the archaic vocabulary he initially essayed, as appropriate to his Spenserian stanzas. ('Whilome in Albion's isle there dwelt a youth, / Who ne in virtue's ways did take delight', stanza 2.) The vocabulary he quickly abandoned. Harold presented more of a problem, one to be triumphantly resolved in Byron's other long poem, *Don Juan*.

Back in England, Byron not only published Cantos I and II and made three speeches in the House of Lords (against the death penalty for workers in Nottinghamshire rioting against the introduction of new industrial machinery, in favour of Catholic emancipation, and in defence of a political reformer) but embroiled himself in a notorious series of affairs: with Lady Caroline Lamb and others, including his own half-sister Augusta, and concluding with his disastrous marriage to the heiress Annabella Milbanke in January 1815. Meanwhile, he was rapidly turning out the first six of his Tales – *The Giaour*, *The Bride of Abydos*, *The Corsair*, *Lara*, *The Siege of Corinth*, and *Parisina*. T. S. Eliot, while admiring the narrative skill of some of them, thought their view of life 'absurd'. Eliot, however, had not had Byron's experiences in the east, or after his return to England, and those experiences to a large extent inform these poems.

The Giaour, for instance, the first of the Turkish Tales, is really a kind of exorcism: Byron's way of confronting something that had actually happened to him on his travels, and needed somehow to be laid to rest. In this 'fragment', as Byron called it, five very different narrators tell the story of a Venetian (not a Greek, as Eliot thought) foreigner who has had a clandestine affair with Leila, a prized inmate of the Turkish Hassan's seraglio. Her infidelity discovered, Hassan has her sewn into a sack and dropped into the depths of the sea. The Giaour (the word means 'infidel') then avenges her by killing Hassan, and ends up as a penitent in a Christian monastery. A surviving letter from Lord Sligo, Byron's companion in Athens for a time, taken together with things Byron later said to Thomas Medwin and others, make it clear that Byron had himself rescued a girl in similar circumstances from a party of Turks about to execute her in this way, and seen her out of Athens to a safe asylum in Thebes. He never liked to discuss the episode (in a journal entry of his own on 5 December 1813 he said merely that his feelings at the time were impossible to describe and it was 'icy' even to recollect them), but he obviously had known Leila's original and in all likelihood had himself been her illicit lover. *The Giaour*, in which the foreigner does not happen to be on the beach at the crucial moment, and the girl is brutally drowned, was for him a way of realizing and coming to terms with a tragedy that almost happened, and with the guilt he would have incurred.

A similar impulse was responsible for *The Bride of Abydos*, Byron's second 'Turkish Tale'. It was written, as he confided to his journal (16 November 1813), 'in four nights to distract my dreams from **. Were it not thus, it had never been composed; and had I not done something at that time I must have gone mad.' The cautious asterisks, like many others in his journals at this time, clearly refer to his half-sister Augusta and their guilty summer affair. *The Bride of Abydos* focuses on the incestuous love of Selim and Zuleika, a love that ends tragically, despite their discovery that they are not siblings after all, merely first cousins. The poem, partly it may be because of the rapidity of its composition, is less impressive than *The Giaour*. Certainly its narrative is handled with less originality and skill. That would also be true of *Parisina* (1816), set in Ferrara, in which the incest theme returns, again tragically, but now involving a wife and her husband's bastard son. As for *The Corsair* (one of Byron's greatest publishing successes) and *The Siege of Corinth*, they too evoke Greece under Ottoman rule, *The Corsair* being remarkable (apart from its compelling narrative) for Byron's refusal to tell his readers what finally became either of the Corsair himself or of Gulnare, the woman who saved his life by murdering her Turkish master. Another kind of reticence marks *Lara*, a tale Byron insisted might as well be set on the moon, which remains teasingly enigmatic throughout as to its characters' motives and the individual pasts which have engendered them. The early Tales come across now as a very mixed bag: good, bad, and indifferent. They were largely responsible, however, for that cult of the Byronic hero – a man gloomy and mysterious, subject to passionate impulses and extremes – which in Byron's lifetime and beyond spread not only in England but throughout Europe.

Childe Harold Cantos III and IV

On 17 November 1813 Byron confessed to his journal that he had recently begun both a comedy and a novel, but had burnt them because they 'ran into *reality*'. 'In rhyme', he felt, 'I can keep more away from facts.' The comedy, presumably in prose, Byron never again essayed, nor the novel – although in the case of the latter, it is possible, strangely enough, to deduce what it might have been like by reading the extraordinary sequence of letters Byron sent to his friend and confidante Lady Melbourne detailing the day-by-day progress of his (ultimately abortive) affair with Lady Frances Wedderburn Webster, in whose husband's country house he was staying for much of the time between 21 September and the end of October 1813. These letters, sent off as soon as written, never corrected or shaped as a whole, read nevertheless like part of an epistolary novel such as Laclos's *Les liaisons dangereuses*. Byron was, of course, a brilliant letter writer, one of the best in the English language, but the complex position this particular sequence occupies between reality and art is very special.

Byron's marriage to Annabella Milbanke foundered in just over a year. She left his house and returned to her parents, taking their infant daughter

Ada with her, and later explained that she believed her husband was going mad. Byron was forced to agree to a legal separation. The resulting scandal – incorporating rumours about his relationship with Augusta – was considerable, and in April Byron left England for the continent, never to return. He would not see his wife or their child again. On board the ship taking him to Ostend, he embarked on *Childe Harold* Canto III, writing its opening five stanzas at sea. He continued the poem after arriving in Belgium, where he visited the field of Waterloo, and then while proceeding up the Rhine to Switzerland, where he settled for a time on the shores of Lake Leman, and made the acquaintance of Shelley, who soon became an important influence and friend.

It is with *Childe Harold* Cantos III and IV that Byron's real power and originality as a poet first declare themselves. Significantly, by stanza 6 of the continuation he already felt impelled to explain – to readers and also to himself – why he needed to write:

> 'Tis to create, and in creating live
> A being more intense, that we endow
> With form our fancy, gaining as we give
> The life we image, even as I do now.

He needed, in effect, to heighten the experiences he himself had, to give them a shapeliness and order they would otherwise not possess. (G. Wilson Knight was percipient when he observed that Byron was a man always trying to find in life the qualities of great art.[6]) Less persuasive (and less honest) are the concluding lines of this stanza – 'What am I? Nothing, but not so art thou, / Soul of my thought with whom I traverse earth' – in which Byron tried to claim for his eponymous hero a centrality and distinction from himself that once again would not be realized. After stanza 18, Harold disappears, making a perfunctory re-appearance in stanzas 52–5, and then (less than halfway through the canto) vanishing altogether. In his Preface to Canto IV, in which Harold's appearances are even less frequent, Byron admitted that here 'there will be found less of the pilgrim than in any of the preceding, and that little slightly, if at all, separated from the author speaking in his own person'. He went on to explain, rather less persuasively, that this was because, despite all his efforts, readers had stubbornly refused to distinguish between the two.

It was said at the time that Byron was probably the only man who could have stood on the field of Waterloo so soon after the battle and made his presence there, and what he wrote about the place, significant. An indication of his celebrity now both in Europe and England, it was also a testimony to the freshness and impact of his writing. His account of the ball in Brussels the night before the battle ('There was a sound of revelry by night') became an anthology piece. At least as striking, however, was his complex response to the place itself and what had happened there. T. S. Eliot may not have admired the line 'How that red rain hath made the harvest grow!' (stanza 17), but, chilling in itself, it is integral to Byron's experience of Waterloo, where the plough had now been over the site, the grain sown and, fertilized by so much human blood drenching the earth, already flourishing in the spring sun. Apart from his young cousin Major Howard, who died at Waterloo on an identifiable spot, Byron refuses to distinguish between the opponents: 'Rider and horse – friend, foe – in one red burial blent' (stanza 28). Byron was later to caricature Wellington as 'Villainton'. Here, he chose simply to ignore him, and the English victory itself – except in so far as it was bound up with the deplorable Congress of Vienna and its restoration of the Bourbon monarchy. For Napoleon, by contrast, then wearing out his days on St Helena, he had more time. Byron, while always fascinated by Napoleon, was never uncritical. Here, as in his 1814 'Ode to Napoleon Buonaparte' and later poems, he treats him as a deeply flawed and self-divided tragic hero: a liberator turned tyrant, who then ignominiously accepted imprisonment and did not take his own life, as Byron thought he should have done.

From Waterloo, Byron journeyed up the Rhine, observing as he went the many decaying feudal fortresses perched high above the river, once the strongholds of warring chiefs, but now 'all tenantless, save to the crannying wind' (stanza 47). It is the Rhine itself that he celebrates here, not its human history, in verse that looks forward to what he would shortly be writing about the Swiss Alps. That landscape Byron found overwhelming – responding to it especially when convulsed by storms – in ways that owed little to Wordsworth or to Shelley, his neighbour on the shores of Lake Leman. With Shelley, Byron sailed around the lake and visited places associated with Voltaire, Gibbon, and Rousseau: 'gigantic minds', as he thought, whose 'daring doubts' were so titanic as to assail Heaven itself (stanza 105). He also visited (twice) the castle/prison of Chillon, and was moved by what he saw there to write *The Prisoner of Chillon*, yet another verse tale in octosyllabic couplets, but significantly different from its predecessors – not least because it is an unbroken monologue throughout, and because Bonivard, the man who tells this story of persecution, confinement, and pain, was an historical figure, unjustly imprisoned.

Switzerland and its mountains also produced *Manfred*, the first of Byron's completed plays, and one of the most mysterious. Full of deliberate lacunae and reticences – things intimated but not directly said – it worries again at the theme of brother-and-sister incest, but now in a Faustian context (although

Byron strenuously denied any influence either from Marlowe or from Goethe). Like all of Byron's plays – with the partial exception of *Werner*, begun while he was still in England and on the Drury Lane Theatre Committee, but completed much later – it was not intended for the stage: a fact which has not (any more than it has with the others) prevented the occasional theatrical realization. Switzerland during the 'lost summer' of 1816, when a huge volcanic explosion on the other side of the world temporarily dimmed the sun across Europe, and there was snow in New England during August, also produced that chillingly prophetic poem 'Darkness', about a cosmic catastrophe responsible for the destruction of all life on planet Earth.

Byron's thoughts, however, even before he reached the end of Canto III of *Childe Harold*, were already turning to Italy, where he journeyed next, and where he would remain – principally in Venice, and then in Ravenna, Pisa, and finally Genoa – until August 1823, when he departed for Greece. It was in Italy, that 'paradise of exiles', as Shelley called it in 'Julian and Maddalo', that Byron wrote his greatest poems and plays: Canto IV of *Childe Harold*, the neo-classical tragedies *Marino Faliero*, *The Two Foscari*, and *Sardanapalus*, his incendiary biblical play *Cain*, the unfinished but superb *The Deformed Transformed*, and, most important of all, the *ottava rima* poems: *Beppo*, *The Vision of Judgement*, and his masterpiece, the sadly uncompleted *Don Juan*.

These works seem to us now Byron's finest achievement. They met, however, with a mixed and often openly hostile reaction from contemporaries. In *Don Juan* he would claim ruefully that although he had once been reckoned 'the grand Napoleon of the realms of rhyme' (Canto XI, stanza 55), what he published now looked more like Napoleon's retreat from Moscow (*Juan*) or his defeats at Leipzig (*Marino Faliero*) and Waterloo (*Cain*). Byron was even obliged to break with his long-time publisher John Murray in these later years, turning instead to the radical John Hunt. It is a measure of the importance poetry now had for him, despite his early disclaimers, that he should have persisted in writing works that not only the general public but (after the death of Shelley) his closest associates and friends deplored. His last mistress, the Countess Guiccioli, even managed to extract a promise that he would not continue *Don Juan* beyond Canto V, but the promise was broken after little more than a year. He had come to recognize and accept not only the importance of poetry for himself but the idea, as he would state in Canto III of *Don Juan*, that

> words are things, and a small drop of ink
> Falling like dew, upon a thought, produces
> That which makes thousands – perhaps millions – think.
>
> (stanza 88)

Italy – and more especially Venice, the city with which Canto IV begins, and Rome, where it ends – produced some of Byron's most passionate poetry. He responded immediately to the Italian landscape, and to its language, 'that soft bastard Latin', as he would describe it in *Beppo* (stanza 45). It was a language he took pains to learn (unlike French and German) until he could speak and write it fluently. To the country's painting and sculpture he paid only cursory attention as he journeyed south in 1817, in the company of his friend John Cam Hobhouse, much more to its architecture, in particular St Peter's and the Colosseum. Rome – 'my country! city of the soul!', as he called it in Canto IV (stanza 78) – affected him in particular, but everywhere he was drawn to Italy's historical past and to places associated both with her own great poets – Dante, Petrarch, Tasso, Boiardo, Ariosto, Pulci, and Boccaccio – and with those foreigners like himself who had celebrated this land across many centuries. Venice was the direct inspiration for two of Byron's neo-classical political plays, *Marino Faliero* and *The Two Foscari*. Arnold, the protagonist of *The Deformed Transformed*, gravitates to Rome as surely as Byron had himself. It was, however, in *Beppo*, not only in *Childe Harold* Canto IV, that his love-affair with Italy – even an Italy suffering now under an Austrian rule that Byron deplored – declared itself fully.

Beppo, The Vision of Judgement, and *Don Juan*

Beppo, the first of Byron's *ottava rima* poems, is really less of a tale (despite a subtitle announcing it as one) than an account of Byron's love-affair with Italy in general and Venice in particular. Beppo himself speaks only eleven words in all, and those near the end, when he returns in Turkish dress to the city, during its Carnival, after years of mysterious absence abroad, and reclaims Laura from her long-established lover the Count: '"Sir", quoth the Turk, "'tis no mistake at all, / That Lady is *my Wife*"' (stanzas 88–9). Laura herself has rather more to say during this momentous encounter, but basically the one voice that sounds throughout the 792 lines of the poem is that of Byron himself – a Byron cheerfully willing to concede in the course of his seemingly endless digressions that 'this story keeps on slipping through my fingers' (stanza 63).

Ottava rima, a verse-form that Byron told Thomas Moore, in a letter of 1 September 1821, was as 'old as the hills in Italy', requires eight decasyllabic lines rhyming *abababcc*. It is far easier to write in Italian than in English. (W. H. Auden, no mean versifier, confessed in his 'Letter to Lord Byron' that although *ottava rima* would have been 'the proper instrument on which to pay / My compliments', he had not attempted it, because 'I should come a cropper; / Rhyme-royal's difficult enough to play' (Part I, stanza 22).) *Ottava rima* requires considerable ingenuity in finding three *a* and three interlocking *b* rhymes in each stanza, a task made harder by the fact that Italian possesses more rhyme-words than English and is also as strongly biased towards feminine endings as English is towards masculine ones. Two-syllable rhymes in Italian are the norm, and even three-syllable ones rarely seem unusual or forced. In English, by contrast, the latter tend to come across as comic, something Byron exploited to the full, above all in *Don Juan*, where 'Laureate', for instance, is made to rhyme with 'Tory at' in the opening lines of the Dedication to Southey, and 'intellectual' later finds itself paired outrageously with 'hen-peck'd you all' (Canto I, stanza 22).

There had been scattered English experiments with *ottava rima* (by Wyatt, Spenser, and Drayton) before Byron took it up. His immediate inspiration, however, was *Whistlecraft*, a poem by John Hookham Frere (itself an adaptation of the *Morgante Maggiore* by the fifteenth-century Italian poet Pulci), a copy of which reached Byron in Venice in 1817. This poetic form, both demanding and relaxed, encouraging digression, appealed to him at once. *Beppo*, his original experiment with it, led inevitably to *Don Juan* – the greatest of his poems – left unfinished in its fragmentary seventeenth canto when the combination of marsh fever and a pair of incompetent doctors killed off Byron and his Spanish hero together in the middle of breakfast at the poem's Norman Abbey.

Byron began *Don Juan* in Venice on 3 July 1818. He took it lightly at first – a poem meant, as he confided to his journal on 19 September 1819, merely 'to be a little quietly facetious upon everything'. As he went on writing it, however, and as it increasingly became the subject of opprobrium from friends, associates, and the reading public, he came to regard it stubbornly as not only a serious work, beneath all the fun, but a fundamentally moral one: a satire on the current abuses of society. Its progress was constantly interrupted, even before his final journey to Greece: by an involvement with Italian politics, by personal calamities, and also by the composition during this period of immense poetic fertility of his last two verse tales, almost all the plays, and in 1821 by that stunning satire *The Vision of Judgement*, the third of his important *ottava rima* poems.

Southey's *A Vision of Judgement*, a copy of which reached Byron in Ravenna shortly after its publication, was calculated to sting Byron into a response, not only because of Southey's barely concealed attack on *Don Juan* in its Preface, but because the recently deceased George III, whose triumphal reception into heaven the Laureate's poem celebrates, in lumbering hexameters, had in truth (especially in his foreign policies) been a disastrous king. Byron's replacement of Southey's indefinite article 'A' with 'The' in his own title is indicative of the subtlety and restraint of his own approach.

Neither Southey nor George III is despatched to hell as a result of the altercation at heaven's gate over the latter's suitability for admission. Southey and his hexameters merely end up dumped together into his own lake, Derwentwater, by celestial beings exasperated by his verses, while the king slips gratefully and almost unnoticed into paradise. Even those immemorial antagonists St Michael and Sathan (the latter compared at one point to 'an old Castilian / Poor noble' (stanza 36) – certainly a far cry from the horned and tailed grotesque Byron had presented some eight years earlier in 'The Devil's Drive') greet each other with courtesy: 'between his Darkness and his Brightness / There passed a mutual glance of great politeness' (stanza 35). The poem is good-tempered throughout, and its satire all the more telling for that reason.

As for *Don Juan*, despite the manifold interruptions in its progress between 1818 and 1824, and its piece-by-piece publication, it reads now as a remarkably consistent and sure-footed long poem. Its one false move Byron corrected almost at once. He began by employing a fictional narrator, in the form of that bumbling Spanish gentleman who tries to interfere, 'and with the best / Intentions' in the troubled marital affairs of Don Jose and Donna Inez, and has 'a pail of housemaid's water' thrown over him down the stairs by little Juan as thanks for his pains (stanza 24). The presence of this narrator, however, quickly proved constricting, and Byron jettisoned him after stanza 82 of Canto I. Thereafter, the narrator of this 'versified Aurora Borealis' of a poem, 'Which flashes o'er a waste and icy clime' (Canto VII, stanza 2), would be unequivocally Byron himself, speaking in his own person.

In abandoning the fictional narrator, Byron also did what he had failed to do for much of *Childe Harold*: establish the poem's eponymous hero, the Juan who sets out from Spain, is shipwrecked into love on a Greek island, sold into slavery in Constantinople, where he has to fend off the amorous advances of the Sultan's wife, participates in the siege of Ismail, becomes an object of the Empress Catherine's desire in Russia, and then her ambassador to England, as a fictional character impossible to confuse with his creator. Indeed, they are strikingly unlike. Where Juan is uncomplicated, rarely reflecting or even speaking in the course of his many adventures, Byron, the mercurial master of many moods, both talks and reflects constantly, imposing his own complex personality upon the poem as a whole, but not upon the protagonist whose adventures he chronicles – a Don Juan who, surprisingly, is far less the predatory seducer of women than their prey.

Apart from Russia, where he had never been, Byron was acquainted with all the various countries in which Juan finds himself. He debated teasingly at one point whether to make his hero end traditionally in hell, or in an unhappy marriage, claiming not to know which was worse, or alternatively, to have him guillotined in France during the Terror. In the event Juan's story breaks off in the Regency England of Byron's own years of fame, where the young Spaniard finds himself torn at a country house party between the attractions of his bored hostess Lady Adeline, those of the virginal Catholic heiress Aurora Raby, and the unabashed sexual rapacity of the Duchess of Fitz-Fulke. These English cantos (X–XVII) are set off from their predecessors by detailed social observation, almost novelistic at times, and by a combination of nostalgia for a world Byron had known well and would never see again and mockery of it. They are sometimes singled out as the finest section of the poem. *Don Juan* asks, however, to be read as a whole, in all its complexity and varying moods, from its beginning in Seville through the idyll with Haidee in the Cyclades to the party at Norman Abbey. Readers who do so can comprehend Byron's extraordinary mind and poetic talents more fully, in all their range and depth, than is possible anywhere else.

NOTES

1 *Lord Byron: The Complete Poetical Works*, eds Jerome J. McGann and Barry Weller, 7 vols (Oxford: Clarendon Press, 1980–93). All quotations from Byron's poems refer to this edition and are identified in the text by stanza or line number. Readers may also like to consult the ongoing edition of the poems prepared by Peter Cochran and available online, through the International Byron Society.
2 See the footnote to the poem in McGann's edition, I, p. 261.
3 Coleridge, *Biographia Literaria* (1817), ch. 13; eds James Engell and W. J. Bate, 2 vols (Princeton: Princeton University Press, 1983).
4 *Byron's Letters and Journals*, ed. Leslie A. Marchand, 13 vols (London: John Murray, 1973–94). All quotations refer to this edition and are identified in the text by the date of the letter or journal entry.
5 See Thomas Moore, *Letters and Journals of Lord Byron with Notices of his Life* (London: John Murray, 1830), I, pp. 346–7.
6 G. Wilson Knight, *Lord Byron: Christian Virtues* (London: Oxford University Press, 1953), p. 176.

SELECTED FURTHER READING

Editions

Lord Byron: The Complete Poetical Works, eds J. McGann and Barry Weller, 7 vols, Oxford, Clarendon Press, 1980–93

Byron's Letters and Journals, ed. Leslie A. Marchand, 13 vols, London, John Murray, 1973–94

Byron: The Complete Miscellaneous Prose, ed. Andrew Nicholson, Oxford, Clarendon Press, 1991

The Letters of John Murray to Lord Byron, ed. Andrew Nicholson, Liverpool, Liverpool University Press, 2007

Secondary works

Auden, W. H., 'Letter to Lord Byron', in *The English Auden: Poems, Essays and Dramatic Writings*, ed. Edward Mendelson, London, Faber and Faber, 1977, pp. 1027–39

Barton, Anne, *Byron: Don Juan*, Cambridge, Cambridge University Press, 1992; paperback edn 2008

Bone, Drummond (ed.), *The Cambridge Companion to Byron*, Cambridge, Cambridge University Press, 2004

Graham, Peter W., *Don Juan and Regency England*, Charlottesville, University Press of Virginia 1990

Guiccioli, Teresa, *Lord Byron's Life in Italy*, trans. Michael Rees, ed. Peter Cochran, Cranbury, NJ, Associated University Presses, 2005

Joseph, M. K., *Byron the Poet*, London, Gollancz, 1964

Lovell, E. J. (ed.), *His Very Self and Voice: Collected Conversations of Lord Byron*, New York, Macmillan, 1954

Marchand, Leslie A., *Byron: A Biography*, 3 vols, New York, Knopf, 1957

Byron: A Portrait, New York, Knopf, 1970

McGann, J., *Fiery Dust: Byron's Poetic Development*, Chicago, University of Chcago Press, 1968

Rutherford, Andrew (ed.), *Byron: Augustan and Romantic*, Basingstoke, Macmillan, 1990

Stabler, Jane, *Byron, Poetics and History*, Cambridge, Cambridge University Press, 2002

18

JAMES CHANDLER

Percy Bysshe Shelley

Percy Bysshe Shelley was born on 4 August 1792, a month and a half before the proclamation of the First French Republic and three years to the day after the momentous Declaration of the Rights of Man and Citizen by the National Assembly in revolutionary Paris. Since Shelley was the scion of an aristocratic family with whose values he was ever at odds, this latter event has special resonance in his life and work. Unlike the 1776 American Declaration of Independence, with which it is often compared, the 1789 French Declaration involved an abjuration of special political prerogatives on the part of the very persons who held them: the French nobility. Coming of age in England in the post-Revolution period, Shelley, too, attempted very explicitly to live a life of aristocratic self-renunciation, and this intention shaped much of his writing. It is true that if we look at Shelley from the point of view of those around him, allies and enemies alike, we discover he was not entirely successful in this effort. Lord Byron's intimate friendship with him was almost certainly predicated on the recognition that, like himself, Shelley was well-born. Conversely, William Hazlitt, one of the earliest and harshest of Shelley's critics, seems to have concluded that, whatever Shelley's protests to the contrary, he was ultimately a part of England's aristocratic order. Those protests began early, however, and they lasted Shelley's brief lifetime.

In 1811, before his twentieth birthday, Shelley would be expelled from Oxford for producing a pamphlet entitled *The Necessity of Atheism*. He would later write to his free-thinking friend Elizabeth Hitchener: 'I am no aristocrat, no "crat" at all, but vehemently long for the time when men may dare to live in accordance with Nature and Reason – in consequence, with Virtue, to which I firmly believe that Religion and its establishments, Polity and its establishments, are the formidable though destructible barriers.'[1] Shelley was an 'anti-establishment' writer long before the term had become a cliché, and his profound scepticism towards the dominant institutions of his time is everywhere evident in his thought and work. In Shelley's view of history, institutions inevitably lag behind the affective development of the society they structure. It is important to remain vigilant in recognizing this gap, ready at any given juncture to develop its productive possibilities. As he put it in his quasi-utilitarian inquiry of 1819, *A Philosophical View of Reform*, social progress is driven by 'a desire of change arising from the profound sentiment of the exceeding inefficiency of the existing institutions to provide for the physical and intellectual happiness of the people' (VII, p. 20). Church and state, law and finance, the rules governing the disposition of property and the arrangements of marriage – Shelley systematically disrespected them all, and he encouraged others to follow in this high-minded campaign.

Shelley's commitment to bringing down the barriers of Religion and Polity can fairly be said to have cost him a great deal, most obviously in respect of personal wealth. Instead of enjoying the fruits of his considerable hereditary expectations, he lived much of his life in difficult financial straits, often in serious debt, and his debts caused hardships for his dependents as well. An 1818 poem, 'Stanzas Written in Dejection Near Naples', records a moment of self-consciously staged self-indulgence in which the poet talks about the many ways in which his life can be found wanting:

> Alas! I have nor hope nor health,
> Nor peace within nor calm around,
> Nor that content surpassing wealth
> The sage in meditation found,
> And walked with inward glory crowned –
> Nor fame, nor power, nor love, nor leisure.
> Others I see whom these surround –
> Smiling they live, and call life pleasure;
> To me that cup has been dealt in another measure.
>
> (lines 19–27)[2]

The record, even beyond the poetic record, suggests that Shelley lived much of the time under the shadow of severe anxiety and dejection. His effect on the lives of others, moreover, especially those to whom he was most attached, was often nothing short of disastrous. Shelley travelled much – in Britain, Ireland, France, Switzerland, Italy – and everywhere he left a trail of personal destruction and despondency, including the deaths of more than one child and the suicide of his first wife, Harriet Westbrook. Though his second wife, Mary Wollstonecraft Godwin Shelley, remained loyal to his memory and became a faithful editor of his work, the strains in their marriage were severe, and differently registered in *Frankenstein* and his 'Epipsychidion', a late love-poem to another woman. Shelley was inordinately prone to risk, and in late 1818, just before composing the 'Dejection' stanzas, his recklessness about enforcing an arduous travel itinerary on his family probably contributed to the death of his newly born daughter Clara. The untimeliness of his own death, in a boating accident in 1822, would almost certainly have been avoided with greater prudence.

All that said, Shelley was also one of the most intelligent and intellectually accomplished of the English poets, and one of the finest. Like Milton, who lived twice as long (and then some), Shelley seems to have committed himself to knowing all there was to be known in his time. He read omnivorously in many fields (philosophy, history, political economy, classics, mythology, and the sciences) and many languages (Greek, Latin, French, Italian, Spanish). He translated Spinoza and Calderón. His translation of Plato's *Symposium* was a standard one until the twentieth century. As to the quality of his poetry, we have the unlikely testimonial of William Wordsworth, a stern critic at the best of times and a writer quite explicitly identified later in Shelley's published work as a poet of the establishment. Wordsworth is supposed to have called Shelley 'one of the best artists of us all: I mean in workmanship of style'.[3] Moreover, Shelley's accomplishment 'in workmanship of style' did not depend on narrowing his subjects, or on limiting the variety of his verse repertoire, or yet on staying strictly within the rules of the genres in which he wrote. He wrote in an enormous variety of poetic kinds, and experimented daringly within them. The result of all this learning, talent, and reckless abandon was a poetic legacy striking at once for its brilliance and for its contradictions. For example, Shelley would become, just after his death, the acknowledged laureate of the mid-nineteenth-century British labour movement known as Chartism, and yet would also eventually be recognized as the avatar of a notion of poetic refinement so highly subtilized as to vanish, for some readers, into the airy thinness of what he called 'the intense inane'.

As with many great poets of his age, Shelley's early ambition did not point to a career in writing verse. His early student activities and interests seemed rather to argue for a vocation in science – or natural philosophy, as it was then called. At Eton College and later at Oxford, Shelley was exposed to influential teachers of chemistry, a domain of study that clearly fascinated him. Much has been written about Shelley's early involvements in the natural sciences. These involvements include a calamitous experiment that he conducted at Oxford when, in an effort to cure his sister's chilblains, he caused an explosion in his rooms in University College. It is not clear that Alfred North Whitehead was entirely on firm ground when he maintained, in *Science and the Modern World*, that if Shelley had continued with his scientific studies he would have become 'a Newton among Chemists'.[4] There is no question, however, but that Shelley's interest in the scientific issues of his time was keen. And it is likewise clear that some of the principles of modern scientific method, as it had developed over the course of the previous century and a half, profoundly influenced his later work.

Shelley ranked the age of the scientific revolution as the pivot in the history of western thought, as he would later explain in *A Philosophical View of Reform*. The very images of Shelley's major poetry can often be traced to his reading in the literature of science, especially (and appropriately) in his epic drama about the thief of fire/knowledge, *Prometheus Unbound* (1820). Some of its visionary sequences were in effect versified passages from contemporary scientific accounts of such natural phenomena as the structure of the molecule and the will-o'-the-wisp. Both Shelley and his wife Mary also interested themselves in the vitalist controversies of his day, such as debates about the origin of life that informed the composition of *Frankenstein, or The Modern Prometheus* (1818). It is important to recall that the question on which his final poem ('The Triumph of Life') is broken off – 'Then, what is Life?' – is strongly inflected with contemporary developments in the new field of biology.

For some time after his departure from Oxford, it was by no means obvious that Shelley was bound to be a poet, certainly not the kind of poet he turned out to be. In 1812, he wrote the first of many political pamphlets, *A Letter to Lord Ellenborough*, in defence of Daniel Isaac Eaton, one of many reform-minded booksellers to suffer prosecution in Regency England. That same year Shelley also wrote two pamphlets advocating Catholic emancipation in Ireland, and travelled to Dublin to have them distributed by his servant, Dan Healy, who was arrested and served six months in jail. After Dublin, Shelley lived briefly in north Wales, where he became involved with a project to build a dyke to protect a model village built on land reclaimed from the marshes of the Glaslyn River estuary. Indeed, when the young Shelley did turn from political activism and pamphleteering to writing what we now call 'imaginative literature', he was as likely to produce some pages of prose fiction as poetry. By 1811, he had already published two gothic novels, *Zastrozzi* and *St. Irvyne*, and in these early years he also left unfinished a political romance about the French Revolution.

Nonetheless, Shelley's was an age in which great talents were drawn from other pursuits to the field of poetry. There was a strong sense in the air, already established by the generation of poets who preceded Shelley, that poetry did make something happen. It was Shelley himself, of course, who would write a few years later that poets were the 'unacknowledged legislators of the world'. By 1812, he had completed his first major poem, *Queen Mab*. Coming so early in so brief and rapid an intellectual maturation, *Queen Mab* holds a curious place in the story of Shelley's poetry. It is a relentlessly didactic poem, a performance best placed in the tradition of poetry that is primarily intended to convey wisdom or information, such as Lucretius's *De Rerum Natura* and Erasmus Darwin's scientific verse of the 1790s. In just a few years, Shelley would not only move away from the didactic mode of *Queen Mab*. He would also come to refuse it on principle, indeed to insist that true poetry necessarily eschews didactic methods and presuppositions, whether taken from natural philosophy or from moral philosophy. Of the latter in particular, Shelley would write as follows in his 1821 *Defence of Poetry*:

> Ethical science arranges the elements which poetry has created, and propounds schemes and proposes examples of civil and domestic life: nor is it for want of admirable doctrines that men hate, and despise, and censure, and deceive, and subjugate one another. But Poetry acts in another and a diviner manner. It awakens and enlarges the mind by rendering it the receptacle of a thousand unapprehended combinations of thought. (p. 517)

Thus, the scientific imagery that later appears in *Prometheus Unbound* is worked into the aesthetic fabric of the play's millenarian vision. Unlike that of *Queen Mab*, it is fashioned in such a way as to become one of the 'elements which poetry has created'. Like most of Shelley's work *Queen Mab* was published in small print runs mostly for elite audiences, in this case for private distribution. But intellectual piracy was rampant among booksellers, and, from as early as 1821, *Queen Mab* circulated in illegal editions that gave it a disproportionate impact on British readership, especially among the Chartists.[5] So it happened, that, though he wrote it long before he arrived at his central aesthetic principles, *Queen Mab* ironically became the poem on which Shelley's nineteenth-century reputation was most decisively established.

About halfway between the time when *Queen Mab* was completed and the time it was pirated, Shelley had begun to find the distinctive voice and vitality of his mature poetry. They are clearly in evidence for the first time in *Alastor and Other Poems*, published in early 1816. Shelley was hurried forward on this rapid course of development, in part through an intense series of life experiences, some of them occasioned by his anti-establishment views, but also in part through a strenuous engagement with the writings and conversation of his contemporaries. In the *Defence of Poetry*, he would declare: 'we live among such philosophers and poets as surpass beyond comparison any who have appeared since the last national struggle for civil and religious liberty [i.e., in the seventeenth century]' (p. 535). Even before his joining Byron in Geneva in mid-1816, Shelley's life was extraordinarily eventful in both its intellectual encounters and its domestic éclats.

By the end of 1811, he had already met Robert Southey, about to become Poet Laureate, whom he judged an apostate to his early political principles. Through Southey he learned that the philosopher and novelist William Godwin, whom he admired greatly but had presumed dead, was still alive. Shelley then contrived to meet the great man (widower of Mary Wollstonecraft), and that encounter in turn led to his introduction to their daughter Mary, not yet sixteen years of age. Though Mary's parents finally married shortly before her mother died giving birth to her, they were also, in Shelley's sense, anti-establishment writers; Godwin had published anarchist arguments against promises and contracts of all sorts, and the marriage contract was one to which they had both entertained longstanding objections. Young Mary Wollstonecraft Godwin shared her parents' views in a way that brought her conception of romantic love into line with Shelley's own. In 1814, two years into his marriage with Harriet Westbrook, Shelley and Mary eloped to the continent. They returned there in 1816, accompanied by Mary's seventeen-year-old half-sister Claire Claremont, who was at this point already pregnant by Byron.

In addition to Southey, Godwin, and Mary Shelley, the years between the publications of *Queen Mab* and *Alastor* also brought Shelley into contact with other key figures. One was Thomas Love Peacock, who later published a thinly veiled and trenchantly humorous caricature of Shelley in the character of Scythrop Glowry, in *Nightmare Abbey*. It was Peacock's later essay on 'The Four Ages of Poetry' that prompted Shelley to rebuttal in *A Defence of Poetry*, one of a handful of truly magnificent pieces of literary criticism in the English language. Shelley also at this time began to follow the work of Leigh Hunt, who became John Keats's patron in 1816, and who would subsequently introduce those two young poets to one another. Hunt would later collaborate with Shelley and Byron on an ill-fated journal called the *Liberal*, and he would eventually write one of the most influential accounts of this generation of English poets just a few years after they all had perished: *Lord Byron and Some of His Contemporaries* (1828).

It was partly through the mediation of the Hunt circle that Shelley began to develop a more complicated sense of the relation between 'politics and poetics', to borrow the precocious title phrase of one of Hunt's early poems. Hunt's stock was high among politically conscious young poets like Shelley and Keats, for he too, like Daniel Isaac Eaton, had been imprisoned for what he published. Hunt's weekly newspaper the *Examiner* became a key organ in the campaign to promote the poetry of both Shelley and Keats. Shelley would publish 'Hymn to Intellectual Beauty' in these pages in 1816, and the famous sonnet 'Ozymandias' there in 1818. Hunt grew to be one of Shelley's most important correspondents during the Italian years, and the

Examiner also became a prime source of news from England. It was from the *Examiner* that Shelley learned about the Peterloo Massacre (16 August 1819) a few weeks after it took place. And it was to Hunt that Shelley sent some of his poetic responses to that event, including a complex allegorical poem in the form of a popular protest ballad, 'The Mask of Anarchy', and the scrambled sonnet 'England in 1819'.

One of the reasons that the question of poetry and politics surfaced in the way that it did in the years between the publication of *Queen Mab* and the publication of *Alastor* in early 1816 was that the Napoleonic Wars were winding down. Many writers could sense that the period that had opened so gloriously with the Declaration of the Rights of Man and Citizen in Paris in 1789 was coming to a more ambiguous kind of closure. The fate of the 1790s reform movement hung in the balance. In literary Britain, much attention centred on the poetic and political reputations of a group of poets who came to be thought of as a kind of school, the Lake Poets – Wordsworth, Coleridge, and Southey. Each had been a radical in the 1790s, but none remained so. It was Shelley's engagement with this group that most clearly defined his own poetic practice and his own solution to the problem of 'politics and poetics' as it was posed in his time. At stake was the relation between poetic genius and political good faith. What did it mean that such poets, giants all in the eyes of both Shelley and Keats, could have lost their way?

Around 1815, Wordsworth emerged as a particular key to this issue, in part because of his own ambitious bid to establish himself as the greatest English poet in decades, the Milton of his time. He made this bid with two major publications: *The Excursion* (1814) and the meticulously arranged, self-monumentalizing *Poems* of 1815, in two volumes. The ambition of these volumes was patent in their prefatory materials. *The Excursion*, in particular, announced itself as part of an epic work-in-progress, *The Recluse*, a politico-psychological epic for the post-revolutionary period. The reception of *The Excursion*, however, was not all that Wordsworth hoped. In the prestigious *Edinburgh Review*, Wordsworth's old nemesis Francis Jeffrey opened his review with deflationary terseness: 'This will never do.' Mary and Percy Shelley read the poem at about the same time, and their comment was even more laconic, and even more damning: 'He is a slave.'

But 'he' was also, undeniably, a genius, and Shelley would spend no small amount of his precious time over the next years sorting out this deep paradox. That long engagement led to the views summarized in *A Defence of Poetry*, but it began with *Alastor and Other Poems*, a volume in which Wordsworth and the Lake Poets, the triumphs of their poetic genius and their loss of political faith, became central topics. The most explicit of the poems engaging with the poetry and politics of Shelley's great predecessors is a sonnet entitled, simply, 'To Wordsworth':

> Poet of Nature, thou hast wept to know
> That things depart which never may return:
> Childhood and youth, friendship and love's first glow,
> Have fled like sweet dreams, leaving thee to mourn.
> These common woes I feel. One loss is mine
> Which thou too feel'st, yet I alone deplore.
> ...
> In honored poverty thy voice did weave
> Songs consecrate to truth and liberty, –
> Deserting these, thou leavest me to grieve,
> Thus having been, that thou shouldst cease to be.
> (lines 1–6, 11–14)

No reader familiar with Wordsworth's great lyrics, especially the 'Immortality Ode', could fail to register how Shelley frames his critique of the elder poet in terms taken from his own most characteristic themes: youth's lost passions and dreams compensated for by the sober, Stoic reflections of maturity.

This poem supplies keys for reading 'Alastor', the richer and more complicated narrative poem that lends its name to the title of the volume. This is the story of a promising young poet whose genius fatally turned inward, away from the world and from fellow human beings and towards himself, dissolving in an act of narcissistic quietism that is pointedly emblematized by way of reference to the narcissus flower and to the famous myth that stands behind it. The poem is studded with signature lines and phrases borrowed from the poetry of the Lake Poets, especially Wordsworth:

> It is a woe too 'deep for tears' when all
> Is reft at once, when some surpassing Spirit,
> Whose light adorned the world around it, leaves
> Those who remain behind, not sobs or groans,
> The passionate tumult of a clinging hope;
> But pale despair and cold tranquillity,
> Nature's vast frame, the web of human things,
> Birth and the grave, that are not as they were. (lines 713–20)

In drawing the 'Immortality Ode' to a close, Wordsworth wrote that he would find 'strength in what remains behind' long after the passions and hopes, the glory and the dream, of his younger days had fled. He wrote that the more sober, tranquil spirit of his later years – what he called 'the philosophic mind' – would enable him to discover 'thoughts that do often lie too deep for tears', even in the meanest flower that blows. Here as in the accompanying sonnet, Shelley suggests that, in capitulating to such sentiments, Wordsworth loses himself and is therefore likewise lost to Shelley. The crucial difference between them, however, is that Shelley feels the loss keenly, while Wordsworth has anaesthetized himself to it, thus compounding its implications.

Sharp as this criticism seems, however, it is strongly tempered by both the verse preamble and the prose preface that introduces the poet's story, for there the speaking 'I' of the poem not only expresses sympathy for the fate of the Wordsworthian Poet but markedly identifies with Wordsworth by emulating his characteristic diction and blank verse rhythms:

> I wait thy breath, Great Parent, that my strain
> May modulate with murmurs of the air,
> And motions of the forests and the sea,
> And voices of living beings, and woven hymns
> Of night and day, and the deep heart of man. (lines 45–9)

The 'I' here is the poem's narrator, the one who tells the story of the Wordsworthian Poet's moral and political collapse. Yet the style of the poem's preamble is so obviously an homage to the sublime meditation in 'Tintern Abbey' that the poem's eventual critique of Wordsworth stands revealed as immanent: that is, it is undertaken from a standpoint of thorough identification with its ostensible target.

This complex engagement with the legacy of Wordsworth and his contemporaries would set the terms for Shelley's developing sense of the relation of 'politics and poetics' over his remaining years. Soon after the publication of the *Alastor* volume, the Shelleys would travel to Geneva, where they would begin their vexed and productive friendship with Lord Byron. In the summer of 1816, though already very much of Byron's circle, Shelley would compose two more poems in the Lake Poets' idiom. One of these, 'Hymn to Intellectual Beauty', was yet another reworking of the terms of Wordsworth's 'Immortality Ode'. Here, the Platonism that Wordsworth merely flirts with in his Ode – see his famous note about Plato's myth of pre-existence – is given a deeply constitutive role by Shelley. The other poem, 'Mont Blanc', refashioned the sublime landscape vision of the Lake Poets – especially Coleridge's 'Hymn Before Sunrise in the Vale of Chamouni'. For Coleridge, the Alpine landscape is portrayed as an inherent hierarchy. Everything points upwards to heaven, to the powerful God of the Judaeo-Christian Bible, underwriter of political and social hierarchies. Shelley challenged this structure. On a visit to Mont Blanc not long before writing the poem, he had notoriously identified himself in Greek as 'Atheist' in the visitors' book at the viewing station. In his 'Mont Blanc', the sublime landscape is represented not as a sign of hierarchy but as an overture to a concert of mind and matter. Its sense of 'nature' is both inward and outward, a double-edged power mediated by poetry's 'subtler language'. Rightly imagined, this power need not oppress. Indeed, it could 'repeal large codes of fraud and woe'.

Shelley's last strenuous engagement with the poetry and politics of the Lake School came three years later, after he and Mary had moved briefly back to England and returned to settle again with Byron, now in Italy. Byron had by this point developed his neo-Popeian brand of poetic satire, and, in the Dedicatory Stanzas to *Don Juan* (1819), had made the Lake Poets the butt of many of his most telling jokes. In that same year, Shelley got word that Wordsworth planned to publish *Peter Bell*, a new 'lyrical ballad' two decades in the making, and that John Hamilton Reynolds, Keats's friend, had published a satire of it even before it appeared. Shelley then had the inspired idea of publishing his own version, *Peter Bell the Third*, a satiric representation of Wordsworth's own life-history in over 150 ballad stanzas divided into seven faux-allegorical parts: Death, The Devil, Hell, Sin, Grace, Damnation, Double Damnation. The poem is less simple than it might appear. On the one hand, it unmistakably parrots Byron's whimsical condemnations of Wordsworth's ponderous egotism:

> He was a mighty poet – and
> A subtle-souled Psychologist;
> All things he seemed to understand
> Of old or new – of sea or land –
> But his own mind – which was a mist. (p. 353)

On the other, it strongly intimates that Wordsworth's problems derive in part from just such unsympathetic responses as one finds typified in the Byronic critique – and by implication in Shelley's own participation in such a failure of generosity. Wordsworth may have become a kind of monster, as the poem suggests, but the cause of this is unclear. As with the creature created by Victor Frankenstein in Mary Shelley's novel of the year before (to which Shelley himself contributed), we cannot say to what degree no one sympathizes with him because he is a monster and to what degree he is a monster because no one sympathizes with him.

Shelley would propose a similarly complex argument in *Adonais*, the great elegy he wrote for Keats in 1821. There, at least for the purpose of framing his posthumous tribute, he seemed to accept the legend then circulating that Keats's death owed something to a critical attack on *Endymion* in the *Quarterly Review*, the legend that had led Byron himself to quip: 'Tis strange that life, that fiery particle, / Should let itself be snuffed out by an article.' Byron was generally contemptuous of Keats, and he and Shelley must have discussed Keats often, no doubt sometimes critically. In *Adonais*, Shelley depicts himself as one of those who, like Byron, passes before the bier of the dead poet with an uneasy sense of having contributed in some way to Keats's premature demise.

This complex strategy of self-implication even shapes the outcome of *Julian and Maddalo* (1818), Shelley's depiction of his conversations with Byron during their first months in Venice after Shelley's final trip to England. A narrative poem in heroic couplets, it is about a madman whom Julian (the poem's speaker) and Maddalo (the Byron figure) have invoked to test their respective philosophies of life: Julian's the more optimist-idealist, Maddalo's the more pessimist-sceptical. It falls into three parts: the philosophical dispute carried on by the two friends while riding on Lido Beach; their visit to the Madman's cell, where they listen to his rant; and finally a brief conclusion in which Julian reports that, after many years, he returned to Venice (only to find Maddalo away) and pressed Maddalo's now-grown daughter for details of the fate of the Madman, which he refuses to narrate: 'I urged and questioned still, she told me how / All happened – but the bold world shall not know' (lines 616–17). The effect of this conclusion is to leave the Madman's monologue suspended, much as Shelley's great admirer Robert Browning would learn to do in shaping his own dramatic monologues, and again to situate and circumscribe the poem's speaking 'I' – the transparently autobiographical figure of Julian.

In his work with shorter lyrics, one can see something of the same tendency – to install the (male) romantic ego at the centre of the poem but also to gain distance on it – but achieved by technical means appropriate to the brief space and greater intensity of tighter forms. One recurring technique involves delaying or displacing the appearance of the lyric's speaking 'I'. This strategy gains its leverage from what had become a convention of the Romantic lyric as Shelley inherited it, especially from the hands of Wordsworth and Coleridge: the immediate and naturalized use of the first-person singular pronoun to identify the poet-speaker. Thus, in Coleridge's so-called conversation poems, which set the template for a certain kind of lyric practice in the period, we find that the first-person lyric tends to appear in the poem's first sentences. Think of the opening of 'This Lime-Tree Bower My Prison' – 'Well, they are gone and here must I remain' – or that of 'Frost at Midnight':

> The inmates of my cottage all at rest
> Have left me to that solitude that suits
> Abstruser musings.

In 'Tintern Abbey', Wordsworth follows suit:

> Five years have passed, five summers with the length
> Of five long winters, and again I …

He does so again both in his famous lyric about the daffodils, 'I wandered lonely as a cloud', and in 'I travelled among unknown men'. In Shelley's 'Mont Blanc', by contrast, a poem that pointedly engages the Wordsworthian-Coleridgian nature lyric, the speaking 'I' is withheld until midway through the poem's second part, at line 35: 'And when I gaze on thee'. In 'Hymn to Intellectual Beauty', the speaking 'I' is withheld until the beginning of the poem's fifth stanza: 'While yet a boy I sought for ghosts' (line 49).

There is method in this madness, design in these deferrals and displacements. To see how, we can return to 'Stanzas Written in Dejection Near Naples', which employs the strategy of the delayed first-person pronoun. I cited stanza 3 above as evidence of Shelley's staged self-indulgence. Here are the poem's first two stanzas:

> The sun is warm, the sky is clear,
> The waves are dancing fast and bright,
> Blue isles and snowy mountains wear
> The purple noon's transparent might,
> The breath of the moist earth is light,
> Around its unexpanded buds;
> Like many a voice of one delight,
> The winds, the birds, the ocean floods,
> The City's voice itself, is soft like Solitude's.
>
> I see the Deep's untrampled floor
> With green and purple seaweeds strown;
> I see the waves upon the shore,
> Like light dissolved in star-showers, thrown:
> I sit upon the sands alone, –
> The lightning of the noontide ocean
> Is flashing round me, and a tone
> Arises from its measured motion,
> How sweet! did any heart now share in my emotion.
>
> (lines 1–18)

The poem's first stanza follows so insistently methodical a procedure that it warns us against taking its deferral of the 'I' too casually. It advances in a geometrical progression: two clauses per line, then one clause per line, then one clause for two lines. What comes next is one clause for four lines, but in a way that involves a syntactical ambiguity – the 'Like …' phrase in lines 7–8 – by which they might also be linked forward to line 9. The lines that introduce the ambiguity into the geometrical progression are also the ones that introduce 'voice' into the poem, lines where 'breath' becomes first the indefinite 'many a voice', then the more definite 'The City's voice itself'.

Voice is thus introduced as a theme in the poem before its utterance is identified with the first-person pronoun. However, this happens in a way that also seems to lead to that identification, right at the start of stanza 2. The poem's speaker no longer just describes 'the waves dancing fast and bright'. Instead, stanza 2 lists acts of perception by a speaking agent: 'I see' the floor of the ocean and 'the waves upon the shore'. The poet knows that, certainly by the Stoic conventions involved in stanza 3's reference to Marcus Aurelius, his complaints in stanzas 2–4 make him even less likely to attract the sympathy of others. Thus the final stanza pointedly returns to the contrast between the ego-less description of 'the day' in stanza 1 and the subsequent lamentation of the 'I' who belatedly enters the poem in stanza 2. Indeed, that final stanza turns on a complex comparison of how observers might respond comparatively to the passing of the poet and the passing of the beautiful day he has described:

Some might lament that I were cold,
As I, when this sweet day is gone
Which my lost heart, too soon grown old,
Insults with this untimely moan –
They might lament – for I am one
Whom men love not, and yet regret:
Unlike this day, which, when the Sun
Shall on its cloudless glory set,
Will linger though enjoyed, like joy in Memory yet.

(lines 37–45)

Typical of Shelley's occasional obscurity is the syntactic ambiguity, continued from stanza 4, around the repetition of 'yet': 'and yet regret', 'like joy in memory yet'. Indeed, this final stanza supplies an example of Shelley's syntax at its most elliptical and most difficult, the sort of passage that leads editors of Shelley's poems to supply explanatory footnotes. Line 38, for instance, elicits this explication in the standard edition of Shelley's poems: 'I.e. Some might mourn (or regret, line 42) my death, as I shall regret the passing of this sweet day.' The note is rightly judged and also accurate in its paraphrase. The larger point to be recognized, however, is that the poem ultimately draws an explicit comparison between the 'day' described in stanza 1 and the 'I' who appears in stanza 2 as the poem's speaking subject. The poem thus 'objectifies' this subject even as it invests a large measure of pathos in him.

We find a similar pattern to that of the 'Stanzas' in perhaps Shelley's most important single lyric, the virtuoso performance in Dantesque *terza rima* stanzas he called 'Ode to the West Wind'. Here again, before the identification of the poem's speaking voice with a first-person pronoun, we have a 'breath' that we are invited to imagine as 'inspiring' the poem itself. It happens in the famous opening lines:

> O wild West Wind, though breath of Autumn's being,
> Thou from whose unseen presence the leaves dead
> Are driven, like ghosts from an enchanter fleeing.

The breath is energetic and energizing here in a way that is not true of the light 'breath of the moist earth' in the 'Dejection' stanzas. In spite of the poem's driving velocity, however, the appearance of the speaking 'I' in this case is delayed even longer than in the 'Dejection' stanzas, indeed until the fourth of the poem's five parts:

> If I were a dead leaf thou mightest bear;
> If I were a swift cloud to fly with thee;
> A wave to pant beneath thy power, and share
>
> The impulse of thy strength, only less free
> Than thou, O uncontrollable ...
>
> ... I would ne'er have striven
>
> As thus with thee in prayer in my sore need.
> Oh, lift me as a wave, a leaf, a cloud!
> I fall upon the thorns of life! I bleed! (lines 43–7, 51–4)

As in the 'Dejection' stanzas, the speaking subject is compared to what the opening of the poem describes: in this case the power of the West Wind. And as in that earlier poem, the status of the speaker hovers between subject and object, a fact registered in the play with objective and subjective cases towards the end of the stanza: 'Oh, lift me ... ! I fall ... '.

The question of how the speaker is to be imagined in the larger frame of the poem is complicated by an extraordinary series of superimposed and interlocking patterns in the 'Ode'. It depends in part on Shelley's way of building the four colours of the autumn leaves – 'yellow, and black, and pale, and hectic red' – into a palimpsest of quartets. The four races of human beings are superimposed on the four humours of ancient medical theory: yellow bile, black bile, phlegm, and blood (each associated with a different personality trait). These quartets in turn are mapped onto the four ancient elements. The first stanza shows the effect of the wind on the land (earth), the second on the clouds (air), the third on the sea (water). We might expect 'fire' to appear in stanza 4, but it does not appear until stanza 5, with the command to the wind to 'Scatter, as from an unextinguished hearth / Ashes and sparks, my words among mankind!' Instead of fire in stanza 4 we have the introduction of the speaker, who in this case is the Promethean poet and bearer of fire. (Shelley had spent much of the year in which he composed the 'Ode' at work on *Prometheus Unbound*.[6])

Like so many other Shelley lyrics – 'To a Skylark', for example, with its shifting sequence of metaphors – the 'Ode' situates its autobiographical speaker in a larger scheme. It does so in the spirit of Shelley's enlightened commitment to systematic inquiry, but it also recasts the whole ensemble in a fresh act of imagination. In these complex gestures lies the key to Shelley's response to the poetic personae of the Lake Poets, and to seeing how Shelley would have us imagine the larger political implications of their poetry, of all poetry. In the extraordinary conclusion to *A Defence of Poetry*, Shelley observed that periods that produce great poetry, such as his own, are marked by 'an accumulation of the power of communicating and receiving intense and impassioned conceptions respecting man and nature' (p. 535). The apparently awkward impersonality of this formulation is deliberate, as quickly becomes clear: 'The persons in whom this power resides, may often, as far as regards many portions of their nature, have little apparent correspondence with that spirit of good of which they are the ministers.' They can indeed themselves be 'the most sincerely astonished at its manifestations'. For Shelley this power is both responsive to and responsible for the gap he had earlier described between the existing state of public institutions and their perceived adequacy to human needs. It is for this reason that he believed that the 'most unfailing herald, companion, and follower of the awakening of a great people to work a beneficial change in opinion or institution, is Poetry'. It is for this reason that he believed that 'Poets are the unacknowledged legislators of the World'.

NOTES

1 *The Complete Works of Percy Bysshe Shelley*, eds Roger Ingpen and Walter E. Peck, 10 vols (London: Ernest Benn, and New York, Charles Scribner's Sons, 1926–30), VIII, p.116. Subsequent references to this edition by volume and page number in the text.

2 *Shelley's Poetry and Prose*, eds Donald H. Reiman and Neil Fraistat, 2nd edn (New York: W. W. Norton, 2002). Subsequent references to Shelley's poetry by line number to this edition. References to *A Defence of Poetry* by page number to this edition.

3 Christopher Wordsworth, *Memoirs of William Wordsworth*, 2 vols (London: E. Moxon, 1851), II, p. 474.

4 A. N. Whitehead, *Science and the Modern World* (New York: Macmillan, 1925), p. 84.

5 William St Clair, *The Reading Nation in the Romantic Period* (Cambridge: Cambridge University Press, 2004), pp. 317–22.

6 In 'Ozymandias', the lyric 'I' appears at the very start of the poem: 'I met a traveller from an antique land', but significantly, this speaking 'I' is immediately displaced by another voice, which is sustained to the end of the poem.

SELECTED FURTHER READING

Editions

Shelley's Poetry and Prose, eds Donald H. Reiman and Neil Fraistat, 2nd edn, New York, W. W. Norton, 2002

Percy Bysshe Shelley, Letters, ed. Frederick L. Jones, 2 vols, Cambridge, MA, Harvard University Press, 1958

Shelley: Poetical Works, ed. Thomas Hutchinson, corr. G. M. Matthews, London, Oxford, and New York, Oxford University Press, 1970

The Complete Works of Percy Bysshe Shelley, eds Roger Ingpen and Walter E. Peck, 10 vols, London, Ernest Benn, and New York, Charles Scribner's Sons, 1926–30

Shelley and his Circle, 1773–1822, eds Kenneth Neill Cameron and Donald H. Reiman, 10 vols, Cambridge, MA, Harvard University Press, 1961–

The Poems of Shelley, eds Kelvin Everest and Geoffrey Matthews, 2 vols to date, Harlow, Longman/Pearson Education, 1989–

Secondary works

Butler, Marilyn, *Romantics, Rebels and Reactionaries*, Oxford, Oxford University Press, 1982

Cameron, Kenneth Neill, *The Young Shelley*, New York, Macmillan, 1950

Shelley: The Golden Years, Cambridge, MA, Harvard University Press, 1974

Carlson, Julie A., *England's First Family of Writers*, Baltimore, Johns Hopkins University Press, 2007

Chandler, James, *England in 1819*, Chicago, University of Chicago Press, 1998

Ferber, Michael, *The Poetry of Shelley*, New York, Penguin, 1993

Holmes, Richard, *Shelley: The Pursuit*, London, Weidenfeld and Nicolson, 1974

Keach, William, *Shelley's Style*, New York, Methuen, 1984

Leighton, Angela, *Shelley and the Sublime*, Cambridge, Cambridge University Press, 1984

O'Neill, Michael, *The Human Mind's Imaginings*, Oxford, Clarendon Press, 1989

St Clair, William, *The Godwins and the Shelleys*, London, Faber and Faber, 1989

Tomalin, Claire, *Shelley and His World*, Harmondsworth, Penguin, 1992

Wasserman, Earl, *Shelley: A Critical Reading*, Baltimore, Johns Hopkins University Press, 1971

19

SUSAN J. WOLFSON

John Keats

'I think I shall be among the English poets after my death', wrote this English poet, 14 October 1818, just shy of his twenty-third birthday.[1] John Keats was not so much tendering a modest boast as attending to wounding reviews of his debut volume, *Poems* (1817), and a second bid, the longest poem he would ever write, *Endymion: A Poetic Romance* (1818). The assailants, in quick succession, were two noteworthy periodicals: a newcomer, *Blackwood's Edinburgh Magazine* (August), and the establishment *Quarterly Review* (September[2]), published by William Blackwood's associate in London, John Murray, prime mover in the publishing world, Tory ally of church and crown. Keats was stung not just by ridicule of his poetry and his aspirations, but also by his targeting in politically fuelled culture-warfare.

Blackwood's, launched in 1817 to contest the liberal *Edinburgh Review*, flaunted nasty attacks on a new poetry that, in overturning neo-classical protocols, seemed complicit with an insurgent new politics. *Blackwood's* reviewer 'Z' had been jabbing gleefully at Leigh Hunt, editor of the radical weekly the *Examiner*, as headmaster of a 'Cockney School of Poetry' and 'Cockney School of Politics'. Insinuating vulgarity, effeminacy, and suburban affectation, 'Cockney' would stick for a century to Hunt and associates, including the protégé tagged for future treatment in a satiric epigraph-verse at the top of Z's first paper: 'KEATS, / The Muses' son of promise … what feats / He yet may do' (*Blackwood's Edinburgh Magazine*, 2, 38; October 1817). The *Examiner* had hosted Keats's first publication, a sonnet *To Solitude*, 5 May 1816; and in a December issue an article by Hunt trumpeted three 'Young Poets' (Shelley, J. H. Reynolds, Keats) and introduced Keats's sonnet 'On first looking into Chapman's Homer'.

Hunt's essay was tuned in part to herald Keats's *Poems* (due in March, from Shelley's publishers); February *Examiner*s offered two more sonnets. Yet for all this previewing and some ebullient first reviews from Hunt's circle, Z's promise impended and would land with force. The real sensation of December 1816, moreover, was not Hunt's parade of 'Young Poets', but Murray's white-hot sale of latest volumes from England's expatriate celebrity, Lord Byron: *The Prisoner of Chillon &c* and *Childe Harold's Pilgrimage, Canto III* (electric sequel to the instantly successful first two, 1812), each quickly selling 7,000. Even Wordsworth, whose self-canonizing collected *Poems* of 1815 proposed him as England's most important living poet in residence, was jealous.

Keats didn't let Z's promise defeat his hopes, and by mid-April 1817 was busy with *Endymion*. 'I have asked myself so often why I should be a Poet more than other Men', he confided to Hunt as it was under way, and gave eager answer: 'What a thing to be in the Mouth of Fame' (May 1817; *K* 50). To vigorously epic painter B. R. Haydon, he confessed swings of hope, anxiety, ambition, and confidence: now 'a horrid Morbidity of Temper', now a hearkening to 'The Trumpet of Fame', now chastisement for 'self delusion' (May; *K* 52–4). Further into his 'Romance', he shared dreams of 'being a Poet' with a friend and his brother George: *Endymion* was to be a 'test, a trial of my Powers of Imagination and chiefly of my invention ... by which I must make 4000 Lines of one bare circumstance' (*K* 61–2) – this in October 1817, just as Z's first attack on Hunt lit up *Blackwood's*. Keats was skewered the next August, a few months after *Endymion* appeared. Then the *Quarterly*: 'Mr Keats', it scoffed, 'if that be his real name, for we almost doubt that any man in his sense would put his real name to such a rhapsody' (*K* 203).

Keats assured allies of his equanimity. To his new publishers (Shelley's had unloaded him), he wrote, 'Praise or blame has but a momentary effect on the man whose love of beauty in the abstract makes him a severe critic of his own Works' (October 1818; *K* 206) – half-alluding to *Endymion*'s (now-famous) opening lines: 'A thing of beauty is a joy for ever: / Its loveliness increases; it will never / Pass into nothingness.' 'My own domestic criticism has given me pain without comparison beyond what Blackwood or the Quarterly could possibly inflict', he continued, in tandem with the reciprocal: 'no external praise can give me such a glow as my own solitary reperception & ratification of what is fine' (*K* 207). But he feared that for all the fine beauty of his lines, their poet would pass precipitously into nothingness.

Beauty is a Keatsian key word: an aesthetic ideal, but also an affective 'intensity' (another key word) at once intellectual, emotional, and sensuous. 'What the imagination seizes as Beauty must be truth', Keats speculated (November 1817; *K* 69); for poetry, 'touches of Beauty should never be half way' (February 1818; *K* 113). Sceptical of absolutes, he proposed to a theology-student friend that 'every mental pursuit takes its reality and worth from the ardour of the pursuer – being in itself a nothing'; those

'Nothings ... made Great and dignified by an ardent pursuit' (March 1818; *K* 114). Keats's poetry is the intensity of this pursuit. Its very phrases are memorable, summoned to the walls of libraries and reading rooms, endowing book titles and popular songs: 'Much have I travel'd in the realms of gold'; 'tender is the night'; 'fanatics have their dreams'; 'season of mists and mellow fruitfulness'; 'Beauty is truth; truth Beauty'. With no schooling in liberal arts beyond his early teenage years, how did this voracious reader, lover of beauty, devotee of poetry, and aspirant to poetic fame, this medical apprentice, this proto-existential philosopher, this intensity of adolescence and genius, become 'John Keats'?

He wrote his first poem in 1814; his last, perhaps a revision of his 'Bright star' sonnet, in September 1820, en route to Italy, where, desperately ill, he wouldn't survive half a year. 'Oh, for ten years, that I may overwhelm / Myself in poesy', he exclaimed in 1816 ('Sleep and Poetry', lines 96–7); it was all but over in less than half that span. At twenty-five Chaucer, Spenser, Dryden, and Swift had written nothing known of, Shakespeare's fame was *The Comedy of Errors* and *Love's Labour's Lost,* Jonson's *The Isle of Dogs*, Marvell's some courtly Greek and Latin poems. Carlyle was also born in 1795; what if Keats had had his years, up to 1881? The fascination of Keats is this poignancy of unheard melodies, unknown potential. Would he have stayed with poetry, having hit his stride with the 1820 volume that issued 'The Eve of St. Agnes', 'Ode to a Nightingale', 'Ode on a Grecian Urn', 'Ode on Melancholy', 'To Autumn', and the spectacular fragment of *Hyperion*? Would he have realized a declared ambition in drama? Or written liberal-opinion journalism (another thought), or personal essays (the genre of friends Hunt, Lamb, and Hazlitt), or even, with his wry sense of character and social behaviour, novels?

His origins were modest. John was the eldest of four, their father the proprietor of a suburban London livery stable. When he died from a riding accident, their mother quickly remarried. Her affection for her children was as erratic as it was doting, and John was devastated when she disappeared from a miserable second marriage, leaving the children to their grandmother. She returned four long years later, wracked with consumption; John devoted himself to her care, and watched her die when he was fourteen. The turbulence of these events would mark the series of adored, adoring, inconstant women in Keats's poetry, all versions of 'La Belle Dame sans Merci'. He drafted a ballad with this iconic title some eight months after he confessed to a close friend,

> I have not a right feeling towards Women ... When I am among women I have evil thoughts, malice spleen ... put all this perversity to my being disappointed since Boyhood ... I must absolutely get over this – but how? ... an obstinate

> Prejudice can seldom be produced but from a gordian complication of feelings, which must take time to unravel and care to keep unravelled. (July 1818; *K* 191–2)

The very love of his life, teenage Fanny Brawne, whom he met August 1818, would bear the brunt of this prejudice, constant as she was.

The Keats boys were being educated at the progressive Enfield Academy, and all the orphans fell under the control of a legal guardian, a businessman whose chief concern was to train the boys for trade and keep their little sister Fanny (now his ward) from their influence. Keats was apprenticed to a surgeon in the grim days before anaesthesia, and was soon studying at the progressive Guy's Hospital in south London. While at Enfield, he had been mentored and befriended by the headmaster's son, who introduced him to literature, music, and theatre – and eventually to Hunt and his avant-garde circle. Though he earned his licence as apothecary and surgeon's assistant, his heart was in poetry – reading it, writing it, dreaming of 'poetical fame'. He revelled in Chaucer, Spenser, Shakespeare, Milton, Chatterton, and, among his contemporaries, Hunt, Wordsworth, and Byron. He was thrilled when Haydon sent one of his sonnets to Wordsworth and received a complimentary response. Reaching legal adulthood in October 1816, and encouraged by Hunt and his friends, Keats gave up medicine for poetry.

Early poetry and *Poems* (1817)

In February 1814, Byron's pirate-romance, *The Corsair*, sold 10,000 copies off the press, 20,000 within a fortnight;[3] in August Wordsworth ushered in his great poem, *The Excursion*, nine books in expensive quarto, only to see it coolly reviewed at best – though one rejoicer was Keats, who had begun writing poetry that year, during his apprenticeship. His first effort was 'Imitation of Spenser', three lush Spenserian stanzas, in homage to *The Faerie Queene* but mindful of Byron's success with this stanza in *Childe Harold*. Amidst medical studies in 1815, he added sonnets, odes, and lyrics; by 1816, encouraged by Hunt, Reynolds, Shelley, and the excitements of a new movement in poetry (*Blackwood's* Z called it *Metromanie*), he was composing in earnest: verse epistles (to a friend, a mentor, and a brother), prospects of a romance or two, and still longer ventures of aspiration and playful imagination.

The title-page of the 1817 *Poems* featured a profile of Spenser, laurel-wreathed, and verse from his *Fate of the Butterfly*: 'What more felicity can fall to creature, / Than to enjoy delight with liberty?' (lines 209–10). Keats meant by this epigraph a friendly quarrel with Wordsworth's signature assignment of 'delight and liberty' to 'the simple creed of Childhood', which subsided into manhood's sober 'philosophic mind' ('Immortality Ode', 1815, lines 137–8). It mattered that Spenser's question qualified delight with liberty (his butterfly is fated to fall to a spider). In Keats's day *liberty* was not just affective discourse; it was also political, indicating opposition to tyranny, especially monarchal. If Wordsworth's *Ode* was shaded by elegy for the childhood or dawn of the French Revolution, Keats wanted to honour its still enduring champions. The last poem he drafted for *Poems* was a 'Dedication' to Hunt: a poet of 'delight' also revered as 'Libertas' for his fearless *Examiner* essays. One of these, 'libelling' the Prince Regent, reaped a steep fine of £500 and a prison term; Keats included in the volume proper his sonnet 'Written on the day that Mr. Leigh Hunt left Prison'. His opening poem set a line from Hunt's *Story of Rimini* in place of any title: 'Places of nestling green for Poets made' – the bower in which Paolo and Francesca, hotly reading about Lancelot and Guinevere, read no more that day. As Keats knew, Hunt's sympathy for these adulterous lovers had riled Z no end.

This opening poem, 'I stood tip-toe', further defied propriety with 242 lines of loose (lawless, some said), 'romance' couplets, flouting neo-classical metre with rhythms of pleasure and passion, feminine rhymes (*wandering/pondering*), and outrageous enjambments, some across a half-dozen lines. Overall, *Poems* is an aspirant's performance, complementing its political marks with tributes to great poets and poetic greatness, romances of imagination and refurbished classical mythology, commemorations of intimate occasions, all to display a poet's skill and versatility. A unit of verse epistles was followed by a unit of seventeen sonnets, full of experimental play with the formal traditions (Petrarchan, Shakespearean). Keats would write sonnets throughout his career; even his long poems in couplets and blank verse include sonnet stanzas, and his ode stanzas are imprinted with sonnet consciousness. One sonnet, drafted in May 1819 just for exercise rather than publication, begins, 'If by dull rhymes our english must be chaind', to address the tradition itself, with a nonce-title in its letter source: 'Incipit altera Sonneta'; Keats means to indicate 'another' in a run of poems, but he obliquely suggests 'altered' (*K* 254).

Keats met his hero Hunt in October 1816, and honoured him with the closing and longest work in *Poems*: 'Sleep and Poetry', heralded with a separate title-page. It was an essay on the aims and ideals of the new poetry, with Keats's personal imprint: another extravaganza of romance couplets, feminine rhymes, irregular metres, the whole subversion of neo-classical formalism abetted by satires of its poets, their 'foppery and barbarism', 'musty laws', and 'wretched rule' (lines 162–206). Hunt loved it; Haydon praised the bolt of lightning; Byron, who esteemed Pope, despised the upstart; and the Tory reviewers lay in wait.

Endymion: A Poetic Romance (1818)

Published May 1818, *Endymion* was hatched in a contest with Hunt and Shelley to finish a 4,000-line poem by the end of 1817. Working diligently from April to December, Keats was the only one to succeed. 'I stood tip-toe' had tendered a brief allegory of imagination in Endymion's rapture with the moonlight world (lines 181–205). *Endymion* extended the fable along various vectors, from the practical and worldly to the ideal and visionary, working its 'trial of imagination' by theorizing poetic imagination itself – its ideals, its frustrations, its successes. Yet over its course, Keats's aim to celebrate poetry as an eternal thing of beauty in a dark world, an inspired product of eroticized visionary imagination, dissipated. Rather than any consolidated argument, *Endymion* issued into an array of local images, figural scenes, sensual poetics, speculations – all spun on a love of 'fine Phrases' (*K* 264). This was Keats's poetic pulse. Writing in August 1820 to Shelley about *The Cenci*, Keats said he wouldn't judge the murderous characters (Shelley's preoccupation), only 'the Poetry, and dramatic effect': 'an artist must serve Mammon', he argued; 'You ... might curb your magnanimity and be more of an artist, and "load every rift" of your subject with ore' (*K* 426) – the quotations drawn from the Cave of Mammon in *The Faerie Queene*.

It is a prognosis in Keats's forecast of 4,000 lines as 'a little Region' which 'Lovers of Poetry' may 'wander in where they may pick and choose, and in which the images are so numerous that many are forgotten and found new in a second Reading' (*K* 61), that *Endymion* became, in effect, a lyric anthology. It struck its first reviewers, both loving and unloving, as an overstuffed jewel cabinet. Victorians Swinburne and Tennyson ridiculed an unmanly sensuality ('Those lips, O slippery blisses', II. 758), while its defenders discerned a religion of Beauty in neo Platonic answer to the quest-death of Shelley's *Alastor*. What is most manifest across its thousands of romance couplets, however, is Keats's recurrent uncertainty about visionary desire, its erotic embodiment, its social and psychological fallout, its pathology, its self-indulgence, its comedy – and not the least, its poetry. Much of this effect registers in relays of key tropes and topoi. There are scenes of dreaming as inspiration, as obsession, as disease, as death-charmed; bowers as paradise, as baby-beds, as parodies of paradise, as prisons, as tombs; and a gallery of dreamy, dreaming young men who mirror and qualify one another: Endymion; the poet-narrator; his dedicatee, suicidal Chatterton; infantilized, embowered Adonis; foolish Glaucus; and the boyish population of myths and legend – Pan, Apollo, Ganymede, Hyacinth, Narcissus. Although the hero Endymion (after ordeals in earth, the lower world, and heaven, and a near vanishing into alienated Childe-Harold melancholy) secures immortality with his dream goddess, Keats had become disaffected with the 'Poetic Romance', and said so in his Preface, describing, with 'regret', a work of 'inexperience, immaturity', a 'failure'.[4]

Was this an honest confession, or a pre-emptive defence? No matter: the reviewers who had satirized *Poems* were waiting to savage *Endymion*, spurred by the anti-monarchal verse at the top of Book III. But Keats had already moved on. *Endymion* would be his last poem to end in lovers' blissful meeting. As he was proofreading in January 1818, he was also 'sitting down to read *King Lear* once again', and wrote a sonnet to commemorate the occasion: his determination to leave 'golden-tongued Romance', that 'Queen of far-away', to 'burn through' the searing, 'fierce dispute' of tragedy, the terrain of Shakespeare, the 'chief Poet' (*K* 92). He didn't publish this, perhaps because he knew that the inspiration of a world ever young, gorgeously full of ease and love, was a vision he couldn't really let go of. In many ways, Keats's career is a serial repetition of the enchantments and disenchantments.

1818 and *Hyperion*

Almost by reflex, Keats reads himself by what he is reading – *King Lear*, Chapman's Homer, *The Faerie Queene* – and the "character" of people, scenes, and society. Late in 1817 he articulated a (now famous) principle, which Shakespearean drama epitomized and Wordsworthian 'philosophy' and Coleridgean discontent with 'half-knowledge' did not: '*negative capability*, that is, ... capable of being in uncertainties, mysteries, doubts, without any irritable reaching after fact & reason' (*K* 78). Wordsworth (he murmured to fellow-poet Reynolds, February 1818) seemed to 'brood and peacock over' his speculations (Keats was the first to verb the bird), leaving one feeling 'bullied into a certain Philosophy engendered in the whims of an Egotist' (*K* 99). By October, he was indexing a 'wordsworthian or egotistical sublime' as foil to his own 'poetical Character' (persona, and the imprint of personal identity): Keats calls himself a 'camelion Poet' of 'no self ... no Identity', 'continually in for – and filling some other Body', capable of (sometimes, unable to avoid) living in the intensity of a mood, a character, a disposition, the 'gusto' of 'light and shade, ... foul or fair, high or low, rich or poor, mean or elevated' (*K* 214). 'The only means of strengthening one's intellect is to make up ones mind about nothing – to let the mind be a thoroughfare for all thoughts', he said to a friend in early autumn 1819 (*K* 276), as if giving a thesis on poetry writing, and poetry reading.

With care for these poetic values (gusto, intensity of feeling and image, fine phrasing, negative capability), Keats was rereading Wordsworth,

Shakespeare (always, soon and late), and *Paradise Lost*, and discovering Dante's *Divine Comedy* in H. F. Cary's recent translation. In a playful-serious verse letter to Reynolds, March 1818, he seemed to satirize *Endymion* in a campy lament, 'O that our dreamings all of sleep or wake / Would all their colours from the sunset take: / From something of material sublime, / Rather than shadow our own Soul's daytime / In the dark void of Night'. Doubting any 'lore of good and ill', he wondered whether this disposition was philosophical honesty ('Things cannot to the will be settled / But they tease us out of thought' – reprised in the last stanza of 'Ode on a Grecian Urn'), or the incapacity of 'Imagination brought / Beyond its proper bound, yet still confined' to discern 'any standard law / Of either earth or heaven'. At the end of the epistle, he promised to take refuge from detested moodiness in a 'new Romance' (lines 67–82, 111; *K* 120–1).

This was *Isabella; or The Pot of Basil*, a tale elaborated from Boccaccio's *Decameron*, and written in *ottava rima*, the verse-form of Byron's satiric Italian romance *Beppo* (just published, in February). On this cue, Keats produced a romance about the genre of 'Romance', with more than a few anti-Romance moments. Across a gothic tale of doomed lovers, murder, ghoulish dreaming, graveyard exhumation, corpse decapitation, pathological fetish, and fatal melancholy, the poet-narrator comments on romance conventions and illusions – starkly embedding the 'rich' pleasures of 'old Romance' (XLIX), literary and social, in a global economy of miserable labour. If Karl Marx had sat in the British Library 'writing a poem instead of a treatise on Capital', commented George Bernard Shaw, it would have been *Isabella*.[5] Every thing and every person is commodity, and the luxury of romance (genre and sentiment both) is implicated in brutal oppression. Reynolds urged Keats to rush *Isabella* into print to refute the reviews of too-dreamy *Endymion*, but Keats wondered if even *Isabella* was 'smokeable' – that is, open to ridicule (September 1819; *K* 267).

Throughout winter 1818 he was attending Hazlitt's lectures on the English poets. Hazlitt, too, disparaged Wordsworth's egotism, but praised the pathos. Keats had new respect for Wordsworth's feeling for 'the burden of the Mystery' (a phrase from 'Tintern Abbey'), admiring the profoundly existential sense of the 'Misery and Heartbreak, pain, sickness and oppression' to which no 'Romance', not even Milton's 'sure points of Reasoning' (so he mapped the argument of *Paradise Lost*), was adequate. It is in the 'dark Passages', not his 'philosophy', that Wordsworth's 'genius' shines (May 1818; *K* 129–31). As he wrote this appreciation, Keats's tubercular younger brother Tom had been spitting blood.

Keats's new attempt at a long poem in 1818, *Hyperion*, opens in scenes of mortal suffering: the Titans' fall, 'Deep in the shady sadness of a vale, / Far sunken from the healthy breath of morn' (I. 1–2), expelled by the new generation of Olympian gods – an idiom of classical mythology not answerable to the biblical logic of *Paradise Lost*. The hero was to be Titan Hyperion's successor, Apollo, god of knowledge, poetry, medicine – a manifold dear to Keats. Yet the most powerful and most deeply felt poetry of the 'Fragment' (in the most dazzling blank verse since Milton's) gave compelling 'camelion' sympathy not to rising Apollo, but to the Titans' pained bewilderment, especially to sole-unfallen Hyperion's anxiety as he realizes the doom of his brothers, and senses his impending fate: 'His flaming robes stream'd out beyond his heels, / And gave a roar, as if of earthly fire' (I. 214–15). The *as if* already writes the fall to come, and Keats coined new negatives for the agon: Saturn's 'realmless' eyes (I. 19) versus Apollo's 'gloomless' eyes across the 'liegeless' air that awaits his rule (III. 80, 92). When Keats turned, in Book III, to Apollo, he couldn't imagine anything more heroic than a deified Endymion. The 'Knowledge enormous' that the godling acquires 'all at once' (III. 113–20), against Keats's turmoil in nursing Tom, dying in the next room, was a 'hateful siege of contraries' – a sympathy with Satan's psychology of irrevocable doom.[6]

1819: new 'romances', odes, *The Fall of Hyperion*

Tom died in December 1818, and Keats abandoned *Hyperion*. Then, in a year-long inspiration, he produced the poetry (death-haunted, all) that would secure his fame, if not immediately when it was first published, then across the century: 'The Eve of St. Agnes', 'La Belle Dame sans Mercy' (the title of the first, and only lifetime, publication in Hunt's *Indicator*), 'Lamia', and all the famous 'Great Odes'.

Early in winter 1819, Keats wrote his most admired, and now most durably anthologized, romance: 'The Eve of St. Agnes'. Though the legend of St Agnes is severe (a fourth-century martyr, saved by a miracle from a sentence to a night of rape in the brothels on the eve of execution), Keats's tale sets the lovers' meeting as the sensuously lush, hot centre of a winter world fraught with Romeo-and-Juliet-like family feuds, a storm into which the lovers fled away, 'ages long ago' (line 370), with unknown consequence. He reprised the Spenserian stanza (idle since that first 'Imitation'), to spin a romance as ironic as it was beautiful – indulging the generic pleasures (passion, sensuous gusto, spiritual aspiration) with a playful, sometimes satiric, sometimes darkly shaded perspective on the genre. He didn't stint on the sexual heat. When his publisher, worried about indecency and offence to female readers, made him revise, Keats complied with angry reluctance ('he says he does not want ladies to read his poetry: – that he writes for men'[7]);

but the imagery of stars and flowers in the consummation is both deftly suggestive, and qualified by the surrounding night:

> Beyond a mortal man impassion'd far
> At these voluptuous accents, he arose,
> Ethereal, flush'd, and like a throbbing star
> Seen mid the sapphire heaven's deep repose;
> Into her dream he melted, as the rose
> Blendeth its odour with the violet, –
> Solution sweet: meantime the frost-wind blows
> Like Love's alarum, pattering the sharp sleet
> Against the window-panes; St. Agnes' moon hath set.
>
> (stanza xxxvi)

Keats wanted this poem, in all its gorgeous complexity, to lead off in the 1820 volume.

Yet neither it, nor the now-famous Odes, was headlined by his publishers, who titled the volume *Lamia, Isabella, The Eve of St. Agnes, and Other Poems*, and identified Keats on the title-page as 'Author of *Endymion*' (which they still had in stock). They admired the *Hyperion*-fragment, and put it at the back with a distinct title-page, saying in an 'Advertisement' at the front of the volume that its inclusion was their doing, 'contrary to the wish of the Author', who was too 'discouraged' by 'the reception' of *Endymion* to proceed. Keats was furious. In a copy for an acquaintance, he crossed out the Advertisement, writing at the top, 'This is none of my doing – I was ill at the time', and after the last sentence about *Endymion*, 'This is a lie.'[8] The publishers meant well, but weren't certain how to brand Keats: a promising poet of epic, the 'Author of *Endymion*', or the author of *Lamia*, a caustic swerve from *Endymion*?

'I am certain there is that sort of fire in it which must take hold of people in some way – give them either pleasant or unpleasant sensation', Keats said of 'Lamia', with no warm view of the reading public: 'What they want is sensation of some sort' (*K* 272). Even so, he told Reynolds, 'I have great hopes of success, because I make use of my Judgment more deliberately than I yet have done' (11 July 1819; *L* II, p. 128), feeling that *Endymion* had been launched '*without Judgment*' (*K* 207). He was enjoying Dryden's verse fables and legends, their crisp heroic couplets spiced with triple rhymes and alexandrine extravagances. Not just in these measures but also in key characterizations and circumstances, *Lamia* is saturated with corrosives to 'golden Romance': its locale, Corinth, was famed for erotic hedonism; Lycius (a young man about Keats's age) is a blind visionary, then a tyrant, then a subject of catastrophic disenchantment; his rejected mentor, the philosopher Apollonius, is a deformation of Apollo; and gorgeous Lamia is the latest twist in Keats's 'gordian complication' of feelings on women. She shares a name with fabled she-vampires, predatory snakes disguised as lovely, alluring maids. But she also seems cursed: perhaps a woman imprisoned in a snake. Keats's conclusion is a dark parody of romance endings, a figuring of 'romance' that cannot survive cold, philosophical scrutiny. On Lycius's wedding day to Lamia, Apollonius cries 'Serpent!', Lamia vanishes, and Lycius swoons to death, his 'arms ... empty of delight' (2. 305–7).

Keats wrote odes early and late, from 'Ode to Apollo' (1814) to 'Ode to Fanny' (1820). At the back of the *Lamia* volume, in a section of various 'Poems', appear 'Ode on a Grecian Urn', 'Ode to a Nightingale', 'To Autumn', 'Ode on Melancholy', and 'Ode to Psyche' – scarcely remarked in first reviews, not really admired until after R. M. Milnes's *Life, Letters, and Literary Remains, of John Keats* in 1848 (which introduced 'Ode on Indolence'), now regarded as the essence of Keats. Writing these odes from spring to fall 1819, Keats drew brilliantly on sonnet resources (quatrains, sestets, an occasional couplet), in varying metres and stanzas (often ten lines), to play the lyric genre into a dramatic staging of 'negative capability'. A 'Question is the best beacon toward a little Speculation', he once said; he clearly liked the workout of 'question and answer – a little pro and con'.[9] The odes are the very poetics of questioning: 'But who wast thou?', the poet greets Psyche, goddess of his mind and soul. 'Was it a vision, or a waking dream? / Fled is that music: – Do I wake or sleep?' is the residue of an 'Ode to a Nightingale' that has been 'half in love with easeful Death'; 'What leaf-fringed legend haunts about thy shape?' is the fascination that stirs fantasies about shapes on a Grecian Urn; 'Where are the songs of spring?' softly sounds *ubi sunt*, a question as old as poetry itself. The odes play out a 'pro and con' of imaginations: a poet's mind as a 'rosy sanctuary' or a place of mere 'shadowy thought'; birdsong that evokes 'full-throated ease' and 'easeful death'; urn-imagery that seems eternal spring and endures in marble as 'Cold Pastoral'; a Melancholy of 'aching Pleasure' ... / Turning to poison while the bee-mouth sips'; a languorous 'indolence' that cannot keep 'sheltered from annoy' of busy thoughts; an autumn of prolonged 'mellow fruitfulness' vibrating with sensations of temporality.

The odes glance at several contexts – the Elgin Marbles, the pharmacology of opium, social misery and political unrest, the loss of Tom to death and George to America, Keats's exquisite sense of his own mortality – and the language is rich with echo and allusion, as complex as it is casual, ranging through the Bible, Keats's earlier poetry and its hostile reviews, and his favourite poets. Nineteenth-century readers prized the beauty and sensuous intensity: 'The murmurous haunt of flies on summer eves'; 'the wealth of globed peonies'; 'whose strenuous tongue / Can burst Joy's grape against his palate fine'. Twentieth-century 'New Criticism' found perfect artefacts for close analysis of a deft linguistic density: the way each ode weaves a field of nuance, reverberation, and imagery across a flux and reflux of desire, speculation, argument, self-correction. From this admiration of 'internal debate', of 'paradox and 'contradiction', later critics described a poetics of 'indeterminacy' and a comprehensive 'rhetoric of irony'. The poet of 'Ode to Psyche' pledges 'to build a fane' in the mind that soon rhymes in sound and sense with an ironizing 'all the gardener Fancy e'er could feign'. The poet of 'Ode to a Nightingale' yearns to escape what his language keeps recalling: 'Here, where men sit and hear each other groan ... / Where youth grown pale, and spectre-thin and dies' – where *here* is a place to *hear,* and *groan* inseparable from *grown.* 'Ode on a Grecian Urn' pursues 'unheard' melodies: 'Not to the sensual ear, but, more endear'd, / Pipe to the spirit ditties of no tone.' Yet it is the sensual tones and textures of poetry that audition this spirit-ear, literally end*ear*'d. 'Ode on Melancholy' distils an intensity of 'Beauty that must die': 'glut thy sorrow on a morning rose' – the brief *morning* already sounding *mourning.* Even as the odist of 'To Autumn' abjures 'the songs of Spring' he can't help but see 'barred clouds bloom the soft-dying day, / And touch the stubble-plains with rosy hue' – as if spring were still on, still in the yearning mind.

Hyperion's story of a fall had turned into a prolonged lyric stasis: intensely realized tableaux of suffering, grief, anxiety, and anticipation, with one god's sudden transformation. The logic of irresolution to which the genre of ode was more apt nagged at Keats in this narrative project. Despite his satires of philosophizing 'certainties', he was rethinking this antipathy, even his prized 'pro and con' pleasures: 'Though a quarrel in the streets is a thing to be hated, the energies displayed in it are fine; the commonest Man shows a grace in his quarrel – By a superior being our reasoning[s] may take the same tone – though erroneous they may be fine – This is the very thing in which consists poetry; and if so it is not so fine a thing as philosophy – For the same reason that an eagle is not so fine a thing as a truth' (*K* 243). He wrote this fine thought in March 1819, in the same journal-letter (to George and Georgiana) that, a month on, would sketch 'a grander system of salvation than the chrystain' one of body/soul, life/immortality dualism – one that 'does not affront our reason and humanity'. This was a regard of mortal life as a 'vale of Soul-making', a 'Place where the heart must feel and suffer in a thousand diverse ways!' – a 'World of pains and troubles' designed 'to school an Intelligence and make it a soul' (*K* 250–2). The 'Philosopher', he would tell his theologist friend that August, is a 'human friend', second only to 'a fine writer' (*K* 264).

Wanting to vindicate poetry and philosophy, or poetry as modern soul-making philosophy, Keats returned to *Hyperion* that autumn, recasting it from the unavailing Miltonic paradigm of 'paradise lost' (by no sin do the Titans fall from Heaven, just inevitable progress) into a Dantean dream-vision, *The Fall of Hyperion: A Dream*. As if sitting down to re-read his *Hyperion* once again, Keats postponed the fragment with a prelude. This *Dream* unfolds the poet's own dream-fall, from a belated Eden into a wide wasteland (mirroring *Purgatorio*), where he experiences, with agonizing sensation, his own near death. He then meets the agent of his ordeal, goddess Moneta, sole remnant of the Titans, her memory forever bearing their trauma. There is no Apollonian god of poetry, only this human poet, whom she accuses of being no poet, just a uselessly fevered dreamer. To his protests, she offers a test, taking him into the theatre of her memory (and back to the text and world of *Hyperion*) to the mortal misery of the Titans, an exquisitely severe vale of Soul-making. Burdened with her knowledge (and the memory of his own near death), the poet bears witness to the agony of the newly mortal Titans, and Hyperion's awakening anxiety. It was 'camelion' poetics with a vengeance. Keats stopped writing at the threshold of Hyperion's doom, halting at his 'bright', fierce resistance to the premonition: 'on he flared – ' (II. 61).

When he broke off, Keats said it was because he was unable to differentiate a 'false beauty proceeding from art' from 'the true voice of feeling' (September 1819; *K* 267). Even so, this art wrought (yet more) new phrasings for feeling: *faulture*: fault and failure; *soother*: smoother, soothing, and sooth (truth); *mourn* as a noun; *immortal sickness*, a paradox wrung from the medical term, *mortal sickness*; Moneta's *visionless* eyes. When *The Fall of Hyperion* was published in 1856 by Milnes in *Miscellanies of the Philobiblion Society* as *Another Version of Hyperion*, it was taken to be the draft from which *Hyperion* was sprung, and was recruited to the Victorian debates, with reference to the Romantic generation, about the relevance of poets, poetic vision, and poetic idealism to the concerns of the modern age.

Unlike most Romantics, Keats wrote no polemics (only that self-deprecating Preface to *Endymion*), no critical essays (just a review of Edmund Kean's *Richard III*); but he did write letters, with a critical intelligence as brilliant as the poetic talent. From their first publication (some by Hunt in 1828; many more by Milnes in 1848), these have been enjoyed for their wit and playfulness, their generosity and candour, their insight and critical penetration, and casually fine, poetic things: 'the most unhappy hours in our lives are those in which we recollect times past to our own blushing – If we are immortal that must be the Hell' (April 1818; *K* 125–6); 'Talking of Pleasure, this moment I was writing with one hand, and with the other holding to my

Mouth a Nectarine – good god how fine – It went down soft pulpy, slushy, oozy' (September 1819; *K* 269).

Keats's last poems reflect more anxious luxuries, involved with Fanny Brawne, the girl next door, whom he met in summer 1818, pledged himself to in December, and hoped to marry when eligible. These include three sonnets, 'The day is gone', 'I cry your mercy', and a revision of 'Bright star'; two odes, 'To Fanny' ('Physician Nature') and 'What can I do?' (the verse houses a sonnet stanza); and a ghoulish, enigmatic fragment, 'This living hand'. Keats was desperately in love, frustrated by fame, and struggling with finances and failing health. With no design of publication, he used poetry to grapple with erotic passion in conflict with poetic self-possession and autonomy, risking, or revisiting, the aesthetic mastery epitomized in the odes and 'The Eve of St. Agnes'. 'I have two luxuries to brood over in my walk, your Loveliness and the hour of my death', he sighed to his love in July 1819, adding, 'O that I could have possession of them both in the same minute' (*K* 263).

Early in 1820 Keats suffered a major pulmonary haemorrhage. With his medical training, he read his fate. Everyone knew he couldn't survive another English winter, so in September 1820, with help from friends and publishers, writing his will and signing away his copyrights, Keats sailed for the warm south. He died in Rome, at the end of the next February – far from beloved Fanny, his family, and his friends, and so defeated by fame, despite some late favourable reviews, that he asked for his epitaph to be 'Here lies one whose name was writ in water.'[10] Yet the fable of a young, sensitive poet slain by hostile reviews that Shelley retailed in *Adonais*, though retold throughout the nineteenth century as if documentary truth, could not have been further from it. 'I must choose between despair & Energy – I choose the latter', a still healthy Keats declared to a friend, and implicitly himself, in May 1819 (*K* 256).

In his last letter, he wrote half-ruefully, half-comically about the existential contradiction of a prized poetic value: 'the knowledge of contrast, feeling for light and shade, all that information (primitive sense) necessary for a poem are great enemies to the recovery of the stomach'. He wrote this not just in solitary sorrow, but in energy and friendship, signing off with a figure of wry self-regard: 'I always made an awkward bow' (30 November 1820; *K* 433).

NOTES

1 To his brother George and wife Georgiana, in America; *John Keats*, ed. S. Wolfson, Longman Cultural Edition (New York: Pearson, 2006), p. 209. Quotations,

unless otherwise indicated, are from this edition, keyed by *K* and page. Poetry is identified by line numbers. Letters are identified by month and year, and when of interest, date and correspondent; Rollins's edition (*The Letters of John Keats, 1814–1821*, ed. H. E. Rollins, 2 vols (Cambridge, MA: Harvard University Press, 1958) is identified by *L*.

2 Unsigned, this review of *Endymion* was by notorious scourge J. W. Croker; *Quarterly* XIX is dated April, but did not publish until September.

3 This statistic is reported by Byron to publisher John Hunt (Leigh's brother), 29 April 1823 (*Byron's Letters and Journals. Vol. X*, ed. L. Marchand (Cambridge, MA: Harvard University Press, 1980), p. 161); the first, Murray to Byron, 3 February 1814 (S. Smiles, *A Publisher and His Friends: Memoir and Correspondence of the Late John Murray*, 2 vols (London: John Murray, 1891), I, p. 223).

4 *K* 138–40; the first draft, which he was urged to revise, was even worse (*K* 116–17).

5 *John Keats Memorial Volume*, ed. G. C. Williamson (London: John Lane, 1921), p. 175.

6 To C. W. Dilke, 21–2 September 1818 (*K* 200); in his *Paradise Lost*, Keats underlined this description of Satan's agony, in the heart of Eden (IX. 121–2).

7 R. Woodhouse (literary adviser) to J. Taylor; *L* 2, pp. 162–3; for the cancelled lines, see the footnotes in Wolfson, *John Keats*.

8 Amy Lowell, *John Keats*, 2 vols (Boston: Houghton Mifflin, 1925), vol. 2, plate facing p. 424.

9 *L* I, p. 175 (to Bailey, 30 October 1817); I, p. 153 (to his sister).

10 The tombstone bears a version; see W. Bate, *John Keats* (Cambridge, MA: Harvard University Press, 1963), p. 694.

SELECTED FURTHER READING

Editions

John Keats, ed. S. Wolfson, Longman Cultural Edition, New York, Pearson, 2006. Poetry, letters, prose, along with reviews and reactions, contextual materials

Complete Poems, ed. J. Barnard, Oxford, Oxford University Press, 1973

The Poems of John Keats, ed. J. Stillinger, Cambridge, MA, Harvard University Press, 1978. With complete information on textual issues; leaner reading edition, 1982

Facsimiles of *Poems* (1817); *Endymion* (1818); *Lamia, Isabella, The Eve of St. Agnes &c* (1819), intro. J. Wordsworth, Oxford, Woodstock Press, 1989, 1990, 1991. Original publications now all available on Google Books

John Keats: Poetry Manuscripts at Harvard, ed. J. Stillinger, intro. H. Vendler, Cambridge, MA, Harvard University Press, 1990

The Letters of John Keats, 1814–1821, ed. H. E. Rollins, 2 vols, Cambridge, MA, Harvard University Press, 1958

Selected Letters of John Keats, ed. G. F. Scott, Cambridge, MA, Harvard University Press, 2002

John Keats: Selected Letters, ed. R. Gittings, rev. J. Mee, Oxford, Oxford University Press, 2002
For images of editions and manuscripts in the Houghton Library, Harvard University: http://hcl.harvard.edu/libraries/houghton/collections/modern/Keats.cfm

Secondary works

Barnard, J., *John Keats*, Cambridge, Cambridge University Press, 1987
Bate, W. *John Keats*, Cambridge, MA, Harvard University Press, 1963
Blades, J., *John Keats: The Poems*, Palgrave, 2002
Brooks, C., 'Keats's Sylvan Historian: History without Footnotes', in *The Well Wrought Urn*, New York, Harcourt, 1947
Hebron, S., *John Keats*, British Library Writers' Lives, New York, Oxford University Press, 2002
Hirst, W., *John Keats*, New York, Twayne, 1981
Homans, M., 'Keats Reading Women, Women Reading Keats', *Studies in Romanticism* 29 (1990), 341–70
Marquess, W., *Lives of the Poet: The First Century of Keats Biography*, London, Pennsylvania State University Press, 1985
Matthews, G. (ed.), *Keats: The Critical Heritage*, New York, Barnes & Noble, 1971
McGann, J., 'Keats and the Historical Method in Literary Criticism', in *The Beauty of Inflections*, Oxford, Clarendon Press, 1988, pp. 17–65
Motion, A., *Keats*, London, Farrar, Straus and Giroux, 1997
O'Rourke, J. (ed.), *Ode on a Grecian Urn: Hypercanonicity and Pedagogy*, www.rc.umd.edu/praxis, 2003
Perkins, D., *The Quest for Permanence: The Symbolism of Wordsworth, Shelley, and Keats*, Cambridge, MA, Harvard University Press, 1959
Rajan, T., *Dark Interpreter: The Discourse of Romanticism*, Ithaca, NY, Cornell University Press, 1980
Ricks, C., *Keats and Embarrassment*, Oxford, Oxford University Press, 1976
Roe, N., *John Keats and the Culture of Dissent*, Oxford, Clarendon Press, 1997
Sperry, S., *Keats the Poet*, Princeton, Princeton University Press, 1973
Stillinger, J., *'The Hoodwinking of Madeline' and Other Essays on Keats's Poems*, Urbana, University of Illinois Press, 1971
Whale, J., *John Keats: Critical Issues*, New York, Palgrave, 2005
Wolfson, S., *Formal Charges: The Shaping of Poetry in British Romanticism*, Stanford, Stanford University Press, 1999
The Questioning Presence, Ithaca, NY, Cornell University Press, 1986
(ed.), *Cambridge Companion to John Keats*, Cambridge, Cambridge University Press, 2002
Borderlines: The Shiftings of Gender in British Romanticism, Stanford, Stanford University Press, 2006

20

HERBERT F. TUCKER

Alfred Lord Tennyson

You take up Tennyson for either of two reasons. One is the depth of his appeal as a superb artist, the other is the breadth of his historical pertinence as a pre-eminent Victorian. You stay with Tennyson, though, for both reasons, because it is a peculiarity of his achievement to have contrived their interdependence. His staying power derives from the care with which he tended, and the persistence with which his poems treat, the relationship between the terms of his art and the conditions of his fame. If a sweet tooth for words attracts you to a voice that can do this –

> Myriads of rivulets hurrying thro' the lawn,
> The moan of doves in immemorial elms,
> And murmuring of innumerable bees

– or if an ear for broken-hearted alienation awakens to the likes of this –

> He is not here; but far away
> The noise of life begins again,
> And ghastly thro' the drizzling rain
> On the bald street breaks the blank day

– then it is just a matter of time until acquaintance with such sheer beauty ripens into an understanding that *The Princess* (1847) and *In Memoriam* (1850) not only flex verbal power but also reflect on how that power may conspire with cultural power of other kinds: Victorian gender hierarchy, say, or the routinization of urban daily living. Conversely, if an interest in Victorian modernization is what draws you to Tennyson on the evolutionary struggle between science and faith, the massive dislocation of custom that was wrought by industrialization, or the globe-sweeping hubris of empire, what holds you there is the haunted and cadenced decorum with which he articulated such developments. Even phrases you already knew, like 'Their's not to wonder why, / Their's but to do and die' ('The Charge of the Light Brigade', 1854), rehearse in the passage from coinage into cliché the Tennysonian embroilment of private affection with public interest.

Born in 1809 into the midst of a large and mainly gloomy gentleman-cleric's family in rural Lincolnshire, Alfred Tennyson followed his unprosperous father's path of least resistance to Cambridge. At that then-moribund university he failed to complete his degree, but got an education all the same among a brilliant set of young men who were to grow into Victorian Britain's best and brightest scholars, bishops, and cabinet ministers. The Apostles, as they called themselves, incubated new ideas about cultural leadership on the part of an elite who – not unlike themselves in prospect – might wield the power of myth and public imagery to move a modern people. They cherished what in the 1820s were still fire-new Romantic convictions that poetry owned special access to that power, and they hailed in Tennyson's remarkable verbal imagination evidence that a wizard suited to the age's dawning occasions was at hand.

In a sense the rest is history. Tennyson's career would constitute a spectacular fulfilment, at national and then imperial scale, of just these undergraduate predictions; and to follow its trajectory as we shall do here is to stay close to the braiding of personal with collective motives. First, however, we need to shake off the aura of inevitability that hindsight has a way of projecting, and to approach Tennyson's unrivalled Victorian spokesmanship as not an entailment but a feat. We need to appreciate the dissonance between most of what we hear about the Victorian Era and much of what, given this poet's temper of heart and ear, we should expect an Age of Tennyson to be. That can-do epoch demanded extroverted uplift. Yet what this poet, left to his own temperament and devices, was likeliest to lift up was the very opposite of uplift. The torch song of a melancholy prostration was his muse's first motion and default theme, and it ballasts the Tennysonian repertoire from earliest moony lament to last elderly jeremiad. Where Victorians hungered for greatness of exhibition and monumental permanence, Tennyson indulged a lifelong fascination with evanescence, flux, and the humiliation to which man and his little systems must submit within the wheelings of aeonic time and the flittings of ever-recessive astral or submolecular space.

To some extent this conspicuous mismatch may be ascribed to the handicap under which poetry labours under modernity. An optional accessory to the business of getting on, a badge of coterie affiliation, a flywheel taking up surplus energy thrown off by the socioeconomic machine, or a therapeutic programme for souls whom that machinery has hurt: poetry conceived in such terms has been driven to the wall, and hung there as a curious trophy, for a long time now. This luxury status has taken its toll not only on poetry but *in* it. At least since the mid-eighteenth century, an impassioned minority who deem poetry's relegation to the sidelines lamentable have so embraced the lament as to make that genre definitive of poetry as such. The Romantic assertion that flowered at the turn of the nineteenth century seems in the long view a gallant exception to the prevailing rule, which typifies the poet as an introverted loser within a tradition that arose with poets of the Age of Sensibility like Gray and Collins, and that reasserted itself with force during the early 1820s when Keats, Shelley, and Byron died in rapid succession. Once the teenage Tennyson had carved 'Byron is dead' on a Somersby boulder, it was the domestic genius Felicia Hemans who ruled the poetic roost; accordingly it was to her hearth-throbs that the forward youth tuned his aspiration. A permanent lien on Tennyson's endowment was held throughout his career by tender, misprized souls abandoned by circumstances to the eloquence of mood, who without provocation break, break, break (up, down, out), or curl 'Into some still cavern deep, / There to weep, and weep, and weep' (*Maud*, 1855). Partly this was a matter of sheer temperament, but it also expressed the poet's acknowledgment of the marginal terms on which poetry was to be heard at all in his day.

Yet, for all this, Tennyson's is as strong a case as we shall find of a poet's discerning in the minority status of his chosen art a major opportunity to move that art from the cultural margin towards the centre. This poet seized on a multiplex codependency between the melodious expression of loss and all that in his culture strove hardest after gain. He cultivated varieties of symbiosis between deplored wrong, hopeless nostalgia, and frustrated yearning on the one hand, and on the other the drive for betterment, the compulsive goal-orientation, and the greed for innovation that typified Victorian progressivism. And he did so by grasping in the calculus of want – where lack precipitates desire – a common denominator between what his contemporaries missed in the lapsed transmission of their inheritance and what they hungered after by way of compensation. In Tennyson's grasp of this essential connection it is hard to know where intuitive tact left off and conscious exploitation began. His Apostolic formation at Cambridge provided a fund of sponsoring ideas that was supplemented for the rest of his life by conscientious reading in science, history, and the theory that accompanied these emergent disciplines. At the same time, however, and in keeping with the irrationality of Victorian cultural drives, there remains something uncanny about Tennyson's knack for putting those obscure drives to work.

Become a name: the lyricist's progress

Major poetic careers don't just happen; they bespeak sustained acts of will. The way Tennyson made a name for himself in Victorian society and in the canon of major poets left a clear trace across his oeuvre through the importance his oeuvre gives to the making of names. If we think of the *name* as a fixed mark of identity – a noun's noun – and of the *voice* as a medium in which the name is constituted – a vehicle by which, verb-like, the name is actualized – then the interdependence between name and voice in Tennyson emerges as analogous to the interdependence we have been discussing between public and private dimensions of his art. A couple of biographical anecdotes help correlate these two linked terms. One is the poet's disarming confession that the verse he learned earliest to love was his own, at five years old, and as recollected in after years a perfect pentameter at that: 'I hear a voice that's speaking in the wind.' Something more than natural, yet less than a full-blown personification, the windy voice in this line speaks nobody knows what. But speak it does, and with an effect that *finds* the pure 'I', calls it out from the sheer play of force into an identity that consists in the act of vocal attention.

A second, reciprocal anecdote dissolves personal identity back into a transpersonal power. It concerns Tennyson's lifelong habit of 'repeating my own name two or three times to myself silently' and so inducing 'a kind of waking trance' that gave access to a mystic state that was as clear, the poet insisted, as it was indescribable. He drew on this experience in 'The Ancient Sage' (1885), speaking under thin cover as the Chinese philosopher he knew as Laotzee (but left nameless in the text), 'revolving in myself / The word that is the symbol of myself', until 'The mortal limit of the Self was loosed, / And past into the Nameless, as a cloud / Melts into Heaven.' Whether the poet thus inly murmured 'Tennyson', or 'Alfred', or his wife's nickname for him 'Ally' hardly matters, for the whole point of the silent meditative chant was to attain 'loss of Self' by emptying of meaning the name that symbolized it. From force through voice to name, then back through voice to force again: like his own cresting and ebbing king of Camelot, 'From the great deep to the great deep he goes' ('The Passing of Arthur', 1869).

Coming into his own on the wings of voice, Tennyson started with gifts of Miltonic timbre, Spenserian amplitude, and Keatsian manoeuvre for which the best latter-day parallels are to be sought in the signature versatility of Frank Sinatra or Elvis Presley, pop-star heirs of the celebrity tradition that Tennyson inherited from Byron and bequeathed to the twentieth century. (Once Edison had his phonograph machine up and running, the aged Laureate's was one of the first voices he made sure to capture on wax.) In tonal balance and range even Tennyson's juvenilia are remarkably poised performances like these crooners', lavish in display yet consistently implying reserves of untapped power. The river of Tennysonian voice eddied early, moreover, around the focus of the name:

> And thrice my name was syllabled i' the air
> And thrice upon the wave, like that loud voice

Which through the deep dark night i' the olden time
Came sounding o'er the lone Ionian.
(*The Devil and the Lady*, 1823)

Already at fourteen amid the swirl of 'name' and 'voice' the poet makes for – precipitates out of his own vocalic resonance, and alights upon – the fitting and proper name 'Ionian'. 'Mouthing out his hollow oes and aes, / Deep-chested music' ('The Epic', 1842), here in the thick of adolescent pastiche the poet made that music accompany an uncannily prescient allusion to Plutarch's tale about the sea-borne rumour 'Great Pan is dead.' Most of what this allusion implied about the twilight of old gods at the dawn of new histories, and about Pan's declension into a notional myth of totality ('pantheism'), lay beyond the teenage poet's ken – although these themes would ripen during the Cambridge *conversazione* that lay not far ahead, whence he would harvest them again and again, in 'Morte d'Arthur' (1842) and 'Tithonus' (1860), to cite two name-dropping examples written at the top of his form. For now, in the heady promise of the 1820s, name-dropping sufficed for its own sake; a mouth-filling name virtually dictated the content for his most ambitious juvenilia, the prophetic blank verse vision 'Armageddon' (1824?) and its recension 'Timbuctoo', which won the Chancellor's Gold Medal at Cambridge for 1829.

Name localized what voice scattered abroad, and its fixative power operated on a different scale in each of Tennyson's first two collections. *Poems by Two Brothers* (1827) scours the latitudes and centuries for rehearsals of the Great Pan theme, wherein harpers, druids, and prophets on the verge of exile keeningly denounce ethnic defeats from Highlands to Hindostan and Persia to Peru. These choric voices minister to ubiquitous cultural collapse with the exilic incantation of names, which the verse cherishes like family jewels. The scope of *Poems, Chiefly Lyrical* (1830) narrows from anthem to lyric, and from politics to persons, as a gallery of female cameos supplants the collectivities from three years before. But much of the former collection's hauntedness persists into this volume, most famously in Tennyson's first canonical lyric 'Mariana', which like the rest is less a voguish portrait of the album or gift-book sort than it is a distillation of affect that happens to pool in the hollow of a name. Claribel, Lilian, Isabel, Rosaline, Adeline, Oriana: the lady-names of 1830 magnetize a longing that would otherwise drain off like the carol of 'The Dying Swan', in a world where 'The Mystic' hears 'Time flowing in the middle of the night, / And all things creeping to a day of doom', and where the poem-titling propositions 'Nothing Will Die' and 'All Things Must Die' are equally true, and equally depressing. Like the strophic forms with which both volumes experiment, the presiding identities Tennyson chants into being are modal stripes on a melancholy spectrum, not distinct individuals but refined awarenesses. What they are most intimately aware of, what their desertion or fixation or abandonment consistently betokens, is the evanescence in which their life shares.

Drawing this awareness into the open, and reconnecting it with the suspended historical and collective consciousness that had prevailed in the 1827 volume, constituted the chief work of Tennyson's next collection, *Poems* (1832). Now 'Mariana in the South' speaks forth the fate her 1830 sister had abstractedly and laconically endured. Now in the person of 'Oenone' Tennyson replaces sheer mood with consequential attitudes, which breed from erotic dereliction a resolve to act in the world, indeed on the stage of world history in Troy, with sororal voices prophesying war. And now in that minor but genuine Victorian myth 'The Lady of Shalott' the artist's need for recognition is rehearsed in a balked love-plot dooming the isolated weaver to the lot her poet feared was also his. Such fame as comes to the disregarded Lady not only costs her death, but entails her misrecognition by the man, and just behind him the public, she dies for. That the names of these under-responsive objects of attention rhyme with each other, and with the Lady's, constitutes a gravitational destiny that rules Tennyson's stanzaic narrative from the beginning: Shalott, Camelot, Lancelot are hoops of matched sound binding the staves of the poem into strangely mellow hollowness. Going out like Oenone into the world, Tennyson's developing career myth of 1832 suggested, meant going out like a candle, or like the Lady's tapestry as it 'floated wide', or like the Lady herself, who by floating her name as a public brand ('Below the carven stern she wrote / *The Lady of Shalott*') is extinguished into the bargain ('Singing in her song she died').

Germ tissue: the elegist's break

Given this cul-de-sac within his own 'Palace of Art' – another 1832 poem where aesthetic dreams end in blind alleys – no wonder Tennyson lost momentum for ten years and did not publish another book before *Poems* (1842). That is what outwardly happened, but *how* it happened is quite another matter. For the autumn of 1833 brought the career-shaping crisis of Tennyson's life, when his intimate friend, best critic, and affianced brother-in-law Arthur Hallam died suddenly in Vienna of a massive stroke at the age of twenty-two. This blunt early encounter with the random hand of death, brutally close yet a continent away, was the formative event of Tennyson's maturity. It desolated him; it also, by an irony whose bitterness never quite left his tongue, proved the making of him. Within months he had drafted seminal passages ('germs' was his notably ambivalent term) of the works that would preoccupy the rest of his creative life. He had broken new generic ground within the forms of dramatic monologue, narrative idyll, and lyric sequence in which not only he but other Victorian poets would do their most lasting work across the century.

Tennyson did these things, not by discarding the vocally rich dead-endedness at which his work between 1827 and 1832 had arrived, but by espousing that mode with transformative intensity. 'Let Love clasp Grief lest both be drowned': the advice thus recorded in the opening lyric of *In Memoriam* could not, in career terms at least, have been bettered. For the ordeal of 1833 taught Tennyson that to clasp grief hard enough was to crystallize melancholia into mourning, to shape a mood into a vector, to mould a state of feeling into a programme for action. Such a programme might in proof evolve with great deliberateness – grief pays its respects after all by slow, exacting instalment – but the very candour of its reluctant progress would make it accessible as an omnibus with capacity for a host of fellow-mourners. No doubt the first stirrings that would bear fruit in *In Memoriam* and *Maud* and *Idylls of the King* were as blind as they were deep. The poetic rehearsal of a talking cure was a stricken man's fumbling first resort – and desperate expression of fidelity – to the gift whose survival seemed, at times, to keep his fellowship with Hallam alive. But over the course of ten years, then twenty and thirty more, Tennyson learned to regard his affliction as representative of losses and anxieties possessing broad Victorian currency. Learning so to regard it, in fact, formed a crucial step along the therapeutic path from alienation to spokesmanship on which his own feet in the 1830s were set.

The renewed agenda appears unmistakably in 1842 poems that are named for a central figure. Unlike their eavesdropped and bespoken forerunners from the 1830s, they now nearly always speak for themselves, within the dramatic monologue format that Robert Browning was concurrently pioneering. Tennyson's new names are mainly heroes now rather than ladies; and, unlike Browning's eccentrics and stowaways, they tend to be Big Names, figures on the scale of Sir Galahad and Ulysses who, even as they 'yearn to breathe the airs of heaven' or 'sail beyond the sunset', are tracing an arc that departs from social norms only to return and quicken them with the energy of legend. This is the once-and-future circuit of King Arthur (also debuted here), and it describes almost as well the route taken by the 1842 collection's token heroine in 'Godiva', though of course the secret of that naked equestrienne's fame is to triumph exposed and yet unseen. An allied problematic of heroic name-making informs with special force another poem, 'Tiresias', that while not published until 1885 was drafted during Tennyson's germinal 1830s. In this monologue the blind, discredited seer persuades a young man to earn an undying 'name' – the word recurs with hypnotic obsessiveness – by committing patriotic suicide. The ironies of reception that had attended the Lady of Shalott's futile martyrdom yield here to grandeurs of civic inscription set in commemorative stone by the 'song', 'lips', and 'tongue' of a grateful people's voice. 'I am become a name'; 'I am a part of all that I have met': if these phrases lodge Ulysses's complaint, in the same breath they frame his boast too. 'The long day wanes: the slow moon climbs: the deep / Moans round with many voices', and those voices are cheering, Ulysses knows, for him. The old uncanny wind off the lone Ionian still blew fresh for Tennyson in 1842, only now the voice it bore was choral, its burden a collective validation in which the heroic name, the public interest, and the poetic agenda all conspired.

This purpose held by different means along the poet's new endeavours in narrative. From the cosmopolitan pastoral traditions of later classical antiquity he bred a native strain of 'English idylls' that focused upon home themes and rural settings a clutch of concerns that were fetched from around the empire. Often the deep's many voices round off a domestic interest, be it suburban ('Audley Court' and later in 1864 'Enoch Arden') or mythic ('Morte d'Arthur'). Even when planted deeper inland, Tennyson's soothing idylls rock 'a wayward modern mind' ('Edwin Morris', 1851) in a deftly balanced middle style to the percussion of commercial news ('Walking to the Mail'), or to such a report as this:

> He spoke; and, high above, I heard them blast
> The steep slate-quarry, and the great echo flap
> And buffet round the hills, from bluff to bluff.
> ('The Golden Year', 1846)

The labial consonants, in consort with the gathering ambush of muffled vowels, mime to vast applause a mapping of industrial change onto perennial landscape. The Snowdonia slate-quarry here stands to the imperial globe somewhat as the idyll stands to the epic, whose conventions charge the old gesture 'He spoke' (*inquit* in Virgil's tongue, *unquote* in ours) with the ambient roar of public works in which all the country participates.

The better parts of Tennyson's odd next book work this idyllic vein to remarkable effect – or perhaps we should say to special effects. *The Princess* abounds in narrative descriptions whose pyrotechnics lift off from a platform of generalizing ambition, like its own miniature 'fire-balloon' that in the prologue 'Rose gem-like up before the dusky groves / And dropt a fairy parachute and past'. In substance the poem confects a fairytale about women's higher education, experimentally performed by a visionary feminist under an indulgent, then aggravated, and at length militantly reassertive masculine dispensation. Readers since first publication have found this fable of domestic recapture intriguing in prospect and annoying in execution, and it seems agreed that a proper home awaited it in Gilbert and Sullivan's light operetta *Princess Ida* many years later. More engaging than the story is the 'medley' apparatus of its telling, which is serially distributed among seven collegians while their lady escorts chime in with interludes of song. This gendered division of poetic labour schematizes the interplay Tennyson's mature oeuvre sustains between progressive narration and melancholic counter-currents that regressively dwell on 'the days that are no more' ('Tears, Idle Tears') or that 'like a broken purpose waste in air' ('Come Down, O Maid').

This latter, feminized influence spills back into the male narrative preserve with a more than lyrical insistence. The unnamed Prince is an effeminate, climactically invalided blondilocks who is subject to fainting spells that repeatedly dissolve even a storybook regal's grip on things. That this should be the consciousness focalizing Tennyson's entire narrative – a psychic kid glove into which all seven narrators slip without a hitch – is a most suggestive feature of the poem. On the one hand, it enforces a hegemonic cultural narrative about how masculinity supersedes the femininity out of which it develops. On the other, it reveals a persistent condition of male neediness that explains a lot: why the goal of a man's development should be to reclaim the femininity he left behind – in marriage, to which the whole comic plot of *The Princess* arises; in heterosexual intercourse, which several late passages imagine with surprising frankness – and also why a manly confession of lack might elicit, and gratify, a womanly desire.

Joining up: the poet's arrival

Tennyson's great mid-century sequences *In Memoriam* and *Maud* were both assembled piecemeal – the former taking seventeen years, the latter not so many months – from lyric germ tissue incubated since the crisis of 1833. And both wear the trace of this compositional history in the thematic implications of their granular, incremental structure. Confessing himself diaristically from moment to isolated moment along an implied narrative continuum set in contemporary Britain, the speaker in each poem enjoys the authenticating advantages of immediacy, anguished retrospect, and worried foresight but by the same token forfeits the long-range comforts of a coordinating overview. Running questions about how to integrate the constituent parts of the poem stand for questions of another order: How can what one knows, what one feels, and what one believes be squared with each other? How can contemporary life sustain relationship with the standpoints and values, even the rhythm and pace, of the traditional life from which it is hastening away? How can the isolated self that is tormented by such questions coexist with other selves, and by what means can they together form a social body?

Both poems ingeniously make these questions answer one another, but they do so to diametrically different effect. *In Memoriam*, gratefully accepting the solidarity it discovers between personal and public dilemmas, takes a mourner's social reintegration within the fellowship of sorrow as an earnest of, and a model for, the achievement of inward psychic balance. The aggrieved speaker of *Maud*, in contrast, finds such a congruence of private with public pathology literally maddening: current events and the recognitions they incite drive him beyond alienated neurosis into a unified social vision whose hallucinatory clarity is available only from the inside of a madhouse, and for which the only imaginable sequel – and the only cure, if you call it that – is the manichean unison of feeling conferred by enlistment in a regiment shipping off to the Crimean War.

As its lapidary title suggests, *In Memoriam A. H. H.* concerns the establishment of a name. Anonymously published at first in 1850, it undertook to inscribe Hallam in the Victorian honour roll where all who had known his promise agreed he would have belonged had he lived, 'a potent voice of Parliament'. Collaterally with this aim, and without detracting from its sincerity, the poem submitted to public judgement as adroit and cogent an application for the Poet Laureateship as can well be imagined. Its measured, hesitant sequence of chiselled quatrains not only correlates a personal malaise with a cultural syndrome – this much Tennyson had already been doing for years – but stages within the virtual time of the text the poet's stepwise, backsliding, recuperative advance towards a reformed credo: namely, that in just such correlation lay the psychic healing and moral integrity he sought. *In Memoriam*'s status as the testament of a joiner is thrown into high relief by the trenchancy with which its opening twenty lyrics incise all that militates against social belonging. The bereaved poet gropes pathetically for a surrogate listener among personified abstractions, apostrophized (and unresponding) objects picked out from the litter of modern living, and stereotypic fellow-sufferers whose imagined pain if anything augments his own. Eventually – and everything that happens in this sedimentary, antimiraculous poem happens eventually – the stubborn death-borne conviction of his own limitation persuades the poet to account as a net gain the depth of love that he too briefly knew but can still in memory affirm.

Over the course of another hundred lyrics, this long pivot towards acceptance accrues gain of a similar kind from across the Victorian ideological system, although it is important to stress that the force of ideology in *In Memoriam* obtains not as propositional truth (about which the poem is by turns insouciant and apologetic) but as felt meaning. The emotional pragmatism of lowered expectations boosted Tennyson's regard for what *worked* in Victorian culture. It opened his elegiac sequence to a miscellany of coping expedients – tourism, the keeping of Christmas, evolutionary theory, seance spirituality – which the poem does not endorse but instead hails for their partial palliation, and collective validation, of the travails of a chronically heavy heart. What Tennyson gave back in exchange for these remedies was the wide quietness of his superb spokesmanship: now touching the vague or the obscure into articulate dignity, now conceding to cliché and periphrasis their due place in public discourse, he followed the branching veinwork of Victorian mourning so steadfastly that it brought him into his culture's baffled core. Intuitive, tentative, and (like its verse-form) constant in purpose while variable in stance and mood, the poem earned its rights of survivorship both by the generosity of its sympathies and by the scrupulous watch it kept on how grief feels, over a long haul in which traumatic affect is not outlived but grows into the texture of life. When T. S. Eliot depreciated the faith of *In Memoriam* and applauded the quality of its doubt, he was saying nothing Tennyson did not know already, nothing indeed that he had not repeatedly built into the poem.

Tennyson even anticipated a charge that is harsher than Eliot's but that readers may be tempted to lodge against *In Memoriam*: that the poet's faith is bad faith. This charge is absorbed poetically, brooded on, and re-emitted with blistering force in Tennyson's first Laureate book and most permanently disturbing work, the experimental monodrama *Maud*. Here again our focal point is a serial confessant, but the circumspection of *In Memoriam* yields now to hairpin mood swings on a tide of hyperbolic invective, set to a virtuoso range of lyric measures that can all the same feel, in their obsessive drivenness, less varied than the chastened phases of the quatrain in *In Memoriam*. That poem's hard-won vision of social integrity is *Maud*'s point of departure, and the new speaker detests what he sees – not least because he knows himself to be complicit in the corruption and injustice that pass for social order at the middle of the nineteenth century. He reels between denouncing that order and resenting his disenfranchisement from a share in its spoils: a bipolar moral syndrome for which the plot of *Maud* offers no lasting relief, but instead a sequence of expedients that only serve to deepen the diagnosis. Maud seems to offer the speaker an alternative to these things, but loving Maud turns out to mean loving privilege, wealth, and a fantasy of dominion that Tennyson's headlong imagery expands unstoppably from a young man's fancy out through gender, class, and race to imperial scale. Defence of the speaker's honour comes to blows in a murderous duel, which prompts exile, whence springs certifiable madness, which brings on the dizzying standoff between Tennyson's first great lyric of urban anomie ('O that 'twere possible' from the notebooks of 1833) and a bravura satirical passage that, written in a matter of minutes, reduces leading Victorian ideals to the rubble and babble of an asylum compound. Whether the speaker's final ascent from madhouse to Crimea troop ship subverts this totalitarian vision of bad faith or confirms it is a question that continues to exercise readers of *Maud*. It was meant to.

Built to music: the Laureateship of state

The 1850 coincidence among the enthusiastic reception of *In Memoriam*, Tennyson's long-delayed marriage to Emily Sellwood, and his Laureate appointment by the queen culminates for us a poet's courtship and espousal of his public. Add to this consecration the market pressures exerted by cascading profits from the sale of his books, and there is reason to expect with the years a Tennyson who was bound ever more snugly to a centrist poetic project. That both is and is not what we find. True, a list is easily compiled of more or less command performances for state occasions, chauvinistic salvos of newsprint quality, historical costume dramas that convened reverential West End audiences in their day but are since forgotten, and conservative vaticinations against newfangled things in general. Worse, a certain loftiness of port that seemed demanded by the station to which he had been called led routinely in Tennyson's later work to that marmoreal mannerism which Gerard Manley Hopkins skewered as the 'Parnassian' mode – the Laureateship on automatic pilot. As often as not, however, and with a creative edge that is the more appreciable when we bear in mind the forces to which he was subject, Tennyson managed to summon that centrism of his to the bar for an independent investigation that produced real insight. His unique post at the apex of Victorian culture disclosed an unparalleled vantage from which to penetrate essential political mysteries of his moment. Chief among these was the mystery he monodramatized with horrified fascination in *Maud*: the recruitment of freelance, laissez-faire individuality into a national collectivity that transcended elder allegiances such as personal loyalty and regional or class identity. From this stem branched other political phenomena that his Laureate work also addressed, among them the nineteenth-century cult of heroic personality and the establishment of state authority under conditions of democratic transition. Tennyson may have become an oracular Victorian sage, but to his credit he kept interrogating the increasingly mass-cultural power in whose name he was privileged to speak.

His first and most permanently conspicuous Laureate piece, a commissioned 'Ode on the Death of the Duke of Wellington' (1852), hammers at the gong of grandeur to beat the band. What is peculiar about this verse soundtrack for what were, by even a Victorian standard, solemnities of extravagant pomp on behalf of the nation's soldier hero is also peculiarly Tennysonian: the recurrent sounding-forth of the Great Duke's 'name' swelled to paean by the roar of popular acclamation. The syllables 'Wellington' do not occur except in its title, but the ode never tires of flourishing his 'name' as an abstraction to conjure with, marching it thrice past the reviewing stand in a brassy phalanx of lines rhymed with 'fame', 'claim', and half a dozen other monosyllables, all as summons and drill for 'a people's voice / In full acclaim, / A people's voice'. It sounds awful as thus described, yet the orotund cathedral effect is rather awesome in its pageantry of what was, when all is said, the modern political idea. For the power this ode invokes is the power of popular sovereignty to which Wellington, like his defining antagonist Bonaparte, had ministered in spite of himself. Tennyson takes this theme to the declamatory limit, if not over the top, by putting words in the people's mouth that threaten to turn into airy nothing, mere Falstaffian puffery: 'With honour, honour, honour, honour to him, / Eternal honour to his name'. One jaw-droppingly autopoetic line runs, 'Truth-teller was our England's Alfred named.' The truth on which our Alfred here wagered his brand-new Laureate reputation was that 'honour' and 'name' depended on the afflatus that public-image manufacture could pump into its Arthurs and Alfreds, heroized front men of the mass state.

Idylls of the King would show this wager won, and then lost, in the person of a blameless monarch who is also a figurehead exalted by the vagaries of consensus, and then ruined by them. In the course of delivering this modern political analysis on an instalment plan half a century long, Tennyson won and lost some literary battles of his own. 'Morte d'Arthur' and its frame 'The Epic' had in 1842 represented a handsome generic promissory note, yet it was one that the poet proved extremely reluctant to redeem. Doubts about his own powers prompted hesitation; so did doubts about the viability of epic in the era of franchises, railroads, and novels. Yet the unique career pattern we have been examining here virtually mandated that this of all poets should bestow on his culture the dignity of what remained the most prestigious of genres, and not many Laureate years had gone by before the matter of Camelot engaged him again. Tennyson's Arthurian campaign of the 1850s was a failed one, brilliantly conducted yet unavailing, into enemy territory that not even he could capture for poetry: the domain of contemporary domestic fiction. The first *Idylls of the King* so named comprised four lady-titled novellas in exquisite verse that concerned families, marriages, and affairs, especially the entanglements of love. Although the collection sold very well, as all Tennyson's work henceforth would do, the poet himself evidently wasn't buying it; for the *Idylls* project languished another decade in imaginative quarantine, like Arthur on his 1842 barge.

In order to revive the project, Tennyson had to retrench, resupply, and steal a march on fiction by properly epic means, which meant mythologizing Camelot in terms that could speak to his century not only domestically but civically. These terms he forged by reconfiguring his staple tactics of name and voice to fit the mass politics he had more recently imagined in the Wellington Ode and *Maud*. 'The Holy Grail' and adjoining idylls of 1869 and 1872 offered an anatomy of groupthink, casting King Arthur as an ideological cipher subject to his adherents' faith – an uncertain quantity that was in turn subject to gossip and scandal, Tennyson's medievalized equivalents for the Victorian public media in which he was himself, of course, an interested player. Ephemeral, irresistible, and wide open to manipulation through the commonly known secret of Guenevere's adultery with Lancelot, the Camelot rumour mill performed the work of myth that makes *Idylls of the King* in finished form so unexpectedly modern an epic: a study in public relations as the cultural power that makes and breaks celebrity names. The windy mystery of Tennysonian voice came downtown at last as *vox populi vox Dei*, with the hum of a machinery as swift, blank, and pitiless as any the epic tradition had known.

Tennyson's late cultural vision gave peculiar yet apt fulfilment to the Cambridge Apostles' early auguries for him as national spokesman. Great Pan's death was a theme that would sound again in a string of taut heroic epyllia from the final Laureate decades, in which 'Lucretius' (1868), 'Columbus' (1880), 'Demeter and Persephone' (1889) declared the powers-that-be suborned, exploded, dispensed with. Duty, smug Victorian virtue though it can now seem in hindsight, shines out from these monologues with the rugged glamour of an existential claim obstinately staked in a wilderness of banality. Nor at the end of the day did duty suffice for Tennyson himself, who characteristically weighed anchor in 'Crossing the Bar' (1889) for a voyage beyond good and evil in which he could at most, and only at last, 'hope to see my Pilot face to face'.

When the reading public petitioned their Laureate for monumental security, what he latterly offered them resembled the way in to Camelot:

> And there was no gate like it under heaven.
> For barefoot on the keystone, which was lined
> And rippled like an ever-fleeting wave,
> The Lady of the Lake stood: all her dress
> Wept from her sides as water flowing away;
> But like the cross her great and goodly arms
> Stretched under all the cornice and upheld:
> And drops of water fell from either hand;

And down from one a sword was hung, from one
A censer, either worn with wind and storm;
And o'er her breast floated the sacred fish;
And in the space to left of her, and right,
Were Arthur's wars in weird devices done,
New things and old co-twisted, as if Time
Were nothing, so inveterately, that men
Were giddy gazing there. ('Gareth and Lynette', 1872)

Structure as process; vertigo as fixture. The very keystone of the realm is carved to represent flows of force that wear its civic might away as surely, as *weirdly*, as in deep geological time the fluent tracts of earth once brought stone forth to begin with. 'Inveterately', Tennyson's habit of imagination erodes what it erects; and the 'giddy gazing' reader who drops from line to line of these pentameters feels with mounting gravitas how the impending fall of Camelot will be due to the same unmasterable tectonics whereby for a season Arthur has built it up. The legendary architecture of the state, as of the poem that Tennyson so slowly 'co-twisted' with it – between, more or less, the passage of the First Reform Bill opening the franchise a crack (1832) and the Third Reform Bill conferring it on nearly every man in the kingdom (1884) – is grounded on the imagination of a people, which is to say incessantly subject to change, which is to say doomed to disappear.

Within a page or two of the passage quoted here, riddling Merlin will hand wide-eyed Gareth the kind of reassurance that is at the same time a challenge, and that may be the only steadying principle Tennyson's civic vision can honestly claim: 'the city is built / To music, therefore never built at all, / And therefore built for ever'. Camelot is built, accredited, and beholden to the unstable capital of a currency for which the nearest analogue is the fluency of the verse that frames it. *Sunt lacrimae rerum et mentem mortalia tangunt.* So Tennyson's epic model Virgil had written two millennia before, on his hero's first sight of a doomed city in the *Aeneid*. The tears in mortal things sap the empires they nourish. So stark a discrepancy emerges between Tennyson's perennial calling to weep the world away, and the constructive vocation which stirred in him from the outset, that his manifest success in that vocation must leave us in doubt as to what the Victorians in truth wanted their Laureate to say.

SELECTED FURTHER READING

Editions

The Poems of Tennyson, ed. Christopher Ricks, 3 vols, 2nd edn, Harlow, Longman, 1987

Tennyson: A Selected Edition, ed. Christopher Ricks, Harlow, Longman, 1989

The Letters of Alfred Lord Tennyson, eds Cecil Y. Lang and Edgar F. Shannon, Jr, 3 vols, Oxford, Clarendon Press, 1982–90

Secondary works

Biography

Martin, Robert Bernard, *Tennyson: The Unquiet Heart*, Oxford, Clarendon Press, 1980

Tennyson, Hallam, *Alfred Lord Tennyson: A Memoir by his Son*, 2 vols, London, Macmillan, 1897

Criticism

Armstrong, Isobel, *Victorian Poetry: Poetry, Poetics, and Politics*, London, Routledge, 1993

Culler, A. Dwight, *The Poetry of Tennyson*, New Haven, Yale University Press, 1977

Douglas-Fairhurst, Robert, *Victorian Afterlives: The Shaping of Influence in Nineteenth-Century Literature*, Oxford, Oxford University Press, 2002

Eliot, T. S., 'Tennyson's *In Memoriam*' (1936), in *Selected Essays*, 3rd edn, London, Faber and Faber, 1951

Griffiths, Eric, *The Printed Voice of Victorian Poetry*, Oxford, Clarendon Press, 1989

Killham, John (ed.), *Critical Essays on the Poetry of Tennyson*, London, Routledge, 1960

Nicolson, Harold, *Tennyson: Aspects of his Life, Character and Poetry*, London, Constable, 1923

Pattison, Robert, *Tennyson and Tradition*, Cambridge, MA, Harvard University Press, 1979

Pearsall, Cornelia, *Tennyson's Rapture: Transformation in the Victorian Dramatic Monologue*, New York, Oxford University Press, 2008

Peltason, Timothy, *Reading 'In Memoriam'*, Princeton, Princeton University Press, 1985

Reynolds, Matthew, *The Realms of Verse, 1830–1870: English Poetry in a Time of Nation-Building*, Oxford, Oxford University Press, 2001

Ricks, Christopher, *Tennyson*, London, Macmillan, 1972

Rowlinson, Matthew, *Tennyson's Fixations: Psychoanalysis and the Topics of the Early Poetry*, Charlottesville, University Press of Virginia, 1994

Shaw, W. David, *Tennyson's Style*, Ithaca, NY, Cornell University Press, 1976

Tucker, Herbert F., *Tennyson and the Doom of Romanticism*, Cambridge, MA, Harvard University Press, 1988

(ed.), *Critical Essays on Alfred Lord Tennyson*, New York, G. K. Hall, 1993

21

J. HILLIS MILLER

Robert Browning

> A good many oddities and a good many great writers have been entombed in the Abbey; but none of the odd ones have been so great and none of the great ones so odd.
>
> (Henry James, 'Browning in Westminster Abbey')

What James says is right on the mark. Robert Browning is the oddest of the great English poets. His poetry is odd in the sense that it is peculiar, strange, idiosyncratic, even weird, or uncanny. The famous dramatic monologues included in most anthologies and course syllabuses ('My Last Duchess', 'Fra Lippo Lippi', 'Porphyria's Lover', 'Soliloquy of the Spanish Cloister', 'The Bishop Orders His Tomb at Saint Praxed's Church', and so on) hardly give a full sense of that strangeness, though they do have an odd propensity to give voice to deep-dyed villains. The oddness in question is partly due to the psychological peculiarities of those who speak in Browning's poems. Perhaps, however, it most conspicuously lies in his poetry's notorious peculiarities of diction and syntax, as these reflect or represent the psychological oddnesses of imagined characters. 'Imagined' applies even when the speakers are historical personages, such as the Renaissance Italian painter Fra Lippo Lippi. Lippi really existed. Browning learned about him from Vasari's *Le Vite de' Pittori* (*Lives of the Painters*, 1550, 1568). Nevertheless, Browning invented, on this basis, Lippi's speech and the dramatic situation of 'Fra Lippo Lippi'. He did this by trying to imagine what it would have been like to be Fra Lippo Lippi.

Browning's poetry in the edition of 1888–94 takes up seventeen big volumes. The one-volume Riverside edition, copyright 1895 (cited here), which follows the 1888–94 edition, is in over one thousand double-columned pages in almost unreadable tiny type. Browning was an exuberantly abundant poet. That is part of his poetry's strangeness, since so little connection in speaker or poetic form exists between one poem and the next if you read them all in sequence. The reader is thrown more or less violently from one interior life and metric scheme to an entirely different one, across the blank space between poem and poem. Matthew Arnold called this 'confused multitudinousness'. Other critics see it as admirable variety and abundance. Few people beyond specialists have read all Browning's poems, though I can, it happens, claim to have done so. The peculiarities of Browning's poetry are especially salient in the rarely read long early poems and in the rarely read long later poems, with the more famous poems forming a relatively lucid middle phase of shorter and clearer works.

Robert Browning's life has its own oddnesses. That life by no means fully explains his poetry, however. Knowing that Browning had learned about Fra Lippo Lippi by reading Vasari does not predict or account for Browning's great dramatic monologue about Lippi, nor does reading Browning's sources for *Sordello* go far to explaining the murkiness of that outrageously exorbitant poem. Browning's life, however, is interesting in itself. His life-story has been told over and over, in long and short biographies, and in response to one form of that propensity to think historical facts are explanatory of poetic texts that is so much a part of western culture.

Robert Browning was born in Camberwell, a south-east suburb of London, on 7 May 1812. His father was a clerk in the Bank of England. The father was a shy, bookish man. He had a collection of 6,000 books in many different languages. Browning's mother was a Scottish woman, an evangelical Congregationalist. The mother strongly influenced her son, for example his complex relation to Christianity and his interest in ambiguous moments in Christian history (as in 'Saul', 'A Death in the Desert', 'Johannes Agricola in Meditation', and 'Bishop Blougram's Apology'). The poet-to-be was precocious, and an omnivorous reader, especially of his father's books. As a result, his knowledge of recondite historical personages and history's nooks and crannies was amazing. That reading may lie behind Browning's understanding of human beings' (mostly men's) boundless capacity for earnest and selfless pedantry. This is celebrated in 'A Grammarian's Funeral'. Browning's out-of-the-way reading forms the background of many of his poems. It also makes many of them, for example *Sordello*, extremely puzzling if you do not happen to know the historical background.

Browning was educated mostly at home. His outside schooling was somewhat irregular, since he was intellectually so far ahead of his classmates. As a nonconformist, he could not attend Oxford or Cambridge. He dropped out of University College, London, after less than a year. Browning refused to adopt any regular profession. He dedicated himself instead to writing poetry, which he had been doing since childhood. His father paid for the publication of his early poems. Browning travelled widely on the continent in his youth. His earliest published poems, long and forbiddingly difficult,

Pauline (1833), *Paracelsus* (1835), and *Sordello* (1840), were little noticed, except primarily to be reviled, though *Paracelsus* gained him the attention of London literati. All three are disguised autobiography, sometimes, as we say, 'thinly disguised'. *Paracelsus* is ostensibly about the sixteenth-century physician and alchemist named in the title. *Sordello* is ostensibly the life-story of a thirteenth-century Italian troubadour poet who wrote primarily in Provençal, and who appears in Dante's *Purgatorio*. John Stuart Mill, in notes written in his copy of *Pauline* for a review he never wrote, says of the author of *Pauline*: 'With considerable poetic powers, the writer seems to me possessed with a more intense and morbid self-consciousness than I ever knew in any sane human being.' Browning's somewhat unpersuasive defence was to claim that the speaker in *Pauline* is an imaginary personage, not the author. This would make the poem the first of Browning's dramatic monologues.

Three famous anecdotes are told about the obscurity of *Sordello*. Douglas Jerrold, a well-known early Victorian dramatist and writer, tried to read his copy of *Sordello* when he was sick in bed. His wife came in to find him weeping. When his wife told him she could not make head or tail of *Sordello*, Jerrold said, 'Thank God! I thought I had lost my mind.' Tennyson is reported to have said that only two lines in the poem are comprehensible, the first and the last, and both are lies. The lines are: 'Who will, may hear Sordello's story told', and 'Who would has heard Sordello's story told'. Carlyle said that his wife had read all of *Sordello* without being able to tell whether Sordello was a man, a city, or a book. Though Browning, at the earnest solicitation of his friends, made a number of attempts to make *Sordello* more comprehensible, this effort was by no means successful. Even the latest version remains, not to put too fine a point upon it, resolutely obscure. The more or less inscrutable side-bars, such as 'How a poet's soul comes into play', are little help, any more than is Browning's claim that the poem is not straightforward historical narrative, but that his 'stress lay on the incidents in the development of a soul; little else is worth study'. Browning seems to have had, for some reason, an unconquerable resistance to 'coming clean' in this poem, or to saying clearly what he apparently meant. I shall later on try to explain this resistance, if, indeed, it can be explained as other than just a major feature of Browning's 'oddness'.

These three early poems overlapped with Browning's short and only marginally successful career as a dramatist. He also published in the early 1840s two collections of shorter poems: *Dramatic Lyrics* (1842) and *Dramatic Romances and Lyrics* (1845). These volumes already contain, under earlier titles, some of his most successful dramatic monologues, for example 'My Last Duchess', 'Porphyria's Lover', and 'The Bishop Orders

His Tomb'. These volumes, however, received almost no attention when they appeared.

Browning's courtship of the reclusive, invalid poetess Elizabeth Barrett, who was kept in seclusion by a domineering patriarchal father, began in 1844 with a long correspondence. It culminated in 1846 with their secret marriage and elopement to the continent. They settled in Florence at the Casa Guidi. They lived there until Elizabeth Barrett Browning's death in 1861. They had one child, a son nicknamed 'Pen'. Browning dedicated himself to caring for his son for a decade after his wife's death. Browning's love for Elizabeth Barrett, and hers for him, as well as his quasi-betrayals of that love after her death, for example in his unsuccessful proposal of marriage to Louisa Lady Ashburton in 1869, no doubt lie behind his many great poems about licit and illicit love, and about the relation of bodily to spiritual love, *eros* to *agape*: 'The Statue and the Bust', 'Two in the Campagna', 'One Word More', *The Ring and the Book*, *The Inn Album*, *Fifine at the Fair*, and many others. The complexity of male–female love, it can be argued, is Browning's great theme, though that in itself hardly distinguishes his poetry from Victorian literature in general or from western literature as a whole. Browning's 'take' on this theme, however, has his characteristic idiosyncrasies, for example as a part of his interest in abnormal psychology. Before his wife's death, Browning's poems about love most often celebrate the triumphs of successful love-affairs, even when they are illicit, while, after 'Ba's' death, Browning's poems tell over and over some version of a love-triangle that involves unfaithfulness or betrayal. That theme, however, is already foreshadowed in a quite early poem, 'My Last Duchess'.

Before his wife's death Browning published *Men and Women* (1855), the most famous of his collections of short poems, mostly dramatic monologues, including, for example, 'Fra Lippo Lippi', 'Andrea del Sarto', and 'Childe Roland to the Dark Tower Came'. This masterwork was followed three years later, in 1864, by the publication of another such collection, *Dramatis Personae*. This also contains many famous poems: 'Rabbi Ben Ezra', 'Caliban upon Setebos', and 'Mr. Sludge, "The Medium"'.

After his wife's death, Browning moved back to London, where he lived for the rest of his life, except for summers spent on the French coast in Brittany or in Switzerland. He was increasingly a celebrity, especially after the success of *The Ring and the Book* (1868–9). That poem is 21,000 lines long. It is a series of twelve monologues, the first and last by the poet, and the middle ten offering different perspectives by participants and spectators on a seventeenth-century Roman murder case. The telling through contradictory juxtaposed points of view uses something like the technique employed almost a century later in the Japanese film *Rashomon* (1950). *The Ring and the Book* is characteristic of Browning's penchant for giving villains lots of opportunity to justify themselves. Only Guido Franceschini the murderer gets two monologues to himself. The poem is Browning's masterwork in the genre of giving all the available evidence as a way of showing that ethical judgement is never all that easy, however much you know the facts. Guido's wife Pompilia speaks her monologue as she lies on the verge of death after having been mortally stabbed by her jealous husband. Her faithful loving friend, the Canon Giuseppe Caponsacchi, who has helped Pompilia escape from her abusive husband, gets his turn, as do lawyers for the prosecution and defence, spokespersons for three different views of the Roman populace ('Half-Rome', 'The Other Half-Rome', and 'Tertium Quid'), and, not least, the Pope, shown agonizing over his decision to authorize capital punishment. The Pope speaks just before Guido's second monologue, this time in the condemned cell, waiting the imminent appearance of his executioners, with its climactic calling on the wife he has murdered to save him. He cries out in a hierarchical crescendo that puts Pompilia above Christ, the Virgin, and even God himself as sovereign pardon-grantors:

> I was just stark mad, – let the madman live
> Pressed by as many chains as you please pile!
> Don't open! Hold me from them! I am yours,
> I am the Granduke's – no, I am the Pope's!
> Abate, – Cardinal, – Christ, – Maria, – God, ...
> Pompilia, will you let them murder me?

During his later London years, Browning was invited to dinner parties so often that people said he would die in his dinner jacket. Henry James has represented the mysterious contradiction between the urbane diner-out and the author of such strange poems in his short story 'The Private Life'. James imagines that two entirely different Brownings must exist, the affable social lion and the man who sits at the same time at home writing long, hyperbolically obscure poems. Browning and James came to be near neighbours in De Vere Gardens, Kensington, towards the end of Browning's life.

During his later years, Browning reverted to stylistic obscurities somewhat like those of *Sordello*. I shall say something more about that reversion later on. Browning published in the 1870s and 1880s almost one long poem or collection of poems a year, often basing them on the scenery of Brittany and on anecdotes he had heard during his summers there. This is true of *Fifine at the Fair* (1872), *Red Cotton Night-Cap Country* (1873), or *The Inn Album* (1875). The Browning Society, devoted to attempts at elucidating his poems, was founded in 1881, with Browning's wary approval.

An immense secondary literature, including editions of poems and letters, biographies, and critical interpretations, followed and has continued to this day. Browning died in Venice on 12 December 1889, on a visit to his son, who lived there in the Palazzo Rezzonico. Browning was buried in the Poets' Corner of Westminster Abbey on the last day of 1889.

Stuart Holmes long ago (1945) published an essay called 'Browning: Semantic Stutterer'. That phrase is as good a description as any of the strange linguistic sludge (to echo one of his characters' names) of Browning's first and last poems. Their language is like an odd sort of primeval soup from which life arose and to which it may return. The lucidity of the famous dramatic monologues is bounded before by the notorious incomprehensibility of *Sordello* (1840), and after by the return to something like the early stuttering in such late and inordinately long poems as those I have mentioned. The language of these narrative poems tends to be extremely murky. Their stories also tend to be lurid and melodramatic. The hero of *Red Cotton Night-Cap Country* tries to drown himself, later burns off his own hands, and then, finally, jumps to his death from a tower. The climax of *The Inn Album* is the quite abrupt, unexpected (to me at least), and brutal murder of the villain by the hero.

I have used the figure of life forms' evolution from primeval slime. The figure is borrowed from Browning. He is a master of the poetry of small things, living and dead. An example is the wonderful catalogue of edible things in 'The Englishman in Italy'. Browning also gives masterly descriptions of the source of those things in a fecund swamp of potentiality. 'Caliban Upon Setebos; or, Natural Theology in the Island' (1864), for example, is Browning's poem about the origin of species and about primeval man's religious intuitions. Caliban is shown in the opening lines barely emerged from his source in the 'pit's much mire', where he bathes and 'feels about his spine small eft-things course'.

Another wonderful example of Browning's poetry of the originating ooze is 'Sibrandus Schnafnaburgensis'. This is a poem about a boring, pedantic book that the poet has thrown, in revenge for his boredom in reading it, into the stagnating rainwater in a hollow tree. There the book gradually loses its character as a readable printed book and moves towards becoming a mere thing, 'With all the binding all of a blister, / And great blue spots where the ink has run, / And reddish streaks that wink and glister / O'er the page so beautifully yellow'. Browning, personifying the book, takes great pleasure in describing the fate of poor Sibrandus:

> How did he like it when the live creatures
>   Tickled and toused and browsed him all over,

And worm, slug, eft, with serious features,
  Came in, each one, for his right of trover?
...
All that life and fun and romping,
  All that frisking and twisting and coupling,
While slowly our poor friend's leaves were swamping
  And clasps were cracking and covers suppling!

This poem exemplifies my argument even better than 'Caliban', since it relates the clarity of articulate language to the primal ooze. The relative clarity, formal crispness, and focus of Browning's great dramatic monologues rises from the inarticulate murmur or stutter of a nascent language that has not yet evolved or crystallized into grammatical clarity. Browning's poetry then falls back in his later writings to the muttering out of which it originated, as, it may be, has human language generally. This trajectory from disarticulated linguistic fragments to relative coherence and then back to obscurity again constitutes the inner drama of his poetry. Browning's poetic language seems always on the verge of falling back into murmuring mutter or stammering stutter.

This deformation is analogous to the various syntactic, sonorous, and semantic devices that tend to reduce Browning's poetic language to the status of mere materiality. This is the materiality of sound that cannot quite be resolved into straightforward meaning, or the materiality of visible words on the page that the reader reads again and again, trying, not always successfully, to reduce them to syntactic and semantic sense. These poetic 'devices' include the use of grotesque rhymes, often feminine rhymes, in which the last two syllables rhyme (e.g. 'blister/glister') – these work to materialize language and move it towards pure sound; insistent alliterations (e.g. 'pit's much mire') that also highlight sound over sense; syntactic fragments that do not quite complete themselves and are replaced by another such fragment, then another and another, often separated by dashes – Browning is a great poet of the dash; inordinate use of ellipsis, so that the reader has to guess at the missing pronoun, subject, verb, or object; long run-on sentences that may be technically grammatical but that exceed the reader's ability to hold all the elements in mind to make a single sentence of them; interpolated dialogue that is hard to sort out, so that the reader has trouble telling just who is supposed to be speaking the words before his or her eyes; weird digressive metaphors or other figures that are sometimes buried inscrutably in a transferred word or phrase, but sometimes are extended for so long and so elaborately that the reader forgets the literal tenor of which they are supposed to be the vehicle; a tendency towards apparent digression of other kinds, or at any rate towards long interpolated passages whose relevance is not easily identified; a love for strange names that are sometimes historical, sometimes invented, but that are often thick with sludgy consonants and that call attention to themselves as mere sound: 'Sludge', 'Hohenstiel-Schwangau', 'Pacchiorotto', 'Sibrandus Schnafnaburgensis', 'Bloughram', 'Balaustion', and so forth; obscure allusions to persons, places, or events, or the use of phrases in French, Italian, Greek, or Latin that many readers will be puzzled by and will see as nonsensical words on the page until they read the editor's annotations; representation in letters on the page of the inarticulate sounds that speakers of any language often emit ('*Hy, Zy, Hine* ... / 'St, there's Vespers! *Plena gratia*, / *Ave, Virgo*! Gr-r-r – you swine!' ('Soliloquy of the Spanish Cloister'); 'A tiger-flash – yell, spring, and scream: halloo!! / Death's out and on him, has and holds him – ugh!' (*The Inn Album*)). One might argue that all these are normal and allowable poetic devices. When too many of them are used at once, however, they move the poet's words closer and closer to the total opacity to which Tennyson, Carlyle's wife, and Douglas Jerrold testified so memorably. These linguistic features correspond to the thematic content of Browning's poems. This content has, not surprisingly, received most attention from critics over the decades. The distinctive linguistic texture of Browning's poems is as important a feature of his greatness as is his representation of psychological complexities in his imagined characters, or as his notorious penchant for allowing villains, charlatans, and madmen to speak at length in self-justifying seductive casuistry, or as his for gift for telling, or at least implying, lurid tales of violence, murder, seduction, illicit sex, chicanery of all kinds.

Here are two passages, one early, one middle, that exemplify the stylistic trajectory I have described.

The first is from the notoriously incomprehensible *Sordello* (1840). Ezra Pound defended *Sordello* forcefully from its detractors, both in the *Cantos* ('Hang it all, Robert Browning, / there can be but the one "Sordello"'), and in *ABC of Reading*. In the latter, Pound castigates 'Victorian half-wits' who 'used to pride themselves on grinning through the horse-collar' when they complained about the obscurity of the poem. Pound quotes with approval a passage describing marble caryatids holding up a fountain in the castle of Goito. The passage is unusually lucid for this poem, but few readers (me included) can easily figure out what it is doing there, or how it is part of Sordello's story. Caryatids were priestesses of Artemis, dedicated, like Artemis herself, to virginity. Why does the young Sordello go there every day to pray for the release of the caryatids from what he interprets as punishment for some unnamed sin? Probably it is some sexual infraction, since they are all charmingly naked, but what is this supposed to tell the reader about Sordello? Such puzzles abound, even though the reader can usually, with a lot of work, figure out at least the grammatical sense of a given passage. I choose an excerpt that, when deciphered, gives one explanation for the linguistic obscurity of *Sordello*. The passage is necessarily long, like *Sordello* itself, to give Browning a chance to make the muddy clear, and also to give the reader a sense of what *Sordello*'s 5,800 iambic pentameter lines rhyming in couplets are like:

> He left imagining, to try the stuff
> That held the imaged thing, and, let it writhe
> Never so fiercely, scarce allowed a tithe
> To reach the light – his Language. How he sought
> The cause, conceived a cure, and slow re-wrought
> That Language, – welding words into the crude
> Mass from the new speech round him, till a rude
> Armour was hammered out, in time to be
> Approved beyond the Roman panoply
> Melted to make it, – boots not. This obtained
> With some ado, no obstacle remained
> To using it; accordingly he took
> An action with its actors, quite forsook
> Himself to live in such, returned anon
> With the result – a creature, and, by one
> And one, proceeded leisurely to equip
> Its limbs in harness of his workmanship.
> 'Accomplished! Listen, Mantuans!' Fond essay!
> Piece after piece that armour broke away,
> Because perceptions whole, like that he sought
> To clothe, reject so pure a work of thought
> As language: thought may take perception's place
> But hardly co-exist in any case,
> Being its mere presentment – of the whole
> By parts, the simultaneous and the sole
> By the successive and the many.

'Boots not'? Well, if it boots not, why go to all this bother to tell the reader about it? 'Cause' of what? And just what is the 'cure' that Sordello devises? What does it mean to say 'he took / An action with its actors'? Just what is the referent of 'its'? Presumably the referent is Sordello's remade language, but then what are 'its actors'? Does that mean his language acted on its own, or that Sordello represented imaginary personages speaking his remade language? How does the extended figure of poetic language as 'armour' clothing the imaged thing underneath it work? It seems as if Browning is saying that Sordello 'welded' 'his Language' into a 'crude mass' that was like unworked metal. This was then fashioned into the requisite parts of a suit of armour for his 'perceptions' or 'imaginings'. That armour then broke away, 'piece after piece'. The side-bar for this passage says, 'Tries again, is no better satisfied'. This armour figure is pretty weird, if you think about it. Browning begins by asserting that language and imaginings are inseparable. The language that 'writhes' is 'the stuff / That held the imaged thing', but seems somehow to resist 'reaching the light'. Only 10 per cent at most, a 'tithe', does so. Therefore the poet's language has to be melted down into a 'crude mass', whatever that might, literally, mean, and armour then hammered out from that mass. The armour is, apparently, the words that 'clothe' 'thought', 'imaginings', 'perceptions whole'. How can language be both an integral part of thought and at the same time its mere external clothing? The passage bristles with such puzzles. After a considerable effort, with the daunting presentiment that a seemingly endless forest of such passages awaits decipherment later on in this inordinately long poem, the reader can see that the text I have cited says that the young Sordello, like Browning himself, had a big problem fitting language to the 'imaginings', or 'imaged things', or 'perceptions whole' that swarmed in his mind. This required a wholesale remaking of the 'Roman' language (presumably he means 'Italian') that he heard around him in Mantua, though nothing is said about the fact that the historical Sordello wrote mostly in Provençal or Occitan. Provençal was already a fully established poetic language that hardly needed melting down. The passage no doubt describes obliquely Browning's sense of his own poetic task. Browning also ascribes to Sordello his own poetic strategy as expressed in *Pauline*. The new language the poet has devised seems to correspond to the 'actors' that use it. The poet 'quite forsook / Himself to live in each'. The result was a 'creature' clothed in the armour of the poet's new language, that is, something like Sordello himself as a creature of Browning's imagination, or like any of the dozens of other imagined personages that speak in Browning's dramatic monologues.

The passage ends, however, with a more or less lucid explanation of what went wrong with Sordello-Browning's poetic project, that is, why 'piece by piece that armour broke away'. 'Thought', says the poet, 'may take perception's place / But hardly co-exist in any case, / Being its mere presentment – of the whole / By parts, the simultaneous and the sole / By the successive and the many.' 'Thought' here must mean thinking as already embodied in language. The poet's insoluble problem is that 'perception' is 'whole', global, total, simultaneous, an all-at-onceness, whereas language, even the most extravagantly 'writhing' poetic language, is, necessarily, one word after another in temporal or spatial sequence, 'successive' and 'many'. It is therefore a 'mere presentment' of the wholeness of what Browning calls 'perception'. No way exists out of this dilemma. It is, in Browning's expression of it, a permanent and inescapable linguistic impasse for any poet at any time or place, for Browning in nineteenth-century England as much as for Sordello in thirteenth-century Lombardy.

The passage I have been discussing is wonderfully helpful as a way to understand the underlying causes of Browning's semantic stuttering and syntactic incoherence. As soon as his formulations start to become sculptural and lucid, the poet feels that this must mean their woeful inadequacy in relation to that of which they are the intended presentment. He must therefore break off before it is too late. He must then start another syntactic unit. That must be broken off in its turn, and so on ad infinitum, until something like *Sordello*, or *Fifine at the Fair*, or *Red Cotton Night-Cap Country* results, that is, another long, murky poem. All the revision in the world, such as Browning lavished on *Sordello*, will not reconcile these equally peremptory, but contradictory, penchants – towards form and towards formlessness. Browning's triumph as a poet is to have recognized this dilemma and to have spent a lifetime expressing it. Of course the dilemma results from the mistaken assumption that such a thing as a 'whole perception' exists as an entity entirely separate from language.

My second citation is the familiar opening lines of 'My Last Duchess. Ferrara':

> That's my last Duchess painted on the wall,
> Looking as if she were alive. I call
> That piece a wonder, now: Frà Pandolf's hands
> Worked busily a day, and there she stands.
> Will't please you sit and look at her?

What a difference! Compared to the lines I have cited from *Sordello*, these lines are brilliantly lucid. This is particularly so when the reader discovers from the rest of the relatively short poem (just fifty-six lines) that the Duke is speaking to the representative of a Count whose daughter the Duke is negotiating to take as his second wife. He has murdered his first wife because she was too free with her looks and smiles. He speaks to send a warning to the Count that the same thing will happen to his daughter if she steps out of line when she becomes the second Duchess. The triumph of Browning's dramatic monologues is that they devise a way to avoid his chronic 'confused multitudinousness' of language. They do this by focusing on the imagined speech of a single well-defined person at a certain crucial moment of his or her life. Fra Lippo Lippi, for example, speaks in self-defence when the night-guard has caught him out of his monastery having a night on the town. Though 'My Last Duchess' is in strict iambic pentameter lines, rhyming in couplets, nevertheless it admirably catches the rhythm and diction of ordinary colloquial speech.

'My Last Duchess' has its complexities, but they are relatively open to at least approximate mastery by readers, students, and teachers. The poem turns on the analogies between looking as an exposure of the self to others, as in the Duchess's promiscuous smiles; looking at a painting, as the Duke and his visitor do when the Duke draws back the curtain, and as the reader does in imagination; and our 'look' at the Duke as he exposes himself through his speech, just as do all Browning's dramatic monologuists. 'My Last Duchess' is about a portrait, but it is itself a double portrait in words, of the dead Duchess and of the Duke himself.

Browning was especially interested in persons who hide some shameful secret. Perhaps he felt all of us hold some such secret. This secret, for Browning, most often involved a sexual triangle of love and betrayal. 'Two in the Campagna' poignantly expresses the gulf that remains even between ostensibly happy lovers: 'Only I discern – / Infinite passion, and the pain / Of finite hearts that yearn.' Though most husbands would not kill their wives just because they smile at other men, many husbands do suffer from a feeling that they can never fully know or control their wives. 'Peter, Peter, pumpkin-eater / Had a wife and couldn't keep her.' Peter's solution, as we all know, was to put his wife in a pumpkin shell: 'There he kept her very well.' The Duke's solution was to have his wife murdered, just as Guido murdered Pompilia in *The Ring and the Book*, and just as Porphyria's lover strangled her with her own hair as a paradoxically perverse way of taking full possession of her.

Browning, it is clear, suffered much from a sense of the inaccessibility of other persons. 'Never shall I believe any two souls were made / Similar', says Don Juan in *Fifine at the Fair*. The assumptions that each other person is unreachable by me because unique, singular, unlike anyone else, and that each other person is innately guilty, as am I, are unmistakably Protestant in provenance. These assumptions are perhaps displaced features of Browning's Evangelical heritage from his mother, as is his abiding faith in God and in an afterlife. In heaven lovers will become at last fully open to one another, under God's paternal patronage. Don Juan, in *Fifine at the Fair*, expresses this in the image of the way each individual person's hidden idiosyncratic life-fire will be blended into a single white blaze in the afterlife: 'What joy, when each may supplement / The other, changing each, as changed, till, wholly blent, / The old things shall be new, and, what we both ignite, / Fuse, lose the varicolor in achromatic white.'

Though in this life we may never enter into the inner world of another person, the dramatic monologue, as employed by Browning, presupposes that the triumph of poetic language is to achieve in imagination what Charles du Bos, in an admirable formulation in praise of Browning, called *l'introspection d'autrui*, 'the introspection of the other'. Browning had a pretty dark view of what would happen if you succeeded at that.

Well, why did Browning not go on writing wonderfully clear and focused poems like 'My Last Duchess'? Why did the long poems of the decades after *The Ring and the Book* return to the often incomprehensible babble that characterizes *Sordello*? Space does not allow me to demonstrate through citation this return to obscurity. I invite the curious reader, however, to give, for example, *The Inn Album* a try. I must limit myself to a brief example of the staccato stammering, culminating at last in a final rhyming word, full of explosive alliterative consonants, that is characteristic of Browning's late work: 'I must say – or choke in silence – "Howsoever came my fate, / Sorrow did and joy did nowise, – life well weighed, – preponderate"' (*La Saisiaz*, 1878). Yes – weigh that well. Ponder 'preponderate'.

Henry James, in a letter to Ariana Curtis of 30 October 1888, a year before Browning's death, after having re-read in Geneva most of Browning's poetry, heaped generous praise on the poet: 'It seems to me that he is on the whole the writer of our times of whom, in the face of the rest of the world, the English tongue may be most proud – for he has touched *every-thing*, & with a breadth! I put him very high – higher than anyone.' Having myself just recently re-read much of Browning, I am prepared to go along with James. I corroborate also, however, what a younger and brasher James said in a wonderfully joyous putdown in his review of 1876 in the *Nation* of *The Inn Album*:

> This is a decidedly irritating and displeasing performance ... 'The Inn Album' reads like a series of rough notes for a poem – of hasty hieroglyphics and symbols, decipherable only to the author himself. A great poem might perhaps have been made of it, but assuredly it is not a great poem, nor any poem whatsoever. It is hard to say very coherently what it is. Up to a certain point, like everything of Mr. Browning's, it is highly dramatic and vivid, and beyond that point, like all its companions, it is as little dramatic as possible. It is not narrative, for there is not a line of comprehensible, consecutive statement in the two hundred and eleven pages of the volume. It is not lyrical, for there is not a phrase which in any degree does the office of the poetry that comes lawfully into the world – chants itself, images itself, or lingers in the memory ... [W]e can as little imagine a reader (who has not the misfortune to be a reviewer) addressing himself more than once to the perusal of 'The Inn Album', as we can fancy cultivating for conversational purposes the society of a person afflicted with a grievous impediment of speech.

James must have had great fun writing this, as he must have had fun writing that sentence in my epigraph about Browning's combination of oddness and greatness. My basic question remains, however. Why is the early and late poetry of this great poet so odd? How could the poet who wrote the crisp lines of 'My Last Duchess' have also written *Sordello* and *The Inn Album*? Several answers have already been suggested. Browning felt that the one-by-oneness of language could not in any way express 'perceptions whole'. He saw poetry as an impossible struggle against this dilemma, a doomed attempt to say everything at once. Or perhaps Browning began and ended with a sense that the idiosyncrasies of human consciousness and its concomitant complexities of inner speech were so great and so interesting that only an extremely gnarled language could do them justice. If a poem is clear, as many of Browning's best-known dramatic monologues more or less are, it is not 'realistic', not valid as a true representation of inner life. Or perhaps Browning really did have a grievous impediment of speech, some form of aphasia that made him a semantic stutterer. It often seems so. I think, however, that Browning's earliest significant poem, *Pauline* (1833), may still give the best answer to my question. With this I conclude, returning in my end to Browning's beginning.

The speaker of *Pauline*, whom we might as well identify with 'Browning himself', if such a thing existed, makes several related statements about his selfhood in the poem. He defines himself as absolute, detached self-consciousness, empty of content: 'I am made up of an intensest life, / Of a most clear idea of consciousness / Of self, distinct from all its qualities, / From all affections, passions, feelings, powers.' This self-consciousness, though it is mere empty potentiality, nevertheless has a grandiose, even megalomaniac, desire to be everything. His 'I' exists

> as a centre to all things,
> Most potent to create and rule and call
> Upon all things to minister to it;
> And to a principle of restlessness
> That would be all, have, see, know, taste, feel, all –
> This is myself.

How in the world can he satisfy this extravagant need? His soul, he says,

> has strange impulse, tendency, desire,
> Which nowise I account for nor explain,
> But cannot stifle, being bound to trust
> All feelings equally, to hear all sides:
> How can my life indulge them? Yet they live,
> Referring to some state of life unknown.

Browning's way out of his dilemma is clear enough. Elsewhere in *Pauline* he claims that he has a miraculous power to enter into the life of things, animals, and people. This is more a version of Keats's 'negative capability' than anything Browning would have learned from Shelley, the guiding spirit of *Pauline*: 'I can live all the life of plants' and so forth. In a potentially endless series of dramatic monologues, the poet can do in imagination and by way of fictional language what he cannot do in reality, that is, enter into the lives of all the multitude of unique persons who live or have ever lived, not to speak of plants and animals. Since he is in himself nothing, those monologues, including even *Pauline*, as Browning repeatedly claimed of his poems, are 'though often Lyric in expression, always Dramatic in principle, and so many utterances of so many imaginary persons, not mine'. Browning's great monologues seem to be a triumphant linguistic solution to an apparently insoluble existential problem. Why then the murky beginning, in *Sordello*, and then the return at the end to such murmuring, inchoate language?

This oddness has a clear explanation. Browning's initial state of infinite potentiality may be identified with the confusion of a language that says nothing definite by potentially saying everything at once. In even the most focused dramatic monologues, that underlying incomprehensible stutter threatens constantly to break through as the expression of what the poet in truth remains, that is, a nothing that would be all and would be satisfied by nothing less than being all. However many dramatic monologues Browning writes, an infinite number of potential ones remain to be written. That dismaying potential haunts the speech of any imaginary person. As a result Browning falls back in the end to a long-drawn-out garrulousness that tries to speak simultaneously for a definite person in a definite situation and for the origin of all language in the mumble of that initial mutter. Between those two contrary penchants Browning's great, but distinctly odd, poetry remains caught. This is so, even though Browning's abiding religious faith anticipates a time when all existential and linguistic knots will be untied. In that happy consummation, human language, it may be, will no longer be needed at all.

SELECTED FURTHER READING

Editions

Collected editions

Poetical Works, 17 vols, London, Smith, Elder, 1888–94
Complete Poetical Works, ed. Horace E. Scudder, Boston, Houghton Mifflin, 1895
Works, ed. F. G. Kenyon, centenary edn, 10 vols, London, Smith, Elder, 1910
Poetical Works, electronic resource, Cambridge, Chadwyck-Healey, 1992

Paperback selection

Karlin, Daniel (ed.), *Robert Browning: Selected Poems*, London, Penguin, 2004

Correspondence

Browning's correspondence and that of his wife are now scattered in numerous volumes, but a collected edition in 40 vols is in progress, with 15 vols out:

Kelley, Philip, Ronald Hudson, *et al.* (eds.), *The Brownings' Correspondence*, Winfield, KS, Wedgstone Press, 1984–

Secondary works

Biographies

Griffin, W. H., and H. C. Minchin, *The Life of Robert Browning*, 2nd edn, London, Methuen, 1938

Miller, Betty, *Robert Browning: A Portrait*, London, J. Murray, 1952

Orr, Mrs (Alexandra Sutherland), *Life and Letters of Robert Browning*, London, Smith, Elder, 1891

Wood, Sarah, *Robert Browning: A Literary Life*, London, Palgrave, 2001

Critical studies

Chesterton, G. K., *Robert Browning*, London, Macmillan, 1903

DeVane, W. C., *A Browning Handbook*, 2nd edn, New York, Appleton-Century-Crofts, 1955

Hair, Donald S., *Robert Browning's Language*, Toronto, University of Toronto Press, 1999

Holmes, Stuart W., 'Browning: Semantic Stutterer', *Publications of the Modern Language Association of America* 40 (1945), 231–55

James, Henry, *Literary Criticism: Essays on Literature: American Writers: English Writers*, New York, Library of America, 1984

Langbaum, Robert, *The Poetry of Experience*, New York, Random House, 1957

Litzinger, B., and D. Smalley, *Robert Browning: The Critical Heritage*, London, Routledge & Kegan Paul, 1968

Miller, J. Hillis, *The Disappearance of God: Five Nineteenth-Century Writers*, Cambridge, MA, Belknap Press of Harvard University Press, 1963

Pound, Ezra, *A B C of Reading*, Norfolk, CT, New Directions, n.d.

Shaw, W. David, *The Dialectical Temper: The Rhetorical Art of Robert Browning*, Ithaca, NY, Cornell University Press, 1968

Tucker, Herbert F., *Browning's Beginnings: The Art of Disclosure*, Minneapolis, University of Minnesota Press, 1980

22

DINAH BIRCH

Emily Brontë

Ted Hughes, born and bred in West Yorkshire like Emily Brontë, was haunted by her memory. His poetic engagement with her life is stamped with his own creative personality, but in its focus on her singleness, her devotion to the wild moorland, her passionate secrecy, and her early death it draws together the central points of a widely shared perception of Brontë's character as a writer:

> The wind on Crow Hill was her darling.
> His fierce, high tale in her ear was her secret.
> But his kiss was fatal.

As Hughes sees it, Brontë's life was inseparable from a dark affinity with natural energies. The erotic intensity of this connection gave her a unique voice, but also made it impossible for her to live: 'Her death is a baby-cry on the moor.'[1] The popularity of that literary image – Emily Brontë as a free, rebellious spirit, close to nature, and doomed to die young – has given her the status of a kind of anti-Victorian woman, celebrated for her defiance of the conventions of the drawing room. Her admirers, including many who have never read a word of her writing, feel that they know her intimately. She has become a myth.[2]

Remarkably few solid facts about Emily Brontë's life have survived, so that legends have had plenty of room to grow. There is no extensive body of letters, journals, manuscripts, or juvenilia. Three formal notes, addressed to a friend of her sister Charlotte, were preserved, together with several essays written while she was studying in Brussels, four widely spaced 'diary papers', part of an account book, and a few other desultory scraps. She seems to have had no close friends outside the family she grew up with in that famous parsonage at Haworth, on the edge of the Yorkshire moors, where she spent most of her life. Her literary output was not large. Twenty-one poems were published as the work of 'Ellis Bell' in the pseudonymous *Poems by Currer, Ellis, and Acton Bell* (1846), alongside contributions by her sisters, Charlotte ('Currer') and Anne ('Acton'). *Wuthering Heights*, her only novel, appeared in 1847; drafts have never been found, and though there is speculation that she worked on a second novel, no trace of a manuscript has emerged. Two years after Emily's death at the age of thirty, in December 1848, a further seventeen poems under her name were incorporated into a reprint of *Wuthering Heights* with her sister Anne's *Agnes Grey*, in a volume edited by Charlotte Brontë.[3] Fortunately, much of her unpublished poetry was saved, and around 200 poems have now been published, their texts established as the result of the meticulous labours of successive editors.[4] Given the modest proportions of this poetic oeuvre, its impact has been extraordinary, and shows no signs of fading.

Emily Brontë's poems were singled out for praise on their earliest appearance in 1846. The *Athenaeum* thought her the most gifted of the three brothers (as the reviewer supposed the youthful poets Currer, Ellis, and Acton Bell to be), remarking on the evident 'power of wing' in her poetry.[5] 'Power' is a term that emerges in responses to Emily's work from the first. *Wuthering Heights* also earned praise for its 'rugged power', though its narrative experiments also attracted a few hard words – it was 'wild, confused, disjointed, and improbable', according to the *Examiner*.[6] In general, however, there was a clear consensus that 'Ellis Bell' was a writer of real promise. Nevertheless, Charlotte Brontë was hurt and alarmed by these initial comments on Emily's work. The eldest of the surviving Brontë children, and the longest lived, she felt a sense of responsibility for her younger siblings that only grew stronger after their deaths. Much of what we know about Emily, along with some persistent misunderstandings, derives from Charlotte's protective manipulations of her writing and posthumous reputation. What seems to have disturbed Charlotte most was the suggestion that her sister's work was 'coarse', a word that tends to recur alongside 'power' in the early reviews, with implications that were particularly threatening to the reputation of a middle-class woman author.[7] Charlotte's interventions are often intended to deflect this interpretation of Emily's writing.

In her 'Biographical Notice' of Emily and Anne, published in association with her 1850 edition of their fiction and poetry, Charlotte gives the misleading impression that notices of Emily's work had been predominantly hostile. She defends her sister by claiming that Emily was a native genius of a kind that could not be judged by conventional standards, and certainly not by those that might usually be applied to a woman. What she said has had a lasting influence on our approaches to Emily Brontë's work:

> In Emily's nature the extremes of vigour and simplicity seemed to meet. Under an unsophisticated culture, inartificial tastes, and an unpretending outside, lay

> a secret power and fire that might have informed the brain and kindled the veins of a hero; but she had no worldly wisdom; her powers were unadapted to the practical business of life; she would fail to defend her most manifest rights, to consult her most legitimate advantage. An interpreter ought always to have stood between her and the world. Her will was not very flexible, and it generally opposed her interest. Her temper was magnanimous, but warm and sudden; her spirit altogether unbending.[8]

Charlotte's summary of Emily's character is written with such firm and authoritative confidence that readers have hardly found it possible to question its accuracy. Emily is cast in the role of Romantic hero, an artless child of nature, forceful and vulnerable in equal measure. She is in need of an interpreter, and Charlotte is ready to take on the role. The piercing description of Emily's decline and death from consumption in the 'Biographical Notice' has the emotional impact of the climax of a novel. Emily is set apart from common humanity, her mortal weakness transcended, as Charlotte describes it, by the intensity of her will:

> The details of her illness are deep-branded in my memory, but to dwell on them, either in thought or narrative, is not in my power. Never in all her life had she lingered over any task that lay before her, and she did not linger now. She sank rapidly. She made haste to leave us. Yet, while physically she perished, mentally she grew stronger than we had yet known her. Day by day, when I saw with what a front she met suffering, I looked on her with an anguish of wonder and love. I have seen nothing like it; but, indeed, I have never seen her parallel in anything. Stronger than a man, simpler than a child, her nature stood alone.[9]

Charlotte's account is calculated to overwhelm readers, and Emily Brontë's poetry has always been read in its light. But the words are Charlotte's, not Emily's.

More of Charlotte's words found their way into the poetry itself, as it appeared in the 1850 volume. She had, she tells us in the 'Notice', discovered Emily's poetry by chance, persuading her sister to allow its publication only with difficulty:

> One day, in the autumn of 1845, I accidentally lighted on a MS. volume of verse in my sister Emily's handwriting. Of course, I was not surprised, knowing that she could and did write verse: I looked it over, and something more than surprise seized me, – a deep conviction that these were not common effusions, nor at all like poetry women generally write. I thought them condensed and terse, vigorous and genuine. To my ear, they had also a peculiar music – wild, melancholy, and elevating.[10]

In 1850, she selected the poetry that best reflected her own image of Emily as a poet inspired by natural gifts that enabled her to transcend her situation as a simple woman living a retired life in provincial Yorkshire. She did not hesitate to edit Emily's work so that it reflected that image more faithfully, changing words and adding punctuation as she saw fit. She replaced, for instance, 'highlands', 'glens', and 'wandering deer' with 'moorlands', 'crags', and 'sheep', to imply that the poetry was recalling the Yorkshire moors rather than making a literary reference to the Scottish Highlands, which Emily had not visited. She sometimes altered the dates of poems to suggest that they were written years earlier than the dates of the manuscripts would suggest, emphasizing the impression that Emily was an untutored genius. 'The Visionary', one of the most celebrated poems among the group published in 1850, even includes two new concluding stanzas composed by Charlotte herself, emphasizing her view of Emily as removed from common humanity by a mystic imagination, a passive and self-sacrificing figure visited by a 'Strange Power'.

> What I love shall come like visitant of air,
> Safe in secret power from lurking human snare;
> What loves me, no word of mine shall e'er betray,
> Though for faith unstained my life must forfeit pay.
>
> Burn, then, little lamp; glimmer straight and clear –
> Hush! A rustling wing stirs, methinks, the air:
> He for whom I wait, thus ever comes to me;
> Strange Power! I trust thy might; trust thou my constancy.[11]

These additional lines by Charlotte Brontë were still being cited as a key reflection of Emily Brontë's poetic vision in the 1980s.[12] Though we might see such covert interference as an offence to the integrity of scholarship, our indignation would be misplaced. Charlotte was not a professional scholar. She was a writer, and the single survivor of a family of six, and she was coming to terms with her grief through serving her sisters' memory in what she believed to be the most effective way. Emily Brontë's work is firmly rooted in the experiences of her exceptional family. Nevertheless, we sometimes need to disentangle those roots in order to think clearly about her identity as a poet.

Despite the confusion that Charlotte sometimes introduced in her self-appointed role as Emily's interpreter, she was right to suggest that the sources of her sister's work were often hidden, and removed from conventional ideas of what was appropriate to women's writing. The intricate history of the lines from which Charlotte extracted 'The Visionary' in 1850 reflects the complexity of Emily's development as a poet. In its earliest version (dated 1845), this long, dense, and ambitious poem was called 'Julian M — — and A. G. Rochelle —'. Emily herself had selected part of this text for *Poems by*

Currer, Ellis, and Acton Bell, where they were published under the title 'The Prisoner: A Fragment', which is still among her most highly regarded poems. Like many of Emily's works, 'Julian M — — and A. G. Rochelle —' has its origins in the Gondal narrative, the extended account of a fictional island she created in collaboration with Anne, whose characters and conflicts absorbed their attention throughout their lives. The only Gondal writings to have survived are the poems that Emily wrote in connection with the history of the imaginary kingdom. No references to Gondal persist in the texts of Emily's poems as they were first published, including 'The Prisoner: A Fragment' and 'The Visionary'. But in its first form the narrative origins of the poem are clear. The opening lines of 'Julian M — — and A. G. Rochelle —' describe a lonely vigil, as the speaker awaits a forbidden visitor on a winter's night. The situation is conceived as a dramatic one, in which family authority is defied:

> Silent is the House — all are laid asleep;
> One, alone, looks out o'er the snow-wreaths deep;
> Watching every cloud, dreading every breeze
> That whirls the wildering drifts and bends the groaning trees —
>
> Cheerful is the hearth, soft the matted floor
> Not one shivering gust creeps through pane or door
> The little lamp burns straight; its rays shoot strong and far
> I trim it well to be the Wanderers guiding star —
>
> Frown my haughty sire, chide my angry Dame;
> Set your slaves to spy, threaten me with shame;
> But neither sire nor dame, nor prying serf shall know
> What angel nightly tracks that waste of winter snow.[13]

This is a recognizably Romantic scene, and it is expressed in perceptibly Romantic lyric language. The speaker is solitary and rebellious, with resolute desires that must be concealed from an unsympathetic world. The poem's distinctive vocabulary recurs throughout Emily Brontë's work, with its emotional register ('dreading', 'haughty', 'angry', 'shame') and its emphasis on a comfortless natural setting ('snow-wreaths', 'cloud', 'breeze', and 'groaning trees'). Like much of her writing, the poem evokes a natural world whose austerity expresses and also tests the fortitude of the solitary speaker. But if this is the solitude of the Yorkshire moors, it is placed within a consciously literary context. The rhythmical structure of the verse is varied and sophisticated, with its subtle handling of the trochaic rhythms that often appealed to Emily, and its confident use of the alexandrine, the least native of English poetic lines, in the concluding two lines of each stanza.[14] Variations on the theme of the 'Wanderer', here guided by a lamp which 'burns straight', with rays that 'shoot strong and far' (they are replaced with a more tentative 'glimmer' in Charlotte's version of the image), recur in poems by Wordsworth, Shelley, Scott, Byron, and other poets of the period. Emily Brontë had read many such poems. The lonely position of the speaker who watches and waits, at first described at a distance ('One, alone, looks out') and then voicing her own situation ('I trim it well'), is equally familiar. So too is the suggestion, implied in the terms 'sire', 'dame' 'slaves', or 'prying serf', of a proud and overbearing family, located in an indeterminate historical period (there is a faint but unrealized suggestion of medievalism here). John Keats's 'Eve of St. Agnes' is among the poems that come to mind, along with S. T. Coleridge's 'Christabel', a poem known to be significant to Emily.

The poem's network of literary references extends still further. Coleridge's 'The Dungeon', together with Byron's *The Prisoner of Chillon*, two poems which condemn the political tyranny that throws its victims into prison, also reverberate through the poem as it develops. Byron's 'Sonnet on Chillon', with its ringing opening lines, was for Emily a peculiarly important text:

> Eternal Spirit of the chainless Mind!
> Brightest in dungeons, Liberty! thou art,
> For there thy habitation is the heart —
> The heart which love of thee alone can bind.[15]

Having placed the watchful speaker in the 'Silent House', the introductory stanzas of 'Julian M — — and A. G. Rochelle —' move with disconcerting suddenness into a narrative account of the arrogant Lord Julian as he visits the captives he has chained in his 'dungeon crypts'. There he encounters his beautiful prisoner, Rochelle:

> The captive raised her face; it was as soft and mild
> As sculptured marble saint or slumbering, unweaned child
> It was so soft and mild, it was so sweet and fair
> Pain could not trace a line nor greif a shadow there![16]

Like the speaker of the opening verses, the captive defies the forces that constrain her. Julian's tyranny represents a particular human cruelty, but Rochelle's suffering, and her transcendence of that suffering, become an emblem for something larger. Her imprisonment represents the confinement of the soul within the body, a restraint that she evades with a visionary passion that no bonds can contain. Her liberty will come with death:

> 'Yet, tell them, Julian, all, I am not doomed to wear
> 'Year after year in gloom and desolate despair;
> 'A messenger of Hope comes every night to me
> 'And offers, for short life, eternal liberty —

'He comes with western winds, with evening's wandering airs,
'With that clear dusk of heaven that brings the thickest stars;
'Winds take a pensive tone and stars a tender fire
'And visions rise and change which kill me with desire —

'Desire for nothing known in my maturer years
'When joy grew mad with awe at counting future tears;
'When, if my spirit's sky was full of flashes warm,
'I knew not whence they came from sun or thunder storm;

'But first a hush of peace, a soundless calm descends;
'The struggle with distress and feirce impatience ends;
'Mute music sooths my breast — unuttered harmony
'That I could never dream till earth was lost to me.

'Then dawns the Invisible, the Unseen its truth reveals;
'My outward sense is gone, my inward essence feels —
'Its wings are almost free, its home, its harbour found;
'Measuring the gulf it stoops and dares the final bound!

'O, dreadful is the check — intense the agony
'When the ear begins to hear and the eye begins to see;
'When the pulse begins to throb, the brain begins to think again,
'The soul to feel the flesh and the flesh to feel the chain!

'Yet I would lose no sting, would wish no torture less;
'The more that anguish racks the earlier it will bless;
'And robed in fires of Hell, or bright with heavenly shine
'If it but herald Death, the vision is divine — '[17]

These ardent lines cast retrospective light on the poem's opening stanzas. The eagerly awaited 'angel' that nightly tracks the snowy waste might seem to be an earthly lover; but in Rochelle's reverie the 'messenger of Hope' who visits her nightly is a harbinger of death. Imprisonment and a corresponding hunger for freedom are recurrent themes in Emily Brontë's writing, often associated, as in the early poem 'High waveing heather', with the wind moving over the moors:

High waveing heather, 'neath stormy blasts bending
Midnight and moon light and bright shineing stars
Darkness and glory rejoiceingly blending
Earth riseing to heaven and heaven descending
Mans spirit away from its drear dongoen sending
Bursting the fetters and breaking the bars.[18]

In this sense, 'Julian M — — and A. G. Rochelle —' is a poem that develops a central strand in her work, one that had formed her interests from the first.

In the work as she prepared it for publication as 'The Prisoner: A Fragment' in the 1846 *Poems*, the urge to break the bars and fly into heaven is what concludes the poem, as Julian (unnamed in this published version) and his warder, chastened and defeated, leave their prisoner:

> She ceased to speak, and we, unanswering turned to go —
> We had no further power to work the captive woe:
> Her cheek, her gleaming eye, declared that man had given
> A sentence, unapproved, and overruled by Heaven.[19]

But in 'Julian M — — and A. G. Rochelle —', the poem as Emily first wrote it, Rochelle's salvation takes a very different form. Julian, having fallen helplessly in love with his captive, releases her from her bonds – 'With hurried blow on blow I struck the fetters through.'[20] Neglecting his duties on the battlefield, and ignoring his family's scorn, he nurses her back to health. 'I guarded her by day and guarded her by night.' 'Julian M — — and A. G. Rochelle —' ends not with death, or with the longing for death, but with happily satisfied devotion:

> And by the patient strength that could the world defy
> By suffering with calm mind, contempt and calumny;
> By never-doubting love, unswerving constancy,
> Rochelle, I earned at last an equal love from thee![21]

The fearless determination that characterizes all of Brontë's protagonists is here turned to a loving fulfilment, rather than the self-destruction evoked by Ted Hughes, or the life-forfeiting patience that Charlotte Brontë describes. Emily Brontë was a more protean poet than her reputation would sometimes suggest, and more concerned with exploring the possibilities of the different models suggested by her varied literary experience.

One of the few certain facts about Emily Brontë's retired life is that she was an eager reader, with access to a wide range of books and periodicals, and the opportunity to discuss them with her equally well-read siblings. *Blackwood's Magazine* (familiarly known as 'Maga'), a choleric Tory journal founded in 1817 and based in Edinburgh, was a particular favourite, with its lively mixture of polemical satire, reviews, articles, and editorials. Conservative in politics, *Blackwood's* nevertheless provided a broad overview of contemporary literary culture, promoting Percy and Mary Shelley, and publishing Wordsworth and Coleridge. The family's early literary efforts included imitations of these magazines, including, in June 1829, their own version of Blackwood's in 'Branwells Blackwood's Magazine', produced with contributions from Charlotte in the miniaturized, carefully handwritten format that characterized the siblings' first writings. After 1831, the family saw

Fraser's Magazine (later to publish two of Anne Brontë's poems), also Tory in its principles but with very diverse literary interests. The variety of poetry encountered by the young Brontës was remarkable. They knew Thomas Moore's work well, including his biographical work on Byron; they read Milton, Shakespeare, Robert Southey, Ossian (the pen name of the Scottish poet James Macpherson), William Cowper, and Thomas Campbell. Patrick Brontë, who has the undeserved reputation (largely derived from Elizabeth Gaskell's biography) of eccentric autocracy, allowed his children unusual freedom when it came to their reading, making no distinction between his daughters and his son. He was a published writer,[22] and his children were determined to follow suit.

Despite Charlotte's influential view of Emily as an untaught writer, largely inspired by original genius, it is clear that her literary identity was established by these experiences. What she made of her reading, however, remains extremely difficult to categorize. She consistently places the claims of the individual spirit above the demands of social custom, but she does so within shifting and sometimes contradictory patterns of thought. Much of her poetry broods on death:

> O mother I am not regreting
> To leave this wretched world below
> If there be nothing but forgeting
> In that dark land to which I go.[23]

Forgetfulness in death is a necessity and a blessing; but to forget the dead is a denial that the meaning of a life can persist. In 'Song: The linnet in the rocky dells', Brontë sees no need for mourning:

> And if their eyes should whach and weep
> Till sorrows' Source were dry
> She would not in her tranquil sleep
> Return a single Sigh —
>
> Blow, West wind, by the lonely mound
> And murmur, Summer streams;
> There is no need of other sound
> To soothe my Lady's dreams — [24]

This is another Gondal poem, probably written in association with the death of 'A. G. A.', the 'Lady' whose stormy life Emily and Anne had been imagining and recording since childhood. Other poems, like 'Remembrance', resist the fading of memory:

> Cold in the earth and the deep snow piled above thee!
> Far, far removed cold in the dreary grave!

Have I forgot, my Only Love, to love thee,
Severed at last by Time's all-severing wave?[25]

In their lyrical and often hymn-like form, strongly rhythmical, with simple rhyme-schemes and starkly dramatic situations, these poems are characteristic of much of Emily Brontë's writing. An element of her fearlessness as a poet is that she does not shrink from repetition. Her manifold confrontations with love, loss, imprisonment, death, memory, and courage echo from poem to poem, sometimes making it hard to know where one poem begins and another ends. These refracted multiplicities are not a matter of indecisiveness. They reflect her persistent questioning of what it might mean to end, or to die, and whether any ending can properly be understood as final.

Much critical debate has been generated by the question of whether readers should differentiate between the poems that are directly linked to the Gondal cycle of stories and those that are not. But the use of dramatically conceived voices is not confined to the Gondal poems. In 'The Old Stoic', among the poems chosen for publication in 1846, Emily fuses her admiration for the Stoicism of Epictetus (whose writings she seems to have known) with a more personal repudiation of conventional piety:

Riches I hold in light esteem
And Love I laugh to scorn
And Lust of Fame was but a dream
That vanished with the morn —

...

Yes, as my swift days near their goal
'Tis all that I implore —
In Life and death, a chainless soul
With courage to endure! — [26]

Audacious and provocative, this is a poem that confirms Emily's refusal to court social approval. It is a remarkable publication, particularly for a clergyman's daughter in her twenties, and its boldness (her 'too-bold dying song', Matthew Arnold called her verse[27]) sheds some light on what lay behind Charlotte's protective anxieties.

'I see around me tombstones grey', unpublished until 1902, is still more forthright in its rejection of the consolations of orthodox religion. Memory anchors the speaker in an earthly existence:

Let me remember half the woe
I've seen and heard and felt below
And Heaven itself, so pure and blest
Could never give my spirit rest —

Part of a literary generation tormented by the questions surrounding personal immortality, Emily Brontë here declares a startlingly defiant position:

We would not leave our native home
For *any* world beyond the Tomb
No — rather on thy kindly breast
Let us be laid in lasting rest
Or waken but to share with thee
A mutual immortality — [28]

The question of immortality and what it might mean for both the living and the dead recurs throughout her poetry. Elsewhere, she is firm in her assertion of heaven's reality. 'No coward soul is mine' is among Emily Brontë's late poems, though these are not in fact the very last lines she wrote, as Charlotte claimed. The claims of churches and sects are resoundingly rejected, but the enduring life of the soul is affirmed:

No coward soul is mine
No trembler in the world's storm troubled sphere
I see Heaven's glories shine
And Faith shines equal arming me from Fear

O God within my breast
Almighty ever-present Deity
Life, that in me hast rest
As I, — Undying Life, have power in thee

Vain are the thousand creeds
That move men's hearts, unutterably vain,
Worthless as withered weeds
Or idlest froth amid the boundless main

To waken doubt in one
Holding so fast by thy infinity
So surely anchored on
The steadfast rock of Immortality.[29]

The polemical abstraction of this uncompromising poem warns that we cannot simply read it as an autobiographical text. It is legitimate, and inevitable, that we should be interested in what her unusually private life might have concealed, but Emily Brontë's writing amounts to more than a record of its troubled and creative course. Her poems are animated by their engagement with a literary tradition that she encounters on her own terms, using and transforming it to resist every version of the 'dark prison house'.[30] It is in this sense that her voice remains unforgettable.

NOTES

1 Ted Hughes, 'Emily Brontë', lines 1–3, 12, in *Remains of Elmet* (London: Faber and Faber, 1979), p. 96.
2 See Lucasta Miller, *The Brontë Myth* (London: Jonathan Cape, 2001) for a brilliantly engaging account of this process.
3 *Wuthering Heights and Agnes Grey. By Ellis and Acton Bell. A New Edition revised, with a Biographical Notice of the Authors, a Selection from their Literary Remains, and a Preface, by Currer Bell* (London: Smith, Elder, 1850). One of the seventeen poems, 'Often rebuked, yet always back returning', has been persuasively attributed to Charlotte rather than Emily Brontë by Janet Gezari in her *Last Things: Emily Brontë's Poems* (Oxford: Oxford University Press, 2007), pp. 128–9, 140–7.
4 The number varies according to editorial decisions as to how the texts should be divided and presented.
5 *The Brontës: The Critical Heritage*, ed. Miriam Allott (London and Boston: Routledge & Kegan Paul, 1974), p. 61.
6 *Examiner*, 8 January 1848.
7 The *Spectator*, the *American Review*, and the *Examiner* all remarked on this aspect of the book; see Allott, *Critical Heritage*, pp. 217, 222, 236.
8 Charlotte Brontë, 'Biographical Notice of Ellis and Acton Bell', in Emily Brontë, *Wuthering Heights*, ed. Ian Jack (Oxford: Oxford University Press, 2009), p. 306.
9 Ibid., p. 305.
10 Ibid., p. 301.
11 Emily Jane and Charlotte Brontë, 'The Visionary', lines 13–20, see Emily Jane Brontë, *The Complete Poems*, ed. Janet Gezari (Harmondsworth: Penguin, 1992), pp. 218–19, 278.
12 See Miller, *The Brontë Myth*, p. 184.
13 Emily Brontë, 'Julian M —— and A. G. Rochelle —', lines 1–12; dated 9 October 1845. See *The Poems of Emily Brontë*, eds Derek Roper and Edward Chitham (Oxford: Clarendon Press, 1995), p. 176; subsequent quotations are taken from this edition.
14 A trochee is a metrical foot in which a stress is followed by an unstressed syllable; in an iamb, the reverse is true. An alexandrine is a poetic line with six stressed syllables, while a pentameter has five. The Spenserian stanza, popular in longer Romantic poems (e.g. Byron's *Childe Harold's Pilgrimage*, Keats's 'The Eve of St. Agnes', Shelley's *The Revolt of Islam* and *Adonais*, and Scott's *The Vision of Don Roderick*) concludes with an alexandrine.
15 Byron, 'Sonnet on Chillon' (1816), lines 1–4, in *Poetical Works*, eds Frederick Page and John Jump (Oxford: Oxford University Press, 1970), p. 336.
16 'Julian M —— and A. G. Rochelle —', lines 25–8; Roper and Chitham, *Poems*, p. 177. 'Greif' was Emily Brontë's preferred spelling; see 'Emily Brontë's Spelling', Roper and Chitham, *Poems*, pp. 278–9. Her unconventional spelling is reproduced in quotations from the poetry throughout this essay.
17 'Julian M —— and A. G. Rochelle —', lines 65–92; Roper and Chitham, *Poems*, pp. 178–9.
18 'High waveing heather', lines 1–6; dated 13 December 1836; Roper and Chitham, *Poems*, pp. 31–2.

19 'The Prisoner: A Fragment', lines 61–4; Roper and Chitham, *Poems*, p. 183.
20 'Julian M — — and A. G. Rochelle —', line 125; Roper and Chitham, *Poems*, p. 180.
21 'Julian M — — and A. G. Rochelle —', lines 134, 149–52; Roper and Chitham, *Poems*, p. 181.
22 His poems and stories fuse Romantic sentiment with political conservatism; see *Winter-Evening Thoughts. A Miscellaneous Poem* (1810); *Cottage Poems* (1811); *The Rural Minstrel: A Miscellany of Descriptive Poems* (1813); *The Cottage in the Wood; or, the Art of becoming Rich and Happy* (1815); *The Maid of Killarney; or Albion and Flora. A Modern Tale, in which are interwoven some cursory remarks on religion and politics* (1818).
23 'O mother I am not regreting', lines 1–4; dated 14 December 1837; Roper and Chitham, *Poems*, p. 47.
24 'The linnet in the rocky dells', lines 21–8; dated 1 May 1844; Roper and Chitham, *Poems*, pp. 152–3.
25 'Remembrance', lines 1–4; dated 3 March 1845; Roper and Chitham, *Poems*, p. 166.
26 'The Old Stoic', lines 1–12; dated 1 March 1841; Roper and Chitham, *Poems*, pp. 120–1.
27 Matthew Arnold, 'Haworth Churchyard' (1855); see Allott, *The Brontës*, pp. 306–10.
28 'I see around me tombstones grey', lines 11–14, 41–6; dated 17 July 1841; Roper and Chitham, *Poems*, pp. 123–4.
29 'No coward soul is mine', lines 1–16; dated 2 January 1846 (first published in 1850); Roper and Chitham, *Poems*, p. 183.
30 'I paused on the threshold I turned to the sky', line 5; undated fragment; see Roper and Chitham, *Poems*, p. 208.

SELECTED FURTHER READING

Editions

Brontë, Charlotte, *The Letters of Charlotte Brontë*, ed. Margaret Smith, 3 vols, Oxford, Clarendon Press, 1995, 2000, 2004

Brontë, Charlotte, and Emily Brontë, *The Belgian Essays of Charlotte and Emily Brontë: A Bilingual, Annotated, Critical Edition*, ed. and trans. Sue Lonoff, New Haven, Yale University Press, 1996

Brontë, Emily Jane, *The Complete Poems*, ed. Janet Gezari, Harmondsworth, Penguin, 1992

The Poems of Emily Brontë, eds Derek Roper and Edward Chitham, Oxford, Clarendon Press, 1995

Wuthering Heights, eds Hilda Marsden and Ian Jack, Oxford, Clarendon Press, 1976

Secondary works

Alexander, Christine, and Margaret Smith, *The Oxford Companion to the Brontës*, Oxford, Oxford University Press, 2003

Allott, Miriam (ed.), *The Brontës: The Critical Heritage*, London, Routledge & Kegan Paul, 1974
Barker, Juliet, *The Brontës*, London, Weidenfeld and Nicolson, 1994
Chitham, Edward, *A Life of Emily Brontë*, Oxford, Blackwell, 1987
Davies, Stevie, *Emily Brontë: Heretic*, London, Women's Press, 1994
Gaskell, Elizabeth, *The Life of Charlotte Brontë* (1857), ed. Elizabeth Jay, Harmondsworth, Penguin, 1998
Gezari, Janet, *Last Things: Emily Brontë's Poems*, Oxford, Oxford University Press, 2007
Glen, Heather (ed.), *The Cambridge Companion to the Brontës*, Cambridge, Cambridge University Press, 2000
Ingham, Patricia (ed.), *The Brontës: A Critical Reader*, London, Longman, 2003
Miller, Lucasta, *The Brontë Myth*, London, Jonathan Cape, 2001
Pykett, Lyn, *Emily Brontë*, Houndmills, Macmillan, 1989
Ratchford, F. E., *The Brontës' Web of Childhood*, New York, Columbia University Press, 1941
Gondal's Queen: A Novel in Verse by Emily Jane Brontë, Austin, University of Texas Press, 1955
Smith, Anne (ed.), *The Art of Emily Brontë*, London, Vision Press, 1976
Thormählen, Marianne, *The Brontës and Religion*, Cambridge, Cambridge University Press, 1999
The Brontës and Education, Cambridge, Cambridge University Press, 2007
Yablon, G. Anthony, and John R. Turner, *A Brontë Bibliography*, London and Westport, CT, Ian Hodgkins and Meckler Books, 1978

23

LINDA H. PETERSON

Christina Rossetti

When Christina Rossetti died in December 1894, the obituary notices and reviews began the process of canonization. In his 'Reminiscences', Theodore Watts, a friend of the Rossetti family, recalled that Christina 'seemed to breathe a sainthood that must needs express itself in poetry', thus linking her well-known spiritual devotion to her lyrics and grounding her poetic achievement in 'the inspiration of the religious devotee'.[1] Watts was extreme in seeking to canonize both the person and the poet, but his emphasis on Rossetti's religious inspiration, seclusion from the world, and freedom from taint of the marketplace became a common strain. The Catholic poet Katharine Tynan called her 'Santa Christina'.[2] Alice Meynell, a poet with a reputation for being an angel in the house, honoured Rossetti as a 'woman of genius', and as a 'poet and saint'.[3] Alexander Smellie echoed this view in his account of a life 'spent, not in the publicity of the market, but in utter quiet and seclusion', and in his belief that her 'inspiration had its roots in her piety'.[4] In Christina Rossetti's life and work, these reviewers found an antidote to the professionalism of the late Victorian literary market, and an alternative to the writer with an eye on celebrity and commercial success rather than on aesthetic achievement. To nineteenth-century readers Rossetti was a poet's poet, an artist devoted to art. Most considered her to be the finest devotional poet of the century, perhaps second in the English tradition only to George Herbert. Tynan concluded, 'Christina Rossetti stands head and shoulders above all other women who have written English poetry.'[5]

Rossetti's aesthetic achievement secured her modern reputation. Yet, as Edmund Gosse observed in an 1893 review, later expanded in *Critical Kit-Kats* (1896), that reputation was based on more than devotional verse. While echoing the dislike of 'the commercial fervor which is so curious a feature of our new literary life, and which sits so inelegantly on a female figure', Gosse reminded his readers of the range of Rossetti's work – from the juvenile 'City of Statues', with its lush catalogue of ripe fruits; to the elegiac love-lyric, 'When I am dead, my dearest'; to the visionary 'Three Stages', with its longing for eternal rest and keynote of 'hope deferred'.[6] In his view Rossetti was the true poet of the Pre-Raphaelite circle; at her best she achieves 'the union of [a] fixed religious faith with a hold upon beauty and the richer part of nature which allies her with her brother and with their younger friends'.[7] (Meynell made a similar point when, describing Rossetti's poetry, she commented: 'how spiritual and how sensuous'.[8]) These assessments enable us to place Rossetti's work in its historical context and understand its range and motive, even if more recent scholars who share Gosse's admiration for her early phase might emphasize the originality, even dissent of her work from that of her Pre-Raphaelite brothers.

Rossetti's career as a poet began in her youth. She grew up in a household immersed in the work of Dante Alighieri and the early modern Italian poets. All of her siblings, Maria, Dante Gabriel, and William Michael, wrote verse in English and Italian. As a young girl she, too, wrote sonnets and other lyrics, often doing bouts-rimés, a poetry-writing game for which her brothers supplied the end rhymes and she invented the words. By the age of twelve she had become the designated poet of the household, and by age seventeen she had composed enough creditable verse for her grandfather Gaetano Polidori to print a volume, entitled simply *Verses* (1847), at his private press.[9] These juvenilia reveal the same love of nature, attraction to sensual beauty, and fascination with spiritual discipline that would characterize her mature work. In 'The Lotus-Eaters', for instance, a Tennysonian poem in theme and language, Rossetti imagines a land where 'Hemlock groweth, poppy bloweth, / In the fields where no man moweth', but her lotus-land includes details of the rural world she so valued as a child, where 'the hares are all secure, / And the birds are wild no more'. Rossetti's love of the natural world often comes into conflict with her foreknowledge of its ruin or her commitment to a spiritual realm – as in 'Summer', where a gorgeous catalogue of flowers ('Tulips like a glowing fire, / Clematis of milky whiteness, / Sweet geraniums' varied brightness') gives way to decay and death, or in the 'City of Statues', where a vision of 'A fair city of white stone' reveals, on closer inspection, men, women, and children 'turned to stone': 'Yea they were statue-cold.' In many poems, especially narratives of young women, the vision of mortality leads to renunciation of 'life's passing show' ('The Dream') or commitment to a life of spiritual contemplation ('The Novice'). Even at the age of fifteen, Rossetti could write: 'Life is fleeting, joy is fleeting, / Coldness follows love and greeting, / Parting still succeeds to meeting.'

According to her modern biographer, Jan Marsh, the melancholy and renunciatory strains intensified during the mid-1840s when Christina suffered some sort of physical and psychological crisis and simultaneously came under the influence of High Anglican asceticism at Christ Church, Albany Street. She 'lost all stamina and animation, falling into extreme weakness and lassitude', symptoms that Marsh associates with 'hysteria and depression'.[10] The poetry of this adolescent period is marked by anguish, guilt, and desperation; as Marsh notes, it is still painful to read a poem like 'Hope in Grief', the first poem Christina entered into her notebook after her breakdown:

Tell me not that death of grief
Is the only sure relief.
Tell me not that hope when dead
Leaves a void that naught can fill,
Gnawings that may not be fed.

Perhaps fortunately for Rossetti's career, most of this verse remained unpublished during her lifetime, and was omitted from the posthumous *New Poems of Christina Rossetti* (1896), edited by her brother William Michael. While the spiritual anguish would recur throughout her life and become a dominant feature of her later years, the young poet presented to the world in the late 1840s was a different figure: a sweet singer of love and death, a modern Sappho, the beautiful lady of Pre-Raphaelitism.

Indeed, the formation in 1848 of a literary club and then the Pre-Raphaelite Brotherhood, a group of young artists led by Dante Gabriel, seems to have spurred Christina's literary ambition. William Michael placed a poem in the *Athenaeum* in September 1848; Christina followed in October with two poems, 'Death's Chill Between' and 'Heart's Chill Between', signed 'C. G. R.' The first expresses a woman's grief after her beloved's death; the second laments the loss of a faithless lover – themes that would become common in her oeuvre. During the next half year, Rossetti produced twenty-two new pieces, many on similar themes, including the lyric 'Remember' ('Remember me when I am gone away, / Gone far away into the silent land'), a memorializing sonnet 'On Keats', and the revisionary 'What Sappho would have said had her leap cured her instead of killing her', in which she imagines a turn heavenward rather than a suicidal leap from the Leucadian cliff for the lovelorn poetess. Despite their high quality, none was accepted by the *Athenaeum* or any other periodical. Rather, it was in the Pre-Raphaelite magazine, the *Germ*, that Rossetti made her real public debut and published seven poems that established her reputation as a gifted poetess (at least among the London literati). Writing as 'Ellen Allyne', a signature invented by Dante Gabriel, Rossetti took the perspective of the 'fair lady' and developed an alternative perspective on the Pre-Raphaelites' contemplation of 'beauty's body'.

The *Germ* opened its inaugural issue with two pseudo-chivalric poems by Thomas Woolner, 'My Beautiful Lady' and 'Of My Lady in Death'. Both tell of doomed love – one praising the lady's fair, fragile body and soul, the other memorializing her 'dizzy swoon', death, and 'cold decay'. The two views are invariably linked, as the illustration by William Holman Hunt suggests with its diptych of above and below, before and after, the lovers in life and the bereaved male lover after the lady's death. Christina would take this Pre-Raphaelite subject and reverse its perspective, speaking as or about the dead lady. In 'Dream-Land', published in the same issue of the *Germ*, she imagines the lady's 'perfect rest' in death:

Where sunless rivers weep
Their waves into the deep,
She sleeps a charmèd sleep:
Awake her not.
Led by a single star,
She came from very far,
To seek where shadows are
Her pleasant lot.[11]

This poem echoes the PRB's fascination with doomed earthly love, but as Dolores Rosenblum has noted, it also echoes key Romantic lyrics of poetic inspiration: Coleridge's 'Kubla Khan', Keats's 'Ode to a Nightingale', and Shelley's 'Alastor'.[12] Most notably, it takes from Tennyson's 'The Lady of Shalott' its down-river voyage and contrast between the realm of ordinary life and the artist's realm, transforming this into a contrast between life and death:

She left the rosy morn,
She left the fields of corn,
For twilight cold and lorn,
And water springs.

Though 'cold and lorn', the realm that the lady reaches holds the source of her imagination – as the 'water-springs' and 'the nightingale / That sadly sings' suggest. Unlike Tennyson's lady, however, who silently suffers Lancelot's gaze,[13] Rossetti's claims the realm of death as a source of poetic power and expression.

Modern critics have treated Rossetti's dead lady as a symbol 'signifying power in powerlessness', resisting rather than 'reflecting male projections': in Rosenblum's seminal reading, 'it represents the female poet's power to reclaim this image of herself from the male tradition'.[14] Yet the various – and varied – appearances of women, dead or alive, in Rossetti's early verse suggest an ambivalence about poetic power – whether its possession, employment, or consequences. In 'Song', for instance, published in the *Germ*'s second issue, the lyricist disclaims both bodily beauty and poetic achievement:

Oh roses for the flush of youth,
  And laurel for the perfect prime,
But pluck an ivy branch for me
  Grown old before my time.

Oh violets for the grave of youth,
  And bay for those dead in their prime;
Give me the withered leaves I chose
  Before in the olden time.

This female speaker inhabits not an imaginative realm of death, as in 'Dream-Land', but a living death, a death-in-life that sees no possibility of love or poetic success, no 'laurel' or 'bay'. 'A Testimony', also in the second issue, repeats the lesson of Ecclesiastes: that earthly treasure 'every one / Is vanity beneath the sun'. And in 'Repining', published in the third *Germ*, a woman's desire for fulfilment, whether in love or art, is chastened by a spiritual vision of devastation. This poem begins as a rewriting of Tennyson's 'Mariana':

She sat always thro' the long day
Spinning the weary thread away;
And ever said in undertone:
'Come, that I be no more alone.'

Yet unlike Tennyson's Mariana, who laments while knowing that her lover will never come and, indeed, generates her lyric from his absence, Rossetti's lyricist soon finds her plea answered. An unknown man appears, bidding in 'a whispered word':

'Damsel, rise up; be not afraid;
For I am come at last,' it said.

With these biblical words of admonition, the 'unknown speaker' takes the lovelorn woman on a journey that reveals harsh wintry landscapes, ships sinking in a 'cold sea', a city devastated by fire, and a battlefield 'full of bleeding heaps' – all emblems of death that shame the lady for her trivial desires. In a move that Rossetti will repeat in later work, earthly longing is chastened by spiritual vision, worldly desire renounced in favour of Christian commitment, *eros* replaced by *caritas*.

The ambivalence of Rossetti's response to earthly love and fame can be read biographically, either as the doleful influence of her instruction by the Rev. William Dodsworth, 'with its heavy stress on self-abasement',[15] or as the result of her broken engagement to James Collinson, member of the PRB. Poems like 'A Testimony', with its rejection of earthly things, seem to reflect

Dodsworth's sermons on 'the value of eternity and the nothingness of all this world';[16] such teaching worked against Rossetti's ambition as a poet. Poems like 'Remember' ('Remember me when I am gone away, / Gone far away into the silent land') seem to hint at trouble in the engagement, or 'Three Moments' at despair when Collinson's conversion to Roman Catholicism finally ended the love-affair:

> The Woman knelt, but did not pray
> Nor weep nor cry; she only said,
> 'Not this, not this!' and clasped her hands.

The biographical links are evident – as Christina acknowledged when she asked her brother *not* to circulate any manuscript poems that an 'imaginative person could construe into love personals', adding: 'you will feel how (more than ever) intolerable it would (now) be to have my verses regarded as outpourings of a wounded spirit'.[17]

Yet, if Rossetti's lyrics of lost love can be read as 'love personals', they can also be read generically as verse in the neo-Sapphic tradition of Felicia Hemans, Laetitia Landon, and Elizabeth Barrett. In this tradition the woman poet, like the Greek lyricist Sappho, faces a conflict between love and fame, domestic bliss and public acclaim. The appropriate feminine response, as in Hemans's 'Woman and Fame', is to prefer love:

> Happy-happier far than thou,
> With the laurel on thy brow;
> She that makes the humblest hearth,
> Lovely but to one on earth.[18]

Rossetti wrote verse in this neo-Sapphic mode – often critically or ironically, as Margaret Linley has shown in her analysis of *Maude*, an autobiographical fiction composed in 1848–50 about an aspiring poetess who 'implicitly dies of literary ambition'.[19] While Rossetti could critique the outworn mode of the Sapphic poetess, doomed to lose love and lament its loss, she was not able fully to escape its influence. Her early verse shows an affinity, even as the poet tries to redirect erotic desire and poetic ambition to a spiritual end.

In the 1850s the limits on Rossetti's poetic ambition were not only psychological or religious. They became quite practical when the *Germ* folded and Christina was deprived of an outlet for her verse. In the lost decade of 1850–60 Rossetti wrote some of her finest, and now most famous, lyrics – including 'A Birthday', 'Song' ('When I am dead, my dearest'), 'Up-Hill', and 'Passing Away', the third of 'Old and New World Ditties', with its tour-de-force single-*a* rhyme. But she could not place her work. She failed with *Maude* and another short story, *Nick*, which her brothers had sent, via their friend

James Hannay, to the publisher Cundall and Addey. She tried *Blackwood's Edinburgh Magazine*, submitting four poems to the editor William Aytoun with a self-effacing letter in which she describes herself 'a nameless rhymester'; this, too, failed. With the encouragement of the poet Mary Howitt, she placed 'The Summer Evening' in the *Düsseldorf Artist's Album* (1854) and 'O Rose, thou flower of flowers' in the *Pictorial Calendar of the Seasons* (1854).[20] She also placed a story, 'The Lost Titian', in the *Crayon* (1856), an American art magazine for which William Michael served as London correspondent.[21] But in the 1850s much of Rossetti's creative energy was channelled into a London ladies' magazine, the *Bouquet*, funded by subscription and composed by young women who took the names of flowers as pseudonyms (Christina was Calta, Italian for marigold) to protect their gentility. This was amateur work in a negative sense. At this stage in Rossetti's biography, Marsh quotes Elizabeth Barrett's admonition to an aspiring poet, 'It is a mistake to think that a true poet (whatever his gifts!) can sing like a bird; he must work on the contrary like an artist', commenting that 'up to this point, Christina had tended to sing like a bird'.[22]

It's not clear that Rossetti *wasn't* working like an artist during the 1850s. Given her secretive methods of composition and destruction of manuscripts, even family members had little knowledge of her artistic methods (other than that she wrote on the edge of her washstand). But it *is* clear that Rossetti wasn't presenting herself or her work in a professional manner and that her ingrained reclusiveness and easily deflated self-esteem led her to shy away from the literary marketplace – as she did after the *Blackwood's* rejection. Without the savoir-faire and ambition of her brothers on her behalf, Rossetti's poetry might have remained hidden from the world. During the 1850s they tried to place her work, even when she seemed reluctant, in leading periodicals. The paradox of her success with *Goblin Market and Other Poems* (1862) – her breakthrough volume – is that the poet assumes a position of femininity and domesticity sheltered from the world while achieving a public position of literary prominence and critical esteem.

In fact, it was Rossetti's own ambition that led to the publication of her poems in *Macmillan's Magazine* and then to an offer, from Alexander Macmillan himself, to publish a collection of verse. In January 1861, just after her thirtieth birthday, she sent David Masson, *Macmillan's* editor, a letter, self-deprecating but hopeful, with an unknown number of poems. Masson answered positively, and Rossetti's 'Up-Hill' appeared in the magazine's February issue, with 'A Birthday' ('My heart is like a singing bird') following in April and 'An Apple-Gathering' in August.[23] By April she was corresponding with Macmillan about a projected volume and happily acknowledging her desire 'to attain fame (!) and guineas by means of the Magazine'.[24]

It took almost another year for *Goblin Market and Other Poems* to appear (in March 1862) – largely because of Dante Gabriel's delay, after the suicide of his wife, with the frontispiece and title-page illustrations. But when the major periodicals reviewed *Goblin Market*, the delay must have seemed trivial in comparison to the unequivocal praise. From 'the genuine utterance of a richly imaginative mind' in the *London Review* to praise of a 'rare poetic discrimination' in the *Spectator*, from the *Athenaeum*'s official designation of Rossetti as 'a mistress of verbal harmony' to Tennyson's unofficial expression of 'great pleasure', *Goblin Market and Other Poems* established Rossetti as the pre-eminent woman poet of the nineteenth century[25] – not exactly an heir to Elizabeth Barrett, whose work was markedly different, but a replacement.

From a perspective 150 years later, it is interesting to ask why this debut volume met with such success. Certainly, the originality of Rossetti's poems pleased Victorian critics – from Edwin Hood in the *Eclectic Review*, who found them a 'rare delight and refreshment', to the *Athenaeum* reviewer, who similarly praised their difference from run-of-the-mill productions: 'To read these poems after the laboured and skilful but not original verse which has been issued of late, is like passing from a picture gallery, with its well-feigned semblances of nature, to the real nature out-of-doors.'[26] Among High Anglicans, the superiority of Rossetti's devotional verse to other popular volumes, including John Keble's *The Christian Year* and Isaac Williams's *The Altar, The Cathedral*, and *The Baptistery*, was evident. Among fellow-poets, a deft, experimental hand was recognized; while Ruskin may have complained that 'irregular metre is the calamity of modern poetry', younger poets like Algernon Swinburne and Gerard Manley Hopkins admired Rossetti's metrical achievement and adapted her tones and cadences (in Swinburne's case, in his quite undevotional *Poems and Ballads* of 1866).

Nor should we forget that 'Goblin Market' had a timeliness that appealed to the Victorians, even as its tale of temptation, fall, and redemption has a timelessness that still exercises its fascination on modern readers. The tale presents two sisters, Laura and Lizzie, one of whom succumbs to the goblin men's entreaties to eat their fruit and then dwindles with 'cankerous care', the other of whom refuses to eat and braves the goblins' attack while seeking an antidote to save her sister. This tale of sister saving sister emerged from Rossetti's experience – including her work at the Highgate penitentiary for fallen women. The voluntary efforts of young Anglican women in such institutions embodied a new form of social work that sought to redeem rather than reject erring human beings. This work was controversial because 'pure' women were exposed to the 'fallen', but as Mary Carpenter explained in the *English Woman's Journal*, 'a true woman will surmount weakness

[and] know how to keep the privacy of her individual nature guarded by an invisible but impenetrable shield'.[27] In 'Goblin Market' Rossetti was not, of course, writing a treatise on the value of social work, but Lizzie admirably keeps up 'an invisible and impenetrable shield'. The poem finely captures both the motives leading young women to succumb to temptation and those prompting other women to sacrifice themselves in aid of the less fortunate:

Tho' the goblins cuffed and caught her,
Coaxed and fought her,
Bullied and besought her,
Scratched her, pinched her black as ink,
Kicked and knocked her,
Lizzie uttered not a word;
Would not open lip from lip
Lest they should cram a mouthful in:
But laughed in heart to feel the drip
Of juice that syrupped all her face,
And lodged in dimples of her chin,
And streaked her neck which quaked like curd.

Lizzie feels pain but also pleasure in the attack, knowing that she exercises power in refusal; hers is a modern martyrdom. Lizzie feels pleasure, too, in the redemptive act, which in Rossetti's treatment blends physical and spiritual:

She cried 'Laura,' up the garden,
'Did you miss me?
Come and kiss me.
Never mind my bruises,
Hug me, kiss me, suck my juices
Squeezed from goblin fruits for you,
Goblin pulp and goblin dew.
Eat me, drink me, love me;
Laura, make much of me:
For your sake I have braved the glen
And had to do with goblin merchant men.'

This scene repeats the sacrament of the Eucharist, as Laura 'eats' and 'drinks' the elements that redeem her from death.

Rossetti claimed that she did not intend 'Goblin Market' as an allegory, but it has been difficult for readers not to allegorize the poem. It offers an everyday tale of Christian redemption, complete with forbidden fruit, knowledge of death, and a Christ-figure who saves those who have gone astray. It can be read as a tale of female erotic desire, with Laura's attraction to the goblin fruit as heterosexual longing or Laura and Lizzie's embrace as same-sex desire (an interpretation encouraged by Dante Gabriel's illustration 'Golden head by golden head' and taken to extremes in the 1973 *Playboy* treatment of the poem as a 'ribald classic'). It can also be read as a tale exhibiting fear of the racialized or colonial Other, with pure, white English maidenhood triumphing over the dusky, animal bodies of the goblin men. And it can be read as an economic parable of nineteenth-century capitalism threatening the self-sufficiency of rural English life, or of women's ambivalent relations to a new market economy and growing consumerism.[28]

The economic aspects of 'Goblin Market' seem to be expunged in the final lines, where the sisters turn their trials into narrative and tell their tale in a private, domestic setting:

> Laura would call the little ones
> And tell them of her early prime,
> Those pleasant days long gone
> Of not-returning time:
> Would talk about the haunted glen,
> The wicked, quaint fruit-merchant men,
> Their fruits like honey to the throat,
> But poison in the blood.

Yet the economic aspects of art are not fully expunged from the volume itself. The attractive illustrations by Dante Gabriel, the aesthetic cover design, and the publisher's plan to make the book 'an exceedingly pretty little volume' all testify to its immersion in the literary marketplace. This paradox has relevance to an understanding of Rossetti's work within British aestheticism – which posits a split between 'high' art removed from the economic realm and 'popular' art vying for commercial success. Rossetti's poetry seems to remove itself, yet never fully escapes.

With the critical success of *Goblin Market and Other Poems* Rossetti could, however, choose to direct her art to different ends. She contributed poems to religious publications, including fourteen to the Anglican collections *Lyra Eucharistica*, *Lyra Messianica*, and *Lyra Mystica*, never accepting a fee for her work. She contributed to new feminist periodicals, the *Victoria Magazine* and *English Woman's Journal*, and to charitable volumes like the *Victoria Regia*, compiled by fellow-poet Adelaide Procter to raise funds for needy Lancashire workers. These religious and charitable venues gave Rossetti a wider audience than she would have had if limited to those able to purchase her books. But she also kept her eye on commercial venues, continuing to sell poems to *Macmillan's* and planning at her publisher's urging a second volume to match, in format and structure, her first.

That volume, *The Prince's Progress and Other Poems* (1866), received much critical praise, but not like that lavished on *Goblin Market and Other Poems*. The title poem, a 'reverse Cinderella story' as Rossetti called it, lacked the fast pace and fireworks of 'Goblin Market'. Its hero, a dilatory prince 'Strong of limb if of purpose weak', postpones his journey to the castle of his bride in a negative version of *The Pilgrim's Progress*. Like the hireling shepherd of Holman Hunt's painting, the prince gets ensnared by a milkmaid, with whom 'he stretche[s] his length in the apple-tree shade'. Like the quester in Robert Browning's 'Childe Roland', he loses his way in a desert. Unlike Bunyan's Christian, he almost loses his life as he crosses the deep river that represents his final trial. And when he finally reaches his goal, his bride is dead, her heart 'starving all this while / You made it wait'. The attendant women sing in final chorus:

> Too late for love, too late for joy,
> Too late, too late!
> You loitered on the road too long,
> You trifled at the gate.

The poem illustrates the dangers of delay, perhaps with a lesson aimed at Dante Gabriel, who had postponed his marriage to Lizzie Siddal so long that she may well have wasted away for lack of love. The poem also illustrates the dangers of faulty interpretation, of failing to read signs and symbols for their spiritual import. These allegorical features appealed to Victorians, though for modern critics they have made 'The Prince's Progress' less rich than the multi-valenced 'Goblin Market'.

What Victorian critics noticed about the 1866 volume was what Rossetti had privately feared: that it was thinner, less polished than her 1862 debut. As the *Eclectic Review* observed, 'Miss Rossetti' is a poet of 'unquestionable fullness and power', but some 'false notes or feeble words ... mar the effect of verses, which a little more care would have made perfectly beautiful'.[29] Rossetti had struggled with a lack of good material to fill the volume, writing to her brother in 1864: 'Why rush before the public with an immature vol.? I really think of not communicating at all with Mac at present: but waiting the requisite number of months (or years, as the case may be) until I have a sufficiency of quality as well as quantity.'[30] She had done her best – composing new verse, polishing old, and suppressing poems that Dante Gabriel disliked, even though some had impressed her feminist friends and today appeal to modern readers (notably, 'The Lowest Room'). Despite a few nondescript lyrics, *The Prince's Progress and Other Poems* is a strong collection, containing some of Rossetti's most memorable work: 'A Royal Princess', 'L.E.L.', and the agonized devotional meditations 'Despised and Rejected' and 'Good Friday'. Years later, when introduced to the poet, Ellen Proctor would ask, 'Are you Miss Rossetti? Did you really write *Good Friday* ("Am I a stone and not a sheep?")' – as if that lyric, more than any other, represented the height of Rossetti's achievement.[31]

Sensitive to critical response, Rossetti decided not to rush a third volume and waited fifteen years before publishing *A Pageant and Other Poems* (1881). In the interim she wrote fiction, devotional prose, and lighter verse: *Commonplace and Other Stories* (1870); *Sing Song* (1872), a collection of nursery rhymes; *Annus Domini: A Prayer for Each Day* (1874); *Seek and Find: Short Studies of the Benedicite* (1879); and *Called to be Saints* (1881), a collection of devotional prose interspersed with short lyrics. Rossetti's lack of poetic production during the 1870s had physical causes as well, including a life-threatening illness eventually diagnosed as Graves' disease (a form of hyperthyroidism that caused rapid heartbeat, irritability, exhaustion, goitre, and bulging eyes). And she suffered from anxiety after the psychological collapse of Dante Gabriel in 1872 and from deep grief after the death of her sister Maria in 1876. Her turn to devotional writing in the late 1870s reflects a renewed commitment to the religious life, and a new artistic commitment to poetry of spiritual vision.

That turn can be found in the most famous work of *A Pageant and Other Poems* (1881): 'Monna Innominata: A Sonnet of Sonnets'. These fourteen sonnets have been read as Rossetti's 'love personal' to Charles Cayley, the Dante scholar with whom she fell in love but whose proposal of marriage she declined in 1866; according to William Michael's 'Memoir': 'She loved him deeply and permanently, but, on his declaring himself, she must no doubt have probed his faith, and found it either strictly wrong or woefully defective.'[32] Whatever the personal basis, this sonnet-sequence has larger aims: it reverses the position of the silent beloved and gives the woman voice; it comments on the Italian sonnet tradition, taking its epigraphs from Dante and Petrarch and redirecting erotic love to a spiritual end; and it challenges Elizabeth Barrett's *Sonnets from the Portuguese*, suggesting that an 'unhappy' poetess, rather than a happily married one, might produce sonnets 'worthy to occupy a niche beside Beatrice and Laura'.[33] 'Monna Innominata', so entitled to suggest an unnamed lady of the troubadours, moves from first moments –

> I wish I could remember, that first day,
> First hour, first moment of your meeting me,
> If bright or dim the season, it might be
> Summer or Winter for aught I can say;

– to full love –

> Today, tomorrow, world without end;
> To love you much and yet to love you more,

– to renunciation and resolve to trust in God –

> Youth gone and beauty gone, what doth remain?
> The longing of a heart pent up forlorn,
> A silent heart whose silence loves and longs.

While the final sestet might be read as a Sapphic gesture (the poetess hangs up her lyre after losing her lover), it is better seen as a renunciation of earthly love and erotic poetry, and a turn to spiritual love and devotional verse. The sequence 'Later Life: A Double Sonnet of Sonnets', influenced by John Donne's 'Holy Sonnets' and included in the same volume as 'Monna Innominata', reinforces this turn:

> The wise do send their hearts before them to
> Dear blessed Heaven, despite the veil between;
> The foolish nurse their hearts within the screen
> Of this familiar world, where all we do
> Or have is old, for there is nothing new.

Rossetti turned wholly to devotional poetry in her final collection, *Verses* (1893). Whereas the first three volumes published by Macmillan had included both 'secular' and devotional verse (set off by the subtitle 'Devotional Pieces'), this fourth volume was published by the Society for the Promotion of Christian Knowledge (SPCK) and assembled 331 lyrics from prior religious works: *Called to be Saints: The Minor Festivals Devotionally Studied* (1881); *Letter and Spirit: Notes on the Commandments* (1883); and *Time Flies: A Reading Diary* (1885). Rossetti rearranged the poems under eight headings, creating a sequence of spiritual progress, from despair in 'Out of the deep have I called unto thee, O Lord', to reassurance in 'Gifts and Graces', to a vision of 'New Jerusalem and its Citizens', and a final section, 'Songs for Strangers and Pilgrims'. In its day *Verses* was Rossetti's most successful volume in terms of sales and reader response. Rossetti reported to her brother that a friend had called to say that 'by Christmas there was no meeting the demand for "Verses": at one considerable shop she tried at she heard that twenty or thirty applications had had to be negatived for the moment'.[34] Three editions of 1,000 copies sold within a year, and by the 1920s sales had exceeded 20,000 copies.

Paradoxically, *Verses* has been the volume most neglected by modern scholars, perhaps because of its devotional focus. Virginia Woolf may have started (or spurred) the trend when she commented that if she were bringing a case against God, Rossetti would be 'one of the first witnesses I should call': 'She starved herself of love, which also meant life; then of poetry in deference to what she thought her religion demanded.'[35] Like Woolf, many modern critics have been embarrassed by Rossetti's tenacious religious beliefs and blinded to the aesthetic achievement of the late devotional poetry.[36] For in fact *Verses* includes many exquisite sonnets and other demanding lyric forms, including the rondel 'Balm in Gilead':

> Heartsease I found, where Love-lies-bleeding
>   Empurpled all the ground:
> Whatever flowers I missed unheeding,
>   Heartsease I found.
>
>   Yet still my garden mound
> Stood sore in need of watering, weeding,
>   And binding growths unbound.
>
> Ah, when shades fell to light succeeding
>   I scarcely dared look round:
> 'Love-lies-bleeding' was all my pleading,
>   Heartsease I found.

This 1885 poem is just as much a tour de force as 'Passing Away', the lyric Swinburne so admired in Rossetti's debut volume. As it and other late sonnets attest, Gosse's insight that Rossetti's best work represents the *union* of a 'fixed religious faith with a hold upon beauty and the richer part of nature' applies not only to the early aesthetic verse he so admired, but also to the devotional poetry of Rossetti's final phase.[37]

NOTES

1 Theodore Watts[-Dutton], 'Reminiscences of Christina Rossetti', *Nineteenth Century: A Monthly Review* 37 (February 1895), 355–6.
2 Katharine Tynan, 'Santa Christina', *Bookman* 41 (January 1912), 185–90.
3 Alice Meynell, 'Christina Rossetti', *Littell's Living Age* 204 (2 March 1895), 569–72, p. 572, and 'Christina Rossetti', *New Review* 12 (1895), 201–6, p. 206.
4 A[lexander] Smellie, 'Christina Rossetti and her Message', *Wesleyan-Methodist Magazine* 118 (March 1895), 203–6, p. 203.
5 Tynan, 'Santa Christina', p. 190.
6 Gosse wrote with access to the rare volume of Rossetti's juvenilia, *Verses* (London, 1847); 'The City of Statues' was retitled 'The Dead City'.
7 Edmund Gosse, *Century Magazine* 46 (June 1893), 211–17; quotation from *Critical Kit-Kats* (London: William Heinemann, 1896), pp. 137–8.
8 Meynell, 'Christina Rossetti', p. 201.
9 Christina G. Rossetti, *Verses* (London, 1847). The title-page notes that the volume was privately printed at G. Polidori's, no. 15, Park Village East, Regent's Park.
10 Jan Marsh, *Christina Rossetti: A Writer's Life* (London: Viking-Penguin, 1995), p. 51.

11 All quotations of Rossetti's poetry are from the scholarly edition of R. W. Crump, *The Complete Poems of Christina Rossetti*, 3 vols (Baton Rouge and London: Lousiana State University Press, 1979–90).

12 See Dolores Rosenblum, *Christina Rossetti: The Poetry of Endurance* (Carbondale: Southern Illinois University Press, 1986), pp. 128–9.

13 'The Lady of Shalott', in *The Poems of Tennyson*, ed. Christopher Ricks (London: Longman, 1969), p. 361. My comments refer to the 1842 version, most probably the one Rossetti knew.

14 Rosenblum, *Christina Rossetti: The Poetry of Endurance*, p. 126.

15 The phrase is from Marsh, *Christina Rossetti: A Writer's Life*, p. 60, who quotes an 1844 sermon by Pusey in evidence: 'I am scarred all over and seamed with sin, so that I am a monster to myself ... I loathe myself; I can feel of myself only like one covered with leprosy from head to foot.'

16 See Marsh, *Christina Rossetti: A Writer's Life*, pp. 97–8, for a description of Dodsworth's sermons, 'Signs of the Times', as an interpretation of recent 'revolutions, earthquakes, choler, Irish famine, eclipses of the sun and moon – as prophetic of divine visitation'.

17 Letter from Christina G. Rossetti to William Michael Rossetti, 28 April 1849, in *The Letters of Christina Rossetti*, ed. Antony H. Harrison, 4 vols (Charlottesville and London: University of Virginia Press, 1997–2004), I, p. 18.

18 'Woman and Fame', in *Felicia Hemans: Selected Poems, Prose, and Letters*, ed. Gary Kelly (Petersborough, Ont.: Broadview Press, 2002), p. 351. This poem was originally published in a literary annual, the *Amulet; or, Christian and Literary Remembrancer* (1829), and in slightly altered form in *Songs of the Affections* (1830).

19 Margaret Linley, 'Dying to be a Poetess: The Conundrum of Christina Rossetti', in *The Culture of Christina Rossetti: Female Poetics and Victorian Contexts*, eds Mary Arseneau, Antony H. Harrison, and Lorraine Janzen Kooistra (Athens: Ohio Univeristy Press, 1999), p. 292.

20 Letter from Christina G. Rossetti to William Michael Rossetti, 19 September 1853, in Harrison, *Letters*, I, p. 78.

21 See Harrison, *Letters*, I, p. 121 n. 5, p. 305 n. 2.

22 Marsh, *Christina Rossetti: A Writer's Life*, p. 157.

23 Letter from Christina G. Rossetti to David Masson, 19 January [1861], in Harrison, *Letters*, I, p. 141.

24 Letter from Christina G. Rossetti to Alexander Macmillan, 8 [April 1861], in Harrison, *Letters*, I, p. 146.

25 See Marsh, *Christina Rossetti: A Writer's Life*, pp. 281–4, for a summary of the reviews.

26 [Edwin Paxton Hood], *Eclectic Review* n.s. 2 (1862) 493; *Athenaeum* (26 April 1862), 558.

27 Mary Carpenter, quoted in Marsh, *Christina Rossetti: A Writer's Life*, p. 226. Carpenter makes a similar argument for the use of voluntary social workers in 'On the Treatment of Female Convicts', *English Woman's Journal* 12 (1863), 251–9.

28 For these seminal analyses, see Mary Arseneau, 'Incarnation and Interpretation: Christina Rossetti, the Oxford Movement, and Goblin Market', *Victorian Poetry* 31 (1993), 79–93; Lorraine Janzen Kooistra, 'Modern Markets for *Goblin*

Market', *Victorian Poetry* 32 (1994), 249–78; Mary Carpenter, '"Eat me, drink me, love me": The Consumable Female Body in Christina Rossetti's *Goblin Market*', *Victorian Poetry* 29 (1991), 415–34; Terrence Holt, '"Men sell not such in any town": Exchange in Goblin Market', *Victorian Poetry* 28 (1990), 51–67; and Elizabeth K. Helsinger, 'Consumer Power and the Utopia of Desire: Christina Rossetti's *Goblin Market*', *English Literary History* 50 (1991), 403–33.

29 [Edwin Paxton Hood], 'Miss Rossetti's Poems', *Eclectic Review* n.s. 11 (1866), 125.

30 Letter from Christina G. Rossetti to Dante Gabriel Rossetti [7 May 1864], in Harrison, *Letters*, I, p. 196.

31 Ellen A. Proctor, *A Brief Memoir of Christina Rossetti* (London: Society for the Promotion of Christian Knowledge, 1895).

32 William Michael Rossetti, 'Memoir', in *The Poetical Works of Christina Georgina Rossetti* (London: Macmillan, 1904), p. liii.

33 This final phrase comes from Rossetti's prefatory comments to 'Monna Innominata'.

34 Letter from Christina G. Rossetti to William Michael Rossetti, [29 December 1893], in Harrison, *Letters*, IV, p. 364.

35 Virginia Woolf, entry for Monday, 4 August 1918, in *A Writer's Diary*, ed. Leonard Woolf (New York and London: Harcourt Brace Jovanovich, 1953), p. 1.

36 This trend is being reversed in recent studies such as Mary Arseneau's *Recovering Christina Rossetti: Female Community and Incarnational Poetics* (Basingstoke: Palgrave Macmillan, 2004) and Dinah Roe's *Christina Rossetti's Faithful Imagination: The Devotional Poetry and Prose* (Basingstoke: Palgrave Macmillan, 2006).

37 Gosse, *Critical Kit-Kats*, p. 148.

SELECTED FURTHER READING

Editions

The Complete Poems of Christina Rossetti, ed. R. W. Crump, 3 vols, Baton Rouge and London, Louisiana State University Press, 1979–90

Christina Rossetti: The Complete Poems, ed. R. W. Crump, London, Penguin, 2001

Christina Rossetti: Poems and Prose, ed. Jan Marsh, London, Everyman, 1994

The Poetical Works of Christina Georgina Rossetti, ed. William Michael Rossetti, London, Macmillan, 1904

Secondary works

Arseneau, Mary, *Recovering Christina Rossetti: Female Community and Incarnational Poetics*, Basingstoke, Palgrave Macmillan, 2004

Arsenau, Mary, Antony H. Harrison, and Lorraine Janzen Kooistra (eds.), *The Culture of Christina Rossetti: Female Poetics and Victorian Contexts*, Athens, Ohio University Press, 1999

Battiscombe, Georgina, *Christina Rossetti: A Divided Life*, London, Longmans, Green, 1965

Bell, Mackenzie, *Christina Rossetti: A Biographical and Critical Study*, London, Hurst and Blackett, 1898
Chapman, Alison, *The Afterlife of Christina Rossetti*, London, Macmillan, 2000
D'Amico, Diane, *Christina Rossetti: Faith, Gender, and Time*, Baton Rouge and London, Louisiana State University Press, 1999
Harrison, Antony H., *Christina Rossetti in Context*, Chapel Hill and London, University of North Carolina Press, 1988
(ed.), 'Centennial of Christina Rossetti, 1830–1894', Special Issue, *Victorian Poetry* 32 (1994)
(ed.), *The Letters of Christina Rossetti*, 4 vols, Charlottesville and London, University of Virginia Press, 1997–2004
Hassett, Constance W., *Christina Rossetti: The Patience of Style*, Charlottesville, University of Virginia Press, 2005
Kent, David A. (ed.), *The Achievement of Christina Rossetti*, Ithaca, NY, and London, Cornell University Press, 1987
Leighton, Angela, *Victorian Women Poets: Writing Against the Heart*, Charlottesville and London, University of Virginia Press, 1992
Marsh, Jan, *Christina Rossetti: A Writer's Life*, London, Viking-Penguin, 1995
Mayberry, Katherine J., *Christina Rossetti and the Poetry of Discovery*, Baton Rouge, Louisiana State University Press, 1989
Psomiades, Kathy Alexis, *Beauty's Body: Femininity and Representation in British Aestheticism*, Stanford, Stanford University Press, 1997
Roe, Dinah, *Christina Rossetti's Faithful Imagination: The Devotional Poetry and Prose,* Basingstoke, Palgrave Macmillan, 2006
Rosenblum, Dolores, *Christina Rossetti: The Poetry of Endurance*, Carbondale, Southern Illinois University Press, 1986
Smulders, Sharon, *Christina Rossetti Revisited,* New York, Twayne, 1996
Sonstroem, David, *Rossetti and the Fair Lady*, Middletown, CT, Wesleyan University Press, 1970

24

PETER ROBINSON

Thomas Hardy

William Empson held views on modern poetry's stylized discontinuities when expected to perform a Matthew Arnold-like 'application of ideas to life' (II, p. 320).[1] In a review of *The Waste Land* manuscripts, he identifies a Dickensian thread: 'but then, if Eliot was imitating Dickens, he was bound to scold ... The difference is that Dickens had a plot, which allowed him to show adequate reasons for his scolding ... but to scold without even a residual plot, as a Symbolist, is bound to feel self-regarding.'[2] Among Victorian novelists who combined scolding with plot was Thomas Hardy, who published his sixth poetry collection, *Late Lyrics and Earlier* (1922), in the same year T. S. Eliot's *The Waste Land* first appeared. Born in 1840, Hardy was largely shaped in his poetic tastes by Palgrave's *Golden Treasury* (1861). On 12 August 1895, he wrote to Florence Henniker that 'A good book for carrying on a long journey is the G. Treasury – as it contains so much in a small compass.'[3] Hardy's *Collected Poems* (1930), published in a fourth edition two years after his death, follows the anthology in its miscellany of light songs, sonnets, ballads both lyrical and narrative, love-poems, and elegies, its mixing of dialect, folk, literary, private, public, and historical materials. Bringing fictional skills, learned in part from balladry and folk song, to the writing of poetry, Hardy might exemplify Empson's preferred poetics. Why then did Empson not admire the poet more?

Reviewing a selection of Hardy's poetry in 1940, Empson expresses irritation at the 'flat contradictions' of the philosophy, dwelling upon his 'complacence', his seeing 'no need to try and reconcile the contradictions'. This was 'the same complacence which could be satisfied with a clumsy piece of padding to make a lyric out of a twaddling reflection'. He speculates that Hardy 'needed this quality to win through as he did. Most people who are admired for "unpretentious integrity" have it.'[4] We can enjoy the good ('you want their honesty and find their beauty'[5]) because the poet had to produce the padded ones. Empson knew short poems on relationships could be 'unjust ... without a prose book. / A lyric from a fact is bound to cook.'[6]

Poets attempting honesty risk dishonesty in being, as they must, economical with the truth, especially if they access honesty by telling stories.

Meeting Hardy late in life, Arthur Compton Rickett 'expressed regret at his abandonment of fiction. "Why?" said Hardy. "Surely there's no tale worth the telling that can't be told better in verse than in prose".'[7] In a 3 April 1901 letter, he asked 'what you think of my opinion' that 'Her Death and After' (I, pp. 51–6) and 'The Dance at the Phoenix' (I, pp. 57–62) were 'as good stories as I have ever told.'[8] To Sir Frederick Macmillan, on 22 September 1910, he wrote that 'narrative poems, like the Trampwoman's Tragedy' (I, pp. 243–7), 'seem to be liked most, & I can do them with ease'.[9] But Ford Madox Hueffer (later Ford Madox Ford) published 'A Sunday Morning Tragedy' (I, pp. 250–5) in the *English Review* after its rejection for impropriety by the *Fortnightly Review* in October 1907. Its subject, the death of a pregnant girl obliged to have an abortion, was criticized in the *Spectator* (5 December 1908) for its 'extreme unpleasantness' (iii, 331; iv, 28). 'A Sunday Morning Tragedy' is one of many such self-evidently story-telling ballads in Hardy's poetic oeuvre.

Yet his poems, however long or short, can rarely get on without explicit or implicit plot and tale. He could recount the perverse crime in 'Her Second Husband Hears her Story' (III, pp. 194–5), for example, or make 'A January Night' (II, pp. 204–5) from a hint of narrative and an ominous coincidence. In an act of Hardyesque grotesquerie the poet's heart was removed after death, to be buried with his first wife in Stinsford churchyard, Wessex, while the heartless corpse was laid to rest in Poets' Corner, Westminster Abbey. In what follows, I look at the heart of his poetic art, its need for story, within the corpus not of his narrative ballads (where you would expect to find it), but in his much-loved lyric poems.

'The Garden Seat', for instance, is a ghost story, describing in the first of three quatrains how soon the piece of furniture 'will break down unaware' (II, p. 331, lines 3 and 4), in the second picturing its past occupants: 'Those who once sat thereon come back; / Quite a row of them sitting there' (lines 6–7), and then, after the repeat of line seven in eight, here comes the twist:

> With them the seat does not break down,
> Nor winter freeze them, nor floods drown,
> For they are as light as upper air,
> They are as light as upper air! (lines 9–12)

Hardy's fictive account of the garden seat articulates an emotion the object inspired, an emblem for his being haunted by an invisible past. The echo of each quatrain's line three in four could be thought padding, though this device reinforces the rhyme-sounds that resonate into the third verse. Perhaps 'nor floods drown', a revision fulfilling the rhyme with 'down', is a stop-gap. Yet the poem mysteriously lifts with that final line, its airy rhyme and confirming repetition having a weightlessness that mimics those harmlessly dead sitters.

Hardy could use the same twist twice, as in the timidities of 'A Thunderstorm in Town' (II, p. 18) and 'Faintheart in a Railway Train' (II, p. 329). The same stanza-form, a quatrain of four-stress lines followed by one of three, shapes the shift into each poem's pathetic might-have-been: 'I should have kissed her if the rain / Had lasted a minute more' (II, p. 18, lines 9–10). The story tells us what didn't happen (the speaker didn't kiss one woman, or get off the train to accost another) thanks to a self-frustrating reserve. The regular rhyming form's predictability interprets the narrative: though painful to tell, this is how it had to be. Despite the speaker's claim to be upset, we sense a relief at the desired thing's not happening. Such an implication might render the poems self-unknowing – their tales revealing less than they might have, thus more colloquially 'pathetic'. Yet Hardy's form both comments and musically reassures, implying at least a subliminal awareness of that very relief.

'Snow in the Suburbs', first collected in 1925, has been thought an 'Imagist equation',[10] associating it with the movement formed by Ezra Pound in 1912. Pound wrote a postcard to Amy Lowell in 1914 suggesting that Hardy be in an anthology associated with the movement.[11] The poem begins: 'Every branch big with it, / Bent every twig with it ... The palings are glued together like a wall, / And there is no waft of wind with the fleecy fall' (III, pp. 42–3, lines 1–2, 7–8). Yet, despite this picture-making, its second and third verses plot a care for the animal kingdom in the incident of a sparrow upon whom 'A snow-lump thrice his own slight size / Descends on him and showers his head and eyes, / And overturns him, / And near inurns him' (lines 11–14), while in the last:

> The steps are a blanched slope,
> Up which, with feeble hope,
> A black cat comes, wide-eyed and thin;
> And we take him in. (III, p. 43, lines 17–20)

This can be distinguished from Imagist poetry by its narrative inhabiting the creatures' viewpoints and giving them the temporal perspectives of a fate. Both mini-plots are articulated around rhyme-words: for the sparrow, it is there in the neologism 'inurns him' while for the cat it's in the anthropomorphism of a 'feeble hope'. In Hardy everything can tell a story. 'Green Slates' ends by having them 'Cry out: "Our home was where you saw her / Standing in the quarry!"' (III, p. 20, lines 15–16).

Empson expects unresolved contradictions to encourage an effortful cohesion of ideas. He believes the contradictions are parts of a monism, the name for any philosophical doctrine that posits, in contrast to dualistic or pluralistic theories, the unity or singleness of its subject-matter[12] – as in 'The Convergence of the Twain', Hardy's account of how the *Titanic* and its iceberg are wedded by fate, when 'consummation comes, and jars two hemispheres' (II, p. 13, line 33). Empson thinks the monism may be true; nevertheless, random or vicious switches across the contradiction's terms reveal an intellectual complacency. They don't constitute an integrated vision of life, but rather a convenient mechanism for producing ironic reversals and disappointments. These risk complacency in expecting life to be perversely spiteful, while simultaneously relieving human agents of responsibility. Hardy's philosophy is a plot device for embodying a clutch of folk attitudes and received wisdoms. He can deploy his satires of circumstance ad infinitum if not ad nauseam.

Yet alongside asserting towards the close of 'In Tenebris (II)' that 'if way to the Better there be, it exacts a full look at the Worst' (I, p. 208, line 14), Hardy staged flights of enchanted singing. Though inclined to be reassured by expecting the worst and not being surprised, he also knew that life could not continue without hope and bets against odds. In 'After a Romantic Day' the poet reconfigures the adjectives in Tennyson's grief-flattened 'On the bald street breaks the blank day'.[13] Hardy admitted to Henry Newbolt on 16 January 1909 that 'I am one of those you allude to as undervaluing "In Memoriam", though I did my duty in adoring it in years past.'[14] His redeployment of Tennyson's adjectives matches such faded adoration:

And the blank lack of any charm
    Of landscape did no harm.
The bald steep cutting, rigid, rough,
    And moon-lit, was enough
For poetry of place: its weathered face
Formed a convenient sheet whereon
The visions of his mind were drawn.

(II, pp. 417–18, lines 7–13)

Perhaps 'rigid, rough' are metrical filler to prepare a confirming rhyme on 'enough'; but, doing so, they echo the moonlight's falling 'like a liquid ditty' and make a love-lyric exemplifying the deleted epigraph from Joel 2:27: 'Your young men shall see visions.' To retain such a sense of life into his eighties, aware that 'The contradictions cover such a range',[15] looks less complacent than Empson claimed. The honesty and beauty of Hardy's best verse are in its rhythms, ones attuned to the contrasting terms of the predictable and the unforeseen. They can figure enchantment or disaffection, but also, on occasion, effect a re-enchantment.

Like his novels, the poems frequently turn on people, places, and things gaining or losing meaning.[16] Though Hardy's art depends upon the former, it is better known for the latter, as at the close of 'Neutral Tones' (1867):

> Since then, keen lessons that love deceives,
> And wrings with wrong, have shaped to me
> Your face, and the God-curst sun, and a tree,
> And a pond edged with grayish leaves.
>
> (I, p. 13, lines 13–16)

Commas locate the lovers' predicament among objects, and their disenchantment is an aspect of rhythm. In 'Since then, keen lessons', the first four syllables claim prominence, resisting a cantabile lift or fall. The comma at the first line end and at the mid-line caesura in two are not required for sense. The contrast between the two-syllable, rising stressed, iambic feet of line two and the three-syllable (two weak followed by a stronger stressed) anapaests at second and fourth position in the third line combine with the stress cluster of 'God-curst sun' and the commas to slow the line to a near stop. Hardy's closing line underscores this with its repeat of 'and a' and its double-stressed 'pond edged'. G. M. Young opined that 'any young man who had read Browning and Swinburne might have written it'. Dr Johnson-fashion, Empson refuted him thus: 'Swinburne my foot.'[17]

Criticized for his technique, as on 11 January 1902 in the *Saturday Review*, which remarked that 'Mr. Hardy has never written with flowing rhythms ... and his verse often halts',[18] the poet appeared to be the purveyor of an untimely pessimism: grimly irreligious visions enacted in what was thought to be clumsy verse. Yet the sestet of 'A Church Romance' steadily crescendoes:

> Thus their hearts' bond began, in due time signed.
> And long years thence, when Age had scared Romance,
> At some old attitude of his or glance
> That gallery-scene would break upon her mind,
> With him as minstrel, ardent, young, and trim,
> Bowing 'New Sabbath' or 'Mount Ephraim'.
>
> (I, p. 306, lines 9–14)

Hardy slows the penultimate line to its end with separated adjectives, releasing the flow in an unstopped final cadence whose rhyme is revealed from within that unpredictable last word, coming home in surprising affirmation. Rhythmic form models social bonding and generational continuity (the poem evokes Hardy's mother's first sight of his father). Both entail the checking of passion by time and memory's unexpected re-enchantment. If the poem is among those which he thought 'quite "churchy" in fact' when writing to his publisher about *Time's Laughingstocks and Other Verses*, the purpose of the letter was to ask for opinions about publishing 'Panthera' (I, pp. 337–43), a dramatic monologue spoken by the centurion who thought himself Jesus's father. Hardy's rhythmic sense (and 'Panthera' is a less successful work) could equally dramatize the tensions between his advanced thinking and his imaginative loyalty to culturally embedded ways of life.[19]

Hardy *had* of course read Swinburne when he wrote 'Neutral Tones'. Born on 5 April 1837, the poet was 'between three and four years'[20] senior to Hardy. Their different writing lives are implied in the third stanza of 'A Singer Asleep' when Hardy recalls encountering *Poems and Ballads* (1866): 'down a terraced street whose pavements lay / Glassing the sunshine into my bent eyes, / I walked and read with a quick glad surprise / New words, in classic guise' (II, p. 31, lines 13–16). Writing to Swinburne on 1 April 1897, Hardy describes himself reading the book at 'imminent risk of being knocked down'.[21] In the poem, his 'with a quick glad surprise' recalls 'with a wild surmise' in the penultimate line of 'On First Looking into Chapman's Homer'. Hardy suggested to Amy Lowell on 6 March 1925 that 'pure serene' in the same sonnet was 'an unconscious memory of the line in Gray's Elegy ending, "purest ray serene"'.[22] Keats's sonnet, on being inspired by a classic author in Elizabethan guise, has a triple rhyme in its sestet on the same sound as Hardy's: 'skies ... eyes ... surmise' pre-echoing 'eyes ... surprise ... guise'. The twenty-six-year-old architectural apprentice may have been 'Silent' then, but he too would eventually be inspired to 'speak out loud and bold'.[23]

Moreover, 'classic' acknowledges Swinburne's sources in Sappho, whose ghost meets his own later in the monody. Hardy was to prove more gothic in the 'cunning irregularity' of his rhythms and forms.[24] 'A Singer Asleep' recalls how a 'fulth of numbers freaked with musical closes' dropped 'Upon Victoria's formal middle time / His leaves of rhythm and rhyme' (II, p. 31, lines 9–11). Yet the rhythms and rhymes of Swinburne and Hardy differently orientate their poems in figuring experience. Swinburne's metrics enfold him in oceanic feelings like being touched all over. His rhymes are un-emphatic, minimizing pauses at them, sustaining thus his music's flow over many lines. As with the three-syllable rhymes in 'The Voice', 'listlessness' and 'wistlessness' being among the more notorious (II, p. 56, lines 9 and 11), Hardy's rhymes tend to require pauses at the line end.

Though he was described as 'Being – like Swinburne – a swimmer',[25] Hardy's rhythms mark separations, eschew physical contact: he 'tried also to avoid being touched by his playmates ... This peculiarity never left him, and to the end of his life he disliked even the most friendly hand being laid on his arm or his shoulder.'[26] 'Let me view you, then', he writes in 'The Voice' (II, p. 56, line 5); and such dwelling on visual detail requires focal distance. His poems succumb to rapture only in carefully occasioned situations. He locates feelings with more incident and story than in Swinburne's rhapsodies. In a letter to Florence Henniker on 11 October 1899 Hardy wrote that 'Swinburne's sonnet in to-day's *Times* disappoints me.'[27] One difference between 'The Transvaal', dated 9 October 1899, and Hardy's Boer War poems is the latter's emphasis on narrated individual perspective, which, in 'Embarkation', 'Drummer Hodge', or 'A Wife in London' (I, pp. 116, 122, 123), prevents them from succumbing to the jingoistic tones of Swinburne's pre-emptive 'Strike, England, and strike home.'[28]

The poet who helped Eliot complete the work Empson criticized for want of explanatory story, Ezra Pound, was also an admirer of Hardy's verse,[29] and especially the benefit in its having been produced, as Pound believed, after the fiction: '20 novels form as good a gradus ad Parnassum as does metrical exercise' and 'After novel writing he wrote verse narrative.'[30] But Hardy did metrical exercises too.[31] He also wrote poems at intervals through his years as a novelist, telling Edmund Gosse on 27 December 1898, after *Wessex Poems* had appeared, that 'the poems were lying about' and 'to indulge rhymes was my original weakness'.[32] He was similarly revising and proofreading a new edition of his fiction in the months before writing the 'Poems of 1912–1913'. Hardy didn't so much give up writing novels to compose poetry as shift the emphasis between his intertwined genres: the fiction suffused with poetic language, the poems constructed around story. Pound, praising their 'clean wording', takes Hardy as exemplifying Ford Madox Ford's belief that 'poetry should be at least as well written as prose';[33] his works make others weigh their own 'for fustian, for the foolish word, for the word upholstered'.[34] Empson's accusation of padding appeared two years later: he may have had Pound's praise in his sights as well. Yet Hardy's wording is 'clean' neither in poetry nor in prose. It's vividly crabbed, twisted with mannerism, as his defence of 'cunning irregularity' indicates. Hardy's directness required both indirect plotting and expression.

'Thoughts of Phena', the poem Philip Larkin said helped him abate his Celtic fever,[35] is neither plain nor straightforward. Its complex syntax turns upon negations and inversions:

> Not a line of her writing have I,
> Not a thread of her hair,
> No mark of her late time as dame in her dwelling, whereby
> I might picture her there;

And in vain do I urge my unsight
To conceive my lost prize
At her close, whom I knew when her dreams were upbrimming with light,
And with laughter her eyes. (I, p. 81, lines 1–8)

Its lucidity is not a feature of style, but of articulated situation, given in the subtitle 'At News of Her Death'. The plot twist is that he has a clearer vision of the now dead Tryphena Sparks because he has none of her writing. Implicit in this story is its being told by both a writer *and* a poet. In 'At Waking' he describes why such a girl's writing might have been so relevant, but then edits out the explanation. If 'Thoughts of Phena' concerns regaining meaning after a death, 'At Waking' explores meaning-loss in life: 'When night was lifting, / And dawn had crept under its shade, / Amid cold clouds drifting / Dead-white as a corpse outlaid' (I, p. 274, lines 1–4). This lack, the 'Dead-white' of the clouds at dawn, includes hints of a letter's white paper – ones characteristically half-revealed and half-concealed: 'With a sudden scare / I seemed to behold / My Love in bare / Hard lines unfold' (lines 5–8). The trace of a lovers' communication remains in the 'Hard lines' that conclude this opening verse. In the published version, it's *as if* he were reading a letter. A manuscript draft of line 10 has 'Those words she had written awry': Hardy's earlier version glances at a written piece of paper that 'Killed her old endowment / And gifts that had cheapened all nigh' (I, p. 274 n).

Concealing this judgement about her handwriting and replacing it with a visual perception, he relocates the loss in himself: 'An insight that would not die / Killed her old endowment / Of charm that had capped all nigh' (lines 10–12). In draft, this is caused by critically reacting to a sign of insufficient literary education. In revision, it's the speaker's vision, for which he appears not wholly responsible, underlined by the change from 'gifts' to 'charm'. The reader has three whites: the 'cold clouds drifting' in the dawn; the face or body of 'My Love in bare / Hard lines'; and the letter, a trace of it surviving in those 'lines'. These whites, with their associated emptiness, are condensed in the concluding verse:

O vision appalling
When the one believed-in thing
Is seen falling, falling,
With all to which hope can cling.
Off: it is not true;
For it cannot be
That the prize I drew
Is a blank to me! (lines 25–32)

This 'blank' is a lottery ticket. Pieces of paper are picked at random, and if a 'prize' has been won it will be written there; if not, the paper will be empty. So Hardy is romantically punning on 'prize', a word that also appears in 'Thoughts of Phena'. The woman shadowed in the poem had been 'the one believed-in thing', yet now seems 'but one / Of the common crowd' and 'a sample / Of earth's poor average kind' (lines 15–16, 17–18). Painfully sad for her, yet the poem concentrates on its speaker's predicament, his problem being perhaps that, as his 'one believed-in thing', she must mean too much. The anguish is produced by a change in perceived value. Reading 'Thoughts of Phena' beside 'At Waking', the phrase 'my lost prize' hints at self-blame for the loss that 'Thoughts of Phena' expresses without narrating. Hardy's gain from the fiction is not lucidity of style; rather, narrative structure makes feeling, event, or opinion seemingly plain – by managing a pointed selection of detail. There is a 'cunning irregularity' too in his not explaining how the prize was lost or in cutting those 'words ... written awry'.[36]

Hardy denied overarching narrative in his lyrics; yet the ironically malign tale he regularly allowed concealed other stories. The 'Apology' from *Late Lyrics and Earlier* describes the poems as 'really a series of fugitive impressions which I have never tried to co-ordinate' (II, p. 319). Story can provide distancing and exclude intimate detail, producing gains in lucidity by articulating familiar contrasts and contradictions as explanations for specific common experience. In more personal lyrics, Hardy's narrative skills shape selected detail to reserve full story, half-keeping a secret by telling us he has one – as in 'After the Visit' (II, pp. 14–15), dedicated to the woman who would be his second wife before the death of his first, or 'Standing by the Mantelpiece' (III, p. 226), on the suicide of his mentor Horace Moule, or the many poems on his marriage, such as 'Wives in the Sere' (I, pp. 182–3) or 'We Sat at the Window' (II, p. 161). Compelled to be honest, the poet is forced to be discreet.

Some of Hardy's best-loved poems, 'Midnight on the Great Western' (II, p. 262), for instance, are composed from a need for story when it's to be intuited; while another railway poem, 'On the Departure Platform', is fatally weakened by the requirement of two morals laboriously tagged to the last stanzas: 'she will appear again ... But never as then!' and ' – O friend, nought happens twice thus; why, / I cannot tell!' (I, p. 271, lines 18, 20, 23–4) In his poorer poems idea is pushed too hard by story; or story doesn't open up to reflection, but insists on illustrating a grimly platitudinous attitude. The leeringly crude 'Satires of Circumstance' sequence not only occupies the same collection as 'Poems of 1912–1913', acknowledged as among Hardy's best achievements; the former provides the book's title. Life has its little ironies, but the reversals in his finest poems outstrip his routine twists. Yet even his greatest sequence includes 'A Circular', a circumstantial satire where the poet, 'As "legal representative"', opens a fashion catalogue sent to his wife. The second verse, essential padding for the final one, simply describes how: 'Here figure blouses, gowns for tea, / And presentation-trains of state, / Charming ball-dresses, millinery, / Warranted up to date' (II, p. 58, lines 1, and 5–8). The ending turns on the already known fact that the recipient is dead:

> And this gay-pictured, spring-time shout
> Of Fashion, hails what lady proud?
> Her who before last year ebbed out
> Was costumed in a shroud. (lines 9–12)

Such poems nevertheless prepare the ground for his magisterial transformations. The 'Poems of 1912–1913' offer scenes from a story, one of *Life's Little Ironies*, as it were; but it's a tale in which the knife twists are mainly at the expense of the lyrical subject, the grieving old man.

The story in the elegies for Emma helps provide their oddly detached note. Hardy had imagined experiencing your wife's sudden death in 'Fellow-Townsmen' (1880), a story where the main character discovers his unloved spouse has drowned.[37] Yet he notices signs of life in her and, against hope of escape from a loveless marriage, has her revived. On the unexpected death of Emma in November 1912, Hardy wrote poems first to resurrect her, then definitively to bury her. He gives her death and his life at the time a narrative shape as if borrowed from one of his own fictions. The surges of rhythmic assurance in 'Beeny Cliff' (II, pp. 62–3) or 'The Phantom Horsewoman' (II, pp. 65–6) are probably indebted to his re-reading poems by Swinburne in the wake of his death in 1909. That poet's 'A Forsaken Garden' provided hints for 'After a Journey' with its seaboard setting and affirmative close, an intimately voiced revision of Swinburne's final 'Death lies dead', echoing as it does Donne's 'Death thou shalt die': [38]

> Ignorant of what there is flitting here to see,
> The waked birds preen and the seals flop lazily,
> Soon you will have, Dear, to vanish from me,
> For the stars close their shutters and the dawn whitens hazily.
> Trust me, I mind not, though Life lours,
> The bringing me here; nay, bring me here again!
> I am just the same as when
> Our days were a joy and our paths through flowers.
> (II, p. 60, lines 25–32)

That 'Dear' links the poem's last lines with 'A Mere Interlude', a story in which the much older Mr Heddegan writes to Baptista, his betrothed, about 'their future housekeeping, and his preparations for the same, with innumerable "my dears" sprinkled in disconnectedly, to show the depth of his affection without the inconveniences of syntax'.[39] Hardy, more expressively, places the 'Dear' against rhythmic and syntactical expectations to emphasize a controlled affective effort. He deploys the word 'Dear' at more usual positions in 'The Division' (I, p. 270, lines 5, 11) and 'When Dead' (III, p. 29, line 3). The benefit of novel-writing lies in his fictionalizing lyric material to place the poet-figure askance to his experience, providing narrative shape and tacit characters. 'At Castle Boterel' deploys multiplied time-schemes to underline contrasting narratives. Hardy describes how 'What we did as we climbed, and what we talked of / Matters not much, nor to what it led' (II, p. 63, lines 11–12) and:

> It filled but a minute. But was there ever
>   A time of such quality, since or before,
> In that hill's story? To one mind never,
>   Though it has been climbed, foot-swift, foot-sore,
>   By thousands more. (lines 16–20)

The lyrical figure and interlocutor are treated as characters in one tale, their own, but placed against 'this hill's story'. At the end, the poet character 'shall traverse old love's domain / Never again' (lines 34–5), meaning that he won't return to the part of Cornwall where they had met in youth. Yet the poet was to retread the paths of his relations with Emma in life and death many more times. Hardy had a professional writer's ability to detach a work from a body of feeling without exhausting its source. This too may derive from his use of disguised personal experience for fiction. When he uses it for lyric poems both detachment and manipulation come into play. Hardy never appears to get over a thing: another likely consequence of the unresolved contradictions Empson noticed.

Hardy's stories and incidents serve to justify cultural beliefs and values, ones that allow rapid switches between contrasting views. When he stages two together in one of his most famous poems, critics are divided about whether the lyric concludes by opting for hope, or ironically disparaging it.[40] Called 'By the Century's Deathbed' when published in the *Graphic* on 29 December 1900, a title which fits its opening sixteen lines where no birds sing, 'The Darkling Thrush' begins with an unstressed first-person singular pronoun, 'I leant upon a coppice gate', and ends its second stanza with the same pronoun, now a rhyme-word stressed for emphasis: 'fervourless as I' (I, pp. 187–8, lines 1, 16). These 'I' pronouns seal the first two stanzas in self-concern.

The clutter of 'ands' in verse two ('germ and birth' inertly echoed in 'hard and dry' and followed by 'And every spirit', lines 13–16) produces a 'fervourless' sound that Hardy made less rhythmically varied by deleting three commas from lines thirteen and fourteen after the *Graphic* publication, where the phrase read: 'The ancient pulse of germ and birth, / Was shrunken, hard, and dry' (lines 13–14). The regular expectations of a punctuated pause at the end of lines two, six, ten, and fourteen, and a stopped sentence close at lines four, eight, twelve, and sixteen, are minimally varied by the comma at the end of line eleven. Such neat patterning over two-line grammatical units includes phrases that form complete clauses at line endings: 'I leant upon a coppice gate' could stand alone, but gains an additional clause with 'When Frost was spectre-gray', again making an autonomous syntactic unit. Line three begins with 'And', as do lines seven and fifteen. Only one of the four quatrain-length sentences doesn't begin its third line with the conjunction. Each of these introduces a phrase that must reach the next line's end to conclude its sense. These studied regularities sap energy from the verse, exemplifying lack of fervour and deathliness not only in the winter landscape and the nineteenth century, but also in the sixty-year-old poet character bracketing the scene.

These verses hardly sing, and indicate why they mayn't burst into song. The simile characterizing the 'tangled bine-stems' puns on musical notation and recalls the traditional instrument of the Greek poets: 'The tangled bine-stems scored the sky / Like strings of broken lyres' (lines 5–6). In 'The Eolian Harp' (1796–1834), Coleridge imagined how 'the breeze warbles, and the mute still air / Is music slumbering on her instrument'. Hardy's 'broken lyres' suggest that the century or so which had passed since Coleridge penned them had given ample reason for fearing that 'if all of animated nature / Be but organic harps',[41] then the storm clouds of the nineteenth century, as Ruskin saw them, have broken the harp-strings. Hardy's ghost world is recalled with the ambiguities in 'all mankind that haunted nigh', and 'every spirit upon earth'. The first two verses of 'The Darkling Thrush' are a stiffly metred exercise using paratactic sentences (ones with no subordinate clauses) so as to evoke the funereal scenery; they also ask if the music of poetry is dying with Victoria's century. The title word 'Darkling' combines the memory of a second-generation Romantic poet being stirred by a bird in the spring of 1819 with that of a Victorian cultural critic looking out upon a far darker scene on his honeymoon at mid-century. 'The Darkling Thrush' is an occasional poem about the spirit of an age, its loss of spirit and the poet's own tiredness, dramatized as a crisis of inspiration in its adopting an adjective used by, for instance, Shakespeare, Milton, Johnson, Byron, Keats, Arnold, and Swinburne.[42]

To mid-point 'The Darkling Thrush' articulates its theme in routine rhythms and simple grammar; but with the appearance of the thrush's song, the poem changes its tune. Now an energetic syntax flows, with pointed pausing at line five, over four-line units:

At once a voice arose among
The bleak twigs overhead
In a full-hearted evensong
Of joy illimited;
An aged thrush, frail, gaunt, and small,
In blast-beruffled plume,
Had chosen thus to fling his soul
Upon the growing gloom. (I, p. 188, lines 17–24)

The interruption of the poem's mood by the song of the thrush had been imagined as more dramatic. In the manuscript and early printings, the opening of the third verse read: 'At once a voice outburst among'. In the final verse's eight-line syntactical structure, both 'I' pronouns are stressed to contrast the subject's view and that attributed to the thrush:

So little cause for carolings
Of such ecstatic sound
Was written on terrestrial things
Afar or nigh around,
That I could think there trembled through
His happy good-night air
Some blessed Hope, whereof he knew
And I was unaware. (lines 25–32)

If the first stressed 'I' emphasizes the poet figure's singularity and the situational precariousness of his thought, the second contrastively underlines an incapacity that he describes himself as mindfully unconscious of. The doubling of implication in first-person denials is a further source of Hardy's complex indirectness. James Longenbach has written that the poem 'refuses any effort to merge the human soul with the bird's song'.[43] Yet that other 'I', the cunningly self-effacing poet, sings in tune with the thrush by composing a poem that itself carols the voice of the bird. This is why, however much it notes the depredations to nature, humanity, and art in its century, 'The Darkling Thrush' choruses a hope that vigorous rhythmic continuities may still be heard and so recovered.

'In Time of "The Breaking of Nations"' uses rhythm and minimal narrative to effect a reversal upon how worldly powers prefer their stories told, by offering an overlooked, a more resilient truth:

I
Only a man harrowing clods
In a slow silent walk

With an old horse that stumbles and nods
  Half asleep as they stalk.

II

Only thin smoke without flame
  From the heaps of couch-grass;
Yet this will go onward the same
  Though Dynasties pass.

III

Yonder a maid and her wight
  Come whispering by:
War's annals will cloud into night
  Ere their story die. (II, pp. 295–6, lines 1–12)

Without main verbs either in the first verse sentence, or in the first half of verse two, the poem underlines its apparent slightness of inspiration. Verbs start coming only with the introduction of the contrastive story, that of the 'Dynasties' that 'pass' or of 'War's annals' that will 'cloud into night / Ere their story die'. Like 'At Castle Boterel', the poem counterpoises kinds of 'story'. Though dated 1915, it was prompted by incidents Hardy observed at the time of the Franco-Prussian War in 1870.[44] That he was courting in Cornwall when he saw the original of the 'man harrowing clods' from St Juliot Rectory garden hints that the 'maid and her wight' (not mentioned in Hardy's note of the time) might be the young Emma and Thomas themselves.[45] The poem stages a reversal of fortunes between the apparently weak or insignificant, and the greater powers that would shape the world. Counter-intuitive in its placing of these anonymous and barely recorded stories against those of 'Dynasties' and 'War's annals', Hardy's rhythmic skill makes the reversal entirely convincing, while his stark shaping of the contrasting terms renders his task that much the harder.

Hardy's reversals can, then, be socially critical examples of redress, of emblematic reparation for the world's violence, achieved here by narrating the viewpoints of more enduring temporal perspectives. The poet's allusion, though, doesn't support that romantic story: his poem opposes the biblical verses alluded to in its title. Jeremiah 51:20–3 prophesies how God will 'break in pieces the nations' *and* 'break in pieces the young man and the maid' in revenge for mistreatments of Israel. Hardy's poem disdains such indiscriminate fury. The tale of 'the maid and her wight' that will not die (such as we may read storied in 'Poems of 1912–1913') equally rebukes the violence of the prophet. Remembering perhaps his own romance, Hardy fulfils Empson's desire to have story justify cultural outlook and critical conviction.

Yet there is a repetition-compulsion in Hardy's writing, for recalling 1870 in 1915 he is yet again traversing 'old love's domain' in imagination and memory. This repetition-compulsion recalls not only the 'will' defined in Schopenhauer's *The World as Will and Representation* (1818), but also the philosopher's allowing art a palliative function in its occasioning releases from that will's impositions. Hardy rejects pessimism in the conclusion to his 'Apology', arguing that if we are moving ominously backward it may be '*pour mieux sauter*', and adding: 'I repeat that I forlornly hope so, notwithstanding the supercilious regard of hope by Schopenhauer ... and other philosophers ... who have my respect' (II, p. 325). Prising apart stories that tell of the world's determining will upon us and those which figure a determined sense of human hope in passion, Hardy's poetic oeuvre forms a homeopathic remedy of some thousand small doses, a salve for its own mechanical ironies, to which his many readers have found themselves repeatedly returning.

NOTES

1 Cited in 'Apology', *Late Lyrics and Earlier*. Volume and page numbers in parentheses refer to *The Complete Poetical Works of Thomas Hardy*, ed. Samuel Hynes, 5 vols (Oxford: Oxford University Press, 1982–95).

2 William Empson, *Using Biography* (London: Chatto and Windus, 1984), pp. 189.

3 Thomas Hardy, *The Collected Letters*, eds Richard L. Purdy and Michael Millgate, 7 vols (Oxford: Oxford University Press, 1978–88), ii, p. 85.

4 William Empson, 'Selected Poems of Thomas Hardy', in *Argufying: Essays on Literature and Culture*, ed. John Haffenden (London: Chatto and Windus, 1987), p. 421.

5 Ibid., p. 423.

6 William Empson, lines cut from 'Aubade', in *The Complete Poems*, ed. John Haffenden (London: Allen Lane, 2000), p. 319.

7 Arthur Compton Rickett, 'I Want to be Remembered as a Poet', in *Thomas Hardy Remembered*, ed. Martin Ray (Aldershot: Ashgate, 2007), p. 290.

8 To Sir George Douglas, 3 April 1901 (*Letters*, ii, p. 283).

9 *Letters*, iv, p. 117.

10 Donald Davie, *Thomas Hardy and British Poetry* (London: Routledge & Kegan Paul, 1973), p. 47. See Peter Jones (ed.), *Imagist Poetry* (Harmondsworth: Penguin, 1972).

11 Ezra Pound, *The Selected Letters of Ezra Pound 1907–1941*, ed. D. D. Paige (New York: New Directions, 1950), p. 40.

12 See Thomas Mautner (ed.), *The Penguin Dictionary of Philosophy* (Harmondsworth: Penguin, 1997), p. 362.

13 'In Memoriam', in *The Poems of Tennyson*, ed. Christopher Ricks, 3 vols, 2nd edn (London: Longman, 1987), II, p. 326.

14 *Letters*, iv, p. 5.

15 Empson, 'Let It Go', in *The Complete Poems*, p. 99.
16 See my '"A blank to me": Thomas Hardy and the Loss of Meaning', *Shiron* 24 (2004), pp. 57–74.
17 Empson, 'Selected Poems of Thomas Hardy', p. 422.
18 R. G. Cox (ed.), *Thomas Hardy: The Critical Heritage* (London: Routledge & Kegan Paul, 1970), p. 331.
19 *Letters*, iv, p. 47.
20 See *Letters*, iv, pp. 15–16, for Hardy's views on Swinburne at his death.
21 *Letters*, ii, p. 158.
22 *Letters*, vi, p. 313.
23 John Keats, 'On First Looking into Chapman's Homer', in *Keats: The Complete Poems*, ed. Miriam Allott (Harlow: Longman, 1970), p. 62.
24 For Hardy's defence of his versification, see F. E. Hardy, *The Later Years of Thomas Hardy 1892–1928* (London: Macmillan, 1930), pp. 78–9, discussed in my 'In Another's Words: Hardy's Poetry', in *In the Circumstances: About Poems and Poets* (Oxford: Oxford University Press, 1992), pp. 58–82.
25 F. E. Hardy, *The Early Life of Thomas Hardy 1840–1891* (London: Macmillan, 1928), p. 84.
26 Ibid, p. 32.
27 *Letters*, ii, p. 232.
28 Algernon Charles Swinburne, *The Poems*, 6 vols (London: Chatto and Windus, 1912), VI, p. 385. See Matthew Bevis, 'Fighting Talk: Victorian War Poetry', and Ralph Pite, '"Graver things ... braver things": Hardy's War Poetry', in *The Oxford Handbook of British and Irish War Poetry*, Tim Kendall, ed. (Oxford: Oxford University Press, 2007), pp. 29–31, 39–43.
29 See Hardy to Ezra Pound, 28 November and 3 December 1920, 18 March 1921, for his responses to *Quia Pauper Amavi* and *Hugh Selwyn Mauberley* (*Letters*, vi, pp. 47, 49, 77).
30 Ezra Pound, *Guide to Kulchur* (1938; London: Peter Owen, 1966), p. 293. See Ezra Pound and Marcella Spann, eds, *Confucius to Cummings* (New York: New Directions, 1964), pp. 283–6, 325–9.
31 See Dennis Taylor, *Hardy's Metres and Victorian Prosody* (Oxford: Clarendon Press, 1988).
32 *Letters*, ii, p. 208.
33 See Max Saunders, *Ford Madox Ford: A Dual Life*, 2 vols (Oxford: Oxford University Press, 1996), I, p. 343. See also Ezra Pound, 'The Prose Tradition in Verse', in *Literary Essays of Ezra Pound*, ed. T. S. Eliot (London: Faber and Faber, 1960), pp. 371–7.
34 Pound, *Guide to Kulchur*, p. 287.
35 Philip Larkin, 'Introduction to *The North Ship*', in *Required Writing: Miscellaneous Pieces 1955–1982* (London: Faber and Faber, 1983), pp. 29–30.
36 See Ralph Pite, *Thomas Hardy: The Guarded Life* (London: Picador, 2006), pp. 164–5.
37 Thomas Hardy, *The Withered Arm and Other Stories*, ed. Kristin Brady (Harmondsworth: Penguin, 1999), p. 109.
38 Swinburne, *Poems*, III, pp. 25. John Donne, 'Divine Meditations', 10, in *The Complete English Poems*, ed. A. J. Smith (Harmondsworth: Penguin, 1973), p. 313.

39 Thomas Hardy, *The Distracted Preacher and Other Tales*, ed. Susan Hill (Harmondsworth: Penguin, 1979), pp. 101–2.
40 Compare, for example, Davie, *Thomas Hardy and British Poetry*, p. 38, Tom Paulin, *Thomas Hardy: The Poetry of Perception* (London: Macmillan, 1975), p. 152, and John Bayley, *An Essay on Hardy* (Cambridge: Cambridge University Press, 1978), p. 39.
41 Samuel Taylor Coleridge, *The Complete Poems*, ed. William Keach (Harmondsworth: Penguin, 1997), pp. 86–8.
42 See *Antony and Cleopatra* IV. xv. 10, *King Lear* I. iv. 237; *Paradise Lost* III. 39; Johnson, 'The Vanity of Human Wishes', line 346; Byron, 'Darkness', line 3; Keats, 'Ode to a Nightingale', line 51; Arnold, 'Dover Beach', line 35; Swinburne, 'Ave Atque Vale', line 134.
43 James Longenbach, 'Modern Poetry', in *The Cambridge Companion to Modernism*, ed. Michael Levenson (Cambridge: Cambridge University Press, 1999), p. 104.
44 See F. E. Hardy, *The Later Years*, p. 178.
45 See Michael Millgate, *Thomas Hardy: A Biography Revisited* (Oxford: Oxford University Press, 2004), p. 119.

SELECTED FURTHER READING

Editions

The Complete Poems of Thomas Hardy, ed. James Gibson, Basingstoke, Macmillan, 1976

The Variorum Edition of the Complete Poems of Thomas Hardy, ed. James Gibson, Basingstoke, Macmillan, 1978

The Complete Poetical Works of Thomas Hardy, ed. Samuel Hynes, 5 vols, Oxford, Oxford University Press, 1982–95.

The Collected Letters, eds Richard L. Purdy and Michael Millgate, 7 vols, Oxford, Oxford University Press, 1978–88

Selected Letters of Thomas Hardy, ed. Michael Millgate, Oxford, Oxford University Press, 1990

Secondary works

Biographies

Hardy, F. E., *The Early Life of Thomas Hardy 1840–1891*, London, Macmillan, 1928

The Later Years of Thomas Hardy 1892–1928, London, Macmillan, 1930

Millgate, Michael, *Thomas Hardy: A Biography Revisited*, Oxford, Oxford University Press, 2004

Pite, Ralph, *Thomas Hardy: The Guarded Life*, London, Picador, 2006

Tomalin, Claire, *Thomas Hardy: The Time-Torn Man*, Harmondsworth, Penguin, 2006

Critical studies

Bailey, J. O., *The Poetry of Thomas Hardy*, Chapel Hill, University of North Carolina Press, 1970

Bayley, John, *An Essay on Hardy*, Cambridge, Cambridge University Press, 1978

Blackmur, R. P., 'The Shorter Poems of Thomas Hardy', in *Language as Gesture*, New York, Harcourt, Brace, 1952, pp. 51–79

Brodsky, Joseph, 'Wooing the Inanimate: Four Poems by Thomas Hardy', in *On Grief and Reason: Essays*, New York, Farrar, Straus and Giroux, 1995, pp. 312–75

Davie, Donald, 'Hardy's Virgilian Purples', *Agenda: Thomas Hardy Special Issue*, 10.2–3 (1972), pp. 138–56

Thomas Hardy and British Poetry, London, Routledge & Kegan Paul, 1973

Gunn, Thom, 'Hardy and the Ballads', in Clive Wilmer (ed.), *The Occasions of Poetry*, London, Faber and Faber, 1982, pp. 77–105

Hynes, Samuel, *The Pattern of Hardy's Poetry*, Chapel Hill, University of North Carolina Press, 1961

Paulin, Tom, *Thomas Hardy: The Poetry of Perception*, London, Macmillan, 1975

Richardson, James, *Thomas Hardy: The Poetry of Necessity*, Chicago, University of Chicago Press, 1977

Robinson, Peter, 'In Another's Words: Hardy's Poetry', in *In the Circumstances: About Poems and Poets*, Oxford, Oxford University Press, 1992, pp. 58–82

Taylor, Dennis, *Hardy's Metres and Victorian Prosody*, Oxford, Clarendon Press, 1988

Hardy's Poetry 1860–1928, 2nd edn, Basingstoke, Macmillan, 1989

25

JAMES LONGENBACH

William Butler Yeats

Whatever else he was, Yeats was a great Victorian poet who lived long enough to become a great modern poet. Notoriously, like Beethoven, he was an artist who changed. Sometimes Yeats was forced to change by the events of his time but, more profoundly, Yeats forced change upon himself, refusing ever to sound the same way twice but never sounding like anyone other than Yeats.

This is how the twenty-seven-year-old Yeats sounded in 1892, when he published his second book of poems, *The Countess Kathleen and Various Legends and Lyrics*. The poem is called 'The Sorrow of Love'.

The quarrel of the sparrows in the eaves,
The full round moon and the star-laden sky,
And the loud song of the ever-singing leaves
Had hid away earth's old and weary cry.

And then you came with those red mournful lips,
And with you came the whole of the world's tears,
And all the sorrows of her labouring ships,
And all burden of her myriad years.

And now the sparrows warring in the eaves,
The crumbling moon, the white stars in the sky,
And the loud chanting of the unquiet leaves,
Are shaken with earth's old and weary cry.[1]

This poet has absorbed the music of Rossetti and Swinburne, late nineteenth-century English poets who shied away from the gregariousness of Tennyson and Browning, preferring an incantatory utterance distilled from the larger discursive pool of the dramatic monologue. This poet is also aware of contemporary French poetry, of Mallarmé's call for a poetry of suggestion, of Verlaine's desire to wring the neck of rhetoric. At the same time, this poet is trying to figure out what it means to be neither English nor French but Irish: not a poet who writes in Gaelic (a language Yeats did not know) but a poet who by making a distinctive noise in English wants to capture that language for himself and, by implication, for his country.

That is an enormous ambition, one that could never be achieved lightly or for long. Listen to the way Yeats sounded thirty-three years later, when he rewrote 'The Sorrow of Love' for inclusion in *Early Poems and Stories*.

> The brawling of a sparrow in the eaves,
> The brilliant moon and all the milky sky,
> And all that famous harmony of leaves,
> Had blotted out man's image and his cry.
>
> A girl arose that had red mournful lips
> And seemed the greatness of the world in tears,
> Doomed like Odysseus and the labouring ships
> And proud as Priam murdered with his peers;
>
> Arose, and on the instant clamorous eaves,
> A climbing moon upon an empty sky,
> And all that lamentation of the leaves,
> Could but compose man's image and his cry. (p. 40)[2]

What has changed? In the first stanza, the 'quarrel' has become a 'brawl', the new word more viscerally physical, less immediately amenable to association. Similarly, the once 'star-laden' sky is now 'milky'. In the second stanza, a poem addressed to an unidentified 'you' has become a poem about a particular 'girl'. She still bears the familiar badges of European love-poetry, the 'red mournful lips' passed from Petrarch to Shakespeare to Keats; but her once whispered alliance with mythic grandeur is now declared adamantly: 'Doomed like Odysseus and the labouring ships'. More crucially, the stanza sounds adamant. In the early version, Yeats coveted the hovering stillness of paratactic syntax, the coordinating conjunction linking a variety of clauses and phrases: 'And then you came with those red mournful lips, / And with you came the whole of the world's tears.' In the new version, Yeats discards his compound sentence, substituting a complex sentence that careens beyond the second stanza to encompass the entire third stanza as well. While in the first version of the poem we receive a spooky list of the repercussions of the girl's appearance, in the second version we inhabit the muscular unfolding of those repercussions in a syntax of cause and effect. The poem feels like a brawl.

Is one version of 'The Sorrow of Love' better than the other? For many years, readers needed to understand the changes Yeats wrought upon his style as an allegory for what happened to poetry between 1892 and 1925: a general movement away from dreamy languorousness towards concrete vigour. These were the years of what we now call modernism. Both *The Waste*

Land and *Ulysses* were published in 1922, and, at that moment, Eliot's poem and Joyce's novel could not seem anything but revolutionary, a violent turn against nineteenth-century taste. And since Eliot and Joyce created the taste by which they were subsequently judged, twentieth-century taste demanded that great modernist writers represent an advance on their Victorian predecessors. By this logic, Eliot and Joyce were not simply different from Whitman and Dickens; they were better, the world in which they walked more challengingly complex.

This narrative, popularized by the literary critical movement known as the New Criticism, transformed Yeats's career into a paradigm. Having been born in 1865, two decades earlier than Eliot or Joyce, Yeats supposedly had to be dragged into the twentieth century. Moreover, he was not strong enough to drag himself: Ezra Pound supposedly applied the muscle, pushing the dreamy Yeats towards a starker, meaner sound. But even if this narrative made any sense (Pound's poems were dreamier than Yeats's at this early point in his career), the narrative would still confuse the big terms of art with the niggling terms of taste. As he changed, Yeats was not remaking literary history; he was remaking himself – remaking the sound of himself in English diction and syntax.

Yeats was not only a poet; no poet is only a poet. As his most meticulous biographer reminds us, Yeats was also 'a playwright, journalist, occultist, apprentice politician, revolutionary, stage-manager, diner-out, dedicated friend'.[3] The list could go on. If Yeats had only written his plays or autobiographies he would occupy a crucial place in literary history; if he had only collected folklore or directed the Abbey Theatre he would occupy a crucial place in Irish cultural history. That Yeats was also appointed a Senator of the newly created Irish Free State in 1922 says more about Ireland than about the essential relationship between literary achievement and cultural power. 'Do not be elected to the Senate of your country', said the Irish Yeats to the American Pound, sweetly oblivious to the fact that no poet could ever be elected to such a position in the United States – much less a poet who let it be known that he attended séances.[4] In Ireland, where poetry occupied a much more prominent position, Yeats could write poems that seemed simultaneously public and private, and he could do so with an inevitability that an English or American poet might covet. But this ease was also a burden, since recognizably public poems speak in a recognizably public idiom. Yeats continually changed the way he wrote in order to make his work harder – to liberate himself (and, by implication, his readers) from any received notion of what relevance might sound like.

Yeats's primary allegiance was to language: whatever his goal, he achieved it in the English language that was his medium, working with syntax, rhythm, and diction in the way that over a long lifetime a painter works with paint, continually rediscovering its textures.

> The friends that have it I do wrong
> When ever I remake a song,

said Yeats in a quatrain written to accompany his *Collected Works in Verse and Prose* of 1908,

> Should know what issue is at stake:
> It is myself that I remake. (p. 551)

Notice that date: 1908. Before anything we could call modernist literature existed, before the Easter Rebellion (the swiftly aborted uprising of 1916) provoked him to say that the world was 'changed utterly' (p. 180), Yeats was already a notorious remaker of himself – someone who could not be satisfied with a single identity; someone who existed among alternatives; someone who valued dialogue, dialectic, opposition, multiplicity. However much Yeats changed, his faith in change did not waver, and of one thing we may always be sure: if Yeats states a position strongly in a particular poem, he will somewhere else contradict it. Not that Yeats was facile with ideas; far from it. The impulse that drove him to remake himself stylistically was a signature component of his way of thinking, his way of being in the world. From the beginning of his career to its end, Yeats harnessed this inclination, making works of art that depend for their effect on the formal and thematic dramatization of conflict. 'We make out of the quarrel with others, rhetoric', he wrote in his prose meditation 'Per Amica Silentia Lunae' (1917), 'but of the quarrel with ourselves, poetry.'[5]

Tentatively, without transforming the identification of difference into hierarchy, it can be useful to think of Yeats's career as divided into several style periods, much as we are accustomed to thinking of Beethoven's career. I've already suggested something about the sound of early Yeats by glancing at the first version of 'The Sorrow of Love'. Throughout this initial period of his career, culminating in *The Wind among the Reeds* (1899), Yeats cultivated a languorous tone, avoiding the adamant music of the English pentameter he also employed. 'I will arise and go now and go to Innisfree', begins 'The Lake Isle of Innisfree', the most famous poem of this period.

> I will arise and go now, and go to Innisfree,
> And a small cabin build there, of clay and wattles made:
> Nine bean-rows will I have there, a hive for the honey-bee,
> And live alone in the bee-loud glade. (p. 39)

'I will arise and go to Innisfree' would be a tougher opening line, an unwavering pentameter, but the early Yeats didn't want to sound tough. He wanted to sound equivocal, seduced rather than driven.

This sound became very popular; it was much imitated; Yeats would still be honoured as the author of 'The Lake Isle of Innisfree' when he won the Nobel Prize.

> You say, as I have often given tongue
> In praise of what another's said or sung,

wrote Yeats in 'To a Poet, who would have me Praise certain Bad Poets, Imitators of His and Mine' (1910),

> 'Twere politic to do the like by these;
> But was there ever dog that praised his fleas? (pp. 94–5)

These lines epitomize the sound of Yeats's second style period, culminating in *Responsibilities* (1914): impatient, epigrammatic, terse. One doesn't need to move beyond the sound of the titles to know that *Responsibilities* is a book calculatedly different from *The Wind among the Reeds*, that 'To a Poet, who would have me Praise certain Bad Poets, Imitators of His and Mine' is a poem different from 'The Lake Isle of Innisfree'. Although the opening stanza of 'The Lake Isle' delineates a world complete with wattles, bean-rows, and honey-bees, these nouns immediately feel emblematic, part of a dreamed landscape rather than a real one. Because of the more insistent rhythm of 'To a Poet', in contrast, the poem's fleas feel like fleas, despite being an obvious figure for the poet's imitators. Yeats sounds not equivocal but defiant, driven to turn against a self he no longer owns and a country he no longer recognizes.

This sound was not much imitated; it was met with bafflement – as if a great poet had gone off. At times, Yeats acknowledged the bafflement, though he would not countenance it. In 'Reconciliation' (1910) he addressed Maud Gonne (the Irish actress and activist whom he loved and then mythologized for many years), suggesting that her repeated rejection of him had produced the new barrenness of his verse.

> Some may have blamed you that you took away
> The verses that could move them on the day
> When, the ears being deafened, the sight of the eyes blind
> With lightning, you went from me, and I could find
> Nothing to make a song about but kings,
> Helmets, and swords, and half-forgotten things
> That were like memories of you – but now
> We'll out, for the world lives as long ago;

And while we're in our laughing, weeping fit,
Hurl helmets, crowns, and swords into the pit.
But, dear, cling close to me; since you were gone,
My barren thoughts have chilled me to the bone. (p. 91)

Here, Yeats not only writes unwavering pentameter lines but organizes them into a shape that feels like a sonnet without exactly being a sonnet: the volta or turn occurs near the end of the seventh line ('but now'), rather than at the beginning of the ninth line, and the poem concludes at the twelfth line, rather than completing the requisite fourteen. The rhymes, organized in couplets, are monosyllabic, starkly insistent, and the whole poem feels wilfully condensed, at war with its own formal expectations, argumentative rather than suggestive.

Yeats wrote this poem just before he met Pound, who came to London with the sole intention of meeting the author of 'The Lake Isle of Innisfree'. When Pound met the author of 'Reconciliation' instead, he wrote excitedly that Yeats had 'come out of the shadows & has declared for life'. Yeats's transformation transformed Pound in turn, not only stylistically but emotionally, since the younger poet felt suddenly that he was participating in an unprecedented moment in literary culture. In a poem of his own called 'The Fault of It', Pound quoted the first line of Yeats's 'Reconciliation' as an epigraph before declaring his allegiance to the new Yeats: 'Some may have blamed us that we cease to speak / Of things we spoke of in our verses early.'[6] What was for Yeats a personal transformation became, in Pound's adoption of its metaphors, the beginning of a movement: Yeats's 'I' became Pound's 'we'.

How large is that 'we'? In retrospect, Yeats has often seemed a part of the modernist movement we associate with Pound, Eliot, and Joyce. But Yeats always considered himself one of the 'last romantics' (p. 245), an artist whose most important affiliations were with great artists of the past or with close friends such as Augusta Gregory, not a great artist but someone who exerted a crucial influence on Yeats's life and work, focusing his attention on a particular vision of Irish culture and heritage. Yeats always feels more excessive, more various than any particular movement with which he might otherwise responsibly be associated. And if the arrogant tone of much of the work of his second style period chimes with the avant-garde sensibility we associate with Pound, Yeats soon transformed himself again, turning against his own need to turn. While never ceasing to be a poet of political awareness, Yeats became in this third phase a visionary poet of unprecedented strangeness.

Publicly, these were the years of the Great War and the Irish Revolution and Civil War. Privately, these were the years of Yeats's marriage to Georgie

Hyde-Lees, with whom he would embark on an occult journey culminating in *A Vision* (1925), a systemization of the information gleaned from their detailed conversations with spirits of the afterworld. Much of what Yeats already believed about history and identity had been described more epigrammatically in 'Per Amica Silentia Lunae', but through his wife's trances and automatic writings Yeats found his deepest inclinations uncannily confirmed. 'We have come to give you metaphors for poetry', said the spirits to Yeats, and the metaphors accounted for the world beyond the poems.[7]

Yeats's most resolutely political poems from this period sound wildly visionary. The final lines of 'Easter 1916', Yeats's harrowing response to the Easter Rebellion, the quickly aborted declaration of an Irish republic, make the simple recitation of the revolutionaries' names feel like incantation.

> I write it out in a verse –
> MacDonagh and MacBride
> And Connolly and Pearse
> Now and in time to be,
> Wherever green is worn,
> Are changed, changed utterly,
> A terrible beauty is born. (p. 182)

The final two lines of 'Easter 1916' (which recur throughout the poem as a refrain) speak with mesmerizing vagueness of a momentous event (cataclysm? rebirth?), yet this event has been engendered by people with ordinary names like MacDonagh and MacBride, the latter a 'drunken, vainglorious lout', the man who married Maud Gonne. Nowhere else does Yeats indulge in a shamrock-and-leprechaun vision of Ireland – 'Wherever green is worn': in 'Easter 1916' even this familiar cliché feels transmuted into something rich and strange.

The assumption of poetry's prominence in Irish culture cannot account fully for the power of 'Easter 1916': Yeats also resists the assumption, folding a familiar event into his idiosyncratic mythology so that readers are forced to reinhabit the event's unmanageable authority. Similarly, his drafts for 'The Second Coming' (1920) show that the poem originally contained references to the Russian Revolution, and, while all such contemporary reference is leeched from the final version of the poem, these uncanny lines none the less feel intimate with the chaos of the world as Yeats experienced it.

> Things fall apart; the centre cannot hold;
> Mere anarchy is loosed upon the world,
> The blood-dimmed tide is loosed, and everywhere
> The ceremony of innocence is drowned;

> The best lack all conviction, while the worst
> Are full of passionate intensity. (p. 187)

'The Second Coming' would be a different kind of poem if Yeats had retained lines like 'The Germans are now to Russia come', but the ghostly presence of such lines behind the poem's weirdly unspecific metaphors ('things') feels inevitable, hardly surprising.[8] The resolutely logical syntax ('The best lack all ... while the worst / Are full') plays off the evasive diction to make the poem feel oracular, as if no human voice could possibly speak it.

'The Second Coming' and 'Easter 1916' retain something of the other-worldliness of Yeats's earliest poems and something of the insistence of his second period, but they also feel unprecedented, forged from the unforeseeable confluence of public and private events. To listen to the final stanza of 'Sailing to Byzantium', the opening poem in *The Tower* (1928), is to experience a poem at once deeply idiosyncratic and yet conversant with the entire history of poetry in the English language. The poem is cast in ottava rima, the eight-line stanza (rhyming *abababcc*) that Byron employed for comic narratives. In Yeats's hands, the stanza becomes a vehicle for highly compressed meditation, the final rhymed couplet embodying the concluded process of thinking.

> Once out of nature I shall never take
> My bodily form from any natural thing,
> But such a form as Grecian goldsmiths make
> Of hammered gold and gold enamelling
> To keep a drowsy Emperor awake;
> Or set upon a golden bough to sing
> To lords and ladies of Byzantium
> Of what is past, or passing, or to come. (p. 194)

As he often did, Yeats forged this stanza out of a single sentence, playing a perspicuously natural syntax against the complicated rhyme-scheme. Throughout *The Tower*, the culminating volume of this third phase of his poetic development, such stanzas roll forward with an inevitability that seems aimed not at us (as in 'was there ever dog that praised his fleas?') but beyond us, as if the poet were communicating most directly with the world by imagining another world in its place. 'That is no country for old men', begins 'Sailing to Byzantium', wiping away the Ireland to which Yeats also remained devoted.

The Yeats who published *The Tower* was sixty-three years old; he had presented his first collected works twenty years earlier. What can an artist do after such a career-crowning achievement? What could Beethoven do after the Seventh Symphony? What could Yeats do after *The Tower*?

There is something wrong with these questions, an insensitivity to what compels an artist to push his medium in one direction rather than another. When Yeats revised the early 'Sorrow of Love' in 1925, a poem distinguished by a languorous accumulation of phrases, uninfected by the will –

> And now the sparrows warring in the eaves,
> The crumbling moon, the white stars in the sky,
> And the loud chanting of the unquiet leaves
> Are shaken with earth's old and weary cry

– became energized by the strategic delay of predication, making the stanza feel pressurized, extruded into existence, as the stanzas of 'Sailing to Byzantium' do.

> Arose, and on the instant clamorous eaves,
> A climbing moon upon an empty sky,
> And all that lamentation of the leaves,
> Could but compose man's image and his cry.

This manner of writing, a manner epitomized better by 'Sailing to Byzantium', was for many years held up by Yeats's New Critical expositors as a paradigm for what makes poetry great; in a sense, poems like 'Sailing to Byzantium' were the perfect New Critical poems, since they so richly reward the desire to find dramatic tension in the language of poetry. But when the poet Louis MacNeice examined the versions of 'The Sorrow of Love' in *The Poetry of W. B. Yeats* (1941), still one of the most acute studies of Yeats's career, he came to a different conclusion. 'The poem is no longer languid', said MacNeice of the second version. 'But perhaps this poem ought to be languid. There is no law which demands that all poems should be close-knit or vigorous or virile.'[9]

This response to Yeats's revision reminds us that the poet is not, in the act of writing, attempting to change taste or to foster a movement or even to write more brilliantly than he has in the past (though any of these things might happen incidentally). The poet is trying to discover what the language of a particular poem requires, and his eye is focused on the smallest details, not the overarching narratives of poetic development or literary or cultural history through which subsequent readers might inevitably read those details. So when Yeats began turning from *The Tower* to the poems of his final decade, he was doing again what he'd always done: becoming himself by asking to be different from himself. 'I think all happiness depends on the energy to assume the mask of some other life', wrote Yeats in 'Per Amica Silentia Lunae', 'on a re-birth as something not one's self, something created in a moment and perpetually renewed.'[10]

Yeats in his fourth and final stage can sound startlingly abrupt, even simple-minded in his dependence on the rhythms of nursery rhyme and popular song. 'Crazy Jane Talks to the Bishop', from the sequence 'Words for Music Perhaps' in *The Winding Stair* (1933), seems initially to have thrown over all of the melodious sophistication of 'Sailing to Byzantium'.

'A woman can be proud and stiff
When on love intent;
But Love has pitched his mansion in
The place of excrement;
For nothing can be sole or whole
That has not been rent.' (pp. 259–60)

Because these clauses are joined by semi-colons, they comprise one sentence; but the stanza doesn't feel like one sentence. The three clauses stomp down the page with outrageous regularity, their alternating tetrameter and trimeter lines filled out almost exclusively with monosyllabic words of Anglo-Saxon origin. The most flagrant exception to this blunted sonic decorum ('excrement') ends up reinforcing it, since we feel the heavily accented rhyme of its final syllable chime so brazenly with 'rent' and 'intent'.

This sonic and thematic coarseness represents one more style, not a rejection of stylishness; its potency depends in part on our feeling its tension with the transcendental impulse that distinguishes other poems. While Yeats longs in 'Sailing to Byzantium' to be released from the 'dying animal' that is an old man's body, he asserts in the later 'Dialogue of Self and Soul' his willingness to 'live it all again', even if 'it be life to pitch / Into the frog-spawn of a blind man's ditch'. The Soul argues in this dialogue that we should 'scorn the earth', but the Self stands with Crazy Jane in its allegiance to earthly pleasure.

I am content to follow to its source
Every event in action or in thought;
Measure the lot; forgive myself the lot!
When such as I cast out remorse
So great a sweetness flows into the breast
We must laugh and we must sing,
We are blest by everything,
Everything we look upon is blest. (p. 236)

Unlike Crazy Jane, the Self speaks with some of the syntactical elegance we associate with 'Sailing to Byzantium'. But while this ecstatic stanza is a variation on ottava rima, rhymed *abbacddc*, the sonic effect of the stanza is different. The second four lines replicate the rhyme-scheme of the first four lines, enclosing a rhymed couplet with an envelope rhyme, but Yeats reduces the line-length of the second couplet from pentameter to tetrameter: 'We must laugh and we must sing, / We are blest by everything'. The rhymes strike our ears more quickly in these tetrameter lines, speeding up the stanza before we're returned to the full music of pentameter in the final line: 'Everything we look upon is blest.' This is the sound of affirmation aimed not beyond us but squarely at us.

Yeats designed 'Sailing to Byzantium' and 'A Dialogue of Self and Soul' as companion poems. He wants us to read them in dialogue with each other, just as he wants us to read the volumes containing them, *The Tower* and *The Winding Stair*, in dialogue with each other. But while the Self does have the last word in 'A Dialogue of Self and Soul', we shouldn't feel that the Self's eloquence is easily won: the poem is a contest between two potent forces, neither of which may be underestimated. Is 'Sailing to Byzantium' similarly divided against itself? What happens to our experience of dialogue *between* the poems once we notice that Yeats also wants us to recognize the dialogue – conflict, argument, ambiguity – that transpires *within* the poems?

Look again at the final stanza of 'Sailing to Byzantium'.

> Once out of nature I shall never take
> My bodily form from any natural thing,
> But such a form as Grecian goldsmiths make
> Of hammered gold and gold enamelling
> To keep a drowsy Emperor awake;
> Or set upon a golden bough to sing
> To lords and ladies of Byzantium
> Of what is past, or passing, or to come. (p. 194)

Having begun the poem by declaring his alienation from natural processes ('Whatever is begotten, born, and dies'), Yeats reiterates in each stanza his intention to sail to Byzantium, a mythical city where he might live in art rather than the body. But Yeats never arrives; he merely reiterates his desire to arise and go. What's more, when he imagines himself as an eternal work of art in the holy city of Byzantium – a golden bird that sings upon a golden bough – he none the less imagines himself possessed by the great drama of mortal life. Delivered from human time, he will paradoxically sing of what is begotten, born, and dies – 'what is past, or passing, or to come'. What else is there to sing about?

> I think if I could be given a month of Antiquity and leave to spend it where I chose, I would spend it in Byzantium a little before Justinian opened the St. Sophia and closed the Academy of Plato. I think I could find in some little wine-shop some philosophical worker in mosaic who could answer all my questions, the supernatural descending nearer to him than to Plotinus even, for

> the pride of his delicate skill would make what was an instrument of power to princes and clerics, a murderous madness in the mob, show as a lovely flexible presence like that of a perfect human body.[11]

In this account of his fascination with Byzantium in *A Vision*, Yeats begins by emphasizing that the ancient city functions for him as a site of supernatural wonder. But as in 'Sailing to Byzantium', Yeats is incapable of leaving the natural world behind. The scene he imagines here is rife with sensual pleasures (a conversation with a mosaic maker over a glass of wine), and the supernatural descends with a simple inevitability that can only be compared to the human body. 'Seek out reality, leave things that seem', says the Soul in 'Vacillation', implying that reality exists beyond the senses. 'What, be a singer born and lack a theme', responds the irrepressible Heart, asserting what 'Sailing to Byzantium' implies – that art is inevitably and essentially sensual (p. 252).

In *A Vision* and throughout the later years of his career generally, Yeats attempted to organize his lifelong inclinations towards conflict into a system that aspires to account for both human personality and human history: like any particular person, any historical moment assumes its shape because of its relationship with an opposite moment in the past, a moment with which it is inevitably in dialogue. Some of Yeats's poems, such as 'The Phases of the Moon', demand to be read within the context of his esoteric system.[12] But it's more important simply to recognize that Yeats's poems are riven, systematically or not, with conflict. They are dramatizations of the process of thought rather than presentations of finished thought.

Look again at the early 'Lake Isle of Innisfree', a poem read easily on its own. Yeats insists several times in this poem that he is about to abandon the drab city, the burden of human life, for the dreamy freedom of Innisfree. But as in 'Sailing to Byzantium', he never leaves.

> I will arise and go now, for always night and day
> I hear lake water lapping with low sounds by the shore;
> While I stand on the roadway, or on the pavements grey,
> I hear it in the deep heart's core. (p. 39)

Here, in the final stanza, Yeats still insists that he is about to arise and go, and, even more potently, he confirms that Innisfree is indeed not a place with bean-rows and honey-bees but a place of the mind. The final lines suggest that he is empowered to imagine Innisfree because he stands on the dreary pavement: the magical place exists because of its conflict with the real, and any resolution of the conflict would destroy the place. Similarly, in 'Sailing to Byzantium', the realized desire to reach Byzantium would transform the visionary poet into a weak nostalgist, capable of imagining only what he once possessed.

Once we notice that 'Sailing to Byzantium' is highly conflicted about its own urge to transcend human experience, then our sense of the poem's dialogue with 'A Dialogue of Self and Soul' becomes richer, less clearly oppositional and more ambiguously reticulated. For while the sound of Yeats's poetry changes over the course of his career, his thematic obsessions remain startlingly consistent – but only in the sense that this consistency is distinguished at all moments by self-doubt, equivocation, interrogation. Having provisionally divided Yeats's career into four style periods, we must also remember that these periods are not fully coherent. Having noticed the tensions between individual poems, we inevitably notice the tension within individual poems. It is no accident that poems so utterly suited to New Critical analysis (stressing the internal unities of poetic language) were subsequently so amenable to deconstructive analysis (stressing the splintering disunities of poetic language).[13]

Consider Yeats's placement of 'A Prayer for my Daughter' after 'The Second Coming' in *Michael Robartes and the Dancer* (1921). 'The Second Coming' concludes with a much-quoted vision of the world to come.

> The darkness drops again; but now I know
> That twenty centuries of stony sleep
> Were vexed to nightmare by a rocking cradle,
> And what rough beast, its hour come round at last,
> Slouches towards Bethlehem to be born? (p. 187)

It's important to recognize that this sentence is a question. Just as the previous age was determined by the birth of Jesus, so will the tenor of the next age be determined by a similarly momentous birth – but of what? The uncertainty is riveting, and the temptation to read 'The Second Coming' as a prophetic condemnation is intense.

But turn the page to 'A Prayer for my Daughter', in which Yeats asks us to interrogate the metaphors that constitute this prophecy.

> Once more the storm is howling, and half hid
> Under this cradle-hood and coverlid
> My child sleeps on. There is no obstacle
> But Gregory's wood and one bare hill
> Whereby the haystack- and roof-leveling wind,
> Bred on the Atlantic, can be stayed;
> And for an hour I have walked and prayed
> Because of the great gloom that is in my mind. (p. 188)

With these lines we are suddenly dropped from prophetic to domestic utterance: the apocalyptic cradle of 'The Second Coming' becomes the simple cradle in which a particular child, Anne Yeats, is sleeping. Outside, the weather is bad. A father is worrying about the safety of his child. Does the future look grim simply because a sleeping baby looks vulnerable, because a storm is blowing off the Atlantic? Or does the future look grim because the human mind, trapped in its own 'great gloom', imposes immense metaphorical significance on these ordinary events – events that happen every night, not just at the inauguration of a new age?

The questions provoked by 'A Prayer for my Daughter' send us back to 'The Second Coming'. Notice how the final stanza of 'The Second Coming' begins: having declared so charismatically that 'things fall apart', the prophetic voice begins to interpret its own declarations – but not very carefully.

> Surely some revelation is at hand;
> Surely the Second Coming is at hand.
> The Second Coming! Hardly are those words out
> When a vast image out of *Spiritus Mundi*
> Troubles my sight.

These lines embody the slippery process by which observation becomes prophecy. In the first line the voice insists that 'surely' these events portend 'some' revelation – it doesn't know what revelation. In the second line the voice suddenly suggests that this revelation must be the Second Coming, and the reiteration of the syntactical pattern ('surely ... is at hand') makes this quick association sound considered. The voice even registers its own surprise at this association ('The Second Coming!') – as if the poem doesn't actually consider its titular subject until it's half over. After these words tumble from the mouth of the speaker, the stanza abandons its shaky logic for a confident vision of the world's fate.

> Somewhere in sands of the desert
> A shape with lion body and the head of a man,
> A gaze blank and pitiless as the sun,
> Is moving its slow thighs, while all about it
> Reel shadows of the indignant desert birds.
> The darkness drops again; but now I know
> That twenty centuries of stony sleep
> Were vexed to nightmare by a rocking cradle,
> And what rough beast, its hour come round at last,
> Slouches towards Bethlehem to be born?

No longer is this voice speculating that 'some' revelation is at hand. 'Now I know', says the voice, but what exactly does it know? On what evidence does this knowledge depend? The phrase 'rough beast' is powerfully suggestive because it is also (like so much of the poem) strategically evasive, and our attitude towards this apocalyptic figure is largely determined by the brilliantly precise verb 'slouches'. To imagine that our unknowable fate 'slouches' towards us suggests a great deal more about our state of expectation than about future events to come.

'The Second Coming' was provoked by Yeats's acute sense of the violence and uncertainty of Europe during the Great War, but the poem does not simply render a judgement (though it is often quoted as if it did). 'The Second Coming' is a dramatization of the route through which a mind might come, responsibly or irresponsibly, to apocalyptic conclusions in response to violence and uncertainty. Yeats was himself attracted to apocalyptic rhetoric at times, but in 'The Second Coming' he is as troubled by the need to leap to conclusions as he is by a chaotic world that may (or may not) support them. To read the poem in conjunction with 'A Prayer for my Daughter', as Yeats asks us to do, first allows us to see that the poems question each other. Then we may see that 'The Second Coming' questions itself, turning against what might initially seem to be its own most charismatic ideas.

This is how Yeats's poems work. 'I have felt when re-writing every poem – "The Sorrow of Love" for instance', he wrote in a 1929 journal, 'that by assuming a self of past years, as remote from that of today as some dramatic creation, I touched a stronger passion, a greater confidence than I possess, or ever did possess.'[14] Yeats was not a compulsive reviser like W. H. Auden or Marianne Moore, poets who tried over a lifetime to get the poem right; Yeats wanted to discover something unprecedented, something that could never merely be willed, in the act of remaking his language. The source of his strongest passion, Yeats suggests, lies not in the poet he has become or in the poet he once was but in the energy between them. By interrogating each other, his poems interrogate themselves, making individual poems feel double.

Listen one last time to Yeats the Victorian poet, writing in the 1890s.

> The road-side trees keep murmuring:
> Ah, wherefore murmur ye,
> As in the old days long gone by,
> Green oak and poplar tree?
> The well-known faces are all gone
> And the fret lies on me.[15]

Listen to Yeats the modern poet, writing in the 1920s.

> There's not a woman turns her face
> Upon a broken tree,
> And yet the beauties that I loved
> Are in my memory;

I spit into the face of Time
That has transfigured me. (p. 46)

Both of these stanzas address a subject that preoccupied Yeats throughout his entire life: the vicissitudes of old age. Both stanzas are cast in ballad measure (alternating tetrameter and trimeter lines), but the first recalls the languorousness of 'The Lake Isle of Innisfree', while the second recalls the devil-may-care toughness of 'Crazy Jane Talks to the Bishop'. Both stanzas conclude the poems to which they belong, and the two poems are distinct. Yet they are also the same poem: Yeats published the first version of 'The Lamentation of the Old Pensioner' in *The Countess Kathleen and Various Legends and Lyrics* (1892), the second version in *Early Poems and Stories* (1925), where it masquerades as an early poem. It perpetuates this masquerade in Yeats's *Collected Poems*.

The second version of 'The Lamentation of the Old Pensioner' is not what we usually think of as a revision: it is a distinct performance – no phrase from the first version survives. The subject-matter is consistent, but the attitude towards it has altered drastically. The form of the stanzas is consistent, but the stanzas sound completely different from each other, 'murmur' superseded by 'spit'. And while 'The Lamentation of the Old Pensioner' represents Yeats's most drastic act of remaking, the energy between the two versions feels typical, not exceptional.

All that I have said and done,
Now that I am old and ill,

wrote Yeats in 'The Man and the Echo' (1939), one of his last poems,

Turns into a question till
I lie awake night after night
And never get the answers right. (p. 345)

These lines may at first sound frustrated, but they are in fact driven by joy – the joy of having more to say, more to do, each conclusion transformed into a fresh question. Yeats's deepest fear is getting it right.

NOTES

1 See *The Variorum Edition of the Poems of W. B. Yeats*, eds Peter Allt and Russell K. Alspach (New York: Macmillan, 1957), pp. 119–20. While this edition of Yeats's poems has been superseded, earlier versions of the poems may usefully be reconstructed by using the editorial apparatus.

2 All page numbers refer to W. B. Yeats, *The Poems*, ed. Richard J. Finneran (New York: Macmillan, 1989).

3 R. F. Foster, *W. B. Yeats: A Life*, 2 vols (New York: Oxford University Press, 1997–2003), vol. 1, p. xxvi.

4 W. B. Yeats, *A Vision* (New York: Macmillan, 1956), p. 26.
5 W. B. Yeats, *Later Essays*, eds William H. O'Donnell and Elizabeth Bergmann Loizeaux (New York: Scribner, 1994), p. 8.
6 See James Longenbach, *Stone Cottage: Pound, Yeats, and Modernism* (New York: Oxford University Press, 1988), pp. 17–18.
7 Yeats, *A Vision*, p. 8.
8 This manuscript draft of 'The Second Coming' is printed in Jon Stallworthy, *Between the Lines: Yeats's Poetry in the Making* (Oxford: Clarendon Press, 1971), p. 17.
9 Louis MacNeice, *The Poetry of W. B. Yeats* (London: Faber and Faber, 1967), p. 71.
10 Yeats, *Later Essays*, p. 10.
11 Yeats, *A Vision*, p. 279.
12 The best introduction to the esoteric system is Yeats's 'Per Amica Silentia Lunae'. For help with the headier mysteries of *A Vision*, see Helen Vendler, *Yeats's Vision and the Later Plays* (Cambridge, MA: Harvard University Press, 1963).
13 See Paul de Man, 'Image and Emblem in Yeats', in *The Rhetoric of Romanticism* (New York: Columbia University Press, 1984), pp. 145–238.
14 Quoted in Richard Ellmann, *The Identity of Yeats* (New York: Oxford University Press, 1964), pp. 239–40.
15 Yeats, *Variorum Edition*, p. 131.

SELECTED FURTHER READING

Editions

Autobiographies, eds William H. O'Donnell and Douglas N. Archibald, New York, Scribner, 1999
Collected Letters, eds John Kelly *et al.*, New York, Oxford University Press, 1986–
Early Essays, eds Richard J. Finneran and George Bornstein, New York, Scribner, 2007
Later Essays, eds William H. O'Donnell and Elizabeth Bergmann Loizeaux, New York, Scribner, 1994
The Letters of W. B. Yeats, ed. Allan Wade, London, Hart-Davis, 1954
Plays, eds David R. Clark and Rosalind E. Clark, New York, Scribner, 2001
Poems, ed. Richard J. Finneran, New York, Macmillan, 1989
Variorum Edition of the Poems of W. B. Yeats, eds Peter Allt and Russell K. Alspach, New York, Macmillan, 1957
A Vision, New York, Macmillan, 1956
The Yeats Reader, ed. Richard J. Finneran, New York, Scribner, 1997

Secondary works

Bloom, Harold, *Yeats*, New York, Oxford University Press, 1970
Cullingford, Elizabeth, *Yeats, Ireland and Fascism*, London, Macmillan, 1981
Ellmann, Richard, *The Identity of Yeats*, New York, Oxford University Press, 1964.
Yeats: The Man and the Masks, New York, W. W. Norton, 1978

Foster, R. F., *W. B. Yeats: A Life*, 2 vols, New York, Oxford University Press, 1997–2003

Henn, T. R., *The Lonely Tower: Studies in the Poetry of W. B. Yeats*, London, Methuen, 1965.

Howes, Marjorie, *Yeats's Nations: Gender, Class, and Irishness*, New York, Cambridge University Press, 1996

Longenbach, James, *Stone Cottage: Pound, Yeats, and Modernism*, New York, Oxford University Press, 1988

MacNeice, Louis, *The Poetry of W. B. Yeats*, London, Faber and Faber, 1967

de Man, Paul, *The Rhetoric of Romanticism*, New York, Columbia University Press, 1984

Stallworthy, Jon, *Between the Lines: Yeats's Poetry in the Making*, Oxford, Clarendon Press, 1971

Vendler, Helen, *Yeats's Vision and the Later Plays*, Cambridge, MA, Harvard University Press, 1963

26

MARJORIE PERLOFF

D. H. Lawrence

Primarily a novelist – the author of *Sons and Lovers* (1913), *Women in Love* (1920), and other well-known novels – D. H. Lawrence (1885–1930) was also a highly original poet, whose early lyrics not only found a wide audience but won the praise of such unlikely fellow-poets as Edward Thomas, Ezra Pound, and Conrad Aiken. 'Mr. Lawrence', declared Pound in a review of *Love Poems and Others* (1913), 'almost alone among the younger poets, has realized that contemporary poetry must be as good as contemporary prose if it is to justify its publication.'[1] The 'prose' in question – perhaps Lawrence's own – was praised for its vivid imagery and uncanny accuracy of observation: Pound's friend Ford Madox Ford, then editor of the influential *English Review*, remarked that only an especially 'observant' writer would call a short story 'Odour of Chrysanthemums', for 'The majority of people do not even know that chrysanthemums have an odour.'[2]

Yet by the time of Lawrence's untimely death from tuberculosis in 1930, the reaction had set in. In 1927, T. S. Eliot, who denounced Lawrence's treatment of sexual love, declared that 'Mr. Lawrence is ... a natural and unsophisticated demoniac with a gospel ... [his characters] seem to reascend the metamorphoses of evolution, passing backward beyond ape and fish to some hideous coition of protoplasm.'[3] And by 1935, the American critic R. P. Blackmur characterized Lawrence's poetry as suffering from the 'fallacy of expressive form' – the fallacy that 'if a thing is only intensely enough felt its mere expression in words will give it satisfactory form, the dogma ... that once material becomes words it is its own best form'.[4] This charge – an absence of adequate *form* to contain the poetry's often overwrought, if not hysterical, content – has continued to dog Lawrence ever since. Add to this the feminist critique of Lawrentian authoritarianism and patriarchal politics that began with Kate Millett's *Sexual Politics* (1970), and it is not surprising that today Lawrence's poetry is little read. In anthologies, Lawrence is typically – and cautiously – represented by his early elegies for his mother – 'My love looks like a girl to-night, / But she is old' ('The Bride') – and by memory poems like the well-known 'Piano' (1918), which begins:

> Softly, in the dusk, a woman is singing to me
> Taking me back down the vista of years, till I see
> A child sitting under the piano, in the boom of the tingling strings
> And pressing the small poised feet of a mother who smiles as she sings.

When one compares these lyrics to the memory poems in Yeats's *The Wild Swans at Coole*, which date from the same period, the accomplishment may indeed seem minor.

But there is another Lawrence – a Lawrence who, far from casting his 'manhood ... down in the flood of remembrance', as does the sentimental protagonist of 'Piano', is the tough-minded and self-possessed ironist we meet in Lawrence's best volume of poems *Birds, Beasts and Flowers* (1922). Indeed, if we ignore the poet's own claim that 'my real demon would now and then get hold of me and shake ... real poems out of me', or that 'free verse is, or should be, direct utterance from the instant, whole man',[5] we will understand that Lawrence is, for all his talk of the 'insurgent naked throb of the instant moment', much less an expressivist than a performative poet – a brilliant rhetorician whose theatrical self-presentation is highly contrived and constructed. Alternately rapt witness and bemused sceptic, this Lawrence is overheard in dialogue with mosquitoes and tortoises, pomegranates and figs, as well as with himself or an unnamed companion, in the process of trying to place himself in relation to all that is Other in his world.

Beginnings

David Herbert Lawrence was born and grew up in the coalmining town of Eastwood, Nottinghamshire, not far from Sheffield. He was the fourth child of Arthur John Lawrence, a barely literate miner, and Lydia Beardsall, a former schoolmistress. The incompatibility of his parents – his mother fancied herself a *lady* and tried desperately to bring her children up in genteel circumstances, even as her husband, frequently coming home drunk, was abusive – provides the raw material for *Sons and Lovers*. As in the novel, the real Lawrence usually sided with his 'proper' mother but had his father's sensual temperament: the conflict between the two everywhere animates Lawrence's work. The young Lawrence won a scholarship to Nottingham High School and then, while working as a schoolteacher in London, began to write short stories and poems. Jessie Chambers, the Miriam of *Sons and Lovers*, who was Lawrence's first – but unsatisfactory – love, secretly sent these writings to Ford, who published them in the *English Review*. Thus Lawrence's career was launched.

In an unpublished draft of the Preface to the *Collected Poems* (1928), Lawrence recalls composing, when he was nineteen, his first two poems – 'Guelder Roses' and 'Campions' – concluding that 'most young ladies would have done better: at least I hope so' (*CP*, p. 849). But it is doubtful that a young lady would have written these opening lines:

> The guelder rose-bush is hung with coronets
> Gently issuing from the massèd green;
> Pale dreamy chaplets; a grey nun-sister sets
> Such on the virgin hair of dead sixteen. (*CP*, p. 853)

Despite its name, the guelder rose is not a species of rose at all but a deciduous woodland shrub, whose sterile white flowers develop into clusters of drooping, juicy red berries. The transformation – or lack thereof – provides Lawrence with the perfect emblem of his Miriam figure – so virginal that she can't provide him with those 'heavy nodding clusters of crimson red' he refers to in the final stanza. 'Guelder Roses' has numerous rhythmic and verbal infelicities – for example, the melodramatic 'virgin hair of dead sixteen' – but it already testifies to Lawrence's ability to give Romantic *Einfühlung* – a Keatsian or Whitmanian empathy with non-human life – a peculiarly Modernist twist. In his nervous, edgy reinvention of Romantic lyric, it is not a field of daffodils or violet by a mossy stone (Wordsworth), not West Wind or autumn leaf (Shelley), that are to be read emblematically, but rather some quirky or lesser-known aspect of botanical or zoological life that most observers would overlook – in this case the contrast between white flower and red berry. A related poem, this time one Lawrence chose to include in *Love Poems*, is 'Cherry Robbers'. Here are the first two of the poem's three stanzas:

> Under the long dark boughs, like jewels red
> In the hair of an Eastern girl
> Hang strings of crimson cherries, as if had bled
> Blood-drops beneath each curl.
>
> Under the glistening cherries, with folded wings
> Three dead birds lie:
> Pale-breasted throstles and a blackbird, robberlings
> Stained with red dye. (*CP*, p. 36)

Here the ballad stanza, with its alternating five- and three-stress lines and simple rhymes (girl/curl, me/see), seems conventional enough, as does the comparison of cherries in the dark foliage to jewels in the girl's dark hair in the opening stanza, as well as the image in the third stanza of the laughing girl, 'Cherries hung round her ears', offering the narrator 'her scarlet fruit'. But, despite the girl's laughter, this is hardly a ballad about a happy night of love under the cherry trees. For in the centre of the poem the 'crimson' cherries turn into 'blood-drops beneath each curl' and then the scene shifts to the three dead birds under the tree 'stained with red dye'. We don't know how these birds got here or why, but when, in the third stanza, the laughing girl offers him 'Cherries hung round her ears', it is clear that the dead birds – those 'pale-breasted throstles [song thrushes] and blackbird' – refer to the girl herself, whose 'cherry' has been 'robbed' by her lover. Indeed, like the cherry-picking scene in *Sons and Lovers*, which immediately precedes the first sexual encounter between Miriam and Paul, 'Cherry Robbers' obliquely presents love-making, not as pleasurable but as deathly.

Lawrence's early lyric is rarely as carefully structured as this. *Love Poems* contains too many ungainly poems like 'Sigh No More' (*CP*, p. 65):

> The cuckoo and the coo-dove's ceaseless calling,
> Calling,
> Of a meaningless monotony is palling
> All my morning's pleasure in the sun-fleck-scattered wood.

What is soon 'palling' here is the insistent onomatopoeic feminine rhyming ('falling', 'scrawling', 'enthralling') that carries on for another twenty lines. 'Reading Lawrence's early poems', W. H. Auden remarked, in his seminal essay on the poet, 'one is continually struck by the originality of the sensibility and the conventionality of the expressive means.'[6] This is true enough of *Love Poems*, but when, in his next volume *Look! We Have Come Through!*, the situation is reversed, the results, to my mind, are not much more satisfactory. If, as Lawrence himself insisted, the constriction of fixed verse-forms was inhibiting, the direct, unmediated exposure of the poet's 'I' proved to be equally problematic.

Look! We Have Come Through!

Lawrence's next book of poems (1917) was conceived as a narrative sequence with an 'Argument' placed in the frontispiece:

> After much struggling and loss in love and in the world of man, the protagonist throws in his lot with a woman who is already married. Together they go into another country, she perforce leaving her children behind. The conflict of love and hate goes on between the man and the woman, and between these two and the world around them, till it reaches some sort of conclusion, they transcend into some condition of blessedness. (*CP*, p. 191)

The reference here is to Lawrence's elopement, in 1912, with Frieda von Richthofen Weekley, the German wife of an English professor of modern languages at Nottingham University, with whom Lawrence had briefly studied. Frieda, six years older than Lawrence, was bored with her marriage and had already had brief affairs with other men when Lawrence fell under her spell. For him, she represented the uninhibited sexuality he had not been able to find in Miriam or other girls, and he also loved the idea that Frieda was a member of the aristocracy (however minor), so unlike the bourgeoisie that Lawrence, as a working-class writer, never stopped resenting. The story of their tumultuous love-affair has been told by countless witnesses as well as by Frieda herself in her rather melodramatic *Not I but the Wind* (1934), which takes its title from Lawrence's 'Song of a Man Who Has Come Through', with its rather histrionic opening, 'Not I, not I, but the wind that blows through me! / A fine wind is blowing the new direction of Time' (*CP*, p. 250). Despite the visionary rhetoric here and elsewhere, the reality was less glorious. No sooner had the lovers eloped to Germany than Frieda wanted to return to England to see her three children, and she and Lawrence began to quarrel bitterly – a pattern that lasted from then on until Lawrence's death. The war years (1914–18) were a special nightmare: married to a German, Lawrence was subject to constant harassment by the British military authorities. After the war, the Lawrences began their life in exile – what Lawrence called his 'savage pilgrimage' – an exile that took them to Italy, Ceylon, Australia, Mexico, Taos, New Mexico, and Vence on the French Riviera, where Lawrence died.

For all Lawrence's talk of the 'condition of blessedness' finally attained by the lovers, most of the poems in *Look! We Have Come Through!* deal with conflict, misery, and misunderstanding. 'The night was a failure', begins 'First Morning', 'but why not – ?' And the poet then explains, in a straightforward diaristic passage, 'In the darkness / with the pale dawn seething at the window / through the black frame / I could not be free, / not free myself from the past, those others – / and our love was a confusion, / there was a horror, / you recoiled away from me' (*CP*, p. 204). The reader feels like a voyeur, having to witness Lawrence's confession of impotence, followed by a slightly happier mood of the following morning, when the lovers 'sit in the sunshine', staring at the dandelions that 'stand upright' and rekindle 'our love'. Similarly, in 'Frohnleichnam' (the title is the name of a Bavarian village, but perhaps Lawrence chose it because *Leiche* means 'corpse') Lawrence begins with straight confession (*CP*, p. 209):

> You have come your way, I have come my way;
> You have stepped across your people, carelessly, hurting them all;
> I have stepped across my people, and hurt them in spite of our care.

And although the mood shifts in the course of the poem, the language tracing these shifts remains curiously inert, as in 'Shameless and callous I love you; / Out of indifference I love you / Out of mockery we dance together' (p. 210), and so on. 'Oh my God', we read in 'Mutilation', 'how it aches / Where she is cut off from me! / Perhaps she will go back to England' (p. 212).

Critics and anthologists have preferred to these often embarrassing confessions the short imagist lyrics like 'Green', 'River Roses', and 'Gloire de Dijon'. 'Green', for example, abandons the loose free verse characteristic of the *Look! We Have Come Through!* sequence; it has two tercets, rhyming *aba*:

> The dawn was apple-green,
>   The sky was green wine held up in the sun,
> The moon was a golden petal between.
>
> She opened her eyes, and green
>   They shone, clear like flowers undone
> For the first time, now for the first time seen. (*CP*, p. 216)

This is a lovely descriptive lyric, what with its Edenic green and gold, its communion with moon and sky, and its depiction of the woman's eyes, opening to her lover even as a flower unfolds itself. At the same time it lacks definition as a link in the larger sequence; the words give no indication as to how this golden moment relates to the moods that precede and follow. More effective, to my mind, are the volume's conversation poems, which, even when addressed to Frieda ('you'), are more properly understood as dialogues of self and soul. 'Bei Hennef', for example, begins with concrete images like 'Green', but quickly moves to undercut them:

> The little river twittering in the twilight,
> The wan, wondering look of the pale sky,
>   This is almost bliss. (*CP*, p. 203)

The 'almost' will become a Lawrentian signature: it signals the poet's ability to step back and look at himself from an external perspective. After some more description of the peaceful twilight and the 'soft "Sh!" of the river / That will last for ever', Lawrence launches into one of his abstract disquisitions – 'at last I know my love for you is here', culminating in the much-cited passage:

> You are the call, and I am the answer,
> You are the wish, and I the fulfilment,
> You are the night, and I the day.

But just when the reader wonders how much more of this bombast – what Lawrence himself burlesqued, with reference to Walt Whitman's lapses, as 'CHUFF! CHUFF! CHUFF!'[7] – one can take, Lawrence adds:

What else? it is perfect enough.
It is perfectly complete,
You and I,
What more – ?

Strange, how we suffer in spite of this! (*CP*, p. 203)

The final deflationary turn nicely punctures the balloon of Lawrence's self-important rhetoric. Here, as in such related poems as 'On the Balcony', where the assertive 'still we have each other!' gives way to the uncertainty of 'what have we but each other?' (*CP*, p. 209), Lawrence recognizes that, as Yeats put it, 'A poet writes always of his personal life ... [but] he never speaks directly as to someone at the breakfast table, there is always a phantasmagoria.'[8] For Lawrence's own phantasmagoria to be realized, he had to distance himself both from his obsession with Frieda and also from his attraction to young men, which, long latent, began to manifest itself in the later war years. Ironically, it was only when Lawrence began to question the very possibility of the sexual fulfilment his 'demon' had long idealized that he could write brilliant poems about erotic encounters – this time his encounters with the non-human.

Birds, Beasts and Flowers

The title of what Lawrence himself considered his 'best book of poems' (see *CP*, p. 995) comes from the familiar 'Evening Hymn':

Now the darkness gathers,
    Stars begin to peep,
Birds and beasts and flowers
    Soon will be asleep.

The hymn connection is not coincidental. One of Lawrence's most delightful essays, 'Hymns in a Man's Life' (1928), pays tribute to the 'rather banal Noncomformist hymns that penetrated through and through my childhood'. He cites 'Each gentle dove', which culminates in the refrain 'O Galilee, sweet Galilee, / Come sing thy songs again to me!'[9] The poet responds: 'To me the word Galilee has a wonderful sound. The Lake of Galilee! I don't want to know where it is. I never want to go to Palestine. Galilee is one of those lovely, glamorous worlds, not places, that exist in the golden haze of a child's half-formed imagination.' And the essay goes on to define *wonder* – the wonder that makes names like Galilee or the image of the moon continue to have resonance for those not yet jaded by the twin evils of knowledge and boredom.

It is a Wordsworthian theme, but in highly ironized form: 'I *never cared* about the Crucifixion one way or another', says Lawrence, 'yet the *wonder* of it penetrated very deep in me.'[10] Wonder: it is the quality that animates the poems of *Birds, Beasts and Flowers*. 'Peach', for example, begins:

> Would you like to throw a stone at me?
> Here, take all that's left of my peach.
> Blood-red, deep;
> Heaven knows how it came to pass.
> Someone's pound of flesh rendered up. (*CP*, p. 279)

Lawrence's free verse has often been compared to Whitman's, but there is, in fact, little that is Whitmanesque in these jagged, nervous, conversational lines, with their abrupt, disjointed phrasing and aggressive mode of address.

In Italy, where he wrote these poems, Lawrence had been studying such Futurist manifestos as F. T. Marinetti's 'Down with Tango and Parsifal', and indeed, 'Peach' begins on a note of Marinettian buffoonery with the speaker as mock-victim, challenging his interlocutor(s) to cast the first stone. The identification with Christ is quickly undermined – 'Here, take all that's left of my peach' – and we recall that a peach stone – a single seed encased in hard wood – is, in fact, large enough to throw at someone and cause pain. One can swallow a plum pit but not a peach stone.

Indeed, what makes 'Peach', like the poem 'Pomegranate' that precedes it,[11] so distinctive is that, unlike most poets, Lawrence *knows* his fruit, botanically, historically, and even, so to speak, sexually. Thus the imagery of lines 3–5 refers to the fact that the flesh of the round peach is very soft and delicate (like breasts? buttocks?) but also easily bruised and hence, like Shylock's mandated 'pound of flesh', associated with pain. The paradox of 'peachness' is now brilliantly rendered:

> Wrinkled with secrets
> And hard with the intention to keep them.
>
> Why from silvery peach-bloom,
> From that shallow-silvery wine-glass on a short stem
> This rolling, dropping, heavy globule?
> I am thinking, of course, of the peach before I ate it.

The peach tree, native to China, has always had exotic connotations in the west: think of the 'nectarine, and curious peach' in Andrew Marvell's enticing garden. Poets and painters have often wanted to capture its 'silvery peach-bloom', here nicely compared to a 'shallow-silvery wine-glass on a short stem'. But Lawrence's posturing is closer to the histrionic 'Do I dare to eat a peach?' of T. S. Eliot's 'Love Song of J. Alfred Prufrock' than to the prettiness of an Amy Lowell: no sooner has he mentioned the silvery peach-blossom than he reminds himself that soon it will give way to the 'rolling, dropping, heavy globule' – the thick liquid drop of the ripe fruit when bitten into. And when over-ripe, the peach's skin, like a vain lady's, is 'wrinkled with secrets / And hard with the intention to keep them'. It is 'hard', Lawrence suggests, punning on the word, for peaches to stay hard and hide those wrinkles, for wrinkled fruit is usually soft and mushy to the touch. Uniquely, perhaps the peach briefly keeps the secret.

In Marvell's 'The Garden', the poet 'ensnared by melons ... fall[s] on grass'. In Lawrence's poem, ensnarement takes on an absurdist edge as the poet questions the peach's identity:

> Why so velvety, why so voluptuous heavy?
> Why hanging with such inordinate weight?
>
> Why so indented?
>
> Why the groove?
> Why the lovely, bivalve roundnesses?
> Why the ripple down the sphere?
> Why the suggestion of incision?

In this insistent series of rhetorical questions, Lawrence concentrates on the actual botanical attributes of the peach – the 'groove' down the centre or 'ripple down the sphere', which, when pressed, makes an incision into two 'lovely, bivalve roundnesses'. One of the peach's great appeals, evidently, is its mystery: when you see it whole, with its velvety surface and thin groove down the centre, it looks totally enchanting. But the incision spoils it all, revealing the heavy stone inside:

> Why was not my peach round and finished like a billiard ball?
> It would have been if man had made it.
> Though I've eaten it now.
>
> But it wasn't round and finished like a billiard ball.
> And because I say so, you would like to throw something at me.
>
> Here, you can have my peach stone.

It's the 'groove', the 'incision', that differentiates the body of the peach – and by implication the human body, specifically the female – from the 'perfection' of the machine, the man-made product. It's that little indent at the centre of the groove that makes the difference. Men, Lawrence implies, are given to making 'perfect' billiard balls; they prefer inanimate things to living matter. But no one wants to hear this truth, and so in a final ironic gesture, the poet proffers his auditor, not the peach, but the peach stone. This, he implies, half-jestingly, is all we deserve.

The peach has often been a symbol of beauty and sensuousness, of Edenic pleasure; it functions in endless metaphors about girls who are peaches. But Lawrence is interested not in what peaches look like or what they signify, but in what they *are* and how they operate in our discourse. The tone of the poem is at once aggressive and bemused, belligerent and light-hearted, the poet shifting voice and address so as to keep the reader riveted. It is a bravura performance.

'Peach', 'Pomegranate', 'Fig': these provide the paradigm for *Birds, Beasts and Flowers*. 'Come up, thou red thing', the poet addresses the moon in 'Southern Night', a lyric composed in Taormina, 'Come up, and be called a moon' (*CP*, p. 302). Or again, the twigs of the 'bare fig-trees' are chastised for 'over-reaching' themselves 'like the snakes on Medusa's head' (p. 300). And the insect, fish, and reptile poems are especially remarkable. 'Lawrence never forgets', Auden reminds us, 'that a plant or an animal has its own kind of existence which is unlike and uncomprehending of man's.'[12] The point is made forcefully in Lawrence's 1927 essay 'The Nightingale'. The flaw of 'Ode to a Nightingale', he declares with mock solemnity, is that Keats thinks he can somehow enter the world of the nightingale, a world actually wholly *other*:

> The viewless wings of Poesy carry [Keats] only into the bushes, not into the nightingale world. He is still outside.
>
> Darkling I listen: and for many a time
> I have been half in love with easeful death ...
>
> The nightingale never made any man in love with easeful death, except by contrast ...
>
> To cease upon the midnight with no pain,
> While thou art pouring forth thy soul abroad
> In such an ecstasy!
> Still wouldst thou sing, and I have ears in vain,--
> To thy high requiem become a sod.
>
> How astonished the nightingale would be if he could be made to realize what sort of answer the poet was answering to his song. He would fall off the bough with amazement. Because a nightingale, when you answer him back, only shouts and sings louder.[13]

This is the no-nonsense Lawrence who knows that chrysanthemums have an odour, who, having killed the mosquito in a poem by that title, remarks, 'Queer, what a big stain my sucked blood makes / Beside the infinitesimal faint smear of you!' (*CP*, p. 334). 'Whenever', Auden remarks, '[Lawrence] forgets about men and women with proper names and describes the anonymous life of stones, waters, forests, animals, flowers ... his bad temper and his dogmatism immediately vanish and he becomes the most enchanting companion imaginable, tender, intelligent, funny and, above all, happy.'[14]

'Happy' may be exaggerated – Lawrence is never happy for long – but the mercurial, playful language of the animal poems is certainly unique. One of the finest in the collection is the long poem 'Fish' (*CP*, pp. 334–40), a witty, sardonic exercise in perspectivism, in which subject and object, far from remaining discrete identities as, say, in Elizabeth Bishop's 'The Fish' ('I caught a tremendous fish'), have a curious symbiosis. Sometimes the poet addresses fish – a particular fish – directly –

> Your life a sluice of sensation along your sides,
> A flush at the flails of your fins, down the whorl of your tail,
> And water wetly on fire in the grates of your gills;
> Fixed water-eyes.

Sometimes, talking to himself, he refers to the fish in the third person, trying to explain certain movements:

> Himself,
> And the element.
> Food, of course!

Sometimes. assuming the voice of the prophet, he poses fish questions to the multitudes:

> Who is it ejects his sperm in the naked flood?
> In the wave-mother?
> Who swims enwombed? ...
>
> What price *his* bread upon the waters?

And sometimes, as observer, the poet corrects himself: 'Food and fear, and joie de vivre, / Without love. / The other way about: / Joie de vivre and fear and food, / All without love.'

At the climax of the poem (*CP*, p. 337), the 'I' tries to *become* a fish:

> To have the element under one, like a lover;
> And to spring away with a curvetting click in the air,
> Provocative,
> Dropping back with a slap on the face of the flood,
> And merging oneself!
>
> To be a fish!

But, no, there can be no such loss of consciousness. Suddenly, the poem shifts ground, the narrator moving outside the frame and now referring to fish in the third-person plural: 'Admitted, they swim in companies, / Fishes ... They exchange no word, no spasm, not even anger. / Not one touch.' And, such distance having been achieved, the poet returns to his everyday self:

> But sitting in a boat on the Zeller lake
> And watching the fishes in the breathing waters
> Live and swim and go their way –
>
> I said to my heart, *who are these?*
> And my heart couldn't own them.

Once that recognition sinks in, the poet defines himself as just another fish-killer:

> I have waited with a long rod
> And suddenly pulled a gold-and-greenish, lucent fish from below,
> And had him fly like a halo round my head,
> Lunging in the air on the line,
>
> Unhooking his gorping, water-horny mouth,
> And seen his horror-tilted eye.

And the fisherman's heart sinks, knowing what he has done: 'And I, a many-fingered horror of daylight to him, / Have made him die.'

Lawrence does not moralize the situation. Having seen the fish from just about every perspective possible, including the desire to *be a fish* and avoid all human touch, the poet now distances himself from 'Fishes / With their gold, red eyes, and green-pure gleam, and undergold', and places both himself and his 'fish' in a larger cultural and religious context:

> Cats, and the Neapolitans,
> Sulphur sun-beasts,
> Thirst for fish as for more-than-water;
> Water-alive
> To quench their over-sulphureous lusts.
>
> But I, I only wonder
> And don't know.
> I don't know fishes.
>
> In the beginning
> Jesus was called The Fish ...
> And in the end. (*CP*, p. 340)

Here the absurdist cataloguing of those who lust ('Cats and the Neapolitans') after fish is juxtaposed with the final apotheosis of fish as Jesus. Lawrence knows perfectly well that the familiar symbolism of Christ as fish has nothing to do with questions of virginity or immortality. The origin of the symbol is that the initial Greek letters of *Iesous Christos Theou Yios Soter* ('Jesus Christ of God Son Saviour') spell out the word *Ichthys*, fish. But by the end of this long, kaleidoscopic poem, we are convinced that fish can, in fact, play the role of Christ the Saviour 'In the beginning ... And in the end'. And only a poet with the erudition, panache, and familiarity with the range of cultural and mythic fish symbolism could have brought it off.

The late poetry

In his last seven years – years of illness and trauma – Lawrence continued to write poems, collected in *Pansies* (1929), *Nettles* (1930), and the posthumously published *Last Poems and More Pansies* (1932). 'This little bunch of fragments', wrote Lawrence in his Introduction to *Pansies*, 'is offered as a bunch of *pensées* ... a handful of thoughts. Or if you will have the other derivation of pansy, from *panser*, to dress or soothe a wound ... Each little piece is a thought; not a bare idea or an opinion or a didactic statement, but a true thought, which comes as much from the heart and the genitals as from the head' (*CP*, p. 417).

But despite this disclaimer, the bulk of Lawrence's 'pansies' *are* direct statements, opinionated and often shrill. They express all of the poet's pet peeves – his scorn of chastity on the one hand, 'mental' sex on the other, his contempt for the middle class ('How Beastly the Bourgeois Is'), his mistrust of 'True Democracy' and true love, his hatred of technology and the modern city. Aphorism, condensation, pithy statement: these had never been Lawrence's forte, and his *pensées* tend to be written in fairly flat prose, divided into line-lengths so as to look like lyric. 'Self-Pity' is typical:

> I never saw a wild thing
> sorry for itself
> A small bird will drop frozen dead from a bough
> Without ever having felt sorry for itself. (*CP*, p. 467)

The point here is that of course we human beings do feel sorry for ourselves. But the poem makes its statement – period. And 'pansy' after 'pansy' begins with lines like 'Since we have become so cerebral / we can't bear to touch or be touched' (*CP*, p. 468), or 'We've made a great mess of love / since we made an ideal of it' (p. 472), or 'The jealousy of an ego-bound woman / is hideous and fearful' (p. 475).

Every now and then, however, the quirky brilliance of *Birds, Beasts and Flowers* returns. Critics usually single out 'Bavarian Gentians' (*CP*, p. 697), with its stately retelling of the Persephone myth, or the solemnly psalm-like 'Ship of Death', as Lawrence's last great lyrics, but I prefer such less 'finished' poems as 'Andraitx – Pomegranate Flowers' (pp. 605–6), a kind of coda to the earlier 'Pomegranate', where the flowers' 'short gasps of flame in the green of night' shade into the 'red flamelets', emerging 'out of the foliage of the secret loins', and 'there reveal / a man, a woman there'. Another compelling poem is 'The Sea, The Sea', which presents the death–rebirth cycle in terms of sugar/salt imagery:

> Once the moon comes down
> and the sea gets hold of us
> cities dissolve like rock-salt
> and the sugar melts out of life
> iron washes away like an old blood-stain
> gold goes out into a green shadow
> money makes even no sediment
> and only the heart
> glitters in salty triumph
> over all it has known, that has gone now
>   into salty nothingness. (*CP*, pp. 454–5)

Here sea-salt is seen as a kind of Shelleyan destroyer and preserver, having the power to dissolve the mineral world – even gold and silver, not to mention iron – and so the heart can 'glitter in salty triumph / over all it has known, that has gone now' – the adverb 'now', in this complex assonantal pattern, no longer a part of 'k*now*n' and reversing the *o-n* of 'g*on*e' to yield 'nothingness'.

Lawrence's great gift – and we find traces of it even in these late poems – is his Wordsworthian ability to 'see into the life of things', even though his nervous, edgy, self-conscious 'I' is always stepping back and mocking the possibility of such a Romantic project. His animal and flower poems have been a model for post-World War II poets like Theodore Roethke, Ted Hughes, and the Sylvia Plath of 'The Rabbit Catcher' and 'Blue Moles'. But these later poets never quite matched Lawrence's ability to surprise and shock the reader. I conclude with the last stanza of 'Bare Almond-Trees', a poem that inverts the biblical, Koranic, and Kabbalistic imagery of almond tree and almond blossom as well as the commonplaces in travel literature extolling the beauties of Taormina:

> Sicily, December's Sicily in a mass of rain
> With iron branching blackly, rusted like old, twisted implements
> And brandishing and stooping over earth's wintry fledge,
>   Climbing the slopes
> Of uneatable soft green! (*CP*, p. 300)

The irony of that last line is quintessentially – and brilliantly – Lawrentian. How seductively 'soft', the poet notes, is the 'green' of those mountain slopes. But don't be fooled. It is also, for us humans, 'uneatable'.

NOTES

1 Ezra Pound, review of Lawrence, *Love Poems and Others*, in *New Freewoman* (1 September 1913), rptd in *D. H. Lawrence: The Critical Heritage*, ed. R. P. Draper (London: Routledge, 1970), pp. 53–4.
2 Ford Madox Ford, 'D. H. Lawrence', in *Portraits from Life* (New York: Houghton Mifflin, 1937), rptd in *D. H. Lawrence: A Composite Biography*, ed. Edward Nehls, 3 vols (Madison: University of Wisconsin Press, 1957–59; rptd 1977), vol. 1, pp. 107–8.
3 T. S. Eliot, 'The Contemporary Novel', *La Nouvelle Revue Française*, rptd in Draper, *Lawrence: The Critical Heritage*, p. 276.
4 R. P. Blackmur, *Form and Value in Modern Poetry* (New York: Doubleday Anchor, 1957), p. 256.
5 D. H. Lawrence, 'Preface to *Collected Poems*' (1928), in *The Complete Poems of D. H. Lawrence*, eds Vivian de Sola Pinto and Warren Roberts (New York: Viking, 1977; rptd 1994), p. 27; 'Poetry of the Present', Introduction to the American edition of *New Poems* (1918), in ibid., pp. 182–3. This edition of the *Complete Poems* is abbreviated hereafter as *CP*.
6 W. H. Auden, 'D. H. Lawrence', in *'The Dyer's Hand' and Other Essays* (New York: Vintage, 1990), pp. 277–95, 285.
7 D. H. Lawrence, 'Whitman', in *Studies in Classic American Literature*, eds Ezra Greenspan, Lindeth Vasey, and John Worthen (Cambridge: Cambridge University Press, 2003), p. 149.
8 W. B. Yeats, 'A General Introduction for my Work' (1936), in *Essays and Introductions* (New York: Macmillan, 1961), p. 509.
9 D. H. Lawrence, 'Hymns in a Man's Life', in *Phoenix II: Uncollected, Unpublished and Other Prose Works by D. H. Lawrence*, eds Warren Roberts and Harry T. Moore (London: Heinemann, 1968), pp. 597–8.
10 Ibid., p. 601.
11 On 'Pomegranate', see Marjorie Perloff, *Poetic License* (Evanston: Northwestern University Press, 1990), pp. 106–8.
12 Auden, 'D. H. Lawrence', p. 290.
13 D. H. Lawrence, 'The Nightingale', in *Phoenix. The Posthumous Papers of D. H. Lawrence (1936)*, ed. Edward D. McDonald (New York: Viking, 1972), pp. 42–3.
14 Auden, 'D. H. Lawrence', p. 289.

SELECTED FURTHER READING

Editions

The Complete Poems of D. H. Lawrence, eds Vivian de Sola Pinto and Warren Roberts, New York, Viking, 1977; rptd 1994. The Cambridge edition of

Lawrence's poetry is still in preparation, and this, therefore, is the most comprehensive collection currently available.

The Complete Poems of D. H. Lawrence, intro. and notes David Ellis, London, Wordworth Editions, Wordsworth Poetry Library, 2002

Phoenix. The Posthumous Papers of D. H. Lawrence (1936), ed. Edward D. McDonald, New York, Viking, 1972

Phoenix II: Uncollected, Unpublished and Other Prose Works by D. H. Lawrence, eds Warren Roberts and Harry T. Moore, London, Heinemann, 1968

Studies in Classic American Literature, eds Ezra Greenspan, Lindeth Vasey, and John Worthen, Cambridge, Cambridge University Press, 2003

Selected Critical Writings, ed. Michael Herbert, Oxford, Oxford University Press, 1998

Secondary works

Auden, W. H., 'D. H. Lawrence', in '*The Dyer's Hand' and Other Essays*, New York, Vintage, 1990, pp. 277–95

Blackmur, R. P., *Form and Value in Modern Poetry*, New York, Doubleday Anchor, 1957

Chauduri, Amit, *D. H. Lawrence and 'Difference'*, Oxford, Clarendon Press, 2003

Draper, R. P. (ed.), *D. H. Lawrence: The Critical Heritage*, London, Routledge, 1970

Fernihough, Anne (ed.), *The Cambridge Companion to D. H. Lawrence*, Cambridge, Cambridge University Press, 2001

Gilbert, Sandra, *Acts of Attention: The Poems of D. H. Lawrence. 1972*, 2nd edn, Carbondale, Southern Illinois University Press, 1990

Nehls, Edward (ed.), *D. H. Lawrence: A Composite Biography, 3 vols*, Madison, University of Wisconsin Press, 1957–59; rptd 1977

Perloff, Marjorie, *Poetic License*, Evanston, Northwestern University Press, 1990

Sagar, Keith, *D. H. Lawrence: Life into Art*, Athens, GA, University of Georgia Press, 1985

Worthen, John, *D. H. Lawrence: The Life of an Outsider*, Cambridge, MA, Counterpoint, 2007

27

MICHAEL NORTH

T. S. Eliot

Two months before his first book of poems appeared, T. S. Eliot published an essay that dismisses as newfangled nonsense the most prominent poetic innovation of his time. 'Reflections on *Vers Libre*', which appeared in the *New Statesman* in March 1917, was the first piece of literary criticism Eliot published, but in it he already sounds like the aged authority he was to become. Speaking as if from the height of a great poetic achievement, he decrees, 'There is no escape from metre; there is only mastery.' Then, showing his own mastery, Eliot brings his argument to an end with an almost audible snap: 'we conclude that the division between Conservative Verse and *vers libre* does not exist, for there is only good verse, bad verse, and chaos'.[1] In form and in substance, 'Reflections on *Vers Libre*' sounds more like the final words of a lifetime practitioner of Conservative Verse than the first literary essay of a poet soon to be famous for revolutionizing his craft.

Even as he lays down the law, however, Eliot lets something a little uncanny back into the closed system of his essay. To formulate the relationship between rhythmic variation and metrical order in verse, he chooses what seems an odd and inappropriate metaphor: 'the ghost of some simple metre should lurk behind the arras in even the "freest" verse; to advance menacingly as we doze, and withdraw as we rouse. Or, freedom is only truly freedom when it appears against the background of an artificial limitation' (*Selected Prose*, pp. 34–5). The spatial organization of this metaphor, in which freedom is somehow highlighted by something that it hides, is enough by itself to make the head spin. But even stranger is the apparent reference to *Hamlet* III. iv, in which Polonius is discovered hiding behind the arras in Queen Gertrude's chamber. The reference seems strange because Polonius is not a ghost, nor is he respected as a principle of order. He is killed, of course, as a result of Hamlet's misplaced impetuosity.

Eliot's own misplaced impetuosity almost seems to insert another story into the background of his essay. Simply put, Polonius is a rather strange choice as a representative of the regularity and order of traditional forms. In fact, it would be hard to find a less impressive figure of authority or a less likely model of the effective use of language. Even a hint of his presence in the background of an argument in favour of literary convention seems wilfully perverse. Compounding the oddity of the reference is the difficulty of fitting Hamlet into the picture. Hamlet does not respect Polonius as a ghost but turns him into one, quite by mistake. If Hamlet is to be associated somehow with free verse, then that form seems to have not a harmonious but a murderously insane relationship with the past. It almost seems, then, that by writing *Hamlet* into the background of the essay Eliot rewrites his own formula, so that metric regularity appears as a doddering old man, who is easily but quite pointlessly killed. Unable to carry out the instructions of the real ghost in the play, his father, and equally unable to strike out on his own, the young poet can only feign madness.

Distant though it may seem from the expressed intentions of Eliot's essay, it is this parodic version that seems more closely to describe his own early work. These early poems do harbour, behind their generally free verse texture, the ghost of a regular iambic metre, but the relation established there between the free and the regular is almost viciously comic. The fourth of the 'Preludes', for example, begins with knee-jerk iambic lines:

> His soul stretched tight across the skies
> That fade behind a city block,
> Or trampled by insistent feet
> At four and five and six o'clock.[2]

Here it seems the poet's soul has been trampled by insistent feet in more than one sense, as if the tick-tock regularity of city life had been forced on the poetry itself. The odd way in which the verb *stretched* loses its hint of the active as the sentence resolves itself into a series of passive fragments underscores the sense of helplessness in these lines. Imagery and prosody both confess an utter subjection to empty routine, the only resistance to which is to be found in the very exaggeration of the routine, as when children forced to walk in a line swing their arms back and forth like miniature soldiers. The schoolboy pun on *feet*, repeated here from the second 'Prelude', is another such exaggeration, like a self-conscious smirk in the imagery.

Weaker than Hamlet himself, this poet cannot kill even Polonius behind the arras but merely mocks him by exaggerated mimicry. But the self-inflicted wounds resulting from the irony are always visible, especially in the way the early poetry deploys its rhymes. The first section of 'Portrait of a Lady' ends thus:

> – Let us take the air, in a tobacco trance,
> Admire the monuments,

Discuss the late events,
Correct our watches by the public clocks.
Then sit for half an hour and drink our bocks.
(*Collected Poems*, p. 9)

The couplets observe their own version of dead public time, with the silliness of the rhyme to mock the pointlessness of being punctual when there is so little to do. But the mockery creates no real distance, as is demonstrated over and over as the protagonist is forced to complete his lady friend's rhymes, even if silently. Despite himself, he confirms her most fatuous clichés, such as 'youth is cruel, and has no remorse / And smiles at situations which it cannot see', to which he responds not just by smiling but by finishing her rhyme: 'I smile, of course, / And go on drinking tea.'

'Portrait of a Lady' ends, therefore, with the protagonist's rhyming complaint against his own inauthenticity:

And I must borrow every changing shape
To find expression ... dance, dance
Like a dancing bear,
Cry like a parrot, chatter like an ape.
(*Collected Poems*, p. 12)

The speaker accuses himself, in other words, of buffoonery, of a kind of ironic mimicry that carves out a little space by blowing out of all proportion the role it is forced to play. The self-reflexive humour of this is evident in the apery of the rhyme itself, a technique that Eliot sums up in the 'dull tom-tom' that 'begins / Absurdly hammering a prelude of its own, / Capricious monotone'. The poet's own name, doubled, becomes a synonym for mindless musical repetition of the kind that appears so often in his own preludes and caprices. Eliot thus names for himself a characteristic prosodic exaggeration, a new kind of irony, that made his poetry seem fresh and interesting even as it was demonstrating the impossibility of freedom in verse.

This is one way, at any rate, of explaining the achievement of a major modern poet, perhaps *the* major modern poet, who did not believe in freedom, for many the defining principle of modernity. For Eliot acted out the basic modern scene of rebellion against authority, but only after ironizing both roles in the drama. His complaint against tradition was that, Polonius-like, it had come down to him in a weakened condition. Thus his repeated declarations, helpfully collected by Christopher Ricks, that 'there was no poet ... who could have been of use to a beginner in 1908'[3] were not so much accusations, as they would have been for Ezra Pound, but lamentations, as of one left in the wilderness. Eliot did not feel it liberating thus to be left alone but all the more limiting, so that all the resistance his characters can muster is to mimic hideously the weakness of the authority that should be sustaining them.

'The Love Song of J. Alfred Prufock' is therefore a complaint against the state of poetry as of 1910, but it is a complaint that turns its expected situation inside out. Where a more forthrightly modern poet might rebel against tradition by avoiding its habits, Eliot castigates by exaggerating them. Thus there is an obvious parallel in the poem between the character's subjection to a life of empty repetition and the poet's chosen subjection to the emptiness of rhyme: 'Have known the evenings, mornings, afternoons, / I have measured out my life with coffee spoons' (*Collected Poems*, p. 4). Though such repetitions are, on both levels, mechanical and routine, there is no escaping them, except perhaps by forcing them into irony. 'Prufrock' thus becomes an extended exercise in prosodic exaggeration, with excessively short lines rhymed with one another, or massively disproportionate words rhymed ('go' and 'Michelangelo'), with the triplets that express such vapidity in 'Portrait of a Lady' extended into triple perfect rhymes and even into quadruple rhymes framed by perfect rhymes ('thin', 'chin', 'pin', 'thin').

Polonius is not behind the arras in a poem like this but out at centre stage:

> No! I am not Prince Hamlet, nor was meant to be;
> Am an attendant lord, one that will do
> To swell a progress, start a scene or two,
> Advise the prince; no doubt, an easy tool,
> Deferential, glad to be of use,
> Politic, cautious, and meticulous;
> Full of high sentence, but a bit obtuse;
> At times, indeed, almost ridiculous –
> Almost, at times, the Fool. (*Collected Poems*, p. 7)

A beautifully modulated piece of poetic clowning, these lines make the reader wait four lines for the expected rhyme of *Fool* with *tool*, putting it off with what is almost but not quite a quadruple rhyme, so that formal equivocation matches the halting rhetoric to create an effect in which putting off the obvious makes it all the more self-evident. The mastery of this is to be found not in subtle deviation from the figure behind the arras, but in devilish mimicry of it.

In his essay on *Hamlet*, first published in 1919, Eliot sees Polonius as one of Shakespeare's own ghosts behind the arras, a bit of material left over from previous versions of the Hamlet story that the playwright simply was not able to assimilate into his own design. Shakespeare's way with such material, according to Eliot, is the same as Hamlet's: 'In the character Hamlet it is the buffoonery of an emotion which can find no outlet in action; in the dramatist it is the buffoonery of an emotion which he cannot express in art' (*Selected Prose*, p. 49). Shakespeare fails, in other words, to find an 'objective correlative' for the feelings he wishes to express, in part because of the interference of material, such as the Polonius story, from other hands. So impressive is Eliot's youthful assurance here in finding fault with Shakespeare that his notion of the objective correlative has often been taken as a positive formula for the analysis of his own imagery. Now that we know that Eliot gathered his early poetry in a notebook entitled *Inventions of the March Hare*, it seems to make more sense to look for buffoonery there instead.

'Prufrock' also establishes its own particular kind of imagery, as subtly different from the prevailing innovations of imagism as its prosody is from free verse. In the founding manifesto of his movement, Ezra Pound had called for 'direct treatment of the "thing" whether subjective or objective',[4] apparently imagining a form in which subjective impressions would appear in poetry only when they could be made as solid as objects. 'Prufrock' may have appealed to him as instantly as it did because it seemed to achieve this ambition. For instance, a simple transferred epithet in the opening description of 'restless nights in one-night cheap hotels', shifting the restlessness of some unnamed sleepers to a more general subject, makes a psychological state seem an aspect of the urban landscape. It might easily seem that the purpose of such a technique is to make the inward and personal outward and objective, but what makes this restlessness so compelling is precisely its disembodied quality. Since it is not transferred to a thing at all, but to a plural noun with a vague and general reference, this restlessness becomes an emotion that is not felt particularly by anyone. If it becomes objective and general at all, it is only by taking leave entirely of the subject that may first have felt it.

Eliot's early poetry is full of such sensations, ones that have not been sensed by anyone in particular. In the first of the 'Preludes', the winter evening 'settles down / With smell of steaks in passageways' (*Collected Poems*, p. 13), where the vivid distinctness of the impression helps us ignore the absence of anyone actually capable of smelling anything. The same tactic is used to begin the next poem in the set, when 'Morning comes to consciousness / Of faint stale smells of beer' (*Collected Poems*, p. 13). The sharp distinctness of the second line jars abruptly with the apparent personification of the first, so that readers willing to imagine that morning can smell something will have further to imagine that it can smell beer. Of course, it is also possible that the lines are supposed to mean that morning smells *like* beer, but that simply raises the further question *to whom*? The rhetorical strategy and even some of the specific images of these early poems can be traced to the poetry of Jules Laforgue or Charles Baudelaire or perhaps to the novels of Charles-Louis Philippe, with which Eliot was impressed during his brief stay in Paris. But what now seems particularly Eliotic is the oddly ironic way in which they satisfy the formula of the objective correlative, which is to say that they are objectified without first having been felt by any subject. As Louis Menand puts it, the pathos of these early poems comes in part from 'the suggestion that the feelings that attach to these images are someone else's'.[5]

As a stylist, Eliot developed his work by promoting this pathos until it became a kind of bitter comedy. As a critic, though, he became widely influential by transforming the pathos into a system. The notion that 'freedom is only truly freedom when it appears against the background of an artificial limitation' seems to express an original predilection of Eliot's, which was always to feel the existence of things only in relation. As a student of philosophy, he was intrigued enough to study at length F. H. Bradley's notion of 'immediate experience', a 'timeless unity' of subject and object so complete that it 'is not as such present either *anywhere* or to *anyone*'.[6] Precisely for this reason, 'immediate experience' was more or less useless outside a strictly theoretical context, as a given that could not and in fact need not be apprehended in practice. It makes no sense, in other words, to try to make experience *more* immediate, since the immediacy of experience to the subject is already absolute and inescapable. This is apparently the sort of absolute relation that Eliot imagines as joining the world's literary objects in 'Tradition and the Individual Talent'. As a whole that is always total and complete, literary tradition never grows, and it is fundamentally the same even when new elements have been integrated within it.

Defined at this level of generality, tradition was a concept as useless as immediate experience, even to Eliot, and he frequently violated his own precepts by writing as if it were possible for one age to be more successfully integrated than another and for certain writers to be more perfectly assimilated into tradition than others, though by the lights of 'Tradition and the Individual Talent' both situations should have been impossible. As a poet, in the 'Preludes' and elsewhere, Eliot often wrote as if the lack of boundary between individual feelings was a pathetic and even tragic fact, a mistake and not a philosophical given. These apparent lapses do not imply, though, that Eliot ever came to believe that, in theory, any age ever came to be independent of any other age, or that any writer could work free of preceding tradition, or that any individual could ever actually have sensations that were quite distinct from all others. He did see quite vividly before him, however, an age that acted as if freedom were an actuality, in purposeful ignorance of the primacy of relation, and the result, in his opinion, was not genuine freedom but a travesty of relation, a return of it not as myth but as farce. Because he felt that farce was also his own, he was able to make it into the defining poem of his time.

Eliot has seemed such an antipathetic figure for so long now that the influence of his criticism and the celebrity of his few works of poetry can seem something of a mystery. The most popular current solution to that mystery is to emphasize the craftiness with which Eliot went about transforming himself from a provincial interloper into the Great Cham of the twentieth century. If Eliot became a calculating careerist, though, it was at least in part because he had to, having first been impetuous. In the space of a few weeks in 1914, he abandoned certain success as an academic philosopher, married a woman he had known only for a few months, and decided to throw in with Ezra Pound in an attempt to remake English poetry. The triumphant success of that effort, in the form of *The Waste Land*, has also been seen as the result of clever marketing, and it is quite remarkable to read through the correspondence, made available by Lawrence Rainey, that shows how Pound and Eliot wheeled and dealed until *The Waste Land* was given the *Dial* award as best poem of 1922. But Pound and Eliot were not so much creating as they were exploiting a demand, one based on the very considerable celebrity Eliot had achieved with eight years of literary labour. When the poem itself appeared it did succeed in overawing quite a number of readers, but where it intimidated it was also often resented, and where it evoked a truly enthusiastic response it was not through its mastery but rather by virtue of its own humiliation.

Publishing *The Waste Land* was actually a significant gamble for a poet who had perfected the style of 'Prufrock' to such an extent that all apparent buffoonery had been refined to savage satire. The poems published together in 1920 as *Ara Vos Prec* in England and as *Poems* in the US were the result of a conscious programme to combat what Pound called 'slosh' in modernist poetry, and the tight quatrains that resulted were so successful that for many readers of the 1920s and 1930s these were the height of Eliot's achievement. It was also apparently much easier in those days to admire what Ronald Schuchard calls the 'savage comic humour' of these poems.[7] Between 'Suite Clownesque', written in 1910, and the quatrain poems of 1920 the comedy has aged and grown fangs. Rhyme is no longer a confessional device but has become a tool of derisive satire. Even in a poem entitled 'Mr. Eliot's Sunday Morning Service', the target of the comedy is not the title character but Sweeney, the villainous fall-guy of the whole collection. It is certainly no accident that controversies over Eliot's anti-Semitism centre on these poems, whose sneering humour seems designed to give offence.

The desperation behind the derisive surface of these poems did not come out until *The Waste Land*, a poem composed amid such acute personal distress that it was completed while Eliot was under psychiatric care. Some of the apparent causes of Eliot's distress, including the overdetermined collapse of his marriage, figure in *The Waste Land* itself. In relation to the poem, though, it seems most useful to note that Dr Roger Vittoz, the Swiss psychiatrist who cared for Eliot in 1921, specialized in treating what he called 'clichés'.[8] By this term, Dr Vittoz apparently meant repeated patterns of behaviour or recurrent thoughts that the patient could not dispel. His patients were suffering, in other words, from reminiscences, the classic affliction of hysteria. For Eliot, putting these reminiscences into his long poem, making it, in fact, a demonstration of the role of involuntary repetition in history and modern society, was apparently part of the therapeutic process.

Before it could be published, though, *The Waste Land* had to be subjected to one of the most remarkable editorial procedures in literary history. Students of the poem were astonished to discover, with the publication of the long-lost manuscript in 1971, that the seemingly inevitable first line had been preceded at one stage by sixty lines of rambling satire, that the fourth section of the poem, now little more than an oracular proverb, had once been a long travelogue, and that Eliot's impulse to add in 'Gerontion' and other free-standing works had been held in check by Ezra Pound, who took his heavy black crayon to the entire text with unrelenting fervour. As relentless as he was, though, Pound tried only to make the poem stand up to its author's best ambitions, and though he did consistently check Eliot's tendency to slip into the brittle iambic satire of *Ara Vos Prec*, he did not try to make the poem into one of his own Cantos. At one point, Pound did help remove the word *like* from between two lines in 'The Fire Sermon', producing a juxtaposition rather like his own imagist verse: 'The barges wash / Drifting logs / Down Greenwich Reach.'[9] For the most part, however, he seemed intent to keep the poem free of anything that would muffle the impact of its innovations.

Publication of the manuscript also inevitably affected interpretations of the poem, partly by exposing the almost haphazard way in which its various parts had come together. When *The Waste Land* was first available, in October 1922, early readers were pathetically grateful for the guidance of critics such as Edmund Wilson, who began to explain it as early as that December. Ever since, *The Waste Land* has been preceded, if not entirely supplanted, by such explanations. Eliot himself seemed to encourage this by supplying for the first publication of the poem in book form a set of notes, which occasioned both interest and derision at the time. Though the notes were, if anything, more motley and disorganized than the poem itself, they did seem to advertise a 'plan' based on the folklore studies of Sir James Frazer and Jessie L. Weston. The title of the poem, according to Eliot's headnote, is taken from Weston's *From Ritual to Romance*, a study tracing the legend of the Holy Grail to ancient fertility rituals, which had been published in 1920. As the manuscript makes clear, though, the notion of a 'plan' is itself an afterthought, since the poem was composed by bringing together disparate fragments, some of them composed even before Weston's book was published. And attention to the Fisher King, the Holy Grail, and fertility ritual, all of which were key elements in Wilson's interpretation, offered in 'The Poetry of Drouth', distracted attention from another possibly more pertinent meaning of the title, in which 'waste' designates excess instead of deficiency.

The waste lands that Eliot had been writing about long before he ever dreamt of the Fisher King were not empty deserts but trashy vacant lots, and the psychological affliction these scenes both occasioned and reflected was not spiritual drought but involuntary repetition. For *The Waste Land*, the city scene of 'Preludes' is expanded in space and time, its atmosphere of disembodied, impersonalized sensations is etherealized even further, and the poetic techniques of that early poetry, dependent as they are on ironic, even ridiculous repetitions, are made to stand as the style of an age of repetition. Eliot's covert sense of himself as a Hamlet doomed to mimic Polonius comes out in *The Waste Land* as the helpless, ironic mimicry of an entire age.

Eliot begins his poem by establishing an unreal situation in which the dead are not buried, despite the title of this first section, but exhumed, a situation in which there is little to depend on but the grammar. The first lines of the poem establish a collective subject, so passive that even its emotions are imposed from without, 'mixing / Memory and desire, stirring / Dull roots with spring rain' (*Collected Poems*, p. 53). Despite the reams of paper used up in discussing the subject, it is not too simplistic to assume that this is the protagonist of the poem, awakened at the outset and forced to experience, or re-experience, the emotions and events to follow. The dead suffer, in other words, from reminiscences, and those reminiscences are what we experience as the collective life of this poem.

At crucial moments, the collective protagonist is so passive it does not even merit a grammatical subject:

> Sighs, short and infrequent, were exhaled,
> And each man fixed his eyes before his feet.
> Flowed up the hill and down King William Street.
>
> (*Collected Poems*, p. 55)

Feet rhyme with street because they have to go where the street leads, as the individual loses his own will in the crowd. The repetition of actions within the crowd rhymes with the repetition of these same actions day by day, as routine, and then century by century, as the scene evokes the famous line from the *Divine Comedy*: 'I had not thought death had undone so many.' Allusions of this kind were first thought to be a kind of showing off, and they are still enough to scare many readers away from this poem. But it seems more likely that this kind of repetition is meant to signal Eliot's own subjection to the automatism he is describing, as the street/feet rhyme, at this point a bit of self-quotation, signals an inevitability in the situation even the poet cannot avoid.

Repetition as automatic as this does not add up but steadily subtracts from a dwindling sum. So the more the members of the crowd are multiplied by one another the more they are reduced to pieces of themselves, eyes and feet in 'Burial of the Dead' and eyes and backs in 'The Fire Sermon'. Time dwindles as well, so that, though there seems to be a great deal of it in the poem, the sameness of it, as of grains in a handful of dust, makes the sum seem less than its parts. Thus Tiresias, who is introduced halfway in as a kind of compendium, 'the most important personage in the poem, uniting all the rest', is not larger but smaller for all he contains, like the Sibyl, quoted in the epigraph of the poem, so weighed down by all the years of her experience that she has actually turned to liquid in a jar. The celebrated fragmentation of *The Waste Land*, in other words, is most certainly a modern condition, one blamed in the poem rather directly on the division of labour, but it is not to be escaped by reference to a tradition exemplified by Tiresias the useless voyeur and the Sibyl lapsed in her jar.

The most immediate symptoms of this life of repetition seem to have been taken from Eliot's own situation in the early 1920s. The competitive sexual struggle of 'A Game of Chess' is most horribly represented by a conversation usually assumed to have been adapted from an original episode acted out between Eliot and his wife. If so, it is also an adaptation of the very similar scene in 'Portrait of a Lady', in which one character harangues another, who seems bottled up in self-protective silence. As in the earlier poem, though, this silent interlocutor is still forced into rhyme despite his silence:

> 'Are you alive, or not? Is there nothing in your head?'
> But
> O O O O that Shakespeherian Rag –
> It's so elegant
> So intelligent. (*Collected Poems*, p. 57)

In this case, though, the rhyme is not just personal but cultural, as the silent character is forced to echo not just his partner but a whole culture, which turns out itself to be a culture of empty rhymes. Recorded music is a model for a certain sort of empty modern conversation, but even the consciousness that shuns that conversation ends up repeating it.

Whatever escape *The Waste Land* does offer must be contained in its fifth section, which seems, rather remarkably, to have been written out more or less as it stands. What is also remarkable is how consistent Eliot remains even as he turns his poem in the general direction of consolation. For the bit of hope that is offered here is to be found precisely within the human deficiencies so harshly described in the first three sections. The story of the road to Emmaus, taken from Luke 24, seems the key here, in so far as it describes the utter oblivion of the disciples to the risen Christ walking between them. The resurrection is an event so far beyond ordinary human consciousness that even physical evidence of it does not make an impression. Eliot is not yet prescribing belief, as he will later, but he is suggesting that the very partiality, confusion, and smallness of human consciousness imply that there must be much that escapes it. The grand, inhuman 'DA' that comes down with the thunder seems divine precisely because it is incomprehensible, and the promise of it begins to die out as that single syllable is parsed, interpreted, and translated into human terms. The poem's final word, 'Shantih', meaning 'The Peace which passeth understanding', suggests that human fragmentation and confusion are not to be transcended or escaped, which is impossible in any case, but embraced, as the best possible evidence that the simple truth is, in every sense, beyond us.

In its own time, *The Waste Land* was seen by at least a few readers as a call to political revolution, one so insistent that John Cornford is reported to have joined the Communist Party after reading it. Needless to say, such readers were confused and confounded by Eliot's announcement, included in the preface to *For Lancelot Andrewes* in 1928, that he had become 'a royalist in politics, and anglo-catholic in religion'. Eliot had in fact joined the Church of England and become a British subject, two acts he apparently considered more or less synonymous. Though this dual conversion is often represented as part of a convoluted attempt to dominate English literary society by disappearing into it, the church hardly represented the high road to literary influence, even in 1928. To call oneself a royalist in a country where the crown has very little practical power is hardly to stake out an influential position.

Despite appearances, Eliot's political conversion was apparently the conclusion of a long intellectual process, going back at least to 1915. And the religion he came to practise, though it was outwardly almost painfully conventional, had at its heart a sceptically negative theology not very far at all from the conclusion of *The Waste Land*. For Eliot, the essential error of the modern age was its wilful ignorance of human damnation, for with it modernity had also lost the possibility of any state beyond the human. By these lights, even a deep-dyed blasphemer like Baudelaire was preferable to the vulgar humanist, for confirming the existence of evil at least helped to sustain belief in the spiritual. So it was not so much to avoid pain and complication as to embrace it that Eliot joined the church, as the weird unsteadiness of his work in the 1930s shows. On one hand, the tomfoolery of the earlier poetry ripens into something truly macabre in *Sweeney Agonistes*, while the riddling fragments of *Ash-Wednesday* accumulated towards the late purposely prosaic style that was to take up so much of *Four Quartets*. Though there doesn't seem to be much connection between Sweeney's brutal assurance that 'Any man has to, needs to, wants to / Once in a lifetime, do a girl in' (*Collected Poems*, p. 122) and *Ash-Wednesday*'s 'Lady of silences', it was Eliot's poetic ambition to reconcile them.

Though he had assumed an influential position as editor at Faber and Gwyer (later Faber and Faber), while also editing his own magazine, the *Criterion*, and had thus become a pillar of the British literary establishment, Eliot's personal life was unsettled in these years. In 1932, he took the occasion of a lecture tour of the United States to separate from his wife, who was certified insane a few years later. At the same time, Eliot revived his acquaintance with an old flame, Emily Hale, who was now teaching in California. He was apparently strongly tempted to make a new life with Hale, perhaps even in California, though the exact nature of their relationship will remain obscure until their letters become available. In any case, it is obvious that Eliot was struck, as people in middle age often are, by the odd series of accidents that had determined his life, which might so easily have been led at Harvard, in the field of philosophy, with Hale as his happy wife. Eliot's last considerable work of poetry emerged fitfully from these feelings of bewildered half-regret.

Appropriately, *Four Quartets* began, not with a magnificent plan, but with an accidental lyric, a bit of extra business Eliot was asked to provide for *Murder in the Cathedral*. When these few lines were first elaborated into an entire poem, the result, 'Burnt Norton', stood as the final item in the *Collected Poems* of 1936, where it provided a baffling conclusion to what seemed a very different body of work. Louis Martz reports feeling that 'Burnt Norton' stood 'in stark isolation at the end of the book', too odd to be interpreted in light of the other poems, too strange to suggest a direction for future work.[10] In fact, it seems quite likely that Eliot himself had no notion of following 'Burnt Norton' with anything similar until World War II presented him with an unavoidable topic.

As Eliot proceeded to elaborate what had begun as a chance composition, he turned what had been the more or less adventitious design of

'Burnt Norton' into a grand symmetrical structure. Each of the poems has five parts, rather like *The Waste Land*, which might very easily have had four or six or even more parts, depending on the outcome of negotiations between Eliot and Pound. There may even have been an attempt to mimic the general shape of *The Waste Land*'s five parts, since the fourth in each case is much shorter than the others. There are other symmetries as well, so that the second part of each of the quartets is a pastiche, while the fifth usually includes a self-conscious essay about the limitations of poetic language. These similarities are complemented by carefully patterned differences between the poems. The four quartets, already squaring the number four in their very title, multiply it further by taking up the four elements and the four seasons. Thus a poetic project that had begun purely by chance, and which was extended by the grand accidents of war, became by its end a tightly constricted diagram, one that Eliot finally felt it rather painful to fill in.

In its very form, then, *Four Quartets* confronts a fundamental ideological tension between contingency and fate. In one sense, it is as modern a series of poems as *The Waste Land*, in so far as it responds to the breaks and accidents that seem to make up modern time. According to Donald Davie, readers of the last three of the quartets received them as timely comments on the war, and even now this seems their chief appeal to contemporary readers.[11] But Eliot also attempts to sense, or even to will into existence, a pattern beyond this kind of contingency. The basic decision behind the whole sequence, to express the passage of time by describing different places, tends to stabilize by spatializing the otherwise liquid progress of history. Creating a tension between individual words and the eternal Word, between ordinary desire and divine love, Eliot tries to manage the tension between the commonplace world of chance and the eternity implied beyond it.

Naming his sequence after a musical form must have been meant to focus attention on the sound of the poems, and one of Eliot's motives in constructing the individual poems as he did was the desire to work with different metrical forms. 'East Coker' thus contains a section in octosyllabics, while 'Dry Salvages' has an altered sestina. Even so, it is hard to find among critics or readers any real appreciation for the actual poetry of the quartets. Davie, who once seriously proposed that part of 'Dry Salvages' was badly written on purpose, still comes in his last words on the subject to find the sequence uneven. For many readers, the simple fact that much of the poetry is, as Davie puts it, 'very markedly explicit and discursive',[12] makes it that much less exciting than *The Waste Land*. There are quite a few moments in the *Quartets* when the poet tells us explicitly or implicitly that 'the poetry does not matter', but there are also moments, especially in the fourth sections, which tend to be allegorical, where the poetry seems to matter too much. Thus the *Quartets* can be and have been criticized for a purposeful prosiness – 'That was a way of putting it' – and for artificial poeticizing: 'The wounded surgeon plies the steel / That questions the distempered part' (*Collected Poems*, pp. 184, 187).

One source of some unhappiness with Eliot's style in the *Quartets* has been his insistence on working only negatively towards the affirmative:

You say that I am repeating
Something I have said before. I shall say it again.
Shall I say it again? In order to arrive there,
To arrive where you are, to get from where you are not,
You must go by a way in which there is no ecstasy.
(*Collected Poems*, p. 187)

It may be passages like this that Ronald Bush has in mind when he calls *Four Quartets* 'a masterpiece of deferred immediacy'.[13] But the negative route is the only honest one that Eliot can imagine from the contingent to the eternal, and if this necessarily involves the ecstatic in a lot of prosy nonsense it is a price he seems willing to pay.

Eliot's success in his gamble is greatest where the difficulty is most visible, in 'Little Gidding', which begins with a pilgrimage to the site of a religious retreat established by English Catholics in the seventeenth century, and ends, at least chronologically, with one of Eliot's foot patrols as fire warden during the Blitz. Though the poem concludes on the assurance that the fire of the Blitz and the historical English rose 'are one', even this assurance would make little sense unless there were a great deal of difficulty in the reconciliation. Thus the ghostly figure who accosts the poet in the ruins of a bombing raid, and who seems to have a lot in common with the recently deceased W. B. Yeats, brings a fairly bitter message back with him from the dead: 'From wrong to wrong the exasperated spirit / Proceeds, unless restored by that refining fire' (*Collected Poems*, p. 205). The message of the lines is contained in the real challenge of the metaphor itself, for Eliot is telling his wartime readers that the loss they are suffering under German bombs is a necessary one, part of a process of detachment from people, things, and country, that will bring them all back in a higher and better relation. The immediate and actual fire of the Blitz is itself refined in Dante's Purgatorial fire to become a Pentecostal tongue of flame.

Though it sounds like consolation, Eliot's solution also insists on the reality of accident and loss, and the trick of the poem, especially as it nears its end, is to make this tension balance without making it disappear. There are moments of unembarrassed simplicity when it seems to succeed:

> We die with the dying:
> See, they depart, and we go with them.
> We are born with the dead:
> See, they return, and bring us with them.
>
> (*Collected Poems*, p. 208)

There is something touching and even a little bold in the allusion here to 'The Return', an early poem by Pound, who was at this time acting in open defiance of the laws against treason. It is also a little eerie to see in these lines a return to the opening of *The Waste Land*, with its involuntary exhumation of the dead, and to realize that Eliot is attempting here to transfigure the very repetition that makes life so hellish in the world of that poem. To be able to see that repetition as a return, to admit the inauthentic and the redundant as an inevitable and even a useful part of any life, must have meant for Eliot a reconciliation with the materials of his own poetry. It seems a fitting end, even if it meant that Eliot never felt the need to write anything substantial again.

As the last major poem of a poet who was to win the Nobel Prize in 1948, *Four Quartets* exerted considerable influence, especially on literary scholars. Metaphors taken from it, like the Chinese jar that 'moves perpetually in its stillness', became touchstones of the New Criticism, and Eliot's poetry, especially as it was presented in anthologies like Cleanth Brooks and Robert Penn Warren's *Understanding Poetry*, became the privileged object of academic literary study as it was reorganized after World War II. All this influence and all of Eliot's very considerable personal authority now exists mainly in inverted forms, and the resentment that naturally attaches to any dictatorship has sometimes made it difficult to estimate fairly the real achievement of the poetry. Still, 'Prufrock' continues to stun first-time readers as it stunned Ezra Pound almost a century ago, and this seems some warrant that whatever was new in Eliot's work then remains new enough even now.

NOTES

1 *Selected Prose of T. S. Eliot*, ed. Frank Kermode (New York: Harcourt Brace Jovanovich/Farrar, Straus and Giroux, 1975), pp. 35, 36.

2 T. S. Eliot, *Collected Poems 1909–1962* (London, Faber and Faber, and New York: Harcourt Brace & World, 1963), p. 14.

3 T. S. Eliot, *Inventions of the March Hare: Poems 1909–1917*, ed. Christopher Ricks (New York: Harcourt Brace, 1996), p. 388.

4 *Literary Essays of Ezra Pound*, ed. T. S. Eliot (New York: New Directions, 1968), p. 3.

5 Louis Menand, *Discovering Modernism: T. S. Eliot and His Context*, 2nd edn (New York: Oxford University Press, 2007), p. 17.

6 T. S. Eliot, *Knowledge and Experience in the Philosophy of F. H. Bradley* (New York: Columbia University Press, 1964), pp. 29, 31.
7 Ronald Schuchard, *Eliot's Dark Angel: Intersections of Life and Art* (New York: Oxford University Press, 1999), p. 89.
8 Lyndall Gordon, *T. S. Eliot: An Imperfect Life* (New York: Norton, 1999), p. 171.
9 T. S. Eliot, *The Waste Land: A Facsimile and Transcript of the Original Drafts Including the Annotations of Ezra Pound*, ed. Valerie Eliot (London: Faber and Faber, and New York: Harcourt Brace Jovanovich, 1971), pp. 48–9.
10 Louis Martz, 'Origins of Form in *Four Quartets*', in *Words in Time: New Essays on Eliot's Four Quartets*, ed. Edward Lobb (Ann Arbor: University of Michigan Press, 1993), p. 189.
11 Donald Davie, *Modernist Essays: Yeats, Pound, Eliot*, ed. Clive Wilmer (Manchester: Carcanet, 2004), p. 149.
12 Davie, *Modernist Essays*, p. 151.
13 Ronald Bush, *T. S. Eliot: A Study in Character and Style* (New York: Oxford University Press, 1984), p. ix.

SELECTED FURTHER READING

Editions

Inventions of the March Hare: Poems 1909–1917, ed. Christopher Ricks, London, Faber and Faber, and New York, Harcourt, Brace, 1996

Collected Poems 1909–1962, London, Faber and Faber, and New York, Harcourt, Brace & World, 1963

The Complete Poems and Plays of T. S. Eliot, London, Faber and Faber, 1969

Selected Prose of T. S. Eliot, ed. Frank Kermode, New York, Harcourt Brace Jovanovich/Farrar, Straus and Giroux, 1975

The Waste Land, ed. Michael North, Norton Critical Edition, New York, W. W. Norton, 2001

The Waste Land: A Facsimile and Transcript of the Original Drafts Including the Annotations of Ezra Pound, ed. Valerie Eliot, London, Faber and Faber and New York, Harcourt Brace Jovanovich, 1971

Secondary works

Bedient, Calvin, *He Do the Police in Different Voices: 'The Waste Land' and Its Protagonist*, Chicago, University of Chicago Press, 1986

Bush, Ronald, *T. S. Eliot: A Study in Character and Style,* New York, Oxford University Press, 1984

Ellmann, Maud, *The Poetics of Impersonality: T. S. Eliot and Ezra Pound*, Brighton, Harvester, 1987

Levenson, Michael, *A Genealogy of Modernism: A Study of English Literary Doctrine, 1908–1922*, Cambridge, Cambridge University Press, 1984

Menand, Louis, *Discovering Modernism: T. S. Eliot and His Context*, 2nd edn, New York, Oxford University Press, 2007

Moody, A. D., *Thomas Stearns Eliot: Poet*, Cambridge, Cambridge University Press, 1979

Rainey, Lawrence, *Institutions of Modernism: Literary Elites and Public Culture*, New Haven, Yale University Press, 1998
Ricks, Christopher, *T. S. Eliot and Prejudice*, Berkeley, University of California Press, 1988
Schuchard, Ronald, *Eliot's Dark Angel: Intersections of Life and Art*, New York, Oxford University Press, 1999
Wilson, Edmund, 'The Poetry of Drouth', *Dial* 73 (1922), 611–16

28

EDWARD MENDELSON

W. H. Auden

Auden thought of poetry as a form of personal speech, spoken by one unique individual to another, even when poet and reader were divided across space and time. In this, as in much else, he differed from his great modernist predecessors such as W. B. Yeats and T. S. Eliot, who often thought of poetry as embodying the collective voice of a culture or nation, either as it actually was or as it ought ideally to become. Much of Auden's uniqueness and variety derives from his way of thinking about poetry and personal voice. He sometimes said that he thought of himself as a comic poet, but he believed that a comic poet could be a greater and ultimately more serious poet than a tragic or solemn one.

Auden's personal voice, like every personal voice, spoke in a variety of moods and styles, ranging from laconic understatement to overstated extravagance, from casual gossip to solemn oratory, and in tones that ranged from agitated and anxious to discursive and meditative. A personal voice, in Auden's view, was unique to the person who spoke it. Yet the only way anyone learns to speak is by imitating other people's voices, so even the most authentic-sounding voice is always more or less artificial. 'Human beings', he wrote, 'are necessarily actors who cannot become something before they have pretended to be it; and they can be divided, not into the hypocritical and the sincere, but into the sane who know they are acting and the mad who do not.'[1]

For some of his poems, Auden felt impelled to create new styles and forms, but for other poems he was content to borrow from other poets ranging from the *Beowulf*-poet through to William Carlos Williams. He was sceptical about Ezra Pound's slogan, 'Make it new', because, in his reading of the poetry of the past, much of it had never grown old.

T. S. Eliot argued in an essay, 'Reflections on *Vers Libre*' (1917), that verse-forms were products of their societies; most traditional verse-forms – the sonnet, for example – were now obsolete because they could thrive only in a coherent society, and modern society was an incoherent chaos. Auden seems to have read this essay early in his career, and suddenly began writing sonnets. He was not merely rebelling against Eliot's authority but affirming his conviction that verse-forms were shaped by individual poets as much as by impersonal social forces, and that poets had far more freedom to choose than Eliot imagined.

Auden wrote poems on modern themes in archaic forms ranging from the Pindaric ode through the Dantesque *canzone* and the Icelandic *dróttkvætt* to the French villanelle, and he often used older forms when writing about subjects entirely different from those for which the forms had first been invented. After writing a sonnet-sequence on personal love, the traditional sonnet subject, he wrote another sonnet-sequence, 'In Time of War', which began with a summary history of civilization and ended with reflections on modern politics.

The great writers of the past two centuries regarded art as the highest human activity, and thought their mastery over language made them, in Shelley's phrase, 'unacknowledged legislators of the world'. Auden was more than once tempted by this idea but always regretted it, especially when the poems that he wrote while tempted became widely admired. He thought art was at best a way of pointing towards truths larger and greater than art; that any work of art that claimed to embody rather than point towards truth was unintentionally comic – foolishly comic, not profoundly so – because it made grandiose claims of power that only artists could imagine to be true.

'All the poems I have written were written for love', Auden wrote.[2] He was referring both to personal love and to his love for the English language. Early reviewers tended to describe his work as intellectual and analytical; some decades passed before critics recognized that most of his short lyrics were love-poems and that his long poems on historical, literary, philosophical, and religious themes turned into love-poetry in their closing lines.

What may have misled the reviewers was the reticent style of his love-lyrics, in which he tried to represent the emotions of real lovers, not the theatrical display of much romantic poetry, nor the public airing of private sentiment that W. B. Yeats, for example, used when one of his love-poems, 'Adam's Curse', said in a pretend whisper, 'I had a thought for no one's but your ear.' Auden's love-poems were more indirect and more conscious of mixed feelings. Late in his career he wrote a long prose poem titled 'Dichtung und Wahrheit' ('poetry and truth' – the title of Goethe's autobiography) about the total impossibility of writing a poem that expressed exactly what he meant by 'I love you.'

Auden's background and temperament predisposed him to prefer truth-telling to imagination. His father was a psychoanalytically expert physician and professor of public health who published learned essays on archaeology and the classics. His mother, unusally for women of her generation, had a university degree and had trained to be a nurse. Both parents were Anglo-Catholics, members of the most ritualistic wing of the Anglican church, and as a child Auden enjoyed the magical excitement of church services.

Auden, born in 1907, was his parents' third child, and enjoyed the traditional folk tales in which the ignored third son finally triumphs. From six to twelve, he spent much of his waking life in a private imaginary landscape based on the lead mines that his family had visited in the north of England. As he filled this imaginary landscape with mining machinery he had seen in books, he sometimes had to choose between two machines that performed the same purpose – one that seemed more aesthetically satisfying, another that was more practical. He felt obliged to choose the more practical one, and experienced this choice as a moral one, a preference for truth over beauty.

As an adult, he thought of himself as making comparable choices between writing poems in ways that were dazzling and resonant or in ways that pointed towards moral and emotional reality. Truth-telling verse, he thought, had a less visceral impact than verse that tells magnificent fictions, but its effect is deeper, more lasting, and ultimately more satisfying. Auden wrote: 'Poetry is not magic. In so far as poetry, or any other of the arts, can be said to have an ulterior purpose, it is, by telling the truth, to disenchant and disintoxicate.'[3]

Until adolescence, Auden had no special interest in poetry, but through his interest in geology and mining he had also become interested in language, and cherished the names of minerals and the exotic names of lead mines in northern England, such as Redam, Thackmoss, and Pity Mea. When he was fifteen, a friend was embarrassed to learn that Auden was religious and changed the subject by asking if he wrote poetry. At that moment, Auden said later, he discovered his vocation as a poet.

During the next three years he wrote poems in traditional styles learned from Romantic and Victorian poets, from Wordsworth to A. E. Housman, and mostly from Thomas Hardy. Poetry gave him a sense of magical excitement like the excitement he had found in church ritual, and he lost interest in religion except as an historical curiosity. When he went to Oxford in 1925 he planned to study natural science, but switched to English. Towards the end of his first year he discovered T. S. Eliot's poetry, and his romantic style transformed almost overnight into this sort of modernist fantasia:

> Inexorable Rembrandt rays, which stab
> Through clouds as through a rotting factory floor,
> Make chiaroscuro in a day now over,

And cart-ruts bloody as if Grendel lately
Had shambled dripping back into his marshes.
('Thomas Epilogizes', 1926)[4]

His allusion to Grendel, the monster in *Beowulf*, is an early trace of the English literary past that he brought into his poetry throughout his career. Auden was tempted at first to think of his literary past as the past of his nation – the past of England – but he renounced this idea for a less politically charged idea of a linguistic past – the past of English, wherever and by whomever it was spoken.

In 1927, at twenty, he wrote his first poem in what he later recognized as his own voice, not one that exaggeratedly imitated someone else's. The poem begins:

Who stands, the crux left of the watershed,
On the wet road between the chafing grass
Below him sees dismantled washing floors,
Snatches of tramline running to a wood,
An industry already comatose,
Yet sparsely living. ('The Watershed', 1927)

This style has the laconic dryness and almost casual obscurity characteristic of Auden's first adult poems. A reader needs a moment or two to make sense of the scene; 'Who stands' is not a question but means 'The one who stands'; the watershed is the ridge that divides waters flowing into different river basins; the 'crux' that seems to be to the left of it, from the observer's perspective, is either a roadside cross or a crossroad – it is impossible to decide – but a 'crux' is also a difficult problem. After establishing a stylistic world where decisions are difficult, the poem proceeds to explore the difficulties of personal decision-making, in a tone of quiet uncertainty.

Much of Auden's work from 1927 through to 1933 was similarly obscure and laconic. But he was surprised when reviewers of his first published book, *Poems* (1930), complained of its obscurity, because he had never intended to be obscure. He later implied that he wrote his early poems with a sense of magical excitement in his own words, without thinking about readers. After his first book made him famous, at the age of twenty-three, he began to think more deeply about the relation of writer and reader and about the temptations open to both.

In 1930 he began working as a schoolmaster, and for the rest of his life he earned his living alternately by teaching at a school or college and by writing freelance essays and reviews. He preferred to teach literary or intellectual history, and except when teaching very young pupils, never taught writing. Teaching, like poetry, was for him a means of truth-telling, and he was always conscious of the temptation felt by both teachers and writers to dazzle an audience with flattering untruths.

In 1931 he wrote a book-length poem called *The Orators: An English Study* which explored these questions in a manner more clear to himself than to his readers. The 'orators' are teachers, writers, leaders, all those who address a collective audience rather than an individual. The first of the book's three parts contains prose speeches by four voices, each about a different phase of the speakers' membership in a group focused on a leader; the group sometimes seems to be a boarding-school class, sometimes a tribal band, sometimes a proto-fascist nation. The second part, 'Journal of an Airman', is the prose diary of an airman-leader who goes mad through his psychological isolation from those he leads. The third section, 'Six Odes', is a set of exuberant verse meditations on leadership, including an ironic hymn to a friend's newborn child in the same tones that fascist propaganda used when praising a leader. 'The central theme of *The Orators*', Auden later wrote, 'seems to be Hero-worship.'[5] What was not visible to readers, though Auden himself was aware of it, was that he was lampooning his own temptation to become a cultural leader through the power of his verse.

The Great Depression and the rise of fascism prompted many writers of Auden's generation to become active in left-wing politics. In 1932 Auden began writing poems on revolutionary themes, often in accessible, rhymed forms borrowed from popular ballads, but he was divided between the idea of a political revolution and the idea of change brought about through an inner psychological revolution, a 'change of heart'.

In 1933 he wrote 'A Summer Night', in a lively stanza-form taken from Robert Burns, about the kind of revolution that he both hoped for and feared. It begins by celebrating the comforts of his life and work, 'The bathing hours and the bare arms'. Then, in the middle of the poem, after praising the equality and affection he enjoys with his friends, he remembers the outside world, where political and economic miseries are far more painful than the 'tyranny of love' that he and his friends sigh over. Like all who share their comfort and safety, he and his friends 'do not care to know' about the violence outside, 'Nor ask what doubtful act allows / Our freedom in this English house, / Our picnics in the sun'.

The poem proceeds to imagine a revolutionary flood toppling his class and his comforts, and acknowledges the justice of the uprising. But the poem ends by hoping that the warmth he and his friends now share may be part of the different political spirit of the future:

> May this for which we dread to lose
> Our privacy, need no excuse
>   But to that strength belong;

As through a child's rash happy cries
The drowned voices of his parents rise
In unlamenting song.

After discharges of alarm,
All unpredicted may it calm
The pulse of nervous nations:
Forgive the murderer in his glass,
Tough in its patience to surpass
The tigress her swift motions.[6]

(The Anglo-Saxon possessive form 'tigress her', instead of the modern 'tigress's', is another trace of Auden's sense of an English literary past still available for present-day use.)

The poem never makes clear what Auden means by 'this for which we dread to lose / our privacy' or, in the final stanza, 'it'. The poem suggests that 'it' is the warmth he shares with his friend, but in an essay thirty years later Auden identified it more precisely as a 'vision of agape', a sense of shared unerotic love. He wrote that on a summer night in 1933, when he was sitting on a lawn with three colleagues, 'For the first time in my life I knew exactly – because, thanks to the power, I was doing it – what it means to love one's neighbour as oneself ... My personal feelings towards them were unchanged – they were still colleagues, not intimate friends – but I felt their existence as themselves to be of infinite value and rejoiced in it.'[7]

For the rest of the 1930s Auden's work was divided between his private sense that what mattered most was loving one's neighbour as oneself and his public role as a political poet whose work was a weapon against fascism. This public role was half invented by journalists, half encouraged by himself.

He stepped into the political limelight partly by writing half-propagandistic plays in prose and verse in collaboration with his friend (and occasional lover) the novelist Christopher Isherwood. Two of their plays, *The Dog Beneath the Skin* (1935) and *The Ascent of F6* (1936), were surprisingly successful, but Isherwood's simplistic politics, and Auden's uncertainty over his public tone, soon made them forgettable. Auden's political reputation grew when he published a few poems that expressed the Marxist idea of history as an impersonal force moving inevitably towards revolution; individuals could either join in history's predetermined triumph or make a futile effort to resist it. The poem that made this argument most explicitly was Auden's birthday poem for Isherwood in 1935, which ended:

And all sway forward on the dangerous flood
Of history, that never sleeps or dies,
And, held one moment, burns the hand.
('August for the People', 1935)[8]

Meanwhile, much of his lyric poetry still took the form of meditative lyrics that had nothing do with the simplicities he was writing in collaboration with Isherwood. 'Fish in the Unruffled Lakes', a typical example, contrasts the instinctive, unconscious beauty of the animals – fish, lion, and swan – with conscious, guilt-ridden human anxieties, but ends in gratitude that the same consciousness that produces human envy and regret also permits the voluntary decision to love:

> But I must bless, I must praise
> That you, my swan, who have
> All gifts that to the swan
> Impulsive Nature gave,
> The majesty and pride,
> Last night should add
> Your voluntary love.
>
> ('Fish in the Unruffled Lakes', 1936)

'Bless', 'praise', and 'voluntary' are the characteristic vocabulary of Auden's love-poetry, which took less interest in a beloved's beauty than in the voluntary relation that issued in 'a lover's Yes' (a phrase from a 1955 poem, 'Homage to Clio').

In 1936, in the verse and prose he wrote for *Letters from Iceland* (a travel book written in collaboration with the poet Louis MacNeice), Auden explicitly renounced the idea of history that he had endorsed in his poem to Isherwood a year earlier; one of the verse letters in the book warned himself against the error of seeing vast forces rather than unique persons and unique places, the error that occurs when the real glacier that he was visiting in Iceland seems 'no glacial flood / But history, hostile, Time the destroyer / Everywhere washing our will' ('Letter to R.H.S. Crossman, Esq.').

His decision to renounce impersonal history and political generalizations was shattered when, also during his visit to Iceland, he heard that civil war had broken out in Spain, and the first battle had begun in what seemed certain to become a second world war. Early in 1937 he went to Spain hoping to drive an ambulance for the Spanish Republic, the first freely elected socialist government in Europe; his departure was front-page news in a left-wing London newspaper.

In Spain, he found that the realities of the Civil War were not the simple struggle between good and evil that he had hoped for. The Spanish Republic was worth defending because its defeat would strengthen the evil of Hitler, but he could not bring himself to write about the Republic as if it embodied moral good in a battle against evil. Writing against his own convictions, he wrote a propaganda poem, 'Spain', in which both warring sides are projections of inner psychological states onto the outer world of action. The fascist insurgents are the projection of our neuroses and hatreds; the defenders of the Republic are the projections of our generosity and love. The closing lines, however, present a subtly different choice, not a moral or emotional one, but a practical choice of victory or defeat:

The stars are dead. The animals will not look.
We are left alone with our day, and the time is short, and
  History to the defeated
May say Alas but cannot help nor pardon.

Auden later wrote that these lines, which say that defeat is unforgivable, 'equate goodness with success',[9] and he dropped the poem from his collected editions. Critics who had been stirred by the poem protested that the lines meant merely that failure was irreversible, that history cannot be undone. Auden, however, knew what he meant when he was writing it, and was convinced that a poet was personally responsible for his own words, and that he was morally obliged not to seduce readers into believing something he knew was false. About the ending of 'Spain' he wrote: 'It would have been bad enough if I had ever held this wicked doctrine, but that I should have stated it simply because it sounded to me rhetorically effective is quite inexcusable.'[10]

During the late 1930s Auden divided his work between grand, rhetorical performances like 'Spain', and self-deprecatingly modest lyrics that pointed indirectly towards his real beliefs. 'As I Walked Out One Evening', written in the traditional ballad stanza, sounds as unsophisticated as the anonymous American ballad on which it is modelled, 'As I Walked Out in the Streets of Laredo', but Auden's poem probes moral and intellectual depths that 'Spain' never acknowledges. It begins with an image of city crowds 'like fields of harvest wheat', unaware of the apocalyptic harvest to come. A lover proclaims his perfect constancy in bad rhymes:

'The years shall run like rabbits
  For in my arms I hold
The Flower of the Ages
  And the first love of the world.'

To this fantasy of an unchanging love, the clocks respond: 'O let not Time deceive you, / You cannot conquer Time.' The clocks insist on the realities of uncertainty, anxiety, and change – everything ignored by the lover's fantasies. The clocks end with a commandment:

'O stand, stand at the window
  As the tears scald and start;

You shall love your crooked neighbour
With your crooked heart.'

This is an explanation, not a contradiction, of the biblical command to love one's neighbour as oneself, and the point is that the commandment applies to imperfect human beings; it is not obeyed by fantasizing oneself or one's beloved as perfect or even good.

The poem never suggests that anyone obeys or even notices what the clocks command. A commandment, by its nature, cannot be enforced, only spoken. Auden disliked the political justification of art based on the idea that art 'makes you think' in any particular way; to Auden, a work of art is both a source of pleasure and a reminder of those aspects of reality that we prefer to ignore.

By 1938, when he was thirty-one, Auden had begun to feel self-disgust about his fame as a poetic spokesman for political causes. While returning across North America from a reporting tour to the Sino-Japanese War, he decided to move to the United States; he left Britain, he thought permanently, early in 1939. (His trip to China was the subject of his final collaboration with Isherwood, *Journey to a War*, with prose by Isherwood and verse by Auden.)

Settling in New York, he was no longer the newspaper celebrity he had been in Britain. He continued the behind-the-scenes work he had taken on in England, raising funds for refugees from Hitler, but after one or two experiences that left him annoyed with himself, he stopped speaking at political events. He had overcome his temptation to enjoy the fame that came to writers who identified themselves with political causes, but he had not yet overcome the temptation to become another kind of leader. He wrote about poets as non-political visionaries whose art could teach the ultimate reality behind the confused jumble of appearances.

W. B. Yeats died a few days after Auden arrived in New York, and Auden inherited the status of the greatest living poet born in the British Isles. He wrote a poem 'In Memory of W. B. Yeats', which was less a eulogy for Yeats than a programme for his own poetic future. The first part quickly disposes of Yeats himself, who is merely dead, transformed into admirers who remember the poems, not the poet. In the second part, poetry outlives the poet's deeds; the verse-form tightens from the loose, irregular lines of the first part into more regular lines, which look like, but aren't quite, iambic pentameter. This second part celebrates the poetic 'gift' that made Yeats's poetry greater than the man himself: 'You were silly like us. Your gift survived it all.' The gift survives, but has no power over events: 'Poetry makes nothing happen'; the world is as dangerous and chaotic a place as it was when Yeats was alive.

Then, in the drumbeat rhythms of the third and final section – echoing Blake's visionary mode in 'The Tyger' – the poem addresses an unnamed 'Poet' who will follow Yeats into the realms of death, then rise again to teach the way out of despair:

> Follow, poet, follow right
> To the bottom of the night,
> With your unconstraining voice
> Still persuade us to rejoice ...
>
> In the deserts of the heart
> Let the healing fountains start,
> In the prison of his days
> Teach the free man how to praise.

Poetry '*makes* nothing happen' – it *forces* nothing to occur – but it can teach the free to make their own triumphant choices.

Once again, he was making inspiring rhetorical gestures on public themes while, in his other poems, he was writing a very different kind of meditative poetry on private themes. Shortly after arriving in America he fell in love with a young poet named Chester Kallman, and thought that for the first time he had made a permanent, faithful relationship that was morally if not legally a marriage. (Their sexual relation ended after two years because Kallman refused to be the faithful partner Auden wanted, but they remained companions, usually sharing a home, for the rest of their lives.) Auden wrote lyrics that combined gratified wonder at this new experience with a realist's sense of human limitation. A poem that begins as a meditation on the many meanings of 'law' ends by identifying it with love:

> Like love we don't know where or why
> Like love we can't compel or fly
> Like love we often weep
> Like love we seldom keep. ('Law Like Love', 1939)

Auden was as convinced as ever of the absolute evil of Nazism, but for a few months around the start of World War II in September 1939 he convinced himself he was a pacifist. He justified pacifism to himself by trying to believe in a revised version of the Marxist idea that history leads inevitably to violent revolution; in Auden's pacifist variation on this idea in 1939, history leads inevitably to a reign of reason and peace, and the killing required by war is more likely to hinder than help its arrival.

This was the idea that Auden knew he had expressed in 'September 1, 1939', and which he later found morally repugnant. The poem adopts the tone and metre of Yeats's best-known poem on public themes, 'Easter 1916', which commemorates a failed uprising by Irish nationalists, and it applies

Yeats's manner to a far greater crisis. After cataloguing the private and public disasters 'From Luther until now', disasters already understood by 'Exiled Thucydides', the poem ends by affirming the poet's special power to clarify and explain:

> All I have is a voice
> To undo the folded lie,
> The romantic lie in the brain ...
> There is no such thing as the State
> And no one exists alone;
> Hunger allows no choice
> To the citizen or the police;
> We must love one another or die.

Auden knew that when he wrote 'We must love one another or die' he meant something like this: love is an instinct like hunger, and human beings who refuse to satisfy hunger and love must die – and therefore a loving society must inevitably be the result of natural selection, however unloving our society is now. Within a few weeks, Auden recognized the whole idea of an inevitably just society and an irresistible instinct towards love as a dangerous, self-defeating delusion. Love was a matter of choice, not instinct. If human beings prefer hatred and tyranny to justice and love, then no instinct, no inevitable force, will intervene to save them. If love were an instinct like hunger, then the clocks in 'As I Walked Out One Evening' need not have commanded, 'You shall love your crooked neighbour'; no one needs to be commanded to satisfy an instinct. Some years later Auden ended another poem, entitled 'First Things First', with the line: 'Thousands have lived without love, not one without water.'

When Auden gave up his fantasy of a just society as the irresistible outcome of history, he also gave up pacifism, which now seemed to him a form of moral selfishness. He began as well to return to the Anglican church, although he now adopted an intellectual religion based on modern Protestant theology, with its severe sense of human guilt and inadequacy, unlike the ritual magic he had enjoyed in childhood.

During the next few years, he wrote poems that gave him no opening to present himself as a visionary leader or prophet. He continued to write lyrics, but most of his energy in the 1940s went into long dramatic poems in which the voices were not his own, but those of invented characters. The first of these long poems was 'For the Time Being: A Christmas Oratorio' (1941–2), which retells the Christmas story as if it had occurred in the contemporary world: the wise men are scientists and economists, the shepherds are industrial workers, Joseph worries in a bar, the Holy

Family's flight through the desert takes them through the landscape of sophisticated modern civilization. The whole poem has a formulaic, slightly mechanical air as if Auden had written it to solve a problem he had set for himself.

His next long dramatic poem, 'The Sea and the Mirror: A Commentary on Shakespeare's *The Tempest*', written in 1942–4, has nothing mechanical about it, although Auden may have begun it as a technical exercise in dramatic poetry. The poem is a series of monologues spoken by the characters in *The Tempest* following a performance of Shakespeare's play. Prospero soliloquizes to Ariel about having given up his artistic and magical powers. The nobles and sailors describe, in a virtuoso range of verse-forms, the lessons they have or haven't taken away from their experience. Finally, Caliban addresses the audience in a long prose poem written in the expansive, artificial style of the later Henry James, because Auden was playing with the idea that Shakespeare's Caliban is the embodiment of pure instinct – the same force named Eros or the Id in mythical and psychoanalytic writings – which has no natural voice of its own and can only speak in a borrowed, artificial voice like that of James's novels.

'The Sea and the Mirror' manages to be artificial and moving at the same time. It is partly a study in the temptations felt by all artists to reshape real events and real human beings for their own purposes, and the temptations felt by everyone to treat others as objects to be used for one's own purposes. In its themes, and in its three-part form and mixture of verse and prose, it is Auden's rewriting of *The Orators*, and his whole later career is marked by works that revise earlier ones by returning to the same themes in more profound and artistically subtle ways.

Prospero, in the first part of 'The Sea and the Mirror', renounces the power he has exercised through art, but never perceives that he retains his disdain for the objects of his power. He asks himself about his daughter and future son-in-law:

> Will Ferdinand be as fond of Miranda
> Familiar as a stocking? Will a Miranda who is
> No longer a silly lovesick little goose,
> When Ferdinand and his brave world are all her profession,
> Go into raptures over existing at all?

Prospero sounds clear-headed here, as he does throughout his speech, but the second part of 'The Sea and the Mirror', in which the other characters speak in their own voices, proves him wrong. Ferdinand and Miranda understand the complexities and temptations of their love in ways that Prospero cannot imagine, and all the other characters achieve similar depths of moral and emotional understanding, even if, like the villainous Antonio, they refuse to act on what they know.

The third of Auden's long dramatic poems was *The Age of Anxiety: A Baroque Eclogue* (1946–8), written mostly in the alliterative metre of *Beowulf*, and set in a bar in wartime New York. Auden had become an American citizen in 1946, and his voice and style, like his subject-matter, had become almost insistently American. The four characters in *The Age of Anxiety* are simultaneously four individual persons and four aspects of everyone's personality; as they talk, they explore the world of memory and, in a waking dream-vision, of the symbolic landscape of the human body and the primitive psychological needs associated with it. The poem's title gave a name to its era, but the poem itself comes to life only near the end, where the two characters with religious beliefs, a Jewish woman and a Christian man, briefly overcome anxiety by confronting the rebukes and obligations imposed on them by faith.

In *The Age of Anxiety* Auden wrote about the human body in terms of what it symbolized – mountains, not breasts; forests, not hair. In the late 1940s Auden grew impatient with the inward-looking themes and styles he had used in recent years, when he was reacting against his own public styles from the 1930s. In 1948 he began to return to Europe from America for half of every year, starting with ten summers in southern Italy, followed by fifteen in rural Austria.

When he began visiting Italy, he also began writing about the human body in ways very different from those of his modernist predecessors. The modernists had typically represented the body as mystically exalted, as in D. H. Lawrence, or as sordidly degraded, as in T. S. Eliot, or as transformable through vision into unearthly beauty, as in W. B. Yeats. Auden cared about the body in its ordinariness, its quiet insistence on breathing and eating rather than fantasizing or conquering, its indifference to anything larger or smaller than ordinary human scale. As Auden saw the limits of the severe Protestantism that he had adopted around 1940, he began to explore a more Catholic theology of the flesh. Auden's religion and his poetry now focused increasingly on what he called 'the sacred importance of the body'.[11]

'In Praise of Limestone' (1948) presents itself as a meditation on the limestone landscapes of Italy and England, which Auden thought of as the most human of all landscapes – unlike the hostility of mountains, or the emptiness of plains. But the poem is also about the human body: 'Mark these rounded slopes / With their surface fragrance of thyme and beneath / A secret system of caves and conduits.' (The pun of 'thyme' and 'time' is an understated way of making the same point about the changing reality of human life that the clocks had made in 'As I Walked Out One Evening'.) The poem also makes a political point about the claims of ordinary human existence in a world divided by ideology into vast armed camps, and increasingly perceived in statistical terms rather than personal ones.

The poem's form is syllabic verse, in which each line has a set number of syllables, unlike the normal accentual verse of English poetry, in which each line is built on a pattern of stressed and unstressed syllables. 'In Praise of Limestone' uses alternating lines of thirteen and eleven syllables, counted according to an arbitrary rule that treats two adjacent vowels (or a vowel adjacent to an initial 'h') as one, so that 'the earth' and 'the house' each count as one syllable not two:

> Dear, I know nothing of
> Either, but when I try to imagine a faultless love
> Or the life to come, what I hear is the murmur
> Of underground streams, what I see is a limestone landscape.

Since 1940 Auden had been using syllabic verse in order to create verse-forms that had the regularity and shapeliness of older forms without being backward-looking imitations. Irregular 'free verse' of the kind pioneered by T. S. Eliot and Ezra Pound had the merit of being up to date, and Auden used it in some of his poems, but he wanted to write poems that combined dynamic and unpredictable changes in content with balanced and symmetrical forms, and free verse made that impossible. Adding to his repertory of syllabic and accentual forms, he began in the 1960s to write the compressed Japanese syllable-counting forms of haiku and tanka.

In the 1930s he and Christopher Isherwood had written political plays. Starting in the late 1940s he and Chester Kallman wrote opera libretti on moral and psychological themes. Opera gave him a medium in which to write with a theatrical intensity and extravagance that had eluded him in the stage plays he had written earlier.

In the 1940s he had written three long dramatic poems in the voices of fictional characters; in the 1950s and 1960s he wrote three sequences of linked poems, with each poem in each sequence adopting a different tone and manner, though all were variations on his own voice. His sequence 'Horae Canonicae' (1949–54) was a series of seven Good Friday meditations, each keyed to one of the traditional hours of prayer. Each of the poems takes a different approach to questions of private guilt and public responsibility. Their tone ranges from the guilty intensity of the syllabic verse in 'Nones':

> What we know to be not possible,
> Though time after time foretold
> By wild hermits, by shaman and sybil
> Gibbering in their trances,

Or revealed to a child in some chance rhyme
  Like *will* and *kill*, comes to pass
Before we realize it

to the calm near-comedy of the prose in 'Vespers', in which the aesthetically minded poet, whose deepest political wish is to be left alone, encounters his politically minded opposite who wants to manage everyone else's lives:

Both simultaneously recognize his Anti-type: that I am an Arcadian, that he is a Utopian.

He notes, with contempt, my Aquarian belly: I note, with alarm, his Scorpion's mouth.

He would like to see me cleaning latrines: I would like to see him removed to some other planet.

Auden paired this sequence with another entitled 'Bucolics' (1952–3), seven poems which expand on the theme of 'In Praise of Limestone' that different human qualities go with different landscapes – from the complacent cosiness of 'Lakes' to the isolating vanity of 'Islands'.

After Auden bought a summer house in Austria – he wept with joy to own a home for the first time – he began a sequence of fifteen poems, 'Thanksgiving for a Habitat' (1958–64), which treated the rooms of his converted farmhouse as he had treated the landscapes of 'Bucolics', each room with a special set of emotions and memories. (Auden claimed that the poem about the lavatory, 'The Geography of the House', was the only serious poem ever written about that subject.)

In the late 1950s Auden had a second experience of fame in Britain when he served for five years as professor of poetry at Oxford – the only professorship chosen by a majority vote of Oxford graduates. He spent only a few weeks each year in Oxford, but was lionized by newspapers and was popular among undergraduates. He enjoyed the experience far more than he had enjoyed his public role in the 1930s, but was again glad to escape when it was over. He wrote a poem, 'A Change of Air', about this second withdrawal from public life, although no one seems to have recognized at the time that the poem was about himself; it seems instead to be about Goethe's abrupt departure for Italy in mid-career, but Auden had by now perfected the art of writing about his deepest experiences while pretending to write about someone else's. The poem opens with the conflict between a public 'name' and an inner self:

Corns, heartburn, sinus headaches, such minor ailments
Tell of estrangement between your name and you,
Advise a change of air; heed them, but let

The modesty of their discomfort warn you
Against the flashy errands of your dreams.

Instead of flashy errands and dramatic gestures, the poem advises an inner change so secret and effective that the only external trace noticed by others is that 'you seem less amusing than you were'.

Auden had long been interested in the 'late style' of great artists, the stage when they care little about reaching an audience and much about their own experiments. Auden's late style included poems that looked back in summary form over his own life, as in 'Prologue at Sixty', or over any human life, as in 'River Profile', which traced the course of a life as if it were the course of a river. The river begins in a sexualized storm that issues in a small mountain stream, descends through remote farms and sophisticated cities until it ends in a final

act of surrender, effacement, atonement
in a huge amorphous aggregate no cuddled
attractive child ever dreams of, non-country,
image of death as

a spherical dew-drop of life.

In his last years he aged quickly. In 1972, at sixty-five, he left his winter home in New York to return to Oxford, where he hoped for the same collegial pleasures he had enjoyed as professor of poetry in the 1950s. He and Oxford had both changed, and he was lonely and unhappy. He died on his return trip to Oxford from his summer home in Austria, on 29 September 1973. His last poem, 'Archaeology', is a meditation, in a series of haiku, on the distant past. Echoing the mystical excitement he had experienced in childhood religion and in his adolescent poetry, he speculated that the world exposed by the archaeologist's spade was one where everyone knew (as everyone also knows now) that their myths were fictions, that the ancients knowingly used their myths 'to grant excuses / for ritual actions':

Only in rites
can we renounce our oddities
and be truly entired.

His last poems withdrew into a timeless world of ritual after a life of deep engagement in the world of time.

NOTES

1 *The Age of Anxiety*, part 5, in *Collected Poems*, ed. Edward Mendelson, 3rd edn (New York: Modern Library, 2007), p. 515.
2 *The Dyer's Hand* (New York: Random House, 1962), p. xi.

3 Ibid., p. 27.
4 *Juvenilia: Poems 1922–1928*, ed. Katherine Bucknell (Princeton: Princeton University Press, 1994), p. 186.
5 'Foreword', in *The Orators* (London: Faber and Faber, 1966), pp. vii–viii.
6 This and further quotations from Auden's poetry are from the first versions in book form, as reprinted in Auden's posthumous *Selected Poems*, ed. Edward Mendelson (New York: Vintage Books, 1977; expanded edn, New York: Vintage Books, 2007); see the note on Editions.
7 In *Forewords and Afterwords* (New York: Random House, 1973), p. 69.
8 *The English Auden*, ed. Edward Mendelson (London: Faber and Faber, 1979), p. 155.
9 'Foreword', in *Collected Shorter Poems 1927–1957* (London: Faber and Faber, 1966), p. 15.
10 Ibid.
11 In *Forewords and Afterwords*, p. 68.

SELECTED FURTHER READING

Editions

Auden repeatedly revised or discarded his earlier poems when preparing his later collected editions. *Collected Poems*, ed. Edward Mendelson (3rd edn, New York: Modern Library, 2007) contains the poems he wanted to preserve in their final versions. *Selected Poems*, ed. Edward Mendelson (New York: Vintage Books, 1977; expanded edn, New York: Vintage Books, 2007), restores original versions and discarded poems. Selected prose writings are in *The Dyer's Hand* (New York: Random House, 1962**b**) and *Forewords and Afterwords* (New York: Random House, 1973).

Secondary works

The standard biographies are Humphrey Carpenter, *W. H. Auden: A Biography* (London: Allen and Unwin, 1979), and Richard Davenport-Hines, *Auden* (London: Heinemann, 1995). Useful critical works include John Fuller, *W. H. Auden: A Commentary* (London: Faber and Faber, 1998); Edward Mendelson, *Early Auden* (New York: Viking, 1979) and *Later Auden* (New York: Farrar, Straus and Giroux, 1999); Stan Smith, *W. H. Auden* (Plymouth: Northcote House, 1997); and Tony Sharpe, *W. H. Auden* (London: Routledge, 2007). See also Stan Smith (ed.), *The Cambridge Companion to W. H. Auden* (Cambridge: Cambridge University Press, 2004).

29

ALAN JENKINS

Philip Larkin

Philip Larkin owed his life's work to Thomas Hardy. He himself expressed his debt in general terms, saying that Hardy's poems taught him 'to feel rather than to write ... to have confidence in what one felt', and the feeling they taught him principally to have confidence in was sadness. He recalled, specifically, the importance to him of Hardy's 'Thoughts of Phena at News of her Death', but he could surely also have cited 'In Tenebris (II)': 'Delight is a delicate growth cramped by crookedness, custom, and fear.'

Larkin's promising career seemed to be over by his mid-twenties. A period of intense creativity that began when he graduated from Oxford in 1943 had produced a volume of poems (*The North Ship*, 1945) and two novels (*Jill*, 1946, and *A Girl in Winter*, 1947). Now his attempts to write a third novel stalled, while a second volume of poems failed to attract a publisher. He was working in a provincial library and 'beginning to find out what life was about', or what Hardy had called 'unsuccess'. His poems hitherto, with their aspirations to W. B. Yeats and Dylan Thomas, their exalted sense of himself and of the poetic, had been vague, allegorical, 'euphemistic' (in Barbara Everett's word).[1] Now Hardy showed him the possibilities of directness, and of his own 'commonplace' reality. Even more, Hardy seemed to endorse his vision of life's unfairness, of humanity as a series of oppressions and of 'the solving emptiness / That lies just under all we do' ('Ambulances': all citations of Philip Larkin's poetry here are from the *Collected Poems*, 1988).

The young Larkin was excited by a very different vision, ecstatic and (theoretically) 'something to do with sex'. 'Life', he confidently told a friend, was 'principally suffering *unprovoked* sorrow and joy'. But he also suffered unrequited longing, while joy mostly meant escape from the 'curious tense boredom' of his home, the tyranny of obligation, into art, male friendship, D. H. Lawrence, and jazz. 'The ultimate joy is to be alive in the flesh. Shake that thing', as Larkin put it. (The jazz Larkin liked best, coming directly out of the blues, is joyful music in which sadness is never far away, and Larkin's fellow Oxford undergraduate and lifelong friend Kingsley Amis remembered his 'melodic, delicately bluesy' style of playing the piano.) Writing, another escape, could bring release *and* acceptance, as did the girls'-school fantasies of 'Brunette Coleman', the louche authorial persona Larkin invented to entertain sophisticated Oxford friends, and as it does for John Kemp in *Jill*. The habit of investing difficult circumstances with a more beautiful unreality is one Kemp shares with Katherine, the protagonist of *A Girl in Winter*, but both outsider-artists are punished with painful awakenings, the understanding that 'love died, whether fulfilled or unfulfilled'.

Hardy 'thought suffering was "true"', Larkin later said, and this is the note struck again and again beneath a pattern of dialectical argument in Larkin's poetry from 'Deceptions' (1950) on. In that poem, a young girl who has been drugged and raped wakes to the busy indifference of her Victorian world:

the brisk brief
Worry of wheels along the street outside
Where bridal London bows the other way.

But the ruined girl is, by a less-than-consoling reversal of Ophelia's 'I was the more deceived, my lord', the 'less deceived': less so, anyway, than her attacker, who must confront the desolation of gratified desire. 'As I try to say in ["Deceptions"]', Larkin said, 'the inflicter of suffering may be fooled, the sufferer never is.'

Suffering is inevitable where desire and the exercise of the will are involved, but there may still be suffering even when there is no inflicter: for the widow in 'Love Songs in Age' (1957), say, reminded of 'that much-mentioned brilliance, love', which promised so much and has so comprehensively disappointed. Or the women, 'moustached in flowered frocks', of 'Faith Healing' (1960), made suddenly and terribly aware of 'all they might have done had they been loved', and of (in one of Larkin's saddest cadences and most pointed near-rhymes) 'all time has disproved' – as, presumably, it will disprove the efficacy of healing and of faith. Time that disproves and disappoints, and brings the certainty of loss: these are a kind of suffering inseparable from simply being alive. But being alive, for Larkin, is the supreme value. Reminding us repeatedly of 'what we have as it once was, / Blindingly undiminished', his poems still cherish what we have, or what we have settled for – our place, our unsatisfactory relationships, the weather and the seasons and 'the toad *work*' – since it is *all* we have.

Hardy, Larkin wrote, 'is not a transcendental writer, he's not a Yeats, he's not an Eliot'. These are the very grounds on which Donald Davie *accused* Hardy of having sold poetry short. For Davie, in Yeats's poems as in Eliot's or Pound's, 'quotidian reality is transformed, displaced, supplanted; the alternative reality which their poems create is offered to us as a superior reality, by which the reality of every day is to be judged and governed'. Hardy's poems, instead of 'transforming and displacing ... the reality of common sense, are on the contrary just so many glosses on that reality, which is conceived of as unchallengeably "given" and final'. This, one suspects, is just what appealed so strongly to Larkin. 'The influence of another poet is not primarily on the choice of words but on the choice of subject', he told one interviewer. A new subject brings a new vocabulary; but does it make sense to talk of choice at all, when so much in Larkin's poems – as in Hardy's, as in life – has not been chosen?

> Whether or not we use it, it goes,
> And leaves what something hidden from us chose,
> Then age, and then the only end of age.
>
> ('Dockery and Son', 1963)

Life narrows our options until we arrive at 'that vague age that proclaims / The end of choice, the last of hope': at the greatest unfairness of all, physical decline and death. If these things are not 'unchallengeably given and final', what are they? Larkin's anguish in the face of them and his inability to transcend it is what gives his art its distinctive pungency and plangency, its air, beneath a sociable, generalizing tone, of confidences shared – as the anguish is one we may perhaps share.

In Larkin's view Hardy 'associated sensitivity to suffering and awareness of the causes of pain with superior spiritual character'. In Larkin, this awareness is all that stands between us and the brute indifference of our biological destiny, or between us and brute socioeconomic fact – even, or perhaps especially, when these allow for the sort of happiness money can buy: 'goods and sex'.

> I listen to money singing. It's like looking down
> From long French windows at a provincial town,
> The slums, the canal, the churches ornate and mad
> In the evening sun. It is intensely sad. ('Money', 1973)

Windows can be looked up from too, as at the end of 'High Windows' (1967), in whose lengthening perspective the casual, consequence-free sex-lives of the young, at first wearily, disdainfully envied, become just another delusory freedom, like that which a generation earlier saw Larkin and 'his lot' excused the religious terrors that tormented *their* elders. And,

> Rather than words comes the thought of high windows:
> The sun-comprehending glass,
> And beyond it, the deep blue air, that shows
> Nothing, and is nowhere, and is endless.

Barbara Everett ingeniously links this poem with Raymond Chandler's novel *The High Window* (1943);[2] no less persuasively, Richard D. Jackson has invoked *John Inglesant* (1881), by Joseph Henry Shorthouse.[3] This novel about religious life in the seventeenth century contains a sentence, 'From those high windows beyond the flowerpots young girls have looked out upon life, which their instincts told them was made for pleasure but which year after year convinced them was, somehow or other, given over to pain', that Hardy copied into one of his notebooks, and echoes at the close of *The Mayor of Casterbridge* (1886) when Elizabeth-Jane Newson reflects that she is someone 'whose youth had seemed to teach that happiness was but the occasional episode in a general drama of pain'. A Darwinian and an atheist, Hardy in old age still believed that 'pain to all upon [the earth], tongued or dumb, shall be kept down to a minimum by loving-kindness, operating through scientific knowledge'; while Shorthouse's novel declares 'Nothing but the infinite Pity is sufficient for the infinite pathos of human life.' Larkin glossed his own poem, 'One longs for infinity and absence, the beauty of somewhere you're not ... one wants to be somewhere where there's neither oppressed nor oppressor, just freedom.' But it's possible that he had read Shorthouse's novel as well as Hardy's; that in showing nothing, being nowhere, the deep blue air also shows not just 'a state of mind essentially beyond words', as Jackson says, but something that might have been thought to be there, once.

More broadly, the poet who as a young man worshipped art and beauty ('I need', he wrote as an undergraduate, 'a friend who accepts mystery at the bottom of things ... the kind of artist who is perpetually kneeling in his heart') and who later described himself as an 'Anglican agnostic' is haunted by the lost shared certainties of earlier times. 'No-one', he told an interviewer, 'could help hoping Christianity was true, or at least the happy ending – rising from the dead and all our sins forgiven.' The analogy he offered for the ample, ornate stanzas of the poems he wanted to write (and did write) was wandering around in a cathedral. 'Church Going' (1954) is explicit about our need for somewhere appropriate to rites of passage: 'marriage, and birth, / And death, and thoughts of these', and a church is hallowed by tradition if nothing else.

Nearly twenty years after 'Church Going' Larkin wrote 'The Building', a poem of sixty-four lines (to 'Church Going''s sixty-three): nine linked, seven-line stanzas, plus one line hanging in the void, nine 'rooms' which contain other rooms, and the frightened people in them. This Building is a hospital, a monument to 'loving-kindness, operating through scientific knowledge' which also harbours our weakness and fosters our hopes, no less than a church does, or did. But it cannot overcome death, any more than churches can, or could: not, that is, 'unless its powers / Outbuild cathedrals'. All in 'The Building' are 'here to confess that something has gone wrong'. Approximately mid-way in time between it and 'Church Going' comes the much shorter 'Ambulances': ambulances are hospitals in microcosm, and in this poem they are 'closed like confessionals'. By the time of 'Aubade' (1977), religion is a 'vast moth-eaten musical brocade' and all that can be seen in the pre-dawn dark is 'The total emptiness for ever', a 'glare' the mind 'blanks at':

> Not in remorse –
> The good not done, the love not given, time
> Torn off unused – nor wretchedly because
> An only life can take so long to climb
> Clear of its wrong beginnings, and may never.

'Not ... not ... not ... nor ... never', if they do not quite cancel each other out, fail to prevent the stirring of remorse and wretchedness here, at once definite and shadowy, as in all those poems of Larkin's which both reveal and conceal what he knew to be the corrosive and unassimilable, 'unworkable' element in his make-up. It too had something to do with sex, and it started early.

Larkin was a shy, short-sighted boy, with a debilitating stammer, whose parents' marriage convinced him that 'human beings should not live together and children should be taken from their parents at an early age'. In 'Coming' (1950) the imminence of spring prompts the response,

> And I, whose childhood
> Is a forgotten boredom,
> Feel like a child
> Who comes on a scene
> Of adult reconciling,
> And can understand nothing
> But the unusual laughter,
> And starts to be happy.

That the laughter is unusual, the reconciling an occasion of happiness, implies the more uncomfortable status quo. Several poems that Larkin chose not to publish in his lifetime, but which appear in the 1988 *Collected Poems*, suggest (along with several of his letters, which throw light – or darkness – on those poems' sources) that as well as boredom, the legacy of his childhood included rage, embarrassment, guilt, resentment, and, perhaps above all, shame. 'Wedding-Wind', from 1946, whose speaker is a newly-wed farmer's wife, suggests how overpoweringly being alive in the flesh, fulfilment, and marriage were once present to Larkin's imagination; but it remains a triumph of a kind he did not try for again. 'To My Wife' ('Now you become my boredom and my failure') and 'Marriages' ('Adder-faced singularity / Espouses a nailed-up childhood'), both 1951, neither published by Larkin, come closer to touching the central nerve.

That nerve, a 'soft horror of life', was well developed by adolescence, and Oxford in wartime seems not to have provided much to set against it. 'At an age when self-importance would have been normal', Larkin recalled in the introduction he wrote for *Jill* when it was reissued in 1964, 'events cut us ruthlessly down to size.' In fact, for all his beery debunking and obscenities, he was full of self-importance, took his artistic vocation seriously, and adopted a pose of supreme irritation at the war as a threat to his creative freedom. (He was medically unfit for service.) By 1947, when he wrote 'Waiting for Breakfast', the war was over but a threat to creative freedom remained: women, with their demands on his time and money, their desire for marriage. 'Waiting for Breakfast', though it turns boredom to tenderness and self-importance to self-irony, ends on a clear-sighted view of the price to be paid for preferring poetry to love, the muse to a flesh-and-blood woman:

> Will you refuse to come till I have sent
> Her terribly away, importantly live
> Part invalid, part baby and part saint?

'Waiting for Breakfast' remained unpublished until 1966: long enough, Larkin must have hoped, for its appearance not to wound the woman with whom he had finally broken off a long engagement fifteen years earlier. 'Long Roots Moor Summer', an unpublished poem from 1954, sets up a painful contrast between his own purely verbal response to summer's fullness, its 'green / River-fresh castles of unresting leaf', its 'vast flowering', and a woman's more appropriate 'reply': 'to be married' – to someone else. In his letters Larkin kept up a grim comedy of bachelor grumbles, but vulnerability and fear underlie the plain closing statements of 'Sad Steps', a poem of his later middle age in which a moon ghosted by the moons of Sir Philip Sidney and Hardy confronts the bachelor-poet with a singleness stronger than his own:

> One shivers slightly, looking up there.
> The hardness and the brightness and the plain
> Far reaching singleness of that wide stare
>
> Is a reminder of the strength and pain
> Of being young; that it can't come again,
> But is for others undiminished somewhere.

Even the verbs take singular forms, where we might expect plural. Then later still (1979), in the small hours of 'Love Again', the focus is intently narrowed: to a woman imagined while 'Someone else' is

> feeling her breasts and cunt,
> Someone else drowned in that lash-wide stare.

Symptoms of love in this miniature confessional masterpiece are 'wanking at ten past three' and pangs of jealousy, indistinguishable from those of the ageing prostate: 'the usual pain, like dysentery'. Weariness and futility bring the poem up short, self-irony has hardened to self-hatred:

> But why put it into words?
> Isolate rather this element
>
> That spreads through other lives like a tree
> And sways them on in a kind of sense
> And say why it never worked for me:
> Something to do with violence
> A long way back, and wrong rewards,
> And arrogant eternity.

Georges Simenon called writing 'a vocation of unhappiness', and in letters Larkin presents himself as not so much saved by poetry as doomed to it. (He was also given to citing another French novelist, Henry de Montherlant: 'Happiness writes white.') Here, in the last substantial poem he wrote, that vocation has a Yeatsian glamour ('arrogant eternity') next to the more plain-spoken or Hardyesque 'violence a long way back' and 'wrong rewards', but all equally have brought him to this domestically scaled-down hell, a 'bedroom hot as a bakery'. It is for others to be swayed on by the tree of life, those 'river-fresh castles of unresting leaf' whose rustling is heard once more in 'The Trees' (1967), this time urging an impossible new start ('Still the unresting castles thresh ... / Begin afresh, afresh, afresh'), and for a final time in 'Aubade', where it is death that is 'unresting' and

> the dread
> Of dying, and being dead
> Flashes afresh to hold and horrify.

Remorse and regret like time and suffering and death may be 'true', but 'to write well', Larkin knew, 'entails enjoying what you are writing, and there is not much pleasure to be got from the truth about things'. Poetry that gives no pleasure cannot meet the needs of either reader or writer – though such pleasure may be inseparable from an exacting truthfulness. Larkin's breakthrough came with the realization that these need not be mutually exclusive, that his poems could tell 'the truth about things' while taking and offering pleasure in shapeliness and musicality, and in the kind of everyday social detail that had seemed the preserve of the novelist. Moving away from his early style and its standard 1940s vatic pretensions, he realized the poetic potential in the much more subtly expressive accents of everyday speech – though without its imprecisions or inconsequentiality.

In this register Larkin found the voice for his own unexceptional experience and feeling – 'bored, uninformed' in 'Church Going', sceptical and self-deflating in 'Reasons for Attendance' or 'I Remember, I Remember'. What were most admired in these and all Larkin's work of the 1950s were wit, diffidence, wariness towards the large statement, the ability to delineate fine shades of distrust, exclusion, or defeat. (A reviewer of Larkin's recorded reading from *The Less Deceived* (1955) noted his voice's 'hesitant, ironic quality, in which certain words are, as it were, singled out and underlined for pejorative mention'.) These qualities were not lost. But what is perhaps clearer now, and is anyway more marked in the two later volumes, *The Whitsun Weddings* (1964) and *High Windows* (1974), is a willingness to be overwhelmed: by ungainsayable and perhaps unsayable emotion, like the simultaneous swelling and falling-off in the last lines of 'The Whitsun Weddings' itself; by broad, undesiring, wordless vistas, as at the end of 'Here' or 'High Windows'.

Yet Larkin's 'immensements' depend, equally, on verbal exactitudes. 'Un-' words in particular – an 'unemphasized, enthralled' catching of happiness, a 'strong / Unhindered moon', 'unfenced existence ... untalkative', 'uncontradicting solitude', 'unmolesting meadows', above all anything unnoticed or undiminished – express a momentary liberation or exemption from the oppressive norm, and can themselves be liberatingly beautiful. Larkin said that his poems, when read, should sound 'like someone talking', which seems a modest ambition until one remembers what it would have meant to him to overcome his stammer to that degree. (This did not happen until he was in his forties.) The fluent speaking voice with all its shifts of tone and register sustained in his mostly iambic lines and rhyming stanzas, the long sentences winding through the final two quatrains of 'Mr Bleaney' or the first three stanzas of 'Here' – twenty-four lines, 'and after that it's all consonants', as Larkin said – represent a special triumph, for the stammerer. It is an even more defiant kind of release we hear in, say, '*D*eath is no *d*ifferent *wh*ined at than *w*ithstood' from 'Aubade', in 'The brisk brief / Worry of wheels' and Larkin's evident enjoyment of alliteration generally. Alliteration is a kind of stylized stammer, turning involuntary repetition into expressive music: exact in the 'mugfaced middle-aged wives' with husbands 'watchful as weasels' and 'car-tuning curt-haired sons' of 'Show Saturday' (1973); snarling with derision at

[the] way I spent youth:
Tracing the trite, untransferable
Truss-advertisement, truth

in 'Send No Money' (1962) or 'The shit in the shuttered château' in 'The Life With a Hole in It' (1974); wistful and flirtatious in a letter to the novelist Barbara Pym: 'Why are single rooms *so much worse* than double ones? Fewer, further, frowstier? Damper, darker, dingier? Noisier, narrower, nastier?'; plangent in

The decades of a different life
That opened past your inch-close eyes
Belonged to others, lavished, lost;
('When First We Faced', 1975)

and despairing in the 'wasteful, weak, propitiatory flowers' that cannot help the inhabitants of 'The Building'.

Alliteration, compounds, the negative prefix, in different combinations are for Larkin forms of a verbal exactness that is also pleasure: the cry 'Hanging unhushed' and the 'Unmolesting meadows' of 'At Grass', or

the balls that bounce, the dogs that bark,
The branch-arrested mist of leaf, and me
Threading my pursed-up way across the park

in 'Spring' (both 1950), or his anathema on modern jazz: 'the cobra-coaxing cacophonies of Calcutta'. Both early and late, there are whole short poems given over to brief, consolatory glimpses of natural and human regeneration. But Larkin's poems grow in stature as the impulses to pleasure and truthfulness are more fully developed and balanced in them: supremely in 'The Whitsun Weddings', 'The Old Fools', and 'Aubade' – the first swelling with the only happiness to which 'normal' life aspires and the second raging quietly at the sad caricature to which happiness and unhappiness alike decline, while the last achieves an appalled, literal clarity as to the way death, 'the sure extinction that we travel to', for someone who lives in terror of it 'slows each impulse down to indecision'.

Indecision, deepening to despair – *what's the point of this?* – eventually, in Larkin, defeated the impulse to write poetry. It also paralysed him with regard to unpublished poems, papers, and letters that would survive him. Thinking once more, perhaps, of Hardy, Larkin declared that one should 'burn everything', but he didn't; nor did he leave clear instructions to his executors that they should either. In consequence the years since his own extinction have seen him enjoying an afterlife he might have thought a mixed blessing: not just the letters and biography, but a substantial outgrowth of the slender, carefully shaped body of lyric poetry by which he was known in his lifetime. As Ian Hamilton, reviewing the *Collected Poems*, put it (and since then there has been a further, generous volume of *Early Poems and Juvenilia*), 'It's as if this most bachelor of poets had suddenly acquired a slightly messy family life.'[4]

Surprising as the quantity of Larkin's trial runs, 'botch-ups, immaturities and fragments' may be, they reveal not just his steady absorption, refinement, or rejection of his early models (Auden and John Betjeman as well as Yeats and Dylan Thomas), but how merciless the mature poet was in cutting off unwanted relations, poems that seemed to him not quite 'true or right or real': even a poem as thoroughly, delicately Larkinesque in tone and feeling as his elegy for his father, 'An April Sunday Brings the Snow', from 1948. By common consent it was two years later, with 'At Grass', that he came into his own, suggesting, as Kingsley Amis said, 'in the vividly drawn picture of a pair of old racehorses, the evanescence of glory, of active life and of life itself'. True: these horses are more or less distant relations of so many of the people in Larkin's poems, pushed 'to the side of their own lives'. But they have also been released from a life of exploitation by humans, from 'faint afternoons / Of Cups and Stakes and Handicaps'. The elegiac sadness that so gracefully tinges them seems mostly to concern *us*; while *they* 'gallop for what must be joy'.

In his polemical introduction to *The New Poetry* (1962) A. Alvarez compared 'At Grass' with Ted Hughes's 'A Dream of Horses', using the latter as a stick with which to beat all that was dry, decent, and decorous about English poetry of the 1950s, and invoking a very different English sensibility, Lawrentian, violent, and 'serious', while Larkin's 'elegant and unpretentious' poem belonged emotionally 'to the world of the RSPCA' (Royal Society for the Prevention of Cruelty to Animals). Larkin's first literary passion was for Lawrence – albeit a Lawrence whose 'beliefs [were] pure (in the sense of utter, sensitive and refined) aestheticism'. Many years later, in his opening address at an exhibition devoted to Lawrence at Nottingham University, he reminded his audience of 'the sense [Lawrence] gives that, in his own words, this is not only a world of men, but a vivid epiphany of life in all its alternatives, of which humanity is only one, and perhaps not the best one at that'. This is the unspoken implication of several of Larkin's poems, while at least four suggest the sharpness of his sympathy for the sufferings of animals at the hands of humans. One of his very last, about his remorse at having accidentally killed a hedgehog in 'The Mower' (1979), draws the wider inference:

> we should be careful
> Of each other, we should be kind
> While there is still time.

Larkin had no real practical interest in politics, but his precocious adolescent reading – George Bernard Shaw and Cyril Connolly as well as Lawrence – fed his dislike of the bourgeois ethos in which he was brought up (Larkin's father was a city treasurer who, while he encouraged his son's intellectual curiosity, also evinced an excruciating admiration for Hitler's Germany), and his conviction that institutionalized arrangements falsified people's real desires: that men and women only wanted sex from each other, free of emotional or domestic obligations, for example. As Larkin grew older the conservatism of that ethos steadily reasserted itself, in art as in life. He stayed in one job, in one place – as librarian at the University of Hull – from 1955 until his death thirty years later. He had arrived in his twenties or thirties at positions which he saw little subsequent need to revise: behind all art was the impulse to preserve; a poem was 'a verbal device that will preserve and reproduce any given feeling or set of feelings indefinitely'; poetry was a matter of emotion, imagination, and intelligence, but not the will; and – a dictum of Leslie Stephen's that had meant so much to Hardy – 'The ultimate aim of the poet should be to touch our hearts by showing his own, and not to exhibit his learning, or his fine taste, or his skill in mimicking the notes of his predecessors.' In the jazz and book reviews he wrote from the 1950s until shortly before his death, and in *The Oxford Book of Twentieth-Century Verse* he edited, Larkin campaigned steadily for the pleasure principle and against those irresponsible modernist experiments ('Parker, Pound and Picasso') that had put a barrier of mystification and outrage between jazz and its audience, poetry and its readers. The academic 'industry' was, at best an irrelevance, at worst another obstacle: poetry was to be read, not studied; as Samuel Johnson had said, it should help us to enjoy life, or endure it.

Being funny could help, too, and Larkin was a very funny man – in print and, by all accounts, in person. He glossed one of his most famous lines ('to prove / Our almost instinct almost true: / What will survive of us is love'; 'An Arundel Tomb', 1956): 'I think what survives of us is love, whether in the simple biological sense or just in terms of responding to life, making it happier, even if it's only making a joke.' His letters are full of glum jokes, part defensive but also part generous, as are the interviews in which he was apt to do a funny, nuanced, disingenuous turn as himself. Then in his last years, as Ian Hamilton wrote, 'Larkin was known to have gone a bit funny, but all this was reckoned to be amiably bufferish ... Only a few people knew that there was nothing at all funny about the way Larkin had gone funny, that his conservatism was tinged with the same vehemence that marked his ever-deepening self-hatred and despair.'[5]

In thirty years Larkin had published three volumes of verse whose standing with critics and the reading public alike was succinctly summed up by his biographer Andrew Motion: '*The Less Deceived* made his name; *The Whitsun Weddings* made him famous; *High Windows* turned him into a national monument.'[6] Easily the most popular English poet after Betjeman, he was widely expected to succeed his friend as Poet Laureate. He had received many honorary doctorates, prizes, and awards, including the Queen's Gold Medal for Poetry and the Hamburg Shakespeare Prize – to collect which Larkin made his one trip outside the British Isles as an adult. But celebrity had arrived at the very moment he felt himself to be 'a gross imposture, a turned-off tap'. What had been an 'uncontradicting' solitude, devoted to poetry or jazz or immersion in Barbara Pym's fictional world, all post-war Anglican gentility and restraint and 'small blameless comforts', as Larkin put it, or the more brutal, masculine world of Dick Francis's horse-racing thrillers, became, once creativity had deserted him, a dismal isolation, exacerbated by deafness. 'I used to believe that I should perfect the work and life could fuck itself. Now I'm not doing anything, all I've got is a fucked-up life', he told his biographer: a final reversion to Yeats.

Larkin was protective of his own and others' privacies, and professed to find his poems 'shamingly' revealing (which is not the same thing as being ashamed of what they revealed). There is sadness in the way his last years left him so exposed in his fear and dislike of a world no longer his, and in the fact that these became common knowledge after his death. But his poems were written for those readers whom they might help to enjoy life, or endure it. His will included a bequest to the RSPCA.

NOTES

1 Barbara Everett, *London Review of Books*, 11 May 2006.
2 Ibid.
3 Richard D. Jackson, *Times Literary Supplement*, 29 April 2005.
4 Ian Hamilton, 'Philip Larkin: 1. The Collected Poems', in *The Trouble With Money and Other Essays* (London: Bloomsbury, 1998).
5 Hamilton, 'Philip Larkin: 3. The Biography', in *The Trouble With Money and Other Essays*.
6 Andrew Motion, *Philip Larkin: A Writer's Life* (London: Faber and Faber, 1993).

SELECTED FURTHER READING

Editions

Collected Poems, ed. Anthony Thwaite, London, Faber and Faber, 1988
Early Poems and Juvenilia, ed. A. T. Tolley, London, Faber and Faber, 2005
Jill, London, Faber and Faber, 1975
A Girl in Winter,London, Faber and Faber, 1975

Trouble at Willow Gables and Other Fictions, 1943–1953, ed. James Booth, London, Faber and Faber, 2002
Required Writing: Miscellaneous Pieces 1955–1982, London, Faber and Faber, 1983
Further Requirements: Interviews, Broadcasts, Statements and Book Reviews, ed. Anthony Thwaite, London, Faber and Faber, 2001
Selected Letters of Philip Larkin 1940–1985, ed. Anthony Thwaite, London, Faber and Faber, 1992

Secondary works

Biographical

Brennan, Maeve, *The Philip Larkin I Knew*, Manchester, Manchester University Press, 2002
Hartley, Jean, *Philip Larkin, The Marvell Press and Me*, Manchester, Carcanet Press, 1989
Motion, Andrew, *Philip Larkin: A Writer's Life*, London, Faber and Faber, 1993

Critical

Amis, Martin, 'Philip Larkin', in *The War Against Cliché: Essays and Reviews 1971–2000*, London, Jonathan Cape, 2001
Booth, James, *Philip Larkin, Writer*, Hemel Hempstead, Harvester Wheatsheaf, 1992
(ed.), *New Larkins for Old: Critical Essays*, Basingstoke and London, Macmillan, 2000
Brownjohn, Alan, *Philip Larkin*, London, Longman, 1975
Cooper, Stephen, *Philip Larkin, Subversive Writer*, Brighton, Sussex Academic Press, 2004
Davie, Donald, *Thomas Hardy and British Poetry*, London, Routledge & Kegan Paul, 1973
Hamilton, Ian, 'Philip Larkin: 1. The Collected Poems', 'Philip Larkin: 2. The Selected Letters', 'Philip Larkin: 3. The Biography', in *The Trouble With Money and Other Essays*, London, Bloomsbury, 1998
Heaney, Seamus, 'Joy or Night: Last Things in the Poetry of W. B. Yeats and Philip Larkin', in *The Redress of Poetry: Oxford Lectures*, London, Faber and Faber, 1995
Morrison, Blake, *The Movement: English Poetry and Fiction of the 1950s*, Oxford, Oxford University Press, 1980
Thwaite, Anthony (ed.), *Larkin at Sixty*, London, Faber and Faber, 1982

FURTHER READING

1. Poets on poetry

Horace, *Ars Poetica* (*c.* 10 BC)
Sir Philip Sidney, *A Defence of Poesie* (1595)
Ben Jonson, *Conversations with William Drummond of Hawthornden* (1619)
John Milton, 'The Verse' (1668)
John Dryden and Sir William Soame, *The Art of Poetry Written in French by The Sieur de Boileau, Made English* (1683)
Alexander Pope, *An Essay on Criticism* (1711)
Samuel Johnson, *Lives of the Most Eminent English Poets* (1779–81)
William Wordsworth, Prefaces (etc.) to *Lyrical Ballads* (1798–), in *Lyrical Ballads*, 2nd edn, ed. Michael Mason, London, Longman, 2007
Samuel Taylor Coleridge, *Biographia Literaria* (1817)
Percy Bysshe Shelley, *A Defence of Poetry* (1821)
John Keats, *Letters*, ed. Hyder Edward Rollins, Cambridge, MA, Harvard University Press, 1958
Matthew Arnold, 'The Study of Poetry', in *Essays in Criticism*, 2nd series (1888)
W. B. Yeats, 'The Symbolism of Poetry' (1900), in *Essays and Introductions*, London, Macmillan, 1961
Letters on Poetry from W. B. Yeats to Lady Dorothy Wellesley, London, Oxford University Press, 1940
William Empson, *Seven Types of Ambiguity*, London, Chatto and Windus, 1930
T. S. Eliot, *Selected Essays, 1917–1932*, London, Faber and Faber, 1932
The Use of Poetry and the Use of Criticism, London, Faber and Faber, 1933
A. E. Housman, *The Name and Nature of Poetry*, Cambridge, Cambridge University Press, 1933
Ezra Pound, *The ABC of Reading*, London, Routledge, 1934
Louis MacNeice, *Modern Poetry: A Personal Essay*, London, Oxford University Press, 1938
Donald Davie, *Purity of Diction in English Verse*, London, Chatto and Windus, 1952
Articulate Energy: An Enquiry into the Syntax of English Poetry, London, Routledge, 1955
Randall Jarrell, *Poetry and the Age*, New York, Knopf, 1953
W. H. Auden, *The Dyer's Hand, and Other Essays*, New York, Random House, 1962
Seamus Heaney, *The Government of the Tongue*, London, Faber, 1988

The Redress of Poetry, London, Faber, 1995
Geoffrey Hill, *Collected Critical Writings*, ed. K. Hayman, Oxford, Oxford University Press, 2008
The Routledge Anthology of Poets on Poets: Poetic Responses to English Poetry from Chaucer to Yeats, ed. David Hopkins, London, Routledge, 1990

2. *Critics*

Abrams, M. H., *The Mirror and the Lamp: Romantic Theory and the Critical Tradition*, New York, Oxford University Press, 1953
Natural Supernaturalism: Tradition and Revolution in Romantic Literature, New York, W. W. Norton, 1971
Attridge, Derek, *The Rhythms of English Poetry*, London, Longman, 1982
Poetic Rhythm: An Introduction, Cambridge, Cambridge University Press, 1995
Bate, W. J., *The Burden of the Past and the English Poet*, Cambridge, MA, Belknap Press, 1970
Bloom, Harold, *The Anxiety of Influence*, New York, Oxford University Press, 1973
A Map of Misreading, New York, Oxford University Press, 1975
Brooks, Cleanth, *The Well Wrought Urn: Studies in the Structure of Poetry*, New York, Reyna and Hitchcock, 1947
Brower, R. A., *The Fields of Light: An Experiment in Critical Reading*, New York, Oxford University Press, 1951
Alexander Pope: The Poetry of Allusion, Oxford, Clarendon Press, 1959
Eagleton, Terry, *How to Read a Poem*, Oxford, Blackwell, 2007
Elliott, Robert C., *The Power of Satire: Magic, Ritual, Art*, Princeton, Princeton University Press, 1960
Everett, Barbara, *Poets in their Time: Essays on English Poetry from Donne to Larkin*, London, Faber, 1986
Forrest-Thomson, Veronica, *Poetic Artifice: A Theory of Twentieth-Century Poetry*, Manchester, Manchester University Press, 1978
Fowler, Alastair, *Triumphal Forms: Structural Patterns in Elizabethan Poetry*, Cambridge, Cambridge University Press, 1970
Kinds of Literature: An Introduction to the Theory of Genres and Modes, Cambridge, MA, Harvard University Press, 1982
Frye, Northrop, *An Anatomy of Criticism*, Princeton, Princeton University Press, 1957
Fussell, Paul, *Poetic Meter and Poetic Form* (1965), rev. edn, New York, Random House, 1979
Griffiths, Eric, *The Printed Voice of Victorian Poetry*, Oxford, Clarendon Press, 1989
Hartman, Geoffrey, *Beyond Formalism: Literary Essays 1958–1970*, New Haven, Yale University Press, 1970
Hollander, John, *The Untuning of the Sky: Ideas of Music in English Poetry, 1500–1700* (1961), rptd Hamden, CT, Archon, 1993
Rhyme's Reason: A Guide to English Verse (1981), 3rd edn, New Haven, Yale University Press, 2001

Hosek, Chaviva, and Patricia Parker (eds), *Lyric Poetry: Beyond New Criticism*, Ithaca, NY, Cornell University Press, 1985

Kermode, Frank, *Romantic Image*, London, Routledge, 1957

Leavis, F. R., *Revaluation: Tradition and Development in English Poetry*, London, Chatto and Windus, 1947

Leighton, Angela, *On Form: Poetry, Aestheticism, and the Legacy of a Word*, Oxford, Oxford University Press, 2007

Ricks, Christopher, *Allusion to the Poets*, Oxford, Oxford University Press, 2002

Smith, Barbara Herenstein, *Poetic Closure: A Study of How Poems End*, Chicago, University of Chicago Press, 1968

Stewart, Garrett, *Reading Voices: Literature and the Phonotext*, Berkeley, University of California Press, 1990

Stewart, Susan, *Poetry and the Fate of the Senses*, Chicago, University of Chicago Press, 2002

Tuve, Rosemond, *Elizabethan and Metaphysical Imagery: Renaissance Poetic and Twentieth-Century Critics*, Chicago, University of Chicago Press, 1957

Vendler, Helen, *The Music of What Happens: Poems, Poets, Critics*, Cambridge, MA, Harvard University Press, 1988

Wesling, Donald, *The Chances of Rhyme: Device and Modernity*, Berkeley, University of California Press, 1980

The Scissors of Meter: Grammetrics and Reading, Ann Arbor, University of Michigan Press, 1996

Wimsatt, W. K., *The Verbal Icon: Studies in the Meaning of Poetry*, Lexington, University of Kentucky Press, 1954

INDEX

Cambridge Companions to ...

AUTHORS

Edward Albee edited by Stephen J. Bottoms
Margaret Atwood edited by Coral Ann Howells
W. H. Auden edited by Stan Smith
Jane Austen edited by Edward Copeland and Juliet McMaster
Beckett edited by John Pilling
Bede edited by Scott DeGregorio
Aphra Behn edited by Derek Hughes and Janet Todd
Walter Benjamin edited by David S. Ferris
William Blake edited by Morris Eaves
Brecht edited by Peter Thomson and Glendyr Sacks (second edition)
The Brontës edited by Heather Glen
Frances Burney edited by Peter Sabor
Byron edited by Drummond Bone
Albert Camus edited by Edward J. Hughes
Willa Cather edited by Marilee Lindemann
Cervantes edited by Anthony J. Cascardi
Chaucer edited by Piero Boitani and Jill Mann (second edition)
Chekhov edited by Vera Gottlieb and Paul Allain
Kate Chopin edited by Janet Beer
Caryl Churchill edited by Elaine Aston and Elin Diamond
Coleridge edited by Lucy Newlyn
Wilkie Collins edited by Jenny Bourne Taylor
Joseph Conrad edited by J. H. Stape
Dante edited by Rachel Jacoff (second edition)
Daniel Defoe edited by John Richetti
Don DeLillo edited by John N. Duvall
Charles Dickens edited by John O. Jordan
Emily Dickinson edited by Wendy Martin
John Donne edited by Achsah Guibbory
Dostoevskii edited by W. J. Leatherbarrow
Theodore Dreiser edited by Leonard Cassuto and Clare Virginia Eby
John Dryden edited by Steven N. Zwicker
W. E. B. Du Bois edited by Shamoon Zamir
George Eliot edited by George Levine
T. S. Eliot edited by A. David Moody
Ralph Ellison edited by Ross Posnock
Ralph Waldo Emerson edited by Joel Porte and Saundra Morris
William Faulkner edited by Philip M. Weinstein
Henry Fielding edited by Claude Rawson
F. Scott Fitzgerald edited by Ruth Prigozy
Flaubert edited by Timothy Unwin
E. M. Forster edited by David Bradshaw
Benjamin Franklin edited by Carla Mulford
Brian Friel edited by Anthony Roche
Robert Frost edited by Robert Faggen
Gabriel García Márquez edited by Philip Swanson
Elizabeth Gaskell edited by Jill L. Matus
Goethe edited by Lesley Sharpe
Günter Grass edited by Stuart Taberner
Thomas Hardy edited by Dale Kramer
David Hare edited by Richard Boon
Nathaniel Hawthorne edited by Richard Millington
Seamus Heaney edited by Bernard O'Donoghue
Ernest Hemingway edited by Scott Donaldson
Homer edited by Robert Fowler
Horace edited by Stephen Harrison
Ibsen edited by James McFarlane
Henry James edited by Jonathan Freedman
Samuel Johnson edited by Greg Clingham
Ben Jonson edited by Richard Harp and Stanley Stewart
James Joyce edited by Derek Attridge (second edition)
Kafka edited by Julian Preece
Keats edited by Susan J. Wolfson
Lacan edited by Jean-Michel Rabaté
D. H. Lawrence edited by Anne Fernihough
Primo Levi edited by Robert Gordon
Lucretius edited by Stuart Gillespie and Philip Hardie
Machiavelli edited by John M. Najemy
David Mamet edited by Christopher Bigsby
Thomas Mann edited by Ritchie Robertson
Christopher Marlowe edited by Patrick Cheney
Herman Melville edited by Robert S. Levine

Arthur Miller edited by Christopher Bigsby (second edition)

Milton edited by Dennis Danielson (second edition)

Molière edited by David Bradby and Andrew Calder

Toni Morrison edited by Justine Tally

Nabokov edited by Julian W. Connolly

Eugene O'Neill edited by Michael Manheim

George Orwell edited by John Rodden

Ovid edited by Philip Hardie

Harold Pinter edited by Peter Raby (second edition)

Sylvia Plath edited by Jo Gill

Edgar Allan Poe edited by Kevin J. Hayes

Alexander Pope edited by Pat Rogers

Ezra Pound edited by Ira B. Nadel

Proust edited by Richard Bales

Pushkin edited by Andrew Kahn

Rabelais edited by John O'Brien

Rilke edited by Karen Leeder and Robert Vilain

Philip Roth edited by Timothy Parrish

Salman Rushdie edited by Abdulrazak Gurnah

Shakespeare edited by Margareta de Grazia and Stanley Wells (second edition)

Shakespearean Comedy edited by Alexander Leggatt

Shakespeare on Film edited by Russell Jackson (second edition)

Shakespeare's History Plays edited by Michael Hattaway

Shakespeare's Last Plays edited by Catherine M. S. Alexander

Shakespeare's Poetry edited by Patrick Cheney

Shakespeare and Popular Culture edited by Robert Shaughnessy

Shakespeare on Stage edited by Stanley Wells and Sarah Stanton

Shakespearean Tragedy edited by Claire McEachern

George Bernard Shaw edited by Christopher Innes

Mary Shelley edited by Esther Schor

Shelley edited by Timothy Morton

Sam Shepard edited by Matthew C. Roudané

Spenser edited by Andrew Hadfield

Laurence Sterne edited by Thomas Keymer

Wallace Stevens edited by John N. Serio

Tom Stoppard edited by Katherine E. Kelly

Harriet Beecher Stowe edited by Cindy Weinstein

August Strindberg edited by Michael Robinson

Jonathan Swift edited by Christopher Fox

J. M. Synge edited by P. J. Mathews

Tacitus edited by A. J. Woodman

Henry David Thoreau edited by Joel Myerson

Tolstoy edited by Donna Tussing Orwin

Anthony Trollope edited by Carolyn Dever and Lisa Niles

Mark Twain edited by Forrest G. Robinson

Virgil edited by Charles Martindale

Voltaire edited by Nicholas Cronk

Edith Wharton edited by Millicent Bell

Walt Whitman edited by Ezra Greenspan

Oscar Wilde edited by Peter Raby

Tennessee Williams edited by Matthew C. Roudané

August Wilson edited by Christopher Bigsby

Mary Wollstonecraft edited by Claudia L. Johnson

Virginia Woolf edited by Susan Sellers (second edition)

Wordsworth edited by Stephen Gill

W. B. Yeats edited by Marjorie Howes and John Kelly

Zola edited by Brian Nelson

TOPICS

The Actress edited by Maggie B. Gale and John Stokes

The African American Novel edited by Maryemma Graham

The African American Slave Narrative edited by Audrey A. Fisch

Allegory edited by Rita Copeland and Peter Struck

American Modernism edited by Walter Kalaidjian

American Realism and Naturalism edited by Donald Pizer

American Travel Writing edited by Alfred Bendixen and Judith Hamera

American Women Playwrights edited by Brenda Murphy

Ancient Rhetoric edited by Erik Gunderson

Arthurian Legend edited by Elizabeth Archibald and Ad Putter

Australian Literature edited by Elizabeth Webby

British Romanticism edited by Stuart Curran (second edition)

British Romantic Poetry edited by James Chandler and Maureen N. McLane

British Theatre, 1730–1830 edited by Jane Moody and Daniel O'Quinn

Canadian Literature edited by Eva-Marie Kröller

Children's Literature edited by M. O. Grenby and Andrea Immel

The Classic Russian Novel edited by Malcolm V. Jones and Robin Feuer Miller

Contemporary Irish Poetry edited by Matthew Campbell

Crime Fiction edited by Martin Priestman

Early Modern Women's Writing edited by Laura Lunger Knoppers

The Eighteenth-Century Novel edited by John Richetti

Eighteenth-Century Poetry edited by John Sitter

English Literature, 1500–1600 edited by Arthur F. Kinney

English Literature, 1650–1740 edited by Steven N. Zwicker

English Literature, 1740–1830 edited by Thomas Keymer and Jon Mee

English Literature, 1830–1914 edited by Joanne Shattock

English Novelists edited by Adrian Poole

English Poets edited by Claude Rawson

English Poetry, Donne to Marvell edited by Thomas N. Corns

English Renaissance Drama edited by A. R. Braunmuller and Michael Hattaway (second edition)

English Renaissance Tragedy edited by Emma Smith and Garrett A. Sullivan Jr.

English Restoration Theatre edited by Deborah C. Payne Fisk

The Epic edited by Catherine Bates

Feminist Literary Theory edited by Ellen Rooney

Fiction in the Romantic Period edited by Richard Maxwell and Katie Trumpener

The Fin de Siècle edited by Gail Marshall

The French Novel: from 1800 to the Present edited by Timothy Unwin

German Romanticism edited by Nicholas Saul

Gothic Fiction edited by Jerrold E. Hogle

The Greek and Roman Novel edited by Tim Whitmarsh

Greek and Roman Theatre edited by Marianne McDonald and J. Michael Walton

Greek Lyric edited by Felix Budelmann

Greek Mythology edited by Roger D. Woodard

Greek Tragedy edited by P. E. Easterling

The Harlem Renaissance edited by George Hutchinson

The Irish Novel edited by John Wilson Foster

The Italian Novel edited by Peter Bondanella and Andrea Ciccarelli

Jewish American Literature edited by Hana Wirth-Nesher and Michael P. Kramer

The Latin American Novel edited by Efraín Kristal

The Literature of Los Angeles edited by Kevin R. McNamara

The Literature of New York edited by Cyrus Patell and Bryan Waterman

The Literature of the First World War edited by Vincent Sherry

The Literature of World War II edited by Marina MacKay

Literature on Screen edited by Deborah Cartmell and Imelda Whelehan

Medieval English Literature edited by Larry Scanlon

Medieval English Theatre edited by Richard Beadle and Alan J. Fletcher (second edition)

Medieval French Literature edited by Simon Gaunt and Sarah Kay

Medieval Romance edited by Roberta L. Krueger

Medieval Women's Writing edited by Carolyn Dinshaw and David Wallace

Modern American Culture edited by Christopher Bigsby

Modern British Women Playwrights edited by Elaine Aston and Janelle Reinelt

Modern French Culture edited by Nicholas Hewitt

Modern German Culture edited by Eva Kolinsky and Wilfried van der Will

The Modern German Novel edited by Graham Bartram

Modern Irish Culture edited by Joe Cleary and Claire Connolly

Modern Italian Culture edited by Zygmunt G. Baranski and Rebecca J. West

Modern Latin American Culture edited by John King

Modern Russian Culture edited by Nicholas Rzhevsky

Modern Spanish Culture edited by David T. Gies

Modernism edited by Michael Levenson

The Modernist Novel edited by Morag Shiach

Modernist Poetry edited by Alex Davis and Lee M. Jenkins

Narrative edited by David Herman

Native American Literature edited by Joy Porter and Kenneth M. Roemer

Nineteenth-Century American Women's Writing edited by Dale M. Bauer and Philip Gould

Old English Literature edited by Malcolm Godden and Michael Lapidge

Performance Studies edited by Tracy C. Davis

Postcolonial Literary Studies edited by Neil Lazarus

Postmodernism edited by Steven Connor

Renaissance Humanism edited by Jill Kraye

The Roman Historians edited by Andrew Feldherr

Roman Satire edited by Kirk Freudenburg

Science Fiction edited by Edward James and Farah Mendlesohn

The Spanish Novel: from 1600 to the Present edited by Harriet Turner and Adelaida López de Martínez

Travel Writing edited by Peter Hulme and Tim Youngs

The Twentieth-Century English Novel edited by Robert L. Caserio

Twentieth-Century English Poetry edited by Neil Corcoran

Twentieth-Century Irish Drama edited by Shaun Richards

Utopian Literature edited by Gregory Claeys

Victorian and Edwardian Theatre edited by Kerry Powell

The Victorian Novel edited by Deirdre David

Victorian Poetry edited by Joseph Bristow

War Writing edited by Kate McLoughlin

Writing of the English Revolution edited by N. H. Keeble